FAMILY GUIDE TO EMOTIONAL WELLNESS

PROVEN SELF-HELP TECHNIQUES AND EXERCISES FOR DEALING WITH COMMON PROBLEMS AND BUILDING CRUCIAL LIFE SKILLS

EDITED BY PATRICK FANNING AND MATTHEW MCKAY, PH.D.
WITH A FOREWORD BY MARY ELLEN COPELAND, M.S., M.A.

NEW HARBINGER PUBLICATIONS, INC.

Publisher's Note

Distributed in the U.S.A. by Publishers Group West; in Canada by Raincoast Books; in Great Britain by Airlift Book Company, Ltd.; in South Africa by Real Books, Ltd.; in Australia by Boobook; and in New Zealand by Tandem Press.

Copyright © 2000 by New Harbinger Publications, Inc.
5674 Shattuck Avenue
Oakland, CA 94609

Cover design by SHELBY DESIGNS AND ILLUSTRATES
Edited by Angela Watrous
Text design by Michele Waters

ISBN 1-57224-207-8 Paperback

Printed in the United States of America

New Harbinger Publications' Web site address: www.newharbinger.com

02   01   00

10   9   8   7   6   5   4   3   2   1

First printing

To our readers, who make it all worthwhile.

Contents

Preface

by Mary Ellen Copeland

I am excited that New Harbinger Publications has developed this comprehensive *Family Guide to Emotional Wellness*. Through my years of doing ongoing research, teaching, and writing books on mental health issues, I have become acutely aware of the strong connection between family and personal emotional well-being. I have seen repeated evidence of the powerful potential for healing when family members know how to deal effectively with emotional problems and issues. When one or several people in the family are having a difficult time, as inevitably will happen sometimes, family members often don't know how to deal effectively with emotional problems and issues. We all need to work to change this. This book meets the need for a resource book that families can use when they want to work on helping themselves feel better. Whether a person is trying to deal with their own feelings and behaviors or those of other family members, such a compendium is invaluable.

If you have children in your life, I hope you will share this book with them as well as with all family members. Promote open discussions in your family. Learn these strategies together, and use them together to brainstorm solutions to problems in the family. Support each other as you work together to learn new techniques. Remind each other of how effective they are. As family members use these skills and strategies, the quality of life for everyone in your family will get better and better.

With guidance and support, even very small children can learn to distract themselves with things as simple as drawing a picture when they are feeling bad, or breathing deeply to help them feel more relaxed. As they get older they can work on maintaining or raising their own self-esteem, giving themselves positive self-talk, and using the many other simple and safe strategies to deal with the complexities of life. These skills will serve them well throughout each developmental stage of life—through adolescence, into adulthood and into their senior years. It's never too early or too late in your life to begin learning and using these methods. The journey becomes easier, each step you take and at any age, for you and everyone that is important in your life.

My thinking on these concepts has come together as I have worked on the Raising Healthy Children Project. The project was developed as a result of research that shows that the children of parents who experience major depression are at high risk for a wide range of emotional disturbances and troubling behavior. The goal of this project was to help the children deal with their parents' problems in ways that would keep them emotionally stable. In addition it was hoped that the parents would learn skills and strategies that would help them to keep their symptoms at bay and respond to their children's needs more positively—a win-win situation for everyone in the family. In this project, thirty families, where at least one parent experiences major depression (including ninety children between the ages of seven and eighteen), came to five all-day educational workshops that were focused on teaching participants strategies and skills to help themselves feel better—the kinds of things that are described so well in this book. It was hoped that by teaching the children positive ways of coping with their parents' depression, and by teaching the parents how to relieve their own uncomfortable and troubling symptoms, the children might fare better over the long term. Ongoing study of these children and their parents is showing this to be the case.

My Story

For most of my life I have believed that if you don't feel well, if you don't like the way your life is, or if you have troubling emotional symptoms, you either just accept the way things are or you reach out to health care professionals. I learned that in my family. I'm sure it is the way serious situations had been addressed in my family for generations. As in most families, difficulties were ignored or "swept under the rug."

I began working with New Harbinger Publications almost ten years ago. In looking back at the years before I wrote my first book, before I realized I could change the way I feel, change the course of my life, and be more supportive of my family, I think of how this book might have helped me—might have relieved some of the suffering, the depression, anxiety, phobias, nightmares, low self-esteem, and other symptoms that made my life so difficult.

Through my childhood and adolescence I was plagued with recurring deep depressions. In those days, the late 1940s and the early 1950s, school officials paid little attention to the shy, well-behaved little girl who never said anything. My family was reeling from the effects of my mother's illness that kept her hospitalized for many years as I was growing up. With no help on how to cope, I often felt very lonely and neglected. Perhaps my siblings also felt this way. We never talked about it. As an adult, these deep depressions were interspersed with times when I could function very well. I began to accept the hard times, difficult as they were, as a part of my life—something that just happened, that I couldn't do anything about. I didn't do anything to help myself feel better. I didn't know there was anything I could do.

Then, in 1976, when I was mothering eight teenagers and directing a small private school for adolescents with special needs, I had a depression that was so deep and so debilitating that family members became concerned about my safety. Finally I went to a doctor. What I wanted—and what I got—from that doctor was a pill that would fix me right away. He gave me several pills in fact, and in a short time I felt much better. But we didn't talk about creating some change in my life that night help relieve these horrible symptoms. And for another ten years, by faithfully taking those pills, I got by. My life wasn't great. I made some bad decisions. I didn't take good care of myself. But I got by.

Then in 1985 all of that changed. I developed some side effects to the medications that made it impossible for me to use them. When I stopped taking them, my symptoms quickly got totally out of control. I had deep suicidal depressions. I developed psychosis. My self-esteem plummeted. I was repeatedly hospitalized in psychiatric facilities. My world fell apart. My family was told I would never get well.

After several years of that, I asked my psychiatrist how people with these kinds of symptoms get well, how they get their lives back. He promised he would have that information for our next visit. When he told me that no such information existed, I got angry. I got so angry that I decided to take matters into my own hands. With the help of a vocational rehabilitation counselor, I began to study how people with all kinds of emotional symptoms relieve these symptoms, how they get well and how they get on with their lives. As I learned from others, I began to use some of their ideas. I began to help myself. And the more I did that, the more I took responsibility for my own wellness, the better I felt.

Since that time I have written ten books based on the findings of my studies and on other pertinent mental health issues. I keep up with a strenuous schedule of lectures and seminars. Instead of living in a housing complex for the elderly and disabled, my husband and I have a small farm in the country. And this change is the result of taking responsibility for my own life, using the kinds of skills and strategies described in this book. In fact, I have read and reread many of the authors who have contributed to this book.

This book is full of great ideas that will help you and your loved ones. I wish I had known many of these skills and techniques when I was younger. Life would have been much easier for me and my family.

Mary Ellen Copeland, M.S., is the author of:

- *The Depression Workbook: A Guide to Living with Depression and Manic Depression*

- *Living without Depression and Manic Depression: A Guide to Maintaining Mood Stability*

- *Wellness Recovery Action Plan*

- *The Adolescent Depression Workbook*

- *The Worry Control Workbook*

- *Healing the Trauma of Abuse*

- *The Loneliness Workbook*

- video: *Coping with Depression*

- audio tapes: *Strategies for Living with Depression and Manic Depression* and *Winning Against Relapse Program*

Acknowledgments

We would like to thank all the dedicated, wise, inspiring authors who over the years have entrusted their manuscripts, their ideas, their reputations, and their financial security to the not-always-so-tender mercies of New Harbinger Publications. To them we offer our highest praise: "You make a difference."

Introduction

Congratulations on obtaining the *Family Guide to Emotional Wellness*. This book will provide valuable information on a wide range of topics that are crucial to the happiness and well-being of your family. This book teaches the best self-help techniques for coping with bad moods and painful feelings, and developing the emotional and problem-solving skills you need to optimize your life. It can help parents maintain and improve their relationship, answer frustrating child-rearing questions, control addictions and other bad habits, and cope with the emotional side effects of physical health problems.

This *Family Guide* is written so that real people in real families can read, understand, and use it. We have cut out jargon and taken great care to include clear explanations and simple instructions for all exercises. Although we know from experience that this book will be consulted most often by the more mature family members who function as the emotional caretakers, the book can also be understood and used to advantage by younger adults and adolescents still in school.

A First Aid Manual for the Heart and Mind

The time has come for every family to have this reference in their home. The openness of modern society has removed most of the stigma formerly attached to stress-related illnesses, marital discord, child development problems, emotional distress, and mental illness. In this more open climate, new therapies and self-help techniques have been developed for a wider and wider range of psychological and health problems.

This book is more than just a handy reference to the many techniques now available for self-improvement, emotional regulation, and interpersonal success. This book is a first aid manual for the heart and mind. It will teach you the crisis management information and skills you need to handle the first days or weeks of an emotional problem. It will provide you with the information you need to determine the nature of a family crisis, the likely cause of emotional pain, and the best way to solve a wide range of problems. In many cases, that will be all you need to get back on track. If you need more help, there are chapters on seeking therapy and medications. Also, the Further Reading section at the end of the book refers you to specific full text books providing information on ongoing care.

How to Use This Book

Look first in the table of contents preceeding this Introduction. Find the chapter most pertinent to your current problem and consult that first. There you will also discover cross-references to other chapters. For example, if you go first to the chapter on chronic illness, you may eventually also be led to the chapters on depression, relaxation, and medication.

At the end of each chapter, the source book is cited with its full title, subtitle, and authors. For full bibliographic and ordering information, consult the Further Reading section at the end of the book.

Warning

A self-help approach is not appropriate for all problems. Some situations are too urgent, dangerous, or complex to be resolved by reading this or any book. Seek professional help immediately if your situation involves:

- suspected child abuse of any kind

- anger with violence and the threat of serious injury

- deep depression with suicidal thoughts

- severe psychosis or personality disorders

About the Authors and Publishers

This book is born out of a unique series of self-help psychology and health books published over the last twenty years by New Harbinger Publications. In 1979, we invented a new kind of self-help psychology book, different from the typical self-help bestseller of the time. Most of that genre relied on a sensationalized exposé of a given problem, with most of the book devoted to stories about how awful it is to be depressed or anxious or under stress. A final chapter or two might have some superficial advice about treatment, but most of the books were devoted to "informing" the public with scary and amazing stories.

Other titles that focused on a single technique, such as self-hypnosis or visualization, were inspirational or "conversion experience" books intended to motivate readers and convince them of the universal applicability of the author's pet techniques. In the late seventies there was plenty of gee whiz and snake oil, but little that was objective or practical.

Our first self-help title was *The Relaxation & Stress Reduction Workbook,* a ground-breaking manual for reducing stress on your own, using many techniques that were innovative then and have now become standard practice.

By 2000 we had published nearly 200 self-help titles in the psychology and health fields. We have helped millions of readers reduce stress, fight depression, reduce anxiety, conquer anger, increase self-esteem, raise healthy kids, and improve their relationships. It's gratifying to receive letters and gifts from satisfied readers who have been able to cope with agoraphobia, graduate from school, reconnect with loved ones, or survive suicidal depression thanks to reading our books.

This book you have in your hands, *The Family Guide to Emotional Wellness*, is the summation of our work over the past twenty years. This book represents the best of the best. In it we have exerpted and adapted the most essential and helpful parts of our most effective and powerful self-help books.

We hope you enjoy and profit from this unique volume, and we welcome your comments and suggestions as you use it to guide your family through the coming years.

Patrick Fanning
Matthew McKay
Oakland, California
June 2000

PART I

GETTING ALONG

Getting along with those close to you is always a challenge. Over time, you can grow apart from your partner. The honeymoon phase lapses into routine, passionate sex cools, minor disagreements heat up into major fights, long talks dwindle into silence, other people and a different life start to look appealing. Or you may have been recently thrust into new or changing relationships by divorce, remarriage, or taking care of a sick parent.

This section helps with troublesome adult interactions of all kinds:

Couple Skills explains the ins and outs of listening, self-expression, and negotiation in intimate relationships.

Sex teaches the sensate focus technique for overcoming the fear, pain, or boredom that may be keeping you from experiencing a comfortable, rewarding sexual relationship.

Anger gives guidelines for controlling and changing your anger trigger thoughts.

Communication helps in expressing your thoughts and feelings assertively, getting your needs met, and dealing with criticism.

Step Families shows how to cope with the most common difficulties encountered by both adults and children in blended families.

Infidelity explains the different types, causes, and outcomes of infidelity, as well as how to survive the pain and upset, whether you are the trnasgressor or the victim.

Caregiving helps family caregivers assess and cope with the pressures of caring for a loved one.

CHAPTER 1

Couple Skills

Being in an intimate relationship can be one of the keenest human joys and one of the greatest sources of pain. Love begins with so much hope: the dream of one day feeling known, accepted to the core; the dream of belonging, of protecting and being safe; the dream of deep passion; the dream of a lasting bond. But hope collides with the realities of love: needs do not fit, anger divides, judgments erode the once easy acceptance, loneliness fills parallel but distant lives.

Relationships that endure and deepen are formed by couples who know and practice basic interpersonal skills: listening, clear communication, negotiation, handling anger appropriately, and so on. This chapter will help you develop and polish the basic skills you need to keep love alive.

Listening

It's hard to really listen to your partner. It's easier to space out, to rehearse your reply, to filter the content for danger signs, to collect evidence for your own opinions, to pass judgment, and so on.

But listening is the most important of all the communication skills that can create and preserve intimacy. When you listen well, you understand your partner better, you stay closely in tune, you enjoy the relationship more, and you know without mind reading why your partner says and does things.

Listening is a commitment and a compliment. It is a commitment to understanding and empathy, to putting aside your own interests, needs, and prejudices long enough to see your relationship through your partner's eyes. Listening is a compliment to your partner because it says, "I care about you. I want to know what you think and feel and need."

Read the following "Blocks to Listening" and check the ones that apply to you:

Blocks to Listening

- **Mind reading.** You are mind reading when you disregard or distrust what your partner is actually saying and instead try to figure out what he or she "really means." Mind readers give too much importance to subtle cues such as tone of voice, facial expressions, and posture. They ignore the actual content of what their partner is saying in favor of their own assumptions and hunches.

  Mind reading is deadly to intimacy because it ignores the obvious in favor of the imaginary. Paul says to Peggy, "I think you look good in both dresses—wear either one." Peggy tells herself, "He really means I'm so skinny and flat-chested that I wouldn't look good in anything."

- **Rehearsing.** You're so busy rehearsing what you'll say next that you never really hear what your partner is telling you. Sometimes you may rehearse whole chains of dialogue: "I'll say ... then my partner will say ... then I'll say ... "

  Susie is telling Sebastian why he should be the one who takes their son to his piano recital on Saturday, but Sebastian isn't listening. He's rehearsing his objection to the idea, because he wants to go to the ball game. He completely misses Susie's deeper concerns about him spending more time with his son.

- **Filtering.** Filtering means that you listen to some things but not others. You may listen for signs that your partner is angry or sad or anxious and then tune out when you sense that your partner is okay and that you aren't expected to respond to some emotional trouble.

  Filtering can also work to exclude things you don't want to hear. For example, your ears might work fine until your partner starts talking about your drinking, your mother-in-law, or moving out-of-state.

- **Judging.** Judging means that you have stopped listening to your partner because of some negative judgment, or that you only listen for the purpose of assigning blame and putting negative labels on your partner. If you think that your partner is stupid or bigoted or crazy, you stop listening. Or you listen only to gather fresh evidence of your partner's stupidity, bigotry, or craziness.

  Randy thought Kirk was an egomaniac, so he seldom listened when Kirk talked about himself. This negative judgment kept Randy from really getting to know Kirk for who he was.

- **Daydreaming.** Everyone's attention wanders. When you've been with someone for many years, it's especially easy to stop listening and drift away into your own fantasies. If you find it harder and harder to pay attention to your partner, it may be a danger sign that you are avoiding contact or certain topics.

  Ralph spaced out nearly every time Gloria talked about her art class. He ultimately realized that he was resentful of the time she spent in class and was avoiding a confrontation by daydreaming.

- **Advising.** Your partner barely has time to speak a complete sentence before you jump in with your advice. Your search for the right solution and your urge to fix everything deafens you to your partner's simple need to be heard.

  When George started telling Marie about his frustrations and despondency over his dead-end job, she was all over him: "You need to get into a whole new line of work. Why don't you go over to the junior college and get some career counseling? Or you could set up some informational interviews with executives in interesting fields." George felt even more overwhelmed. What he really wanted was sympathy and permission to just be a little depressed for a while.

- **Sparring.** You listen only to disagree, argue, and debate. You take a position and defend it, regardless of what your partner says. In many troubled relationships, sparring is the standard mode of communication.

    Whatever topic Joyce brings up—the kids, money, relatives—Ted starts a tirade, repeating his party line regardless of any new ideas his wife tries to explain. Ted is so argumentative that he is incapable of listening.

- **Being right.** This block protects you from hearing anything that suggests you are less than perfect. To avoid any suggestion that you are wrong, you will lie, shout, change the subject, justify, quibble, make excuses, accuse, or otherwise fight off criticism.

    Jennifer expressed concern about overdue notices and asked Rudy if he had paid the dentist bill or if she should pay it. He took this as an implied criticism and blustered that paying bills on time was stupid. "Let them wait—we'll keep the money and collect interest till after the second notice. Now give it a rest." Rudy never heard how anxious Jennifer felt getting the overdue notices.

- **Derailing.** You change the subject or joke it off whenever the conversation becomes too personal or threatening. By misdirection or humor you avoid listening to your partner's serious concerns.

    Sylvia said that she thought Anne should cut down on her drinking and staying up late. Anne laughed it off by saying, "Hey, with my stress, I'd be crazy not to drink. And late nights are the only times I have to unwind."

- **Placating.** You are too quick to agree. As soon as your partner expresses doubt, irritation, or anxiety, you jump in with "Yes . . . you're right . . . I know . . . I'm sorry . . . I'll fix it." You are so concerned with being nice, supportive, and agreeable that you don't give your partner enough time to fully express his or her thought.

    Molly tried three times to tell Jeff why she was fed up with his old cars blocking their driveway. He would "apologize her to death," and shuffle one or two cars into the street for a couple of days. He never got the message that she wanted him to get rid of them if he wasn't going to restore them in the near future.

Assessing Your Listening Blocks

On a separate sheet of paper, describe three situations where communication broke down between you and your partner. Indicate which blocks kept you from really listening to your partner. You may find that you used two or three different blocks in the course of the same conversation.

Use this format:

Situation	Blocks to Listening

Over the next two days, notice how often you use your favorite listening blocks. Review every conversation with your partner.

Which blocks do you use most consistently?

Are the situations similar?

What topics do you have the most trouble listening to?

Do you block other people as well as your partner?

Did your greater awareness of listening blocks change your usual style of listening?

Active Listening

It's not enough to shut your mouth and open your ears. Your brain must also be actively engaged in listening. There's really no such thing as a passive listener. Communication is a two-way, collaborative process, even when one person is ostensibly doing all the talking. To listen actively, you must paraphrase, clarify, and give feedback.

Paraphrasing

Whenever your partner says something important to you, you should state in your own words what you think your partner just said. This is the most important part of good listening. If you learn only one thing from this chapter, learn to paraphrase.

You can preface your paraphrase with lead-ins such as "What I hear you saying is that . . . In other words . . . Let me get this straight . . . So you felt that . . . If I understand you correctly . . . Do you mean . . . Would you say that . . . "

If you consistently paraphrase, you will:

- Prevent most listening blocks.
- Correct false assumptions and misinterpretations on the spot.
- Give your partner the priceless gift of being heard and acknowledged.
- Keep angry feelings from escalating.
- Help yourself remember what was said.

Try paraphrasing the next time your partner tells you anything of note. You may be surprised at how long it takes to completely understand even the simplest statement. For example, Joel decided to paraphrase what Cindy was telling him about her mother:

Cindy: My mother wants to come up and stay with us over Easter break.

Joel: Your mother asked if she could come up for Easter?

Cindy: Yeah. Well, she didn't ask—I suggested it, and she thought it sounded like a good idea.

Joel: You want your mother to come up.

Cindy: Sure.

Joel: And stay with us.

Cindy: Well, she usually stays with Cathy, but I want her here, so we can have more time.

Joel:	You're hoping for more time with her than usual?
Cindy:	Uh huh. We could relax for a few days, play with the kids, and—you know—just talk.
Joel:	Just hang out.
Cindy:	And talk about how things are going with her. Being alone down there.
Joel:	You want to talk about her loneliness?
Cindy:	Yes, she's all by herself in that big house. If she moved up here, she could be close to us, close to her grandkids.
Joel:	You want her to move in with us for good, not just Easter?
Cindy:	Well, not with us forever. Just a trial week, to see if she likes it, how it works out. Then look for a place nearby.

As you can see, Joel's gentle paraphrasing has uncovered an agenda much vaster than a simple Easter visit. If he had not been a good listener, this issue could have lain dormant and unexplored.

Clarifying

Paraphrasing leads naturally to clarifying. You tell your partner what you thought you heard, find out you were wrong, and start asking questions to clarify. In phrasing your questions, remember that your intention is to understand, enjoy, learn, or help. Your intention must not be to interrogate, to pressure for your own point of view, to blame, to belittle, or to manipulate in any way.

Asking questions will give you a broader picture that includes more specific details, finer shades of feeling, and greater understanding of your partner's point of view. Ask for the facts—who, what, where, when, how. And also ask questions like "How did you feel about that?" and "What were you thinking then?"

Feedback

Feedback comes after you have paraphrased what your partner said and asked questions to clarify your understanding. Then you "feed back" your own reactions. You calmly relate, without judgment, your own thoughts, feelings, opinions, desires, and so on. You share your inner experience of your partner's account, without falling back into listening blocks such as sparring or advising.

Feedback accomplishes three things. First, it is another chance to check out your perceptions with your partner, so that he or she can correct any misconceptions. Second, your feedback provides your partner with information about the accuracy and effects of his or her communication. Third, your partner gets the benefit of your fresh point of view.

Good feedback is immediate, honest, and supportive.

Immediate means that you don't waste any time. As soon as you think you understand your partner's story through paraphrasing and asking for clarification, give your feedback right away. A delay of even an hour will lessen the impact.

Honest means that you have to give your real reaction, undistorted by fears of offending, desires to manipulate, or unwillingness to reveal your own feelings. For example, if you think your partner is wrong or you feel threatened, you need to say so in your feedback.

Supportive means that your honesty must not become brutality. You need to find ways to soften negative opinions without destroying their meaning. For example, you might say "I think maybe you made a mistake" instead of "You really blew it this time." Or you could say "I'm feeling insecure about you leaving" instead of "I'll die if you leave me."

Exercises

Listening with Your Body

Your body can encourage your partner by conveying that you're listening. The next time your partner starts to talk to you, follow these simple instructions:

1. Maintain eye contact.

2. Move closer or lean slightly forward.

3. Nod or interject a "yes" or an "uh huh."

4. Smile or frown in sympathy with what is being said.

5. Keep your posture open, facing your partner, arms unfolded and uncrossed.

6. Actively move away from distractions. Turn the radio down, put the magazine away, and so on.

Reciprocal Communication

This simple but powerful exercise may seem very structured and artificial, but try it anyway. Agree to discuss a topic that is a source of mild conflict between you. Take turns being the speaker and the listener.

When you are the speaker:

1. Explain your point of view briefly and succinctly.

2. Talk in terms of yourself and your experience. Use "I" statements to express your feelings and needs.

3. Avoid blame and name calling. No "you" statements about your partner's failings.

Stop after five minutes. Your partner will summarize what you just said. Let your partner know if anything is left out.

When you are the listener:
Pay close attention to really understand your partner's feelings, opinions, and needs.
No disagreeing, arguing, correcting, or talking back.
You may ask questions for clarification only.
After your partner speaks for five minutes, summarize your partner's experience as you heard it. Your partner will add anything you left out, or clarify anything you may have misunderstood. Keep going back and forth until the speaker feels that he or she has been completely heard and understood.

Now switch places, letting the one who was the listener become the speaker and vice versa. Follow the same instructions until the second speaker has been thoroughly listened to and understood.

This is how Art and Evie did this exercise.

Evie:	When I found out that your mom left us ten thousand dollars, I was overjoyed. It felt like we could have some cushion at last. We could pay off the credit cards, get the car fixed, and have something in the bank instead of living from week to week.
Art:	Do you feel like we've been living from week to week?
Evie:	Yes. I know we both make good money, and we don't have any kids to put through college or anything, but it seems like we always spend just a little more than we make. It feels to me like we're always in the red, always a bit behind. That's why I don't want to go to Hawaii or Jamaica or any of those expensive places. I love trips, but I'd love some money in the bank even more. I also feel a little guilty about dragging my feet whenever you bring up the idea of a trip. I mean, she was your mom and in that sense, it's your money to do with what you want.
Art:	Hey, it's a community property state.
Evie:	That's a comment, not a question.
Art:	Sorry.
Evie:	That's okay. I was finished anyway.
Art:	So let me summarize this: You feel nervous about living week-to-week. You want to save the money and not blow it all on trips and stuff. But you feel guilty about telling me what to do with my mom's money.
Evie:	You got the feelings right, but not the plans. I want to pay down the credit cards and get my car fixed. To me that would be money well spent.
Art:	And you'd like to save what's left.
Evie:	Yes. Even if it's enough to go to some exotic beach place, I'd rather save it.
Art:	I got it.

Then it was Art's turn. He explained that his desire to get away wasn't entirely frivolous. After the expense and worry of his mom's illness, he felt drained. He wanted to go somewhere warm and just sit around for a while, get in touch with his grief, and think about being an "orphan" in the world now that both his parents were dead. He also explained that he didn't feel much pressure about being somewhat in debt, since he had a secure job with good chances of advancement.

This exercise was the first time Art really listened to Evie's insecurities about money. And it was the first hint Evie had of how much Art was affected by his mother's death. They eventually compromised by catching up on bills, taking a more modest vacation, and investing some of the money in a mutual fund.

Empathy

Empathy helps you understand your partner's position more clearly. To increase your empathy, consider that both of you are just trying to survive physically and emotionally. Everything you both do—including the violent, inconsiderate, outrageous, or stupid things—is done to minimize pain or threat and maximize pleasure or safety. From this point of view, everything people do is some kind of coping strategy. Some coping strategies are better or more appropriate than others. Some are clearly self-destructive. But all serve the same purpose—to ensure the survival of the self.

In the space below, describe and analyze a disagreement that you frequently have with your partner.

My Position	My Partner's Position

My Coping Strategies	My Partner's Coping Strategies

My Needs	My Partner's Needs

My Fears	My Partner's Fears

Here's how David did this exercise:

My Position	My Partner's Position
I want to stay home and work on my motorcycle this weekend.	Lisa wants us to go away and visit friends.

My Coping Strategies	My Partner's Coping Strategies
I delay talking about it, complain about the expense, get angry, sulk.	Lisa hints, whines, nags, cries, threatens to go without me (without ever intending to).

My Needs	My Partner's Needs
I need relaxation, and time alone, but don't want to look like I'm being selfish.	Lisa needs to be with friends, be with me, feel connected.

My Fears	My Partner's Fears
If I go, I'll be bored, restless, stressed out. If I stay, I'll be guilty.	If we stay home, she'll feel lonely, isolated, unloved, angry. If we go, she'll feel guilty about forcing me.

David shared his analysis with Lisa. His description cleared the air by showing that they both had real and legitimate needs that they were trying to meet and real fears that made them fight desperately for emotional survival. They were able to hear each other better and stay calm enough to compromise and take turns getting what they wanted.

Expressing Feelings and Scripting Needs

This section teaches two related but distinct skills. Expressing feelings is a matter of first identifying and then giving appropriate voice to your emotions. Scripting needs means planning in advance how you will ask for what you want, so that you can be assertive rather than passive or aggressive.

If you are weak in one of these skills, your relationship will be impaired. If you lack both, it may be doomed.

For example, Bill often felt vaguely irritated by the toys and junk mail all over the living room, but he never examined his feelings or tried to express them to his wife Sally. But about every other month he would express his need for more order in his life by going on a rampage. He would shout, "This place is a pigsty!" and then scoop up toys and papers at random and toss them into the trash. Sally and the kids would invariably respond with tears and rage at his uncaring impulses. Remorse would set in and Bill would retire to the garage to cool down. Until the next time.

Identifying Your Feelings

Good or bad? Sometimes a situation makes you feel something, but it's hard to say what that feeling is. In those cases, begin with the simple question, "Is it good or bad?"

Close your eyes, take several slow, deep breaths, and focus on the experience that causes the ambiguous feeling. Is the overall sensation positive or negative? Are you drawn toward the situation or repelled?

Location, size, shape, and color? Once you have decided whether the feeling is good or bad, try to give it a location in your body. Close your eyes again, focus on your breathing, and relax. Scan your body while feeling the feeling. Does it seem to reside in your chest, your stomach, your hands, your neck?

Now concentrate on that area most closely associated with the feeling. How much space does the feeling take up? Is it large or small?

As you begin to get an idea of the size, try to sense a shape. In your mind's eyes, trace the feeling's all-around shape. Is it a regular shape, like a ball or a cone? Or irregular?

What color comes to mind as you contemplate your feeling? Is it a warm red or orange? A cool blue or green?

Don't evaluate or judge your feeling or your performance in this exercise. Just observe whatever comes up for you when you try to identify location, size, shape, and color.

What does it say? Imagine that your feeling can talk by itself. What does it say? Let words come spontaneously, without forcing or judging them. You may hear meaningful clues to the nature of your feeling such as the words loss, gone, unfair, sad, bad, and so on. Or you may hear only silence, or a phrase whose meaning eludes you.

What do you want to do? When you feel this feeling, what action are you drawn to? What do you see yourself doing—running, hugging, hitting, hiding, crying, shaking, screaming? Imagine that you are performing the action. This is just fantasy, so you don't have to restrain your actions the way you might in real life. Let your imagination go.

The action urged by your feeling is a good clue to the nature of the feeling. If you want to hug or comfort someone, you may be feeling sympathy, remorse, love, or desire. If you want to hit or shake someone, you're probably feeling anger or frustration. If you want to cry, hide, or turn away, you may be feeling sadness, depression, or anxiety.

What past experience does it remind you of? Have you had this same feeling before? Let your mind drift to the past and focus on a time when you felt something similar. Who were you with? What was happening? Were you able to identify the feeling? How did you express or fail to express this feeling in the past?

Sometimes it's easier to identify feelings by looking for a repeated pattern in your life. For example, Mary Jean felt ill at ease and distracted. Her husband Bob was out of town and she had a million things to do, but no energy or motivation to do them. She looked into her past and remembered feeling the same way when her college roommate moved away. She realized that she was feeling lonely and abandoned, even though her intellect knew that Bob's business trip was a necessary absence from home.

Name your feelings. By now you should be able to give your feeling a name. The list following can help by reminding you of the many words available to describe feelings. Don't be surprised if you need several words to accurately describe your feeling. Most feelings are combinations of several component feelings.

Go through the list slowly and put a check next to the words that best describe your feeling.

Feelings List

Affectionate	Contemptuous	Enraged	Hopeless
Afraid	Controlled	Exasperated	Horrified
Amused	Curious	Excited	Hostile
Angry	Defeated	Fearful	Impatient
Annoyed	Dejected	Frantic	Inhibited
Anxious	Delighted	Frustrated	Irritated
Apprehensive	Depressed	Fulfilled	Isolated
Bitter	Desirable	Furious	Joyful
Bored	Despairing	Generous	Lonely
Calm	Desperate	Glad	Loved
Capable	Determined	Gloomy	Loving
Cheerful	Devastated	Grateful	Loyal
Comfortable	Disappointed	Great	Melancholy
Competent	Discouraged	Guilty	Miserable
Concerned	Disgusted	Happy	Muddled
Confident	Distrustful	Hateful	Needy
Confused	Embarrassed	Helpless	Nervous

Out of control	Put down	Supportive	Unloved
Outraged	Relaxed	Sympathetic	Upset
Overwhelmed	Relieved	Tender	Uptight
Panicky	Resentful	Terrified	Used
Passionate	Resigned	Threatened	Useless
Peaceful	Sad	Thrilled	Victimized
Pessimistic	Safe	Touchy	Violated
Playful	Satisfied	Trapped	Vulnerable
Pleased	Secure	Troubled	Wonderful
Powerful	Sexy	Unappreciated	Worn out
Prejudiced	Silly	Uncertain	Worried
Pressured	Strong	Understood	Worthwhile
Proud	Stubborn	Uneasy	Yearning
Provoked	Stuck	Unfulfilled	

Feelings diary. For the next week, make a note each time you interact with your partner or think about your partner and you are aware of a particular feeling. This practice will train you in noticing and clarifying your feelings from moment to moment. Here's how Diane kept her diary.

Date	Situation	Feeling
8/3	Keith mowed over my poppies	Enraged, sad
8/4	Keith brought me flowers to apologize for mowing the poppies	Loved, tender, resigned
8/4	Wanting to visit my nieces upstate, knowing Keith won't want to go	Nervous, apprehensive, irritated
8/5	Talking about visiting nieces	Upset, put down, guilty
8/7	Driving upstate alone	Determined, guilty, lonely
8/8	Taking nieces to the zoo, thinking about how much more fun it would be if Keith were with us	Sad, depressed
8/9	Explaining why Uncle Keith didn't come	Embarrassed
8/10	Back home, telling Keith how much fun I had, how I missed him, trying not to beg him to come with me next time	Nervous, suppressed anger

Find a notebook or pad you can carry around with you for a week. You can use the three-column technique that Diane used, or any other format that pleases you.

Expressing Your Feelings

The Key Affective Word

"Affective" means emotional. The first step in expressing your feelings is to pick the key word that describes your emotional state: depressed, angry, anxious, guilty, worried, and so on. The feelings list presented earlier can help in this.

Modifiers

One word does not expression make. You need to expand on the key affective word to define what it means to you, to explain the intensity of your feelings, the duration, the context, and any historical information that will help your partner understand precisely how you feel.

1. Definition. When Joan says "upset," she means that she is very worried and frightened. When her partner Gail says "upset," she means that she feels angry and irritated. You have to define your key affective word to clarify your meaning. Pick synonyms that will make your meaning clear: "I'm annoyed . . . irritated and stressed out." "I feel depressed . . . sad and lonely and not interested in anything." "I'm worried about my job . . . concerned that the company isn't doing well, afraid I'll get laid off."

2. Intensity. Use modifying words or synonyms to express the intensity of your feelings. If you are a little angry, say "a little" or "slightly." Choose synonyms that denote mild anger: "annoyed, irritated." If you are extremely angry, say so, or choose synonyms that make the intensity of your anger clear: "enraged, outraged, furious."

3. Duration. Explain how long you have been feeling this way: "all my life," "since last week," or "after I got up this morning." Seeing your feelings in a time frame can be another indicator that helps your partner gauge the seriousness or intensity of your feelings.

4. Cause and context. Avoid describing your partner as the cause of your feelings:

"You made me so mad."

"I'm worried about your reckless spending habits."

"You left me here all alone and I got depressed."

It's very tempting to blame your partner for any negative feelings you may be experiencing. This is especially true if your bad feelings really do stem directly from some unfair or inconsiderate action by your partner. But blame never solves problems. When you identify your partner as the cause of your unhappiness, your partner hears only the blame, not the unhappy feelings. Your partner is moved to self-defense, not sympathy and problem solving.

It's better to choose your words carefully so that you describe the context of your feelings without directly ascribing blame or causation:

"I felt mad after you broke the dishes."

"When I get an overdraft notice from the bank, I get very worried."

"When I was home alone today, I started to get depressed."

5. Historical precedents. Often it is helpful to share what this feeling reminds you of—some time in your past when you felt the same way.

"It feels like the time my first wife left me."

"I haven't been this confused since I was applying to graduate school."

"I remember feeling like this when my mother was in the hospital."

6. Putting it all together. Here's how Alicia put these steps together.

"I feel very angry (key affective word). I'm upset and disappointed and I really feel let down (definition). This trip was a big deal for me (intensity). The moment I realized that you had forgotten to make the reservations (duration), I had this sinking feeling, just like when my sister didn't show up for my birthday (historical precedent). When I don't get something I've been counting on (context), it really hits me hard."

Exercise

In the space below, express one of your common feelings fully, using the key affective word and each type of modifier. Write in short, complete sentences and in a conversational style. Don't hesitate to connect modifier sentences that go together in the same way that Alicia did with her expression. Imagine that your statement is a short speech you'll be making. Read the complete statement out loud to see how it sounds.

Key affective word:

Definition:

Intensity:

Duration:

Cause and context:

Historical precedents:

Guidelines for Expressing Your Feelings

These four guidelines are the best insurance that you will express your feelings clearly and that your partner will remain receptive.

1. Use "I" statements. Take responsibility for your feelings by using "I" statements rather than "you" statements. Notice how blaming these "you" statements sound:

"You make me furious."

"You're driving me crazy."

"You never let me get a word in."

Recast as "I" statements, these versions are less inflammatory, put responsibility for the feelings on the speaker, and are much more likely to be heard:

"I'm furious."

"I feel confused and crazy."

"I want to talk now."

Beware of the "you" statement in "I" statement clothing: "I feel that you are a jerk" does not qualify as a legitimate "I" statement. When you hear the word "that" in an "I" statement, it is usually a disguised "you" statement.

Take a moment right now to change the following "you" statements into "I" statements in the space provided.

"You never pay any attention to me."

"I feel that you are an hysterical nitpicker."

"Your careless spending habits make me furious."

2. Be honest. It is tempting to describe dinner with your in-laws as "fine, very pleasant," when actually you were bored and irritated the whole evening. It is tempting to say that you're tired and just want to go to bed when actually you are worried about the kids and afraid to broach the subject. It is tempting to invent important work you must do in the office when actually you just want to be alone.

Resist the temptation to describe your feelings in ways that manipulate or distort or hide the truth. When you cut your partner off from your true feelings, you also cut yourself off and make it that much harder to genuinely express emotions.

3. Be congruent. It's very confusing when your tone of voice and body language don't match your words. If you say "I'm sad" while you're smiling and dancing around, which is your partner supposed to believe, your words or your actions?

If you notice that your body language is incongruent with your statements, this may indicate that you actually do feel differently about the topic than you think you do. Spend some more time looking inside and see how you really feel. On the other hand, you may just have developed a habit of smiling when you deliver bad news or frowning when joking or some other incongruent style. If necessary, practice in front of a mirror until your posture, tone of voice, gestures, and so on match the way you feel.

Scripting Your Needs

You have a right to ask for the things you need in your relationship. In fact, you have a responsibility to yourself and to your partner to be clear about your needs. You are the expert on yourself. No one else, not even your partner, can read your mind and know what you need in the way of support, intimate contact, time alone, domestic order, independence, sex, love, financial security, and so on.

On the other hand, everyone else, especially your partner, is trying to get his or her own needs met. Your needs don't have automatic priority. You have a right to ask, but that doesn't necessarily mean that you are entitled to everything you ask for. You have to balance your right to seek your needs with your partner's right. Your needs may at times be in conflict: you want the sedan and your partner wants the pickup, you want another child and your partner thinks that two are enough, you want to move for better employment opportunities and your partner wants to stay in the same neighborhood. Compromise and cooperation are often the essential keys to resolving conflicting needs.

Exercise

It's best to write out your request ahead of time. This sounds very artificial, but it's important. When you have a serious need that you want your partner's help in satisfying, it's always worth the time it takes to write out your request first. You will get things clear in your mind, and, most importantly, you can make sure that your communication has all the elements of a good request. Use the needs script that follows to make sure that you have included the situation, your feelings, your request for behavior change, and your self-care alternative if appropriate.

Needs Script

Situation (specific, objective description of facts):

Feelings (non-blaming "I" statements):

Request (for behavior change):

Self-care alternative (how you could take care of yourself):

Guidelines for Scripting Your Needs

The situation. Be very objective. Describe just the facts, without analysis or interpretation. Avoid inflammatory language. Don't say, "This place is a dump." Instead, just say, "Sometimes there are dirty dishes in the sink and dirty clothes on the floor."

Feelings. Apply all you have learned in the first part of this chapter to clearly express your feelings.

Request. Ask for a change in behavior only. This is a very important rule. Don't expect your partner to change his or her values, attitudes, desires, motivations, or feelings. These characteristics are very hard to change. It's like asking someone to be taller or more intelligent. People feel personally threatened if you ask them to try to change intangibles that are seen as part of their very nature and largely beyond their conscious control. For example, what does it mean to ask someone to be "more loving" or "less critical" or "neater"? These kinds of requests are heard as attacks, and little real change is likely to result.

Stick to observable behavior. If you want your spouse to be more loving, describe the actions that loving means to you: "Hug me when I come in the door." "Sit next to me on the couch when we watch TV." "Take me out for dinner on my birthday." If you want your partner to be less critical, you're going to have to spell out the desired behavior: "Don't kid me about the phone bill or my driving when other people are around." "Don't comment on my driving in the car, and help me pay the bills this month so we can balance the checkbook together." If you want someone to be neater, put it in terms of desired behaviors: "Put all dirty clothes in the hamper, hang up the tools when you're done with them, and bundle all the newspapers by Wednesday night."

Don't ask for too much all at once. Sigmund told his longtime girlfriend Robin that he was willing to marry her if she would do 135 sit-ups a day to tighten her stomach muscles, allow him to buy her a more stylish wardrobe, read fewer novels so she could pay more attention to him, and send her son to therapy. His excessive demands broke up the relationship.

You have to stick to one situation and just one or two behavioral changes at a time. A laundry list of changes will be overwhelming to your partner. Concentrate on one request, get agreement, and try the new arrangement for a while before you go on to ask for something else.

Your self-care alternative. This is otherwise known as the "or else." Your self-care alternative is what you intend to do for yourself if your partner isn't willing to grant your needs request. For example, if you are tired of doing the dishes by yourself every night, but your partner doesn't agree to help you, your self-care alternative might be to stop going out to the movies on Fridays and use the savings to buy a dishwasher.

A self-care alternative isn't meant to be a punitive ultimatum. Your alternative is meant to be your plan for solving a problem if you can't get your partner's help in a preferred solution.

Don't spring your alternative right away. Save it until you see how negotiations are proceeding. But have an alternative ready, just in case.

Here is how Ben scripted his need for time alone.

Situation: Since we started the tax-preparing business, we've been spending almost all our time together. I notice that I don't read or listen to music by myself like I used to.

Feelings: I really enjoy working together, and I feel like we're closer than we've been in years. But I've also been feeling a little stressed out and nervous, like I'm on stage all the time or under pressure.

Request: I need a little time each week by myself. What do you think about reserving one morning or one afternoon a week for things we can do separately? For instance, I'd like to get my camera out on Saturday and go off to take some pictures.

There are several things to notice about Ben's statements:

- He keeps the facts of the situation separate from the feelings.

- There is no blame. He uses "I" statements that take responsibility for his feelings.

- His request is specific and behavioral in nature. Rather than saying "I want you to stop breathing down my neck and talking about the business all the time," he requests an afternoon off.

- Although he didn't need to mention it, he had a self-care alternative in mind. If necessary, he planned to enroll in a meditation class so that he would have a set time each week to be off on his own without his partner.

When you have your request polished and ready, pick a time to talk to your partner. Make sure that he or she has the time and is in the frame of mind to listen attentively to your request. Commit yourself to a calm, cool request. Any tone of anger or irritation will severely limit your chances of getting what you want.

If you run into resistance with your first request and your self-care alternative doesn't work, see the chapter on negotiation for help in resolving conflicts.

Reciprocal Reinforcement

Relationships can gradually run down. Early pleasures become commonplace and boring. Minor flaws become major faults. Charming eccentricities become incredibly irritating. To counteract this trend, you need to give each other new pleasures from time to time. Reciprocal reinforcement can help.

Reciprocal reinforcement simply means that each person does more of the things that the other person likes—small, obvious things such as back rubs, washing dishes, giving flowers, fixing a lamp, making a favorite dessert, or returning a video tape.

This sounds too simple to be a serious therapeutic technique, but it works. If your relationship has become boring, irritating, and unsatisfying, reciprocal reinforcement may be the ideal starting place. It has five advantages:

1. It establishes collaboration—you will both be working together to make improvements.

2. It works fast, increasing pleasure, commitment, and caring immediately.

3. It builds confidence by giving each of you a sense of control over the relationship.

4. It's easy—you don't have to learn any new skills. You already know how to cook favorite dishes, give a hug, make a phone call, or attend a PTA meeting.

5. It can set the stage for future change on more significant, long-standing issues.

Week One—Make Pleasers List

For one week, carry around a piece of paper and a pen. Keep a running list of what pleases you and what pleases your partner. Add to your list whenever you think of something. If you forget during the day, be sure to add something to your list before retiring each night.

Look for pleasers in these areas of your relationship:

Considerate acts

Sensuality, touching

Communications process

Leisure activities

Child care

Household management

Financial decision making

Employment

Education

Personal habits

Appearance

Independence

Guidelines for Reciprocal Reinforcement

1. Omit items that have been areas of serious conflict for you. If most of your arguments involve money, leave out financial matters.

2. Cross out items involving giant expenses or effort. The ideal pleaser costs nothing and is easy to do, like a kiss. New cars, losing weight, and major remodeling should not be on your pleasers list.

3. Don't include anything you are not really willing to do. For example, don't plan to visit your mother-in-law in a rest home daily or to itemize all your personal expenses unless you are really willing to do those things.

4. Add details to be more specific. For example, "Refinish the green dresser" is more detailed than "Spruce up the house." "Shave Saturday and Sunday mornings" is more specific than "Improve grooming."

5. Use wording that focuses on behaviors, not attitudes. For instance, "Hug her when I come in the door" is a specific behavior, while "Be more loving" is a vague attitude. "Consult him on New Year's party plans" is an obvious behavior that you can remember to perform, whereas "Be less bossy" describes a change in attitude that is much harder to act on.

Keep track of what pleases you and your partner until you have at least ten items for each of you. Rank each item according to this scale:

1 = Nice

2 = Better

3 = Great

Example. Rod and Linda developed the following lists over the course of a week.

Rod's List

Pleases me

Offer a drink and a hug when I come home   3

Leave me alone in front of TV for 15 minutes before dinner   3

Dump garbage daily   1

Keep cat out of our bedroom   3

Kiss good night   2

Leave notes—where she's gone, when she will return   3

Write full information in checkbook   2

Wear my favorite perfume   1

Dance together in the living room   2

Pleases her

Fix things   3

Hugs   2

Eat more veggies   2

Pay attention to her stories   1

Birthday and anniversary gifts   3

Refinish dresser   2

Wax her car   2

Notice her outfits, give compliments   2

Support her Weight Watchers efforts   2

Make my own breakfast   1

Do recycling   2

Be nice to her sister   3

Linda's List

Pleases me

Hugs   2

Compliments   3

Pay attention, check in daily   3

Keep up yard   1

Listen to my opinions and let me know he understands what I'm saying   2

Cook his own breakfast   1

Clean up closet   1

Keep books and magazines off couch   3

More affectionate touches that don't lead to sex   3

Take cooking course   2

Notice when I look good   3

More balanced meals when he cooks   3

Pleases him

Perfume   3

Initiate sex   2

Meat and potatoes   3

Balance my own checkbook   3

Hugs and kisses   1

Neck rub   1

Keep kitchen tidier   2

Help with yard work   3

Watch TV with him   1

Be quiet when he's reading   2

Return his library books   1

Don't share your lists with each other until the end of week two. Unexpected pleasures are doubly satisfying. And at this stage you shouldn't raise your partner's expectations about what you plan to do, just in case you forget to provide some of the pleasers you have planned.

Week Two—Provide Pleasers

Based on your revised list, pick four or five highly rated items that you are willing to provide. Look for things that you have not been doing recently, pleasers that it will be easy for you to give. Every day of the next week, give your partner at least one item from your list that you think will be most pleasing.

Set a modest target number of pleasers that is a little higher than the number you were providing before. For example, if you usually do three things a week that your partner likes, plan to do one thing per day for this week. Start slow and don't try to become a perfect mate overnight.

Keep track. At the end of each day, write down the pleasers you performed and the ones you received. Don't try to second-guess yourself or your partner—include everything pleasing that you do or have done for you, even things that you and your partner "would have done anyway."

Keep track, but don't keep score. There may be discrepancies in the average number of pleasers already existing or being added in this week. There is really no way to tell if this is a reflection of one person putting out more effort, or a perception problem on the part of the other partner. Don't compare rates and make it a cause for argument. Assume that any apparent discrepancy is a mutual problem: one partner has trouble giving enough pleasers and the other has trouble perceiving and reinforcing pleasers. Concentrate on meeting your own target. You can depend on the fact that when you find the pleasers that really work, you will start getting pleasers coming back from your partner.

Don't tell each other what you have picked from your lists. Just give what you think will be pleasing to your partner and see what happens for a week.

In the second week of their experiment with reciprocal reinforcement, Rod hugged Linda several times, complimented her on how well she was doing with her Weight Watchers program, fixed a vegetarian meal, repaired her umbrella, and washed her Pontiac. Linda helped with some yard work, gave Rod a neck rub, made two meat and potato meals, joined Rod in front of the TV news, and kissed him good night when she went to bed first.

Feedback. At the end of week two, give honest feedback to each other about which pleasers you noticed and appreciated the most. It's important to let your partner know which pleasers worked and that you appreciate the effort in general. Giving positive feedback is essential to keep the flow of satisfaction coming your way. If you find giving feedback awkward or can't remember everything that happened, just read your daily lists of pleasers received to each other.

When Linda and Rod gave each other feedback, they learned some interesting things. They both appreciated the hugs. Linda especially valued Rod's vegetarian dinner, but she didn't even notice that Rod had fixed her umbrella. Rod appreciated help with the yard work and the neck rub, but found that watching the TV news together was irrelevant to him. He realized that his TV watching was a way of avoiding contact with Linda, not a relaxing activity in itself.

Week Three—Ask for Pleasers

At the beginning of this week, each of you gets to ask for three special things that you want the other to do during the next seven days. Be sure to follow these important guidelines:

1. The items should come from your lists. If you must ask for a new, untried pleaser, it should be very similar to the pleasers you already know are satisfying and easy to give.

2. Be specific. "Put all dirty clothes in the hamper and shoes away in the closet" is better than "Keep the bedroom neater."

3. Ask for behaviors, not attitudes. "Give me a nicely wrapped birthday present, with a card, on time" is better than "Be more caring."

4. No blaming. Be careful to make your requests in a way that doesn't imply blame. "Keep a running balance in the checkbook" is better than "Stop throwing away money we don't even have."

5. Pick behaviors that have no negative emotional history. Reciprocal reinforcement will improve your day-to-day relationship and prepare you to tackle your heaviest problems, but it will not solve them by itself.

6. Pick behaviors that can be performed at minimal cost and effort.

7. No negotiating at this point. When your partner asks you to do something, just say whether you are willing and how likely you are to do it. If you are unlikely to do it, your partner should pick another item. If your partner is unwilling or unlikely to do what you would like, don't press, don't even ask why. Just pick something else.

When Rod and Linda made their requests, Linda opted for compliments about things she does around the house, more affectionate touches, and for Rod to make his own breakfast. Rod wanted a hug when he got home, the cat kept out of the bedroom, and notes left by Linda whenever she would be gone.

Evaluation. At the end of the week, evaluate by asking yourselves these questions:

• Was each requested pleaser carried out?

• Was it satisfying?

• How did each of you feel?

• If it wasn't done or wasn't satisfying, why not?

• Did one of you do something to undermine the interaction?

• Did you ask for something you didn't really care about?

• Did you agree to something you weren't really willing to do?

• Did you discount a pleaser because it was done by agreement and not spontaneously?

If a pleaser didn't pan out, don't blame anybody. Just don't ask for it again. Save it for later problem solving at a time when your relationship is stronger. There is probably some underlying conflict that prevents easy reciprocal reinforcement.

When Linda and Rod evaluated their week, they had managed to perform all their pleasers, and most were satisfying. Rod noticed that he actually enjoyed the touching without sex, although he had assumed it would be meaningless or frustrating. Linda found that leaving notes about where she was and when she'd be back was difficult. At first it felt like she was giving up some of her independence. Then Rod thanked her for making it easier for him to plan his activities and explained that he felt more secure knowing how to find her in an emergency. Linda realized that the notes were a communication tool, not a way of controlling or judging her. Rod realized that to keep getting the notes, he had to express his appreciation once in a while and refrain from criticizing how she spent her time.

Week Four—Exchange Contracts

You now have a repertoire of pleasers that you both enjoy receiving and are willing and able to give. You are ready to codify your best pleasers in the form of a contract. List what you will do and when and how often you will do it. Limit your contract to two or three really important behaviors at first. Put your contract where you will see it frequently and be reminded of your agreement. Keep the contract in force for a week, then open it up for renegotiation. Change or add pleasers.

Here is the contract that Rod and Linda developed:

I, Rod, will compliment Linda on her dress or appearance and things she does around the house. I'll cook my own breakfast. I will listen to Linda without interruption when she has an opinion and I'll let her know that I understand what she's saying.

I, Linda, will keep the cat out of the bedroom, give Rod a hug when he gets home, and give him time to relax quietly right after work.

They posted their contract on the inside of their medicine cabinet door, where they would see it a couple of times every day. Note that some of the items had changed from week three because they wanted to try some new things from their lists.

Week Five—Mutual Pleasers

If your exchange contract works out, you're ready to move up to mutual pleasers. Plan to do more activities together that both of you consider pleasurable. This can be the most powerful form of reciprocal reinforcement because you are working with each other rather than for each other. Mutual pleasers are especially good for busy people with divergent interests and those who have been avoiding each other to avoid conflict.

Start by each writing down possible activities on a list and then combine the lists into one list. The rules of brainstorming apply here: anything goes on the list at first, no matter how crazy or unlikely. No criticism is allowed. Just generate as many ideas as you can, regardless of their apparent merit. Often two poor ideas can be combined into one good idea, or a wildly impractical notion might make you think of a really creative and more likely activity. Don't hold back in fear of sounding ridiculous and don't ridicule your partner's suggestions.

When looking for mutual pleasers, consider things you used to enjoy together but haven't done in a long time. For instance, if you met on the horse trail but haven't been riding in years, try a short ride together.

Another promising area is to look for new hobbies and avocations you can explore together—things neither of you has done before: antique collecting, skin diving, tennis, singing, political action, and so on. Learning and exploring something new can be less threatening than just planning to be alone together, with no particular focus. Also, a new activity will have no history of failure or contention for you as a couple.

Avoid things you have tried recently that didn't work. If you have been fighting every time you attend one of your daughter's soccer games, don't choose your children's sporting activities as a mutual interest to develop. Let such activities slide in favor of something genuinely interesting to both of you.

Once you have settled on a shared activity to try, nail down the details: when, where, how long, baby-sitting, rescheduling time conflicts, making reservations, how you will pay for it, and so on. It's all too easy to agree to go on a bird-watching hike some time, then never get around to it.

There are a few hurdles that you may need to watch out for:

1. If one of you typically makes all the social arrangements, make sure that the other one takes some active role in setting up your mutual pleaser.

2. If one or both of you tend to agree just to be agreeable, make sure you each genuinely want to do the activity you choose. It won't work if one of you "goes along" with the other's plan, or if one of you says yes to an activity just because it is too hard to say no.

3. Watch out for hidden agendas. Rachel got Henry to go for a long walk in the woods, ostensibly to get some exercise and enjoy nature together. Rachel's hidden agenda was to use the time alone to quiz Henry about his level of commitment to their relationship. Henry ended up feeling trapped and fooled and angry. Rachel ended up feeling sneaky and disappointed.

Excerpted and adapted with permission from *Couple Skills: Making Your Relationship Work* by Matthew McKay, Ph.D., Patrick Fanning, and Kim Paleg, Ph.D. For more information on this and related books, see the "Further Reading" section in the back of the book.

CHAPTER 2

Sex

Sensual and sexual activity is one important way to express feelings toward a partner. Whether you want to enhance your sexual intimacy or you want to address sexual difficulties you are facing, the exercises in this chapter can be of great benefit.

Sensate Focus Exercises

Sensate focus means to focus your attention on the sensations you experience during sensual or sexual activity. Sensate focus exercises are designed to gradually teach a series of erotic, stimulating, and pleasurable experiences in touch during sexual activity. They were first developed in the 1960s by Masters and Johnson as part of a treatment program for couples experiencing sexual problems. Since then, many clinicians have elaborated on the original exercises. With sensate focus, the couple practices a series of exercises in the privacy of their home consisting of physical touching and caressing with gradually increasing levels of sexual arousal. These exercises are deceptively simple and straightforward, but they often evoke strong emotional responses from one or both partners. The couple discusses their reactions to the exercises in order to tease apart the different components of sexuality, as well as to identify sexual strengths and difficulties. As the couple continues to do sensate focus exercises, the sexual problem is further illuminated, including its origins relative to each partner, the couple's behaviors that maintain it, and the resources required to fix it.

One purpose of sensate focus is to decrease, or eliminate, the anxiety that results from having to perform sexually. A therapist will sometimes recommend a ban on sexual intercourse and orgasm for a short while to remove the pressure to perform. In this way, sensual pleasure becomes the focus of sexual activity and fear of failure is removed.

Why is this ban so important? With goal-directed sex, everything you do is part of the plan to reach the end of the sexual experience with simultaneous orgasm during intercourse. This unrealistic expectation creates pressure and anxiety for both partners. Without performance goals, partners can focus on the emotional and sensual experience.

It is often helpful to use the relaxation techniques described in the chapter on stress in part V before attempting the sensate focus exercises. Deep muscle relaxation and deep breathing will help you achieve a state of relaxed but energized openness to these sensual experiences.

Sometimes relaxation techniques are also helpful if you become anxious during an exercise. If this should happen, you can stop and take several relaxing breaths during which you focus on the part of your body where you notice tension, pain, or unpleasant sensations. Imagine sending your breath to the place where you hold the unpleasant sensations; often this will relax you enough to continue with the sensate focus.

Sensate focus does not have to involve a total ban on sexual activity, but should initially be kept separate from regular lovemaking. You will find that the relaxation and serene pleasure of sensate focus can eventually be integrated with regular sexual activity as anxiety and fear of failure are removed.

A second purpose of sensate focus is for partners to learn how to touch each other in pleasurable, erotic ways. The most common complaint that women have about making love is that their partners do not spend enough time with foreplay. As couples progress with sensate focus, they also learn how to both give and receive sensual pleasure. This mutuality is important for couples who normally approach sex with rigid roles that prescribe which partner does what to whom. It also helps restore balance to any power struggles during sex, making it easier for both partners to share sensual touches on equal footing.

Despite the initial appeal of sensate focus exercises to most couples, at some point one or both partners may resist carrying them out or cooperating with each other. Discussion of this resistance often reveals previously unrecognized emotions about sex, one's self, and one's partner. Take note of sensory numbing, fleeting thoughts and feelings, distracting images, body sensations, and negative feelings and attitudes that occur during sensate focus. If there is a clear pattern to the way in which one partner reports their reactions or resists sensate focus, a characteristic defense mechanism may be revealed. For example, one partner may always blame the other for lack of progress, when in reality they are defending themselves against performance anxiety or self-blame by projecting it onto the partner. As the sensate focus exercises continue, the origins and progression of sexual problems become more clear.

Many people are able to use these steps toward the goal of sexual pleasure without the help of a therapist. However, others need the help of an objective person to understand the roadblocks standing in the way of progress. A sex therapist will help to maximize the benefit of these exercises—by selecting an approach, adding or subtracting elements, and adjusting the pace and structure of learning to fit each individual person.

Who initiates sex? Who follows?

Before you begin sensate focus exercises, you will have to talk about who initiates activity in general, who follows, who opposes, and/or who refuses to engage. All couples have a process, often out of their conscious awareness, by which they relate to each other both sexually and nonsexually. For instance, if one person always initiates social plans and the other always says no, that may occur sexually as well. There are many ways to learn about how your process works; first try the following exercise.

1. Who usually initiates sex—you or your partner? What percentage of the time do each of you initiate sexual activity?

2. Has your role changed over the course of the relationship? If so, how?

_____

_____

3. What factors affect your role and your partner's role both as initiator and as follower?

_____

_____

4. Role-play with your partner: Each of you take turns going through the motions of initiating sexual activity. What do you do? Do you ask for sex? Do you start with actions, such as a caress or a kiss? Is there no clear pattern?

_____

_____

5. Switch roles and try to imitate, in a respectful way, how you think your partner initiates sex. This gives both of you a chance to see what the experience is like for the other. What did you learn?

_____

_____

6. Demonstrate how you both would like the other to initiate sex. Then show each other how you would like to be turned down. This can avoid a sequence of hurt feelings and emotional withdrawal.

_____

_____

7. Practice how you would ask for affectionate touch only, with no sex to follow. How does this feel?

_____

_____

8. Take turns describing what you experience when you are the follower and when you are the initiator.

_____

_____

9. Write down how you feel about the following situations. Refer to the list of possible emotional reactions or use your own descriptions:

Sample emotions: happy, elated, excited, apprehensive, nervous, fearful, upset, numb, sad, angry, confused, furious, horny, turned off, put off.

Initiating sex

You: _____

Your Partner: _____

Being asked for sex

You: _____

Your Partner: _____

Agreeing to sex

You: _____

Your Partner: _____

Refusing sex

You: _____

Your Partner: _____

Being turned down

You: _____

Your Partner: _____

It is very important to be clear when you are asking for physical affection only, as opposed to when you would welcome a sexual encounter. Often people mix up these two activities and cut themselves off from the pleasures of hugging, holding, kissing, and caressing because they worry it will lead to sex. Some couples have nonverbal signals, while others have a private language to make it clear. But for couples having trouble with sex, it is especially important to let your partner know what you do and don't want. In sex therapy, the therapist helps a couple work out the details of initiating and responding. Decisions are made about how often to do the exercises, who will start, and how to say "yes" or "no" to a partner's request. If a person has a low sex drive, this may be due partly to not noticing internal as well as external cues that might increase desire. A partner with low desire may need to be willing to begin a sensate focus assignment even when they do not feel interested in sex. As these sensual exercises progress, interest usually grows.

Many couples often feel pressure to move quickly through these exercises, hoping for an instant cure to their problem. We caution against this attitude. In the beginning it is best to err on the side of being conservative, in order to enhance relaxation and de-emphasize sexual goals. Taking small steps is always more successful than attempting huge leaps and possibly failing. You will probably try to go too fast sometimes and then feel disappointed. If this happens, break down the exercise into smaller components. For example, if touching the whole body is too much, start with a neck or hand massage.

You should negotiate a contract with your partner, with respect to how you will initiate the sensate focus exercises, how often, when and where, and under what circumstances. It is critical to determine this before beginning and to allow some flexibility. Plans can temporarily go awry, but the important thing is that you do it at some point or another. Realistically, you should be able to find time at least once a week, preferably for an hour. If possible, three times a week is optimal. Weekends usually offer more flexible time schedules. Do not worry about spontaneity for these exercises: you may even find it is best to "schedule" an exercise like you would schedule any appointment.

Sensate Focus I—Nonsexual Touching Exercises

The first level of sensate focus is an experience of nonsexual touching and an emotional and physical experience of mutual trust. Sensate focus I is designed to provide a relaxing time for you and your partner with no pressure to perform. This exercise does not include sexual touching or intercourse. As with any intimate experience, you need time to make the transition into close connection. Before you begin, select a comfortable, warm, quiet, and private place in your home.

Consider taking the phone off the hook and lowering the lights. Set a relaxing mood, perhaps with soft music, candles, a warm breeze from a window—anything that you both find comforting. Most people like to shower or bathe beforehand, either separately or together. For some couples, feeling fresh and clean will enhance the moment. Warm water relaxes the body and eases tension. It is common to feel uneasy when you do this exercise.

If you decide to shower or bathe together, take your time, and be playful, close, tender, and affectionate, finding your own special way to relate to each other. You may want to start the first exercise being fully clothed or perhaps wearing what you wear to sleep. If you usually sleep together nude, you can start that way. When you have settled into your comfortable space and have eliminated distractions, you are ready to begin.

Once you begin, use this experience as a nonverbal way to feel connected. Keep talk to a minimum. Decide who will be the first giver. Lie together for a few moments to slow down and try to settle into the experience. This exercise does not lead to sexual touching or intercourse. You may experience a sense of uneasiness as you begin to open yourself up to intimate or tender feelings. This is a normal feeling for anyone as they learn new things, especially as they allow themselves to surrender to an intimate exchange. Paying attention to your breathing can help you focus on the exercise at hand. Begin selecting a giver and a receiver.

Instructions for the Giver

The giver should begin by rubbing their hands together to warm them and generate energy. Caress your partner gently, starting with the head and touching the entire body to the feet. This touching is meant to be sensuous, not sexual. In other words, it is meant to stimulate in a comfortable and pleasurable, but not directly sexual, way. Take your time as you touch and caress your partner. Try a variety of touches: use both the palms and the backs of your hands, gently scratch with your nails, caress with your hair or lips, or use your whole body to touch your partner. You can start with long, deep strokes at first, gradually lightening the touch. Use your fingertip like a feather, touching lightly over your partner's body, barely stroking the skin with light touches. Pay attention to the rhythms of your touch. Give full attention to the face and neck, touching behind the ears, on the eyelids, on the lips, and on the neck. Touch the palms of their hands, bottoms of their feet, backs of their knees, backs of their elbows—every delicate place you can find. Avoid the genitals and specific body regions that are potentially sexually arousing (such as breasts, inner buttocks, and inner thighs) even if you feel ready for such stimulation. The point of this first exercise is to eliminate any sense that sexual excitement is the goal.

To end this exercise, use a massage technique to integrate the whole experience. Starting at the top of the head and using your fingers loosely relaxed, stroke down over all the surfaces of your partner's body. Think of your hands as gentle, soft brooms, sweeping delightful energy evenly over your partner's body. End with their hands and feet. This first sensate focus exercise is not a test of your massage abilities, nor is it an endurance contest. Maintain awareness of your own experience. Focus on your own feelings rather than on whether your partner is enjoying the touching. The receiver will give you feedback if necessary.

If you find yourself getting distracted or bored, shift to a different stroke. Think about what feelings you would have if you removed the boredom. Pay attention to the energy you feel coming from your partner and notice their muscle tension and strength, skin texture, hair, and the soft contours of their body.

Sometimes touching causes worry to surface in either the giver or receiver. If you feel tense, notice where you hold the tension in your body, and then breathe in through your nose while you imagine your breath is carrying healing energy and relaxation to those areas. Focus on relaxing the tension and notice how you feel more alive to touch as you relax. Use your breathing to stay in touch with your partner and yourself. If you slow down and concentrate on your own experience, chances are your partner will like it. It is often the case that when a receiver complains, it is because the giver has not been actually focusing on the touching, but thinking, worrying, or daydreaming about something else.

Instructions for the Receiver

The receiver should lie on their stomach and focus on the feelings of the moment. Let the distractions of the day go. Sometimes breathing easily and focusing attention on the exact place you are being touched helps keep your relaxed focus. Don't worry that the giver is getting tired or bored. Stay with your physical sensations. Tell your partner to change only if what is happening is unpleasant or hurts. Many women are accustomed to gritting their teeth or cringing if they don't like a particular sexual touch, waiting for it to be over. If you do this you may feel resentful and end up focusing on angry feelings instead of your experience. In this exercise, you have an opportunity to learn new responses. Giving your partner feedback in a way that is not hurtful is an important skill in achieving good sexual relations. Instead of making only a negative comment, try to also suggest something you would like. If you are feeling ticklish, show your partner how to touch you more slowly and firmly, with a deeper pressure.

Using soft tones and gentle language helps let your partner know that it's the touch you're uncomfortable with, not them. For example, suppose the giver touches you in an uncomfortable way. An aversive response would be "Stop that!" or "That hurts!" or "Come on!" This can anger or upset the giver—even when you don't mean it that way. It is hard to relax and enjoy something when you feel angry or rejected. A gentler response would be something like, "Honey, I like it best when you are very gentle on that spot," or "My shoulder is a little sensitive there—try rubbing softly." You must provide the giver with gentle feedback and this can require some practice.

Jenny and Steven

Talking it out beforehand, Jenny complained that Steven's touch felt like a "window wiper," and her skin began to hurt when he didn't move his hand from her abdomen. Steven realized that he was anxious because Jenny never gave any indication of how he was doing, so he felt too nervous to experiment. They agreed that she would moan and sigh enough so he could tell he was on the right track. This was hard at first for Jenny who had always been embarrassed to make any noises during sex. She started off by making noises very quietly, until she felt comfortable to be more audible. Steven felt more relaxed and confident with his touching since he knew what Jenny liked. It was a new and exciting thrill for him to know that he was pleasing her. Before long, both felt at ease and agreed that touching had become a wonderfully satisfying experience.

Remember, the giver will succeed most by focusing on their own experience of touching. Here is a suggested model for the exercise in which Jenny and Steven are receiving and giving touch:

Jenny lies on her stomach. Steven massages for ten minutes.

Steven lies on his stomach. Jenny massages for ten minutes.

Jenny lies on her back. Steven massages for ten minutes.

Steven lies on his back. Jenny massages for ten minutes.

They engage in pillow talk for ten minutes (see the following section on pillow talk).

Alternative: Steven massages both sides of Jenny for a total of twenty minutes, and then they switch.

If you wish, change places and do the exercise a second time. The suggested times are only that—feel free to agree on your own timetable. We do recommend spending at least forty-five minutes on the exercise.

Pillow Talk

After completing each of the sensate focus exercises, it is important to talk about the experience for ten to fifteen minutes to provide each other with feedback. This talking can increase intimacy, improve communication, and build confidence. If either of you have difficulty with the exercise, you may need to discuss this with a therapist. Again, this exercise can reveal many of the reasons why you are having sexual fear or pain. Resistance and roadblocks should be greeted as opportunities and challenges to learn more about yourself and your partner and to work toward a resolution.

Here is a chance for you to be honest about what you feel. Try to speak in the first person, so that your partner will not feel hurt or insulted. Here are several examples:

Instead of saying . . .	Try saying . . .
That tickles!	*I feel ticklish.*
Ouch! That hurts!	*It hurts when you touch my neck that way.*
Quit making me feel nervous.	*I feel nervous about doing this.*
You're bothering me and making me angry.	*I feel angry and I want to stop and talk.*

This type of communication accomplishes several things. First, it removes the accusation directed at your partner and doesn't put them on the defensive. It makes you responsible for your own feelings, helping you to identify and own them. Then your partner may feel less rejected and more willing to listen and respond to your needs and requests. It is important to give both positive and negative feedback, usually starting with the positive. Often it seems difficult to tell your partner something negative, so to ensure that you are sharing true feelings, plan to mention at least two pleasant and two unpleasant types of touch. This will lead to increased intimacy if both of you can trust each other's honest responses. This is an improvement on "Everything you do feels great."

Typical Responses

Some people have a positive experience with these exercises and feel closer to their partner. They may even feel stirrings of sexual excitement that they haven't felt for a long time. If you do feel excitement, it is best not to act on it yet. Try to just enjoy the feelings and trust they will return.

Some people are surprised to discover that they have a negative response. If either you or your partner feels anxious, you may find that you begin to avoid the exercise, either by having a fight, being too busy, or feeling too tired. You may also feel bored, foolish, angry, or ashamed. You might begin to discover that you dislike your body or have a poor body image. You may blame your partner for being insensitive or awkward. You may also feel obligated to turn a sensuous experience into a sexual one, and this focus on sexual goals may cause anxiety, anger, or resentment. If you do have a negative reaction, use some of your relaxation skills. Take several deep, relaxing breaths and breathe into the part of your body where you feel most uncomfortable. Ask your partner to stop for a moment as you breathe. If your eyes were closed, open them and look around to orient yourself to time and place. Stay focused on your feelings and the images that arise, and ask yourself how they contribute to your sexual problem. If you can continue with the exercise, do so. But if you have a strong negative reaction you may need to stop. Never continue with a sexual experience if you are afraid or in pain. Try to discuss the experience with your partner later.

Your Responses to Sensate Focus I

For both partners: In the grids below or on a separate sheet of paper, record your reactions to the sensate focus exercise in your roles as both giver and receiver. What feelings came to mind? What did you like about it? What difficulties arose? Then, write down what you imagine your partner was thinking during the exercises as giver or receiver.

The following is a sample response from a couple.

Your name Leslie

Role	How did you feel?	What worked well?	Problems
Giver	I felt tense and then I gradually relaxed	I liked using different strokes on his back	Couldn't tell if Mike enjoyed it
Receiver	I felt embarrassed	Liked scalp massage	Felt ticklish
Partner as giver	He felt bored	He seemed to enjoy touching me	He thinks I'm fat
Partner as receiver	I don't know	He liked back massage	I don't know

Partner's name Mike

Role	How did you feel?	What worked well?	Problems
Giver	Tense mostly	I liked her softness	I didn't know what to do when she felt tickled
Receiver	Felt great	I liked the whole massage	None
Partner as giver	Happy	She was really creative	No problems
Partner as receiver	She never wants to receive	She relaxed with the scalp massage	She was so ticklish it was hard to touch her

Your name _____

Role	How did you feel?	What worked well?	Problems
Giver			
Receiver			
Partner as giver			
Partner as receiver			

Partner's name _____

Role	How did you feel?	What worked well?	Problems
Giver			
Receiver			
Partner as giver			
Partner as receiver			

After completing these grids, exchange them with your partner and discuss your reactions. Are you surprised? Are there areas of agreement? disagreement? Talking about the exercise, either alone or in therapy, will help clarify what each of you are experiencing. Try to do this without blaming the other. You may find ways to modulate the exercise, perhaps by adding or subtracting parts or dividing it into smaller segments, to meet your individual needs. Review the following case vignettes for some suggestions:

Plan to do the nonsexual exercises at least twice a week for two to three weeks, or until you both feel relaxed and comfortable during the entire exercise. Don't move on until you have settled into a mutually comfortable pattern of nonsexual touching and communication. There is no time limit. Some couples may feel ready in two weeks—others in two months. You are ready to move on when you begin to feel relaxed enough to focus on your own sensations and enjoy the exercise. If this is not happening, you need to stick with the first exercise and reassess which area needs more work.

Sensate Focus II—Genital Touching to Explore and Arouse

We recommend that you begin sensate focus II like the earlier exercises, by gradually transitioning into a safe haven and leaving other concerns and distractions behind as you focus on the relaxed awareness of sensual touching. You may want to start with a bath or shower for two reasons. Generally, people feel more comfortable if they are clean before they engage in sexual contact. Also, the time you are bathing acts as a transition, allowing you to slow down and get in touch with each other emotionally and physically. Warm water relaxes muscles and eases body tension. Washing your hands and face and brushing your teeth can help you feel clean and refreshed. Some couples make this into a small ritual, using scented soaps or body lotions and wearing special nightclothes or lingerie. The goal is to prepare yourselves for a special, private time. Once you are ready to begin the exercise, lie together and connect at an emotional level before moving into touching. Men and women may differ about the timing of genital touch. Some men say they like genital touch immediately. Most women report that they want other types of caresses first and feel hurried if they don't receive touching all over before their partners begin focusing on their genital areas.

Looking at Each Other's Genitals

This exercise involves a visual examination of each other's genitals. Use a hand mirror so that you both can see the other's genital structures. As you take turns looking at each other, decide what names or labels you want to use; this will facilitate your communication. Some people are comfortable with clinical names, while others prefer to use names they have read or heard, or use private nicknames. There are dozens of words for male genitals, but fewer to describe the different parts of women's genitals. Be creative. Kim named her vagina her "jewel case," and Mary Ann referred to her genitals as her "pretties." These names should have positive connotations—avoid derogatory labels that reinforce unpleasant thoughts or feelings. If your names inspire laughter, such humor may help both of you relax and will lighten the experience. This exercise can improve your communication and reinforce your understanding of genital anatomy. It may also reveal new difficulties: fear of exposure, shame, embarrassment, squeamishness, etc. Take time to discuss problems that arise and ways to resolve them before moving on. Once you both feel comfortable with this exercise, you can move on.

Genital Touching and Exploration

In this exercise, you and your partner will begin a tactile exploration of your bodies. Start with the whole body and gradually focus on the genitals. Basically, you will be repeating the earlier exercise, but you will now include the genital regions. This touching is meant to explore and not to arouse. If you feel aroused, just let it be; arousal will diminish if you don't actively pursue it. Allow yourself to enjoy the sensations of touch without a goal. If you find yourself feeling anxious, ashamed, or other negative emotions, try "breathing into" the area being touched. See if you can stay with the sensations and make the negative feeling diminish. After the exercise is completed, share your experiences. Follow the same schedule you used for sensate focus I, and repeat the same pillow talk exercises.

The Sexological Examination

In this exercise, you will take turns with slow and gentle exploration of each other's genital regions and discover the wide variety of touch available to you. The purpose of this exercise is to teach each other what you like or don't like. This exercise was developed to give people a simple way of expressing their experiences without talking, since it is hard to concentrate on your bodily sensations when you talk. You can indicate what you like with sighs or moans, but it's best not to use this time to chat or converse. As the giver touches a spot, the receiver will give immediate feedback as to the level of pleasure of this touch using the scale shown below. At first, the receiver may need to adjust their mind to the task by comparing several touches before being able to assign a number. But, in time it becomes easier.

Sexological Exam Scale

+3   The most pleasurable touch you can imagine

+2   Touch that feels very good

+1   Touch that is mildly pleasurable

 0   Neither pleasurable nor unpleasant—neutral

-1   Touch that is slightly unpleasant

-2   Touch that is quite unpleasant

-3   Touch that is very unpleasant and causes physical or psychological pain

The giver begins by touching an area an inch or so from the genitals with their fingertip. When the receiver is female, start at the pubic mound or vulva and gently stroke or pull the outermost pubic hair. The receiver will then express a number based on the Sexological Exam Scale. The giver should then move to another part of the vulva, such as the outer lips on the right and the receiver again gives the touch a rating. Touch both sides of the vulva separately. Many people are surprised to discover that one side is more sensitive than the other. Continue in small increments of touch, progressing from the outer to the inner labia, to the region around the clitoral hood, and then to spots encompassing the entire genital area. Avoid touching the clitoris or inserting a finger into the vaginal vestibule at this point. Avoid the sensitive urethral and anal regions for now (many individuals find these areas too sensitive for sexual contact at any point). If the receiver is male, begin in the pubic hair and progress along the shaft of the penis, again avoiding the sensitive opening to the urethra. Lightly stroke the scrotum below. Remember that the underside of the tip of the penis is the most sensitive and sexually arousing location.

As the receiver feels more aroused, go over the same areas again, trying less or more pressure and faster or slower touch. The receiver will help the giver map out areas and types of touch that feel good. If there are negative numbers, move outward and use a gentler touch. As long as you have completed earlier sensate focus exercises, you will usually be able to find many areas that are erotic and exciting when touched. To enhance the experience, add a water-soluble lubricant such as Astroglide or KY jelly. This will change the experience and usually make it more erotic. If the receiver feels too sensitive, consider touching through a sheer panty or light cloth.

When you have each completed the initial exploration, consider a more in-depth exploration for the female receiver. Insert a finger into the opening of the vagina, delicately stroking in and out once. Think of the opening as the face of a clock. The receiver will notice different sensations as a finger touches twelve, three, six, nine, and again twelve o'clock. Add another level of experience by touching two places at once, such as the six o'clock position at the opening of the vagina and the twelve o'clock position at the hood of the clitoris. Or make a circling motion around a nipple as you touch a certain spot. After you have finished the exercise, change places. When you are done, rest in each other's arms and breathe slowly and comfortably together.

As long as you both feel comfortable (a lot of plus 1s through plus 3s), feel free to experiment. You will slowly create an internal image of comfortable, pleasurable, and arousing spots to guide you in future exercises. Remember that everyone has both comfortable and sensitive areas when stimulated. Everyone has times when they want to be touched and other times when they don't. Be aware of your physical experience and let your partner know what you want. You are both learning when, where, and in what manner you like to be touched. It is important to repeat the pillow talk exercises after every sensate focus. This will allow you to refocus your touching and find solutions to resistance and difficulties.

Sensate focus with genital exploration might prove to be a major hurdle for some women with sexual pain disorders. Vulvar pain might make it difficult if not impossible at times to complete the exercise. Dyspareunia and vaginismus might make vaginal insertion too difficult. If this is the case, we suggest the following:

1. Spend more time on earlier sensate focus exercises; focus on light genital stroking and visualization.

2. Share your feelings with your partner as you do the genital exploration to explain where the area is sensitive. This will help lower anxiety for both people. For instance, if you have a firm agreement not to try penetration, the receiver who is fearful of penetration might relax and be able to enjoy stimulation very much.

3. Be flexible in terms of the amount of time you explore. Better to go slowly than not at all.

4. Speak to your doctor or gynecologist about appropriate medication for vulvar disorders.

5. Discuss with your gynecologist the use of a biofeedback to break the pain loop and a tricyclic medication (such as Disiprimine, Nortripiline, or GavaPectin) to change the pain signals by stabilizing the dorsal horn. In Boston, Dr. Elizabeth Stewart at Harvard Vangard has successfully treated many patients this way.

Sometimes couples abort their efforts when they start an exercise and run into a major problem. For example, if you experienced pain during genital touching, you might have jumped out of bed and asked to cancel the exercise. These incidents can easily create anger, discouragement, or even hopelessness in both partners and can lead to arguments.

How should you deal with such an occurrence? First, try to understand what is happening: the pain or fear has just overwhelmed one partner, activated the sympathetic nervous system, and led to the fight-or-flight reaction. In other words, the sexual dysfunction has just been recreated within the exercise. This will happen at points along the way—so expect it and don't be discouraged. Reframe your perspective; instead of seeing it as a problem, look at it as a challenge; instead of letting it stall your progress, think of ways to move beyond it. To do this, take a break from the exercise and spend ten to fifteen minutes on a relaxation exercise. This will deactivate sympathetic nervous arousal and restore a state of calm. Then try to repeat part of an earlier sensate focus exercise that worked well, such as nonsexual touching. When you and your partner are feeling calmer and more confident, discuss the problem and try to find a solution. Perhaps gentler touching is needed or slower movements toward the genitals. There are always ways to salvage exercises.

Finally, your sexual relationship may be affected by unrelated emotional problems of either partner. See also the chapters in part V on low self-esteem, anxiety, traumatic experiences, and depression.

Excerpted and adapted for both genders with permission from *A Woman's Guide to Overcoming Sexual Fear and Pain* by Aurelie Jones Goodwin, Ed.D., and Marc E. Argronin, M.D. For more information on this and related books, see the "Further Reading" section in the back of the book.

CHAPTER 3

Anger

Sometimes your emotions and the expression of those emotions can adversely affect your relationships with others. One such emotion is anger. While anger is a natural and healthy emotion that everyone sometimes experiences, anger can become a problem if it becomes a frequent or overwhelming feeling. The exercises in this chapter can help you assess and address problems with anger.

Combating Anger Trigger Thoughts

A young woman sank back into the client's chair and began her story. "I can't control my anger at my children," she said. "I scream, I shake them sometimes. It's hurting our relationship, and down the line I think it will affect their self-esteem. With my eldest I'm the worst. Totally nuts at times. I feel like slapping and slapping him till he shuts up."

"What are you thinking when you get so angry at your son?" the therapist asked.

"What a brat, what a selfish brat. He's trying to get back at me because I want a little order in my life."

"Does it feel like he's doing something to you, something to hurt you?"

"In those moments I feel like he's trying to drive me to despair, like he wants to destroy me."

"So you're saying to yourself that he's a selfish brat, that he wants to get back at you, that he wants to destroy you and drive you to despair. Let me ask you a question. Suppose, after his misbehaving, you said something like this to yourself: 'He's unhappy and he's trying to get my attention. His behavior is unpleasant, but he's just trying to take care of his needs.'"

"But I don't believe that, I think he's trying to . . ."

"I understand that, but we are speaking hypothetically. Suppose you were to say to yourself what I suggested. Would you feel as angry?"

"No, I don't think I would. I think I'd feel differently."

"Here is something very important, then, that we have to talk about. You do have control over your anger. What you think, what you say to yourself triggers your anger. You can gain control of your anger by changing your thoughts, beliefs, and assumptions about your boy's behavior."

There is nothing automatic about getting angry. Pain, unfairness, and other people do not make you angry. Thoughts make you angry; beliefs and assumptions make you angry. This chapter is an opportunity for you to examine the traditional beliefs and assumptions that are the cognitive foundations for anger and the necessary prerequisites for every angry outburst you have ever experienced.

The cognitive triggers for anger fall into one of two categories: shoulds and blamers. What follows is an exploration of how both shoulds and blamers create a distorted, anger-inciting picture of reality that leaves you feeling victimized and controlled by others. This chapter will help you to identify your trigger thoughts and replace them with new, more forgiving awarenesses.

Shoulds

If you listened carefully to the inner monologue with which you analyze and interpret your experience, you would notice that many times each day you are judging the behavior of others. These judgments are based on a set of rules about how people should and should not act. People who behave according to the rules are right, and those who break the rules are wrong. You assume that people know and accept your rules. When they violate your shoulds, their behavior seems like a deliberate break with what is correct, intelligent, reasonable, or moral.

While waiting in line at the toll plaza, John deeply resents drivers who use the carpool lane to get ahead of the jam and then cut in front of him. He believes that people should wait their turn, and those who don't should be punished. Samantha has had a recent hysterectomy and is enormously angry that her husband rarely checks in about how she feels and even more rarely helps with any household jobs. Her should is that a spouse ought to show his concern by checking in and doing things to help. The problem with John's and Samantha's shoulds is that the other people don't agree with them. This is almost always the case. Others don't see reality as you do. Their perception of a situation is colored by their own needs, feelings, and history.

The drivers who cut in think it's perfectly fine to do so, and Samantha's husband feels very righteous because he's given up golf and poker to be home with her. It never occurs to him to be more helpful or inquiring.

So the first problem with shoulds is that the people with whom you feel angry rarely agree with you. Their perception of the situation leaves them blameless and justified. Their rules and beliefs always seem to exempt them from the judgments you think they deserve. And the more you try to convince them of their wrongness and their failure, the more indignant and defensive they become.

The second problem with shoulds is that people never do what they should do. They only do what is reinforcing and rewarding for them to do. Shoulds are your values and needs imposed on someone with different values and needs. The most complex human behavior can be looked at in terms of a very simple formula: strength of need minus strength of inhibition. If the strength of the inhibition is equal to or greater than the need, the person does not act. If the need surpasses the strength of the inhibition, some behavior will be enacted. Consider the drivers who keep cutting in front of John. Their need to get ahead and save time is greater than the sum of all inhibiting factors—fear of disapproval or reprisal, fear of a traffic ticket, guilt for not waiting their turn, and so on. The same is true for Samantha's husband. His need to watch television, sleep or read, or do whatever else he does instead of helping Samantha must be presumed greater than his inhibitions—fear of Samantha's disapproval, his self-rebuke for violating values of helpfulness and caring behavior, and so on.

When you demand that people behave according to your rules, you are violating reality in two ways. First, in most cases others will not agree with your values and rules. Their unique history and needs shape their perception in a way that justifies their behavior. Since you can rarely get others to agree that they are wrong, applying your shoulds to their behavior is an exercise in futility. Second, since behavior is shaped by the formula of needs minus inhibitions, shoulds have almost nothing to do with it. Judging behavior according to your own arbitrary standard of right and wrong really seems to miss the point. The real issue is how much does this person need to act this way and what inhibiting influences, if any, might stop him.

Exercise 1. Stand in their shoes. When you're angry at someone, answer these four questions.

1. What needs influence him or her to act this way?

2. What beliefs or values influence him or her to act this way?

3. What aspects of his or her history (hurts, losses, successes, failures, rewards) influence this behavior?

4. What limitations (fears, health problems, lack of skills) influence this behavior?

Answer each question as completely as possible. If you don't have all the information, make up something that seems likely. The purpose of this exercise is to explain the behavior you don't like from the other person's point of view.

Exercise 2. Accurate empathy. In his excellent book, *Feeling Good*, David Burns suggests an exercise to help you cope with shoulds. Imagine a dialogue between yourself and the person with whom you feel angry. Start out by accusing him or her of acting wrongly, of violating some basic rule of conduct. Really try to articulate your should. State it as clearly and persuasively as you can. Now imagine yourself as the other person, trying to answer your attack. Do your best to really become this individual, to see the world from his or her point of view. After you've answered as the other person, go back to your original feeling of anger and expand on your accusations. Keep up the attack. Now go back again and answer as the other person, really explaining his or her viewpoint. Shuttle back and forth between your accusing voice and the other person's defense at least three times. Notice how your feelings begin to change as you acknowledge the other person's unique experience.

While any kind of should can trigger anger, the five specific types of should statements covered below are extremely damaging in intimate relationships.

The Entitlement Fallacy

The entitlement fallacy is based on this simple belief: because I want something very much, I ought to have it. The basic idea is that the degree of your need justifies the demand that someone else provide it. The feeling is that there are certain things you are entitled to. Many people feel they are entitled to be sexually fulfilled, or feel emotionally and physically safe, or have a certain standard of living. Some people feel they are entitled to always rest when they are tired, or never be alone, or to have their work appreciated, or to have their needs known without asking. The list of possible entitlements is endless.

Sabrina was thirty-eight and very much wanted a child. Her husband remained ambivalent and was extremely fearful about losing a sense of spontaneity and freedom if they had children.

Sabrina harbored a belief that if she wanted something this much, he should help her have it. Her anger with his ambivalence was so great that each discussion of the issue soon developed into an escalating series of accusations.

Sam wants his son to go on a fishing trip. After all, he pays for the boy's college education, he's his father, the boy can jolly well give up a few days chasing girls to keep his old man company. Sam is in a rage when his son tells him that he'd rather make a demo tape with his band.

The entitlement fallacy confuses desire with obligation. It says, "When I want something this much, you have no right to say no." Strong feelings of entitlement deny others the freedom to choose. And this is how entitlement damages relationships. It demands that the other person give up his or her limits and boundaries for you. It says your need and your pain must come first, that the function of the relationship is to serve you.

Now, most of the time you would deny feeling that way and be quite offended if anyone were to accuse you of demanding that your needs come first. But the feeling of entitlement waxes and wanes. Sometimes you have no awareness of it. But when the needs are very strong, when the feeling of longing begins to engulf you, all you care about is getting what you want. And for a little while the other person may become only an instrument to provide for you. These painful feelings of need may periodically tempt you to forget the other person's equally important needs, his or her right to say no and set boundaries.

Exercise. Remember times you had to say no to another person's strong desire—a time when someone was in love with you, wanted to sleep with you, wanted your money, your support, your energy. His or her desire felt as real and vital and legitimate and necessary as yours does to you. Now try to remember why you said no. Remember the ways that your needs were different or conflicted. Remember how important it was for you to set your limits and clarify what you were and were not willing to do. You knew you had a right to your limits, you knew you had to say no because you needed something else.

Coping statements. These are things you can say to yourself when you find you are falling into the entitlement trap.

1. "I am free to want, but he or she is free to say no."

2. "I have my limits, and you have your limits."

3. "I have the right to say no, and so do you."

4. "My desire doesn't obligate you to meet it."

The Fallacy of Fairness

This belief hinges on the application of legal and contractual rules to the vagaries of interpersonal relationships. The idea is that there is some absolute standard of correct and fair behavior which people should know and live up to. The conviction that relationships must be fair reduces the complex give-and-take of friendship or marriage to a set of entries in privately kept books. Your books tell you whether you are in the red or in the black, whether you are getting as much as you give, whether you are owed something for all the sacrifices you have made. The difficulty is that no two people agree on what fairness is and in personal relationships there is no court or arbiter to help them. The measurement of what is fair is totally subjective and depends entirely on what you expect, need, or hope for from the other person. Fairness can be so conveniently defined, so temptingly self-serving that people can literally call anything fair or unfair. And as the debate rages, each person gets locked into his or her fortress of conviction. Each person is the victim, the bearer of injustice.

Joan was convinced that she had been victimized. "I supported him through grad school, and that was his dream. Now I want to buy a house—that's my dream—and he won't do it. It isn't fair." Anthony complains, "Ninety percent of the time we go to her place, ten percent to mine. She doesn't care if it's fair or not."

Joan and Anthony no doubt heard their parents appeal to the concept of fairness when they were children. "Be fair to your brother, let him play with the toys. . . . That's not fair, let her have some of the ice cream too. . . . I played with you now be fair and let Daddy read for a while." Fairness is sometimes a useful concept for controlling the behavior of children (after all, there is an adult present to be the final judge of all such matters). But as an adult, the concept is just too dangerous to use. The word "fair" turns out to be nothing more than a disguise for personal preferences and wants. What you want is fair, what the other person wants or does is unfair.

When you say, "This is fair," what you're really saying is my needs are more legitimate than yours. No one wants to hear this. People resist and defend against such assertions. A better approach is to throw out the concept of fairness altogether. Reframe the situation as one of competing needs or preferences. Each person's need is of equal importance and value. Each person's need is equally legitimate.

When you finally put away the idea of fairness, you can begin to negotiate as peers who have competing wants and somehow must resolve the problem. Joan wants a house, her husband doesn't. Instead of arguing about what's fair, they can negotiate from a position that each need has equal weight. Maybe they will buy a smaller house than Joan had originally envisioned, maybe they will put off buying till a specific date, maybe they'll buy a country place, maybe they'll continue to rent but invest in real estate. Anthony and his girlfriend can adjust the percentage of time spent in each house, or they may work out special compensations or accommodations and keep the current lopsided percentage. Once fairness is thrown out, real negotiation can begin.

Exercise. If you are struggling with the issue of fairness, try reframing the problem as competing, but equal needs. Then attempt to make a clear, unbiased description of the other person's need. Don't try to evaluate whether it is more or less significant than yours.

Coping Statements

1. "Our needs are equally important."

2. "Each need is legitimate, we can negotiate as peers."

The Fallacy of Change

The fallacy of change is based on the assumption that you really can have control over the behavior of others. While sometimes people do change if you ask them, the fallacy of change reflects the belief that you can make people different if you just apply sufficient pressure. Richard expects that if he criticizes and belittles his wife enough, she will change into someone who is interested in discussing world affairs and political and social ideas. Leanne thinks that if she complains enough and gets angry enough she can change her husband's preoccupation with his job, his hobbies, and his personal experience (he keeps a detailed diary of his dreams and childhood memories).

The problem for both Richard and Leanne is that they are ignorant of one basic fact of human behavior: people change only when they are reinforced to change and capable of the change. In other words, people change when they want to, not when you want them to. Richard and Leanne find that their spouses are not changing, and the reason is that people do what is rewarding for them to do. Richard's wife finds it more rewarding to talk about the psychology of her friends than the relationship between the Druze and the Phalangists in Lebanon. Until Richard can make such discussions rewarding and fun for her, she will resist participating. Leanne has the same problem. Her husband is highly reinforced to keep doing the things he does. He won't change until she can make it more rewarding for him to spend time with her. Her current strategy of getting angry is having the opposite effect. He finds it more and more aversive to be with her and hence takes refuge in his hobbies and dream journal.

Expecting people to change leads to frustration and disillusion. If you can't find a way to make them want to change, you have undertaken a quixotic mission. You are tilting at windmills.

Exercise. Think about and answer the following questions:

1. How many times have you made a major change and sustained it because someone pressured you to do so?

2. What percentage of the people you have known have made a major metamorphosis to satisfy the needs of someone else?

3. How often have you succeeded in changing someone by pressuring him or her with anger?

Coping Statements

1. "The amount of support, help, and nourishment I am now getting is all I can get, given the strategies I am using."

2. "People will change only when they are reinforced to change and capable of change."

3. "People only change when they want to."

Conditional Assumptions

Conditional asumptions are based on a syllogism like this:

"If you loved me, you'd pick me up at the subway station after work (or do the dishes, or show more sexual interest, or get home earlier, or help me when I'm tired, or spell me with caring for the kids, or fix things in the house, or finish school so you could get a real job)."

Other variations include:

"If you were a real friend, you'd help me lay the bricks for my patio (or initiate more often, or just spend time with me rather than always having to do something, or take more interest in my problems)."

And a last one:

"If they valued my work here, they'd get me a nicer desk (or give me a raise, or give me a better secretary, or ask what happened when I was sick last week)."

It's possible to love or care for someone and still not meet his or her needs. Disappointing others doesn't make one uncaring, and caring doesn't obligate one never to disappoint. No matter how much someone loves you, that person is still responsible for taking care of his or her own basic needs. That person is still responsible for saying no, setting boundaries, and protecting his or her own limits. "If they cared, if they loved me," is a setup to make you feel righteous and make the other person feel bad. Truthfully, it's a strategy for manipulation. But the result is rarely what you might hope. In the long run, making others feel bad doesn't reinforce them to do what you want. It makes them want to run away, to avoid you.

Exercise 1. List the times you have disappointed someone you loved or cared for. Remember the times you have had to make difficult choices, when you decided to take care of your needs over someone else's. As you think back, notice how little your choice had to do with how much you loved, but rather with how much you needed, or how much you were afraid, or how much energy you had.

Exercise 2. As you did with the fallacy of fairness, reframe your conditional assumptions as a collision of equally legitimate needs. Define your need, and then carefully describe the needs, as you understand them, of the other person. See the problem as two peers, working to negotiate. Read the Communication chapter in part I and apply the assertive communication skills discussed there to a process of compromise and accommodation so that each of you gets some of what he or she needs.

Coping Statements

1. "Disappointing someone doesn't mean you don't care."

2. "Our biggest task, no matter how much we love, is to take care of ourselves."

3. "His or her needs are as legitimate as mine, and we can negotiate."

The Letting It Out Fallacy

This fallacy rests on the belief that people who hurt you or cause you pain should be punished. It often feels very good to express anger when you're frustrated and hurting. It helps to discharge the pain. And it functions as a kind of revenge for any perceived injustice.

The underlying belief is that you are not responsible for your pain. Someone else is. That person must have done wrong in order for you to feel so badly. Therefore, he or she deserves every bit of anger you feel like expressing. Maybe he or she will learn to do better in the future.

The problem with this whole line of reasoning is that you are responsible for your pain. And taking care of yourself is always your first responsibility. Pain and pleasure are essentially private experiences. You are the only one who really feels your hurt, you are the only one who experiences your joy. No one else can be held accountable or responsible for your private experience. You know it and you feel it. Therefore, you are the only one who can be responsible for it. If someone is frustrating or hurting you or causing you pain, your job is to either negotiate for your needs or let go of the relationship.

The second problem with letting it out is that anger destroys relationships. (This is particularly true for anger used as revenge.) When the object of your anger is to inflict the same degree of hurt that you are feeling on someone else, people begin to erect psychological barriers to protect themselves from you. The tissue of a relationship gets thickened and scarred. And finally you both become insensitive to pain and pleasure. This is how anger kills love: it makes you thick-skinned, untouchable. You no longer feel the warmth, the caress.

The last reason letting it out doesn't work is that anger rarely gets you what you want. What you want is to be listened to, appreciated, cared for. Anger gets you coldness, withdrawal, and anger in return. Letting it out feels good. But it's like smoking crack: a five-minute high, followed by depression, pain, and emotional bankruptcy.

Exercise. When you are tempted to let it out, first review the positive and negative consequences of using anger with this particular person in the past. Make four columns down a piece of paper. Over two of the columns write "short-term consequences" and over the other two write "long-term consequences." Label the two short-term consequences columns "positive" and "negative." Do the same with the long-term columns. Write down all the long- and short-term consequences of anger that you can think of, both positive and negative. At the end of the exercise, ask yourself this question: "Did anger get me what I wanted?"

Blamers

They did it to you. You are lonely, hurt, frightened, and they did it. Blaming triggers anger by making your pain someone else's responsibility. In intimate relationships, blaming leads to the development of negative cognitive sets in which you begin to label, classify, and interpret a person's behavior in consistently negative ways. He is controlling or uncaring or selfish or insensitive. And as this negative cognitive set hardens, so do your assumptions about the other person. Even neutral or ambiguous behavior gets a negative label. More and more parts of the relationship are tainted by the consistently negative way that you interpret and evaluate the other person.

The problem with blaming is that it denies reality in two ways. First, blaming assumes that you are not responsible for your pain, someone else is. In reality, however, you should view yourself and only yourself as responsible for your experience. The second way that blaming denies reality is by constructing a world in which people are deliberately doing bad things. People do not do "bad" things. As Plato observed, people always choose the good. Each of us will choose the action that seems most likely to meet our own needs. The potential benefits of the action you choose, at least at the moment of choice, seem to outweigh the foreseeable disadvantages. Obviously, the action that seems best at the time depends on your awareness. Awareness is the degree of clarity with which you perceive and understand, consciously or unconsciously, all the factors relating to the need at hand. At any moment in time, your awareness is a product of your innate intelligence, your constitution, your physiological state, your emotional state, your beliefs, your needs, your total life experience and conditioning, and your skills and competencies. All of that goes into making a decision. And the decision you make is the very best one available at that moment in time. Good or bad is nothing more than a label you apply to decisions after you have observed their consequences for yourself and others. But at the moment the decision was made, those consequences were unknown. And it was therefore the best choice available.

Now you may be thinking that sometimes people know better but do the wrong thing anyway. "My son knows I'll be upset and that he diminishes his chances for college when he brings home Cs and Ds. He knows better, but he does it anyway." But "knowing better" is not sufficient to "do better" if the boy's awareness at the time is focused on stronger and opposing motivations. If his need to play football or go out with girls or rebel against the family rules is larger than his need to please you or his long-range concerns about college, then grades will be a low priority. It all comes down to what is most important at the time.

So blaming doesn't make sense. It labels people and behavior as bad when in fact each person makes the best choice available. By blaming, you end up punishing people for actions they could not help performing.

Exercise. The components of awareness. Think of someone you know well, someone you have at various times blamed. Think of a decision that person made that angered you. Now here's the hard part. Try to reconstruct the decision from that person's point of view. What do you know of his or her constitution or physiological state, emotional state, beliefs, needs, conditioning, competencies, or limitations? Try to see how these factors could combine so that his or her decision was the best choice available.

Good-Bad Dichotomizing

If you do a lot of blaming, you're beginning to repaint the world in black and white. People are good or bad, right or wrong. You don't see any shades of gray or any continuum between the polar opposites.

Once you start labeling people as bad, the problem with cognitive sets comes in. You develop a kind of tunnel vision that blocks out every behavior that doesn't fit your assumption of badness. You simply don't see the things that are kind or generous or loving. Jim very often sees Martha as selfish and uncaring. Even though she frequently gives him little hugs, does his laundry, and invites his friends to dinner, he fails to notice these as loving or generous acts. Jim is missing a big part of the relationship because his cognitive sets blind him to seeing the way Martha expresses her caring feelings.

Exercise: Finding shades of gray. Write a complete description of someone you know well, someone you care for but with whom you also feel angry. Read over your description. How many of the items are judgments, implying that some aspect of his or her personality is either good or bad? How much of your description is either pejorative or praising? Now try rewriting the description without any hint of judgment. As best you can, make the descriptions neutral. Instead of saying that he's fat, say that he weighs two hundred and fifty pounds. Instead of saying that she has a beautiful face, say that she has even features and smooth skin. Stick to the facts. Don't embellish with your value judgments. How does it feel to think about people without judgment? Does the description feel more accurate or less accurate when it is nonpejorative?

Coping Statements

1. "I make no judgments."

2. "People are coping with pain and stress in the best way they can, given their level of awareness."

3. "It is merely a problem that our needs conflict; he is not wrong, and I am not right."

Assumed Intent

This is mind reading, the tendency to make inferences about how people feel and think. Assumed intent triggers anger when you conclude that your pain is a consequence of someone's deliberate effort to do you harm. Jill lost track of her nine-year-old son at the county fair. She assumed that he had deliberately disappeared to scare her. Joshua believed that the waitress was being deliberately slow and inattentive because he had asked for extra cream and wanted his eggs done a special way.

Notice that assumed intent must include two important concepts to make you angry. First, that you are in pain through the fault of someone else. Secondly, that you are being deliberately harmed. Few people would get angry if a pine cone fell and scratched their car. But a child throwing pine cones would be a different story. Now the two elements necessary for anger are present: harm and deliberate intent.

There are several problems with assuming intent. It is very difficult to accurately assess the true motives of another person. The word "assume" means that you think you know, but you never asked. Mind reading is so often dead wrong, yet it is probably the greatest source of anger. Claudette thought that a friend had deliberately excluded her from a luncheon "as a kind of slap." She was irate until she learned that the lunch had honored an unknown co-worker of her friend's. Reese thought that his girlfriend was trying to hurt him by deciding to spend fewer nights together. After first withdrawing, then picking several fights, he discovered that her very deep feelings of love and dependence were frightening her. The motive that he had assumed was quite the opposite from the facts. It was her positive feelings rather than any attempt to harm that lay behind her decision.

Exercise. Try this process for one day. Make a commitment to yourself that you will make absolutely no assumptions about the motivations of others unless you check out your assumption with the other person. In other words, you have to ask, "Is it true that you're being slow getting ready for the movie because I didn't wash the car today?" "I have a feeling you're being a little withdrawn because I spent the day with Rich. Is there anything to that?" "When you said the potatoes were overcooked, I felt like you were mad at me or something, is that true?" "You're driving so fast, I wonder if you're trying to scare me?" Your rule for yourself for this day will be that you either avoid assumptions or find out if they're true.

If you succeeded in doing the exercise for a day, try extending it to a week. The more you avoid mind reading, the healthier your communications will be.

Coping Statements

1. "Assume nothing or check it out."

2. "I don't guess at the motives of others."

3. "No mind reading."

Magnifying

When you magnify, you make things worse than they are. You use words like terrible, awful, disgusting, horrendous. You overgeneralize by using words such as always, all, every, and never. Jill complains about her boss: "He's always handing me things at the last minute. He's awful with the whole support staff. Never a kind word, never a smile. He's just a lousy person to work for." Art complains about his neighbor: "He's always piling crap in my walkway. He never asks, he never even talks to me. It's terrible to live next to somebody who doesn't give a damn."

Both Jill and Art are magnifying. Jill's boss doesn't always give her things at the last minute. It isn't true that he never smiles. Art's neighbor isn't always piling things in the walkway. Nor does he never speak to Art. These magnifications crank up your sense of being victimized. By exaggerating the problematic behavior, you generate a feeling of being deeply wronged. They're bad and you're innocent.

Magnifying your trigger thoughts is like throwing gasoline on a fire. Your anger explodes because you feel so wronged, so righteous, so justified.

Exercise. For one day, eliminate these words from your vocabulary: all, always, every, never, terrible, awful, disgusting, horrible, sickening, and so on. Commit yourself to describing people and events without magnifying. Strive for accuracy rather than exaggeration. Give the exact frequency: "Three times in the last two weeks . . ." "The second time this quarter . . ." "Once a month we chat for five minutes." Avoid using generalized pejoratives like terrible and awful. Instead, stick to simple conclusions like "I don't like it . . ." "I'd prefer he didn't hand things to me after four o'clock."

Coping Statements

1. "No more always and never."

2. "Accuracy, nonexaggeration."

3. "Let the facts speak for themselves."

Global Labeling

Your office mate is an imbecile. Your roommate's neurotic. Your father's stupid. The grocery checker is a jerk. Your lover's a selfish asshole. Your landlord is a ripoff artist. Your cousin is a blabbermouth. Global labels fuel your anger by turning the other person into someone who is totally bad and worthless. Instead of disliking specific behavior, you indict the entire person. Global labels are always false because they focus on a single characteristic or behavior, but imply that it's the whole picture.

It's much easier to get angry at an ogre, a despicable person, than it is to rage at one specific behavior. It's hard to really work yourself into a true feeling of victimization if you're only responding to one unfortunate event. But if you decide you've been mistreated by a selfish jerk, you anger comes to a quicker boil.

Exercise. The antidote for global labeling is specificity. The next time you catch yourself using pejorative labels, shift into a specific description of the offensive behavior. Leave the person out of it. Describe what he does, not who he is.

Coping Statement

1. "No labels. Be specific."

Changing Your Trigger Thoughts

Changing a long-standing pattern of thinking is no easy task. But it's absolutely necessary. If you don't find ways to combat your trigger thoughts, your shoulds and blamers, they will continue to ignite anger.

It'll take hard work and discipline to change what seems second nature now. But there is a way. Aaron Beck, one of the founders of cognitive behavioral therapy, devised an extremely effective process for confronting your distorted thoughts. It's called the three-column technique. Divide a sheet of paper into three columns. Whenever you feel angry, write down in column A what you're saying to yourself. In column B write down the kind of trigger thought you were using (some are listed below as a memory aid). In column C, rewrite your original statement so that it no longer contains the distorted trigger thought.

Shoulds	Blamers
Entitlement fallacy	Good-bad dichotomizing
Fallacy of fairness	Assumed intent
Fallacy of change	Magnifying
Conditional assumptions	Global labeling
Letting it out fallacy	

Here's an example of how you can use the three-column technique.

Ann's Diary

That jerk's keeping me waiting	Assuming intention, Magnifying	I don't like waiting.
Yard duty again. The principal always does this to me.	Conditional assumptions	I assume he's doing the best he can, but it's quite inconvenient for me.
Why doesn't he learn to sit down and behave?	Fallacy of change	He'll learn to sit down when I figure out how to reinforce him to do so.
If she was any kind of a friend, she wouldn't stick me with the whole damn thing.	Conditional assumptions	It's a conflict of needs. I've got to negotiate this with her. Neither of us wants to do it.
Why do these people keep me waiting?	Shoulds	People never do what they should do, only what they're reinforced to do.
Why do I have to live in this closet when my ex-husband is still living in the house?	Entitlement fallacy	Just because I want that house doesn't mean I can afford it. He owns a plumbing business, I'm just a teacher. There is no reason why he should give up a house just because I want it.

As you can see, the third column is the most important. That's where you talk back to the trigger thoughts and begin to modify your anger. Here's another example.

Harold's Diary

Now she's off to yoga and aerobics. We'll lose the whole morning, God damn her, she's avoiding me.	Letting it out fallacy, Assuming intention	Blowing up won't get me what I want. I'll stop assuming and find out what her needs are.
She consented to have breakfast. Big deal. I work all week so she can go to school, and I have to talk her into breakfast.	Fallacy of fairness	Okay, both our needs are important. She doesn't owe me anything. Her needs are as legitimate as mine.
Why do they always screw up my photos every time I bring them here?	Good-bad dichotomizing, Magnifying, Global labeling	They're not that bad. They're doing the best they can. They don't always screw up. This is 4 out of 36 negatives.
Why can't she wear something sexy to bed?	Entitlement fallacy	Just because I want it doesn't mean she has to do it. She has her own needs and limits. If I want to work on this, I can find out what her needs and fears are and negotiate some compromise.

Now it's time for you to try some on your own. In Column A you'll find a list of trigger thoughts. Name the distortion in Column B. In column C, rewrite or refute the distortion so it no longer triggers anger.

Column A	Column B	Column C
1. Are you stupid? How can you forget your homework?		
2. He should stop the damned gambling. It's destroying our marriage.		
3. If she cared about me, she'd come home earlier.		
4. He never listens when I'm upset about something.		
5. He should have walked me to the car in this neighborhood.		
6. I took care of her when she had a cold last week. Now I have a toothache and she doesn't even ask how I am.		
7. He's walking this trail when he knows very well I'm afraid of heights.		

Suggested Answers:

1. *Global labeling.* "I don't like you forgetting your homework. How can we help you remember it? Perhaps you can stay up a half hour later if you remember your homework."

2. *Shoulds, fallacy of change.* "He'll only stop if he's reinforced to change and capable of changing. Pressure from me isn't working. I have to decide whether to live with this or let go."

3. *Conditional assumptions.* "Love has nothing to do with it. This is a conflict of needs. I have to find out what needs or fears keep her working late and negotiate some sort of compromise."

4. *Magnifying.* "Be specific. He listens maybe _____ percent of the time. How can I take responsibility to reinforce him to listen more?"

5. *Shoulds.* "That's my value and need, not his. He doesn't do what I think he should, only what his values and needs dictate."

6. *Fallacy of fairness.* "She has her own needs at this moment. Both our needs are equally legitimate. It is my responsibility to ask her for what I want."

7. *Assumed intent.* "I'm assuming things. I don't really know why he's walking here. Better check it out. I have to negotiate for my own needs."

Here are the main points to remember when you are writing your refutations to the trigger thoughts:

1. Be specific, not global.

2. Be nonpejorative, nonjudging.

3. Punishment and revenge won't get you what you want.

4. Check out all assumptions.

5. You, and only you, are responsible for your needs.

6. Recognize that people do the best they can given their level of awareness at the moment of choice.

7. Recognize that people do what is reinforcing for them to do. You can only get them to change by negotiating for and reinforcing new behavior.

Whenever you feel anger, continue to use the three-column technique to confront your trigger thoughts in your anger journal. It's essential that you make a commitment to keep at this. It is difficult, arduous work to keep examining your thoughts, to keep questioning and rebutting what seemed so natural, so reasonable. But getting control of your anger requires that you become more and more aware of how trigger thoughts create upsetting feelings. It will take at least three months of consistent effort monitoring and confronting your angry cognitions before you begin to feel the tide turn. Gradually they will become less automatic. Gradually you will find yourself experiencing more and more discomfort when the old trigger thoughts pop up. They will no longer sound so right, so convincing. In fact, you will begin to recognize them for what they are—excuses to discharge pain, deceptions that trigger destructive aggression. As you keep talking back to the shoulds and blamers, you will find your new attitudes and beliefs beginning to take hold. As you accept more responsibility for your needs, you will move beyond anger to problem solving, negotiating, and exploring the needs of others.

Excerpted and adapted with permission from *When Anger Hurts: Quieting the Storm Within* by Matthew McKay, Ph.D., Peter D. Rogers, Ph.D., and Judith McKay, R.N. For more information on this and related books, see the "Further Reading" section in the back of the book.

CHAPTER 4

Communication

Introduction

See the chapter on Couple Skills, for basic communication skills—listening, expressing feelings, and scripting needs. This section focuses on assertiveness, a key communication skill.

Assertiveness training teaches you to express your feelings, thoughts, and wishes, and to stand up for your legitimate rights without violating the rights of others. Assertiveness is a skill you can acquire, not a personality trait that some people are born with and others are not. Like aggression and passivity, assertiveness is a social behavior that can be learned.

Nobody is consistently assertive. You may be assertive with your children in one instance, aggressive with them in another, and passive in still another. You might have no trouble being assertive with your family, yet find it almost impossible to be assertive with strangers. Assertiveness training can expand the number of social situations in which you can respond assertively rather than passively or aggressively.

Learning to be assertive doesn't mean that you must always behave assertively. There are times when it is entirely appropriate to be aggressive, as it is when your life or property is being threatened. There are also times when it's appropriate to be passive, such as when a judge is lecturing you. Learning to be assertive means that you can choose when and where to assert yourself.

Your Legitimate Rights

You learned a set of beliefs early in your life to help guide your social conduct. These beliefs are essentially a set of rules about "good" and "bad" behavior passed on to you by your parents and later role models. While these rules helped you get along with the people you grew up with, they are not cast in bronze and lightning won't strike you down if you decide to act differently.

Read the following list of traditional assumptions. Do any of them remind you of rules you learned as a child? Do you still believe that they apply to you as an adult? Listed beside each traditional assumption is a statement of your legitimate right as an adult. These rights are a reminder that you have a choice about what you believe and that you are no longer an unquestioning child, but rather an adult with alternatives.

Mistaken Traditional Assumptions	Your Legitimate Rights
1. It is selfish to put your needs before others' needs.	You have a right to put yourself first, sometimes.
2. It is shameful to make mistakes. You should have an appropriate response for every occasion.	You have a right to make mistakes.
3. If you can't convince others that your feelings are reasonable, then your feelings must be wrong.	You have a right to be the final judge of your feelings and accept them as legitimate.
4. You should respect the views of others, especially if they are in a position of authority. Keep your differences of opinion to yourself. Listen and learn.	You have a right to have your own opinions and convictions.
5. You should always try to be logical and consistent.	You have a right to change your mind or decide on a different course of action.
6. You should never interrupt people. Asking questions reveals your stupidity to others.	You have a right to interrupt in order to ask for clarification.
7. Things could get even worse, don't rock the boat.	You have a right to negotiate for change.
8. You shouldn't take up others' valuable time with your problems.	You have a right to ask for help or emotional support.
9. People don't want to hear that you feel bad, so keep it to yourself.	You have a right to feel and express pain.
10. When someone takes the time to give you advice, you should take it very seriously. They are often right.	You have a right to ignore the advice of others.
11. Knowing that you did something well is its own reward. People don't like showoffs. Successful people are secretly disliked and envied. Be modest when complimented.	You have a right to receive recognition for your work and achievements.
12. Don't be antisocial. People are going to think you don't like them if you say you'd rather be alone instead of with them.	You have a right to be alone, even if others would prefer your company.
13. When someone is in trouble, you should always help them.	You have a right not to take responsibility for someone else's problem.
14. You should be sensitive to the needs and wishes of others, even when they are unable to tell you what they want.	You have a right not to have to anticipate others' needs and wishes.

Identifying the Three Basic Styles of Communication

The first step in assertiveness training is learning to distinguish between assertive, aggressive, and passive behaviors.

Passive Style

When you are communicating passively, you don't directly express your feelings, thoughts, and wishes. You may try to communicate them indirectly by frowning, crying, or whispering something under your breath. Or you may withhold your feelings and wishes entirely.

In the passive style you tend to smile a lot and subordinate your needs to those of others. You also probably do more than your share of listening. If you do speak up directly, you make disclaimers such as "I'm no expert. . . . I'm really not sure. . . . I really shouldn't be saying this, but . . . " You find it very difficult to make requests. When someone asks you to do something that you don't want to do, you're inclined to do it or make an excuse rather than say no.

A passive speaking style includes a soft, weak, even wavering voice. Pauses and hesitations are common. You are likely to be at a loss for words. You may ramble, be vague, and use the phrases "I mean" and "you know" often. You frequently rely on others to guess what you want to say. Your posture is likely to be slouched, and perhaps you will lean against something for support. Your hands are apt to be cold, sweaty, and fidgety. Eye contact is difficult for you; you tend to look down or away. Because you are often not saying what you mean, you don't look like you mean what you say.

Aggressive Style

In the aggressive style, you are quite capable of stating how you feel, what you think, and what you want, but often at the expense of others' rights and feelings. You tend to humiliate others by using sarcasm or humorous put-downs. You are likely to go on the attack when you don't get your way, and you stir up guilt and resentment in others by pointing a finger of blame. Your sentences often begin with "You . . . " followed by an attack or a negative label. You use absolute terms such as "always" and "never" and describe things in a way that implies that you're always right and superior.

When you are behaving aggressively, you tend to move with an air of superiority and strength. Your style may run the gamut from cold and "deadly quiet" to flippant and sarcastic to loud and shrill. Your eyes are narrowed and expressionless. Your posture is that of a solid rock: feet planted apart, hands on hips, jaw clenched and jutting out, gestures rigid, abrupt, and intimidating. Sometimes you point your finger or make a fist. You are so intent on being right that you don't really hear what others are saying, even when you ask them a direct question.

Assertive Style

When you communicate assertively, you make direct statements regarding your feelings, thoughts, and wishes. You stand up for your rights and take into account the rights and feelings of others. You listen attentively, and let other people know that you have heard them. You are open to negotiation and compromise, but not at the expense of your own rights and dignity. You can make direct requests and direct refusals. You can give and receive compliments. You can start and stop a conversation. You can deal effectively with criticism, without becoming hostile or defensive.

When you are behaving assertively, you convey an air of assured strength and empathy. Your voice is relaxed, well-modulated, and firm. While you are comfortable with direct eye contact, you don't stare. Your eyes communicate openness and honesty. Your posture is balanced and erect.

Assertive Goals

List at least five assertive goals in terms of social situations in which you would like to be assertive. Write down specifically how you would like to *behave* differently, not how you would like to feel or be. Include the people with whom you would like to behave assertively in each situation. For example, you might write:

1. I want to be able to say "no" to members of my family when they ask me to fix their cars.

2. I want to tell my husband not to change the TV channel when I am watching a program in the den.

3. I want to present my ideas on a new product in a business meeting with my boss and colleagues.

4. I want to tell my mother how I feel when she criticizes me on the phone.

5. I want to take back defective items I have bought in the store and get my money back.

Your assertive goals:

1.

2.

3.

4.

5.

Assertive Expression

If you're like most people, you tend to be fairly indirect about expressing your feelings and needs. Perhaps you were told as a child that it was self-centered to talk a lot about yourself or to overuse the pronoun "I." Or maybe you're afraid how people will react if you are direct.

When you share your thoughts indirectly, you often call on the invisible expert: "They say the economy is getting worse. Of course, some say it's getting better. But you never know who you can trust."

When you state your feelings indirectly you are apt to sound something like this: "They just laid our whole department off. Makes a man feel kind of . . . you know. You work all those years, then it's all gone in a moment. It's frustrating, but what can you do? You just go home and wait."

When you can't express your wants directly, you have to hint: "It looks like a nice day for an outing . . . what do you think?" Or worse: "The newspaper mentioned an airshow this Sunday. . . . " Or even worse: "Gee, it sure is nice out. . . . "

If you're lucky and happen to have a very attentive listener, he or she may understand your feelings and wishes. Assertive expression, however, doesn't leave communication to chance.

An assertive statement has three parts:

1. Your perspective of the situation.

2. Your feelings about the situation.

3. Your wants regarding the situation.

Here are some examples using the three components of an assertive statement:

"When I think about giving a speech I get nervous. I've been feeling butterflies in my stomach since yesterday when I told you I would talk at the next general board meeting. I realize that I don't want to give that talk. Please find someone else."

"I think we have a lot in common. Spending the evening with you has been a lot of fun. I want to get to know you better, and I'd like to go out with you again next Friday night."

"We spend a lot of time talking about your situation at work. I feel irritated and a bit bored when you come home and only discuss office politics. I'd like to have time to tell you about my day. And also to talk about us, how we're feeling about being together."

Notice that assertive statements don't blame and don't use attacking labels. When describing the situation, try to describe it objectively. Don't stack the deck so that the other person sounds like a jerk. State the facts—what happened and what was done—without slipping into negative judgments. In an assertive statement, any feelings—positive or negative—belong to the speaker. "I feel that you're self-centered" is an accusing "you statement," not a feeling, and it would never pass as an assertive expression.

When you state what you want, be specific. The more you hedge, the easier it will be to have your message ignored or misunderstood.

Exercise: For each of the situations described in your assertive goals, write three assertive "I" messages:

1. I think _____

    I feel _____

    I want _____

2. I think _____

    I feel _____

    I want _____

3. I think _____

    I feel _____

I want _____

4. I think _____

   I feel _____

   I want _____

5. I think _____

   I feel _____

   I want _____

Assertive Listening

When you listen assertively, you concentrate your attention exclusively on the other person, without interrupting, so that you accurately hear feelings, opinions, and wishes. There are three steps in assertive listening:

1. Prepare. Tune into your own feelings and needs to find out if you are ready to listen. Check to be sure that the other person is also ready to speak.

2. Listen. Put your full attention on the other person. Try to hear feelings and what is wanted. If you are uncertain about the other person's feelings or wishes, ask him or her for more expression. For example, "I'm not really sure how you feel about that . . . can you tell me more? What is it that you want?"

3. Acknowledge. Let the other person know that you heard his or her feelings and wants. For example, "I hear that you are exhausted from a hard day, and want to spend an hour before dinner taking a nap." You may want to acknowledge the other person's feelings by sharing your feelings about what has been said. For example, "I'm angry to hear that you had to do so much extra work today."

Combining Assertive Expressing and Listening

When you're in conflict with someone and you both have strong feelings, the two of you can take turns using assertive listening and expressing.

Many problems can be solved simply by stating clearly what you each feel, think, and want. Misunderstandings are often cleared up, or solutions to problems quickly appear. Here's an example:

Paul: This house is a mess! It's maddening to come home to chaos after a long day at work.

Mary: I don't understand. . . . What's upsetting you?

Paul: I get really pissed off when I come home to a cluttered, noisy house. I want some peace and quiet when I first get in. I want to be able to walk into my study without tripping over toys and I want to spend some time alone.

Mary: I hear that you're angry because the house is noisy and chaotic when you first get home, and that you need to have some quiet time alone, and that you wish that the place could be picked up.

Paul: Yes, that's right.

Mary: Well, I have my own perspective on the problem. Ever since I took that part-time job, I haven't had time to keep this place spotless. I get exhausted and frustrated trying to work, take care of the kids, keep house, and do all my errands. I want you to help me more with the housework and the errands.

Paul: I wasn't aware you were feeling overworked to the point of exhaustion. What exactly do you want me to do?

Paul and Mary make a deal: he'll do the vacuuming and fold the clothes if she'll have the living room picked up and give him an hour to decompress when he gets home.

Exercise: With a friend or family member, practice combining the assertive listening and expressing skills. Begin practicing on a small issue such as what to do next weekend. When you feel comfortable with the skills, try using them with more emotionally laden problems.

Responding to Criticism

One of the major reasons people have difficulty being assertive is that they experience criticism as rejection. This is often a leftover from childhood, when you faced criticism from a one-down position. Each time you erred, your critical parents or teachers would pass judgment on you. You were wrong. And therefore you were bad. In time you learned to feel bad each time you were criticized. You may even have learned to use criticism as a club to beat yourself until you felt guilty and wrong.

Because criticism can be so painful, you may have developed special strategies to minimize the hurts. You may respond to criticism by verbally blowing up. Or you may respond in kind, bringing up old sins to fault your critic. Couples are particularly good at this: "You say I'm a spendthrift? Why, you bought yourself a whole new wardrobe last year and then put on 30 pounds so you couldn't wear a stitch of it!" Some partners respond to criticism with sarcasm: "Look at Mr. Perfect who knows so much!"

If you respond to criticism passively, you may become silent, turn red, cry, or try to escape your critic as soon as possible. You might either pretend you didn't hear what was said or in order to avoid conflict quickly agree with everything the critic says. When you respond passively, you hold in your anger and hurt. As a result, you run the risk of developing such physical symptoms as headaches, gastritis, ulcers, and spastic colitis. Sitting on your feelings is also a very good way to get depressed.

Storing resentments and hurts can propel you into the "getting even" syndrome. Either consciously or unconsciously you start "forgetting" important dates, procrastinating, arriving late, going too slow or too fast, being silent, or talking nonstop in an annoying whine . . . whatever will most irritate your critic. The advantage of this tactic is that you don't have to take responsibility for how you feel and what you do. When challenged, you can respond innocently: "Who me? You've got to be kidding. You're too sensitive," or "I'm sorry, I didn't mean it." The major disadvantage of this tactic is that your feelings and wants often get lost in the process of rationalizing and defending. Your little revenges also tend to alienate your critic and bring on more criticism.

Both the passive and the aggressive strategies for dealing with criticism can seriously disrupt your relations with others. An assertive response to criticism is based on the assumption that you are the final judge regarding your feelings, thoughts, wants, and behavior. You are also responsible for their consequences. Each individual has a different genetic heritage and life history, and therefore different expectations, likes and dislikes, and values. Your set of rules is likely to differ from those of other people, so it's understandable that you will not always agree with them. Ultimately, you are the best person to decide what's best for you.

There are three good strategies for assertively responding to criticism: acknowledgment, clouding, and probing.

Acknowledgment

Constructive criticism can help you improve yourself. When you make a mistake, feedback can assist you in learning how not to repeat the error. Sometimes the criticism you receive is not constructive, yet it is accurate. The other person, for his or her own reasons, is letting you know that you did something wrong.

When you receive criticism with which you agree, whether it is constructive criticism or just an unnecessary reminder, acknowledge that the critic is right. For example, "You're right, boss, I do misspell a lot of words, and I could use a dictionary at my desk." "Yes, I don't have the report in that was due last week." "Yes, I was half an hour late for work today."

Don't fall into the trap of making excuses or apologizing for your behavior. This is an automatic response left over from childhood when you accidentally spilled milk, soiled your clothes, or came home fifteen minutes late, and your parents asked, "Why did you do that?" They expected a reasonable answer, and you learned to supply an excuse. As an adult, you choose sometimes to give an explanation for your actions, but you don't have to. Stop and ask yourself if you really want to, or if you are just reacting out of an old habit. For example, you might say, "Yes, Jack, I haven't submitted that report that was due last week," and decide not to give Jack any explanation, since he's your peer and not in charge of when you get your work done.

On the other hand, when responding to your boss you wouldn't merely acknowledge that you were "half an hour late this morning." Since you value your job, you hasten to explain: "My car battery was dead and I had to ask a neighbor to jump it."

Clouding

Clouding is a useful technique for dealing with nonconstructive, manipulative criticism with which you disagree. It provides a quick way to dispense with statements that have a grain of truth in them but are intended mostly as put-downs. When you use clouding you find something in the critical comment to agree with while inwardly sticking to your own point of view. This calms critics down and gets them out of the "win/lose" game so that you can either communicate about more important things or end the conversation.

You may think that clouding is manipulative. It is. But it's better than the aggressive or passive alternatives. Although it does not require elaborate rehearsal, it does require that you listen carefully to find something that you can honestly agree with. There are three ways that you can agree with your critic:

Agreeing in part. Find some part of what the critic is saying that you agree with, and acknowledge that they are right about that part. Ignore the rest of the criticism. Modify any words the critic uses that are sheer exaggeration, such as "always" and "never." Rephrase the sentences that you almost agree with, but do not distort the essence of the critic's original meaning.

Critic:	You're always working. You think the world would fall apart if you took a day off.
You:	Yes, I do work a lot.
Critic:	You never have time for your friends anymore. You've become driven and obsessed by work.
You:	You're right, I don't have much time for my friends right now.

Agreeing in probability. You agree in probability when there's some chance that your critic is right. Even if the odds are one in a thousand, you can make replies such as "It may be. . . . " or "You could be right. . . . " Using the last example, you could respond to the critic with "It may be that I work too much," or "It could be that I don't have time for my friends anymore."

Agreeing in principle. Sometimes you can agree with the logic of your critic, without agreeing with his premise. You can agree that "If X, then Y" and still not admit that X is true.

Critic: If you don't study more than you do, you're going to fail your classes.

You: You're right, if I don't study, I will fail my classes.

Probing

Assertive probing is useful when you can't tell if the criticism is constructive or manipulative, when you don't understand the criticism, or when you think you're not getting the whole story. Criticism is often a way of avoiding important feelings or wishes, so if you're confused by a critical comment, probe for what's underneath it.

To use probing, pick out the part of the criticism that you think the critic feels most strongly about. Generally this will be something that affects his or her self-interest. Ask, "What is it that bothers you about . . . ?" and then restate the part of the criticism you think is most important to the critic. If necessary, ask the critic to provide a specific example. Listen to the critic's response carefully to determine what he or she feels, thinks, and wants. Continue to probe, saying, "What is it that bothers you about . . . ?" until you are satisfied that you understand the critic's intent. Don't use phrases such as "So what's the matter this time?", "What's wrong with what I did?", or "What's bothering you?" These make you sound defensive and will deter the critic from expressing authentic feelings and wants.

Here's an example of effective probing:

Critic: You're just not pulling your weight around here. Your work is half-assed.

You: What is it about my work that bothers you?

Critic: Well, everybody else is working like a dog, doing overtime. You waltz out of here every night at five o'clock.

You: What is it that bothers you about me leaving the office on time when other people work overtime?

Critic: I hate working overtime myself. But the work has to be done. I'm responsible to see that it is, and I get angry when I see you just working by the clock.

You: What is it that bothers you when I work by the clock?

Critic: When you leave, somebody else has to finish your work. I want you to stick around until it's done.

You: I see. I appreciate you explaining the situation to me.

In this case, probing got you to a clear understanding of the critic's gripe, and a clear request for you to do something about it. If your critic had continued to put you down in vague terms, you could have turned to clouding.

Possible responses:

Acknowledgment: "You're right. I don't seem to get deeply involved with anyone."

Clouding: "It's true that arguing and anger frighten me."

Probing: "What bothers you about my not getting involved?"

Special Assertive Strategies

Broken Record

The broken record is a useful technique to use when you want to say no or otherwise set limits with someone who is having difficulty getting your message. You can use it to say no to your five-year-old, to tell a door-to-door salesperson that you're not interested in buying the product, or to inform your enthusiastic hostess that you really don't want a drink. The broken record can also be an effective way of telling others what you want when their own wishes are blinding them to seeing yours—for instance, when telling your husband that you prefer to go out for French food instead of Mexican, when telling your teenaged son that you want him home by midnight, or when you want to tell your landlord to fix the leaky plumbing.

The broken record is most handy in situations where an explanation would provide the other person with an opportunity to drag out a pointless argument. It has five steps:

1. Clarify in your own mind exactly what you want or don't want. Be aware of your feelings, your thoughts about the situation, and your rights.

2. Formulate a short, specific, easy-to-understand statement about what you want. Keep it to one sentence if you can. Offer no excuses, no explanations. Avoid saying "I can't. . . ." This is an excuse of the worst kind. The other person will probably return with "Of course you can," and then proceed to tell you how. It's much simpler, more direct, and more honest to say "I don't want to. . . ." Review your statement in your mind. Try to get rid of any loopholes which the other person could use to further his or her own argument.

3. Use body language to support your statement. Stand or sit erect, look the other person in the eye, keep your hands quietly at your sides.

4. Calmly and firmly repeat your statement as many times as necessary for the person to get your message and to realize that you won't change your mind. The other person will probably come up with several excuses for not going along with your wishes. He or she may simply say no again and again. But most people run out of no's and excuses eventually. Children and salespersons are particularly persistent, but even they will bow to a consistently repeated clear statement. Don't change your broken record unless the other person finds a serious loophole in it.

5. You may choose to briefly acknowledge the other person's ideas, feelings, or wishes before returning to your broken record. "I understand you're upset, but I don't want to work any more overtime." "I hear what you want, but I don't want to do any more overtime." Don't allow yourself to become sidetracked by the other person's statements.

Here's a dialogue that exemplifies the broken record:

Customer: I bought this blouse here a couple of weeks ago and I want to return it and get my money back.

Salesperson: Do you have a receipt?

Customer: Yes. (She shows it to the salesperson.)

Salesperson: It says you bought the blouse over a month ago. That's too long. How can you expect us to take back something you bought so long ago?

Customer: I understand I bought it a month ago and I want to return it and get my money back.

Salesperson: This is highly irregular. Our store policy is that all returns must be made within one week.

Customer: I understand that and I want to return this blouse and get my money back.

Salesperson: Given the policy, I would feel uncomfortable authorizing your return.

Customer: I can appreciate your feeling uncomfortable about accepting it, but I want to return this blouse and get my money back.

Salesperson: I could lose my job for doing such a thing.

Customer: I hear your worry about losing your job and I still want to return this blouse and get my money back.

Salesperson: Look, I don't want to take any chances. Why don't you return it tomorrow when the manager is here.

Customer: I hear you would rather have me come back tomorrow, but I want to return this blouse and get my money back now.

Salesperson: You sound like a broken record. You're unreal.

Customer: I know I sound that way, but I want to return this blouse and get my money back now.

Salesperson: Okay, okay, okay. Gimme the blouse.

In this example, there was no compromising. However, if the other person changes their position somewhat and you think that a workable compromise can be reached, offer an alternative.

Always prepare your broken record in advance. If you have difficulty saying no to solicitors or to family or friends who ask you for favors, prepare your broken record now. If you want something but are afraid to ask, jot it down in a simple sentence: "I want you to clean up your room right now," or "I want to sit down and discuss the bills with you tonight after dinner." A good rule of thumb is to try the broken record at least four times. You will feel awkward practicing this technique at first, especially if people respond by telling you that you sound like a broken record. But the results you get from this simple but powerful skill will convince you that it's worth the initial discomfort.

Content-to-Process Shift

When you think that the focus of a conversation is drifting away from the topic you want to talk about, use the content-to-process shift. You simply shift from the actual subject being discussed (the content) to what is going on between you and the other person (the process). For instance, you could say, "We've drifted away from what we agreed to discuss into talking about old history." "I realize that I'm doing all the talking on this subject, and you're being very quiet."

A content-to-process shift often involves some self-disclosure about how you are feeling or thinking in the interaction at that very moment. "I'm afraid to go on talking about this. You're turning red and grinding your teeth." "I'm feeling uncomfortable discussing this issue in a public place, and I notice that we're both whispering." "I feel great about getting this problem resolved. We're really communicating! I feel very positive about you right now."

Content-to-process shift is especially helpful when voices are being raised and both people are angry: "I see we're both getting upset. It's a touchy issue," or "We're talking a lot louder and seem squared off for combat." The trick is to comment on what's going on between you in a neutral, dispassionate way, so that your statement won't be experienced as an attack.

Momentary Delay

You may feel compelled to respond immediately to any situation. If asked a question, you feel you have to answer right away. As a result, you may often end up doing or saying something you regret. If you don't take time to check your own feelings and needs, you may be letting others make your decisions for you.

Momentary delays let you make sure that you understand the other person, analyze what has been said, go inside and become aware of what you feel, think, and want in this situation, and consciously influence the situation so that you are more likely to get the outcome you want. Momentary delay is very helpful when you are just learning to use the other assertive techniques presented in this chapter. It gives you time to think and prepare.

Here are some examples:

"Slow down! This is too important to race through."

"That's interesting. Let me think about that for a moment."

"I don't quite understand that. Would you please say it in a different way?"

"This seems important. Would you repeat it?"

"Did I get what you were saying?" (You repeat what you think you heard while you take time to digest it and reflect.)

"I must be getting tired. Let's go over this again, only more slowly."

"Wait a minute. I want to give you my honest answer."

"There may be something to what you are saying . . . let me think about it for a little bit."

Time Out

When you know that what you're discussing is important, but the discussion is at an impasse, delay the conversation until another time. Time out is valuable when the interaction is too passive or too aggressive. One of you may be silent, tearful, or frozen into agreeing with everything the other says. Or one of you may be acting hurtful, name calling, and dragging up antique complaints.

Time out can also be used when you just want some room to think. For example, you're having difficulty deciding which car to buy and the car salesperson is pressuring you. Or your girlfriend has just told you that she loves you and wants to know how you feel about her. Or you've just been invited to spend the weekend at your in-laws' beach house.

These are typical examples of time-out situations:

In response to an inflexible, blaming co-worker, you say: "I think what we're talking about is important, and I'd like to discuss it with you tomorrow."

You're about to dissolve into tears or rage, or you're feeling very anxious. Further discussion would be fruitless or just too painful. So you say: "Time out. I'm upset right now. I know that I will be able to deal with this issue much more effectively tomorrow."

You are feeling pressured to do something that you're not sure you want to do. You say: "I want to sleep on it." "I'll get back to you next week." "I want to talk to my spouse (attorney, accountant, friend) about this before I make a decision." "This is important; when's a good time for you next week to discuss it?"

Don't abuse time out by using it repeatedly to avoid a difficult problem. Set up a specific time in the near future to continue your discussion.

Assertive Skills Practice

Using these assertive skills will feel awkward at first. Ideally you will practice these skills with a sympathetic friend or another student before you apply them in your daily life. If you are learning these skills on your own, you will find the "empty chair" technique helpful in rehearsing them:

Imagine that the person with whom you want to be assertive is sitting in a chair facing you. See the person's face in your mind's eye. How are they sitting, how are they dressed? Try to see as clear a picture as you can.

Now make your assertive statement as though the person were really in the chair listening.

When you are finished, move to the empty chair. Pretend you are the other person and respond as you think that person would respond.

Return to your own chair and notice how you feel and what you think of the other person's response. Make an appropriate assertive statement.

Continue this process, moving back and forth between the two chairs until you have finished the interaction.

If you feel too self-conscious using this empty chair technique, try going through its steps in your imagination. Or write out a script with your statements and the responses of the other person set down as in our examples. Many people find it helpful to rehearse their assertive lines in front of a mirror in order to make sure that their body language is consistent with what they're saying. Tape recording an imaginary assertive conversation can also be very useful. All of these techniques give you an opportunity to slowly integrate the assertive skills into your everyday life.

Excerpted and adapted with permission from *Messages: The Communication Skills Book* by Matthew McKay, Ph.D., Martha Davis, Ph.D., and Patrick Fanning. For more information on this and related books, see the "Further Reading" section in the back of the book.

CHAPTER 5

Stepfamilies

Stepfamily life can be wonderful or miserable. There are many reasons for this. While all families are complex and have many difficult challenges and problems to face, this is even more so in stepfamilies.

The simplistic notion that a stepfamily is like a first-time family has trapped countless adults and children, who often face, for the second time, the disintegration of their world and their dreams.

Why do hopes dry up and dreams not come true for so many people who enter stepfamily life with optimism and joyful anticipation? Why does the "second time around" appear to be even more difficult for many couples than the "first time around"?

It is because stepfamily life presents many *unique and complex challenges*. If these are to be successfully confronted and overcome, people need to have even more knowledge, understanding, skill and maturity than first-time families demand. This is not understood by most people.

A stepfamily is one in which at least one partner has at least one child from a previous relationship. These families come in many different shapes and sizes. They have many different living arrangements and patterns of interaction.

In spite of this, however, many of the problems they face are similar. This is irrespective of whether

- the parents of the stepfamily are legally married

- the "ex" lives nearby or far away

- an ex-partner keeps in touch

- a stepparent was previously widowed or divorced

- the children live at home or are adults themselves

Stepfamilies *are* different from other families in many ways. Let's now look at some of these differences.

Why Stepfamilies Are Different

- At least one partner has experienced marriage and parenthood before or a partner who is a parent has never been married.

- Stepparents who have never married or lived with a partner are unaccustomed to family life (apart from their family of origin).

- Adults and children come into the relationship at the outset.

- The parent and stepparent often do not have time together alone before having children live with them.

- Stepparents have to live with, care for and/or relate to stepchildren with whom they have no "history." There is a lack of bonding.

- Single-parent family life often precedes stepfamily life.

- There is at least one "intruder" in the stepfamily unit.

- Children often lose contact with a parent from the previous family—sometimes this is a loss of daily contact, other times it is forever.

- Children often have two homes with two sets of rules, conditions, discipline, etc.

- Visiting children/stepchildren have to be accommodated into the stepfamily from time to time.

- Family members may experience relocation of home, school, job, activities, etc.

- New responsibilities may emerge.

- Unfinished business from a past marriage (anger, grief, guilt, anxiety) can come into stepfamily life.

- Suspicion and lack of trust between stepparent and stepchildren may exist.

- Surnames of children can be different and create a sense of not belonging.

- There are more people, all at once, having to get used to each other.

- There is no legal relationship between stepparent and stepchild.

- Socioeconomic conditions might change; money can be tight.

- Sibling order might change so the oldest, for example, could now be a middle child.

- There might be less space or territory for each person.

- At least one person has to adjust to living in a different home—with different family rules, etc.

For a stepfamily to reach maturity and its full potential, it typically passes through various stages as the years unfold. These are part of the overall unique process of the growth of a stepfamily. Within this process, the marriage relationship is the pivotal point. It too encounters natural stages which affect the whole stepfamily.

Stages in Stepfamily Growth

1. The Fantasy Stage

There is a lack of reality in the shared belief of the husband and wife that with this marriage all dreams of happy family life will come true. In some cases stepsiblings are excited about having each other and look forward to fun times together. Sometimes children look forward to living with a "mother" or "father" again. There is idealism and, to a certain degree, illusion and delusion. In this stage the parent and stepparent do not really know each other—they have not lived together long enough for the idealism of their relationship to wane. Many, if not most, of the people involved put their best foot forward so as to be liked and even loved.

2. The Confusion Stage

In this stage differences begin to emerge and there is a growing awareness that the happiness and joy that have previously been experienced and expected are slipping away. There is typically a denial of many signs of impending trouble. This stage is characterized by a growing tension. For the parents, the romantic phase of their relationship may have run its course; the novelty for the children has worn off (if ever it was there); there is fear that this family is not going to make it; many issues are unidentified or unresolved.

3. The Conflict Stage

In stepfamilies, as within marriage, this stage may involve open or hidden expressions of anger and aggression. Either way it creates tension, stress and the breakdown of relationships and family life unless conflict resolution skills are used. In this stage family members become aware that some or many of their own needs are not being met. Up until now these needs might not have seemed important. Power struggles ensue. The conflict stage is a normal and natural stage and has to be negotiated with skill for the maturity of stepfamily life to be achieved. The "blending" or "curdling" of the stepfamily is determined by the way in which this inevitable stage is handled.

4. The Coming-Together Stage

Gradually the stepfamily moves into a stage where emotionality is not as intense, family members are learning how to resolve issues and there is, among stepfamily members, a growing awareness that they are, in fact, a family. Relationships, even if not ideal, are becoming comfortably familiar. The family system is operating smoothly or at least is able to get back on balance after an upset. This stage is an important phase in the growth of a stepfamiy and one where hope is renewed.

5. The Resolution Stage

When this stage is reached there is relief that the bad times have passed. Optimism returns and the future looks better. Family members are more able to be themselves and to accept each other for better or worse. Family ties are now growing as familiarity develops. Methods for resolving conflict have been learned and will, of course, need to be used again and again. When a stepfamily reaches this stage, the original myths have been dispelled and dreams begin to come true.

If you are beginning to have a sense of despair and are saying to yourself, "Help! I married for all the wrong reasons. This isn't what I expected!" you are probably going through a stage that most step-couples experience. You are going through a "normal" stage of stepfamily growth.

Blending or Curdling Stepfamilies

Stepfamilies are often referred to as blended families. This term probably refers to the union, or coming together, of three or more people who form a family that is not a first-time family. They have blended to form another sort of family. If, however, the word blended is meant to imply a harmonious union, then the word is a misnomer.

Given that stepfamily life, *like that of any family*, involves an ongoing process, it makes more sense to refer to successful stepfamilies as blending families. If, on the other hand, stepfamily life becomes embroiled in difficulties and unhappiness, the process may well be one of curdling.

A blending stepfamily is one in which the overall experience is one of increasing joy—in spite of the inevitable hurdles along the way.

A curdling stepfamily is one in which the process of blending has become stuck, and the overall experience is one of increasing despair. There is an accompanying inability to resolve the issues and difficulties that are normally encountered in stepfamily life.

The goal is not to be a blended stepfamily as such, but to be able to reach the resolution stage, wherein the blending process is successfully continuing.

The measure of blending is the degree to which family members can resolve their issues and continue to develop their relationships in a positive way.

Positive Possibilities for Stepfamilies

The image of the "Brady Bunch" type of family is a myth. This television series, and others like it, have led many people to think that stepfamily bliss can be easily experienced. Many couples have been tricked by the happy antics and warm fuzzy feelings of these television families into believing that this joy awaits them once they embark on stepfamily life. Such beliefs are a trap, and one from which many people never escape.

They are unaware of the forces in stepfamilies that, if not dealt with constructively and with skill, create a tangled mass (and mess!) of mixed emotions. This lack of awareness results in misery and confusion for everyone, and leads to the curdling and disintegration of stepfamily life.

On the bright side, these same forces can be utilized for the creation of a unique, united and truly blending stepfamily. You need information, the opportunity to think and learn about yourself and your family, and a willingness to learn new skills.

If you, your partner and your families embark on this journey of blending, everyone will experience happiness along the way. In fact, this is what happiness is all about—succeeding day in and day out in the process of overcoming obstacles, and seeking new joys with each other. While there may be difficult times along the way, the overall feeling can be one of pleasure that you are moving ahead in the blending process.

How Stepfamilies Work

A family is sometimes referred to as a family "system." This system consists of different parts or persons. It always operates (unconsciously) to maintain a familiarity which keeps it in a state of balance. If this familiarity goes, the family is thrown off balance and strives to find a new balance.

When a family experiences death, separation, divorce, or remarriage, family members have to adjust to the change and find a new balance. This is usually a painful process and may take many years. This balance is really an *emotional balance* which is experienced as security—or a feeling of comfort—in family members.

When a stepfamily system forms, it encounters all of the forces that operate in other families, but because of its added complexities, family members usually take longer to find a state of balance within this system.

They also encounter barriers to establishing an identity of their own. For first-time families, upon marriage and with the addition of each child, identities are established naturally. This process is the goal of stepfamily life and yet often proves to be very difficult—if not impossible.

Any group of two or more people within the family system forms a subsystem. Here are some subsystems that can exist in stepfamilies:

a. The ex-partners (parents of the children)

b. Husband and wife (one or two step-couples)

c. Husband and his children (from the first-time family)

d. Wife and her children (from the first-time family)

e. The children of the husband (from the first time family)

f. The children of the wife (from the first-time family)

g. All the children (from parent and stepparent)

These additional subsystems in stepfamilies make the process of finding a balance, and an identity, far more complex than in first-time families.

"Triangling" in the Family System

A common interaction between family members is when a third person becomes involved in a matter concerning two other family members. This is called "triangling," and is very dangerous in families.

A person may "triangle in" on others without permission, or that person may be invited to do it. Here are some examples of the triangling that took place in the lives of Matthew and Patricia and their children:

Triangling without Being Asked

- Matthew heard his daughter on the telephone pleading with his ex-wife Pat to take her out. Pat remained firm. Matthew became angry and took over, accusing Pat of being selfish and uncaring. (Matthew triangled in on an interaction between his daughter and her mother.)

- When Pat left Matthew and the children, Matthew's parents went to see Pat and demanded that she return. (Matthew's parents triangled in on an issue that was between Pat and Matthew.)

- Matthew could not restrain himself in his new stepfamily from telling his stepson that he was ungrateful and lazy and no help at all to his mother. (Matthew triangled in on an issue between his stepson and the boy's mother.)

Being Asked to Triangle in on Someone Else's Issue

- Matthew and Pat's youngest daughter asked her mother to tell her father to make sure he didn't get her to softball late. (Pat was asked by her daughter to triangle in on an issue that existed between the child and her father.)

- Matthew arranged to meet Pat's second husband and asked him to make sure that Pat kept in regular contact with their children. (Pat's second husband was triangled in by Matthew so that he became involved in an issue between Matthew, Pat and their children.)

- Pat phoned Matthew's brother and asked him to talk to Matthew about the way Matthew spoiled the children. She had tried unsuccessfully herself to do this. (Matthew's brother was triangled in by Pat to become involved in an issue that was certainly not his.)

Triangling is dynamite! Here are two rules to follow if you want to work toward the blending of your stepfamily:

1. *Never* triangle in on anyone else's issue—even if you are asked to do so (unless you think someone's personal safety is involved).

2. *Never* ask anyone to triangle in on your issues. Try to resolve them yourself. Sometimes an impartial person, such as a therapist, is needed to help couples and families resolve conflict.

Three Key Factors in Stepfamilies

When two people and one or more children come together to form a stepfamily, there are three very important factors operating:

1. Individual differences that exist between them.

2. The force of togetherness, or "we-ness"—a natural, instinctual drive which pulls people together.

3. The drive of separateness, or "I-ness"—a natural instinctual drive to be an individual.

These very powerful influences are present in every family, but in stepfamilies they are even more complex.

Individual Differences

Stepfamily members are very different from each other—much more different than they usually realize. Each person has his or her own individual package of characteristics. The following list shows some of what each person brings into the stepfamily:

- His or her own genetic inheritance.

- Family of origin influences that have been handed down through many generations.

- Values, attitudes, beliefs about all sorts of life issues (for example: health, discipline, loyalty, honesty, family, tidiness, friendship, enjoyment, education, spirituality, punctuality, home ownership, children, finance and so on).

- Traditions and rituals.

- Behaviors that are culturally determined (for example: ethnic, socioeconomic, family, etc.).

- Religious convictions.

- Political convictions.

- Individual traits and ways of thinking.

- Life experiences (from birth to the present time).

- Decisions about how to live life.

- Order of birth (for example: first child, middle child, fourth of five, youngest of nine children).

- Exposure to different role models (mother, father, etc.).

- Experiences and learned behaviors as husband or wife (in first or previous marriage(s)).

- Unfinished (emotional) business from first or previous marriage(s).

- Current situation (for partners) with regard to parental status.

- Unfinished (emotional) business from childhood.

- Communication patterns.

- Conflict resolution methods.

- Expressions of sexuality.

- Degree of comfort with intimacy (verbal and nonverbal).

- Social life, hobbies, interests.

- Educational background and achievement.

- State of health.

- Physical energy and cycles of energy.

- Wealth and social class factors.

- Food traditions and preferences.

And so on. . . .

With all these differences it's a wonder that people get together in the first place. The interesting thing is that instead of recognizing all that is so different between them, when two people enter a relationship they are more inclined to think they are similar.

Think about your relationship and the differences between you and your partner—especially at the time you met each other. Did you know then that there were many differences between the two of you? In what areas have you become more similar? Are there any factors that apply to you that are not mentioned in the above list? Which of the above do you think applied to the children in your stepfamily at the time it was formed? What differences exist between them now?

The Force of Togetherness

In every family there exists an instinctual "togetherness force," or drive that pulls family members together. Its "motor" has two elements: one is each person's genetically programmed instinct to do this, the other is the unconscious self of each family member.

This togetherness force operates most strongly between related family members. To a lesser degree, it is also present between couples, in stepfamilies, in groups and even in nations. This drive, or force, pulls people together and gives them a sense of we-ness through similar belief systems, attitudes, values, desires, ways of behaving and even similar emotional reactions to different life situations.

First of all we will look at what happens in marriage relationships with respect to seeking sameness. Even though people are so different from each other, at the start of their relationship they become focused on their similarities. This involves denial and is what makes them believe they are made for each other. Some or all of their differences are hidden or unknown. This is because it is more comfortable for them if they seem to "be the same"—operating out of their pseudo selves and agreeing about all sorts of things (even if they don't!), thus gaining the approval (and love) of each other.

Even if differences are noticed in these early days, there is a denial of these—so great is the need to seem to be the same. This is why romantic love is often referred to as being blind.

Sooner or later, when the illusory romantic phase of the relationship has waned and differences are now being acknowledged, the drive for togetherness or *the need to be the same* gets into gear. Each partner now operates more out of his or her real self. Bit by bit pressure is applied by each one to *make the partner the same as him or her*. "Why don't you pick up your clothes?" (the way I do); "Gosh, don't you like curry? Try it" (my family loves curry); "For goodness sake, close the door!" (the way I was taught to).

If the differences between partners create discomfort, either the togetherness force begins to operate between them or, alternatively, they distance themselves from each other.

When two people enter a second marriage, they have experienced life in two families: their family of origin and their first marriage. In each of these families the togetherness needs have shaped the personality and behavior of these people.

Seeking Sameness with Children in Stepfamilies

Much like adults, children who enter stepfamily life usually find that they have to adapt to a new set of rules, values, beliefs, behaviors and so on. They frequently resist any attempt to behave as their stepparent wants them to. "Mom doesn't make me eat my peas." "Dad used to clean my shoes." The greater the enforcement of rules by these newcomers in their lives, the greater might be their resistance.

What often evolves in stepfamilies is an "I'm going to win at any cost" attitude. This cost is often the marriage and stepfamily. For many people the thought of giving in is unthinkable. On and on they go, trying to make people be the way they want them to be. They are driven by unconscious forces, seeking security in the name of sameness or togetherness.

(*Note:* If this is what you do, it will be constructive for you and your stepfamily if you think deeply and try to find out what drives you to push this way. Your conscious mind can do a lot of thinking and exploring, and maybe in the process will retrieve some information out of your past which may shed light on what your behavior is about.)

Here is what one stepfather did when he became aware that his attempts to get his stepchildren to do as he asked were unsuccessful and causing much conflict in his stepfamily:

> Bruce was constantly at war with his stepchildren, Amy and Eliza. He wanted them to sit up straight at the dinner table, to finish everything on their plate, and not to interrupt when he or his wife were speaking. Furthermore, he expected them to clear the dinner table and help their mother in the kitchen every night.
>
> For quite a while he blamed his new wife for not having raised these children "correctly" and was determined to "teach" them the right way. Many awful fights had erupted over these issues, and still Bruce continued to try to make his stepchildren behave the way his own children had been taught to behave. In reality, when he started to think deeply about all of this, he was trying to make them behave as he had been made to behave when he was a child. He now realized how he had hated his father for controlling him in this way! He began to realize he had a lot of anger toward his father about this, which he was taking out on his stepchildren (displacement). He also realized that he felt guilty that he wasn't with his own children, and this was affecting his behavior too. Once he had these realizations, he was able to "own" the problem as his and gradually was able to relax and allow his stepchildren more freedom.

Take Time

Think about the pressures you put on others to do things your way. Ask yourself: "Where did I learn that this (value, behavior, attitude) is important?" "What would be the worst thing that might happen if I don't get my way?"

Teenagers in Stepfamilies

When small children come into stepfamilies, they are more likely to adapt to new rules and family behaviors than are older children. When teenagers enter stepfamily life, additional problems are likely, however skilled the parent and stepparent are at parenting and relating.

This is because at the very time that the togetherness force begins to exert its strength in the creation of the new family, the teenager has reached the natural developmental stage in life when he or she seeks to separate in order to seek his or her identity. The question "Who am I?" becomes a burning psychological issue, and original family and stepfamily values are frequently challenged and flaunted. (It's interesting that often the adolescent does this by striving to be the same as his or her peers at school.)

This can be a very difficult time for parents, stepparents and children. In many ways, however, the difficulties are no different from those in first-time families when children enter the teenage years, although it is probably true to say that stepfamily life, together with unresolved issues from the family of origin, combine to make this time quite turbulent for many adolescents and their families.

Some Strategies That Are Used in Stepfamilies to Force Togetherness

Here are some of the things that people might do to force togetherness in stepfamilies:

- Mealtimes all together, all the time (terrible for most teenagers).

- Disagreements not allowed.

- Children told to "be nice" to other members of the stepfamily.

- Family outings together, even if a child wants to do something else.

- Insistence that a child kiss his or her stepparent good night.

- Dressing stepsiblings alike so they look as though they belong to each other.

- Stepparent told by partner to inquire after his (her) child's day.

- Over-involvement in many areas of children's life—especially by stepparent who wants to be involved.

- Name change so that all family members match.

- Stepparent to be called "Mom" or "Dad."

- Stepchildren to call step-grandparents "Grandma," "Grandpa" or whatever the natural children call them.

- Stepsiblings sent to the same school, so as to be together.

- Pressure put on children to play happily together and love each other.

While some of these strategies might contribute to stepfamily happiness, depending on how they are implemented, they might just manipulate stepfamily members to fit in with someone's dream of being one happy family. Usually the effects of this are damaging to the stepfamily and contribute to the curdling process.

Some Characteristics of Stepfamilies Where *Positive* Togetherness Behaviors are Predominant

- Family members know each other and accept differences between themselves.

- There is a feeling of security because family members care for each other by nurturing each other in a nonthreatening way.

- Family members are interested in the lives of each other but do not interfere.

- Family members give support and comfort to each other.

- There is love, devotion and compassion between family members.

- A sense of belonging, but having freedom at the same time, is experienced by family members.

- Family members are there for each other: for example, at times of crisis or rejoicing.

- Cooperation rather than competition exists.

- Family members communicate honestly with each other.

- There is a working together toward the goal of blending.

- There is enjoyment at being together.

- When family members experience conflict between themselves they are able to resolve it.

- Family members share rituals, traditions and family celebrations.

- There is respect for each other.

- A strong sense of trust and loyalty exists.

- There is a lack of gossip about each other.

- Family members are united, yet retain a strong sense of their own identity.

The Force of Separateness

The two forces of togetherness and separateness push and pull against each other and underlie your interactions in relationships at home, at work and at play. In stepfamilies that are striving for a sense of togetherness, each member is also striving to maintain or achieve a sense of being a separate person, with his or her individual way of thinking, feeling and being in the world.

The challenge in living with others and getting along with them is trying to achieve a balance between these two instinctual drives. It is natural to seek closeness, that feeling of we-ness, at the same time that you seek to be your own separate person, with a sense of "I-ness."

The two-year-old's tantrum demonstrates the power of the force of separateness. This behavior is well-known to many parents and often to other family members as well. The two-year-old is asserting him- or herself to get his or her own way. This is very interesting, because no one teaches a toddler to have a trantrum. It is instinctual and the drive is so strong that no one has any control over it, let alone the child.

Even before the age of two, children have learned that they are separate human beings. This is one of the first major lessons that babies instinctively learn: that they are not part of mother but that they exist alone in the world.

When children have pressure put on them to be as others want them to be, they often rebel.

Melissa, age eight, had recently started to live in her new stepfamily with her father and two brothers. Her stepmother did not like the way she spoke to her brothers. She wanted her to "be respectful and polite." The more she insisted that Melissa change her ways, the more Melissa had to fight for her own sense of self. She did this by being even more disrespectful to her brothers—and her stepmother!

(*Note:* Melissa's stepmother is driven by the togetherness force to make her stepdaughter conform to her values, and Melissa is driven by the separateness force to resist. This resistance helps her retain and even reinforce her sense of who she is: her identity or sense of self.)

Older children often rebel, too, when they experience pressure from others to conform.

Albert and Jenny sat around the dinner table with their respective children discussing politics. One of the children, now at voting age, was explaining why she would vote differently from her stepfamily at the next election. All hell broke loose. She was criticized as being ignorant, foolish, rebellious. . . . But (fortunately for her) she remained steadfast and true to herself in the face of this onslaught.

(*Note:* In seeking a sense of I-ness a certain amount of rebellion in children is healthy. Some children, however, learn to be more compliant than rebellious. This is because they feel safer—perhaps because of punishment, conflict or rejection (or the fear of these) should they present a challenge to the authority figures. Children who are overly compliant often grow into adults with a more poorly defined sense of self.)

The greater the pressures are in a stepfamily for a family member to conform to the thoughts, desires or behaviors of other family members, the more likely it is that this person will fight to be different and separate.

Negative and Positive Separateness Behaviors

Given that each one of us is driven to be our own separate and individual person, there are many ways we try to bring this about. We have not been given lessons but instead have developed, in our own unique and creative ways, many different strategies to fulfill this life task. Some of them have had positive outcomes for us and our partners, families and friends and others have had negative outcomes. These outcomes are on a continuum, so that you will probably be able to identify items that apply to you in each of the next two lists. First, here are the negative outcomes:

- Self-centeredness.
- Isolating self by pulling away from others (physically as well as with behaviors that push people away).
- Rebellious attitudes and behaviors.
- Creating disunity (through isolation and rebellion).
- Disrespect for others.
- Lack of interest in the well-being of others.
- Selfishness.
- Being emotionally dead or overemotional.
- Fear of intimacy or close friendship.
- Emotional cutting off.
- Being pseudo rather than real.
- Finding it difficult to trust others.
- Lack of respect for the uniqueness of others.
- Likely to be jealous.
- Discomfort when people disagree.
- Difficulty in giving and receiving love.
- Fearful of losing self (arguing, being defensive).

- Fearful of rejection.

- Low self-esteem as a result of the above.

- The family is disengaged.

Here are the positive outcomes:

- The ability to think, feel and act for oneself.

- The ability to be alone, and to enjoy aloneness.

- Speaking for oneself (comfortable with the use of the word "I").

- Being emotionally separate from family. This means that emotional issues with the family of origin have been resolved. (Although it is said that no one ever completes this task.)

- Being real (true to self) rather than pseudo (seeking approval from others).

- An ability to trust oneself.

- A sense of inner freedom.

- An ability to trust others (many people find this difficult).

- An ability to respect the individuality of others and not try to make them be the same (as oneself).

- Working at the positive aspects of togetherness without losing a sense of self.

- Acting on the basis of thoughts rather than feelings.

- Taking responsibility for oneself (not blaming others).

- Exploring one's life philosophy, courses of action, values, etc., and not relying on what other people think.

- Not minding if someone disagrees.

- Being self-disciplined.

- Not being rebellious—cooperating and compromising when appropriate.

- An ability to love others for who they are.

- An ability to be intimate without fear of losing oneself.

- Developing high self-esteem as a result of all of the above.

Take Time

Which of the above behaviors, in either list, do you think apply to you? Which ones apply to your partner? Your children? Your stepchildren? What can you do to make changes in yourself? Do you want to behave in more positive ways to develop your own individuality and enhance your self-esteem?

For additional information, see the chapters in part I on Couple Skills and Communication, or the chapter on low Self-Esteem in part V.

Excerpted and adapted with permission from *Stepfamily Realities: How to Overcome Difficulties and Have a Happy Family* by Margaret Newman. For more information on this and related books, see the "Further Reading" section in the back of the book.

CHAPTER 6

Infidelity

Our trust in our loved ones, especially our romantic partners, allows us to rely on and support those around us. When that trust is breached, we may have to reassess our relationships with others and with ourselves. This chapter will address how infidelity can affect our relationships.

The word *infidelity* means the breaking of trust. When people marry they pledge before their friends, families, the state, and in most cases, their god, that they will remain faithful to one another until separated by death. Indeed, this expectation of mutual trust is the foundation of their commitment to each other. One significant element of this trust is the unspoken vow that the couple will remain sexually exclusive. Another is that there is a certain level of emotional intimacy that is reserved for the couple, not to be shared with others. Having pledged faithfulness, it is not surprising that the discoverer experiences such shock upon finding that a mate has violated it. *Infidelity occurs when one partner in a relationship continues to believe that the agreement to be faithful is still in force, while the other partner is secretly violating it.*

You do not have to be married to experience infidelity. Many people are in long-term, exclusive relationships. They may remain unmarried, but in some way "wedded." This may be by mutual choice, because one partner refuses to marry, or by necessity (as is often the case with long-term gay or lesbian relationships). Although many of the ideas and studies I've drawn upon have been derived from the study of conventional marriage, unmarried couples in long-term relationships often face the same issues. For this reason, I will sometimes refer specifically to marital issues, and at others to problems affecting all exclusive relationships.

The Moment of Discovery

The moment you realize that your mate has been unfaithful you feel overwhelmed. You are flooded with thoughts: "How long has this been going on?" "Does this mean my relationship is over?" "How many other people know?" "How could I have ever trusted him?" "How could she have ever done such a thing to me?" "How could I ever trust this person again—even if I wanted to?" "Is this the first time it has happened?" "Should I confront him about this right now?" "Should I just ignore it? Maybe it's just a passing thing." "Should I set a trap?" "Should I talk with other people about it? My friend recently went through something like this—maybe it would be a good idea to talk to her about it."

Accompanying these thoughts is a rush of feelings: rage, shame, hurt, jealousy, betrayal, fear, uncertainty. Some people are so overcome at the moment of discovery that they have profound physical reactions. Many of my patients have reported bouts of vomiting or diarrhea. Others, normally the calmest of people, have screamed themselves hoarse, broken objects, or physically attacked the unfaithful mate. Some have considered suicide, others homicide.

Most of my patients report that at the moment of discovery their predominant feeling is that all hope is lost and that the relationship is over. In fact, the majority of marriages that I've treated because of infidelity have not only survived, but improved. As you read this chapter, you will discover that in many instances there are factors that have led to the infidelity, and that if both partners work together to repair these circumstances, their relationship will be greatly enhanced.

Just as the discoverer of infidelity suffers, the mate whose unfaithfulness is discovered may also be filled with painful thoughts and feelings. Unfaithful mates are often not at all sure that they really want to end their relationships. They seem to have put all of their thoughts and feelings about their unfaithfulness in another part of their mind, as if being unfaithful had nothing to do with their long-term relationship. Until their actions are discovered, or they sense that they are on the verge of being revealed, many people never even imagined that they would be found out.

Nor have they imagined the devastating effects on their mates, their children, their families, themselves, or the third parties. The mate who has been discovered may experience feelings and thoughts as intense as those experienced by the discoverer. One patient, Roger, told me, "I am really afraid of destroying my marriage. I can't imagine what it might do to my kids, and I'm not even sure that I really don't love my wife anymore. But I am just as fearful about losing what I've found with Sally [the other woman]. I feel so alive with her—there's so much excitement. I haven't felt like this in years." Roger also told me that he was really worried that Sally might try to retaliate in some way if he tried to cut off the relationship. Roger's fears and confusions are similar to those experienced by many people at or close to the moment of discovery.

Denial

Even though the revelation of an infidelity is overwhelming and shocking to both the discoverer and the discovered, reflection often leads them to recognize a series of actions, hints, and behaviors that preceded not only the discovery, but the infidelity itself. Each partner has been engaged in hiding many other thoughts and feelings from him- or herself, often for a long period of time.

The term describing the ability to hide things from yourself is denial. Denial is an unconscious act. You don't will yourself to deny—it simply happens. It can be defined as a way of resolving emotional conflict and allaying anxiety by the unconscious disavowal of thoughts that would be otherwise unbearable. In most cases, the discoverer has been increasingly plagued with fleeting thoughts that "something is wrong." Somehow these thoughts are so unacceptable that they remain in denial until the weight of evidence is so overwhelming that it must be faced. If you have recently discovered your partner's infidelity, you may now recall a series of circumstances which, with hindsight, indicated that something was going wrong. These might include changes in work habits, sudden and unexplained expenses, and even warnings from friends that they suspected something. At a deeper level, you may have been denying that there was some meaningful decline in the quality of the marriage, one that you may have ignored for a long time and never talked about. You may want to begin keeping a journal to jot down your thoughts and feelings. Use it now to try to figure out what signals you might have been missing before that may help you to understand what was going wrong. The couple mentioned earlier, Roger and his wife Ann, began keeping journals at my suggestion after his affair came to light. Here are some entries:

Ann: For years now, almost all we ever talked about was the kids. Now I remember that whenever he wanted to do something alone with me, the kids were always with us. It's like they were a shield between us. I think he must have felt I was pushing him away. But there was stuff I was ignoring about him, stuff that should have told me something was wrong. All of a sudden his hours were changing, I couldn't get hold of him if I needed to talk to him. He didn't really seem to approach me to make love anymore. I guess because he would do it with me if I approached him, it fooled me into thinking things were okay—but it was really never that way before. He even shaved off his mustache—maybe that should have told me that he was doing it for someone else.

Roger: So many times I wanted to sit Ann down and tell her how boring things were getting between us. Maybe it wasn't true, but when I would come home from work, I felt like she couldn't have cared less. Maybe I should have said something then. I think I just buried all those thoughts. I don't know how to tell Ann when I'm angry. It always seems to make her cry—so I'm gun-shy. Maybe that's why it looked so good with Sally for a while— because I didn't have to explain anything, and I had her attention whenever I wanted it.

Sometimes There Is No Answer

Sometimes an unfaithful mate is such a skilled liar that it is all but unthinkable that an infidelity has occurred. In this situation, the many clues that are ignored when you're in denial can't be discovered, even with the virtue of hindsight. For example, Randi came to me following a discovery that was so shocking to her that she had been hospitalized with what she thought was a heart attack, which turned out to be a severe anxiety reaction. She had been in what she regarded as a "perfect" relationship. Her fiancé was very understanding, extremely thoughtful, affectionate, and considerate. Randi's folks thought that he was a perfect mate for her, and after two years of courtship, she and John had set a wedding date. Announcements were sent out, a hall was rented, and bridesmaids were chosen. A day or two before the wedding, Randi needed to check some details with him, so she decided to drop in at his apartment. She came in to find him in bed with another woman. In the months of therapy that followed, she found it impossible to find any clues that would have predicted his behavior—he had been unfailingly kind and considerate, and they had never had any sort of blowup.

Randi's distrust was so powerful that it was two years before she dared even to say hello to a man. She felt totally unprotected from future betrayal. There was absolutely nothing that she could learn from this experience that would make her a better judge of men. In one session, she told me that she wished that she had been in denial, because then she would have felt more prepared to be alert about possible dishonesty in her next relationship. She wasn't wrong. When you understand what you have denied, you can correct it—if not in your current relationship, at least in the next one.

Compartmentalization

When people are in denial, their unconscious plays a trick on them. It is as if all tracks of the offending thought or feeling have been obliterated. By contrast, there are situations in which people are very conscious of what they are doing, but develop the ability to disconnect that awareness from other aspects of their lives. Patrick's case is a useful example.

Patrick had been married for about ten years. At first he felt he had a perfect marriage. Over time, almost without his awareness, the joy seemed to go out of his and Charlene's relationship. As the children came along, Charlene sensed a sadness that never seemed to leave Patrick. From time to time she would try to confront him. "Is there anything wrong?" she would ask. Or, "I don't know what's the matter with you, Patrick—you used to smile all the time. I think it's been years since I saw a real smile come from deep inside of you." Try as he might, he could never name anything that would account for his sad mood. If anything, her questions simply annoyed him. Patrick wasn't lying. He was numb to his feelings. If he was occasionally aware of some feeling, such as anger at the loss of Charlene's companionship that seemed to come along with motherhood, he would dismiss it, thinking, "I guess this is just normal."

Patrick just didn't see any connection between his sadness and these thoughts. If someone had asked him at this point in his life if his marriage was all right, he would probably have said that it was—maybe not great, but certainly all right. When he drifted into an affair at work, he was mildly surprised. It seemed so out of character for him. He was very excited about the affair, because it provided him with the attention and emotional involvement that he had lost with Charlene. But if someone had asked him he would probably have said, "I just don't see the connection."

Patrick was surprised about something else as well—the energy his affair produced. He could go to work, spend hours slipping notes to his new friend, Connie, and eagerly awaiting her replies. He couldn't get her out of his mind during the workday. Sometimes they would steal away for a couple of hours to go to a motel and make love. He was amazed at how alive he felt—almost like when he had first met Charlene. The strange thing was that when he came home, Connie was all but forgotten. He could make love to Charlene, feeling no guilt or strangeness. It was as if there was one box in his mind for Charlene and another for Connie. The two boxes seemed sealed, each absolutely separate from the other. Some psychologists call this phenomenon compartmentalization. Unlike denial, compartmentalization is a conscious act. Patrick knew that he was having an affair. He knew he was married. He was aware that he was experiencing pleasure in the affair.

Compartmentalization and denial often exist side by side. Beyond the ability to compartmentalize the affair, the mate who has been unfaithful is often also in denial about problems in the marriage. As we have seen, Patrick was quite aware that he was excited about his affair. He remained unaware, however, of his feelings about his marriage. Because he could compartmentalize the affair, he was able to say to Charlene that he couldn't see what his office affair had to do with his marriage. Locked in separate compartments, his marriage and affair seemed to have nothing to do with each other. He believed that nothing he could do in his marriage would remove his need for the affair. Nor could he imagine himself wanting to end either his affair or his marriage.

Patrick's situation is not unusual. When I speak with each mate alone following the discovery of an infidelity, I often find that they have never really talked very much or very well with one another about the satisfactions and the problems that they have been experiencing in the marriage. In some types of infidelity, it is this persistent and shared denial that sets the scene for the subsequent affair. Denial and compartmentalization play different roles in various types of infidelity. We will now examine some of the ways in which infidelity occurs.

Types of Infidelity

Each type of infidelity brings with it its own problems, and each may require different types of help if the situation is to improve. As you read these descriptions, whether you are the discoverer or the discovered, try to determine which type of infidelity best describes your current situation.

One-Night Stands

Anita came to me one day in a highly agitated state. She reported to me that she had recently attended a conference out of town. There she met a man, with whom she had a few drinks and ended up in her hotel room, where they had sex. She reported that by the next morning, she was feeling awful. The night before she had felt excited and powerful, but when she awakened in the morning she felt entirely different. Her mind was racing: "Did anyone see us go off to the room? We were both drunk, and it was a stupid thing to do, as exciting as it seemed last night. What if I got a disease? Should I tell my husband?" She reported that this was the first time that it had happened, and that it was going to be the last. She said, "It's funny—it's like the time I used LSD in college. When I did it, it was kind of exciting and novel. But the next day, it really scared me that I had done it. God knows what could have happened. And because of that feeling, I never tried it again. The difference is, with the LSD I only risked hurting myself. With this thing, I risked hurting my husband and my marriage." Further conversation revealed that she felt her marriage was satisfying for both her and her husband, that their love life was excellent, and they felt, for the most part, very close and could talk easily with one another. Nonetheless, she feared his reaction should she reveal her one-night stand to him.

Philandering

I have never treated a philanderer who came willingly to therapy. Frank was no exception. He said that the only reason he had agreed to come was because his wife Jane had told him that her next move would be to see a divorce lawyer. During the first meeting, Jane could barely contain her rage. She frequently arose from her seat to pace around the room. "You've been playing around for years," she screamed. "You're all wrong," he replied. Suddenly she reached into her bag and flung a set of papers at him. "Here's your little black book," she said. I caught one of the pages. It was a computer printout containing the names of women, the towns in which he'd met them, the hotels in which they'd stayed, and what looked like some kind of rating system. Once he was confronted with this evidence, Frank admitted that Jane was right. He liked to "find, bed, and forget" a woman almost every night he was on the road. He protested (rather meekly) that he truly loved Jane, wanted desperately to continue his marriage, loved his children dearly, and didn't have the vaguest understanding of his compulsion to have these liaisons. He claimed that his love life with Jane was "just fine," and that, for the most part, his conquests brought him little sexual satisfaction. Although he was terribly frightened by Jane's anger and appeared anxious to continue the marriage, he nonetheless maintained that he couldn't understand why it was so important to her since it had no meaning to him, and always occurred "out of her sight." For him, any regret or sorrow he felt was connected only to her discovery, rather than to his actions. Had she not found out, he would have continued his customary behavior untroubled.

Affairs

When I first met Artie and Sarah, they had been married for over twenty years. They came to therapy together. Neither complained of any particular crisis that brought them to my office, but both agreed that they wanted "better communication." They did not seem very strongly motivated to make much change in what they agreed was "an okay, but not a great marriage," as Sarah described it. After a few meetings, and with no particular warning, they stopped therapy. About three years later, I received a desperate call from Artie. He had just discovered that, during the time they had been in treatment, and for several months before, Sarah had been having an affair with a mutual friend, Rich. Worst of all, the affair was on again and was now more open.

When I saw them together, Sarah for the first time admitted that she was in a relationship with Rich and that she felt very confused. She was not sure she wanted to end her marriage. Artie was a good human being, and they had shared many happy experiences. Their son was about to marry, and this seemed a particularly ironic time even to be thinking about ending their twenty-three-year marriage. Yet at the same time, she could not bear the thought of giving up her relationship with Rich.

Artie was equally torn. He felt that he loved Sarah, but was enraged by her relationship with Rich. He felt bewildered and betrayed. How could he not have known? It was the lies that hurt him, even more than the realization that she had been having sex with another man. It had made their whole life together a sham. What had been true and what a lie?

Trauma

One of the common threads running through each of the three types of infidelity outlined above is the experience of trauma by each of the participants. Trauma may be defined as an injury caused by an external event. It derives from the Greek word meaning a wound. It is also related to the word "throe," as in "to be in the throes of a painful struggle." When people feel emotionally traumatized, this is exactly what they report. In the book *Shattered Assumptions* the psychologist Ronnie Janoff-Bulman (1992) described the effects of trauma. She reports that people who experience severe psychological trauma suffer from a shattering of their basic assumptions about the nature of the world. Before the traumatic experience, according to Dr. Janoff-Bulman, such people held three fundamental assumptions:

- The world is benevolent

- The world is meaningful

- The self is worthy

After the trauma, all three of these assumptions are called into question. Many say that their world has fallen apart. The world stinks, nothing seems to make any sense, and the sense that you know who you are and feel reasonably good about yourself is replaced by the feeling that there most be something terribly wrong with you if something so awful has happened to you. People who react to trauma this way are said to be suffering a *post-traumatic stress reaction*.

This loss of a sense of benevolence, meaning and self-worth is easily understood if we take into account most people's assumptions about marriage. Dr. Florence Kaslow (1992) studied a group of people who believed that they had good marriages. She found that the qualities most valued by these couples were "trust in each other that includes fidelity, integrity and feeling safe," and "permanent commitment to the marriage." It is reasonable to believe that most couples expect these same qualities when they marry. People who are not married also may decide to enter a monogamous relationship. For example, most people assume (even if they do not directly discuss it) that if they are engaged to be married, they will be monogamous. Even people involved in unmarried romantic relationships often hold this unspoken assumption of monogamy. High school students who are "going steady" generally expect that their relationship is exclusive and experience secret involvements with others as cheating. People who are living together, whether in heterosexual, gay, or lesbian relationships, also often agree that they are in an exclusive relationship. Cheating in these relationships is also experienced as very traumatic.

Because these assumptions are so deeply rooted in most people's ideals about romantic relationships, it should come as no surprise that their sense of the world's benevolence is severely shaken when infidelity is discovered. If you cannot believe that your own relationship is safe, how can you trust that your job will be safe, your friends will not betray you, and that everything you have trusted and believed in might not prove equally untrustworthy? The meaningfulness of your very life is called into question. People in such a situation often find themselves thinking: "What good did it do me that I was a considerate mate? That I cared for my husband when he was sick? That I comforted my wife when she lost her job? That I tolerated my intolerable in-laws in order to make things easier for my mate?" Finally, many people ask themselves, "What worth did I really have if I could be cast off with such ease?"

Not everyone who has discovered marital unfaithfulness is equally wounded, nor is every person whose infidelity is discovered equally affected. However, if you are reading this, chances are that you, your mate, or someone with whom you are close has experienced the discovery as very traumatic. We do not know all of the reasons that make this event so much more traumatic for some people, while others seem to recover quickly. What we do know is that many people seem to find, at least at first, little strength to ward off this trauma. In fact, their every waking moment seems to be absorbed in pondering this wound and even their sleep is often severely disturbed. Mary-Jane's reaction to Carl's infidelity can help illuminate the nature of the post-traumatic reaction.

Mary-Jane was forty-six years old when I first met her. She had divorced many years ago, and it wasn't long after that she had met Carl, who had never married. Mary-Jane had a daughter, by then three years old. After the divorce, neither Mary-Jane nor her daughter had ever seen the father again. Carl not only loved Mary-Jane, but her daughter Marni as well. He lavished gifts on the little girl, helped care for her when she was ill, and acted in every way as if he was her father. Carl was the product of a divorced home, and told Mary-Jane early on that, given her angry divorce and his own parents' terrible experience, they would do better to live as man and wife but not go through a legal marriage. He even went so far as to sign over his life insurance benefits to Marni. When Mary-Jane discovered that Carl was involved with another woman, she was devastated. Carl was frightened by the intensity of her reaction. He told her that he almost immediately realized how wrong he had been and swore he would end the relationship.

Although they continued living together, she told him that she felt as if she was "living with the enemy." She said that the thought of lying in the same bed with him disgusted her. Almost anything could send her into a bout of rage or tears. Seeing a movie about unfaithfulness could result in days of rage. Hearing about a friend who discovered an infidelity could bring her to endless tears. She told him that, on some level, she knew that he was now telling the truth, but she was still plagued with dreams in which she saw him with the other woman. She relived many times over the moment that she learned of the infidelity. She could still feel the almost electric shock she experienced. She played over the events that preceded the discovery. She would try to get it off her mind, but every attempt to push it away seemed futile—if anything, it came back stronger than ever. One moment she felt that she wanted to end the relationship forever. The next, she couldn't imagine a life without him.

If your experience is similar to Mary-Jane's, and you have two or more of the following symptoms, you are probably in a post-traumatic reaction:

- difficulty falling or staying asleep

- irritability or outbursts of anger

- difficulty concentrating

- excessive vigilance—always feeling on guard

- jumping at the slightest sound

- physical reactions to reminders of the infidelity, such as nausea or shakiness

These symptoms are the usual results of the discovery of infidelity. They are not signs of mental disorder, although if they persist, it is important to see a qualified mental health practitioner in order to obtain some relief. If you are experiencing some of these symptoms now, note them in your journal. For each symptom that you have, assign a rating between one and ten. The lowest rating means that the symptom is absent. As you read on, go back to this journal entry periodically, rating the symptoms again. This will help you to see whether you are getting beyond the traumatic reaction on your own. If not, you may need the help of a mental health practitioner.

Is the Relationship Over?

There is no simple answer to this question. Without a doubt, the discovery of marital infidelity is a crisis for all concerned. As with any crisis, there is an element of danger but also an element of hope. The first thing I tell my patients is that the outcome of this event should ideally be change for all concerned. I explain to them that change means that they will be moving toward a better marriage, or in some instances, a better divorce.

After thousands of hours of work with people struggling through infidelity, I have found that many couples have the capacity to emerge from this experience with new insight and new hope. However, it is very important to be aware that during the time the discoverer is experiencing a post-traumatic reaction, she or he is also probably feeling both depressed and agitated.

When you are feeling depressed, you are likely to see only the dark side of things. It is very important to remember that most people do not know with certainty what the future really holds when an infidelity is discovered. A depressed person is likely to find it hard to imagine any good coming out of this crisis. This can paralyze you, and make it impossible to take any kind of positive steps. People who are positive that their marriages are over are often proved wrong. As they mastered their depressed feelings, they felt more mobilized to take actions that have helped to correct their situation. To help counteract this understandable depression, it is important to remind yourself that the more closed off every path seems to you, the more immobilized you are likely to become. Remember, since there are often issues in the marriage that helped to trigger the infidelity, it is a real possibility that it will now be possible, working together, to correct these problems.

Agitation can also take a considerable toll. People who are agitated do not think clearly and often take very rash and impulsive actions. When the infidelity is first discovered, many people almost immediately begin to blame either their mate, the other party, or themselves. They may feel that someone must be punished, whether one of the other parties or themselves. As long as these rage-filled thoughts predominate, it's all but impossible for the couple even to begin to talk about what has gone wrong and to think about whether it can be made right or made even better than before.

Why Did It Happen?

Perhaps one of the first questions that the discoverer of infidelity asks is, "Why did it happen?" There is no simple answer. Some people are unfaithful for reasons that lie deep in their past, such as a history of infidelity in their parents' marriage. Others are unfaithful because of what they believe about the opposite gender. Men who believe that women are prey to be caught, and women who believe that they are nothing without a man are caught in a way of thinking about the other gender that often leads to unfaithful behavior. For others, infidelity is rooted in the marriage itself. It is important to try to understand why an act of unfaithfulness has occurred, because once you have some sense of why it happened you can begin to consider what to do about it. This is as important for the person who is acting unfaithfully as for the one who has discovered the infidelity and just as important for the third party. One way to try to understand what causes infidelity is by describing various types of extramarital involvement.

Not All Involvements Are the Same

An *affair* takes place over time. It may be very emotionally intense, and it may or may not involve sexual intercourse. In contrast, a sexual involvement with a third party may be part of an emotional attachment, but it may also be free of it, taking little more time than the sexual act itself. People may have an affair without sex, and they may have sex without having the emotional involvement of an affair. *Once a committed relationship is established, if there is a secret sexual and/or romantic involvement outside of the relationship, it is experienced as an infidelity.*

Psychologist Fred Humphrey (1987) has spent many years studying infidelity and extramarital sex. He suggests that we can best understand any particular act by considering the many factors involved. For one thing, you may want to know how long an extramarital affair has been going on. If your partner has been involved with more than one person, how often has it happened and with how many partners? It may also help to know whether there was a strong emotional bond between your mate and the other person. Some people find it very important to know whether there was sexual intercourse; others are much more upset about a strong emotional attachment.

For many people, the secrecy involved in extramarital activities is the most hurtful thing. For others, the discovery that one's mate is secretly involved in a gay or lesbian relationship is especially confusing and painful. Understanding the elements of any particular act of infidelity can shed light on why it happened. The more emotional we feel about something, the less clearly we can think about it. Standing back, examining what has happened, and opening dialogue about it can help an individual or a couple get beyond the initial shock of discovery.

Using this logic, let's examine some examples of extramarital involvements. Dan, for example, had frequent one-night stands with no emotional involvement. Another patient, Laura, was involved in a lengthy emotional but nonsexual affair. These two situations are very different, although each is a type of infidelity. Dan's frequent and secret escapades with many partners may have no emotional meaning for him, but they certainly put him at particular risk for sexually transmitted diseases. While Dan's wife might feel relieved to hear that his extramarital activities were neither emotional nor long-standing, she might well be frightened of contracting a disease from him. She might also feel hurt and angry because of all his lying to cover his adventures. Laura's husband is confronted with a wife who is involved in a long-term relationship with one man. He may need to talk with her not only about his hurt, but also about what emotional needs are being fulfilled in her affair that are not being met in their marriage. He may see her affair as the inevitable end of the marriage. Laura, however, may feel that telling her husband offers one last chance to see how much change the marriage will need in order to be successful for her. Maybe, she thinks, this will finally make him see how much she wants a deeper emotional involvement from him.

Are Men's and Women's Extramarital Involvements Different?

It isn't surprising that Laura is looking for greater emotional involvement, while Dan seems to be looking for a variety of sexual experiences. Men and women often seek different things when they become involved in extramarital activity. Research by two psychologists, Shirley Glass and Thomas Wright (1992), shows that there are important differences that determine why men and women become involved extramaritally. Glass and Wright found that women are more likely to link sex with love, while men's involvements are more often primarily sexual.

This is, of course, not true of all men or all women. Some men view an affair as a return to romance and excitement and an escape from day-to-day responsibilities. Some women feel that extramarital sex, with no emotional entanglement, adds spice to their lives. In many instances, the beliefs that people hold about why people stray make it difficult for a couple to communicate when an infidelity is discovered. For example, Dan's wife may find it hard to accept his explanation that he was simply sexually curious, that his many involvements with other women had nothing to do with love, and certainly were not intended to hurt her. In her mind, sex and emotional commitment are locked so tightly together that she can't imagine one without the other. Similarly, Laura's husband would probably accuse her of lying if she said that she had never had intercourse but craved only the emotional attention and kindness that she had experienced in her affair. He believes that if a man gets close to a woman, he has only one goal in mind—to have sex with her.

So we can see how the beliefs that men and women hold about each other's extramarital activities can get in the way of honest communication. For this reason, it isn't surprising to hear a man who strays claim that his marriage is good—and really mean it. Such a man may see his exploits as a male privilege that has nothing whatever to do with his feelings about his marriage. Women who stray are much more likely to feel great disappointment in the emotional side of their marriage and finally reach a point where they look beyond their marriage for emotional comfort; of course, men too may have an affair because of marital disappointment.

In our attempt to understand why extramarital behavior occurs, let's begin with some of the most frequent reasons given for various types of infidelity. If some of these items ring true for you, use your journal to examine them. If there is an issue that you think is important to your situation that is not on this list, be sure to include it in your own journal entry.

- Not understanding what relational love is

- Inability to communicate feelings or needs

- Not having the verbal skills to solve problems together

- Not being able to accommodate to one another's needs or interests

- Not really knowing the person you married (for example—unaware of some upsetting sexual problem)

- Not being able to cope with cultural or ethnic differences

- Unrealistic expectations about the nature of marriage

- Disappointment that your mate has not grown in the same ways you have

- Sexual curiosity

- Emotional need (feeling lonely in the relationship and looking elsewhere)

- Sexual addiction

- Boredom

- Losing the sense of fun and excitement you once had as a couple

- Getting so caught up in life's daily obligations that you lose sight of one another

As you continue reading, compare your journal entry to the specific explanations that various authorities have proposed, which I've outlined below. You will see later that understanding why an infidelity occurs has many benefits. It will help to determine what the chances are that the relationship will survive the infidelity, what approach the discoverer should take, how the involved partner can resolve his or her own feelings about staying in the marriage, and what kind of treatment would be most helpful. As you read ahead, look for any issue that you think is relevant to your own situation.

The Life Crisis Theory

There is a series of events that most people have either already experienced or will experience in their life time. These include: meeting who you think of as the "ideal person" to spend your life with; mutually deciding to marry or enter a long-term, exclusive relationship; having a child; getting a promotion at work; buying a first house. Many people think of these events as milestones in their lives—events that mark increasing maturity and responsibility. You may also experience other, more painful milestones as you pass through life. These might include: losing a child; feeling rejected by a mate; losing a parent; losing a job.

Each of the above events, whether positive or negative, produces a certain amount of stress. Think first of the negative events. It isn't hard to understand the pain of loss, whether it's losing a parent, a child, or a job. But positive events also can produce stress. One might feel: "Have I really chosen the right mate?" "Am I truly ready for the responsibilities of parenthood?" "Can I really fulfill people's expectations as I undertake this new job?" "Now that our children are grown, what is left of my marriage?"

Thus you can see that either positive or negative life changes can cause stress and anxiety. If both members of a couple are good at talking about these stresses, they usually weather them together, and their relationship becomes even deeper and more satisfying. For example, when Ned received an important promotion he told Beverly, "I know I'm excited about this, but I'm also kind of scared. I hope I've really got the ability to succeed at this. And what if I mess it up? Will I be out of a job?" Beverly listened, accepted his fears, and even shared some of her own concerns. Such a couple is developing a way to get through the first tough weeks of the new job because they can speak openly about it. More than that, because they are talking with each other about an important event in their lives, they are growing closer together. The ability to trust one another enough to talk honestly about what you are feeling, even if it is negative—to reveal yourself safely, to openly express needs, disappointments, longings and pleasure—are all aspects of intimacy.

Another man, filled with the same excitement and the same doubts, says nothing to his wife—perhaps because he doesn't know how to or because he feels it makes him look less of a man. Jack, a thirty-five-year-old stockbroker, came to therapy because his wife discovered that he had been seeing a call girl for several months. As we talked in therapy, it came out that he began his involvement with the call girl the day of his promotion to section manager. He had always prided himself on being a "heavy hitter" financially, and he described himself as the kind of guy who never takes his troubles home. Like his father, he had learned to suppress his anxiety because talking about it might make him seem weak to his wife. He said that when he was with the call girl, he felt absolutely at ease because his every need was attended to, and he didn't have to ask her for anything. He never talked with her about the stress he was under, but he felt that simply being in this situation gave him the relief that he wanted. He also felt ashamed that he had done it and frightened that his wife might leave him over it.

Almost every therapist has encountered a young husband who had sex with someone on the very night that his wife was giving birth. One patient explained to me that he had never felt so alone, incompetent, or useless as he did leaving the hospital following his daughter's birth. He said, "It's like I had no purpose being there. I felt like I was just in the way. It's like, becoming a mother, she was in a different place." He went out, had a few drinks at a local bar, and ended up having drunken sex with a woman he met there. Other men feel rejected by their wives because of the intense bonding they see between their wife and baby, a bonding that seems to squeeze them out. They see their wives as tired, preoccupied, and uninterested in sex. One patient told me that this filled him with despair and led him to an affair that spanned several months. Women are similarly vulnerable after the birth of a child. Annette, a thirty-two-year-old account executive, was thrilled after the birth of her first baby. She found herself increasingly angered, however, by her feeling that her husband Al seemed so uninvolved in caring for the baby. She began to feel that the baby and the home were a second job she had to take on alone. Attempts to talk about this with Al led to angry fights that never seemed to get resolved. When she met a man at work who found her attractive and made no secret about it, it was not long before she was intensely infatuated with him. Soon after, her office romance began.

Mid-Life Crisis

A person's life, like any good story, has a beginning, a middle, and an end. It isn't surprising that many people, as they approach what they think of as the midpoint of their life, undertake a kind of review. You may find yourself thinking, "What have I accomplished, and will I continue to accomplish? Am I satisfied with the course that my life has taken? Can it get better? Am I disappointed in how my life is going? Can I change it? What would be the price of change? For myself? For my mate? For my children?" The more you think, the more questions flood your mind.

The psychologist Dan Levinson (1978) has studied the impact of developmental change on men's lives. He describes this process as "mid-life evaluation." Others call it a mid-life crisis or "male menopause." Although Levinson entitled his book *The Seasons of a Man's Life*, there is reason to believe that as many women as men begin at mid-life to consider these same questions. The psychiatrist Frank Pittman (1989, 1993), an authority on marital infidelity, describes three separate mid-life crises that often trigger an act of infidelity. The first is called the "empty nest" crisis, which occurs as the last child grows up and leaves home. Now that the children are grown, the couple must consider what is left of their marriage. Is the fire out? Can it be relit?

A second mid-life crisis is what Pittman calls "reaching the summit." Men are particularly likely to experience this particular crisis, but as more women enter the competitive world of business and professional life, they also are likely to experience it. Arriving at the summit often includes the feeling that there is no place to go now but down. This often causes feelings of depression or panic in the growing realization that the dizzying pace cannot be maintained forever. Many men have been so trained to succeed that they have no idea what their lives would be like without the degree of power, money, and success that they have finally achieved.

Pittman details a third crisis, which may or may not occur at mid-life, called "the facts of life" crisis. Unlike the summit or the empty nest crises, a sudden awareness of "the facts of life" can occur earlier or later than mid-life, but like these other crises, "the facts of life" crisis is a frequent trigger for extramarital activity. "At some point in the course of the marriage," says Pittman, "people come to grips with several painful realities. They are imperfect, their spouse is imperfect, their children are imperfect, they are not going to conquer the world . . . and it will all get worse." These thoughts have enormous power. Like the empty nest and summit crises, this realization can also cause great anxiety or overwhelming depression. When people are anxious or depressed, they often set upon solutions that, at least for the moment, seem to relieve these feelings. One quick fix is to find a new love; to regain the feeling of a new future, with new possibilities.

Entitlement

The feminist movement has worked hard to increase people's awareness about men's attitudes toward women. Despite these gains, many people still believe that it is perfectly all right for men to eye women, make suggestive remarks to them, and view them as objects rather than as living people. This message is delivered in many ways. We see it in TV advertisements, in magazines, and in the movies. Many people continue to hold the belief that if a woman "gets into trouble" with a man, she somehow has brought it on herself. Men who buy the message that women are their playthings are more likely to have sexual affairs to which they attach no emotional meaning. The psychologists Glass and Wright report that 56 percent of men who had purely sexual extramarital involvements reported that their marriages were happy, as do 33 percent of women. Clearly, there is a group of people who believe that extramarital sex, as opposed to extramarital romance, has nothing to do with their marriage. Men and women who feel this way never find their way into a therapist's office until one of two things happen: they are caught by their partner, or they begin to feel that they are falling in love with someone with whom they have been having sex, and that this means that their long-term relationship or marriage is over.

There is another form of entitlement that seems to strike men and women more equally. This is the belief that marriage should meet all their needs. One such need is for constant attention, another is for consistently great sex. Another belief is that women are responsible for relationships. Those who accept this see a wife's role as keeping her husband content and satisfied. For some women this becomes a full-time occupation. Barbara told me, "I did everything I knew how to keep my husband happy. I learned from my mother that my job was to create a beautiful and serene home, to dress well (meaning the way he liked), to keep myself well groomed, and to protect him from the children's little squabbles." In return, she felt entitled to his continual shows of interest and to his large income, which had given the family many material advantages. Her husband Bob said that he had learned that his job was to be the provider. He felt that he was supposed to handle life outside the home, and that it was her responsibility to make the home a safe and welcome place for him. This was how his parents' marriage had worked, and it seemed good enough for them. Through the years, both Barbara and Bob had played their roles so well that once the children had grown, they felt they barely knew one another and were left with little to share. They came to therapy because each one of them had discovered that the other was having an affair. Both were seeking in their affairs the feelings of closeness and sharing that they had lost through the years.

Sexual Identity Affairs

Many people grow up with very conflicted feelings about their own sexual identity. For many people, the issue reaches crisis proportions during adolescence. A boy may find himself attracted to girls but also to boys. A girl may find herself cold to the advances of boys but feeling a deep crush on another girl. A boy may be plagued by thoughts of having sex with a much younger girl. Adolescents learn quickly that they must be very secretive about these thoughts because they can experience much cruelty from others if these thoughts and impulses are openly admitted. For some, the internal pressure is so strong that it must be acknowledged and dealt with. It is at this point that a person will openly declare, "I am gay," or "I am a lesbian," or "I am bisexual." For others, these thoughts remain deeply buried, coming to light only much later in life. The lessons of secrecy have been well learned. At some point in a person's life, these long-suppressed thoughts may suddenly erupt. The person is forced into exploring these old feelings.

Doug's wife Eunice told me: "The fact that Doug was having a gay relationship hit me like a ton of bricks. He is a minister and, I always thought, a good Christian. He is a good father and a great parson and preacher. Everyone loves him, and the weirdest part is, we always had a good love life—at least I thought we did. He is considerate, gentle, and interested in my pleasure." Doug explained that, as a teenager, he had feelings toward other boys, but he had done nothing about it because he thought it was sinful and wrong. He had never dated much but when he became a seminary student he began to feel that it was important to find the right woman to marry and he had never felt that he did not love and respect her. He said, "In a way, it was like being a sleepwalker. I went through the marriage always trying to be a good husband and a good man but always feeling that, in some way, I was not sure that this was me, at least not the real and true me." At a convention, he met a man to whom he felt deeply attracted. He had a drink or two and found himself in the man's hotel room, where for the first time in his life he had gay sex. He was filled with excitement, shame, and guilt. He said nothing to Eunice, but she noticed that he had come back from the meeting not quite himself. Neither of them is sure that this means the end of their marriage, but it's left each with many questions about Doug's sexual identity.

Adrienne's situation is quite different. She married at sixteen to escape a brutal home life where she was frequently beaten and often saw her mother suffer serious physical injuries at her father's hands. She met Mario, a twenty-eight-year-old man who seemed the answer to her dreams. He always seemed to have money in his pocket, courting her with a stream of expensive gifts. A few times during their whirlwind courtship she suspected that he was playing around with other women, but he assured her that she was mistaken. A couple of times when they were at parties he became jealous. A fight erupted between them and he would hit her, but she thought, "At least it was for a reason—not like my father, who hits for nothing." They married within a few months of meeting and had, within a space of seven years, six children. During this time the fights escalated.

Adrienne gradually became aware that Mario was a compulsive gambler, and that in his gambling episodes, he frequented prostitutes. She also discovered that he was in deep trouble because of gambling debts and had already used up a considerable amount of their savings. With all this, she continued to crave his attention and love, but he seemed increasingly distant. If she pressed for attention, he would disappear for a few days, a week, and finally, for months. One day, during one of Mario's increasingly frequent absences, Adrienne met a woman at a church dinner who seemed kind and attentive, providing a sympathetic ear for stories about Mario and the marriage. The relationship between Adrienne and Florrie gradually deepened.

One day, Florrie called Adrienne and told her that she must see her immediately. She explained to Adrienne that she was a lesbian, that she felt enormously attracted to Adrienne, and could not continue the friendship if it did not include romantic love and affection. Their relationship moved rapidly from exploratory kisses and hugs to a full sexual relationship, and for the very first time in her life, Adrienne experienced orgasm. She felt so confused. Did her affair with Florrie mean that she was a lesbian, or perhaps bisexual?

When Mario discovered the affair, he immediately filed for divorce. It was at this point that Adrienne noticed that her passion for Florrie was ebbing. For the first time, she admitted to herself how many things about Florrie really bothered her, especially how Florrie, very much like Mario, wanted control of her life. Adrienne eventually came to the conclusion that her sexual relationship with Florrie was an experiment that she wished she had made in high school. She felt that what she really craved was a tender relationship with a man, something she had never known. What she learned from Florrie was that, locked within her, was a sexually alive self. A few years later, she found herself in a relationship with a man who respected her and did not control her. Now she knew that she could be safe enough with a man to permit herself to be sexually fulfilled. Speaking about her confusion with a therapist a few years later, she said, "I think my awakening could have come from any one, whether man or woman, who showed me the slightest kindness."

Sexual Addiction and Don Juanism

The term *sexual addiction* refers to a compulsive need to engage in sexual experiences. These experiences are nonrelational—they are not romanticized, as affairs usually are. The psychologists Ralph Earle and Gregory Crowe list a series of attributes that they believe all addicts share. People who are sexually addicted generally show all or most of the following characteristics:

- a tendency to hold low opinions of themselves and to constantly remind themselves of their deficiencies

- distorted or unrealistic beliefs about themselves, their behavior, other people, and the events that occur in the world around them

- a desire to escape from or to suppress unpleasant emotions

- difficulty coping with stress; at least one powerful memory of an intense high experienced at a crucial time in their lives and an ever-present desire to recapture the euphoric feeling

- an uncanny ability to deny that they have a problem

Philanderers crave quick sexual adventures. Romance doesn't interest them at all. Most Don Juans are men, although occasionally we find a woman Dona Juana. People who philander are very different from those who have affairs. In an affair there is a third person who has become an important part of the life of the involved partner. When an affair occurs, the mate can often see some relationship between the way the marriage was going and the onset of the affair. With philandering, however, the quality of the marriage is not the real issue. The problem of Don Juanism lies deep within the Don Juan, and its solution depends upon whether he (in some cases, she) is ready to face it.

Philanderers may appear to be very strong and successful people, but inside, they feel empty. Each conquest leaves them with a fleeting feeling that they are powerful, attractive, and wanted by another human being. The purpose of the philandering is to bring relief to a person who really doesn't feel at all good about him- or herself. Like any other addiction, the initial "hit," whether it is the first sniff of cocaine, the first cigarette, or the first conquest, has a powerful effect. That intensity can never be recaptured. Each subsequent experience is a little weaker in its power to produce the original feeling, but the addict feels ever more drawn to the addiction because it fills the emptiness that is so central to his life.

Don Juans feel compelled to go through the experience of finding some person to "conquer," spend as little time as possible scheming to get them into bed, and then, having accomplished this goal, leave. These sexual partners are seen not as people, but as wanted objects. They have no meaning beyond this. The next day, addicts once again begin their feverish search, although it may be days, weeks, or months before they "score" again. Being "successful," however, only lasts for a while, and they continue to be driven to try with some new person.

Exploratory Affairs

Unlike the "accidental" affairs that we talked about earlier, exploratory affairs have a more deliberate quality. An exploratory affair is more likely to occur when a person becomes deeply aware that a marriage is in trouble but has not yet clearly resolved whether to stay or to leave. Cheryl, for example, had spent years trying to "reform" Cliff. All he seemed to want to do was work, come home, open a bottle of beer, sit on the couch, and watch whatever sports event happened to be on. He was angry with her if the house was not in perfect order and, if the children bothered him while he was watching the TV, he would become so enraged that it scared her. Their love life had come to a grinding halt. "There was a time when he was my friend, and I could talk things over with him—but no more," she said. Cheryl was becoming more discouraged every day. Sitting at her computer one evening, she began to surf the Internet and found herself drawn to a chat line called "Lonely and Looking." "Something clicked in me," she reported. "It seemed like a perfect description of where I was in my life." After a few visits to a chat line, it wasn't long before she began an e-mail correspondence with a man who seemed to be sensitive, interested in her feelings, and as lonely as she.

Eventually a personal meeting was arranged, and she and the man had a brief affair. At first he seemed wonderful and caring, but it wasn't long before she realized that he was a problem drinker. She also learned that, at forty years of age, he still lived with his aging parents. Later she could see that this brief fling, and a few others that followed, gave her a chance to see what it was like "out there." She began to sense that some of the problems she had with her husband could as easily occur with other men. She decided to throw all of her energy into a new attempt to re-examine not only her husband's part in the decline of the marriage, but her own as well.

While some exploratory affairs end with the realization that the marriage can improve, others end in a decision to divorce. One man explained to me that in his exploratory affairs he got his feet wet. When he felt sufficiently strong he was able to end his marriage and move on with his life.

Tripod Affairs

People may choose to stay in an unhappy marriage for a variety of reasons. These include fear of the economic consequences of leaving, fear of the impact on children, worry about the effect of divorce on their status in the community, and concern about its effect on aging parents. In order to maintain a marriage that is so lacking in positive feeling, some people find another person who fulfills the needs that they feel cannot be fulfilled in the marriage. It is as if the marriage couldn't stand on its own two feet, so a third party is added for support, just as the third leg of a tripod adds support. The third party may provide companionship, sexual fulfillment, tenderness, even adventure. Often the affair-involved person believes that it is the affair that holds the marriage together. In some cases this is true. I have treated marriages that have involved a third party for many years. However, in many of these cases, there is evidence that the noninvolved mate is aware of the affair, or at least strongly suspects it, but never directly challenges the mate. In this sort of relationship, the tripod affair seems more like a covert or maybe even an overt agreement by husband and wife to maintain the marriage by means of the affair.

More often, however, the noninvolved mate is not conscious of the affair. As in any protracted affair, there is a chain of lies that supports the second relationship. When the affair is revealed, the noninvolved mate is hurt and enraged. This rage is not lessened by the mate's protestations that the last thing he or she wanted was to end the marriage. In many instances, if the marriage does end, the affair-involved mate almost immediately experiences pressure from the third person to marry. It is often at this point that the new relationship becomes strained. Many tripod relationships then break apart. I have often heard patients tell me, after the breakup of first their marriage, followed by the ending of their tripod affair, that they couldn't believe how blind they had been to the faults of the person with whom they were having the affair. In many instances, people later regret that they couldn't see their affair as an unheeded sign that their marriage was in trouble.

People may also choose to stay in a marriage with a chronically ill or debilitated mate, both for the reasons mentioned above and out of compassion. In such cases, there may be an open agreement, or the ill mate may be so debilitated that communication is not possible.

Retaliatory Affairs

Sometimes the offended mate responds by having an affair as an act of retaliation. It has been my experience that women are more likely to have retaliatory affairs. Perhaps this is because of differences in power between many men and women. A man's act in a similar situation might be to express his anger by leaving the marriage. A woman may feel less able to do so, either because her concept of marriage does not allow leaving it, or because she fears the consequences for herself and her children. For this reason, most retaliatory affairs are expressions of helpless rage and powerlessness. These affairs are particularly joyless. Their purpose is really more to hurt the offending partner than to bring joy to the retaliating person. They usually are not intended to end the marriage, although occasionally the mate's reaction to the retaliation is to seek a divorce. The best that can be said of retaliatory affairs is that, for some people, they seem to even the score. But they do not help the couple resolve the problems that led to either the original affair or the retaliatory affair.

Exit Affairs

You've seen that in exploratory, tripod, and retaliatory affairs, the affair-involved mate may be unsure of whether he or she wants the marriage to end. In an exit affair, the affair-involved mate has already made that decision, although his or her mate may not yet know it. Many therapists have met a couple in the throes of an exit affair. Often a man will bring his wife to therapy, hoping that the therapist can prop her up as he prepares to leave. He will come armed with a list of complaints, including her depression and irritability. It has been my experience that many people involved in exit affairs don't want to be seen as bad people, and so they subtly (or not so subtly) throw the blame onto their mate. As their mate's rage overflows at the moment of discovery, this offers further proof to the offending mate of how bad things have always been. In addition, seeing the other person as "the problem" may also help to justify unethical behavior.

References

Glass, Shirley, and Thomas Wright. 1992. Justifications for extramarital relationships: The association between attitudes, behaviors, and gender. *The Journal of Sex Research* 29:361–387.

Humphrey, Fred. 1987. *The Erotic Silence of the American Wife.* New York: Plume, a Division of Penguin Books, USA.

Janoff-Bulman, Ronnie. 1992. *Shattered Assumptions: Towards a New Psychology of Trauma.* New York: The Free Press.

Kaslow, F., and H. Hammerschmidt. 1992. Long term "good marriages": The seemingly essential ingredients. *Journal of Couples Therapy* 3:15–38.

Levinson, Daniel. 1978. *The Seasons of a Man's Life.* New York: Alfred A. Knopf.

Pittman, Frank. 1989. *Private Lies.* New York: W. W. Norton.

———. 1993. *Man Enough.* New York: G. P. Putnam's Sons.

CHAPTER 7

Caregiving

A caregiver is an individual who provides care for another person who, ordinarily, would not require care. For example, someone may become a caregiver when a spouse or partner suffers an injury or becomes chronically ill. Similarly, parents are usually responsible for the care of their children, but as parents age, their children become their caregivers. In some cases, the label is applied when the care needed goes far beyond what would normally be required, as when a twelve-year-old brain-damaged child needs to be fed, toileted, and bathed.

Caregiving is actually a two-part process, in which the caregiver first must recognize the needs of the care recipient, then figure out how to meet them. Depending on the nature of the problem, helping may require a small amount of work or a great deal. In the latter case, everyday tasks such as bathing or eating can become tedious chores that take extended periods of time to accomplish.

No matter what tasks they perform, caregivers must be sensitive to their care recipients' feelings about being dependent. When some people need help, they accept it graciously and are cooperative. Others, however, may be difficult, angry, or rude. Disgusted with themselves, furious with life, and enraged at their illness or disability, members of this second group may curse and berate the very people who provide the help they need. Care recipients may be whiny and manipulative or stubborn and resistant. Some become possessive and demanding, resentful of any attempts their caregivers make to take time for themselves. If you are a caregiver and wish to remain sane and helpful, you must not only be a planner, innovator, organizer, and helpmate, but a psychologist as well! You must be accepting, forgiving, understanding, and patient. And, while doing all this, you must attend to your own needs, or you run the risk of burnout. Make no mistake about it, caregiving is anything but easy.

Reactions to Being a Caregiver

Although it is impossible to predict with certainty how a person will react to becoming a caregiver, the following variables help determine the ease with which this role can be assumed. In assessing your own reactions, consider each of the following factors.

The Suddenness with Which You Are Thrust into the Role

Did you expect to become a caregiver? If you are thrown into that role without warning or the chance to prepare emotionally, you may have an unusually difficult time. On the other hand, if you take on that role gradually, adjustment is often easier. This was what happened in the L family. Over many years, Mrs. L, who was healthier than her husband, gradually assumed more and more tasks in caring for him. Toward the end of his life, she almost literally became his eyes and ears. A woman of strong will and boundless energy, she managed to provide most of the care he required until she was in her mid-eighties. A home health aide was brought in (and willingly accepted) only when the limits of the elderly woman's strength and endurance made caregiving impossible. The fact that her responsibilities grew incrementally over the years gave her time to adjust emotionally to the role and to develop needed skills. Not all caregivers have that luxury.

The Phase of Your Life Cycle

As partners age, they expect to provide caregiving services for one another. Health problems and minor surgeries become more common, knees wear out, chronic conditions such as arthritis and high blood pressure take their toll. It is quite another matter when a young person must care for an equally young spouse. For example, a thirty-three-year-old woman, with two small children and a career of her own, had to care for her thirty-five-year-old husband when he was diagnosed with inoperable bone cancer. So many demands fell on this young woman's shoulders at the same time that she was almost crushed beneath their weight. "Everything I counted on was falling apart. How could I face losing my husband? What about the children? My career? His parents? My parents?"

There is never a right time to become the caregiver for a chronically ill or disabled person, but some times are worse than others. For example, the early phases of a family's life cycle are typically characterized by the presence of young children and unsettled finances. If the family has relocated recently (not unusual for young couples), they may also have limited knowledge of the new community and its resources. These factors, when added to caregiving responsibilities, may create more stress than they can handle.

The Anticipated Outcome

Short-term caregiving is much easier to accept because the disability is temporary and the anticipated outcome is a happy one. For example, when one partner cares for another following a surgical procedure from which complete recovery is expected, caregiving is usually short-term and upbeat. Taking on the role of caregiver is far more upsetting and terrifying when there can be no happy ending.

The Quality of the Relationship

The presence of love and mutual respect between partners in their normal interactions increases the likelihood of a generous give-and-take in adverse circumstances. By contrast, when genuine caring is absent, a partner's needs may quickly become burdensome. Caregiving is like a litmus test of the health of the relationship. "Our marriage was always a sham," a woman said recently, in the course of discussing her angry reactions to caring for her husband following a serious accident. "I can't stand taking care of Pete. I knew things weren't good, but I didn't realize they were this bad. I guess I just didn't want to face how little we really have between us."

Sometimes, even prior to the onset of formal caregiving, there is a long history of dependency on the part of one spouse. If the dependent partner becomes ill or disabled, his spouse, worn down by everyday, unacknowledged caregiving, may become resentful of the additional burden. In one instance, following a needy spouse's back surgery, his always-patient wife became contemptuous of her husband's disability and she provided care only grudgingly.

The Demands on the Caregiver

Some care recipients need care that is easy to deliver. The caregiver's responsibilities may be limited to providing companionship, reminding a partner to take a pill, and driving him/her to the doctor. On the other hand, care recipients may be completely unable to care for themselves, requiring assistance with walking, showering, and even using the toilet.

One elderly couple brought this point home clearly. They were referred for counseling by a neurologist following a worsening of the husband's symptoms of dementia. The problem for which they were referred, however, was his healthy wife's distress. She was nearly overwhelmed by her husband's illness, and made it quite clear that it was she, not he, who needed support. "I don't know if I can cope any longer," she stated sadly. "How can I take care of him when he can't even remember who I am!"

The Care Recipient's Attitude

Care recipients are often far from cooperative. They may be so angry at being ill or disabled that they cannot acknowledge the help they're receiving, let alone express gratitude for it. Feeling sorry for themselves, consumed by self-pity, they cannot appreciate the efforts made on their behalf.

Ironically, however, gratitude and cooperation don't always make things easier. They may have the opposite effect, inhibiting any feelings of anger and resentment the caregiver may have, thereby making her job even more difficult.

The Caregiver's Temperament

Relaxed, confident, and flexible caregivers are able to assume their burdens with quiet calm, inspiring faith in their care recipients. Conversely, anxious and uncertain caregivers, often edgy themselves, do anything but inspire confidence. Caregivers who know and respect their limitations, and who are willing to ask for help, almost always succeed with less angst than those who feel they must do it all and are unwilling to ask for or accept assistance.

At this point, we would like you to take a few moments to answer some questions about yourself as a caregiver. Throughout this book, we will ask you to respond to questions like these.

Your answers may be used as a starting point for discussion in a caregiver support group or to help you identify problems or plan for changes on your own. To derive full benefit from your reading, we ask that you take the time to answer these questions thoughtfully and honestly, and use them as an opportunity to clarify your feelings and needs.

Your Caregiver Profile

Please answer each of the following questions by checking the appropriate box.

1. Your sex:
   - ❑ M
   - ❑ F

2. Your age:
   - ❑ Under 30
   - ❑ 30–39
   - ❑ 40–49
   - ❑ 50–59
   - ❑ 60 or above

3. Your relationships:
   - ❑ Married or live with partner
   - ❑ Single, divorced, separated, or widowed

4. Your responsibilities in addition to caregiving:
   - ❑ Work inside the home
     - ❑ homemaking
     - ❑ home-based business
     - ❑ care for children under age eighteen
     - ❑ care for children over age eighteen
   - ❑ Work outside the home
     - ❑ part-time employment
     - ❑ full-time employment

5. Percent of caregiving responsibilities that fall on you:
   - ❑ 100 percent (you are the sole caregiver)
   - ❑ You share caregiving responsibilities with others
     - ❑ bulk (more than 50 percent) of caregiving responsibilities fall on you
     - ❑ bulk of caregiving responsibilities fall on one or more other persons

6. The person for whom you provide care:
   - ❑ spouse or partner
   - ❑ child
   - ❑ parent
   - ❑ sibling, friend, relative, or other

Compare your answers to those of the typical caregiver. The following data, collected and reported by both the National Family Caregivers Association (National Family Caregivers Association 1998), indicate that the typical family caregiver is female (82 percent), married (74 percent), and between thirty-six and sixty-five years old. She is likely to be employed (47 percent) and to work more than thirty-one hours a week (71 percent).

Most caregivers care for a spouse or partner (48 percent). A smaller percentage cares for a parent (24 percent). Nineteen percent provide care for children; the remainder (9 percent) care for a sibling, friend, relative, or some other person.

The typical female family caregiver often gets little help. When the care recipients are elderly parents, male siblings are likely to provide moral support and sometimes financial help, but little more. Female siblings sometimes cooperate, although one daughter often assumes the bulk of the responsibility. For example, in one case a dutiful daughter cared for both of her elderly parents while her less responsible sister remained uninvolved, doing little more than calling her parents occasionally and visiting them once in a great while. Sadly, on the few occasions when she and her sister did make time to discuss the disparity in their responsibilities, the uninvolved sibling almost always called her sister a martyr and a fool.

Caregiver Pressures

Family caregivers experience many different pressures. Some can be traced to external factors. Others originate within the caregivers themselves.

Typical External Pressures

Your spouse complains that you are unavailable. He may say that "Even when you're here physically, you're not here emotionally." Your children resent the fact that you're always so busy you have no time for them. Your boss and colleagues tolerate your personal phone calls, occasional absences, late arrivals, and early departures. However, tolerant as they may be, they make it known that they still expect you will fulfill your job responsibilities. Your siblings simply expect that you will be able to do it all. Your friends become impatient with you because you cancel social engagements, fail to return calls, and drop out of touch for long periods of time. In each of these instances, you feel pressure. Whether subtle or direct, it is burdensome.

Unusual External Pressures

Often caregivers must cope with additional stress unrelated to caregiving. Some may be under extreme financial pressure. Others are facing divorce. Still others may have just lost a job. These additional stressors put the caregiver at risk for overload and burnout, and demand special vigilance with regard to self-care. The coping strategies discussed below will be especially useful for caregivers in these potentially explosive situations.

Internal Pressures

In addition to pressures that originate externally, caregivers sometimes impose pressures on themselves. For instance, you may expect that regardless of the number and kinds of responsibilities you must fulfill, you should be able to carry them off without letting anyone down. One woman berated herself for her inability to take care of her ill husband while simultaneously looking after her three children, running a business, and caring for her own elderly parents. Only after she thought about her predicament did she come to realize that she simply could not do all she wished. Other pressures are the result of loneliness and isolation. Friends may drift away because they have never lived through your situation and cannot appreciate the trials you are experiencing.

As a caregiver, you probably live with almost constant feelings of frustration. Coping with a loved one's temporary disability is difficult enough. When age, permanent disability, long-term health problems, a chronic mental disorder, or a terminal illness makes any prospect of recovery impossible, the situation is indeed depressing.

Leisure time is a phrase that may well have lost meaning for you. You are not alone. Many caregivers complain of a lack of leisure and personal time.

The Caregiving Services You Provide

There are different kinds and degrees of caregiving responsibilities. Some caregivers are little more than companions to their care recipients. They may read to their care recipients or bring them lunch. These are relatively simple services—neither physically taxing nor emotionally demanding. On the other hand, the caregiver may become the eyes, ears, and mind of the recipient.

Often, caregiving responsibilities change over time. For example, when you provide care for an aging individual, it's typical for demands to increase as time passes. To gauge the kind of caregiving responsibilities you have, please complete the following questionnaire:

Caregiving Services

Please put a checkmark on the appropriate lines.

1. As a caregiver, I primarily:

____ Provide companionship and show concern through calls and occasional visits

____ Take my care recipient to lunch

____ Shop with my care recipient

____ Arrange for occasional outings

2. As a caregiver, I primarily:

____ Arrange medical appointments, coordinate schedules, etc.

____ Take my care recipient to medical appointments; provide transport for laboratory tests, and take him/her to and from procedures (such as surgeries) performed on an outpatient basis

____ Consult with members of my care recipient's health-care team and make decisions in consultation with my care recipient

____ Shop for my care recipient

____ Prepare some meals for my care recipient

3. As a caregiver, I primarily:

____ Provide homemaking services (do laundry, clean house, etc.)

____ Arrange for home repairs, maintenance, etc.

____ Prepare most or all meals

____ Arrange for care when I can't be there

____ Pay bills

4. As a caregiver, I primarily:

____ Provide help with bathing, dressing, eating, and using the toilet

____ Assist with the management of incontinence

____ Help my care recipient cope despite serious cognitive disabilities (for example, the forgetfulness and lack of orientation characteristic of Alzheimer's disease)

____ Arrange for home-health aides and others to provide help when I am not available

5. As a caregiver, I primarily:

____ Help my care recipient prepare advance directives such as a living will

____ Serve as health care proxy

____ Serve as attorney-in-fact for most or all other matters; manage all financial affairs, etc.

The items in this questionnaire were arranged in five clusters of caregiving activities. Each cluster represents a different degree of responsibility. See the table below:

Cluster Number	Description
1.	Light duty (companionship, socialization)
2.	Medium duty (oversight, transport, consultation, and practical assistance)
3.	Substantial duty
4.	Heavy duty (services essential for living)
5.	Legal, ethical, and moral responsibilities

Items in the higher number or later clusters are usually added to those in the lower number or earlier clusters, rather than simply replacing them. For example, providing companionship does not end when medical oversight and transport are added to your caregiving responsibilities. As time passes, and as a care recipient ages or becomes sicker, the caregiver takes on more and more responsibilities. Little wonder that the death of a recipient sometimes evokes not only sadness, but relief and anxiety as well. "What will I do now?" is a question more than one caregiver has asked herself when her care recipient has died.

How You Became a Caregiver

Why do certain family members become caregivers while others do not? Under what conditions does an individual take on this role? Is the decision made because of social expectations?

Gender? The relationship with the care recipient? Accident or circumstances? Family pressures? Timing? Physical proximity to the person(s) needing care? Consider the following examples:

1. Several years after Rosemary married Carl, he was stricken with myasthenia gravis, a chronic and debilitating condition. Since she was his wife, it seemed most reasonable that she would assume responsibility for his care.

2. When Dr. and Mrs. Shapiro's third child was born with a serious brain disease, it seemed natural that they would serve as her caregivers.

3. When, by second grade, it became clear that Brian was learning disabled, his mother assumed responsibility for advocating on his behalf, attending parent-teacher conferences, and ensuring that he got the extra help he required. Because his father worked outside the home in a job that required frequent travel, his mother, Sharon, seemed the logical person to assume responsibility for his care.

4. As Jose's parents grew older and became infirm, it seemed logical that Jose and his wife would be the ones to care for them; Jose's brother, Manuel, had never been very close to either of his parents. Furthermore, Jose had long been the "good" child in the family.

5. Tahitia had always been considered the "crazy" one in her family: sensitive, deeply feeling, and intelligent, she had never really been understood by her parents or her younger sister, Mavis. Although their father died when the girls were in their late twenties, their mother lived on for many years. Mavis automatically assumed responsibility for her care. The fact that this placed all the responsibility on her shoulders was considered an acceptable price to pay for maintaining peace in the family.

6. When Mrs. Borruso, eighty-one, began showing signs of dementia, her husband, Emil, eighty-three, assumed the role of caregiver. However, despite his good intentions, he was not really up to the task. This placed their daughter in a predicament. Whenever she attempted to intervene, Mr. Borruso rebuffed her efforts. "I had to pretend my father was taking care of Mom," she observed, "while, in fact, the responsibility fell on me."

As these examples illustrate, many circumstances contribute to a person becoming a caregiver. The key factors are: social expectations, relationship quality, self-perceptions, and accident and circumstances. Often, two or more factors combine to determine the decision.

Social Expectations

In most societies, ours included, there are unwritten expectations about who will care for whom in the event that caregiving becomes necessary. For example, if a child is ill, disabled, or born with a birth defect, it is expected that the parents will assume responsibility if at all possible. If a spouse or domestic partner becomes ill or is injured, it is assumed that the able-bodied partner will become the caregiver. Similarly, as a person ages, it is the life partner who usually provides care until that is no longer possible. At that point their children, if there are any, will take on the job of providing care. Institutionalization is socially sanctioned only when the situation becomes unmanageable, and even then, it is often accompanied by recriminations and guilt.

Within the realm of social expectations, gender becomes a factor. In most societies, women are expected to be caregivers as a natural extension of their nurturing role. Although men can be wonderfully compassionate, they are not commonly expected to take on this responsibility.

Convenience is also a factor. It is usually assumed that the person who lives closest to the care recipient and whose schedule is the most flexible will become the caregiver. This may, unfortunately, result in a resentful caregiver who feels boxed in and unable to refuse the role because it makes "so much sense" for her to take it on.

To provide a sense of the rules that govern decisions about who assumes caregiving responsibilities, we have created a decision tree that reflects what we have observed. Our goal is not to include every conceivable situation in which care is required, only the most common ones.

Two other family-related variables play a role. The first one is past behaviors within the family. In every family, some members are simply more solicitous, more accommodating, and more willing to put themselves out for others. If a person has earned that reputation, it's likely he or she will become a caregiver when the need arises.

The second variable is birth order. For one thing, age is often tied to status in families, even among adult children. For that reason, younger adult children, perhaps the youngest, will be charged with caregiving responsibilities. For another, the youngest adult child may still be living at home when the need for caregiving arises and the older siblings may have been on their own for some time.

Relationship Quality

All other things being equal, the person who has the closest and most gratifying relationship with the care recipient is most likely to become the caregiver. Often this is the favorite child. This was the case in the O'Brien family. Margaret was the apple of her parents' eye. Her sister, by contrast, had always been a source of distress. Rebellious and self absorbed, Nora had provided little gratification to her hard-working parents. It was thus logical that when it came time to provide care, Margaret would take on those responsibilities.

Self-Perception

Self-perception almost always plays a part in determining the choice of caregiver. If a person sees herself as caring, devoted, reliable, and so on, she will likely assume the role. Since terms such as "caring," "kind," and "compassionate" are more often applied to women than men, it's not surprising that women are assigned the caregiving role, and that they are also most likely to see themselves as fitting the part perfectly.

It's also likely that a good many caregivers assume that role because it suits them temperamentally. Something in their personality makes them capable of tolerating the demands of caregiving. Indeed, some caregivers take genuine pleasure in their work. Here, for example, is the response of a caregiver who attended one of our workshops. When asked about the rewards of caregiving, she wrote: "I think my caregiving has made me a better person." These are some of the benefits:

1. A new relationship with person being cared for (in her case, it was an elderly mother)

2. A chance to give back

3. A sense of accomplishment

4. Development of new skills, knowledge (e.g., advocacy abilities)

5. Increased compassion and personal growth

6. New relationships with others through support groups

7. The building of memories

Sometimes, however, the motives underlying an apparent desire to provide care are not at all benign. Some caregivers, for example, take perverse pleasure in playing the martyr, simultaneously "upstaging" other family members and inducing guilt. "See what a good child I am," they say by their self-sacrifice. Others do it for more sinister reasons, such as to take financial advantage of the care recipient. It would be unfair to defame all caregivers by assuming they are driven by unhealthy motives. Yet it would be naive to assume that love and compassion are the only motives involved.

Why You Became a Caregiver

Instructions: Please indicate the extent to which, in your opinion, each factor resulted in your becoming a caregiver. Mark each scale at the appropriate point.

1. Social Expectations

I have become a caregiver because of

a. my sex

| 10 | 9 | 8 | 7 | 6 | 5 | 4 | 3 | 2 | 1 |

most
important
factor

moderately
important
factor

least
important
factor

b. family pressures: my role and past experiences in my family made me the most likely
   choice

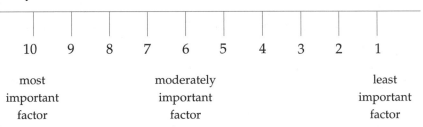

| 10 | 9 | 8 | 7 | 6 | 5 | 4 | 3 | 2 | 1 |

most
important
factor

moderately
important
factor

least
important
factor

c. my age or birth order in my family

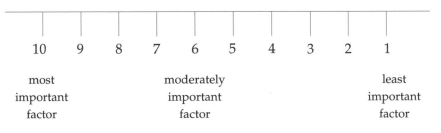

| 10 | 9 | 8 | 7 | 6 | 5 | 4 | 3 | 2 | 1 |

most
important
factor

moderately
important
factor

least
important
factor

d. I live with or nearest to the care recipient

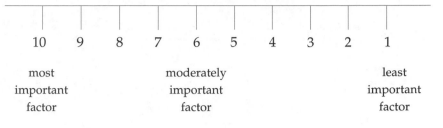

e. I possess special skills or abilities others in my family do not have (for example, you may have been trained in a health field such as nursing)

```
    |    |    |    |    |    |    |    |    |    |
   10    9    8    7    6    5    4    3    2    1

   most             moderately              least
important          important            important
 factor              factor               factor
```

2. Your Relationship Quality

I have become a caregiver because of

my especially close relationship with the care recipient

```
    |    |    |    |    |    |    |    |    |    |
   10    9    8    7    6    5    4    3    2    1

   most             moderately              least
important          important            important
 factor              factor               factor
```

3. Self-Perceptions

I have become a caregiver because

a. I see myself as strong, reliable, and competent

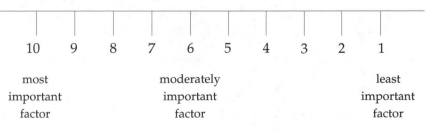

b. I am nurturing and enjoy caring for others

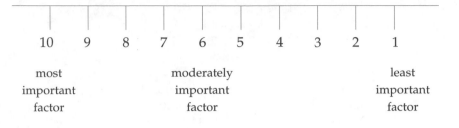

| 10 | 9 | 8 | 7 | 6 | 5 | 4 | 3 | 2 | 1 |

most	moderately	least
important	important	important
factor	factor	factor

c. I enjoy being needed, and take pleasure in being seen as the grateful child or the devoted parent

| 10 | 9 | 8 | 7 | 6 | 5 | 4 | 3 | 2 | 1 |

most	moderately	least
important	important	important
factor	factor	factor

d. I am willing to defer satisfaction of my own needs to help others

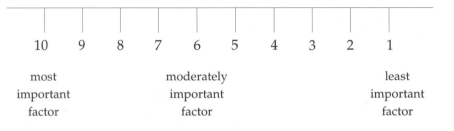

| 10 | 9 | 8 | 7 | 6 | 5 | 4 | 3 | 2 | 1 |

most	moderately	least
important	important	important
factor	factor	factor

4. Accident and Circumstances

I have become a caregiver because of

illness, accident, or other circumstances beyond my control

| 10 | 9 | 8 | 7 | 6 | 5 | 4 | 3 | 2 | 1 |

most	moderately	least
important	important	important
factor	factor	factor

By plotting your scores on each criterion in the box below, you can get a sense of the factors that contributed to your assuming the caregiving role. If your examination of the results of this inventory suggests that you need or want to re-evaluate your position, this is the time to begin thinking about that.

Instructions: Each item in column A corresponds to each question you just completed. in column B, record the numeric score you marked above. Then plot the numbers on the grid that appears at the bottom of this exercise.

Column A Factor	Column B Score You Earned (10 = most important, 1 = least)
1. Social Expectations	
Sex	
Family pressures: roles and past experiences in the family	
Age or birth order	
Physical proximity to care recipient	
Special skills and abilities	
2. Relationship Quality (emotional closeness to care recipient)	
3. Self-Perceptions	
4. Accident and Circumstances	

Now plot on the grid below the number score you wrote on each line:

Sex

Family Pressures

Age

Physical proximity

Special skills

Close relationship

Competence

Nurturance

Being needed

Willing to defer

Circumstances

0　1　2　3　4　5　6　7　8　9　10

Plan of Action

Take a moment now to review your questionnaire results. If you are comfortable with the factors responsible for your becoming a caregiver, and do not resent having taken on this role, then go no further. If, however, this is not true of you, use the Action Plan Example below to plan for some changes. For example, if you care for your mother because you live on the next block, find a way to involve your brother, who lives elsewhere. If you were chosen as caregiver because you are the only "girl" in the family, or the youngest child, address this issue with your siblings and arrange for a more equitable distribution of responsibilities.

Following we have included an example of an Action Plan. It consists of a goal, the means to achieve it, and measures to evaluate outcomes. Use it as a guide for your own planning.

Action Plan Example

1. Things I'd Like to Change (my goal): I need assistance in taking care of my mother.

2. Methods (how I can achieve my goal)

   a. I can call my siblings, spell out what I am doing for Mom, and ask them to help out.

   b. I can call a home health agency and arrange for an aide to come twice a week.

   c. I can arrange for meals-on-wheels so I don't have to cook for Mom as often.

3. Measure(s) of Success (how I will know I have accomplished what I set out to do):

   a. I will have more time for myself and my family.

   b. I will feel better about taking care of Mom.

   c. I'll be less resentful and less tired.

References

National Family Caregivers Association. 1998. A profile of caregiving. *Taking Care* 7:1(Winter): 7–8.

PART II

KIDS

Your relationship with your children is special. You instinctively love them, protect them, and want them to grow up strong, healthy, happy, and successful. And yet, they sometimes seem like space aliens—how could you bring forth such monsters? You may get along well with your spouse, your mom, your dad, your brothers and sisters, but have enormous conflicts with your kids. That's because you have many years to get used to your parents and siblings. And you get to choose lovers and whom you marry. But kids are thrust upon you and you're stuck with them. You can't wait around for a better set of kids, break up with your kids, trade them in, or divorce them.

This section covers the inevitable problems that many parents have in raising their children:

Postpartum Survival gets mothers through the fatigue, anxiety, depression, and other emotional extremes that often mark the first months of parenthood.

Parenting Skills will help you get your kids to cooperate without yelling, nagging, or pleading.

Kids and Anger teaches how to control the anger that all parents sometimes feel toward their children.

Children's Sexuality—What's Normal explains what constitutes normal sexual interest and behavior in children at different ages, as well as what is cause for alarm.

Divorce and Kids shows how divorce affects kids at different ages and explains how to minimize the effects of divorce on children.

Trauma and Kids tells you what you can do and say to help children cope with the aftermath of traumatic experiences such as natural disasters, accidents, violence, and abuse.

Anxiety and Kids gives sound advice on rearing those children who are especially timid, shy, and anxious.

CHAPTER **8**

Postpartum Survival

You Are Not Alone, You Are Not to Blame, and You Can Feel Better

If you're reading this, chances are that there's a postpartum crisis in your life. Whether it's your crisis, or a crisis being experienced by someone close to you, the first thing we'd like to tell you is to take heart! Things will get better. The postpartum period is an overwhelmingly difficult time—and anyone who tells you otherwise is mistaken.

There are measures that you and your family and friends can take to ease your stress, so that you can begin to enjoy your baby and feel like a human being again. Some of these measures may involve counseling and/or medication, depending on your situation. Other coping measures may simply be a matter of changing the way you think about things. Don't underestimate the power of your attitude and expectations. Changing the way you think just a little bit can make the difference between feeling totally out of control and feeling like you're under stress but coping.

Now, before we go on—if you're at the point where you're considering doing harm to yourself or someone else, you need to get professional attention right away. Call your OB/GYN, call a psychologist or social worker, call a suicide or child abuse hotline. You're going to be all right, and your baby will be all right, too—but you both need more help and support just now than can be found in a book.

Motherhood: The Hype, the Reality

Having a baby is supposed to mark one of the happiest times in your life. For nine months, you await your child's emergence with a whole range of emotions, from nervous anticipation to unadulterated joy. Society is quite clear about what your emotions are supposed to be once your baby is born. Television, movies, magazines, newspapers all give you the message that happiness, calm satisfaction, joy, and pride are the norm when a new baby arrives. Family, friends, and medical professionals tell you to "relax and enjoy your baby," as if relaxation played even the smallest role in the drama of life with a brand-new child.

Hardly anyone talks about the enormous physical, emotional, and relationship changes that accompany the birth of a new baby. Maybe it's because no one wants to be the killjoy sounding the notes of grim reality among all the soft-focus hype. But for many women and their families, the experience of having a baby turns out to be very different from their expectations. You may feel devastated when all your beautiful images of motherhood crash in a pile at your feet. "It wasn't supposed to be like this," you want to shake your fist and shout at someone. And the worst part of it is that no one wants to listen—not really. When you report that you're so sleep-deprived that you feel like an eighty-year-old running a marathon, well-meaning friends and health professionals will tell you to sleep when your baby sleeps. Whom do they think they're kidding? When their babies sleep, new mothers tend to their wounded bottoms, or throw some food in the oven, or agonize over the birth announcements they haven't even had time to buy, much less address the envelopes of.

The reality is that becoming a parent is a considerable task. The new mother's body appears to have gone haywire; her hormones fluctuate greatly. She is tired beyond belief, and suffering from sleep deprivation. Sleep deprivation, by the way, is a tried-and-true method for torturing prisoners of war! The new mother is in a physically vulnerable state from these changes and from the enormous physical stress of childbirth. And then, after a couple days' rest, if she's lucky, she is put in charge of meeting another human being's needs before tending to any of her own. Feed the baby, diaper the baby, rock or walk the baby, wash all the clothes that the baby has spit up on, and try to squeeze in your own shower, lunch, or fun. That is without even considering work, in or out of the home.

On top of these physical changes are emotional changes: you are now someone's mother, with all the psychological burden that role carries in our society. And having to put your child's needs first means that every other role you have played must be revised: partner, daughter, friend, worker. You may feel, quite naturally, exhausted, unsure, and overwhelmed. And because of the cultural myth of "this wonderful time," your negative feelings may have taken you completely by surprise. Since it wasn't supposed to be like this, you may find yourself feeling angry, cheated, and depressed. And who wouldn't, when you discover that the bliss and well-being you expected have been lost to feelings of depression, anxiety, and exhaustion?

What is most important to remember is that these negative feelings make sense when you look at the task a new mother is tackling. When you lack sleep, you are going to feel exhausted. When you take on a new job, it's normal to feel scared and uncertain. When you have little time to take care of your own needs for fun, companionship, and order, it's logical that you'd feel frustrated, resentful, and overwhelmed. Yet few sources of information for new mothers include a discussion of these negative feelings, or warn you about what to expect emotionally in the postpartum period. Instead, the myth of maternal bliss endures, leaving many women feeling cheated, depressed, and ashamed.

The Wide Range of "Normal" Postpartum Adjustment

When you ask women what their postpartum adjustment period was like, you will hear a wide range of answers. Some new mothers feel wonderful, in charge, and confident. But many others report feeling rotten. Look at this list of feelings mentioned by women in a postpartum support group:

I am so irritable.

I cry all the time.

I can't sleep.

I can't get going.

I can't think straight.

I feel so worried.

I have panic attacks.

I can't stop eating.

I am nauseated.

I have scary thoughts.

I feel so nervous.

I feel so alone.

I feel so guilty.

I feel so ashamed.

I feel so ugly.

I feel so tired.

I feel like a failure.

I can't feel anything.

I have no interest in sex or other normal activities.

We understand how difficult such feelings can be when you're faced with the myth that your life would be all rainbows. We know, as women and mothers first, and then as psychologists, the sense of guilt and failure when having that new baby in your life feels less than wonderful. In our work as psychologists, we've seen the relief in women's faces when their negative feelings are validated. Women feel crazy for having these feelings. They feel deficient and abnormal and ashamed. If it were possible to put a big motherly hug into words, this is what we'd do for every postpartum mom who picked up this book. In the words of Jane Honikman, founder of Postpartum Support International, we want you to know that **you are not alone, you are not to blame, and you can feel better!**

A Guide to Feeling Better

The process of feeling better begins with letting go of self-blame. You can then tune into your own needs and the location of your anguish. What do you need most of all? How can you balance your own needs and the needs of those who are important to you, from the baby to other family members? What do your symptoms—the negative feelings or behaviors you have—tell you about issues you need to tackle? When you know what your needs are, you can begin to develop a plan to meet those needs. You can learn a new habit of taking care of yourself. We believe taking care of yourself to be critical to your physical and psychological health; it's also an essential skill in becoming a caring and successful parent.

Think of yourself as a pitcher of water. Every time you give to someone, meeting their needs, you are pouring water out of that pitcher. If you rock the baby, you are meeting her need for comfort. A little water pours out of your pitcher. You listen to your partner's report of a frustrating day. That takes a bit more from your pitcher. You take the baby for her checkup, draining the pitcher a bit more. You talk to a friend who had a big fight with her husband. By offering support, you are depleting your pitcher once again. The catch is that you are not a bottomless pitcher. You must stop at some point and do something to fill the pitcher up again. And how do you fill the pitcher? By taking care of yourself.

You can learn what works best to refill your pitcher. Some people like to relax in a hot bath, some people prefer exercise, or reading funny stories, or talking with supportive and nurturing friends. No matter what you do to fill the pitcher, it is essential that you do something. Otherwise, you will soon be empty. When you give and give without paying attention to your own needs, you're in danger of draining yourself dry.

About Breastfeeding

You may want to know about the effects of breastfeeding on your mood. This is a common question among overwhelmed new mothers. After all, breastfeeding involves firing up all those female hormones. Many women want to know if breastfeeding might be making them feel worse. They wonder if they would feel better if they quit breastfeeding.

The answer to that question must be evaluated on an individual basis. Some women do find that they feel much better when they are not solely responsible for providing their baby's food. Nonetheless, the research on postpartum emotional reactions very clearly shows that women who are breastfeeding do not have more negative moods than women who are bottle-feeding their infants. Instead, the hormones involved in the production and let-down of breastmilk often produce feelings of peacefulness and relaxation for the nursing mother. No matter what you may have heard to the contrary, breastfeeding does not mean that you'll have greater postpartum depression or anxiety. Nor does it put you at greater risk for feeling badly. In fact, if you are breastfeeding your baby and wean abruptly, you may find that your mood worsens because of the rapid change in hormone levels. Many women report increased negative feelings, such as depression and anxiety, when they wean their infants. So if you've recently weaned your baby, and were faced with an increase in your negative feelings or an unwanted change in your behavior, rest assured that this is not at all uncommon.

We've seen a disturbing trend in the treatment of postpartum reactions by medical professionals. Many of them appear all too hastily to prescribe antidepressant or anti-anxiety medications for the new mother who is feeling badly. Taking these medications usually requires abrupt weaning from the breast. Certainly, at times, this can be essential for the health of the new mom. But we feel strongly that, for women who are committed to breastfeeding, there are many other options to try before using medication. If breastfeeding is important to you, please know that you do not need to wean your baby, in many cases, if you do not really want to. You can first try the strategies outlined here before taking the more drastic step of weaning so that you can take medication. If your doctor seems cavalier in prescribing drugs, don't forget that you can always get a second opinion. Consult another physician, a lactation specialist, or a La Leche League counselor for support and advice.

To continue to breastfeed or not is your choice. You may need to "shop" to find medical professionals who will work with you to make your choice compatible with the help or treatment you need.

If you are feeling overwhelmed by the demands or difficulty of breastfeeding, you may wish to wean your baby so that you can share the responsibility for his or her nutrition. You may want to try a compromise solution rather than weaning the baby outright. Check with your pediatrician or a lactation consultant about supplementing your breast milk with formula. One or two bottles of formula a day (or during the night!) may give you the breaks you need, while allowing you to continue to nurse your baby. Too often, new mothers may see this issue as black or white (I must nurse exclusively/I need to quit nursing). No matter what anyone else says, there is a gray area in between (I can use formula to supplement and breastfeed, too). Many women who take an all-or-nothing approach and wean the baby because of their negative feelings in the postpartum period later regret having done so.

Postpartum Adjustment Problems

Because childbirth is a major life change, it's natural for you to have some negative feelings about it. The range of feelings different women may go through is much like the spectrum of light in a rainbow: the distinctions between the bands of color are not always clear; one color or category may blend into the next one. This chapter describes each level of negative postpartum reactions, from "the blues," which is the most common and least disruptive, to postpartum psychosis, affecting only 2 out of every 1,000 or so new mothers. We've provided a checklist for each category to help you locate your own feelings along the continuum.

The Blues. This is the term used to describe the common tearfulness, fatigue, insomnia, exhaustion, and irritability of the first two to three days after the birth of a baby. The blues are so common, striking 50 to 80 percent of all new mothers, that most health professionals pay little attention to the phenomenon. Feelings associated with the blues usually go away on their own within a week or two, and tend to be only slightly bothersome to the new mother.

Normal Adjustment. The next level of distress felt by new mothers is categorized as "normal adjustment." "Normal crazy" might be a more accurate description. You may have many of the feelings of the blues, plus anxiety, mood swings, and anger. These feelings are completely normal, but feel crazy because of societal expectations that this should be a wonderful time in your life. In fact, these negative feelings of the normal adjustment period make perfect sense. New mothers are sleep-deprived, exhausted, and typically overwhelmed. They're thrown into a new job for which there's no adequate training available, and are given sole responsibility for a completely vulnerable and complex human being that arrives in the world without an instruction manual. The mother's negative feelings may continue for up to two months, and usually are "on again, off again" in nature, with many good days mixed in with the bad.

Postpartum Mood Reactions. The collection of symptoms called postpartum mood reactions comprises the next step along the continuum. The new mother may be depressed, suffering from an amplified version of the crying, exhaustion, anger, mood swings, irritability, sleep problems, and self-doubt of the previous two categories. In the state called mania, she may have excessive energy, little need to sleep, and extreme irritability. Postpartum mood reactions last longer than either the blues or normal adjustment. The symptoms are much the same, but feel worse and interfere to a greater extent with getting daily tasks done. If you have many of the symptoms of the blues, and your baby is more than six weeks old, you may fit this category.

Spectrum of Postpartum Emotional Reactions

The Baby Blues	Normal Postpartum Adjustments	Postpartum Reactions	Postpartum Thought Reactions
□ Crying	□ Crying, tearfulness	*Depression:*	*Any symptoms from list at left, plus:*
□ Irritability	□ Irritability	□ Worsening of normal adjustment symptoms	□ Debilitating confusion
□ Anger	□ Anger	*Mania:*	□ Hallucinations
□ Insomnia	□ Sleep disturbance	□ Feeling speeded up	□ Delusions
□ Exhaustion	□ Fatigue	□ Decreased need to sleep	
□ Tension	□ Dysphoria (negative mood)	□ Distractibility, pressured speech and thinking, irritability and excitability	
□ Anxiety	□ Appetite changes	*Panic reaction:*	
□ Restlessness	□ Loss of interest in usual activities	□ Panic attacks	
□ Emotionality	□ Anxiety	□ Extreme anxiety	
	□ Emotional lability (mood swings)	□ Physical symptoms—difficulty breathing, dizziness, shaking, etc.	
	□ Feelings of doubt (re: attractiveness, parenting skills, etc.)	*Post-traumatic stress:*	
	Postpartum exhaustion:	□ Panic attacks related to a specific past trauma	
	□ Denial of depression or anxiety	*Obsessive-compulsive reaction:*	
	□ Feeling overwhelmed	□ Disturbing repetitive thoughts	
	□ Inability to sleep or rest		
	□ Physical symptoms (headaches, stomachaches)		

Postpartum Anxiety Reactions. Like mood reactions, postpartum anxiety reactions involve an exaggeration of the negative feelings a woman may have in normal adjustment; but anxiety, worry, and panic are the primary symptoms rather than depression. Women who have anxiety reactions worry a great deal, have scary thoughts which they feel unable to control (this thought pattern is called obsessive-compulsive), or have panic attacks with many physical symptoms such as buzzing in the ears, tingling in hands or limbs, shortness of breath, dizziness, or flushed skin. Often these worries and panicky feelings are so troublesome that the new mother has difficulty getting her daily tasks done at all.

Postpartum Thought Reactions. The rarest form of postpartum emotional reaction is a type of psychosis which occurs only once or twice among every one thousand new mothers. In postpartum thought reactions, the new mother may have any of the problems described in the foregoing categories. But on top of these feelings and symptoms, she also has life-threatening confusion, hallucinations, or delusions that impede her normal functioning. Women with postpartum thought reactions see or hear things that are not there. They believe that what they are experiencing is real rather than illusory; as such, they can pose a great danger to themselves and their baby. Women with these symptoms need immediate medical attention.

Exercise: Two Minutes for Yourself

You may find yourself being extremely self-critical, telling yourself such things as "You are so stupid! What's wrong with you that you can't even take care of your baby? You wanted this baby so badly and now all you can do is cry; get it together! What kind of a deviant person are you to have such terrible thoughts? What a lousy mother you are!"

Acknowledge what you are telling yourself; then imagine instead that you are talking to a child or a close friend who is tormenting herself in this way. What can you tell her to make her feel better? How can you encourage her, and acknowledge all the hard work she's done so far?

Close your eyes, take four deep breaths, then say to yourself, "You are strong and competent, and this is really hard work. Just hang in there! Everything's going to be all right. Things will get easier soon." Draw on your compassionate side, and talk to yourself in the same gentle, supportive manner you'd use to cheer up a child or a friend who was in terrible pain. Do this for *yourself.* You are a special and wonderful person who deserves to be treated kindly.

Am I at Risk?: Biological, Psychological, and Relationship Risk Factors

You may be afraid that you're having postpartum adjustment problems because something is wrong with you as a person. Rest assured that there's nothing wrong with you in particular—but it's easy for the physical and emotional stresses of childbirth to cause imbalances in the body, and your relationships.

For all women, having a child results in enormous biological, psychological, and what we're calling relationship changes. Under the best of circumstances, you're bound to feel tired and at times overwhelmed and uncertain. It may seem as if your world is falling apart. For almost all new parents, it seems as if the world has turned upside down.

Fortunately, a great deal is now known about the factors that contribute to postpartum adjustment problems. There are three main categories of causes: those which are biological, those which are psychological, and those which have to do with relationships.

Biological Causes

Biological causes include:

- Normal physical changes of pregnancy and childbirth

- Hormonal changes of pregnancy and childbirth

- Heredity

- A previous episode of postpartum reaction

- Complications of pregnancy and childbirth

- Breastfeeding and weaning

- Premenstrual Syndrome (PMS) and menstrual problems

- Thyroid imbalance

From what is currently known, if you have experienced a prior postpartum reaction, you have a 50 percent chance of having another one. With regard to heredity, your odds of experiencing a postpartum episode may greatly increase if your mother or another close female relative had a postpartum reaction, or if there's a history of manic-depressive illness in your family. Information about how strongly other biological factors contribute to postpartum problems is less clear, and may vary considerably from woman to woman.

Psychological Causes

Psychological causes include:

- Normal psychological changes accompanying childbirth

- Expectations about motherhood

- Lifestyle patterns

- Previous psychological problems

- Childhood experiences

- Unresolved losses

- Recent stressful life events

- Personal resources for self-care and coping

Experts suggest that up to 70 percent of all women who experience a postpartum reaction have no history of psychological problems. So even if there aren't many psychological factors contributing to your postpartum difficulties, the normal emotional upheaval accompanying childbirth is in itself a risk factor.

A woman's expectations about what her life will be like after having a baby, and what sort of mother she'll be, are of enormous importance to the ease or difficulty of her postpartum adjustment. The more perfection you expect, the more emotional trouble you're likely to experience when you come face to face with the realities of having a baby. Unresolved issues from the past may also complicate your adjustment, particularly if they bothered you just prior to or during your pregnancy. Having a child may cause unresolved issues from the past to surface. Stressful events that occur closely before or after the birth of your child seem to be a larger contributor to postpartum adjustment problems than stressful events from the more distant past.

Relationship Causes

Relationship causes include:

- Normal relationship changes following childbirth

- The quality of your marriage or partnership

- The quality of your social support system

- Being a single mom

- The quality of your relationship with your baby

- Your relationship with your other children

With constant demands on your time and energy, having a new baby can strain even the best of marriages. If relationship problems predate your child's birth, your risk of a postpartum reaction is greatly increased. The weaker your network of close friends and family to lend emotional support and assist you with child care, the more susceptible you'll be to problems after the baby's birth. Although less is definitively known about other relationship factors, the quality of your relationships is crucial to an easy postpartum adjustment.

Exercise: Two Minutes for Yourself

Try to remember a day in your life when you felt happy, peaceful, and self-confident. It doesn't matter if the memory is a recent one or from very long ago. If you don't have an actual memory to draw on, try to imagine what such a day would be like. Are there people around you or are you alone? Are you at the beach, in an office, on a stage, in a restaurant, or snuggled up in bed? Picture as vividly as possible the details of your surroundings. Use all five senses—identify sounds, smells, tastes, textures, and colors. Now pay attention to how your body feels on this wonderful day. What is your breathing like? Can you feel your heartbeat? Do your shoulders feel relaxed? What about your feet and your hair? Can your feel your happiness in the tips of your fingers?

Now take a mental snapshot of this scene. You can return here whenever you need a break, whenever you need to feel refreshed and renewed. It only takes a couple of minutes. You just have to close your eyes and look at the snapshot again. It will all come flooding back to you: the sounds, smells, tastes, textures, colors; the feelings of happiness, peace, and self-confidence radiating out into each part of your body. No one can take this away from you. It's yours to keep and to draw on whenever you're in need.

Taking Care of Yourself

The first step in feeling better is to take care of yourself. The following suggestions can be included in every new mother's plan for self-care:

- Take care of yourself physically—get enough rest, eat right, exercise.

- Develop a support system—make sure you have other new parents to talk to, and make a point of talking to them or seeing them at least once a week.

- Express and accept your negative feelings—know that it's normal to feel bad sometimes when you're adjusting to a new baby. You are still an okay person if you don't feel just wonderful about this new addition to your life.

- Attend to your positive feelings—look for ways in which you do feel good, and pay attention to these too.

- Take breaks—by yourself, with your partner or another adult. No one can do a job non-stop without some time off every day.

- Keep your expectations realistic—no one can "do it all," let alone do it perfectly. Working toward reasonable, achievable goals, whether having to do with your feelings, the cleanliness of your home, the baby's schedule, control of your body, or whatever other issues are important to you now.

- Nurture your sense of humor—there is great value in keeping in touch with the funny side of life. Try to laugh daily, whether at yourself, your situation, or something outside of all this.

- Structure your day—plan loosely how you will spend your day, with time designated for all the items on this list. Plan for when you will talk to another adult, when you will rest, when you will take a break. Keep the plan flexible and realistic, so that you can stick to it.

- Postpone major life changes—your life is full of enough change and stress right now as it is. Avoid moving to a new job, a new home, a new partner—until you feel more settled in your new role of mother.

Once you have your self-care plan in place, and are working to care for yourself as we have just described, you may begin to feel better. Nonetheless, many of the negative feelings and symptoms that have been plaguing you may not disappear just because you begin to focus on your own needs. The remainder of this section is devoted to concrete ideas about what you can do to tackle these problems.

Physical Symptoms

Low energy and fatigue. The lack of energy and extreme fatigue felt by many new mothers is due in large part to sleep deprivation and hormonal imbalances. You probably won't feel fully restored until a certain amount of time passes postpartum—how much time depends on your physical condition and the nature of your birth experience. But certain measures can help.

The old advice to sleep when your baby sleeps is still good advice, even though it can be hard to follow. If you can't sleep, at least designate a rest period of twenty minutes or so to put your feet up with a tall glass of water, juice, or herbal tea within easy reach. Listen to music or read something enjoyable. Do not do chores—remember that this is your official break time. If your baby doesn't sleep sufficiently during the day to allow you to rest, call on your support network to spell you. Someone else can take the baby out in her carriage, or rock her, while you take a nap or relax.

It may seem illogical, but exercise is also an excellent way to gain more energy. With your weary body, it may take a big push to get yourself moving—but the payoff in energy will be well worth the effort. Walking is probably the best thing you can do now. You can build your endurance gradually, you can take your baby with you, and you'll both get fresh air. If the weather's horrible, see if you can find a gym that has an indoor track, or a mall that allows walkers in before or after store hours. As soon as your OB gives you the okay, swimming is also a great way to regain your strength, although you'll have to get someone else to watch the baby.

Pay attention to your diet, too. If you have a doughnut for breakfast and then feel exhausted by midmorning, you're probably having a "sugar crash." You need a balanced diet, including low-fat sources of protein. Try to eat lots of fresh fruits and vegetables, and whole grains such as brown rice, oats, and barley. Even if this isn't a diet you're accustomed to, it's one that will keep your system in working order. Snacking on nutritious foods throughout the day—having six small meals—is actually better for you than three full meals, which may be harder to digest.

A fun activity, or good talk with a friend, can also be energizing. If you're running on empty, and not taking some time for yourself, it's no wonder if you feel burned out and tired.

If your fatigue is due to sleep problems read the section below.

Sleep problems. Sleep problems can take many forms: difficulty falling asleep, either at the start of the evening or after waking to feed the baby; early morning awakening; insomnia; or over-sleeping. If you have trouble falling asleep, check out physical causes first. Caffeine (from coffee, soft drinks, tea, or chocolate) is the most common cause. Having a glass of wine or another alcoholic beverage to try to ease yourself into sleep often backfires: the alcohol may relax you at first, but then acts as a stimulant a few hours later. Medications can keep you from sleeping well; talk with your doctor or pharmacist if you suspect that a drug you're taking is disturbing your sleep. Spicy foods or late-night snacks have been known to interfere with dozing off.

If you rule out stimulants, and you're still not sleeping, try to notice what you're thinking about when you lie awake. Anxiety and worry may be the major cause of insomnia in new mothers. See the suggestions later in this chapter for dealing with anxiety.

If you're not getting adequate sleep, you're probably getting more and more worried about how you'll get through your work the following day. Such worry can set up a vicious cycle of worry and sleeplessness. To tackle insomnia, try to follow these guidelines:

- Stick to a regular schedule, especially a waking time. This can help reset your biological clock if it's gone haywire.

- Avoid naps if you're unable to sleep at night. Rest and relax instead.

- Avoid sleep-disruptive drugs and other stimulants such as caffeine.

- Exercise in the morning or early afternoon, but not late in the day.

- Avoid heavy meals or feeling hungry close to bedtime.

- Sleep in a safe, secure, and quiet setting.

- Don't lie in bed for extended periods when you're not intending to sleep. Don't use your bed as a library or an office. Cultivate a strong association in your mind between going to bed and going to sleep.

- Try to wind down and relax in the evening. (This may be difficult if your baby tends to be fussy in the evening. If this is the case, try to get people in your support network to help out in the evening, so that you can get some time to relax.)

- Go to bed only when you're sleepy. (But try to keep to the same schedule every day.)

- If you are not asleep in ten to fifteen minutes after lying down, go into another room. Do something boring or relaxing—listen to music, read a boring book, listen to a relaxation tape, or imagine a blank screen in your head. Return to bed only when you are sleepy.

Again, the goal is to associate bed with falling asleep quickly. Repeat this process if necessary.

- Make it your goal to stay relaxed, rather than focusing on falling asleep. Visual imagery, such as a picture of a restful beach scene, may help you become, and stay, more relaxed.

- To wind down in the evening, try some breathing exercises.

- Have a glass of warm milk or a high carbohydrate snack (such as bread, cereal, bagel, pasta).

- Soak in the bathtub or take a warm shower before going to bed.

- Set your alarm clock but turn the clock around so that you can't watch it.

- Get up at the same time every day.

If your problem is oversleeping—if you can't get up in the morning or you nap all day—a regular sleep schedule will help you as well. Exercise can energize you, as can high-protein snacks. Not being able to get up may be a sign of depression that you cannot easily tackle on your own. If this applies to you, please see the section on seeking professional help.

Appetite or eating changes. You may find that you suddenly have cravings, or no appetite at all. Keep in mind that a well-balanced diet is essential to your physical and emotional health. Allow yourself reasonable portions of the foods you crave; often, denial of the craved food only makes the craving worse. But try not to binge; and make sure you get adequate portions of all the nutrients you need. If you're nursing, you'll need three hundred to five hundred extra calories a day—get nutritional advice from your doctor or La Leche League publications, or make an appointment to speak to a professional nutritionist.

If you have no appetite, work on identifying a few foods that might taste good. "Comfort foods," which you ate happily in childhood or at other times you recall fondly, are a good place to start. Maybe you can eat small amounts of soup, for instance, gradually adding bread or fruit to broaden your diet. If you find that you cannot force yourself to eat, or you're throwing up after you eat, get professional help right away.

Hyperactivity. Perhaps you feel driven to accomplish everything. You can't stop and rest; you feel very jumpy inside. If you can, force yourself to take rest times, breathe deeply, and reduce the number of things you are trying to accomplish. Make sure you are exercising. Watch your intake of caffeine and sugar; both of these substances can "hype" you up. If you cannot make yourself slow down, you must seek professional help. You may be experiencing postpartum mania, and may be at risk for a more serious postpartum adjustment problem.

Panic symptoms. Hyperventilation, dizziness, shaking, hot or cold flashes, numbness or tingling, and heart palpitations can all be signs of a panic attack. Panic attacks are triggered by biological changes, and can be treated medically. Please see the chapter on Panic Attacks in part V.

Constipation or diarrhea. Exercise and proper diet are essential in maintaining proper bowel function. The soreness from childbirth, hemorrhoids from pregnancy, and little time to oneself can contribute to problems in this area. You may need to get on a schedule, allowing yourself quiet time at home to relax. Take time for yourself alone in the bathroom at this time, even if the baby needs to be put in the swing or the crib for a few minutes alone.

Itchiness. Dry skin can result from hormonal changes. Pamper yourself with some nice lotion; have your partner rub some soothing cream on your back, or soak in a bathtub with baby oil added. Itchiness can also be a sign of emotional turmoil, so pay attention to your feelings and read the relevant sections that follow.

Headaches or spots before the eyes. Headaches and seeing spots or halos can be signs of stress, anxiety, and depression—although you want to be sure to rule out an underlying medical problem before making this assumption. Read the relevant sections that follow, and make sure you get some exercise and adequate time to relax every day. Migraine headaches can be particularly debilitating, but in recent years have been managed through medication, biofeedback, Chinese medicine, and other alternative approaches.

Physical tension, stiff and sore muscles. Without doubt, the hard work of labor and birth can leave you feeling stiff and sore. Gentle exercise and pampering are the key to relieving tension and soreness. Be sure to always warm up before you exercise by bending and stretching. Make the time to have a relaxing bath or massage.

Emotional Symptoms

Crying. Crying and tearfulness in the postpartum period can have any number of causes. Tears can come from feeling overwhelmed, tired, frustrated, depleted, hungry, or sleepy. You may feel a sense of loss about any number of issues: your life as it was before the baby came; the contrast between your dreams of the perfect baby or delivery, and the way things turned out; your figure and how long it's taking you to lose the weight you gained during pregnancy; and so on. Use the suggestions in this chapter for addressing each of these underlying causes: read the recommendations for sleep problems, loss, and trouble coping.

If none of these issues seems to strike a chord for you, and/or you just feel like crying, go ahead and cry. Crying can be beneficial in releasing stress. Set aside fifteen or twenty minutes each day to cry out your feelings. Set the kitchen timer, collect the tissues, and cry. Or cry in the shower.

Confusion or trouble with concentration. It's common in the postpartum period for new mothers to feel "muddled." You may lose your train of thought, forget what you were going to say or do, or even become confused about what day of the week it is. This muddled state of mind is likely caused by a combination of fatigue, concentration on the new job of being a parent, and fluctuating hormones. To remedy this, first make sure that your habits for rest, relaxation, and diet are in good shape. Try to decrease overload and expectations—having fewer jobs to keep track of will help. Make lists and write things down, but keep your lists simple. Many women find it most useful to make their (brief) lists the night before, rather than in the morning when they're feeling groggy. Pick your most alert time, and plan your day then. Using a calendar with reminders, and checking off each day, can orient you about the passage of time. Take rest breaks, when you close your eyes briefly, using your imagination like a TV screen to focus on important tasks or items to remember. If your partner or family members are more organized than you're feeling now, let them call you or write you notes with daily reminders. (But avoid this if their reminders feel more like pressure than help—stay attuned to what works for *you*.)

Trouble coping, feeling overwhelmed or powerless. Everything may be feeling as if it's crashing in on you. You can't get anything done; you feel as if you have little or no control over the day's events and your reactions to them.

First of all, single out one area in which you do have control, and in which you are accomplishing something. This may be as simple as getting the baby's diaper changed when needed. You are succeeding here. Write this down on a notecard and post it somewhere: "I am getting the baby's diapers changed every day." Pat yourself on the back. Reassure yourself that there is nothing wrong with you for feeling overwhelmed with your life.

Slowly add one more task at a time, never adding more than you can reasonably hope to accomplish. Sit down with your partner or a trusted friend or family member and examine your expectations. Throw out any expectations that are unrealistic. Brainstorm about ways to get help getting basic chores done—things that will make your life miserable if they're left undone.

Lack of confidence, feelings of inadequacy. Few people feel like a parent when they take home that new baby. If you find yourself saying, "Where did this baby come from, and what am I supposed to do with him?" you are completely normal. It's a myth that you will suddenly know what your baby needs or what to do to feel like a parent. Reassure yourself, your partner, your baby, and your family (if they are asking) that you certainly can learn to fulfill your role as a parent. What is important is that you know you can, and that you tell yourself this. Write it down and post it on notes around the house if you need reassurance: "I can be a good enough parent." "I can be a person and a parent, too." Read these affirmations to yourself at various times throughout the day.

Sadness or hopelessness. Feelings of sadness tend to well up easily in the postpartum period. This might seem strange to you in the context of everyone saying, "Lucky you—this is the happiest time of your life!" Expectations that your life should be wonderful now only make you feel worse, making you wonder, "What's the matter with me?" In reality, it's not uncommon to feel sad when you have a new baby. If you can identify some of the reasons underlying your sadness, list them on a piece of paper or talk about them with your partner or a trusted friend.

Irritability or hypersensitivity. Fluctuating hormones, fatigue, and the uncertainties that go with being a new parent are all big contributors to the irritability and hypersensitivity that new mothers often feel. Take a look at when your feelings get hurt most quickly, and see if any patterns exist. Does it happen when you are tired, or hungry, or when you've been alone all day? Is it worst in the evening, when you are looking forward to your partner's return, and your expectations of "relief" are high? If you can see factors that trigger your irritability, work to change them. If your partner wants to come home and play with the baby, leaving you feeling neglected, speak up. Give yourself permission to ask for some attention, too.

Taking several deep breaths and counting to ten are old standbys for preventing an all-out fight being triggered. When you give yourself time to think through what bothered you about another person's comment, you can evaluate whether your perceptions are accurate and fair, and you may be able to respond in a more measured and reasonable way.

A lack of feelings toward the baby, anger, or overprotectiveness. The idea that bonding takes place on the delivery bed is an old myth that dies hard. The attachment process is a slow, gradual growth of feeling between you and your baby. As you get to know your child, you will feel stronger feelings—and all of these feelings may not be positive. Feeling angry or overprotective toward your baby may occur as you become attached for many reasons. You may spend more time with the baby than with any other person. The baby may be the source of most of your joy as well as your frustration with your life right now. After all, you did not feel this way before the baby appeared.

Worry, anxiety, or obsessive thoughts. You may find that you are "stuck" on certain worries or thoughts that make you feel anxious. Anxiety and worry frequently plague new parents. Surviving pregnancy and childbirth may give you a new awareness of the fragile nature of human life. You see how small and vulnerable your baby seems. And you are inclined to protect him or her. Seeing how small babies are, and then comparing them to the world of violence and potential harm we live in, it is quite natural to wonder (and worry) about how they'll ever grow to reach adulthood. And then for you to be in charge of that—how overwhelming! It's in this reasoning process that worries tend to surface.

Many events that affect your child are simply not subject to your control. You can't control weather or wars or an uneven pavement that may cause your child to trip and fall. You can't shield your child from every disease-bearing cough or sneeze or handshake. To manage your worries and anxieties, you can first make sure you're taking all the recommended steps to care for your child. Use a car seat, get those vaccinations, feed her well, make sure no one smokes in your household. For your own peace of mind, you may want to quit reading the newspaper or watching the evening news or talk shows for a while. It can be helpful to have a "worry time" set aside each day. Keep a tablet close by throughout the day. When worries surface, jot them down and tell yourself, "I'll think about that later, during my worry time." When the appointed time arrives, get out the tablet and focus on it for twenty or thirty minutes, really allowing yourself to worry and think about possible precautions. When the time is up, switch gears with a distracting activity (exercise, pampering) and begin to put aside your worries for the next session.

Issues

Social support or social withdrawal. Whether you know and talk often with other people who have babies can make a big difference in your life postpartum. Research has shown that those new parents who talk regularly with a person who understands their trials and joys have an easier adjustment than do new parents without such friends. But making new friends, or time for the ones you do have, can seem impossible when you have a new baby and can barely get yourself dressed each day. Making friends as an adult isn't as easy as it was in childhood or college days, when there was a ready supply of prospects at school, and you may have felt more open emotionally, and more willing to take risks. You may have few women who stay at home on your block, or no co-workers with children. If you need to find potential friends, getting out and approaching other mothers you see is essential. Speak to them in the grocery store or the park. Advertise at your pediatrician's office or your church. Take a postpartum exercise class, or a mom-baby class, at your local recreation center. Check with your local mental health association about new mother groups in your area (look in the city or county listings in your phone book under "Mental Health Association").

Once you have spotted a person or two in the same boat, make getting to know that person a priority. Or, if you already know someone, commit to meet with her on a regular basis.

Control and perfectionism. These may seem like two very different issues, but in practice they're intimately related. Control is a matter of wanting everything to be "the right way," which often translates into wanting things to be perfect and wanting things to be your way. When you have a new baby, it's often difficult to accept the many aspects of your life that you can't control. Your life may no longer seem perfect, or as nearly perfect as it was before. You can't make the baby sleep. You can't make yourself sleep at times. Often, you can't make the baby stop crying. You can't control what your partner does or says; he may not be the perfect parent you hoped he'd be. Your formerly lovely house may be a total mess, with laundry and baby things and dirty dishes and wilted flowers everywhere. This all may make you feel extremely out of control, as if you can influence nothing in your life.

Perhaps you've been accustomed to controlling your life to a great extent. You may have finished your education, delaying marriage and having a baby until the time was right. This may mean that you'd finally bought a home, or planned the baby for a certain time of year, or had saved enough money so that you could stay home with the baby for several years. The cold, cruel reality of not being able to control your life to this extent anymore may now be hitting you hard. It may be time to adjust your expectations; time to identify those issues that you can control in your life right now. You have to choose your battles from now on.

You may need to push yourself to make mistakes in order to have a chance to accept them. You will not know that mistakes and imperfection are tolerable, and not life-threatening, unless you actually make them. Experiment with some little things. Put the baby's shirt on backwards or insideout. If you are picking up the toys (or clothes or books and papers) every time the baby goes to sleep, practice leaving them out instead. Don't wear makeup one day. Serve cereal for dinner. All of these small imperfections can broaden your perspective. You "goofed," and life went on.

Anger. Anger may be the feeling that you least expected to have after the birth of your baby. What on earth do you have to feel angry about, you may ask yourself. You may even be asked that question by others. Rest assured that anger is a common postpartum emotion for many women, and it may seem incredibly strong.

There are legitimate reasons to be angry after having a baby. Most of them have to do with expectations. You did not expect to feel so badly. You did not expect to feel so out of control. You did not expect your baby to cry all the time, or be a boy, or girl, or look like your father, or be sick, or colicky, or any number of other things that have come to pass. You did not expect to have the birth experience you had. You did not expect to feel neglected by your partner, parent, friend, etc. You expected your loved ones to be more helpful and involved. You expected to get some rest, and to look and feel better sooner. You may feel cheated about any number of things. And while you may be surprised about having these feelings, there's nothing wrong with you for feeling them. You are not crazy.

Speaking up is also an important way to diffuse anger. Keep in mind that you want your expression of angry feelings to be assertive, not aggressive. You want to speak your mind without hurting others. Use the word "I" rather than "you." Avoid name-calling or accusations. Stick to the event at hand, rather than the last forty anger-provoking events in your life. For example, say, "I was angry when you walked in and right past me to the baby. I want you to greet me first." This will get you to a solution much quicker than saying, "You are so heartless—you ignore me all the time." Try to be specific about what was done, and what you would like to have done differently. And realize that you have a right to express your angry feelings, but so does the other person. Be prepared to listen, and to acknowledge the other person's feelings. "I didn't know you were angry, too," can go a long way toward soothing someone's feelings. Finally, expressing your anger may not accomplish anything more than making you feel better by getting the anger off your chest. Keep your expectations in check here, too. Remember that you're expressing your anger as a way to make yourself feel better. You're not getting your anger out to make someone else feel guilty, or as a way to control someone. Change may come about as a result of your words, but there are no guarantees.

Dysfunctional family of origin. Perhaps in your family of origin your feelings were not respected, or you were not allowed to be yourself. You may feel a deep hurt about wrongs inflicted on you by your family. Your parents may have provided models that you desperately don't want to copy; you may fear imposing their parenting style on your own child. There are many ways in which the family in which you grew up can influence your own transition to parenthood, and you may feel a need to face those family issues once your own baby has arrived.

You may need to do some serious thinking about what needs to be different. If you had a magic wand, what would you change about your family, or its influence at this time in your life? Once you can define a specific goal—such as, "My mother needs to tell me positive—not negative—things about my ability to be a parent"—you can brainstorm about how you might achieve that goal. It is often easier to write letters to family members, telling them what you would like to see change, rather than confronting them in person or by telephone.

Families can be powerful influences in our lives; and it can be very difficult to sort these things out on your own. If confronting your family seems overwhelming, you may want to get the added support of professional counseling.

Uninvolved or absent partner. In many marriages, one partner may in effect be absent because of work demands, travel schedules, or busy lives in general. Perhaps you pictured parenting as a joint venture, but now feel as if you're flying solo. Some new mothers feel this way because of the physical demands of breastfeeding. Mothers, much more often than fathers, take extended leave for infant care. Even though times are changing, many new parents even now have to struggle consciously not to fall into the traditional roles of father as breadwinner and mother as homemaker. We've noticed a tendency in many new fathers to actually increase their time at work postpartum. This appears to be a common way for men to cope with the responsibilities of being a parent.

You may want to begin by setting up a weekly "date." That can be time out of the house for you and your partner together, dinner together after the baby is in bed, or simply a designated "talk time" to keep in touch with each other's lives. Your relationship is the foundation of your new family, and you will now need to devote time to nurturing it, just as you need to nurture your baby. You need to plan time together; otherwise, it can easily get swallowed up by other tasks and activities that seem much more pressing. Sitting together and just listening to music, or cuddling, or taking turns massaging each other's shoulders are other important ways to stay close and keep in touch.

Assigning your partner one specific child-care task each day can also increase his involvement with the baby. You'll get a break as well. Have your partner give the baby a bath each evening, or rock the baby to sleep. It's tempting to have your partner tackle the dishes, rather than a child-care task. But your goal is to involve him with the baby, and to build the infant-parent relationship—as well as to give you a break.

Loss. There are certain losses that are part of being a new parent. You may feel a real loss of freedom—from being able to come and go as you please, to always having to plan for the baby before you go anywhere. You may feel sad about losing your carefree, childless lifestyle. Sleeping until noon on the weekends, staying up late, dancing until dawn may be things of the past. Many women feel that they have lost their "self" and turned into a parent, a person who is foreign to them. "I'm no longer the old me," is a frequent complaint. You may feel sad about losing the specialness of pregnancy. You are no longer the focus of attention and doting; people now smile at the baby, not you. You may feel the loss of the close relationship you had with your physician or midwife. You visit extensively with that person for nine months, trust in them, rely on them, feel cared for by them. Then suddenly that person is "discharging" you, and you will see them only rarely.

You need to allow yourself to acknowledge any of these losses that you feel keenly. They are real. Give yourself permission and time to grieve your losses. Acknowledge the sadness, cry, keep a journal to record your feelings. You need to seek the support of your family in this process as well. You may need to hear from your partner that the loss is real, a confirmation of your need to grieve it, so that you can start to feel better. Don't be afraid to ask for this acknowledgement and support from the people who matter to you.

Guilt. The adjustment of new parents is often complicated by guilt. It's a difficult task to try to maintain your pre-baby life and do a good enough job of meeting your baby's needs as well. You may feel as if you never have enough time for everything you want to do. If you neglect your own needs or your partner or your job, you feel guilty. And you feel guilty if you put any of those priorities above the baby's needs. Guilt just comes with the territory at times. It's normal to want to be at home with the baby if you're at work, and to want a break from the baby if you're at home. Getting yourself on a schedule, so that time is allotted for everyone's needs (including your own), can help. Play with the baby, then do one household task, then take a brief rest break for yourself followed by cuddle time for your partner. Of course, your schedule will be determined by how cooperative or sleepy your baby is, or else on the strength and presence of your support network. You can tell yourself that you are doing it all, just not all at once.

Body image. Your body doesn't feel like yours anymore. You may look in the mirror and wonder who it is you're seeing. What happened to your pre-baby body? Just getting dressed in the morning can trigger all kinds of negative feelings about your current shape and weight. Exercise and proper diet are critical to feeling better, of course. Shop smart, stocking up on low-fat, high energy foods like whole-grain breads, nonfat yogurt, fruit, and vegetables. Plan special low-fat snacks for your break times, and make a point of using a special mug or napkin, or setting a flower in a vase at your place. Take a postpartum exercise class where babies are welcome. Get back to an activity you enjoyed pre-baby, such as tennis, golf, or running.

Exercise and diet are important, but so is what you say to yourself. Stating to yourself, or posting on your fridge, "My body is looking better and better every day," or "I can eat just what I need," can give you the feeling that you can control this part of your life. Look in the mirror, and find one feature that you like in your appearance.

Financial stress. Changing income levels and rising expenses cause financial stress for many new parents. If you and your husband make an effort not to spend more than you take in, the financial strain of having a baby will probably diminish over time. If your financial problems seem overwhelming, you may want to look for the Consumer Credit Counseling Service in your area. This is a nonprofit community agency that can offer advice on budgeting and consolidation of debt.

Attachment. You may worry about the effects of your postpartum adjustment symptoms on the relationship you are developing with your baby. Attachment or bonding with your baby occurs over the course of time, and is influenced by many factors. Your mood is just one of those factors. While you want to do all you can to take care of yourself and improve your mood, you need to remember that how you feel is not the only influence. Your baby's temperament, the involvement of other adults in your baby's life, and the interaction you and the baby have on your good days all affect the bonding process. And the passage of time will help you build the relationship with your baby, as you begin to feel better. There is no "critical period" for human infants when you either have to "bond" or all is lost. If you miss the first few weeks because of severe symptoms, you can work at the mother-infant relationship when you feel better.

Relationship difficulties. One of the major stresses and adjustments in the postpartum period is maintaining the balance in your relationship with your partner. Babies require you to rethink how you have set up your relationship: who takes care of whom, who pays the bills, who makes the money, who has veto power. All the discussions you may have had, and all your expectations and fantasies, often go out the window when you bring the new baby home. The most powerful model in the back of your mind for how a family should be is how your family was when you were growing up. You may be overwhelmed to find yourself in your parents' marriage all of a sudden, acting just as they did and expecting your partner to do the same.

Rather than feeling devastated by these changes in your relationship, be assured that they are completely normal. All couples go through an adjustment period after the birth of a baby. You and your partner need to take it slowly, and realize that you can get back to your previous status if you just don't panic. All the changes that have occurred do not mean that your pre-baby ways of relating are gone for good. They're just lost in the fog for a while. Spend lots of time discussing what you want, how you're feeling, and how you'd like your relationship to be. Stick to wording using "I," not "you." Use concrete examples of behavior you'd like to see. For example,

"I like it when you hug me when you come home," is much more positive than, "You never pay attention to me anymore." Remember that you're in this together, and solutions will only come if you work together.

If you and your partner have a stormy relationship history, your previous problems will likely be magnified after your baby arrives. For instance, feeling that your partner is always critical will likely mushroom into a major issue if you are the least bit insecure about parenting. Expect to have to face these ongoing issues as a couple. Counseling is advisable if you are unable to iron out these differences on your own. Do take your conflicts seriously, and seek outside help if you need it; divorce is not uncommon after the birth of a baby. Use all the stresses and strains of the adjustment period as an excuse to rework your relationship into a stronger and more positive bond.

Self-esteem, self-doubt, and identity. You may find yourself mourning the loss of your "old self" now that you are "just somebody's mother." Questioning who you are or your value as a person is a common concern after the birth of a baby. You may have had a strong identity as a working person, and felt good in that role. But now you may place less emphasis on that part of yourself, or have given it up (for a while or forever) in order to devote more of your energy to parenting. You may feel lost without the old you. Many new mothers feel less valuable without outside income and periodic performance reviews. And caring for an infant does little to bolster self-esteem with the long hours, tiring physical labor, and lack of feedback involved. Your baby never looks up and says, "Good job, Mom!" It's no wonder you may question the whole process, and your importance as a part of it. Our society does not put a high premium on parenting. Evidence of this is found everywhere, from the low pay for teachers and child-care workers, to the lack of available training for parents, to the snub you may have experienced at a social gathering when you say that you are "just a mother."

You need a bumper sticker that says, "Motherhood is a proud profession." Raising children to adulthood is an immensely valuable occupation, whether you are home all day or balancing paid work with full-time parenting. You need to recognize your strengths, as a parent and otherwise.

List your strengths on paper and review them every day. List your accomplishments, too, in parenting and in other arenas. If you feel that you have given up everything to devote yourself to your baby, identify a part of your pre-baby self that you would like to revive. Then do it. Have your partner care for the baby so you can take a class, indulge a hobby, develop or improve a skill. Don't be afraid to ask for recognition or a pat on the back from those around you, whether family, friends, or work associates. Most important is how you talk to yourself, however, and value your own achievements, at home and elsewhere. Tell yourself you did a good enough job, that you are doing the best you can do. If you are proud of yourself, and speak up about it, or even show this in your body language, others will take note and respect you, too. If you have serious doubts about your ability in a certain area, take the plunge to improve yourself. Take a class, do some reading, or just experiment with a new way of doing things. Don't be afraid to make mistakes; you can survive a mistake or two. People who doubt themselves improve fastest when they jump right in and attempt to solve the problem, rather than brooding about it for a long time. Even if they don't solve their problem perfectly the first time, they feel better and stronger for having tackled it.

Excerpted and adapted with permission from *Postpartum Survival Guide* by Anne Dunnewald, Ph.D, and Diane Sanford, Ph.D. For more information on this and related books, see the "Further Reading" section in the back of the book.

CHAPTER 9

Parenting Skills

Take Charge!

King Edward VII, after a trip to America, said, "The thing that impresses me most about America is the way parents obey their children." So often, parents are unknowingly and unconsciously controlled by their children. Parents may wish and hope that their children will behave, but somehow lack the skills and knowledge to follow through on their hopes. Most often, these parents are not even aware of what is happening to them, even when they can point out when it's happening to other parents. These are some examples from a recent trip to the park:

It is a sunny summer day. I decide to take my three children and my sister's two children to the park. As I sit on a park bench and read my book (on parenting, what else?), I occasionally look up to view the parenting styles of other people in the park. I see a mother and daughter (around age nine). The daughter is on the top of the slide and calls out:

Daughter: Ma! I want some of that juice.

Mother: Okay, honey. (*Brings the juice over to the slide, and hands it to her daughter along with a granola bar.*)

Daughter: I just asked for juice. (*Tosses the granola bar back at her mother.*)

Mother: (*Not even noticing the disrespect*) I don't think it's safe for you to be up there with your rollerblades on.

Daughter: I'm fine, Mom.

Mother: I sure wish you'd come down.

Daughter: I'm being careful.

Mother: Oh, okay.

I shake my head and return to my book. A few minutes later, I see two dads with their three-year-old girls. One of the girls takes her shoes off. The other sits down to do the same.

Father: You know our rule: shoes stay on at the park.

Daughter: But Susie has her shoes off!

Father: I know. But that's our rule.

Daughter: (*Starts to cry*) But I want mine off, too!

Father: But you know the rule!

Daughter: (*Crying*) Pleeeeease, Daddy!

Father: (*Shrugging his shoulders*) Oh, I guess it would be all right.

I could just cry! It's sad when a parent starts off so right, but then allows a fussing, whining child to win the battle! How can you be a parent in control of the daily situations that occur with your children?

Say this with me, out loud, three times: **I am the parent. I am in charge**.

Do you believe it? Or do you still feel like your parents' child? Do you still question your decisions? Do you worry a lot about your mistakes? The first step toward improving your situation is to change your attitude. Of course, you will make mistakes, everyone does. But your efforts, your skills, and your love for your child will far outweigh any mistakes you make. An overall solid parenting style will more than compensate for a few mistakes. The problem comes when you repeat a mistake over and over. A very common mistake is allowing a child to be in control.

Decide here and now that you will be in charge. It is not only your right, it is your responsibility. Your children need you to parent them effectively. They are counting on you to guide them into adulthood.

Expect your children to obey you. Your expectation alone will carry weight in the eyes of your children. When you expect your children to obey, you will act differently. You will have an inner strength that your children will rely on. Expecting your children to obey is much different than wishing that your children would obey. Remember the mom with the nine-year-old on the slide with rollerblades? The mom said, *"I don't think it's safe for you to be up there. I sure wish you'd come down."* That's a very typical parental request. Couple it with that hopeful add-on, "Okay?" and you have yourself an ineffective request. Other "wishing" statements start out: "Would you like to . . . ?" or "It would be nice if you . . . " or "Don't you think you should?" When you expect your children to obey, your vocabulary changes. For example, try these alternatives when telling a child to do something.

"It's not safe up there with your rollerblades on. Come down, or take them off."

"Boys, we are leaving the park in 5 minutes."

"Please take out the garbage."

"When you have finished your homework, you may go out and play."

No Guilt, No Explanations

We undermine many of our decisions by allowing guilt to creep in. The dad with the three-year-old in the park who let his daughter take off her shoes despite their "shoes-on-in-the-park" rule gave in because his little girl cried, and her friend had her shoes off. So Dad felt guilty and worried about his daughter's immediate happiness. Is making our children happy our most important job? I don't think so. Consider this:

Our Most Important Job Is Not to Make Our Children Happy, But to Prepare Them for Life

Life is not always fair. Life is not always consistent. Many of our family rules are created because they reflect what we as a family believe in, not what society as a whole believes in. As an example, not all six-year-olds go to bed at the same time. Some go to bed at 8:00. Some at 9:00. Some at 10:00. Some kids are allowed to run around barefoot, some are not. Some kids must make their beds, some don't have to. Some kids walk to school, some ride the bus. Which rules are the right rules? Which are the best rules? They all are. Families are different. Families' needs are different. Families' goals are different. It's okay for families' rules to be different, too.

Once you decide what your family's rules are, you need to feel comfortable enforcing them. Don't worry about what the neighbors are doing. Don't worry if your rules aren't perfect. Don't overthink your decisions: as a matter of fact, if you look hard enough, you can find an expert somewhere who will agree that whatever you have decided is right.

Because I Said So!

Didn't you just hate it when your parents said that? I did, too. Even so, believe it or not, I occasionally use this line on my kids, because, sometimes, it's the only real reason!

Child: Why do I have to come in now?

Parent: Because I said so.

Child: Why can't I have this?

Parent: Because I said so.

Child: Why do I have to go to bed at 8:30?

Parent: Because I said so.

There's another good reason to use this old standby. When kids ask "Why?" usually they don't really want a reason, they want you to change your mind. Typically, the more reasons you give, the harder they fight:

Mom: Time to go now.

Child: Why?

Mom: Because it's getting late. We need to go home.

Child: Why?

Mom: Because I have to make dinner.

Child: I'm not hungry.

Mom: I am.

Child: Can't you have a granola bar?

Mom: I don't want a granola bar, I want dinner.

Child: Well, how about five more minutes? (and on and on and on and on . . .)

Consider instead:

Mom: Time to go now.

Child: Why?

Mom:	Because I said so.

Yes, children need explanations for rules and limits to give them the sense that you're not completely arbitrary. However, they don't need a reason for everything. When is it okay not to explain? One: Your child already knows the reason, and is just asking as a way to stall. Two: The reason is too complex for your child to understand. Three: Giving the reason will just cause an endless argument.

If "Because I said so" sticks in your throat, try one of these alternatives:

Child:	Why?
Parent:	Because I am the parent and it's my job to make this decision.
Child:	Why?
Parent:	Because I am the adult and I have more experience than you do.
Child:	Why?
Parent:	For many reasons that we are not going to discuss right now.

Whatever you say, it's important to acknowledge the fact that as a parent you are ultimately in control. This does not mean, of course, that you will control everything your children do. A very important part of maintaining your control is to understand that your goal is to prepare your children for life—on their own. This means that as your children grow, you need to give them certain freedoms, along with the responsibilities that go with those freedoms.

When a young tree is first planted, it is held up by two sticks and pieces of rope. As the young tree becomes stronger, and is able to stand alone, the sticks must be removed to allow the tree freedom and room to grow strong. A child, like a young tree, must have the support of his parents while young, like the sticks of support for the tree. As time goes on, he must learn to stand alone, but the memory and direction of the sticks of support will determine how well the child, like the tree, grows to his full potential.

Think!

Often, when in the role of parent, the tendency is to go with the flow. That is, parents often make decisions and invent rules on the run. They may never really think in advance about their parenting style, specific skills, or household rules. When they see their children doing something they don't like or that's dangerous, they swoop down and say, "Stop!" When their children make an unreasonable request, they say, "No!" When a repeated misbehavior occurs, they tend to babble, flap, and whine.

The problem with going with the flow is that you often end up in the rapids, and sometimes even go over the waterfall. Someone once said, "If you fail to plan, you plan to fail." This is so very true when raising a child. If you don't think, if you don't plan, then you can get caught up in the emotions of the moment, and your decisions are going to be less than ideal.

When You Say It, Mean It!

Do you want to do a fascinating experiment? All you need is a tape recorder and a blank tape. Put the recorder in the kitchen, and when you are sharing a meal with your children, turn it on. (Even better, let your spouse or a friend turn it on when you are unaware.) Then sit back and really listen to what happens. You will probably be surprised. A typical parent's comments during an hour-long meal might go something like this:

"Kevin, stop poking your brother. . . ."

"I said, stop poking your brother! . . ."

"Kevin! Do you need to go to time out? Stop poking your brother! . . ."

"What is wrong with you today! Stop that poking! . . ."

"Will you stop that! . . ."

With all the empty words this parent was using, it would have been better not to have even mentioned the poking in the first place. I often hear parents ask their children three or four times to do something. Then, when the child has not cooperated, they yell, "Do it now! And I mean it!" I always wonder why they just didn't mean it the first time. Here's a plan for meaning what you say:

Step 1: Think

Think before you talk. Say only what you are willing to follow up on.

Step 2: Warn

Give one warning.

Step 3: Act

Follow through to physically help your child carry out the desired action.
This example will clarify how the plan works:

Parent: (Thinking: We have to leave now. I'll let James play for five more minutes.) James. We are leaving in five minutes.

Parent: (Four minutes later) Please put your shoes on—time to go.

Parent: (One minute later) James, time to go (picks up shoes in one hand, takes James' hand, and walks him to the car in stocking feet).

When you first change to this strategy, you can expect some real resistance on the part of your child. You will be tested. At first, your child won't believe that you have changed. This is a critical juncture: if you don't follow through every time, your child will see that nothing has really changed. If you do follow through every time, your child will catch on that "things are really different around here now!" Soon enough, when you talk you will be heard.

5–3–1–Go!

Go with me now to an indoor kid park with all sorts of wonderful activities and equipment for young children. Let's look in at the play area and watch as various parents try to encourage their children to put on their shoes and leave for home:

"Becky, time to go!" says Nellie Nag. It appears that Becky has not heard her, so Nellie repeats herself, "Becky! Time to go." Becky continues to play with her new friend, Peter. But Peter's mom, Betty Briber, is whispering in his ear, "If you get in the car right now, I'll buy you a box of those cute little cookies you like, and you can eat them on the way home!" Meanwhile, Letty Lecture is looking up the slide at her two kids and saying, "You know, guys, when I take you to this place, I expect you to cooperate when it's time to go. I bring you here because I know you love it. But when I ask you to put your shoes on, I would like you to listen. Last time we came here . . . " Nellie's voice can still be heard over the din: "Becky. It's time to put your shoes on, honey." Meanwhile, Wishy Wanda can be heard wondering about her children's behavior: "I sure wish you kids would put your shoes on. It would be nice if you listened to me." Oh, and in the background: "Becky, don't you have your shoes on yet?" Everyone pauses for a minute as Bret Threat shouts, "Get in that car right now or I'll never let you come here again!" Bret's children hurry out to the car, as they pass Count Casey and hear him say, "If you kids aren't in the car by the time I count to three . . ."

"Becky! Find your shoes, and let's get going," says Nellie Nag. In the meantime, Wilma Whiner sounds like fingernails on a blackboard: "Kiiiiids. Come oooooon. I asked you to put your shoooes ooooon. Will you pleeeeeze listen to meeeee." But her kids aren't really listening to her, because they are busy playing with Becky . . .

Sound familiar? Just listen in on any birthday party, neighborhood park, or gymnastics class, and you'll hear all these parents trying to gain their children's attention and cooperation. So, you want to know, just how do you get them to leave the kid park?

First, let's try to understand what's going on here. When kids are having a good time, it's hard for them to change gears on a dime, which is what we expect. When a kid is in the middle of a great game with a new friend, and Dad walks in and says, "Time to go," it's hard for a child to immediately comply. Actually, it's hard for adults to do this too. Picture yourself at the computer typing away when your spouse calls, "Honey, dinner's ready!" Do you immediately pop off your chair and run to the kitchen? Or do you answer back, "Just a minute," and take the time to finish your paragraph, save your work, tidy up your desk, and—only then—saunter into the kitchen?

What really helps children prepare to finish or change activities is to allow them the time to process the change mentally before they follow through physically. Watch how this happens:

Molly and Austin are happily playing together at the park while Mom is reading on a nearby bench. She looks up at them and says, "Molly! Austin! We're leaving in five minutes," she holds up five very visible fingers. Somewhere in the back of Molly's and Austin's minds the information is filtering through. A few minutes later, Mom says, "Molly! Austin! We're leaving in three minutes." She holds up three fingers. A few minutes later: "Molly! Austin! One minute! Do you want to have one more swing or one more slide?" "Slide!" they shout. After the slide, Mom says, "Time to go. You guys want to run to the car, or hop like bunnies?" And the three of them hop to the car.

A few pointers on 5-3-1-Go! You can adjust this technique to meet your family's needs, your children's ages, or your personality. For instance, for a 16-year-old, you may pop your head in the family room as she's watching TV and say, "Corine, we're leaving at 3:00 sharp. It's 2:45 now." You can use this technique to call your kids to dinner, to the bathtub, or to bed. Keep in mind one very important point: this won't work the first time you use it. And probably not the second. But, by about the third or fourth time, your kids will understand and accept this new way of doing things. From the first, when you say, "Time to go!" you must immediately go. If you don't, this won't be any different from any of the old techniques that don't work.

A student named Mel called to tell me about trying this technique. In a rather grim voice, he told me, "It better work." "You sound angry," I said. "Oh, yes. I took my four-year-old to McDonald's. I said, 'Matthew, five minutes . . . three minutes . . . one minute . . . time to go!' And he jumped into the ball pit. So, I remembered what you said about meaning business when you say Go; and I jumped in the ball pit after him! Do you know how hard it is to get out of one of those things with a screaming, kicking four-year-old under your arm?" (I felt like selling tickets!)

The good news is that, yes, indeed, Mel did stick with the idea, and a few months later reported that it was working like a charm.

Time Out

Time out can be a potent, positive disciplinary tool. It has been used effectively by parents for generations (it has its roots in that old standby, sitting in the corner). Time out works because it interrupts a child's negative behavior with space, time, and quiet. There can be three different purposes for time out. Each has its own method for successful use.

I. Stopping a specific misbehavior.

Time out can be an excellent way to stop a child mid-action. It conveys a strong message that says, "This behavior is unacceptable. It will stop now." The method is especially useful with preschoolers, and is often used with great success in stopping physical violence—hitting, biting, and so on. It's effective because it allows the parent to take control of the situation immediately while still understanding that angry, out-of-control preschoolers often needs an adult's help to gain control of themselves.

Here's an example of how time out can work in this context. Danny and Alisa, brother and sister, are playing together. They begin to fight over a toy. Alisa grabs the toy, and Danny hits her.

Parent:	*(Taking Danny by the hand to the bathroom)* Danny, no hitting. Time out. *(Danny is put in the bathroom for one minute. He's then allowed to return and play with Alisa. After a while, he hits her again.)*
Parent:	*(Taking Danny by the hand to the bathroom)* Danny, no hitting. Time out. *(Danny is returned to the bathroom for two minutes. He's then allowed to return and play with Alisa. Again, he hits her.)*
Parent:	*(Taking Danny by the hand to the bathroom)* Danny, no hitting. Time out. *(Danny is returned to the bathroom for three minutes. He's then allowed to return and play with Alisa. All is peaceful.)*

There are several keys to using time out in this way:

1. Be quick. Catch your child in the act of misbehaving. Time out seldom works when it is delayed.

2. Use a boring place for time out, like a bathroom or a laundry room or the stairs. This is not meant to be fun. (Make sure, though, that the place is a safe one for your child to spend a few minutes alone in. If no safe place is available, your child can have time out in a chair within sight of you.)

3. Use time out for selected behaviors such as hitting or backtalk. If you use time out for every misbehavior, it loses its impact.

4. Use progressive amounts of time for repeated offenses. Stick with it! When you first start using this method to stop a certain behavior, your child may spend the whole day in the bathroom! It's okay! A valuable lesson is being learned by your child ("I cannot win this one").

5. Remember that time out used in this way stops the behavior, but does not teach a child what he should do instead. It is important that you couple time out with teaching the child about other, more peaceable options. For instance, Danny's parents need to teach him how to handle his frustration with his sister in more positive ways. One way to go about this is to watch their play carefully. Typically, when you watch a child's behavior, you can intercede before things escalate to the point of violence. Danny and Alisa are fighting over a toy. Alisa grabs the toy. You can see Danny getting mad. Now is the time to quickly intercede by walking over to Danny and talking to him. Help him by acknowledging his feelings, coach him on alternatives and model positive behavior: "Danny, I can see that you're upset about Alisa grabbing the toy. Say to her, 'Alisa. I don't want you to grab.' Or, Danny, you can give Alisa another toy and ask her, 'Can we trade?'"

2. Giving a child the time and space to cool off and calm down.

Central to using time out to cool off a child is the attitude of the parent and the explanation given the child. Of course, it won't do you much good to lecture a preschooler. But if your children are older, you can let them know your views on the subject: "Everyone needs a time out once in a while to cool off. It helps to have a place to sort out our feelings and get control of our actions. Your angry feelings are okay, but your angry actions must be limited. If your behavior is inappropriate, I will ask you to go to your room. As soon as you feel calm and ready to behave correctly, you may come out." The purpose of using time out in this way is to teach children how to control their angry emotions. This is a valuable life skill that will prevent your children from flying off the handle, and saying—and doing—things they will later regret.

When using time out to calm an angry child, it is usually fine to send the child to his or her room. It doesn't matter whether the child holes up there and listens to the stereo, reads a book, cries, or hits a pillow. The purpose is to allow children to get control of themselves in whatever way works for them, so that they can then re-enter "society" and deal with their problem in a more productive way. Children can learn from their mistakes when adults help them understand, accept, and deal with their strong emotions. (This is an important lesson for most adults as well.)

3. Giving a parent the time and space to cool off and calm down.

There are times when we get so angry at our children that we just want to strangle them or else ground them for life! This is the time to put space between you and your child. Make a brief exit statement: "I'm so angry with you, I need a minute to think!" Then go to your room to calm down, take some deep breaths, and reflect. This will not only help you control yourself, it will provide a good role model for your child to follow.

Allowing yourself a time-out when you need one can help keep your emotions under control, and remove the strain of having to deal with every situation immediately. It is also a wonderful way to model appropriate anger management for your children. (It's also a great technique for keeping a disagreement with your spouse from escalating into a full-blown argument.)

Natural Consequences

Experience is a wonderful teacher. Life has a way of teaching children things in a way that is very objective and straightforward. For example, children who don't wear their mittens will get cold hands. A child who is rude to a friend will find the friend unwilling to spend time with him. Parents would do well to let nature take over more often as their child's teacher. It can save plenty of time, and volumes of lectures, to stand back and let nature takes its course.

> It was a beautiful, snowy day. Vanessa and Angela were in the yard building a snowman when two-year-old David awoke in the morning. Barefoot and in his pajamas, he, of course, wanted to join them. I said, "Sure! Let's put on your boots and coat." Well, David would have none of that. I could tell by the way he put his hands on his hips that he was ready to do battle. This particular morning, I didn't want to fight. So I opened the door and waved him outside. David took two steps out the door, turned around, and said, "Mommy, need boots and coat!"

Do you know, I could have lectured, yelled, and threatened for an hour, and David would have been insistent about not wearing his boots and coat. But when I let natural consequences take over, I found that even a two-year-old can make some pretty smart decisions.

Natural consequences permit children to learn through their own actions (or *lack* of actions!). Children, in essence, become their own teachers. *Valuable learning occurs when a child is allowed to learn the hard way.* And there, in that sentence, is the *key* to the effective use of natural consequences. Read the sentence again, because the key is hidden there. The magic key is expressed in the word . . . (drum roll, please) . . . "allowed." Often parents seem determined to prevent their children from becoming frustrated or unhappy. They step in (or perhaps *rush* in) anytime their child seems ready to take a fall. This mistaken approach prevents a child from learning the many lessons that can only be learned the hard way.

It can, indeed, be difficult to stand back and watch your child suffer through a poor decision. But there are times when the best thing a parent can do is stand by and offer a shoulder and a hug.

> Anna described her nine-year-old daughter, Heather, as "bossy." She was concerned that Heather's abrupt, bossy attitude—especially with her friend Emma—would cause other kids to avoid her company. Anna said she normally "lectured" Heather after Emma's visits about how she should be more sensitive and kind to her friend, but Heather never seemed to hear her. She asked me for advice. I suggested that she just sit back and watch, and let "natural consequences" be the teacher.
>
> A few weeks later Anna called to tell me how things were going between the two friends. She said that the last two times Heather invited Emma over to her house, Emma declined the offer. When Heather pushed her for an explanation, Emma simply said, "I just don't feel like being bossed around, okay?" Heather was crushed, and her mother was close by to comfort her.

Obviously, Heather heard her friend's words far more clearly than all her mother's previous lectures. As painful as it was for Anna to watch this, she agreed that it was important to have her daughter learn a valuable lesson about friendship.

Natural Consequences Are Enough—Keep Your Angry Emotions Out of the Picture

A very important key to letting consequences teach your child is this: use empathy and kindness to support the natural lesson. Often, parents understand the "consequence" part of this process, but miss the opportunity to help their child learn, by changing the focus of a discussion to the parent's anger. When a consequence is rolling along, a child is typically immersed in the process. But when a parent charges in full of anger, with lectures and pointing fingers, and "I told you so's," the child is pulled away from the learning process and forced to deal with the parent's anger.

Logical Consequences

There are times when we cannot allow a natural consequence to occur, because it would be too severe or too expensive. You can't let your child get hit by a car to teach crosswalk safety. And you don't want your child's new bike stolen to teach responsibility. And then there are times when there is no natural consequence that will occur on its own.

At times like these you can make use, instead, of logical consequences. Logical consequences are those that you arrange or enforce as a result of your child's actions or lack of actions. Logical consequences are most effective when a child can clearly see the connection between the behavior and the consequence. For example:

> Michelle and Loren used logical consequences effectively with their ten-year-old daughter, Sarah. It seems that Sarah was using two or three towels after each bath, and filling the hamper with them. Loren had explained that a towel could be re-used several times before washing, but his message wasn't sinking in. Loren and Michelle decided to let logical consequences become the teacher. Sarah was notified that she had a new chore: laundering the towels. Loren reports that the family now has a "towelhawk" who carefully monitors everyone's towel usage!

Excerpted and adapted with permission from *Kid Cooperation: How to Stop Yelling, Nagging and Pleading and Get Kids to Cooperate* by Elizabeth Pantley. For more information on this and related books, see the "Further Reading" section in the back of the book.

CHAPTER 10

Kids and Anger

How to Cope with Anger at Your Kids

Parenting is the hardest job in the world, with long unpaid hours of noisy, messy, repetitive, exhausting, frustrating work. Anyone might occasionally develop feelings of anger when working under such conditions. It would be hard even if parents could focus solely on their job as parents. With all the other competing responsibilities in their lives, anger becomes inevitable.

Studies indicate that many parents are concerned—for good reason—about how frequently and how intensely they express anger toward their children. Of particular concern is corporal (physical) punishment. It's a very small step from excessive anger to abuse, and the growing epidemic of child abuse in this country is frightening.

Even nonabusive anger isn't helpful—especially to children. As you learned in chapter 7, on choices and consequences, anger is frightening and causes children to feel unsafe. They begin to believe that they must be terribly bad people to deserve such treatment. And anger begets more anger. Children who have been exposed to a lot of anger are more likely to express their own anger in aggressive ways than others not exposed to such conditions.

This chapter will help you learn how to cope more effectively with your angry feelings by using such strategies as combating your trigger thoughts, reducing the stress in your life, asking for what you want, and planning ahead.

Why You Get Angry

When you're really stressed, getting angry can actually make you feel better. It can discharge or relieve tension caused by other painful feelings (emotional or physical) or unmet needs or desires. Alternatively, it can also serve to block awareness of such uncomfortable feelings. When you're anxious you feel vulnerable and helpless, whereas when you're angry you feel much more powerful. Therefore feeling angry can seem easier—or at least preferable—to feeling anxious, scared, guilty, or ashamed.

Amelia and John's Story

Amelia was waiting for her ten-year-old son, John, to get home from soccer practice. It was already five o'clock, and he should have been home half an hour ago. As the minutes ticked by, Angela's anxiety grew. She could no longer concentrate on what she was doing. Instead her mind was filled with images of John amid the mangled remains of his bicycle.

At 5:15 she heard the front door open, and John sauntered into the kitchen. Realizing that John was unhurt—and therefore had no excuse for worrying her so much—Amelia's anxiety was immediately discharged by an angry outburst. Her feelings of relief were so fleeting she barely registered them.

John, who had had a flat tire on his bike and was feeling tremendously proud of himself for having changed it by himself, was crushed by his mother's rage. It was a blow not only to his self-esteem, but also to their relationship.

Exercise: Understanding Anger

Think about the last time you got angry with someone. Briefly describe the situation leading up to the anger.

_____

_____

_____

_____

Now, using the assumption that anger serves a purpose by either discharging or blocking awareness of other painful feelings (emotional or physical) or frustrated needs or desires, try to identify the underlying stress. Were you feeling anxious, scared, depressed, hurt, disappointed, guilty, or ashamed? Were you experiencing physical pain, muscle tension, overstimulation, or fatigue? Were needs or desires being frustrated? If so, what were they?

_____

_____

_____

_____

How You Get Angry

What enables the rapid transition from one feeling (anxiety, frustration, disappointment, pain) to another (anger)? Anger has two essential requirements: stress and trigger thoughts.

Trigger thoughts are those that ignite stressful feelings into anger. They usually take one of the following forms:

- They ascribe negative traits to the misbehaving person—"You're so lazy/stubborn/selfish/cruel."

- They assume a negative intent behind his or her behavior—"You're doing this deliberately to hurt me."

- Or they magnify the behavior to intolerable proportions—"I can't stand this, this is unbearable."

Stress by itself is not enough to cause an angry outburst. Without trigger thoughts you simply have stressful feelings. Trigger thoughts allow you to shift responsibility for those painful feelings to someone else—and then to justify your anger toward that person.

For example, if your daughter says she's going to clean up her room and doesn't, you'll probably feel disappointed and maybe a little frustrated—not really angry. But if at the same time you think to yourself, "I can't believe she lied to me again. She's so selfish," you'll notice a rapid transition into anger and outrage.

Another example: If your child throws a temper tantrum in public, your first reaction is probably going to be embarrassment and frustration. Not anger. But combine those stressful feelings with the thought, "He's deliberately trying to humiliate me in public. I won't tolerate this!" and once again you'll experience a rapid escalation into anger and outrage.

Amelia and John

Amelia had been profoundly anxious about John's safety when he hadn't arrived home at the expected time. Had she been willing to endure the anxiety, she probably could have experienced her relief in his safety more fully and gone on to express some of both her relief and her anxiety to John. Together they might have come to some kind of resolution that enhanced their relationship.

Instead, Amelia triggered anger and outrage with the thoughts, "He's so damn selfish and thoughtless. He knows I sit here and worry, and he can't be bothered getting here on time. And then to saunter in as if everything was okay—it drives me crazy." With such thoughts, Amelia could justify her rage at John rather than having to endure her anxiety.

Exercise: Identifying Trigger Thoughts

Look back at the preceding exercise, in which you identified a situation where you were angry and then identified the underlying stressful feelings or frustrated needs or desires. This time try to identify what was going through your head as you were beginning to experience that underlying stress. What were you thinking? Did you ascribe negative traits to the person involved? Did you assume there was a negative intention behind his or her behavior? Did you magnify the seriousness of the actions? Write down these trigger thoughts.

_____

_____

_____

Coping with Anger

First recognizing and then changing your trigger thoughts is an essential part of coping with anger. The following are nine ways to reduce anger. The first four deal specifically with changing your trigger thoughts. The rest have to do with changing the way you act and react.

Develop coping statements. Come up with, and memorize, some brief messages that can help you keep your cool in stressful situations. For example:

- Relax, stay calm.

- I'm staying calm. I don't have to get angry to cope with this.

- He/she is doing the best he/she can right now. He/she is not trying to upset me.

- I may not like what's happening, but I can cope with it without anger.

Remembered and silently repeated whenever you feel yourself beginning to get angry, these coping statements will calm you and help you look for more constructive choices than anger.

Assess the real cause. Parents often assume that their children misbehave deliberately to provoke them—to punish them, to test them, to drive them crazy, to "get at" them. Researchers and child development specialists find that this is rarely the case. Torturing their parents is not often a motive for children. It's important to look at other factors to discover the real cause of your child's behavior. As discussed in chapter 1, one such factor is temperament—the built-in wiring that each child is issued at or before birth—the way he or she tends to respond to life experiences. Characteristics that determine temperament include general activity level, basic disposition, ability to adapt to change, distractibility, and persistence. It doesn't make sense to get angry with a child whose shyness, high activity level, or difficulty with transitions is temperamental.

Another important consideration is that the main task of childhood is to gain independence and autonomy. In order to achieve this goal, a child has to learn to make decisions and choices, experience the consequences of those decisions and choices, and develop a sense of separateness from his or her parents. That means that much of a child's behavior is aimed—appropriately—at demonstrating his or her separateness: testing the limits, disobeying parental rules, and trying to control the outcome of different situations. Again, it doesn't help to get angry with a child who's doing what children are supposed to do.

Finally, when assessing the real cause of the behavior, it's important to remember that children's behavior is primarily an attempt to meet their needs. These needs can range from the more fundamental (to achieve significance, to feel autonomous, to belong) to the more everyday (to get praise, attention, physical nurturing, sleep, food, or help doing something or solving a problem). If you can try to understand and meet those needs, it may lead to a change in the behavior. At the very least, the attempt may distract you from your anger.

Replace negative labels. To reduce your anger, you must avoid those provocative terms that make you see red, such as "lazy," "spoiled," "thoughtless," "cruel," and "stupid." Replacing these labels with a clear, accurate, neutral description of what's happening is hard to do, but it really works. It means sticking to just the facts, as if you were an investigator. When your son doesn't provide you with the information you requested about the school fund-raiser, you could simply label him as selfish and lazy—and chances are you'd rapidly escalate into anger. Instead, ask yourself what exactly is happening here. Then answer with just the facts: "I asked Andrew to provide me with the information today, and he didn't. I don't know why." If you don't have all the facts, ask your child for his or her input. The process will go very differently. Without labels, your anger will be far easier to control.

Assess the magnitude of the problem. How truly serious is the problem? Avoid thinking such things as "It's outrageous," "Completely intolerable," "Totally ridiculous," "I can't believe that . . ." Replace these provocative exaggerations with accurate, behavioral descriptions of exactly what's happening: "Andrew didn't provide me with the information today, and I need it to calculate projected sales for the school. I wish he'd brought it, but since the fund-raiser is still a week away, I can probably manage if I get the necessary data in the next day or so." The absence of trigger thoughts prevents an escalation into anger.

Use a time-out. To prevent the situation from escalating and to think about an appropriate response, take a break. Think about choices and consequences so that you can be clear about what you want from your child and about the consequences of his or her noncompliance. A few minutes apart will give you time to calm down and think about your desired response. Giving the child a time-out—a few minutes in his or her room—can sometimes be a sufficient consequence by itself. Or you can take the time-out yourself. Leave the situation for a few minutes: Go to the bathroom and wash your face. Get yourself a tall glass of water and drink it. Make a cup of tea. Take a deep breath and count to fifty—very slowly.

Practice relaxation. The more stress in your life in general, the easier it is to be provoked into anger. The early signs of anger include increased muscle tension (clenched jaw or fists, a constricted feeling in the chest, butterflies in the stomach), and a shift in breathing pattern (heavy or rapid breathing, feeling short of breath). Breathing deeply requires that your chest and belly expand, and enables the slow, full replenishing of oxygen to the lungs, so it is almost impossible to breathe deeply and maintain a high level of stress.

Deep breathing exercises provide an antidote to stress and therefore a valuable tool in the fight against anger. To practice deep breathing use the following steps:

1. Sit or lie down in a relaxed position and put one hand on your belly.

2. Inhale slowly and deeply, pushing the air down into your belly and making the hand resting there rise.

3. Gently exhale with a slow whooshing sound, keeping your muscles relaxed and saying to yourself "Relax."

4. Continue to take long, slow, deep breaths into your belly and let them out gently. Focus on the sound of your breath and the movement of your belly, and notice how you become more and more relaxed.

The more frequently you practice this breathing exercise, the more impact it will have in your life. A few minutes a day will counteract some of the ups and downs of daily life. And a concentrated effort to use it before responding to a provocative situation will enable you to avoid escalating into anger.

Identify what you need and ask for it. As discussed above, there are often feelings underlying your anger: disappointment, guilt, shame, embarrassment. Once you can identify the feeling, ask yourself what you need to do to take care of it. If you're feeling embarrassed about your child having a tantrum in the supermarket, perhaps you need to remind yourself that you're a good parent. If you're feeling guilty about your two-year-old hitting another child in the playground, perhaps you need to remind yourself that this is a stage that he or she will outgrow with adequate guidance from you and as he or she develops the necessary language skills.

Once you've identified what you need, ask for it assertively. When you see your four-year-old jumping up and down on the new couch, it may take some effort to refrain from screaming at him. But you'll be more successful in the long run if—after lifting him off—you can say something assertive, such as, "I get really nervous when I see you jumping on the new couch. That couch just cost me a lot of money, and I don't want it broken or damaged—or you to get hurt either. You can either sit on it nicely, or go to your room."

Plan ahead. In some cases, if you can anticipate situations that have the potential for triggering anger, you can devise a coping strategy. This reduces the chances of being caught off guard and reacting explosively. The following exercise walks you through the planning process. The steps in planning to head off anger use the strategies discussed above.

Exercise: Heading Off Anger

Think about the ways your child typically behaves that make you angry.
Pick one example of your child's behavior that regularly makes you angry.

_____

_____

_____

Identify your typical trigger thoughts related to that behavior.

_____

_____

_____

Develop some coping statements to say to yourself when it occurs next time.

_____

_____

_____

Think of possible explanations for the behavior other than those negative attributions described in your trigger thoughts.
Temperament:

_____

_____

_____

Could this be age-appropriate behavior?

_____

_____

_____

What needs could your child be trying to meet?

_____

_____

_____

Plan an assertive statement to ask for what you want or need, and determine what choices and consequences you will set, if appropriate.

Assertive statement:

_____

_____

_____

Choices and consequences (if appropriate):

_____

_____

_____

Repeat this process for all the problem behaviors you identified.

A Note on Your Child's Anger

Anger is inevitable at some times for everyone. As you've learned in earlier chapters, there's nothing wrong with your child having angry feelings. However, the way your child chooses to express those feelings may be inappropriate, and might require you to set limits about what is and is not okay behavior. This is no different from setting limits on any other behavior that you deem inappropriate—that is, anytime the problem is yours.

On the other hand, if your child seems to express a lot of anger a lot of the time, you can help your child learn modified versions of the strategies described to cope more effectively with his or her anger. Identifying and changing trigger thoughts, assessing the real cause and magnitude of the problem behavior, learning some relaxation or breathing techniques, asking assertively for what is wanted, and planning ahead are all things that children can incorporate to varying degrees. You will need to adapt the strategies to the child's age and abilities.

Anger is one of the hardest emotions to cope with appropriately. It probably feels at times like you have no control over your anger at all. Yet you live in an age where access to lethal weapons is terrifyingly easy, and giving in to anger can have violent, devastating consequences. Starting with your own small part of the world and taking responsibility for your own anger, you can help decrease the anger and potential violence in the world as a whole. The strategies discussed in this chapter can help you make a significant start in that direction.

Excerpted and adapted with permission from *The Ten Things Every Parent Needs to Know* by Kim Paleg, Ph.D. For more information on this and related books, see the "Further Reading" section in the back of the book.

CHAPTER 11

Children's Sexuality—What Is Normal?

Understanding Children's Sexual Behavior

This chapter will explain natural and healthy childhood sexual behaviors in detail, providing statistical data gathered from adults remembering back to their childhood sexual experiences.

Children's natural and healthy sexual exploration is an *information gathering process*. It involves children exploring and touching their own bodies. When trying to understand their body and sexuality, children naturally use their own bodies as a map. Just as they stick their fingers in their ears, noses, and mouths, children explore what you may call the "private parts" of their bodies.

When you're changing the diapers of your children or bathing them, for instance, you may see your child touch his penis or put her finger on her labia. This is a good opportunity for you to name this part of the body. "That is your penis. That is a private part of your body." "Those are called the labia. That is a private part of your body." It is good for you to take every available opportunity to teach about the body parts and help the children develop an accurate vocabulary. This encourages open discussion about sexual topics.

You may find your child peeking when you're in the bathroom or trying to listen outside your bedroom. This can provide the opportunity to ask if he or she has any questions and indicate your willingness to answer them while also teaching them about privacy: "I will gladly answer any questions you have but everyone deserves not to be spied on." If your child starts to fondle his or her genitals when you're present you can say, "That is for when you are alone."

Forty-eight percent of the college students surveyed said they looked at their body in the mirror when they were between the ages of eleven and twelve, and 23 percent did this when they were between six and ten. Thirty-seven percent of the students said they became more detailed in their exploration and explored their bodies, including their genitals, when they were between eleven and twelve years old. Thirty-one percent said they did this when they were between the ages of six and ten. Twenty-six of the eleven- and twelve-year-olds and 16 percent of the six- to ten-year-olds said they had fondled their genitals.

Looking and Touching Others

As part of their information gathering, children explore each other's bodies by looking and touching. These are the standard ways in which children gather information about each other's bodies. By looking and touching they begin to build an understanding of what the body looks like, what differences exist between boys and girls, and what it feels like to touch another's body. It's not uncommon for children to be caught in the bathroom or in a bedroom or playroom at home examining each other's bodies. Although this often causes teachers and parents dismay, this is a time-honored learning method. Children like to see and touch sand, Jell-O™, mud, caterpillars, sparkly items, penises, and vaginas. Each of these spark an interest in children. The most curious children often do the most exploring—curiosity is at the heart of learning.

In the study of college students, 17 percent said that they "touched or explored the private parts of another child" when they were twelve and younger. In the survey of 352 mental health and child welfare workers, 30 percent said they showed their "private parts" to another child, and 46 percent said that they "played doctor."

Exploring through the Media

As part of their information gathering, children look at *magazines*, *videos*, *books*, explore the *Internet*, and *peek at others*. Such an abundance of material with sexual content has probably never been more available to children. Network television and cable television with music videos, talk shows about sex, and call-in sex shows are an enormous source of information and misinformation. Radio has call-in talk shows whose primary topics are sex. Children with radios and ear phones can listen in the wee hours of the night without detection.

You probably want to try to monitor your children's intake of information from the various media. This is frequently impossible. Therefore, it's helpful for you to have frequent and frank discussions about sexual topics to monitor what your children know. Many parents watch a few shows a week with their children and use what is on the television to stimulate discussion. A lot of shows targeted to children show dating and kissing and other sexual topics. You can use the TV to reinforce values you accept or to point out ones you don't, or ask your child what he or she thinks about what is being portrayed. Television and other media are natural vehicles for talking about sexual topics with children. You can search for "teachable moments."

Be aware of what you watch when your children are around. Not only does this give children permission to watch but it also models what is of interest and what is acceptable to their parents. Children learn from their parents. If you're watching a show or video portraying something you don't approve of, you can use the opportunity to teach your child. "Men should not be mean to women like that. I hope she leaves him. Women should not put up with that kind of abuse." "It looks as if that teenager is getting in a lot of trouble. I wonder if his parents need to help him more. Kids should tell their parents when they have problems. I hope you will tell me or Mommy if you have any worries. We're always here to help. Sometimes kids are afraid to tell if they do something wrong but it's better to tell and get our help. That's what we're here for."

When college students were asked about their primary sources of sex education, 68 percent said friends, 55 percent parents, 54 percent sex education in school, 39 percent said books, 34 percent television. Thirteen percent said sex education came from pornographic material. Forty-four percent of the eleven- to twelve-year-olds said they looked at "dirty pictures," 25 percent of the six- to ten-year-olds did this.

What's All the Fuss About?

In natural and healthy sexual play or exploration children are generally excited and feel silly and giggly. It is fun and enticing. Early on children seem to understand that sexual exploration should be done secretively. It's important for you to try not to make your children feel badly if you catch them exploring. A calm tone of voice and short statements are best.

Unfortunately, some parents make their children feel ashamed about their desire for sexual knowledge and touching. This can cast a negative shadow over their sexual development that may deter them from further exploration. Learning about sex and feeling confident and happy about it is part of healthy sexual development.

Prior to the 1980s when we knew less about the sexual abuse of children, there may have been a more relaxed attitude amongst many parents about their children's sexual behaviors. We now live in a time when many parents worry that if their child is engaging in sexual behaviors the child has been sexually abused.

There is a tension in our society that may infect the sexual play of children. This can be a great loss to children for their sexual development and for their attitude toward sex and sexuality. Sexual curiosity and play should be lighthearted. Children can have a great deal of fun exploring what it means to be a man or woman. If children are looking at each other's bodies and their behavior doesn't fit the problematic characteristics listed later in this chapter, you'll be better off not making a big deal about it.

I am concerned that some children have begun to equate touching private parts with abuse. While this is abuse under certain circumstances, it is not under *all* circumstances. For instance, during childhood many children play doctor or touch another child's private parts: Do we want children to think this is abusive?

In the mid- and late 1980s when it was discovered that children molested other children, there was a surge of *mislabeling sexual exploration* as *sexual molestation*. This concern on the part of adults can find its way to children and diminish their positive feelings about sexual exploration.

When children grow into adolescence they'll likely engage in some genital touching: How will they know that isn't abuse? Some children may even construe sexual contact between adults as abuse.

You can help by listening carefully to any comments or questions your children may have about sex and sexuality to make sure that they're not getting a negative message about sex.

Another concern is that sexual touch is often equated with "bad touch." Some prevention programs leave children with this message. As a result, children may misconstrue their natural curiosity to touch and explore as "bad."

When they were engaging in sexual behaviors alone, 40 percent of the college students said they felt good or fine, 34 percent felt silly or giggly. When they were engaging with other children in sexual behaviors, 37 percent felt good or fine, 48 percent felt silly or giggly. It seems that it is more fun to engage in sexual behaviors with other children. When asked if they felt "excited (not sexually)," 21 percent said "yes" when they engaged in sexual behaviors alone and 24 percent said "yes" for mutual behaviors with one other child. College students also indicated less positive feelings. When participating in sexual behaviors alone, 32 percent felt confused, 30 percent felt guilty, 16 percent felt scared, 13 percent felt bad. When involved in mutual sexual behaviors with one other child, 27 percent felt confused, 21 percent felt guilty, 21 percent felt scared, and 8 percent felt bad. These data indicate that behaving sexually creates a lot of feelings in children and many are not positive. Feelings of confusion and guilt are quite high in children who engage in sexual behaviors. Parents do not want to increase these feelings for natural and healthy sexual exploration.

For example, a colleague who is a psychologist in Michigan described the following scene she witnessed in a preschool. As she was observing the four-year-olds on their playground, she saw three children playing together. They were giggling and having a good time. After a few minutes the little boy kissed each of the girls on the cheek. One of the little girls turned around and shouted "sex abuse" toward where her teacher was standing.

You can be a good model for your children by showing affection in front of them, such as lighthearted kissing and hugging.

Bathroom Humor and Games

Another aspect of typical childhood curiosity is a delight in bathroom humor and games, an interest that sometimes flusters adults. Three ten-year-old boys, for example, threw the staff at one elementary school into conflict when they were discovered playing in the bathroom. One of the children was "creating designs in the toilet bowl with his urine," while his two friends were seeing which boy could stand the farthest away while directing urine from his penis into the bowl. The principal was convinced the behavior was "perverted" and suggested that the children be removed from school (Morgan 1984).

Despite the principal's alarm, this is an excellent example of healthy—if, perhaps, mischievous—childhood behavior. The typical affect of children regarding normal behaviors related to sexuality is lighthearted and spontaneous. These boys were trying out something fun. They were exploring the capabilities of their bodies.

Sex Is Just a Part of the Whole Picture

The sexual behavior of children engaged in the normal process of childhood exploration is balanced with *curiosity about other parts of their universe.* They want to know how babies are made as well as why the sun disappears. They want to explore the physical differences between males and females as well as figure out how to get their homework done quickly so they can play outside. Children often go through periods when they seem to be always interested in sexual things, and then it becomes less prominent. Some children's sexual interest never becomes known to parents and some young children do not become interested.

Which Children Explore?

There are wide differences in the sexual development and interest of children. Some theorists, including Freud, have thought that all children engage in sexual behaviors but this is not the case. In fact, there may be a substantial number of children who don't show any particular interest in sexual topics during childhood.

Fifty-seven percent of the college students said they had engaged in solitary sexual behaviors when they were twelve years and younger and 60 percent said they engaged in sexual behaviors with one other child during this period of childhood. Twenty percent said they engaged in sexual behaviors with two or more children. Therefore, it's obvious that not all children take part in sexual behaviors during their childhood.

The college student data also indicates a wide variation in the number of times they engaged in any of the behaviors. While most of the students only participated in the behaviors one to eight times, four students in the sample indicated engaging in behaviors hundreds of times.

Likewise, children show different levels of interest. If your child is very interested in sexual topics and sexual touch, this may simply be a reflection of his or her inborn drives. If your child has no interest in sexual topics or exploration, this may also be a reflection of inborn characteristics.

Thirteen percent of the college students said they remembered dreaming about sex when they were between eleven and twelve, only 3 percent remembered this when they were between six and ten years old.

Friends

Sexual behaviors occur mainly between children who have an *ongoing mutual play* or *friend* relationship. Childhood friends explore caves, woodlands, video games, how to light matches, make cookies, play football, and play sexually together. This type of exploration does happen between brothers and sisters who are close in age or who don't live near their friends, but it's more likely to occur between friends.

This is the same with sexual contact. There is noncoercive sexual contact between siblings that is still natural and healthy but most children pick someone outside their family with whom they have an ongoing play relationship. Since behaving sexually is taboo to most parents, your children probably want to make sure they aren't going to be told on. This is why they're more likely to sexually experiment with their friend than with a sibling who may get angry with a sibling and tell "Mommy."

Overwhelmingly, when young children engage in mutual sexual behaviors, they choose friends rather than relatives or siblings. The choice of friends is six times more likely than siblings or relatives. It's extremely rare, however, that a child would engage in sexual behavior with someone they didn't know.

Who Are Your Child's Friends?

Children involved in natural and healthy exploration are generally of *similar age, size,* and *developmental level.* The average age difference is about six months between children who are experimenting sexually. For instance, if your child is eight years old he or she will probably engage in sexual behaviors with someone who is between seven-and-a-half and eight-and-a-half years old.

Perhaps your child is large or small for his or her age. In this case, however, size isn't relevant. Likewise, if your child is ten but has an emotional age of six and plays with six-year-olds, this might also be an exception to the age and size difference as most sexual behavior between young children occurs between friends. If your child lives in an area without peer-age friends, he or she may engage in sexual behaviors with nonpeer-age friends.

Checking Out the Gender Roles

Gender roles is an area of high exploration. Children are very interested in male and female roles. The stereotypical male and female roles are beginning to erode but boys playing bad guys, and girls playing with dolls, is still seen in preschools throughout the United States. Trying on gender roles can also move into playing house, with one person playing mommy and the other daddy. This can turn into divorce or the exploration of the roles of mommies and daddies in "baby-making."

Twelve percent of the mental health and child welfare professionals said they engaged in "humping" or simulating intercourse. Eighteen percent of the college students also said they partook in this behavior.

Exploring other gender roles and clothes has become culturally more acceptable for little girls but remains controversial for boys. Boys trying on girls' clothes and exploring their sex role behaviors are not highly uncommon up until the age of about five or six. Once children enter school, boys tend to consolidate their sex role characteristics although they aren't as rigid as they used to be. Boys interested in dance, cooking, poetry, sewing, and other traditionally female-oriented interests are no longer the subject of intense negative appraisal.

If you are worried that your child's sex role development is different than other children's his or her age, you may want to consult your pediatrician or a licensed mental health practitioner with advanced study in child development. Never try to make your children ashamed of who they are or how they behave, and always remember that respect for your child is the most important thing.

If your child is being ridiculed by his or her peers, he or she needs your support. Some children also need to become more aware of their behavior and make choices. Ridicule doesn't generally bring behavioral change (for any behavior) over the long run, yet it manages to destroy self-esteem and the relationship between the person doing the ridiculing and the person ridiculed.

Childhood sexual exploration can be between *same gender* or between *boys* and *girls*. Statistically there are no significant trends. When college students were asked about "showing their privates" to others, it was sometimes with a child of the same gender and sometimes with the other gender. The same was true of "touching the private parts" of other children. Generally, the gender a person prefers to engage in sex with becomes important around puberty. Early childhood exploration is more a matter of who your friends are, who is willing, and who is there when the situation is ripe for experimentation.

Boys and Girls Are Both Curious

There are few differences between the sexual behaviors of young boys and girls. There are many books right now describing male and female adult sexuality as very different—such as John Gray's *Men Are from Mars and Women Are from Venus*. In young children's sexual behaviors, however, there aren't so many differences. In fact little girls seems to engage in about as much sexual behavior as boys. Perhaps male sexuality is more visible than female sexuality, or perhaps socialization has more to do with men's and women's sexuality as they traverse adolescence and young adulthood.

We generally think of adult men as being more sexually oriented than women. It's interesting that in the college student study there were no significant differences between males and females in their sexual behaviors or in their feelings when engaging in the sexual behaviors. For instance, whether alone or with one other child, boys were more likely to behave in a sexual manner, but not significantly more than the girls. Overall 60 percent of the students said they engaged in solitary sexual behaviors. Of this 63 percent were boys and 55 percent were girls. When engaging with one other child overall 57 percent said they did this. Of this number 63 percent were boys and 56 percent were girls. Overall 20 percent of the students said they engaged in sexual behaviors with at least two or more children. Of this number 25 percent were males and 16 percent were females.

Fourteen percent of the students said they were coerced into sexual behaviors. Of the students who said they were coerced 18 percent were males while 12 percent were females. We often think of boys being more aggressive when it comes to most behaviors and sexual behaviors would probably be the same. In the college sample it was 7 percent of the sample who coerced others into sexual behaviors. Of this number 9 percent were males and 4 percent were females. Neither the victimization or coercion of other children was statistically different for males and females.

Pleasure

Many children experience *pleasant sensations* if they touch their own genitals, some children may experience sexual arousal, and some will experience orgasm. At birth and in utero children have all of the sexual apparatus necessary for adult sexual behavior. Infants' vaginas can lubricate, boys can have erections, the clitoris can be stimulated, children can have orgasms, the fallopian tubes are present, and the eggs are all stored and ready to be released at puberty when menstruation begins.

Although all of the apparatus is present most children don't experience sexual orgasms and pleasure similar to that experienced by adults until puberty. With puberty and the major influx of the sexual hormones the body and mind are more driven toward genital contact and erotic pleasure. Children do experience pleasant sensations when their genitals are stimulated but this isn't the same as the orgasmic pleasure, which is more pervasive after puberty.

Thirty-two percent of the mental health and child welfare professionals described feeling "pleasant body sensations" when engaging in sexual behaviors between the ages of eleven to twelve, 27 percent felt "pleasant body sensations" between ages six to ten. When asked if they felt "sexually stimulated as an adult might feel," 21 percent did when they were eleven to twelve, 9 percent when they were six to ten. The college students said they felt more "sexually stimulated as an adult might feel" when engaging in sexual behaviors alone (22 percent) than when engaging in sexual behaviors with other children (17 percent).

Only 17 percent of the students said they had masturbated to orgasm when they were between eleven to twelve years of age, 4 percent said they did this between the ages of six to ten. More girls (17 percent) than boys (8 percent) masturbated to orgasm when twelve and younger. This may be due to girls going through puberty earlier. Orgasm is a far more frequent experience in postpubertal children.

Secrecy

If children are discovered in normal sex play and instructed to stop, the sexual behavior will probably *diminish* or *cease, at least in the sight of adults*, but may arise again during another period of their sexual development. Infants and toddlers show more of their sexual behaviors than when they get to preschool and kindergarten. Adults generally tell children not to do such things as touch their genitals or the private parts of others. Thus the children stop doing it in front of the adults.

Swearing is a good example. Young children around four and five often begin to say words such as "shit." You may react very negatively to your child saying these things—most adults do. So your child may learn to swear in private with their friends or even stop for a while. There are probably very few children who go through their elementary school years without experimenting with lots of "bad" words.

When children become old enough to understand adults' reactions to sexual exploration, secrecy becomes the hallmark of sexual behavior. When asked whether any adult knew about their sexual experiences with other children around the time they engaged in them, 90 percent of the college students said "no." When asked, "Did you tell anyone about your sexual behaviors?", 84 percent of college students said "no."

Coercion

An important aspect of childhood sexual exploration is that it is usually *without pressure*. "I'll show you mine, if you show me yours" is a time-honored phrase. It implies that one child is asking another to explore with him or her. Another phrase is "I'll be your best friend if you'll show me your pee-pee." This implies that the child asking will like the other child more if he or she complies with the request. Between two friends this is not of concern. One child might feel slightly pressured to engage in the behavior, but he or she would also know that the threat probably wouldn't come true for long. A friend would also know that they could refuse to continue if he or she wanted to stop. Friends partake in this type of mild coercion regularly, in the sexual realm and outside of it.

For instance, if a child wants to liberate some of his mother's freshly baked cookies and wants his friend to go with him he might threaten, "If you don't come with me, I won't play with you ever again," or, "If you don't come with me, I won't give you any. I'll eat them all myself."

If a child is using the same types of "threats" with children who have no friends or desperately want to be that particular child's friend but are always rebuffed, these statements can feel very threatening. A vulnerable child may acquiesce out of fear of losing an opportunity for friendship. This is not in the realm of natural and healthy play.

When describing sexual encounters among two or more children, the college students described some of their coercive techniques. At the top of the list were teasing (such as calling the other child a chicken), then begging, bribery, trickery, physical force, verbal threats, and physical pain. The average age at which these experiences occurred was nine years old. Clearly the methods used moved to more aggressive coercion than any child might have been able to withstand whether or not the other child was a friend.

Fourteen percent of the students said they had been tricked, bribed, threatened, forced, or otherwise coerced into sexual behaviors by someone twelve or younger when they were twelve or younger. Seven percent said they had bribed, teased, threatened, physically forced, or otherwise coerced another child twelve or younger to engage in sexual behaviors with them when they were twelve or younger.

Important Points to Consider about Your Child's Sexual Behaviors

There are some points about childhood sexuality that are important for you to consider as you are understanding your child's sexuality.

- *Most behaviors related to sex and sexuality in young children are natural and expectable.* Understanding sexuality is an important area of your growing child's expanding knowledge. Sexual exploration and sexual play are a natural part of your child's development. Accept this and help him or her feel comfortable while also knowing the limits.

- *Your own childhood sexual experiences may have been quite different than your child's.* It's not advisable to use your own childhood experience as the norm for sexual experience. When you do this you may believe that your own experience was the norm. This may not be true at all. If you didn't engage with other children in any sexual behavior, you may think it's not normal to do so. If you didn't talk to other children about their sexual behaviors as a child, you didn't know what other children were doing. If you engaged in some solitary sexual behavior and felt bad about it, you may carry this over to your children. If you were caught and scolded for sexually experimenting, you may feel guilty and bad for the behavior. It's best to look at the facts presented in this chapter and make your assessments based on a wider data pool.

Things have changed. Speaking with other parents and caregivers who have children of similar ages is helpful in determining what is natural and healthy. There is a great deal more sexual stimulation in our culture today, and children have a greater knowledge about sexual behaviors than in previous generations. Your experience was shaped by your culture, your parents, your siblings, the religion in which you were raised, where you lived, as well as other things. These factors are different for your child. Be current.

- *Don't confuse your own adult sexual feelings, fantasies, and behavior with those of children.* Most prepubertal children do not experience sexual arousal and sexual pleasure, but some do. In prepubertal children, the sexual activity generally doesn't represent the desire for sexual gratification as much as exploration of their bodies, other's bodies, and gender roles. Children describe different sensations related to the sexual exploration. Some are sexually arousing and pleasurable; others describe them as weird or funny; others say they are exciting, as in doing something forbidden. Some children whose sexual development has been interfered with by adults describe their genital sensations as "uncomfortable," "icky," "confusing," or "scary."

  Even though children's sexual behaviors may look like adult sexual behaviors, it generally isn't experienced with the erotic and sensual components. This is important information to consider as some adults are disgusted thinking a child is engaging in adult sexual behaviors with the same thoughts and feelings as themselves and then treat the children as disgusting, weird, sinful, and so on.

- *The relationships we have as we grow up are fundamental to our healthy development.* The best foundation for healthy adult relationships is secure attachments to adults and family as your children grow up. A secure relationship or attachment is one in which your relationship to your child is consistent, caring, reliable, and focused on the needs of your child rather than your own. If a child feels insecure in his or her relationships with adults, this will make it more difficult for them to feel secure in adult relationships and to provide this feeling for their children.

  For example, if adults in a child's life have sexualized relationships with him or her, or the child has only seen failed relationships that were sexualized, permissive, aggressive, hurtful, and unfulfilling, this will impact a child's view of the role that sex plays in adult relationships.

- *As we have learned more about the sexual abuse of children, sexual behavior between children sometimes causes too much concern.* What starts out as two children exploring each other's genitals can end up with one or both being interviewed by child protective services and/or the police due to concern that they have been sexually abused. While caution is always necessary, there are many clues to children being sexually abused and sexual behavior is only one of them.

  Sexual behaviors that are indicators of sexual abuse by an adult or an adolescent rarely fit the pattern of natural and healthy sexual development described in this chapter. There are no childhood sexual behaviors that have been seen only by mothers of sexually abused children. There is no single behavior that indicates sexual abuse. The next section lists the characteristics of sexual behaviors that increase the concern that a child has been sexually abused in a hands-on manner or has been exposed to too much adolescent or adult sexuality.

Characteristics of Problematic Sexual Behaviors During Childhood

If your child's sexual behavior can be described by several of the following characteristics, and your parental intervention hasn't curtailed the behavior, and you cannot find a reasonable and healthy explanation for this, your child should be evaluated by a *qualified professional*. Find a professional who is knowledgeable about child sexuality or child abuse. You may also need to have your child medically examined.

There are many reasons that can contribute to a child's sexual development getting confused. Most people think it is always hands-on sexual abuse. This isn't true. Other factors can contribute to a child engaging in problematic sexual behaviors. It will be important for you to not jump to any conclusions about your child as you read. The characteristics toward the beginning of the list are less worrisome than the characteristics toward the end of the list.

1. *The children engaged in the sexual behaviors do not have an ongoing mutual play relationship.* Sexual play between children is an extension of regular play behavior. Just as children prefer to play with children with whom they get along, this is the same with sexual play. As most children are very aware of taboos on sexual play in the open, they pick friends who will keep the secret.

2. *Sexual behaviors that are engaged in by children of different ages or developmental levels.* Unless there are no similar-age children in the neighborhood, most children select playmates of the same age. Yet, developmentally delayed children may choose to play with younger children because their developmental level is more similar. Children with poor social skills may also play with younger children. It's important to assess the availability of peer-age friends, developmental level, and the previous relationship between the children to determine if sexual behaviors among children of different ages are problematic. In general, the wider the age difference, the greater the concern.

3. *Sexual behaviors that are out of balance with other aspects of the child's life and interests.* Children are interested in every aspect of their environment from the sun rising to how babies are made. While children may explore some aspects of their world more extensively at certain periods of their young lives, their interests are generally broad and intermittent.

   Children's sexual behavior follows the same pattern. At one period they may be interested in learning about sexuality and another time about how the dishwasher works or what makes Mommy mad. Many fluctuations occur in a day, a week, and a month. But, when a child is preoccupied with sexuality, this raises concern. If a child prefers to masturbate rather than participate in regular childhood activities, this raises concern.

4. *Children who seem to have too much knowledge about sexuality and behave in ways more consistent with adult sexual expression.* As children develop, they acquire knowledge about sex and sexuality from television, movies, videos, magazines, their parents, relatives, school, and other children. Knowledge gathered in these time-honored ways is generally assimilated, without disruption, into a child's developing understanding of sex and sexuality; this translates into additional natural and healthy sexual interest. When children have been overexposed to explicit adult sexuality, or have been sexually misused, they may engage in or talk about sexual behaviors that are beyond age-appropriate sexual knowledge and interest.

5. *Sexual behaviors that are significantly different than those of other same-age children.* The frequency and type of children's sexual behaviors depend, to a certain extent, on the environment (home, neighborhood, culture, religion) in which they have been raised, their parent's attitudes and actions related to sex and sexuality, and their peers' behaviors. If a child's sexual behavior stands out among his or her neighborhood peers, this raises concern. Teachers from schools who serve neighborhood populations are very good resources to consult to evaluate whether or not a child's sexual behaviors are similar to his or her peers.

6. *Sexual behaviors that continue in spite of consistent and clear requests to stop.* While adults may be inconsistent regarding other behaviors and children may persist in engaging in them, most children learn very quickly that there's a strong taboo on openly sexual behavior. Yet while most adults are consistent about telling children to stop, some aren't. Inconsistent messages regarding sexual behavior may increase, or not decrease, a child's sexual behaviors. For example, if you think it's cute when your child runs around the house naked but punish your child sometimes, it may be hard for him or her to learn the rules.

   Children's sexual behaviors that continue in the view of adults, despite consistent requests to stop or even punishment, may be a conscious or unconscious method of indicating that they need help. When children "cry for help," they may persist in the behavior until adults pay heed, discover, and/or change the causes of the sexual behavior. Sometimes children who are being sexually abused signal the abuse by engaging in persistent sexual behaviors.

   Certain children have learned to "space out" in times of stress. While they're spaced out, they may engage in sexual behavior, which itself is another way to decrease their anxiety. If this is happening, the child may be unaware of the sexual behaviors he or she is doing. Because the child's response to stress is to space out and engage in sexual behaviors, it may happen in spite of consistent requests to stop. Children who space out need help to stay present and cope with their feelings and thoughts that create the anxiety. They need the help of adults who can help figure out what causes them to space out.

7. *Children who appear unable to stop themselves from participating in sexual activities.* Some children appear to feel driven to engage in sexual behaviors even though they'll be punished or admonished. Typically, this type of sexual behavior is in response to things that go on around them or feelings that reawaken memories which are traumatic, painful, overly stimulating, or of which they can't make sense. The child may respond by masturbating or engaging in other sexual experimentation behaviors alone or with children or adults. Hiding the sexual behaviors or finding friends to engage in the behaviors in private may not be possible for these children. Sexual behavior that is driven by anxiety, guilt, or fear often doesn't respond to normal limit setting. The sexual behavior is a way of coping with overwhelming feelings. This type of sexual behavior may not be within the full conscious control of the child.

   Some children may have psychiatric disturbances such as obsessive-compulsive disorder that cause them to partake in repetitive behaviors. These could be sexual as well as other kinds of rituals. Some children may have urinary tract or yeast infections that cause chronic itching or sensations, which look like sexual touching.

8. *Children's sexual behaviors that elicit complaints from other children and/or adversely affect other children.* Generally, children complain when something is annoying or discomforting to them. When a young child complains about another child's sexual behaviors, it's

an indication that the behavior is upsetting to the child and should be taken seriously. In natural and healthy sexual play both children agree directly or indirectly not to tell and are involved in the behavior willingly. It's quite unlikely that either would tell on the other; therefore, if one child is telling, this is a cause for concern.

9. *Children's sexual behaviors that are directed at adults who feel uncomfortable receiving them.* Children hug adults and give them kisses. These are generally spontaneous reflections of caring or because they have been told to kiss the adult (usually a relative) by a parent. When a child continues to touch an adult in a manner more like adult-adult sexual contact, offer themselves as sexual objects, or solicit sexual touch from adults, this may be an indication that someone is teaching the child to engage in age-inappropriate sexual contact. When children are sexually abused, the abuse may take the form of teaching the child to sexually pleasure the adult. Young children may generalize this to their contact with other adults. If children are doing this, it will be important to find out how the child is learning to engage in this type of physical contact. Child protective services can be called if there is a suspicion of child abuse.

10. *Children (four years and older) who do not understand their rights or the rights of others in relation to sexual contact.* Most parents teach their children by their own behavior about emotional, physical, and sexual privacy. Generally, school-age children have developed an awareness of their own and others' personal space. If children are brought up in homes where their personal boundaries are violated, such as in emotional, sexual and/or physical abuse or intrusiveness, they may not learn the unwritten rules regarding personal space violations

11. *Sexual behaviors that progress in frequency, intensity, or intrusiveness over time.* When sexual behavior in young children is natural and healthy, the frequency is generally moderate, the behaviors occur sporadically and mostly occur outside the vision and knowledge of others. As most children grow up there's an increase in the sexual behaviors and they transition from looking to touching. But by elementary school age, children increasingly hide their sexual behaviors from adults. If adults know a lot about the child's sexual behaviors, this may be because either the children are interfering with other children and being reported, they don't understand healthy contact, or they're unable to contain the sexual behaviors. This is uncommon and raises concern.

12. *When fear, anxiety, deep shame, or intense guilt is associated with the sexual behaviors.* Children's feelings regarding sexuality are generally lighthearted, spontaneous, giggly, or silly. In some cases, if a child has been caught engaging in sexual behaviors, the adult's response may have generated embarrassed or guilty feelings in the child. Yet, these feelings are qualitatively different than the deep shame, intense guilt, fear, or anxiety of a child who has been fooled, coerced, bribed, or threatened into sexual behaviors, or overexposed to adult sexuality, particularly sexuality paired with aggressive feelings or actions.

13. *Children who engage in extensive, persistent mutually agreed upon adult-type sexual behaviors with other children.* Children generally engage in a variety of spontaneous and sporadic sexual behaviors with other children for purposes of exploration and the satisfaction of curiosity. Some children who feel alone in the world may turn to other children to decrease their loneliness. These children often do not see adults as sources of emotional warmth and caring. If the children have been prematurely sexualized and/or taught that sex equals caring, they may try to use sex as a way to cope with their loneliness.

14. *Children who manually stimulate or have oral or genital contact with animals.* Children in urban and suburban areas rarely have contact with the genitalia of animals. Children on farms might have some sexual contact with animals but it is limited. Children who engage in repeated sexualized behaviors with animals or who harm animals raise concern.

15. *Children sexualize nonsexual things, or interactions with others, or relationships.* For example, the child imagines "she wants to be my girlfriend," or "he is thinking about doing sex" without any observable basis for thinking this. The child sees everyday objects as sexual or people as sexual objects.

16. *Sexual behaviors that cause physical or emotional pain or discomfort to self or others.* Children who engage in any behaviors, including sexual behaviors, which induce pain or discomfort to themselves or others, cause concern.

17. *Children who use sex to hurt others.* When sex and pain, sex and disappointment, sex and hurt, sex and jealousy, or sex and other negative emotions and experiences have been paired, the children may use sex as a weapon. Angry sexual language and gestures as well as sexual touching becomes a way to get back at people. This can be in much the same way as it has been used against them.

18. *When verbal and/or physical expressions of anger precede, follow, or accompany the sexual behavior.* In healthy development, sexual expression and exploration is accompanied by positive emotions. Verbal or physical aggression that accompanies children's sexual behaviors is a learned response to sexuality. In general, children who repeat this behavior have witnessed repeated instances in which verbally and/or physically aggressive behavior has occurred, in the context of sex. Children may have witnessed their parents or other adults hitting one another when fighting about sexual matters. Some children may have witnessed a parent being sexually misused. Some parents use highly sexual words when verbally assaulting their partners.

19. *Children who use distorted logic to justify their sexual actions. ("She didn't say 'no.'")* When caught doing something wrong, children often try to make an excuse. But when young children make excuses about their sexual behaviors that disregard others' rights or deny responsibility for their troublesome sexual behaviors, this raises concern. For instance, a child who says he was grabbing at a girl's bottom because she had on a short skirt, or the girl who said she was grabbing at the penis of a boy because "all boys like sex stuff"—these are signs of a child using distorted logic.

20. *When coercion, force, bribery, manipulation, or threats are associated with sexual behaviors.* Healthy sexual exploration may include teasing or daring; unhealthy sexual expression involves the use of emotional or physical force or coercion to involve another child in sexual behavior. Children who engage in coercive sexual behavior generally target a child who is emotionally or physically vulnerable. Although infrequent in young children, groups of children may coerce one or more children into doing a sexual behavior.

After reading about the characteristics of children's sexual behaviors that raise concern, you may have found that your child does some. Make sure you have read about healthy sexuality and gauged your child's behavior from that point of view also. Look for the balance of healthy and problematic in your child's behavior. Since parents know their children better than anyone else, you will want to decide if the problematic characteristics you see in your child's behavior need to be modified and how you want to do it. If you have a spouse or partner, you should decide together.

If you decide you need help, you can contact your pediatrician or a licensed mental health professional with experience in child development, child sexuality, or child sexual abuse. He or she will help guide you to modify your child's problematic sexual behavior. If your pediatrician does not know of qualified mental health professionals, you can call your local outpatient mental health agency, the department of mental health, the department of child protective services, your priest or minister, your child's school counselor, or ask your local hospital mental health department.

References

Morgan, S. R. 1984. Counseling with teachers on the sexual acting-out of disturbed children. *Psychology in the Schools* 21(April): 234–243.

Excerpted and adapted with permission from *Understanding Your Child's Sexual Behavior: What's Natural and Healthy* by Toni Cavanagh Johnson, Ph.D. For more information on this and related books, see the "Further Reading" section in the back of the book.

CHAPTER 12

Divorce and Kids

In the course of interviewing more than three hundred children for his book, *Divorced Kids*, Warner Troyer (1979) found that in almost every case the children had received no warning of any kind that their parents were planning to separate. This remarkable discovery was echoed in the findings of the California Children of Divorce Project, a landmark study by Judith Wallerstein and Joan Kelly (1980). After following 131 children of divorce over a period of five years, Wallerstein and Kelly reported that 80 percent of the youngest children studied were completely unprepared for their parents' separations. They were given no assurances of how they would continue to be cared for. In a disturbingly high number of cases, a parent would simply disappear while a child was sleeping or away from home.

One child reported that she had been sent to a neighbor's house on a particular afternoon to play. "They were fighting and I was sent to Martha's. I came home after dinner and Mom said Daddy was gone. I didn't believe her, so she showed me his empty closet." Another child, who had experienced great trouble sleeping since the divorce, told how she'd been awakened one night to a lot of banging and loud whispers. In the morning her father's chair was gone, her parents' bed, and "a lot of other stuff." A week later, her father came to say good-bye. He had moved to a town some seventy miles away.

Why Parents Fear Telling Their Children

Many parents fear that their children are "too young" to be told. As one mother put it, "How could we tell a three-year-old about the pain we felt? How could we burden her with our own fear and anger?" Most professionals agree that if a child is old enough to recognize a parent's existence and has some grasp of language, he or she is old enough to be told. Even preschoolers can understand that Mommy and Daddy have been angry and unhappy. They can grasp that one of you will move and that both of you will continue to provide care, attention, and love. Some parents use the excuse that a child is too young to understand as a way of putting off a painful confrontation. The truth is that a child is almost always aware that something is wrong. And sooner or later the child must endure the trauma of a disrupted family. Your child needs to know what is going to happen and how it will affect him or her.

Many parents delay telling their children because they can't decide on the appropriate time. Should they talk about the separation a day, a week, a month before the actual departure? Should they wait until one parent has actually moved out? The following two guidelines may help with the time element:

1. The best time to tell the children is when a definite decision for separation has been made. Usually the final decision is made a few weeks to a month prior to the event. This allows the children time to ask questions, express feelings, and get important reassurance from both parents. If you decide only the night before, tell the children then. Don't make them wake up to a *fait accompli* the next day. Telling the children too soon, when you are only fantasizing or considering a separation, is also a mistake. Too much lead time contributes to denial. The children will tend to "forget" about the separation and be traumatized all over again when your plans are finally complete.

2. Tell your children when they ask. If they are old enough and concerned enough to ask, they deserve real answers. Without definite information from you, children will simply make up their own answers. And very often the answer will be that they have done something wrong or are being rejected. A little girl named Ginny, in the absence of any definite information, decided that Mommy had left because she was tired of washing the sheets after Ginny wet the bed. George felt that his father had decided to replace him "with a better family somewhere else."

Many parents are confused about how to tell the children—separately or all together, with one or both parents present. The ideal way to tell the children is at a "family meeting" where everyone is present. When both parents participate in telling the children, it gives the message that Mom and Dad will both continue to act as parents despite the separation. As one twelve-year-old put it, "We asked them a lot of questions. We were screaming 'How could you?' and everything. But they hung in and you could tell they were really worried about us."

Telling all of the children at the same time also helps them develop a sense of closeness as they share feelings and ask questions. They can learn how their reactions are similar and different and can begin to give each other a measure of support. Your goal should be to create an ethic of "This is painful, but we're all in it together."

A family meeting to tell the children will obviously not be the final word. Discussions will continue—between the children, between parent and child. In later conversations with individual children, you can make separate explanations that take into account age and personality differences. A very young child may need to hear over and over exactly what arrangements are being made for his/her care. Because safety needs are uppermost for preschoolers, this emphasis on who will feed them, where they will live, how often they will see the second parent, and so on is of primary importance. Older children may need to hear more about your efforts to save the marriage and to be reassured that you won't force them to take sides.

Perhaps the greatest inhibitor when trying to explain separation is the fear of saying too much. Parents are uncertain how to explain the erosion of love or how to describe their hurt and distrust. Sexual problems, affairs, the yearning for growth or freedom, the loneliness, the large and small betrayals—all those things seem too complex and "grown up" to share with children. The time of separation is also typified by a good measure of anger and blame, and it may seem an impossible task to describe your marital problems to the kids nonpejoratively.

Wallerstein and Kelly found that children coped better with divorce when they understood the event that led to the decision. The child's ability to deal with trauma was strengthened when he/she saw that the divorce was purposeful and rationally undertaken and that it was a carefully considered solution to the family's problems.

Telling your child the truth about what led to the separation enhances trust. Deceiving the child or "dressing up" your conflicts leads to confusion and distrust. It's okay to tell a child that Mommy and Daddy had problems in their sexual relationship, or that Daddy became involved with someone else, or that Mommy felt lonely. The description of the problems should be straightforward and nonjudgmental. You should also include information about your attempts to improve and save the marriage.

Jean, a thirty-year-old computer programmer, told how she dealt with the difficult issue of her husband's homosexuality. "We told them that Bob had always been attracted to other men and that sometimes he'd had brief relationships with them. We said that it had affected our own sexual relationship and that I'd withdrawn because I didn't know how to cope with it. Bob said he needed to be free to explore his feelings toward men. We said we'd been in a lot of pain, and while we couldn't stay together, we'd both continue to love and take care of our kids." Notice that Jean didn't blame Bob or turn him into a bad person. She simply stated the facts, while reassuring the children that they wouldn't lose either parent.

You don't need to be explicit about affairs, impotence, or homosexuality, but you can acknowledge these issues if they exist. It's better for children to hear things directly from their parents than to fantasize their own nightmares or hear it from someone else. Your goal should be to give as much accurate information to children as possible, to create an atmosphere of open communication where children can ask questions and get real answers.

A particularly ticklish issue is whether you should reveal which parent initiated the divorce. The initiating parent naturally fears that the children will place all the blame on him or her and that the parent who opposed separation will have an opportunity to appear as the blameless victim. The best policy once again is to be open. Sooner or later the children are bound to learn who precipitated the divorce. And if you don't choose when to tell them, they will probably learn in the context of an angry or resentful attack. Discussing the issue openly, with both parents present, takes away some of its sting. As one child put it, "I know it was Daddy who decided to leave, but he still loves us."

Almost every parent fears the inevitable pain a child will feel when he/she learns of the separation. The most dreaded reaction is anger. A rejecting, enraged child adds enormous stress at a time when emotions are already raw. Wallerstein and Kelly found that fewer than 10 percent of children welcomed the divorce, while 75 percent strongly opposed it. There's no doubt that the children will be unhappy. Some will run screaming through the house, some will retreat to their rooms, some will cry and beg you to reconsider, some will threaten and berate. Fully a third of the younger children will simply deny or ignore what they've been told.

No matter how raw you feel, no matter how hard it is to face your children, it is a job that must be done—not just as an announcement that must be made, but also as the beginning of a process where children can express feelings, get reassurance, and gradually integrate this enormously important change into their lives.

Guidelines for Telling the Children

Here are eight specific suggestions for telling children about your separation plans:

1. Tell the children clearly and directly what divorce means. Tell them in an understandable way what problems and issues have led you to the decision. Be prepared to repeat this information several times before the younger children really acknowledge what's hap-

pened. Try to show them that your decision comes from much careful thought about the marriage and not from whim or impulse.

2. Describe some of your attempts to protect and improve your marriage. One woman explained to her children how four months of counseling had led her to the inescapable feeling that very little would ever change in the marriage.

3. Emphasize that both parents will continue to love and care for the children. Be specific. Share your tentative decisions about visitation or shared custody.

4. Do not assess blame. If the children are told that there was an affair, acknowledge that it was a symptom of the marital unhappiness. Stress that each parent has been hurt in his or her own way and that each has felt pain. If you're angry, acknowledge it, but don't express your rage and blame to the kids. When you blame, you are tacitly asking your children to choose sides, to form a pathological alliance that labels one parent good and the other bad. As a result of such an alliance, a child may not only lose a parent, but also begin rejecting parts of himself that are "just like Daddy" or "just like Mommy."

5. Try to describe any changes the children can expect in their day-to-day experience. Let them know where they will live, whether they'll continue at the same school, how often they will visit or spend the night with the second (noncustodial) parent. Children often worry a great deal about money, so let them know if finances will be pinched in any way that may affect them (guitar lessons, summer camp, Mommy going off to work or working more hours). Warn the children if it looks like their primary parent may become, in some way, less available (going into a school or training program, returning to work, and so on). Give specific reassurance about who will buy and cook the meals, who will drive them to school, who will tuck them into bed. Little children, especially, worry about not having enough to eat and being left alone. Addressing these concerns is very comforting for them. If any living arrangements remain indefinite, frankly admit it. But reassure the children that all decisions will be immediately and openly discussed with them. Let them know that both parents are working to solve the inevitable problems and that order will be restored just as soon as possible.

6. It is important to emphasize that the children in no way caused the divorce and are not responsible for problems between their parents. Explain that you are divorcing each other, not your kids. It is equally important to let children know that nothing they can do can bring about a reconciliation. Little children often harbor fantasies of mending your broken marriage. They plot and scheme and hope. One six-year-old kept moving his father's picture onto his mother's night table. This daily ritual continued until the picture was hidden away. Tell your children very directly that you have made a careful, adult decision to separate and are unlikely to change your minds.

7. Assure your children that they will always remain free to love both parents. No pressure will be brought on them to reject one parent in order to continue being nurtured by the other.

8. Encourage your children to ask questions. Not just at the beginning, but throughout the long process of adjusting to a separation. Allow them to express their feelings. Let them know you are listening by repeating back in your own words the concerns they express to you.

Effects of Divorce on Children

Over 60 percent of couples seeking a divorce have children still living at home. For these children, the breakup of the family begins a period of unparalleled stress and psychological pain. The first acute shock is often followed by intense fears, anger, and grieving. Wallerstein and Kelly, in their California study, found that one-half of all children experienced serious distress and felt their lives to be "completely disrupted" at the time of separation.

Few children in the study were relieved by the decision to separate. This was true despite the fact that 40 percent of the father-child relationships and 25 percent of the mother-child relationships were characterized as extremely poor, marked by neglect and threats of abuse. No matter how dysfunctional the family was, children felt it gave them vital support and protection. Even when children witnessed repeated spouse abuse (as was the case for 25 percent), most still preferred a bitter and violent family to the unknown terrors of a "broken home."

Divorce trauma for children involves far more than the removal of one parent from the house. Many children suffer a sudden and disturbing remoteness from the parent who stays behind. As one mother reported, "I'm depressed, I'm anxious, I'm overwhelmed. It never lets up. And Leah gets the short end of it." Tasks that had been shared by two are now the responsibility of one. As the primary parent struggles to keep emotional balance and still manage the home, children receive less attention and energy. During a time when they need more support and nurturing, they often do without. The children may become depressed and feel concern for the well-being of one or both parents.

Following separation, an income that was sufficient for one household must now be stretched over two. Many women feel compelled either to train for new careers or to resume an old one. The effect on children is that Mom is suddenly much less available. She's not there after school. And all the little afternoon rituals, all those important and nourishing interactions, get lost.

The noncustodial parent is obviously also less available. Despite the critical importance of staying involved, the vast majority of fathers tend to visit infrequently. University of Pennsylvania sociologists Frank Furstenberg and Christina Nord surveyed children between the ages of eleven and sixteen. They found that only 16 percent were visited by their fathers as often as once a week. Wallerstein and Kelly found that 60 percent of the fathers they studied visited less than once a week following separation; 25 percent visited erratically and infrequently (less than once a month). Nine- to twelve-year olds were particularly deprived: one-half of the fathers of children in this age group visited infrequently. A child who is used to seeing a parent every day experiences a deep sense of loss when forced to wait weeks between visits. For most children, and particularly for boys, infrequent and erratic visits deepen the anger and sense of rejection they feel.

In addition to experiencing their parents' increased remoteness and unavailability, children are often forced to contend with frightening displays of blaming and rage. Bad-mouthing and backbiting were common for approximately half of the mothers and fathers in the Wallerstein and Kelly study. In most cases, embittered parents simply failed to shield their children from the emotional chaos surrounding the separation. Children heard their fathers attacked as "liars, bastards, terrible parents, unreliable, disgusting, and crazy." They heard their mothers dismissed as "whores, unfit, drunken bitches, greedy, sexually inadequate, and crazy."

Aside from the trauma of the actual breakup, children are most seriously distressed by the bitterness they are forced to witness and encouraged to join. Children of parents who rage and backbite tend to be extremely anxious. They obsess about the content of the fights, worry about the future, and are torn by their loyalties to both parents.

Major Themes

Wallerstein and Kelly identified six major themes in the responses of the children they studied. These were the following:

1. *A pervasive sense of loss.* One-half of the children were tearful and moody. One-third showed depressive symptoms such as sleeplessness, restlessness, and difficulty concentrating.

2. *Anxiety.* Three-quarters of the children worried that their basic needs would not be attended to. One-third feared that their mothers would abandon them. Most felt that the world had become uncertain and unpredictable. They feared being left alone. They worried about money and about their parents' emotional and physical health.

3. *Feeling rejected.* Half of the children reported feeling rejected by one or both parents.

4. *Loneliness.* Two-thirds of the children longed for the absent father, and many were preoccupied with fantasies of reconciliation. In general, children received less attention from both parents.

5. *Anger.* One-quarter of the children studied showed symptoms of explosive rage. One-third of all children reported feeling extremely angry. For the majority, the anger was directed at the absent father.

6. *Conflicted loyalties.* Two-thirds of the parents studied competed for their children's affection and allegiance. The children walked a tightrope, afraid that enjoyment and intimacy with one parent might seem a betrayal of the other.

Age Differences

Wallerstein and Kelly found that children of different ages had very different responses to divorce. Four age groups were studied: preschoolers, six- to eight-year-olds, nine- to twelve-year-olds, and teenagers. Preschoolers (three- to five-year-olds) were fearful of being abandoned. They often became anxious at bedtime and exhibited disturbed sleep. During the day they were clinging and cranky and showed increased irritability and aggressiveness toward other children. Preschoolers often regressed to earlier habits such as bed-wetting, thumb sucking, or carrying security blankets. Masturbatory activity increased. Some children denied that a parent had left, while others spent hours fantasizing their father's return. Many of the preschoolers blamed themselves for the breakup. One child felt that her play had been too noisy; another thought that Daddy didn't like her dog.

The six- to eight-year-olds felt the most intense sadness of any age group. Unlike younger children, who used denial and fantasy as a defense, these children were often on the brink of tears. A great yearning for the departed parent accompanied their sadness. Half of the children missed their fathers intensely. Many felt abandoned and grieved openly. Although one-quarter of the children were under pressure from their mothers to reject their dads, few criticized or expressed anger to their fathers.

Many of the children in this group worried about being left without a family or of being deprived of food and toys. Half slipped significantly in school performance. In contrast to the younger group, most of these children denied feeling any responsibility for the divorce. But most continued to wish for a reconciliation and clung to such fantasies even after the remarriage of one or both parents.

The reaction of the nine- to twelve-year-olds was predominantly anger. This anger was usually directed toward the parent who appeared responsible for the divorce. One-fifth of the children in this age group were seduced into a strong alliance with one parent against the other. Alignments with the mother occurred in twice as many cases as alignments with the father. Particularly susceptible to being caught up in one parent's anger and rage, this age group became faithful allies and agents in parental wars. The nine- to twelve-year-olds also grieved and felt anxious and lonely, but these feelings were less marked than their anger.

Teenagers (thirteen- to eighteen-year-olds) expressed anger about their parents' dating, which they experienced as competition with their own emerging sexuality. They also felt anxiety about whether the breakup foreshadowed failure in their own relationships. Like the youngest children, many adolescents experienced a deep sense of loss. They reported feelings of emptiness, troubled dreams, difficulty concentrating, and chronic fatigue. These symptoms of mourning reflect a grief for the lost family of childhood.

Approximately one-third of the teenagers used the divorce as a catalyst for growing up. They took on more household responsibilities and helped in the care of younger children. They showed increased sensitivity and maturity in their relationships. Another third reacted by pulling away and distancing themselves from the family crisis. They displayed a marked increase in both social and sexual activities, often as a way of acting out anger toward their parents.

Sex Differences

Boys tend to respond to separation with more grief and sadness than girls of the same age. The impact of divorce is also more pervasive and lasting for boys. This may be so because boys tend to feel very rejected by their fathers. Many see themselves stuck with Mom because Dad doesn't want them anymore. As one boy put it, "I'm here because he wouldn't get an extra room for me."

A second reason for the heavier toll on boys is that divorce often disrupts the process of identification that a boy experiences with his dad. His father, whom he once idealized, has abandoned him and may now be condemned by his mother. To "be like dad" suddenly means being the one who betrayed the family, the one who failed, and continued identification may threaten the boy's relationship with the primary parent.

A third reason noted by Wallerstein and Kelly is that girls were found to be treated with better consideration by their mothers. High levels of bitterness and anger may lead some mothers to perceive male children as similar to the rejected spouse. Some research indicates that boys in single custody perceived more negative feelings directed toward them from their mothers than girls did. She also found that girls in joint custody had higher self-esteem than boys and also felt more positive parental involvement.

In the eighteen-month follow-up to the Wallerstein and Kelly study, girls were clearly the better adjusted. Nearly twice as many girls as boys had improved in overall functioning since the initial assessment. Boys were significantly more stressed in the postdivorce families, as well as more depressed and more focused on hopes of reconciliation. The girls had more friends and used them as a support system.

Five Years Later

Thirty-four percent of the children were doing exceptionally well in the five-year follow-up to the Wallerstein and Kelly study. Twenty-nine percent were thought to be adjusting adequately.

Thirty-seven percent, however, were found to be in poor psychological health. All of the children in this group were moderately to severely depressed.

Anger played a major part in the emotional life of 23 percent of the children—anger linked to school failure, delinquency, and sexual acting-out. In most cases the anger was directed at the father, who was blamed for deteriorated parent-child relationships.

Although 17 percent of the children felt rejected and uncared for by their mothers, the majority felt comfortable with the primary parent. Children who were doing well after five years had a nurturing, dependable relationship with their primary parent (usually the mother). She was psychologically stable and had not displayed chronic depression or unremitting bitterness. The children had not been forced into a pathological alliance against their fathers.

Thirty percent of the children felt rejected and uncared for by their fathers. Twenty percent still yearned for the absent father, and 25 percent were "very disappointed with the visiting relationship." Good father-child relationships were linked to high self-esteem and absence of depression in both sexes. Above the age of nine, however, the boys' adjustment was more correlated with the father-son relationship and the girls' with the mother-daughter relationship. Children who were rarely visited or were left unvisited by the father often felt unloved and unlovable.

Ten Years Later

In their insightful and sobering book, *Second Chances—Men, Women, and Children a Decade after Divorce*, Judith Wallerstein and Sandra Blakeslee revisit 116 of the 131 children studied in *Surviving the Breakup*. The children, harboring the importance of their stories and openly willing to renew their contacts with the interviewers, were thoughtful and exact in their responses. They revealed a subjective, collective identity as "children of divorce"—survivors of a tragedy, whose lives were overshadowed by existential loneliness, tears, sadness, and a sense of being less comforted and cared for than other children. They remembered vividly the *day of separation*.

They projected the bleakness of their experience onto their future children, with the resolve not to have kids until they were sure of marital success. And although they could envision marriages of fidelity, commitment, and enduring love, they expressed great anxiety about realizing those dreams. Only one in eight of them saw their parents find happiness in remarriage. While they retained real anger at their parents' behavior during the breakup, it was tempered with great sympathy. Almost half of these kids had spent the last ten years surrounded by parental anger and conflict and were distressed that the divorce had provided no resolution.

The attitudes of children at the time of the divorce offer no reliable clues to its long-term effect on them, but the age of the child at divorce may greatly affect its influence at the time and over the following ten years. Surprisingly, while preschoolers show the greatest anxiety and fear of abandonment at the time of divorce, they may be better adjusted ten years later than their older siblings.

In contrast to the open willingness of the children, the parents seemed wary of reevaluation, as if they still carried a sense of guilt ten years later. Half the women and a third of the men were still angry, and this anger was a continuing influence on their children. A third of the women and a quarter of the men expressed the sense that life was unfair, disappointing, and lonely.

Women who married young and divorced in their midtwenties often started over, reorganizing their lives around jobs, education, and child care. But for the men who divorced in their twenties, life ten years later was often disorganized. Many had not found a career path and were struggling financially. While most of them remarried within two years, nine out of ten of those second marriages had failed ten years later. The majority of them paid no child support, even though many now had two families for which to provide.

Parenting Problems Immediately after Divorce

The emotional extremes that follow separation confront parents with special problems and challenges. There may be no other time in your relationship with your child when the stakes will be so high and your emotional resources so depleted. Following are some of these special challenges, with suggestions for coping with them:

1. **The angry child.** Most children, and particularly nine- to twelve-year-olds, experience an upsurge of anger and aggression following separation. Much of this anger is directed toward the primary parent, rather than the visiting one. A primary parent can easily feel victimized by this unfairly distributed hostility. It's true, the situation is unfair. As the primary parent, you carry most of the burden and also take most of the flak. Younger children are generally afraid to confront the visiting parent (usually dad) because of the very real possibility that their anger may drive him away. It's also obviously true that you're around to take the heat and the visiting parent isn't. How can you cope? The first step is to recognize that this process is normal and necessary and an experience that many parents endure following separation. The second step is to encourage your children to *talk about their feelings*, rather than dump them. Set aside a time that is just for them to share their feelings with you—not only their frustrations and fears about the things that have changed, but in particular their feelings about you. It isn't always easy to find regular intervals for these "check-ins"; but a consistent effort will reduce the frequency of fights and blowups. As one woman explained, "The tension between us would get so thick you could cut it with a knife. And then we'd have a socko, knockdown fight. Now I sit down with the kids every few days and find out what's bugging them." And it's not enough just to talk. Reassure your kids with lots of hugs and physical affection.

2. **The parent's aggravation cycle.** A primary parent is under enormous stress following separation. He or she is on an emotional roller coaster and also must somehow keep the house running, get food on the table, and continue attending to each child. Irritations may accumulate and then suddenly spill out in angry attacks on the kids. As the rage dissipates, you feel waves of panic ("Am I doing them harm?") and remorse. The irritation-anger-remorse cycle may continue for months as you adjust to all the new stresses.

   This aggravation cycle can be short-circuited in two ways. First, keep track of your level of irritation and stress. Don't let it build up to the point that you become a ticking time bomb. Scan your body for tension and take notice when you are feeling emotionally fragile. These are cues to take time off, to do relaxation exercises (see the chapter on stress in part V), decompress in front of the TV, or play racquetball—whatever works for you. Give yourself a special treat. One woman described how she would start hunching her shoulders as a symptom of stress. "So I'd put the kid in the playpen, open a soda, and put on the earphones for a while. A pleasure break really helped." Second, try relieving your stress with some adult contact. The nonstop demands and natural egocentricity of children can be frazzling. Even if you do no more than make a brief phone call, time with your adult friends can be restorative and renewing.

3. **The overburdened parent.** Kids, work, kids. This routine is hard enough when you have a partner to help. Alone, it's exhausting. The answer is to get as much help as you can. The more emotionally and physically exhausted you become, the poorer you will be at parenting. You have a responsibility to your children and to yourself to arrange your life so you don't go into emotional bankruptcy.

   If you can afford child care, arrange for it. If the second parent is willing to take your children for overnights, set up a regular and predictable schedule that lets you look forward to time off. Join a child care collective, or share child care responsibilities with a neighbor who has children near in age to your kids. Many parents also find that their children can be an important resource. Kids often can take over certain household responsibilities that were once exclusively handled by grown-ups. Don't be afraid to assign shopping, cooking, and cleaning tasks to the older ones.

Being overburdened means being less available. Wallerstein and Kelly found that 25 percent of mothers spent substantially less time with children six months after separation. One way to avoid losing contact with the children is to do many of the household tasks together. Mom washes and Jimmy dries, Susan cleans the tub and Mom does the sink, Ed makes the salad and Dad makes the hamburgers.

4. **Children who won't behave.** An upsurge in mischief, talking back, and problems at school are common following separation. Since it was often the children's father who provided the real discipline at home, mothers may feel uncertain how to establish control. As one woman put it, "They won't listen to me because they know I can't really hurt them. I yell, and they yell back at me."

The answer is to make clear rules with definite sanctions and then stick to them. If you've decreed that the children lose their allowance when they yell at you, then you must take away the allowance when there is an infraction. Giving the children a second chance or letting them ignore your rules teaches them not to take you seriously. Everyone has known a mother who had to call her kids twenty times before they came in. She waited at the front door, hoarse with screaming. If she had understood the principle of consistent reinforcement, she would have had to call only once. Children who didn't come when they were called would lose a valuable privilege. If they did come, they'd get praise and a hug.

Many parents get better cooperation when they encourage the children to participate in creating the house rules. When rules are developed through compromise and consensus, each child feels a part of the decision making. As one mother said, "When the boys have a role in the cleanup decisions, they get the work done without much fuss. When I just lay down the law, they take a month of Sundays to scrub the sink." Problems at school or delinquent behavior should be addressed by both parents. It's hard to face an irate principal alone, and the children's father can be an important support. He can also help reestablish limits when the child has gone temporarily out of control.

5. **Visit anxiety.** Fathers who are no longer part of the daily lives of their children often feel depressed after a visit. They have lost their role of protector and provider and the power of decision making. Dads also go through torture trying to invent fun outings each week. They are reduced to playing the good-time parent who never confronts or disciplines the children.

If you are a second parent, it is recommended that you bring the children to your new apartment as soon as possible. In this way they will learn that you have a real place in the universe. They'll know where you live and what it's like there. Overnights are especially helpful, because they give you a chance to do some real parenting. The visit becomes more than a frenetic trip to Marine World and instead offers a chance for quiet talks and bedtime stories. One father explained it this way: "I was always planning something special. I didn't think they'd want to just be with me. But when I started doing overnights, everything slowed down. We talked quietly instead of screaming over the roar at a baseball game. We could do ordinary things. I felt I could still teach them things."

Introduce the children to your neighborhood. Encourage them to make friends with kids in the area. When your children can play happily in the local park and have made some friends on your block, much of the pressure will be off. You will feel significantly less visit anxiety.

Recommendations

Here are some guidelines to help you protect your children during the first crucial months following separation:

- *Maintain a consistent pattern of frequent visits.* Losing contact with a parent can be a crushing experience for a child, whose immediate response is to feel rejected and unloved. The long-term result is often a lowering of self-esteem. Although children need both parents, a large majority of fathers choose to visit infrequently. Consistency is as important as frequency. A visiting parent must keep his or her promises. Don't fail to show up; try hard not to cancel.

- *Consult your child about the visitation schedule.* Many children complain that they are forced into a pattern designed only for their parents' convenience. The kids resent it and eventually begin finding excuses to avoid the visits. Take the needs of your children into consideration when arranging visitation. Keep the schedule adaptable and flexible.

- *Keep up any child support payments.* Less than 40 percent of women who are eligible for child support receive it. The obvious result is a greater or lesser degree of economic hardship for the children. The less obvious result is loss of contact with Dad. Fathers who stop making child support payments tend to see their children infrequently. As they fall behind, they are criticized by their ex-wives and may be denied visitation privileges. Furstenberg and Nord found that only 8 percent of the children whose fathers were not making payments saw their dads once a week or more. Thirty-five percent had had no contact with their fathers in more than five years.

- *Subject children to as few changes as possible.* In the year following separation, children experience less stress if they can remain in the same home, neighborhood, and school. Explain concretely where, when, how, and with whom a new experience will take place.

- *Don't use the children as messengers or spies.* Try not to ask your kids about the other parent's life. Avoid reporting to your children how angry, lonely, or economically strapped you are in the hope that they will carry this information to your ex-spouse. Communicate directly with the other parent. When you need information, ask for it. If you want to give information, make sure the other parent gets it directly from you.

- *Avoid using children as allies in parental battles.* No child should be forced to choose one parent over another. No matter how much you may hate your ex-spouse, don't let your feelings interfere in any way in your parent-child relationship. Don't encourage a child to share your resentments toward the other parent; don't block visits.

- *Avoid joining in your child's anger toward the other parent.* This kind of rapport is just another way of forming alliances. Encourage your child to talk the problem over with the other parent; let them work it out.

- *Keep kids out of the middle.* Do not denigrate, malign, or badmouth the other parent. Attacking or blaming the other puts children in an untenable position. They must either lie about their feelings in order to agree with you, or bring their feelings into line with yours and basically lose a parent.

- *Stay out of custody battles.* Approximately 10 to 15 percent of divorcing families struggle over their children in court. The only people who win such battles are the lawyers. Often the underlying motive is to take revenge on an offending spouse, and the usual result is that the children become pawns in a shattering legal war. If at all possible, enlist the services of a mediator to help with custody conflicts. Examine coparenting and joint-custody options as ways of sharing the parenting role.

- *Avoid frightening the children with threats or with your worries about eventualities.* Many children have been severely disturbed by parents who threaten suicide or promise that they'll move away or block visitation if a child doesn't behave. Don't share your fears about money until the squeeze brings a concrete change in the child's life. At all costs, give your children the feeling that there will always be enough to eat, that they will always have a place to live, and that they will always have you.

- *Stay in the role of parent.* Be honest with your children and let them know when you feel bad, but don't turn them into emotional props or force them into the grown-up roles of confidant and decision maker. Children need to mature at their own pace. It's natural for them to accept more responsibility following a separation, but those responsibilities should not include being your therapist or soul mate. Reassure the children that you know what you are doing and can take care of them.

- *If you are severely depressed (can't work, can't get out of bed) or dysfunctional (paralyzed by anxiety or bitterness) you should seek professional help.* A child needs a functional mother and father. You owe it to your child to get whatever help you need to recover your parenting effectiveness.

- *If children fail to resume normal development after the first year, they too should receive professional attention.* Signals that help is needed are persistent anger or depression or the presence of serious behavior problems such as excessive aggressiveness or belligerence, promiscuity, or drug use. Any professional help you seek should include family therapy. Children's problems usually develop in response to the family milieu as a whole and are rarely treated effectively without involving at least the primary parent and siblings. Many family therapists also prefer to include the second parent as well.

- *Children sometimes need to grieve.* Take the time to draw them out individually, or encourage them to spend a weekend with loving relatives.

References

Furstenberg, Frank, and Christina Nord. Fff@ssc.upenn.edu or (215) 898-6718.

Troyer, Warner. 1979. *Divorced Kids: A Candid and Compassionate Look at Their Needs.* Buffalo, N.Y.: General Distribution Services, Inc.

Wallerstein, Judith S., and Sandra Blakeslee. 1996. *Second Chances: Men, Women, and Children a Decade after Divorce.* Boston, Mass.: Houghton-Mifflin Co.

Wallerstein, Judith S., and Joan B. Kelly. 1980. *Surviving the Breakup.* New York: Basic Books.

Excerpted and adapted with permission from *The Divorce Book: A Practical and Compassionate Guide* by Matthew McKay, Ph.D., Peter Rogers, Ph.D., Joan Blades, J.D., and Richard Gosse, M.A.. For more information on this and related books, see the "Further Reading" section in the back of the book.

CHAPTER 13

Trauma and Kids

It was the middle of the day, a hot and humid afternoon, when Maria witnessed the brutal murder of her baby-sitter, a woman whom Maria loved deeply. They had just sat down together on the front porch steps with root-beer floats when an angry man approached them with a knife.

Moments later, at the tender age of eight, Maria watched the man—in uncontrollable fury—stab her baby-sitter over thirty times. Maria stood in shock as her baby-sitter lay dying before her eyes. Maria saw her baby-sitter's body twitch as blood poured from her chest. She watched tears streaming down her baby-sitter's cheeks as she lay gasping for air in pools of blood. Overcome by terror, Maria managed to run from the scene, fearing she would be his next victim. Maria ran, but later struggled with a sense of profound shame for having "left" her baby-sitter behind. Maria was haunted by the memory of her baby-sitter's face when their eyes met for the last time.

In the weeks following the murder, Maria became mute. She was the only witness to the crime and detectives on the case were anxious to hear her story. She refused to talk to anyone. Maria and her mother were referred to my office for help.

This young girl taught me many things. The first thing I learned from Maria was that I needed to be able to be mute, too. We spent many sessions sitting in a rocking chair together, saying nothing. Sometimes we rocked and sometimes we sat still. I remember Maria's hands, because we spent hours examining them together. Sometimes she would twist a small piece of her clothing, wringing it tightly. Most of the time, however, her hands did not move. Her body sank limply into the chair and I could see the effort it took her to lift even one finger.

I told Maria that I didn't blame her for being quiet. I told her I believed she would talk again when she was ready. I let her know I felt confident that she would eventually talk like she used to and that she would know when it was the right time to do so. I said I understood why it would be hard to talk about what she saw. I let her know that I would listen to whatever she wanted to say. I explained that when she was ready, telling me about what happened would help her feel better again.

The detective made daily visits to my office, hoping for a "breakthrough." Every day he asked when I thought she'd be ready to talk. I continued to disappoint him; my response was always the same: "She'll tell me what she wants to when she's ready, and I don't have a clue when that will be." Given enough time, I hoped Maria would come to trust me, but the only thing I was certain of was that Maria was the only one who could decide when she would tell her story.

One day in a session with Maria, I wondered aloud what the detective would do if both of us refused to answer his questions. I suggested to Maria that we invite the "pesky" detective in and say nothing together. She spoke her first word to me at last: "Okay."

The detective eagerly entered my office, hope written all over his face. He gently explained what he needed to know. He said he needed Maria to tell the story of what happened so he could "put this bad man away where he could never hurt anyone again." I sensed his urgency and impatience, and I knew he was right to be asking. He wanted a conviction. For a moment, I imagined joining his efforts to coach the information out of her, a fleeting thought sparked by my own contempt for the killer.

The detective grew increasingly uncomfortable with our lack of response to his questions and comments. I finally told him, "We're not talking." Maria and I exchanged a knowing look. We shared a secret now. After he left Maria let out a short giggle. No words or sentences, but it was a sound full of meaning just the same. Trust could start to build now.

Maria and I continued to see each other almost every day. I was grateful every time she stepped through my door, fearing she would grow tired of our appointments before I could help. I told her I liked talking to her even though she still said nothing. One day I asked if she'd be willing to pretend to be my counselor and listen to me talk. I invited her to help me out if I was stuck for words or if I said something she thought wasn't quite right. I told her she could tell me in any way she wanted—by nodding, writing, or using gestures. I began to describe my feelings about what happened to her. I told Maria how sorry I was. I explained the sadness I felt for what she saw and remembered. Thirty seconds later Maria began talking. With hands pushed against her chest, she said, "It hurts inside and out. It hurts in my heart."

Her pain, at last, had a voice. We had connected.

I wanted to embrace her, this delicate yet resilient being. She was so fragile that I was afraid she would shatter if I did. She wrapped her arms around my waist and began to cry. Her feelings finally could be shared. I was able to comfort her.

Maria had a wound so deep it penetrated her heart. In the weeks ahead I learned just how powerful a medicine love would be for her traumatic pain. The healing process could not begin without it.

Trauma Hurts the Heart

Bearing witness to a tragic event is painful. Like Maria, children often hold their hands over their hearts when they show "where it hurts most." It is normal to attach feelings and emotions to the heart. When asked to draw what they feel, many traumatized children draw pictures of broken or blackened hearts.

The pain and heartbreak children feel is complicated by troubling symptoms of stress and fear. In this state of emotional turmoil, children who have been profoundly impacted by trauma often say they feel like they're "going crazy."

The Emotional Balancing Act

Parents and children cope with stress on a daily basis. Lost car keys, a teacher conference, waking up late for work or school, or even something as simple as breaking a glass disrupts a normal routine. Stressful experiences throw you off balance, if even for a few moments.

The majority of people handle the day-to-day stresses that interrupt their lives relatively easily. They regain their balance or sense of emotional equilibrium and usually the rest of the day continues unaffected. But when something traumatic happens, it throws you so far out of balance and out of the normal range of your equilibrium that it is impossible to regain it (Young 1998). I've heard children describe the experience by saying, "I feel like I'm in a nightmare, but I'm not waking up."

The effects of trauma can put children on an emotional roller coaster. One day they're sad, the next day nervous, another day it's forgotten, the next day it's all they think about. Some children say they feel as if they're walking on a tight rope and can't catch their balance. They fear life will fall apart again at any given moment. The ups and downs and anxiety of living on the edge take an emotional toll. Given enough stress, no one is immune to these effects.

When emotional balance is lost, children do not behave, think, act, or feel the same. And how could they? Their lives have shifted out of kilter. You can help them learn ways to find their balance again and hold it. This is how to start:

- Assure children that having frightening or confusing feelings does not mean they are "going crazy." What happened was crazy, but they are not.

- Explain to children that as strange as it may sound, part of what will help them feel better is to let themselves feel out of balance for a while.

- Tell them it's not wrong, bad, or weak to feel the way they do.

- Explain that the way they feel is the same for most kids and adults after an experience like theirs.

- Let them know it is important for them to accept help and support for a while until they feel more like themselves.

- Reassure them that while right now it might take effort and concentration to get normal things done, getting their balance will become easier the more they do it (just like learning to ride a bike).

Like adults, with adequate support and care children will regain their sense of emotional equilibrium. However, when it comes back, it will be in a different place. Children will never be the same. This does not mean life will be worse, it means it will be *different*. Some children even grow stronger with the new balance they acquire.

Trauma changes you. As one child said, "This changed me forever. It's changed everyone who saw it. I don't know how I'll feel ten years from now, but I know I'll be different than I would've been—all because of this."

Depression

When the world falls apart, the shock immediately following the experience can soon give way to depression. Children experience depression in different ways. They can be subdued and withdrawn, becoming mute like Maria, or they can be irritable and explosive, seeming angry rather than sad. The despair children sometimes feel over what they've witnessed or experienced can be so overwhelming that they may need to find ways to forget what they saw. Children may do this by telling you they don't remember or don't want to talk about it. They may also:

- change the subject when it's discussed

- practice behaviors that distract themselves or you from their feelings

- express anger and irritability with you or others

- say it was "no big deal"

- refuse to say anything at all

What You Can Say to Help

Sometimes it's hard to know what to say, but the way you respond to your child's feelings of despair is important. You can offer comfort and support by saying what you feel. Here are some ideas to help you get started:

- I'm sorry it happened.

- I'm glad you're safe.

- Hearts can hurt the same way a broken bone does. Hurting is part of the cure.

- Broken hearts do heal.

- You can't forget or stop the pain because this is something too painful to forget.

- It's normal to feel sad at a time like this.

- Crying over something sad is not the same as acting like a baby.

- People do not die from crying.

- Feelings may change from day to day. You may also feel a lot of different ways at once.

- Feelings can be confusing to people who have been through what you have.

- You can trust your feelings.

- No one can make the pain disappear.

- You can never completely forget what happened, but with time it will feel less frightening to remember.

- You may allow yourself to forget for a while, but you shouldn't be surprised if you get upset when something reminds you.

- It's okay to remember.

- Remembering won't always feel this hard.

- I can see you feel very angry/sad/scared right now. How can I help?

- Let's think of ways you can help yourself feel better (or safer).

- Draw a picture of what you can do to help yourself feel better (or safer).

- Friends, family, counselors, and others can help you learn ways to live with what happened.

- I can listen, even when what you say is sad or hard to share. No matter what you say, I'll always love you.

Your child's sadness may look different from day to day. It may remain constant or not seem obvious at all. Children may be tearful, withdrawn, angry, or depressed. They may appear emotionally "numb." They may exhibit increased energy or decreased energy. Some people notice that their children move in and out of all these symptoms very quickly. Others notice an ongoing pattern of the same predictable behaviors.

Trauma Affects Self-Esteem

Children who carry strong feelings of self-worth and feel good about themselves are generally more hopeful about life. However, self-esteem can take a beating when tragedy strikes. The self-confidence your child once enjoyed may be temporarily buried beneath the emotional rubble that trauma often leaves behind.

The mixed emotions that children are sorting through often interfere with the view they once had of themselves. They may question their strengths and abilities, the same way they now question their sense of security and safety in the world. Self-esteem can be impacted by feelings of guilt or self-blame for what happened. It may cause children to struggle with feelings of self-doubt if they were unable to do the "right" thing under pressure or duress at the time of the incident.

Children may be too fearful, anxious, or sad to approach life with their usual level of energy and enthusiasm. They may stop taking the healthy risks they need in order to feel good about themselves (Krupnick and Horowitz 1980). When children stop trying new skills, expanding their interests, or joining new groups, they lose two important self-esteem builders: the experience of success and accomplishment. Consequently, feelings of self-worth diminish and self-esteem suffers.

Rebuilding Confidence and Self-Worth

You can help change your child's outlook and emotional state by nurturing his or her feelings of confidence and self-worth. Self-esteem nurtures feelings of hope through the positive outlook it cultivates. Maintaining a positive self-esteem through times of trauma will help children better cope with a wide range of emotions and help them persevere through the difficult days ahead.

Here are some ways you can help your children rebuild confidence and feelings of self-worth:

- Always pay attention to what you value about your child and put it into words: "You are so good at taking care of yourself," "Your ideas are important to me," "I admire the way you handled that," "I appreciate your positive outlook," "I can see what a good friend you are."

- Encourage and support friendships that help children feel good about themselves. Help arrange opportunities for your children to spend time with good friends who build them up emotionally and who can be accepting of what they've been through.

- After a trauma it can be empowering for children to put their energy into making a difference in someone else's life or to an important cause. Help children understand that healthy self-esteem is not mere self-absorption.

- Confidence is gained in part by participating in what it is they like to do. Allow children to continue participating in the things they enjoy. You know children are building self-esteem when they are busy having fun and taking pride in what they do or create.

Praise and Reward Your Child

Kids thrive on praise and are motivated by rewards, but since the trauma, your children may not be participating in life like they were before. The stress from trauma can cause children to feel so overwhelmed that they are incapable of performing even the simplest of tasks. When this happens, children lose opportunities to be acknowledged and appreciated.

Now is the time to pay attention to everything your child is able to accomplish. You can actually reduce feelings of stress in children and increase feelings of well-being just by giving them ongoing positive reinforcement.

High levels of praise will benefit your child's mood and help them maintain the behaviors you reward. Of course, not all behaviors are ones you wish to reinforce. Some parents find it difficult to praise and reward children who are deeply distressed and acting out in ways the parents don't approve of. Here are some important points to remember about giving praise:

- Lecturing about behavior you don't like may only increase it. Keep your corrections simple and to the point. Your time will be better spent if you praise your child for the qualities and behaviors you respect and admire.

- Don't worry if the qualities and behaviors you want to see more of are sometimes few and far between. Don't give up. The more you notice and admire the qualities you appreciate, the more you'll find your child expressing them.

- Find something to praise and reward every day. Some families enjoy giving daily written praise to one another through a family journal or a note in a lunch box.

- Don't forget to smile.

- Don't forget to give hugs and show your affection.

- Don't forget to say "I love you."

No matter how small or insignificant it might seem, point out the special qualities and abilities you see in your child. Now more than ever, your child needs your encouragement and admiration. Help children understand that the trauma they endured does not have to change all of who they are or wish to be.

The Gift of Feelings

Trusting Feelings

Children don't know what to do with many of the feelings that have engulfed them since the trauma occurred. To resolve the various emotions that will surface, children must learn how to trust what they feel. To do this they will need you to share the following information.

All Feelings Are Normal

Children need to know that everything they feel is normal. It is important for children to understand that whatever reactions they experienced before, during, and after the trauma were common responses for them to have. Encourage children to tell you about the range of reactions they remember experiencing. Let children know that kids who have been through something similar may feel angry, scared, confused, different, and/or lonely. Tell them that all of their feelings are natural.

Listen to Feelings

Children need to be taught how to listen to their feelings. Following a terrifying experience many children are frightened and perplexed by the range of emotions they experience in the moments before, during, and immediately following the trauma. They may no longer want to listen to what they feel. But children need to know that paying attention to their feelings will help them make sense of what happened. Help children understand that even though their feelings were frightening and can't change what already happened, their feelings *can* help protect and guide them in the future.

In the aftermath of trauma, you can help children tune in to how they feel. The best way to help children learn to listen to feelings is to acknowledge the ways you listen to your own feelings.

An example of this is when I denied my daughter the opportunity to spend the night at a new friend's house. She was understandably disappointed. She repeatedly asked, "But why, Mom?! Why can't I?" I didn't have the usual reason, so she felt confused by my decision. She was accustomed to hearing a straightforward answer like, "We have other plans," "We need to get up early," or "Because chores aren't finished." This time I told her that I made the decision to say no because I didn't feel comfortable having her in a home I didn't know enough about. I told her I had learned to trust my feelings, and that even though they weren't always right, I knew my feelings were important to listen to.

I explained to my daughter that I would not risk having her stay somewhere that might not be safe or healthy. I told her my feelings helped me know how to help protect her and keep her safe. I assured her that she could do the same with her feelings. I helped her understand that listening to them could help her make smart choices and decisions. Surprisingly enough, my daughter readily accepted the decision and my explanation. She told me she later realized she felt the same way I did and was actually relieved when I said she couldn't go. Her own developing intuition was in agreement with mine.

When children are faced with their own choices and decisions, encourage them to identify all the thoughts and feelings they have around their options. Listen to them and point out the doubts or ideas you hear that support or deny a certain direction. You might say, "It sounds like you would like to join your friends because you said they are fun to be with, they are really nice, you like them a lot, and you all enjoy skating. Are there any reasons why you wouldn't want to go?" Or, "It sounds like even though you want to go, there are some good reasons why it might be uncomfortable for you to join this group of friends. You said that you've seen them behave in mean ways to other people and that they don't always tell you the truth. You also said you don't like going with kids you don't know very well. That makes good sense to me. It sounds like you can trust your feelings to know whether this is something that will be fun for you to do or not." Remind children that their feelings can't always control situations or predict the future, but that they can be useful guides when facing new experiences and finding ways to help themselves feel better.

Take Their Feelings Seriously

Children's feelings need to be taken seriously. They need to know their feelings will be respected by you. After trauma, children's mixed-up emotions may be hard for them to explain. If they have the ability and words to verbalize what's inside them, they still may be afraid of sounding silly, crazy, or too babyish.

Children can gain inner strength and confidence by hearing your positive responses to whatever they are able to share. It is a relief for children to be able to tell you how they feel, but if they judge from your words or behaviors that what they say seems silly or unimportant to you, they will learn to stop sharing. When you don't take your child's feelings seriously, they may interpret this to mean:

- What I have to say doesn't matter.

- What I feel about what happened must be wrong.

- Something is wrong with me.

- Everyone knows what I feel better than I do.

- I don't know what I feel.

In order to help prevent your children from feeling these ways, respond to what they disclose in a calm and serious tone. A minimizing or discounting reaction can cause children to discount their ability for personal insight and it can affect the confidence they have in accurately identifying their feelings.

Understanding Feelings

Help children understand why they feel the way they do. It is important for them to understand that it's normal to have many different feelings for all kinds of reasons. Their understanding of some of the reasons behind their feelings may help explain confusing reactions they've had since the trauma. The more children can understand, the easier they can cope with unwanted or distressing emotions.

Children also need to be assured that feelings can't make bad things happen, that they don't have magic. You can explain that feeling angry at someone, even wishing someone would go away and never come back, cannot make that wish happen. They need to know that telling someone "I wish you would die" cannot kill that person. Explain to your children that everyone has feelings that they later feel sorry about or wish they'd never had.

It is important to help children identify and gain an understanding for the feelings and reactions they personally experienced related to the trauma they had to face.

After my family was impacted by a burglary in our home, my seven-year-old daughter went through a period of intense fear and anger. She was finally able to talk about the reason for her outbursts of rage toward us. She told me she didn't know why she felt the way she did, she just did.

I assured my daughter that once we figured it out, her feelings would help her. We would learn what action to take so that she could feel better. We figured out that she hated her feelings of constant worry and fear but didn't know how to feel better. She got angry and frustrated with herself. That only added to her confusion. She knew we didn't like her taking out her anger on the rest of the family, and she felt ashamed of that, too.

She soon learned that what happened to us was bad, and that she wasn't. She learned this because I took the time to explain it to her. Over a coloring book, on a drive in our car, on a walk to the park, I told her that we can't help feeling the way we do, but we can do a lot of things to change the feelings we don't like. I also reassured her that she was reacting in normal ways to something that had been overwhelming to all of us.

The truth is, the crime made us all angry. As my daughter learned to accept the mixed-up feelings inside her, she started talking about what was making her mad. She was angry that her personal belongings were destroyed and stolen. She was angry that her room didn't feel like her room anymore, instead it felt contaminated. Our home no longer represented safety and comfort for her. She was angry that she didn't feel the way she used to. Every night she worried the "mean people" would come back. She had nightmares about fires and men holding knives to her throat. She was tired of being afraid for her life.

Many children have no idea why they feel the way they do. You can help them learn how to express what they feel, and in time they will probably be able to figure it out. It can help to let them know this.

Once you understand what feelings your child is carrying, you can find ways to help meet special needs and provide comfort. You can do things to help calm fears, ease pain, and rebuild hopes for the future. Children need to be told of your confidence in their ability to heal.

Behaviors Are Feelings Disguised

Changes in behavior are normal reactions to being frightened and upset. Sadness and pain are often expressed through behavior. Many parents are alarmed if a child "acts out" in aggressive and violent ways following a trauma. Acting-out behaviors often communicate anxiety, hurt, fears, and/or underlying depression. It may be the child's attempt to numb him or herself to what happened.

The parents of a ten-year-old boy named Alan came to me expressing concern that he had suddenly started drawing "violent and bizarre" pictures and was engaging in "gun play," which he had not done prior to the shooting he witnessed. I assured his parents that Alan's play and increased aggressiveness was a normal response to his confusion surrounding the random crime he experienced.

Rather than punish Alan for this behavior, his parents learned to help him play out his feelings in safe ways. They accepted his make-believe world and joined in when invited. His parents helped Alan understand that his play had a purpose. They told him they believed his games were a smart way to help him feel less sad and afraid. They explained that it was normal to try to figure out all the confusing questions and feelings he might have, even while he played and drew pictures. Together Alan and his parents struggled to find answers to the questions they all had about why the traumatic event had happened, how it could happen, why it wasn't stopped in time, why some people didn't survive, and what they would do if it ever happened again. Alan's parents became a powerful resource in their son's recovery. He was no longer alone in his thoughts and feelings.

Five-year-old Jacob was in my office for the first time when he spontaneously started "flying." Every time his parents attempted to tell me about the robbery they endured in their home, he jumped off his chair and "flew" around the room to each piece of furniture he could safely land on. This otherwise shy and withdrawn little boy became animated, loud, and forceful in his behavior. It was the only way he knew how to stop us from talking about what happened and flee the anxiety it produced in him. He continued to "fly away" through out our subsequent sessions whenever he needed to.

Jacob's behavior was an important way he protected himself from feeling overwhelmed. I suspect it was also a way for him to feel he could escape if he found himself in danger again. His illusion of having a magical flying ability soothed his feelings of helplessness and powerlessness. It is important to respect the ingenious ways children take care of themselves.

Difficult Feelings Take Time to Change

You can tell children their feelings may feel mixed up for a while. Explain that some feelings take time to understand and change. In the meantime, you can reassure them by saying:

- It's okay to feel and act differently for a while.

- There are a lot of safe ways that you can take care of yourself.

- Being different can be better when new behaviors help you take care of yourself (like Jacob's need to "fly away" at times).

- It won't always feel this bad.

- You are smart to do things that help you feel better and safer.

- It's okay if you don't feel like you used to.

- You will feel happy again.

- What happened to you has changed you. That's to be expected.

- Life may never feel the same as it did before, but it will get better.

- It will take time to feel better again.

- In time we'll all feel better. Your scary, sad, and angry feelings will go away.

The Recipe for Understanding

"It just takes time" is a familiar phrase. When you tell a child it will take time to make sense of what happened and to feel better again, it can be helpful to illustrate what this means.

You could compare "taking time" to the process of baking bread or cookies. You can explain that first you have ingredients like flour, salt, and baking soda. They don't taste good separately. You mix them together and they begin to taste better. But it's not until you go through the last step of baking that you have a cookie you can eat or a loaf of bread for your sandwich.

Baking is a process much like that of healing. It involves many different steps and ingredients. It takes time to complete. If you rush the process, your cookies and breads won't be done enough to enjoy.

Every recipe requires different amounts of time. In the same way, people require different amounts of time before they are done healing and can begin to feel better again. Understanding feelings is one step in the healing process, but all the steps are important and necessary to complete. Help kids to take the time they need. Help them learn to be patient with themselves by being patient with them.

Expressing Feelings

It is important to tell children they do not have to be alone in their feelings. Help them learn ways to express what they feel with people they love and trust. Regardless of a child's age, parents often find that their child shares many of the same feelings they have. It can be comforting for children to know this.

Because most children do not know how to express their emotions, they will look to you for how to do this. Here is what you can do to show them how:

- Don't hide your own emotions from your children. Instead, let them see the ways you cope with your feelings.

- Don't hide your tears or pretend you are not in pain when you are. Model acceptance for your feelings and reactions.

- Explain to your children how you feel about what happened.

- Tell them why you feel sad and upset.

- Practice sharing how you feel about many situations, not just those involving the trauma.

- Identify all your feelings such as anger, sadness, excitement, happiness, frustration, and loneliness so they will see how to face their own feelings and make sense of them.

What to Say

Help children understand that talking about the feelings they experienced during and after the trauma can help them feel better. Some kids worry that the feelings they have are wrong or bad. It is difficult for them to express feelings to people who might criticize or punish them for feeling the way they do. Children must know there are no wrong feelings. They also need to hear you say it's okay to talk about anything and everything. Here are some things you might say to convey this:

- You don't have to share your thoughts and feelings with everyone, but it's okay to share them with me, or anyone else you trust, when you're ready to talk.

- It's okay to feel sad and cry by yourself. After you've had time to be alone, it will help to talk about how you feel.

- I can listen to whatever it is you would like to tell me about. Your feelings won't worry or frighten me.

- Nothing you feel is wrong. You can tell me anything.

How to Respond

When children begin to express their feelings, you will want to be ready to respond in helpful ways. Here are some suggestions:

- When children are ready to talk, be ready to listen. Stop and be quiet. Give your undivided attention to what your child is saying.

- Repeat what you think you heard them say. Check out if you are understanding what it is they want you to understand. Don't worry about what your perspective is. Just keep listening to theirs.

- Talk more about it. Encourage your child to keep explaining to you how they feel, without judging them.

- Don't ask why they feel the way they do. For now just accept it. They feel the way they do for a reason. You can ask for help in understanding later, but for now, operate from the assumption that there are good reasons for all their feelings.

- Remember to respond rather than react. If you're angry, shocked, blaming, or questioning with judgments or suspicion, your children will not trust you to understand and they may learn to stop talking. Who needs the third degree when you're trying to explain something important inside you? It's counterproductive to healing wounds of the heart.

Using Feelings

Teach children how to use what they feel. Explain that they can use their feelings to help better understand themselves, others, and the world. Following trauma, help children realize that when they trust, understand, and express emotions, they can discover how to use their feelings to help them heal.

What Feelings Can Tell You

Give your child examples of how feelings can show them what they need in order to feel better and take care of themselves:

- When you're *tired*, you know you need to sleep or slow down.
- When you're *lonely*, you need to ask for company and maybe a hug.
- When you're *sad*, you may need to cry, talk, or be alone.
- When you're *angry*, you need to tell someone why. You may need to express to someone why your feelings are hurt.
- When you're *afraid*, you need to find a way to feel safe.
- When you feel *sick*, you may need to go to a doctor or do special things to take care of yourself.
- When you feel *confused*, you need to think and do your best to figure out why.
- When you feel *disappointed*, you learn life does not always give you what you want.
- When you feel *love*, you sometimes need to express it. You can appreciate what and who you love.
- And when you feel *happy*, you learn what you enjoy about life.

Help children learn how to use their feelings through the healing process. If you can help them understand that all of their feelings are valuable parts of themselves, you will have found an important way to assist their recovery.

From the Eyes to the Listening Heart

It only takes seconds to experience a trauma. In a moment or in a glance, a traumatic event can instantly leave it's indelible mark on the heart of a child. One thing is certain: The emotions that follow can take children on an important path in the healing process. It can be the first path on the road to their recovery.

Maria learned to trust, understand, express, and use her feelings in ways that helped empower her recovery. As the key witness at the trial of her baby-sitter's murderer, she told me the pain in her heart would help her tell the truth. She said it would help her remember why it was important to be there showing the judge who the "bad man" was. She told me her anger would help her tell what happened so the man could never kill or hurt anyone again. Her love inspired her to testify because she knew her baby-sitter would be proud of her. Maria clearly wanted to protect other people from the murderer. She said she was afraid but would do it anyway. She would do it for her baby-sitter.

Maria confronted her fears. She never denied the terror she felt of being in the same room with the assailant, but she learned ways to live with the fear. She expressed her pain and openly grieved her loss all along the way. Maria learned that healing happens even in the hurt. Hurting was part of the cure.

In the end, Maria testified beautifully. It was her testimony that resulted in the conviction of the killer. On that day she focused on those of us in the courtroom who loved and supported her. My own tension transformed when she began to speak. I was quickly filled with respect and admiration for this courageous young girl, who just weeks earlier was determined never to speak again. On that day her voice was loud and clear and powerful. She spoke from her heart.

References

Krupnick, J. L., and M. J. Horowitz. 1980. Victims of violence: Psychological responses, treatment implications. *Evaluation and Change* Special Issue: 42–46.

Young, M. A. 1998. *Responding to Communities in Crisis: The Training Manual of the Crisis Response Team.* Washington, D.C.: NOVA; and Dubuque, Iowa: Kendall/Hunt Publishing Co.

Excerpted and adapted with permission from *Children Changed by Trauma: A Healing Guide* by Debra Whiting Alexander, Ph.D. For more information on this and related books, see the "Further Reading" section in the back of the book.

CHAPTER 14

Anxiety and Kids

Emily had a secret problem. She was twelve years old and was still afraid of the dark. At night, when the family was asleep, she would often hear strange noises outside and panic, imagining that they were being robbed or that they'd all be murdered while they slept. Emily still kept a night-light on in her room and would often run to her parents' room on particularly bad nights and slip into their bed. She'd never take the garbage out at night or go upstairs alone after dark, and she usually insisted on her parents checking her room before she went to sleep. Because of her fear, which was a secret to everyone except her parents, Emily never accepted invitations to sleep over at friends' houses and found excuses to not go to school camp. Emily's parents had tried to push her to face her fears and sleep in the dark, but she became so upset and they had so many fights that eventually they just gave in to her fears. Now her parents feel frustrated at the limitations that Emily's fear causes both in her own life and for everyone else in the family.

Ten-year-old Connor had a different problem. He was extremely shy. At home he would talk freely with his family. At school or with strangers, Connor was different. He was terrified that he would do the wrong thing and make a fool of himself. He hated to speak in front of the class. Even though he could play the piano beautifully, he was too scared to perform at the school concert. In the schoolyard he was usually alone, afraid to join in with the other children.

If you're reading this chapter, the chances are there is a child similar to Emily or Connor in your family. Problems like Emily's and Connor's are common, normal, and quite easily handled. But they can often cause unpleasant and potentially serious interference in children's lives and in the lives of their families.

Fear, worry, and anxiety in children can take many forms. All children experience fears and phobias at particular stages of their lives, and this is a normal part of growing up. For example, we know that infants develop a fear of separating from their mom at the same time they begin to fear strangers and new people. A little later, most children will be scared of the dark and, at some point, many young children begin to imagine monsters under the bed and burglars at the door. In the teenage years, self-consciousness and shyness become a very common and often annoying part of developing maturity. When these fears develop, they're usually just part of the normal developmental process that we all go through. But sometimes, fears and worrying can reach a point where they start to cause a problem for the child. These excessive fears are often temporary and transient, but may still cause such distress that as a parent, you want to help your child hurry through this stage. On the other hand, some children experience fears and worries to a much greater degree than their peers, and some continue to experience fears long after other children their age have outgrown them.

Some fears are very understandable and based on obvious causes. For example, your children may be scared to go to school because they are being bullied; or they may be scared of the dark following a burglary at home. In other cases, the fears and worries that children experience are much harder for parents to understand. For example, the children who worry that they're stupid, even though they may be doing perfectly well in school and elsewhere in life. Or the children who are scared that their mom will be killed in a car accident, though no one they know has ever been in a car accident and their mom always makes sure she picks her children up on time. Or the child who worries about and imagines every possible disaster. In these cases the anxiety may be an entrenched part of the child's personality, and you may feel as though your child has been sensitive and high-strung for all of his or her life.

How Can You Help Manage Your Child's Anxiety?

By the time you've completed this chapter, you will have a good understanding of:

- the way in which you currently deal with your child's anxiety

- the advantages and disadvantages of some of the most common strategies used by parents to handle their children's anxiety

- an effective step-by-step approach to handling your child's anxiety

There are numerous different ways of handling a child's anxiety. Some of the more common strategies are in the following list. As a general rule, some of these strategies are effective in managing child anxiety and some of them are not. Each strategy will be reviewed in more detail in this chapter. Place a check beside each strategy or strategies that you think are characteristic of the way in which you currently handle your child's anxiety. You'll probably find that you use several of these strategies at different times.

- ☐ excessively reassuring a child (for example, repeatedly tell the child that "everything will be all right")

- ☐ telling a child exactly how to handle the situation

- ☐ empathizing with a child's anxiety by discussing in detail what makes you anxious and afraid

- ☐ being tough with a child and not letting him or her avoid the situation

- ☐ removing a child from the feared situation or allowing a child to avoid the situation

- ☐ prompting a child to independently decide how to cope constructively with his or her anxiety

- ☐ ignoring a child's anxiety

- ☐ becoming impatient with a child

Can you think of any other strategies that you use in dealing with your child's anxiety? List any that are relevant in the space below:

_____

_____

_____

In case you're beginning to wonder whether the way in which you parent your child is going to be called into question, rest assured—it's not! The above list has been generated with the help of many parents who also have anxious children. It's not meant to gauge how "good" a parent you are. Rather, it is intended to show that lots of other parents face similar difficulties and often respond to them in similar ways to you.

Being the parent of an anxious child can be really tough, and no doubt there are times when you feel that you just don't know what to do and say in response to your child's anxiety. No doubt there are many times when you feel that nothing that you do or say seems to work. Typically, when an individual is very involved in a particular situation or problem, it's difficult for that person to view the situation in question objectively. Hopefully, this chapter will help you to gain some objectivity in thinking about the strategies that you're currently using to handle your child's anxiety. By carefully considering the advantages and disadvantages associated with each strategy, you'll be able to make informed decisions regarding whether or not a certain strategy is likely to be effective in the long term with your child.

There are no right or wrong ways of handling a child, and every child and every family are different. However, there are some things that parents can do to reduce the anxiety that their child will experience in the long run. On the other hand, sometimes parents and children slip into a pattern that isn't very helpful for the child's anxiety. We will discuss some of the ways in which different strategies may help to maintain or reduce your child's anxiety. In this way, you'll be in a better position to choose how you want to handle your child.

Unhelpful Ways of Dealing with Anxiety in Children

Excessively Reassuring Your Child

Based on parents' reports, this strategy appears to be very commonly used with anxious children. Examples of ways in which parents attempt to reassure their children include physical affection or closeness, and telling the child that "everything will be all right," and that there is "nothing to be afraid of." Within reason, these are all great strategies, and if they feel right for you, you should continue to use them. It's only when you find yourself constantly having to reassure your child that alarm bells might start ringing. Loving children and giving them comfort, security, and reassurance when they're hurt is an important part of parenting, and we would never say that you should not reassure your child. In fact, too little reassurance can be as bad as too much. Children who never get reassurance or comfort from their parents are likely to feel insecure and alone. But because of their personalities, anxious children are often not able to rely on themselves and will ask for reassurance far more than other children. That's when you can start to get into a vicious circle.

Reassurance is a natural parental response to a child's distress. Unfortunately, to an anxious child, reassurance is like water off a duck's back. It has very little effect and they come back asking for more. More importantly, even if reassurance may help to relieve your child's anxiety a little in the short run, in the long run the more reassurance you give as a parent, the more reassurance your child will demand.

Reassurance is a form of positive attention for your child. This means that every time your child gets anxious and you reassure him or her, you are actually rewarding your child's anxiety. In some cases, this might make the anxiety seem almost worthwhile for the child. At the very least, it can help to teach children that they cannot cope by themselves and that they need you to handle difficult situations. For this reason, you may find that for anxious children, you will actually need to hold off your reassurance even more than you would for nonanxious children, simply so that anxious children are forced to learn that they can do things themselves.

So what do you do when your child does seek help or reassurance? The best strategy is to help teach children how they can come up with answers themselves rather than always expecting you to do it for them. One common way of doing this is described in detail later in this chapter (see "Helpful Ways of Dealing with Anxiety in Children"). Another technique is to prompt your child to use detective thinking. In other words, rather than simply giving your child reassurance (e.g. "Don't worry, it'll be all right"), it would be much better to get them to apply their detective thinking to the worry (e.g. "What would Sherlock Holmes say about this? How might you know whether it will be okay?").

When you're dealing with a child who has become used to asking for reassurance a great deal, you may need to begin gradually and then give less and less help over time. For example, if you decide to encourage your child to use his or her own detective thinking rather than coming to you for reassurance, you may need to spend a little time with your child going through the detective thinking the first few times. After a short while, you can gradually expect children to do more and more of the detective thinking for themselves. Eventually, if children come to you seeking reassurance, you should be able simply to tell them to do their own detective thinking about the problem.

If you're going to make a change from always helping your child as much as he or she wants to withdrawing a little, it's very important that you let your child know. A sudden change without explanation might leave your child feeling hurt, unloved, and afraid. No matter how young your child, you should explain clearly what the changes are going to be and why you're making them. It's also a good idea to introduce rewards (and of course lots of praise) when your child successfully solves a problem by him or herself. Finally, it's absolutely essential that you're consistent. No matter how hard it is, it's important not to give in to your child's requests for reassurance (within reason). Don't enter into extended arguments with children. Rather, inform them clearly and calmly that you are confident that they know the answer and you are not going to discuss it anymore. Then ignore any further requests for reassurance. Don't forget to reward and praise your child for successful self-reliance (i.e. for not seeking reassurance).

Kurt's Example

Whenever they're going on a family outing, Kurt bugs his parents with repeated questions about what will be there, who will be there, what they should take, what he should wear, and so on. In the past, Kurt's parents have tried everything to get him to relax and ask fewer questions. Usually, however, they end up answering his questions for a while, eventually losing patience and yelling at him. Finally, Kurt's mother decided that it was time to tackle this problem in a different way (his father was not very interested in the program).

To begin, Kurt's mother sat down with him at a calm time to discuss the issue. She told him that she loved his usual questions and his curiosity, but that when he was worried about things, he would often begin to ask too many questions. She explained that she knew he was very smart and that he was now old enough to answer many of his own questions. She said that the next time he began to worry and ask too many questions, she would help him to do his detective thinking to try to come up with his own answers. After that, Kurt's mother explained, she and his father would ignore any further "worry questions." They would be very pleased with him if he could do his own detective thinking and not ask them any worry questions.

A week later, Kurt's family were invited to a family friend's house for lunch. As the time approaches, Kurt began with some questions. He was particularly worried about whether he would know anyone and about the possibility that the other kids might not like him. As soon as he began to ask questions, his mother sat down with him and went through his detective thinking with him. She encouraged him to think about how many times he had previously been to family friends and had known people, whether other kids had usually found him likable, what he was likely to think (based on previous experience) of the other children there, and so on. After Kurt had been through the evidence, his mother praised him and went about her work. The next time that Kurt asked a question about the visit, she said to him, "You know that we've already talked about this and done the detective thinking. I know that you have the answers and you don't need me to tell you. If you ask again, I'm not going to answer you, but I am very happy to talk about anything else you would like to discuss." When Kurt asked again, his mother simply ignored the question. When he did not ask any questions for ten minutes, she said, "Kurt, do you realize that you haven't asked me anything about our outing today for the last ten minutes? I'm really proud of how brave you're being. Keep up the good work." Kurt asked no more questions about the visit that day. After the visit, Kurt's parents took him to his favorite restaurant to congratulate him for being so brave.

Being Too Directive

When a child is extremely anxious, some parents will try to take over and direct the child. In other words, they will tell the child exactly what to do, how to behave, and what to say in the anxiety-provoking situation, or they will do things on behalf of their child.

Take George's parents, for instance. George becomes very anxious in social situations with other children. On one particular occasion, George and his father went to the birthday party of a younger cousin. George spent most of the time sitting beside his father and not mixing with the other children. At one point, a clown arrived and began handing out candy. George's father could see that George would love to have some sweets but that he was not going to step forward and ask for any because he was too shy. So his father leapt up and went to the clown to get some sweets for George. George blushed from ear to ear, but he was very pleased with the candy.

The manner in which parents sometimes take over for their anxious children is an excellent example of what we call "a vicious circle." Usually, parents only adopt this strategy after the repeated experience of watching their child feel helpless with anxiety. Most parents don't tell their kids what to do in anxiety-provoking situations because they are naturally bossy. Instead, parents behave in this way because they feel so much for their child when the child becomes gripped by fear. In the short run, this strategy helps to reduce the child's fear and gets them what they want. However, if you think about it, this reliance on parental direction is actually a form of avoidance. In the example of the party, George has learned that he is unable to handle the feared situation himself, and that he can only do it with his father's help. This helps to further reduce his self-confidence.

Even though it can be very painful, it's vitally important that you don't do too much for your child. The bottom line is that children often learn best by being allowed to make their own mistakes. Also, children can only learn that situations aren't dangerous and that they can cope if they are forced to experience the situation. It's important for you to think about whether you sometimes become too involved with your child's activities.

So how much involvement is "too much"? Unfortunately, there's no simple answer to this question. There is no way to quantify how involved to be and, of course, every parent and child and every situation will be different. What you need to ask yourself is whether you think that you help your child more than other parents and whether your child relies on himself or herself less than other children of the same age. You may need to think about concrete examples of times when your child has appeared helpless and you felt you had to step in. Talk to other parents and ask what they or their child would do in such situations. And above all, ask yourself, "Did I really need to step in? What would have been the worst thing to happen if I didn't?" As we said earlier, with an anxious child, it's possible that you may need to help less often than you might otherwise.

Permitting or Encouraging Avoidance

Anxious children avoid lots of activities. As a parent, it's hard to continuously nag your child to try everything, so sometimes you might give in to your child's fears and let him or her avoid them. If this happens occasionally, it's understandable. Obviously, in the short run, your child's anxiety and distress will drop and you will also make yourself very popular by allowing your child to get out of doing things that he or she does not want to do. However, if it becomes a common habit, the long-term consequences of permitting and encouraging avoidance in your child are very serious. As long as children continue to avoid, they won't overcome their anxiety. At this point, you don't need to do anything about avoidance, aside from be aware of it. We will discuss how to deal with avoidance in detail in the next two chapters.

Becoming Impatient with Your Child

Unfortunately, as many parents tell us, it's all too easy to become impatient and frustrated with an anxious child. Nothing you do or say seems to help. At times, it can feel as though children are deliberately clinging to their anxiety. Often it feels like "they could do it, if only they would try harder." While it's understandable that you might sometimes lose your patience, obviously becoming angry with your child will only serve to make him or her more frightened and dependent. If you feel yourself losing patience, it is helpful to ask another person (such as your partner) to help or to leave the situation for a short while to gather your thoughts. It can sometimes be useful to try and remind yourself what you are asking your child to do. Imagine having to confront your worst nightmare (perhaps standing naked in front of your colleagues) and you might be able to understand the difficulty that your child is having to face.

Helpful Ways of Dealing with Anxiety in Children

Rewarding Brave, Nonanxious Behavior

All children, no matter how anxious, will at certain times do things that are frightening for them. As a parent, you should look out for any examples of this type of bravery, no matter how small, and reward them. This will make it more likely that they will happen again. Think of it as fanning the small embers of a fire to get it to grow. At first, you need to look for any example of bravery and make a big fuss over it. Later, as your child becomes less anxious, you can reward only the more obvious examples. Make sure you don't set your expectations too high. Remember, what may seem like a small thing to you may be extremely difficult to a nervous child. You will need to make sure you look for behaviors that are brave based on your child's personality, not on anyone else's standards. By pointing to and focusing on successes, you will help your child to build self-confidence as well as help them realize what they are capable of.

In addition to looking for naturally occurring bravery, at times you may want to encourage your child to do things that are a little challenging for him or her. Again, this needs to be rewarded. We will discuss this strategy in much more detail in the next chapter.

Rewards can fall into two broad types—material and nonmaterial. Material rewards are the ones most of us think of immediately. These might include money, food, stickers, or toys. The child is given the reward, say a small toy, after the brave action is noticed. Nonmaterial rewards include praise, attention, and interest from the parent. Parental attention is an extremely powerful reward. Most children, especially younger children, will do almost anything for the approval and praise of their parents. Spending extra time with your child (e.g. playing a game or going for a bike ride) is a great way to reward them for brave, nonanxious behavior. Whenever possible, we suggest the use of nonmaterial rewards because they have the added benefit of giving your child a sense of security and self-esteem.

It's also important to keep your rewards varied. If your child keeps getting the same reward over and over, it will very quickly lose its impact.

There are several points to remember when using rewards:

- In order to be effective, rewards must be meaningful to the child. There is no point rewarding a child with something he or she doesn't like. The easiest way to make sure that the child will work for the reward is to discuss it with your child. Find out what he or she wants most at this moment.

- Communicate with your child about the rewards. There is no point showering rewards on children if they think the rewards came for no reason. It's important that children know exactly why they're getting the reward and how they can get it again. Praise should be clear and specific. You want children to know exactly what they have done that you liked and want them to repeat in the future. For example, saying "David, you were able to go by yourself with Mrs. Jones into class this morning, instead of needing me to come in with you. I was really proud of you," is much more useful than saying, "You were a good boy today, David."

- The rewards must be in keeping with the activity, and you need to make sure that you give the child a reward that is the right size for the difficulty of the activity. For example, if your child is terrified of dogs and has just spent the last half hour with the neighbor's dog, which she or he had never approached before, it's not fair to give only a small token or two minutes of your time. On the other hand, if your child has done something that was only slightly difficult, you're leaving yourself with nowhere to go if you reward them with a new television.

- Most importantly, rewards must be given as soon as possible after the brave action has occurred, and they must be delivered if promised. Consistency is essential for effective parenting. Children will learn very quickly to stop trusting their parent's word if they find that promises are not delivered. If you promise your child a reward, it must be delivered. Similarly, rewards lose their effectiveness the later they are given. If your child does something brave on Monday and you give them a small reward the following Saturday, the whole impact will have been lost. For maximum impact, the reward should be delivered immediately. That is why your own time and attention can be so much better than buying a gift. Of course, there will be times when delivering an immediate reward is just not practical. For example, you may decide to reward your child by going skiing together. Obviously, this can't be done immediately, and may need to wait until the weekend. In this case, it is useful to give some sort of interim reward. For example, you may make up a small voucher that clearly says the reason for earning the voucher on it, and have your child exchange it at the weekend for the ski trip. At the very least, if the reward is delayed, you need to make an immediate fuss and give attention to the brave act and make it very clear that the later reward and the brave act are connected.

- If you have other children, you may find that they become resentful of the extra attention and rewards that your anxious child is getting. One way around this might be to introduce a reward system for all children in the family. You can introduce a star chart where each child can earn rewards, although the rewards might be earned by different behaviors for each child. In this way, you can build bravery in all your children if needed, or you could use the rewards for your other children to increase helpful habits such as obedience, cleaning teeth, tidying their rooms, and so on.

Ignoring Behaviors That You Don't Want

This is really the flip side of the previous strategy. It involves removing your attention from your child's anxious behavior and attending again (and praising) when the anxious behavior has stopped. The idea is that when you notice a behavior that you are not happy with (for example, your child repeatedly complaining about feeling sick before school), you need to stop any interaction with your child as long as she or he is doing that behavior (complaining). Of course, it is essential that your child understand exactly why you are ignoring him or her and exactly what she or he needs to do in order to regain your attention. Using this strategy should be immediately followed by specific praise for something good that the child is doing (e.g. complaining stops for one minute). As we discussed previously, ignoring is a particularly useful strategy for dealing with reassurance seeking. This strategy must always be used carefully and only in relation to a specific behavior. It's important that your child understands that it is the particular behavior in which he or she is engaging that is unacceptable to you and not his or her general character.

Preventing Avoidance

Avoiding feared situations is one of the main causes for anxiety in children. By avoiding feared situations, children never learn that they can cope with their anxiety, that the situation is not really dangerous, and that they are stronger than they had realized. Obviously, you must be satisfied that your child is actually capable of coping in the anxiety-provoking situation. You should not force your child to do something that he or she is not actually able to do. For example, it may not be helpful to encourage your child to enter a singing contest if his or her singing isn't a strong suit. Doing this would set the child up for failure, and would only strengthen the original anxiety. In the same way, it is not helpful to force your child to do something that really is terrifying for him or her. However, you will need to push to some degree so that your child starts to do things that are slightly difficult and gradually builds up the degree of difficulty.

Communicating Your Empathy Effectively

When you are talking with your child about the things that make him or her anxious, it's important that you express your empathy and understanding in a calm and relaxed manner. Children need to feel listened to, understood, and supported, but it's equally important that they're encouraged to constructively solve the problem of their anxiety rather than focusing on how bad they feel.

Prompting Children to Cope Constructively

Parents who use this strategy typically prompt their children to think for themselves about how to constructively handle an anxiety-provoking situation. This is quite different to parents who tell their children exactly what to do in the anxiety-provoking situation.

George's Example

George is highly anxious about a debate he has to take part in at school. He is very upset and imagines the worst possible outcome. George is sure that he will make a mess of his speech and look like a complete idiot. He complains that he has a headache and that his stomach hurts.

George's mom comes and sits down with him. She says to him, "George, I can understand that you feel a bit worried about the debate. But the fact is that you have to do it for class, and at the moment, you're just not helping yourself. You're saying a lot of negative things about how things are going to go, and that must be making you feel worse. Plus, you're talking yourself into feeling sick. What you're doing right now isn't making you feel any better, is it?" George agrees with his mother. She then goes on, "Okay. So, what can you do that might help? What can you do that would make you feel better?" George answers this by saying that staying away from school on the day of his team's debate would help him feel better. His mom points out that George's teacher would probably just postpone his team's debate until he came back to school, and George will have to do more public speaking tasks now that he is in high school, and that if he puts it off now, the next time will be even harder. George can see the logic of this, especially the first point. He suggests that maybe if he practiced the speech with his mom, he might feel better about it. She praises him for coming up with a constructive way of dealing with his anxiety and agrees to practice with him.

In this example, the parent is prompting the child to come up with his own solutions. She is not encouraging him to rely on her by directly intervening. Instead, she is encouraging him to take responsibility for managing his own anxiety in a constructive manner. At the same time, she is firmly not allowing him to avoid the debate.

Encouraging your child to use the detective approach to evaluate the realistic probability of his or her negative, worrying thoughts being true is an important component of this strategy. Prompting your child to independently decide how to cope constructively with his or her anxiety is a good long-term strategy, because it involves showing faith in your child's abilities. You would be surprised at how often children are able to rise to meet their parents' expectations. If you believe that your child possesses the ability to overcome challenges and to solve problems, he or she is more likely to believe this too.

Modeling Brave, Nonanxious Behavior

Children learn how to behave by observing others (most significantly, their parents). Thus, as a parent, everything that you do or say has added significance because you are serving as a model for your child. The very best type of model is a "coping model," that is, models who demonstrate that they experience difficulties and also that they cope constructively with these difficulties. This type of model is more effective than one who apparently never experiences any difficulties. If you believe that you have a problem with anxiety yourself, it may be worth seeking help so that you can begin to model more effective coping to your child.

What to Do When Your Child Becomes Frightened

You may be wondering at this point, how do I stop my child from feeling anxious at those times when he or she suddenly becomes very scared and refuses to do something? The simple answer is, "You don't!" It's not possible to take away all anxiety from a child. We all feel anxious at times, and we all need to learn how to deal with it. Even though it's really hard to see it in our own children, as parents, we sometimes have to accept that our children will feel anxious. The good news, however, is that there are some things you can try to help reduce your child's anxiety.

1. Summarize what your child has said. Check the accuracy of your understanding of the problem, that is, make sure that you know what he or she actually means. Communicate your empathy with your child in a sympathetic but calm way.

2. Summarize the choices open to the child at this point. On the one hand, the child can continue to feel anxious and upset, and to behave in an anxious manner. On the other hand, the child can choose to do something to reduce his or her anxiety.

3. Make sure you don't just take over the task for children. Rather, help them come up with their own suggestions of ways to reduce the anxiety and feel better. Ask children to brainstorm all the possible ways in which their anxiety might be reduced. Praise the child for the ideas that they've generated. Even if the ideas are not actually very useful, praise them for effort. The fact that they're engaging with you in the process of trying to constructively reduce their anxiety is a very positive and important step.

4. Go through each idea or strategy that the child has generated, one by one. For each idea, ask the child, "What would happen if you did this?" If the child does not identify obvious consequences of a strategy, gently point them out to him or her (for instance, you might say, "I wonder if _____ would happen if you did _____ to make yourself feel better. What do you think?"). Remember, your overriding goal is to encourage approach solutions rather than avoidant solutions. Praise the child for trying to generate likely outcomes or consequences for each strategy.

5. Encourage your child to think like a detective and figure out how to reduce anxiety.

6. Prompt the child to select the strategy that is most likely to result in a positive outcome and least likely to result in a negative outcome. Remind your child to remember the evidence he or she has generated with the detective thinking.

Jack's Example

Maggie and Dan are going out to dinner to celebrate their wedding anniversary. Their nine-year-old son, Jack, is extremely anxious about being separated from them, particularly at night. He is crying and clinging to his parents, begging them not to go out.

Step 1: Maggie and Dan sit down with Jack and find out what the problem is.

Maggie:	Jack, we can see that you're very upset about the idea of us going out. Can you tell us exactly what it is that's worrying you?
Jack:	I don't know. I just don't want you to go.
Dan:	Okay, we know that you don't want us to go. But we need you to tell us why. What is it that you're afraid will happen if we go out?
Jack:	You might be in an accident and be hurt.
Maggie:	*[Maggie summarizes and checks her understanding of what Jack has said]* So, you don't want us to go out because you think that we might be in an accident and get hurt. Is that right, Jack? Is that why you're so upset?
Jack:	Yes.

Step 2: Maggie and Dan present Jack with his choices.

Dan:	Okay, Jack, your mother and I are going out tonight. And it's really up to you how you deal with that. You can keep on doing what you're doing right now and feel really bad. Or, you can try and do something to cope with the bad feelings that you're having. Mom and I would really like to help you cope with the bad feelings. Are you willing to give that a try?
Jack:	I want you to stay with me at home. If you stay, I won't have any bad feelings.
Maggie:	Jack, you heard your dad. We're not going to stay at home with you tonight. The decision you have to make is what you're going to do about how you're feeling right now. How about you work with us and we'll try and come up with a plan to make you feel better?
Jack:	I guess . . .
Dan:	Good boy.

Steps 3 and 4: Maggie and Dan prompt Jack to generate suggestions as to how he might cope with his anxiety (that is, what he might do to make himself feel better). Jack is praised for his effort.

Maggie:	Okay, Jack. We need to think of as many things as possible that you can do that might make you feel better. What do you think you could do?
Jack:	What do you mean? I don't understand.
Dan:	Well, for instance, you're worried about us going out because you're saying to yourself that if we go out, we might have an accident. Maybe instead, you could watch a video and take your mind off your worries. Do you see what I mean?
Jack:	I could take your car keys and hide them. Then you wouldn't be able to go.
Maggie:	Well, that's one idea. At this stage, we'll write down all the ideas and then we can decide on one later on.
Jack:	I could go and watch my videos to take my mind off things.
Dan:	Great, Jack. What else could you do?

Jack:	I could write down that thing about you and Mom being good drivers, so that I can remember it later.
Maggie:	You mean your detective thinking—that's really excellent, Jack. You're trying really hard and coming up with some good ideas. Can you think of anything else?

Step 5: Maggie and Dan prompt Jack to identify the likely consequences or outcomes of each of the coping strategies generated.

Dan:	Right. Now Jack, we've got a few different ideas written down here as to what you might do to make yourself feel better about us going out. Let's go through them one at a time and find out what would happen if you actually did each of these things. First of all, there was the idea that you hide the car keys? What do you think would happen if you did that?
Jack:	You might stay home?
Dan:	You know, Jack, I think that if you did that, it's probably more likely that we'd send you to your room and call a taxi to take us out to dinner.
Jack:	Yeah, I guess.
Dan:	How about your idea about watching a video? What would happen if you did that?
Jack:	I'd have fun and I wouldn't be thinking about you and Mom.
Dan:	And how about your idea of writing down that your mom and I are good drivers? What do you think would happen if you did that?
Jack:	It would remind me that you probably wouldn't have an accident, and I might feel better.
Maggie:	Okay, that's the end of our list. Well done, Jack, you're doing a really excellent job of helping yourself get over your bad feelings.

Step 6: Maggie and Dan prompt Jack to choose the most positive and least negative solution.

Dan:	Okay, now the last thing we need to do is to pick one of these ideas. Have a look at the list and the things that would probably happen if you chose each idea. Which one do you think would have the best results for you?
Jack:	Well, that's easy. It would be my idea of watching the video. Plus, I could also write down something about you and Mom being good drivers, to remind myself not to worry.
Maggie:	I think that's an excellent choice. Well done, Jack. Your dad and I are very proud of you for being able to figure out how to cope with your worry in a helpful way.

Note: Assuming that Jack handled his anxiety in a useful way and allowed Dan and Maggie to go out without difficulty, they would praise his efforts the next morning and might organize a special reward, such as playing a favorite game with his parents, to acknowledge his bravery.

Practice

For the situation in which your child becomes most anxious, try to jot down some ideas for each step in the approach outlined above. As you go through this process, try to identify the problems you are most likely to encounter at each step.

The situation is: _____

Step 1: _____

_____

Step 2: _____

_____

Step 3: _____

_____

Step 4: _____

_____

Step 5: _____

_____

Step 6: _____

_____

Step 7: _____

_____

In Summary

- There are many different ways of handling your child's anxiety. Some of these are more effective than others.

- Some methods tend to be less effective and may even increase your child's anxiety. These include: excessively reassuring the child, being too directive, permitting or encouraging avoidance, and becoming impatient with your child.

- The most useful strategies for handling anxiety in children include: not allowing avoidance, helping the child to independently manage his or her anxiety in a constructive manner, and reducing reassurance-seeking by ignoring this behavior.

- When your child becomes anxious about a future event, there are several steps you can follow to help your child to come up with some constructive solutions.

There are several other options, besides altering your parenting style, that can help your anxious child. Cognitive therapy can help reduce catastrophic thinking. Relaxation training can lower physical arousal levels. Modeling assertive social skills can help teach shy children how to interact with others and avoid being pushed around.

Excerpted and adapted with permission from *Helping Your Anxious Child: A Step-by-Step Guide for Parents* by Ronald M. Rapee, Ph.D., Susan H. Spence, Ph.D., Vanessa Cobham, Ph.D., and Ann Wignall, M. Psych. For more information on this and related books, see the "Further Reading" section in the back of the book.

PART III

CONSUMING PASSIONS

234FAMILY GUIDE TO EMOTIONAL WELLNESS

Addiction takes many forms, each characterized by a passion to consume more of something than is good for you, be it food, alcohol, cigarettes, or the Internet. For alcohol, nicotine, and other drugs, the solution has proven over time to be abstinence with group or individual support. For a necessary behavior such as eating or using a computer, you need to learn moderation and control.

This section offers proven solutions to some of the most consuming passions:

Eating Disorders shows you how to recognize, understand, and survive anorexia and bulimia.

Body Image teaches how to counter destructive cultural expectations, accept yourself, and love your body just the way it is.

Alcohol and Drugs outlines how to tell if you have a problem and how to stop your drinking and drugging. A separate section tells what to do when a loved one has a sustance abuse problem.

Smoking explains how to stop smoking safely and permanently.

Internet Addiction asks the question, "Are you a Nethead?" and tells what to do about it if your answer is yes.

CHAPTER 15

Eating Disorders

Panic, handmaid of numbing fear.
—Homer, Illiad, 850 B.C.

The Epidemic of Affluence

Suppose that you opened a newspaper tomorrow morning and read about a disease that was currently affecting 5 percent of the population. The story would be on page one, and it would describe great alarm on the part of public officials. Soon all forms of the media would be carrying daily stories on the problem. The Surgeon General would declare a national emergency. Some sections of the country might even be put under quarantine. People in every state would be in a state of panic lest the disease affect their family.

Yet, as you read these words, an epidemic is happening in the United States which is not affecting just 5 or even 10 percent of the population. The epidemic I am speaking of probably affects 20 percent of females between the ages of thirteen and forty. The National Institute of Mental Health has recently estimated that five million American women suffer from an eating disorder. It is called the Deadly Diet. You probably know it by several of its more popular names: anorexia or bulimia.

The Extent of the Epidemic

Eating disorders are sweeping this country and are rampant on our junior high, high school, and college campuses. It is rare for any young female not to know of someone with an eating disorder. Although the statistics are still being gathered, it appears that at least one in five young women has a serious problem with eating and weight.

The Victims Are Female

The Deadly Diet basically appears to be a female problem. (Females also have a better chance of recovery than males.) Eating disorders are most prevalent in middle to upper middle-class families—the so-called managerial-professional family. Currently the incidence is much lower in females from "blue-collar" families.

Estimates vary as to when this problem typically begins. The Deadly Diet can begin anywhere from the ages of ten to thirty. The peak age for the beginning of the Deadly Diet in females is between eleven and fifteen; the peak age for males is between fifteen and eighteen.

Although much of the information on the Deadly Diet says that it is a problem of teenage girls, our clinic has found that most of the people who come for therapy are in their twenties and thirties. This may be because younger people are generally less likely to seek professional help. Often it is the parent who brings the reluctant child to therapy. Adults who have left home and had to personally grapple with managing their lives usually tend to realize more clearly the need to seek help and make changes.

Is Our Culture to Blame?

Even the most casual observer will notice that our culture places an extremely high value on women being thin. Although some people in the fashion business now claim that today's models are more filled out than those of a few years back, the evidence is difficult to see. An issue of *People* magazine in the winter of 1983 had a cover story on Karen Carpenter and the tragedy of her fight with the Deadly Diet. Yet the same issue had a lengthy story on one of America's top fashion models, with pictures showing a woman five feet, ten inches tall and weighing 110 pounds. The pictures of this model looked little different from those of Karen Carpenter in the few months before her death.

Our society evaluates and admires men for their vocation—what they accomplish and what they achieve. Women are usually evaluated by and accepted for how they look, regardless of what they do. A woman can be incredibly successful and still find that her beauty or lack of it will have more to do with her acceptance than what she is able to accomplish. From the time they are tiny children, most females are taught that beauty is the supreme objective in life. The peer pressure for girls in school to be skinny is often far greater than for boys to make a team. When it is spring, young girls all start thinking, "How am I going to look in my bathing suit? I better take a few more pounds off!"

Another reason that females are more prone to have this problem than males is that the personality characteristics underlying eating disorders are usually found in women. These characteristics, which will be discussed in detail later in this chapter, are probably passed down from generation to generation, from mother to daughter.

Dieting

It has been estimated that 90 percent of all women have dieted at one time or another, while 50 percent are on a diet at any one time. When asked to estimate weight, 90 percent of all women say they are overweight. This is an astonishing statistic. Most professionals consider a person healthy if they are within ten pounds of their preferred weight. Yet women have been forced to believe that they are overweight if they are not exactly at the expected body weight. How many women continue to believe they need to "take off just ten pounds"?

This perception is not limited to adults. Half of all girls start dieting before thirteen years of age. Amazingly, half of all eight- to nine-year-old girls are on a diet of some sort. The professional journal, *Pediatrics*, reported in 1988 that overweight children are subjected to ridicule by their peers at a very early age. Because of this, even thin girls as young as five or six are concerned about bodily image and are afraid of getting fat.

So why do girls become preoccupied with dieting? In 1987, Dr. Drewnowski of the University of Michigan School of Public Health identified three factors which contribute to early dieting: maturation, money, mother.

Girls become more acutely aware of their bodies at puberty. Dr. Drewnowski found a relationship between early maturation and early attempts at dieting. Girls who mature before the age of twelve tend to be heavier than average and therefore, he believes, may have an increased risk of developing an eating disorder.

Children of wealthy parents are inclined to be more anxious about body image and dieting than children of a lower socioeconomic status.

His study also found that about half of all dieting girls were encouraged to do so by their mothers. Although his study did not look at the influence of fathers and brothers, my experience has been that these family members can indirectly encourage dieting by making remarks about how girls look.

When Did It All Start?

Since we've become a wealthy nation and have the ability to eat whatever and whenever we want, we can now choose not to eat. Eating disorders are a problem of affluence and consequently a rare condition in societies where people are starving and don't know when they will eat again. Eating disorders only appear to be a problem in countries where people are well fed.

Mass communication has brought with it an emphasis on making people fit into standard molds. In the flapper era women were seen as desirable if they had no curves but were shaped like a preadolescent girl. The advent of Twiggy firmly implanted in the public's mind that thin was where it was at. We must be careful not to minimize the role of television in the current epidemic of anorexia and bulimia. All of us are aware of the overwhelming influence that TV has had on the American public. The number of American homes with a TV set is currently 99.5 percent and the average on-time is six hours and twenty minutes per day. The average person watches eighteen thousand commercials each year. It is these commercials that tell the Deadly Dieter what to feel, how to look, and whom to want. Advertising executives depend on the ability of TV images to implant themselves in the mind, remain there, and cause people to imitate the characters and behavior in commercials. The Deadly Dieter seems to be particularly vulnerable to this influence.

How Is the Deadly Diet Different from Other Diets?

The Deadly Diet almost always starts off quite innocently as a normal diet. As the person takes off weight, she is praised and congratulated for having so much willpower. When the weight is taken off—and sometimes surprisingly quick—the person begins to think that maybe a few more pounds would be good insurance. Unfortunately, there is never enough "insurance." The pounds continue to slip away. And the person is caught in the unrelenting grip of the Deadly Diet.

From this point on, the Deadly Diet is very different from the average "diet." The average dieter may spend time thinking of weight and food, but with the Deadly Dieter these thoughts are obsessive. Some people have said to me, "Oh, wouldn't it be nice to have anorexia so that you wouldn't have to waste time thinking of your weight or what foods you eat." Nothing could be further from the truth. The Deadly Dieter thinks constantly of food. It is the first thing she thinks about when she awakens in the morning and the last thing she thinks about when she goes to bed at night. The time in between is continually filled with thoughts about food, calories, and weight.

The major difference between the regular dieter and the Deadly Dieter has to do with the issue of control. It is not, as some professionals have stated, that the Deadly Dieter is too much in control and needs to learn to let go. The Deadly Dieter is totally out of control. Even the "perfect" diet itself is out of control. The regular dieter is in control of the diet; the Deadly Dieter is controlled by the diet.

Types of Deadly Dieters

There are five basic types of Deadly Dieter. Although there are probably as many variations of these basic types as there are people in the world, all eating disorders fall into one of these types of Deadly Diets.

Fasting

This type of Deadly Dieter will often try to exist on only five hundred calories per day, even though most nutritionists claim that a starvation diet is no lower than about twelve hundred calories a day. This person can get so distraught over any "extra" calories that she begins to see calories where there are virtually none. For example, I have had people tell me they are afraid to chew one piece of gum for fear they would take in too many calories. One Deadly Dieter was even afraid of the "calories" in a glass of water!

Binging

People who just binge, and consequently are obese, can also be called Deadly Dieters. They, too, are out of control. Their "diet" is constantly on their minds. It begins to kill them—not only in terms of their health, but also socially and personally. Although this book is not geared specifically for this type of Deadly Dieter, the skills and principles can easily be adapted to help the binge eater.

Binging-Purging

These people often begin their Deadly Diet as fasters. They soon learn that fasting also cuts them completely off from most social functions. In our society it is rare when people get together and don't have some type of food available. The solution to "being thin" and yet being able to eat is to get rid of your food after having eaten it. The most common form of purging is vomiting. A much less common method is the use of copious amounts of laxatives.

Fasting-Purging

This form of the Deadly Diet combines the worst of two other categories. The binge-purge individual may at least get some nutrition into her body and might even maintain a normal weight. The faster-purger will throw up her food or take laxatives even while subsisting on 500 calories a day. This devastating combination is what most often kills the Deadly Dieter.

Fasting-Binging

This is the most frustrating category, because the person will often go on a "normal" diet for as long as six months. After staying at a reasonable weight for a period of time, she will go on a binge, which can last another six months. During this time she will put on as much as one hundred pounds. Most people involved in this person's life insist that she has the "willpower" to eat properly "if only she would make a commitment." Unfortunately, this attitude only confuses the issues. The person has the same problem with eating and weight as the other four types of Deadly Dieter—it just looks different on the outside.

For our purposes in this chapter, all five types of Deadly Dieter will be treated as similar. They all share the same problem—the underlying, common denominator of being out of control. EATING IS NOT THE ISSUE! The issue is the lack of control in all areas: physiological, emotional, mental, and behavioral.

Definition of the Deadly Diet

The mental health community has defined two of the five types of Deadly Diet: anorexia and bulimia. The definitions have been very carefully constructed and are good guidelines for determining if you have either disorder.

The "official" definition of anorexia nervosa consists of five components:

1. An intense fear of becoming obese, which does not diminish as weight loss progresses

2. Disturbance of body image, or claiming to "feel fat" even when emaciated

3. Weight loss of at least 25 percent of original body weight

4. Refusal to maintain body weight over a normal weight for age and height

5. No known physical illness that would account for the weight loss

The definition for bulimia (from the Greek words meaning "animal hunger") is also composed of five parts:

1. Recurrent episodes of binge eating

2. Awareness that the eating pattern is abnormal and fear of not being able to stop eating voluntarily

3. Depressed mood and self-deprecating thoughts following eating binges

4. The bulimic episodes are not due to anorexia or any other known physical disorder

5. At least three of the following conditions: (a) consumption of high-caloric, easily digested food during a binge; (b) inconspicuous eating during a binge; (c) termination of such episodes by abdominal pain, sleep, social interruption, or self-induced vomiting; (d) repeated attempts to lose weight by severely restricted diets, self-induced vomiting, or

use of cathartics or diuretics; (e) frequent weight fluctuations greater than ten pounds due to alternating binges and fasts

Physical Problems

In addition to the symptoms above, anorexia and bulimia can also be accompanied by medical side effects. For anorexia, some of these symptoms may include feeling cold even in hot weather, fatigue and lack of energy, loss of menstruation, skin problems, inability to sweat, chilblains, swelling in the face, dehydration, and even gangrene of the fingertips.

Some of the physical symptoms associated with bulimia include sweating, breathlessness, rapid heartbeat, hot flashes, and many of the symptoms associated with anorexia listed above.

But perhaps the most dangerous physical result of any form of the Deadly Diet is the potential for an electrolyte imbalance. This is often discovered as a low potassium level. Low potassium is one of the most common causes of nocturnal cardiac arrest, and many of the deaths associated with the Deadly Diet are the result of cardiac arrest. Since an electrolyte imbalance can literally be a matter of life and death, it is of the utmost importance for anyone with an eating disorder to be under the care of a knowledgeable physician.

For three types of Deadly Diet—Fasting, Fasting-Purging, and Fasting-Binging—starvation is one of the key ingredients. Most people who fast think one thousand calories is the magic number to avoid. Deadly Dieters often go for half of that. In reality, most nutritionists and dieticians designate one thousand two hundred calories as the starvation cut-off.

The problem with fasting is that it dramatically decreases glycogen, fats, and proteins in the body. These elements are vital in the production of glucose, which is the basic energy source for all the body's systems. The body needs energy for its activities including organ function, not just physical exercise. To rob the energy storage areas is similar to living off the principal, rather than the interest, in your savings. If the principal (fat) is sufficient, you can live for a long time. Once the principal is gone, however, the interest is the only thing left and the process of self-destruction is inevitable. When a person decreases her energy input (starvation), the body goes through three fairly well-defined stages.

Stage one begins immediately. The day a person begins fasting the carbohydrate stores in the body begin to become depleted. Low glucose levels trigger a response in the body, which makes the pancreas begin to secrete glucagon in the liver which is then released into the body as glucose. This operation allows the body to continue functioning by keeping the energy at needed levels.

While this mechanism for replacing lost energy in the body is occurring, other events are taking place which are identified as the second stage of starvation. A special type of body fat, lipids, are the primary energy source for most body cells. The liver is one of the major organs for metabolizing fatty acids and when it does, the ketone bodies are produced in large quantities and transported to body and brain cells. Unfortunately, these cells can only use a finite amount of ketones, so the excess spills over into the blood and is known as a condition called ketosis. The excessive ketones in the blood result in a decrease in the pH of the blood. Eventually a problem called metabolic acidosis develops, which causes depression of the central nervous system and can eventually lead to coma. The length of this second stage depends on the amount of stored body fat.

When the fat stores are depleted, the third stage begins. This causes the proteins, which are needed to maintain cellular functioning, to break down as an energy source. When protein stores are depleted to about one-half their normal level, death usually results within twenty-four hours.

Nutrition

Many of my clients appear to be quite knowledgeable in nutrition, some even being nurses, registered dieticians, and nutritionists. In a sponsored study which appeared in the International Journal of Eating Disorders sixty-eight questions concerning nutrition were presented to people with eating disorders and people with normal eating habits. The results showed that Deadly Dieters knew more about nutrition in the areas of macronutrients, roughage, and calories. Both groups were about equally informed regarding questions of vitamins. The researchers concluded that people with eating disorders know how to eat well and care for their bodies. The problem is that they are unable to use information properly.

At the University of Michigan, Dr. Dean Krahn found that people with eating disorders consumed high levels of caffeine. He defined high daily caffeine intake as: fifteen cups of tea, or eight cups of coffee, or sixteen twelve-ounce sodas. His study seemed to indicate that the excessive caffeine might even worsen the behaviors of the Deadly Diet, such as binge eating and vomiting.

As already mentioned, it is very difficult for your body to get the nutrients it needs to maintain good health when you consume fewer than one thousand calories a day. To be sure you get all the nutrition your body requires, eat a diet that includes servings from each of the basic food groups. Rather than eliminating certain food groups or concentrating on just one or two food groups, it is better to keep a variety of foods in your diet but change the portion size. Your body also desperately needs fats in your diet. As you saw above, fats are essential for maintaining proper body functioning. Rather than eliminating them from your foods, you would be wiser to increase physical activity to help control body fat.

Eating Suggestions for Those with Bulimia

- Avoid "trigger foods" (those you associate with a binge) at first. These can be reintroduced later in your treatment. Instead, eat a nutrient-dense replacement that has some of the same pleasant characteristics.

- Eat three planned meals a day, rather than smaller, more frequent meals—this will help you to avoid binges.

- Eat foods that require the use of utensils, rather than eating finger foods. This will slow eating time and help increase meal satisfaction.

- Include generous portions of carbohydrate-containing foods.

- Include low-calorie items in each meal, such as vegetables, broth-based soup, salad, and/or fruit, to prolong the mealtime.

- Include adequate fat, which slows the emptying of food from the stomach to increase meal satisfaction.

- Eat a variety of foods at each meal.

- Eat all meals and snacks sitting down.

- Include hot or warm foods, rather than eating just cold or room-temperature foods.

- Plan meals ahead, using a food diary.

- Use foods that are naturally divided into portions, such as one potato (rather than rice or pasta); 4- and 8-ounce containers of yogurt, ice cream, or cottage cheese; precut steaks or chicken parts; and frozen dinners and entrees.

Eating Suggestions for Those with Anorexia Nervosa

- Eat small frequent meals to help reduce bloating.
- Begin to introduce fat into your diet, because fat is a necessary ingredient of good health.
- Eat foods cold or at room temperature to decrease early feelings of fullness.
- Eat finger foods, or snacks.
- Eat high-fiber foods to encourage good bowel habits.
- Limit fruits and vegetables because the soluble fiber they contain slows the emptying of food from the stomach and may make you feel bloated.
- Limit caffeine intake because it may interfere with normal appetite patterns.
- Take a multivitamin-multimineral supplement, as recommended by your physician or nutrition counselor.

Exercise

How much energy you dissipate during exercise is determined by your age, sex, height, weight, basal metabolic rate, dietary history, and level of physical activity. It is a common illusion among Deadly Dieters that you only burn energy when you are active. The basal metabolic rate is the amount of energy that your body uses when at rest. As you increase physical activity, you increase your basal metabolic rate and your lean tissue mass (muscle).

The best way to measure your basal metabolic rate, determine how many calories you need daily, and the amount of healthy exercise you need is to have yourself water-weighed by a reputable organization. By measuring your weight under water and checking your lung capacity, you can calculate how to be healthy. If you would like to approximate how many calories you need per day, complete the following steps:

Calculating Calories Needed

1. Calculate estimated ideal body weight: _____

    Men: 106 pounds for the first five feet of height plus 6 pounds for each additional inch

    Women: 100 pounds for the first five feet of height plus 5 pounds for each additional inch

2. Adjust your ideal body weight based on your frame size: _____

    Add 10% if you have a larger-than-average frame size

    Subtract 10% if you have a smaller-than-average frame size (keep in mind that this is just an estimation)

3. Daily calorie expenditure: _____ calories

    If sedentary: Ideal body weight x 13

    If moderately active: Ideal body weight x 15

    If active: Ideal body weight x 17

    If very active: Ideal body weight x 19

Deadly Dieter Profile

Our clinic has developed a profile that seems to fit many of the people who come to us for treatment. It should help you see the similarities between yourself and others who have been captured by the Deadly Diet. Complete the following survey and then read carefully the explanation of each profile characteristic.

Eating Disorder Profile

	Yes	No
1. Are you a worrier?	☐	☐
2. Are you a perfectionist?	☐	☐
3. Do you have a lot of stress in your life?	☐	☐
4. Do you ever feel like you're losing control?	☐	☐
5. Do you get nervous when your daily routine is upset?	☐	☐
6. Have you ever had a panic attack?	☐	☐
7. Do you talk to yourself a lot?	☐	☐
8. Do you have a poor self-image?	☐	☐
9. Are you ever concerned about what others think?	☐	☐
10. Which of the following emotions do you experience and how often?	☐	☐

	Never	Sometimes	Frequently
Depression	☐	☐	☐
Guilt	☐	☐	☐
Helplessness	☐	☐	☐
Resentment	☐	☐	☐
Unhealthy Anxiety	☐	☐	☐
Unreasonable Fear	☐	☐	☐

Explanation of the Profile

Worry. Worry is a Deadly Diet characteristic that has escaped professional attention. Yet every client I have seen at the clinic has been a worrier: a constant, chronic, unbelievable worrier. This is not your everyday variety of worry. When this kind of worrier isn't worried, she worries because she's not worrying. When friends are around, nobody else has to worry because the Deadly Dieter worries for everybody. Most clients say to me, "I don't remember a time in my life when I didn't worry. I can remember being four years old and worrying about something."

One of my clients remembered an incident that happened when she was seven years old. An earthquake, which occurred nine hundred miles from where she lived, caused her to worry about earthquakes for an entire year. Even when she was finally shown on a map how far away it had been, she still continued to worry. In fact, many Deadly Dieters grow up thinking that worry is the norm. When they become adults and realize that nobody else worries like they do, they begin to worry about being so different.

Perfectionism. Perfectionism does not mean that you always have a clean house or room all the time. Rather, it is a method of making decisions that stresses extreme options. As a perfectionist, when you have a task to do, you will either try to do it flawlessly or not at all. There is no middle ground. Few Deadly Dieters are full-time perfectionists, but most usually think that in one or two areas of their life things have to be "just so." Often these areas of perfectionism are associated with an overall sense of self-worth. By not allowing mistakes in these few areas, perfectionists can feel good about themselves in general and stay insulated from failures and mistakes in other areas. One woman who came to our clinic was admired by others for being able to get so many things done in a day and still do them so well. During therapy she came to realize this quality was really a manifestation of her wanting to be perfect in everything she did. Unfortunately, the perfectionism was controlling and ruining her life.

Stress. Many of my clients seem to have stress that never goes away. Never—despite yoga, biofeedback, or even hypnosis. In fact, their stress can be so common they learn to live with it and accept it as normal. Sometimes when I ask the question, "Do you have a lot of stress?" they will respond, "No, I don't think I do." With further questioning I find out that they suffer enormous amounts of stress and believe it is an inevitable part of their life. They may have headaches, insomnia, fatigue, or loss of concentration. See also the chapter on Stress in part V.

Control. The issue of control is just beginning to be recognized in psychology as a significant part of human behavior. Many of the therapists who first worked with the Deadly Diet thought that their clients were "too much in control." Even today, some therapists who work with Deadly Dieters think that the eating disorder is deliberately used to "control" or manipulate or use other people. This is the exact opposite of what is really happening. Deadly Dieters are hopelessly out of control; the last thing in the world they are able to control is their eating behavior. The central problem is that the eating controls them. Many of my clients will tell me, "Nobody really understands me when I tell them I feel out of control. They think I'm nuts, and sometimes I begin to wonder if maybe I really am going crazy."

Inflexibility. Many Deadly Dieters find themselves mentally planning their days and nights compulsively around food. When events occur that upset these plans, they get terribly nervous and irritable. It is often difficult for them to act spontaneously. They dread the unexpected for fear that something will happen to make them lose further control. Their ritualistic behavior is a means of trying to keep control of their life. One anoretic man told me that the moment he woke up in the morning he would begin thinking about food. He would mentally plan out his day— every event revolved around food and his avoidance of it. If he had to go some place where there might be food, he creatively figured out how to not get involved in the event. When he went to bed at night he knew that sleep was only a temporary relief from the same process, which would begin all over again the next morning.

Panic attacks. A panic attack is a stress reaction of terrifying proportions. About one-third of Deadly Dieters report having them. Most find that words are inadequate to describe the subjective reaction they have to a panic attack. One client put it this way: "It feels like you're going to die, you know you're not, but you wish you would." Deadly Dieters who have panic attacks find food even more disruptive than other Deadly Dieters. See also the chapter on Panic Attacks in part V.

Internal dialogue. Some of my clients are not initially aware of the mental battle that takes place continuously within their minds, but many do report the feeling of a constant debate going on inside their head. Others report no such internal conversations. With these individuals, the dialogue is so pervasive they are just not aware of it. One client told me that this internal dialogue "went on continually and never stopped," even when she tried hard to force herself to think of other things.

Self-image. When asked if they have a poor self-image, about nine out of ten Deadly Dieters will answer yes. I find this quite ironic, because they tend to have qualities admired by most people. They are often kind, considerate, personable, likable, bright, and creative. Deadly Dieters are very often looked up to and admired by others, and their poor self-image does not fit their high level of achievement. Although some professional therapists still see the Deadly Dieter as manipulative and generally unsuccessful in life, this is simply not true! See also the chapter on Body Image in part III.

Evaluation by others. Constant attention to what others think can become so habitual and obsessive that it often turns into a mental distortion called mind reading—"knowing" what others are thinking without any indication or confirmation from the other person. Of course, these evaluations always turn out to be negative. Even after receiving a compliment, one of my clients thought to herself, "They didn't really mean that. They just said it to be nice."

Destructive emotions. Although not all Deadly Dieters experience all six destructive emotions all of the time, these emotions still tend to be significant factors in the life of the Deadly Dieter. In fact, feelings such as depression are so common that many therapists misdiagnose the Deadly Diet as a depressive disorder. A middle-aged woman said that she had been to three psychiatrists and all of them had told her she was probably depressed and going through her mid-life crisis. They gave her pills to make her feel better. One therapist was so insistent that these emotions were the primary diagnosis that my client never mentioned her eating disorder to him again, even though she continued seeing this therapist for another year.

If, after reading the descriptions of the Deadly Dieter Profile, you have concluded that your eating behavior (or diet, if you prefer) may be controlling you rather than you controlling it, then you need help.

The most helpful treatment for Deadly Dieting is cognitive behavioral therapy. It teaches the Deadly Dieter:

- to accept personal responsibility for his or her actions
- to be a less-than-perfect person
- to effectively and independently solve personal problems
- to correct mental distortions about weight
- to be a growing and maturing individual
- to take risks and be vulnerable to life
- to identify his or her needs and get them met
- to take complete control of his or her life

Eating Disorders as Phobias

Originally, very few people working with Deadly Diet clients noticed the similarity to phobic individuals. Since the early '70s there have been more people who have observed how Deadly Diets tend to be phobic in nature. In 1983 a group of researchers in British Columbia, Canada, did a comparative study between Deadly Dieters, phobics, and people with obsessive-compulsive problems. Although this study concluded that Deadly Diets were more like an obsessive-compulsive disorder, it was apparent from the discussion of what phobias were like that the researchers did not really understand the thoughts and feelings of the person suffering from a severe phobia.

The "official" definition of a phobia is "a persistent, irrational fear of, and compelling desire to avoid, an object or situation." The person using the Deadly Diet is also controlled by an irrational, overwhelming, runaway fear—that of getting fat! If you ask a Deadly Dieter what she fears most in life, she will say, "gaining weight" or "getting fat," even though "fat" may mean only one-half pound. The person with a phobia avoids things that bring on unhealthy anxiety; likewise, the Deadly Dieter avoids things related to food that can bring on extreme anxiety. These anxieties are pervasive and tend to intrude into the person's life on a regular basis.

The similarities between the Deadly Dieter and the person with a severe phobia fall into four categories: mental distortions, high stress levels, destructive emotions, and rituals (avoidance behaviors).

Mental distortions. One of the foremost features common to both problems is the intense worry that characterizes the person's daily thought life. Both Deadly Diets and phobias involve destructive self-statements such as the "what ifs," "shoulds," and the use of absolutist words such as "never" and "always." Both groups of people are intensely worried about what other people think of them. In fact, this one thought is often the driving force behind avoidance behaviors. Perfectionism in phobics and Deadly Dieters results from the mistaken idea that a person's worth is equal to his or her behavior. Therefore, the person cannot allow herself to make a mistake for fear of being proven worthless. Another chronic worry is the conviction of poor self-image. The irony is that while the person is convinced that she is worthless, she compulsively strives to behave "perfectly" in order that others will not see her total imperfection.

High stress. Extreme levels of stress are also common for both Deadly Dieters and people with phobias. The evidence for this stress is often seen in headaches, insomnia, hyperventilation, or panic attacks. The stress makes it difficult for the person with a phobia or Deadly Diet to learn even the most basic skills for working on her problems. Ironically, few people with these problems have tried to do anything about the stress—other than, perhaps, exercise—and some don't even know what techniques are available for the reduction of stress. Some of the more common methods people have tried for dealing with stress are medication, biofeedback, yoga, and meditation. Many times these techniques work for a while and then lose their effectiveness because the person stops practicing the skills.

Destructive emotions. The third similarity between phobias and eating disorders is the presence of destructive emotions. What was pointed out earlier about misdiagnosing depression for the Deadly Diet holds equally for phobias. Many people with phobias have been classified as neurotic, hysterical, depressed, and even "schizoid." In addition to depression, almost all people with phobias and Deadly Diets tend to feel guilty a great portion of the time. They tend to take on the unrealistic expectations of others and society in general. A feeling of helplessness and being trapped is also very common. This feeling occurs when the person's options begin to narrow down so that very few choices are left for everyday decisions. Anxiety and fear are also destructive emotions common to both phobias and Deadly Diets. In fact, all of these emotions are so common that when a Deadly Dieter and a person with a phobia meet for the first time and get beyond their behavioral differences, they are amazed at how similar their problems tend to be. When we combine both populations into a treatment group, the Deadly Dieter can empathize with those who have phobias, while those with phobias can understand what happens internally to those suffering from the Deadly Diet.

Rituals. The final similarity is the existence of ritualistic coping behaviors. These usually involve some type of situational avoidance. In the case of the Deadly Dieter it means avoiding the effects of food on her body. The faster simply doesn't put much in, while the binger-purger tries to take it back out as fast as she puts it in. The phobic will often avoid a broader range of situations: high places, freeways, elevators, large crowds, certain animals or insects. It is not uncommon, however, for both groups of people to avoid many social situations. If the problem has continued for any length of time, social avoidance can be common for both groups of people.

The Control Cycle

As has been stated, being out of control is THE major feature of the Deadly Diet. For some, the feeling of lack of control is just concerned with eating and weight control. For others, it seems that everything in their life is out of control.

Every Deadly Diet consists of five basic components that together comprise the Control Cycle. They are: (1) environmental triggers, (2) destructive thoughts, (3) high stress, (4) ineffective coping behaviors, and (5) destructive emotions. These are interrelated to one another as illustrated in the diagram on the next page.

Situation. The situation refers to anything out there that triggers the Control Cycle. Of course, for the Deadly Dieter the trigger is usually something to do with food. Eating is a large part of our culture that is built into our social habits, and there are a lot of triggers in life for the Deadly Dieter. How many times have you socialized with someone and not had something to eat or drink? These external triggers set off characteristic worries, destructive self-statements, doubts, and self-attacks.

Thoughts. The worry, the kicking of self, the old painful memories that suddenly erupt are a habit that feels like a totally independent entity. It seems independent because people with Deadly Diets tend to be quite intelligent and "know" that most of the worries and irrational thoughts are meaningless. Many people have told me that they wished they didn't worry so much but that they "just can't help it." To even dream of a life without worry is to engage in a fantasy of immense proportions. The chronic worry, in turn, is responsible for two more things happening: stress and destructive emotions.

Stress. You will notice on the diagram that stress is internally generated, not externally generated. In other words, stress comes about because of what you think, not because of what is happening to you. We know this to be true because some people can be relaxed and calm in the most distressing circumstances, while others can be coming apart at the seams in the mildest situations. Remember that stress is not an emotion, but a physiological event that can influence the type of behaviors we use to cope with life.

Emotions. The worry also causes one or more destructive emotions. These emotions in turn add more stress to the body. But they also compel a person to engage in some type of coping behavior to counteract the feelings of unpleasant emotions and high stress.

Behavior. When you are feeling highly emotional and your body is feeling stressed, you are generally in a high discomfort zone. This off-balance experience motivates you to do something in order to "feel better." What you eventually do is get caught in ritualistic behaviors. For example, when you feel bored, your reflex reaction might be to binge; when you have a stress headache, you might be even less likely to eat even your self-imposed five hundred calorie limit. Avoidance behavior is one of the most common rituals. Not eating is an obvious example of avoidance for the faster. The binger-purger is often involved in a double-avoidance ritual. She may eat to avoid "feeling bad" and then purge herself in order to avoid feeling guilty for binging.

Often avoidance becomes an entire lifestyle. The person will avoid anything that presents a conflict, anything that can cause pain. A psychologist from Canada has coined the phrase "discomfort dodging" to describe this experience. Over a period of time, people who tend to avoid life's friction become passive, nonassertive persons, and this avoidance in turn causes them to worry even more.

The problem with Deadly Diets is not primarily the behavior, even though the behavior is what tells others that something is wrong. The problem illustrated by the Control Cycle is that ritual behaviors can bring the person right back to the top of the cycle: more worry, and on around the cycle in a never-ending pattern. For example, after a person has avoided food or binged and purged, she will often engage in a series of destructive evaluations of herself that will continue the cycle indefinitely.

When shown this cycle, people with Deadly Diets say, "That is exactly how I feel. I feel like I am going around in circles, like my life is a merry-go-round and I can't get off." The situation triggers worry, worry triggers stress and destructive emotions, the emotions add to the stress, and then the person spends considerable time ineffectively coping with the problem—which then starts all over again.

Joan had been struggling with bulimia for over five years and had found herself caught up in this vicious cycle of out-of-controlness. Even though she could go for a couple of weeks at a time without binging, when it did happen she felt as if she had absolutely no control of what was taking place. The situational triggers for Joan often revolved around her mother, who tended to call her several times a day from the other side of town and inquire into the private affairs of her family. After some of these conversations, she became very upset but said nothing to her mother. Her husband was finally tired of hearing about the problem and had told her to be more assertive with her mother. When the control cycle was finally analyzed it was found that the telephone conversations with her mother triggered several thematic thoughts: "I resent my mother implying that I don't know how to run my family. But if I were to say anything to her, she would get upset and I would feel guilty. It is sure unfair that my mother and I cannot have a good relationship." These thoughts often were stressful enough to bring on a severe headache, either by itself or along with the feelings of depression, guilt, and helplessness. When either of these things occurred, she would secretly binge and vomit her food. When this ritual was completed, she would start putting herself down for what she had just done and telling herself that she should know better. This in turn triggered more guilt and stress. Joan was now caught up in the vicious out-of-control cycle.

Three Basic Skills

The endless nature of the Control Cycle is what makes Deadly Diets so terrifying. No matter what you do, you wind up in the same place. When you get caught in this vicious cycle, you spend all your energy going around in circles. Life becomes a treadmill, and you live it like a hamster running on a wheel that never goes anywhere.

The goal is to help you break this cycle by teaching you how to change the three points on the circle, which keep perpetuating the problem. Turn back to the diagram of the Control Cycle and refer to it as I discuss these three skills, starting with stress and moving counterclockwise.

Reduce stress. The first skills you will learn will be those you need to reduce stress. Since stress can impair your memory and learning abilities, it is important that this be the first skill you learn and practice. For detailed instructions in Progressive Muscle Relaxation, see the chapter on Stress in part V.

Cognitive change. The next set of skills comes from the new field in psychology called "cognitive therapy." These skills are designed to change the way you think. As you can see from the Control Cycle, your thoughts have tremendous influence over the rest of your life. In fact, they act as a bridge between what is outside of you and what happens inside of you. We all know intuitively that we are what we think, and yet we have never been shown how to change the way we think when it becomes destructive. How many times have you been told to "change your attitude" and felt helpless even though you knew it was a good idea? Mankind has been trying to change attitudes for thousands of years, but it was not until the 1970s that we began to develop the tools to do exactly that. For the first time in the history of the human race we now have the rudimentary tools for making dramatic changes in our lives by learning how to stop our negative and destructive thinking processes. This approach to the Deadly Diet is almost exclusively devoted to changing your thinking. When you change your thinking, your old habitual eating patterns won't change instantly. But they will change. Those thoughts, which filter out what goes on around you and which interpret your experiences, have a direct bearing on your eating behavior.

Behavior change. The last skill you will learn is the one to be the most concerned about. Your eating behavior is public and highly visible. Consequently, most people around you see your behavior as "the problem." How many times have others told you to "just eat more" or "stop that stupid binging and barfing." Yet you know that the eating is not the real problem. Attempts to change that focus only on the behavior are doomed because the other components of the Control Cycle have not been dealt with. To change your behavior without changing your thoughts or stress level would be like trying to put out a fire by throwing gasoline on it. It only gets worse!

The skill of behavior change is also the most scary one because it is the final step in which you have to put all your other skills into practice. It is like moving from the practice session to the stage in front of a real audience. Many people balk at this point because of what we call the plateau effect. By the time you have reached the stage dealing with your actual behavior, much of your emotional pain will have been modified so that your daily life will have reached a plateau of relative comfort. Pain is a wonderful motivator, and without it many people find it difficult to make changes. When you have learned to change your destructive thoughts, it will be tempting to "take a break" from reaching your goal and to subtly and gradually begin to stop working on the problem. Beware! The plateau is not flat, but slopes backward. If you stop work at this point, you are almost assured of having a major setback that will discourage you from continuing your progress.

Three Myths

People on the Deadly Diet generally go through life believing three myths about themselves. These myths are quite powerful and can affect the way you live, your lifestyle, and your relationship to others.

MYTH 1: "I'm the only person in the world with this problem."

Some Deadly Dieters may actually not know at least one other person with the same problem. But with the current media attention focused on this problem, it is difficult to imagine that a person could believe this myth. One reason this myth is still powerful is the high denial factor that exists with Deadly Dieters. It is very common for clients to deny vehemently that they have anorexia or bulimia, while everyone around them can plainly see the problem. Although they deny the presence of the Deadly Diet, they still insist that no one else has a problem like they have, and that consequently no one can really understand or sympathize with them. If finally forced to admit that they are a Deadly Dieter, they will retreat to the conviction that "My problem is unique and totally different from the type of Deadly Diet anyone else has."

The other factor that contributes to this myth is that people don't talk about this problem in public. In many cases, it is now socially acceptable to talk about quite personal and intimate details of our lives. Few people are shocked to hear someone talking about a sexual problem, an intimate detail of their marriage, or surgery they have had. Yet it would be inappropriate for someone at a party to volunteer information about his or her Deadly Diet. This topic is rarely discussed because only another Deadly Dieter really understands it. This lack of understanding in the general population makes the Deadly Diet a very isolating problem. The person on the Deadly Diet usually begins to draw further and further away from social contact, which in turn further reinforces the myth that he or she is the only one with the problem.

MYTH 2: "My problem is incurable."

The word "incurable" is the wrong word here. The Deadly Diet has no "cure" because it is not really a medical problem. Since it is not biological in nature, there is no germ, virus, or bacteria that can be eradicated. The Deadly Diet can have medical side effects, but the basic problem is a learned condition, a psychological condition. The Deadly Dieter can recover by learning to deal with the problem. In this sense, being on the Deadly Diet is similar to having a problem with alcohol. It's an addiction and a handicap that may last a lifetime. But the important thing to remember is this: The solution isn't to "cure" the person, but rather to learn how to cope with the problem. Our work at the clinic has shown beyond a doubt that Deadly Diets can be brought under control.

MYTH 3: "I must be crazy or soon will be."

Once a person is absolutely convinced that she is the only person in the world with this problem and that this problem is untreatable and incurable, this third myth is unavoidable. It is very common for Deadly Dieters to believe that something is drastically wrong with them emotionally. Sometimes they are afraid that if people knew of their problem they would be sent away to a psychiatric hospital. The irony here is that people on the Deadly Diet are not only quite sane, but also generally have qualities that are admired, adored, and coveted by others. They tend to be energetic, bright, intelligent, and imaginative. Many are talented in the arts. Many of the young women with Deadly Diets are excellent students.

If you are a Deadly Dieter, it's very important to know that you are not going to go crazy! You may feel like you are losing your grasp on reality, especially if other people don't understand the problem. But remember—you are a normal person with a very difficult problem.

The most effective treatment for eating disorders is cognitive behavioral therapy. For detailed instructions in this therapy, see the chapters on Uncovering Automatic Thoughts and Changing Patterns of Limited Thinking in part V.

Excerpted and adapted with permission from *The Deadly Diet, Second Edition* by Terrence J. Sandbek, Ph.D. For more information on this and related books, see the "Further Reading" section in the back of the book.

CHAPTER 16

Body Image

The way that we feel about our bodies can positively or negatively affect our self-esteem. While we're bombarded with societal messages about how we should look, it is possible to uncover any negative beliefs we may have about our bodies and challenge those beliefs. This chapter will help you uncover any negative beliefs that are hindering your self-acceptance and enjoyment of your body.

The Psychology of Physical Appearance

A few years ago, I surveyed over a hundred people and asked them: "What do you see when you look in the mirror?" Some typical responses:

What I see is a body I regret to call my own. I wasn't fond of it as a child. I really disliked it as a teenager. My twenty-five adult years have been constant contempt of my ugly fat body. I would trade it in for almost anything.

(White man, age forty-five)

What I see I really hate. I hate my thighs. I hate my butt. My mouth is too big. My eyes are too big. My hair is too straight. I wish I didn't have to spend so much time on my looks. Tomorrow I'll start working out.

(White woman, age twenty-five)

What I try to see (but can't) is what I dream about being: Rich! Rich enough to afford to have plastic surgery on my nose and to have my teeth fixed plus a chin implant. Rich enough to have my makeup and hair done professionally. Then, there are the fashionable clothes. Dream on! I'm always going to be a plain Jane.

(White woman, age thirty-three)

I see an average-looking dude. I wish I was bigger. I wish my hair was fuller. I wish I was a couple of inches taller. Why am I kidding myself? I'm less than an average-looking dude. I'd settle for average.

(African-American man, age twenty-six)

Unfortunately, most of the comments I received didn't reveal a very favorable body image. What about your own reflections? Using the following Helpsheet, carry out a self-discovery exercise in your mirror.

Self-Discovery Helpsheet: Reflections in My Mirror

Alone, in the privacy of your room, stand in front of a full-length mirror. Describe what you see when you look in the mirror.

_____

_____

_____

_____

What thoughts run through your mind as you look at your reflection?

_____

_____

_____

_____

How do you feel as you look at your reflection?

_____

_____

Looking at Looks: The Inside View is What Counts

Being objectively good-looking does not guarantee a positive body image, just as homeliness does not dictate a lifetime of self-loathing. In 1986, I appeared on ABC-TV's *20/20* news program to discuss my research on the psychology of physical appearance. Reporter John Stossel also interviewed professional models, both men and women, about how they felt about their beautiful bodies. Here were people who are prototypes of what many of us wish to look like, yet most of them were self-critical. They zeroed in on specific physical features that really bugged them. Their candid comments and complaints conveyed a fundamental truth that research has also confirmed: Your body image has little to do with your outward appearance. Body image is really a state of mind.

Body image problems spawn other problems in living. The following are some of the most frequent troubles. How much do they apply to you?

- A poor body image often lowers self-esteem. Poor self-esteem means feeling inadequate as a person; it means you have low self-worth. Studies confirm that as much as one-fourth to one-third of your self-esteem is related to how positive or negative your body image is. If you don't like your body, it's difficult to like the person who lives there—you!

- Body image is integral to gender identity—your feelings of manliness or masculinity, or your feelings of womanliness or femininity. Some people believe that they don't have the physical qualities necessary to experience themselves as particularly masculine or feminine. This can diminish their sense of acceptability as a person.

- A negative body image can cause interpersonal anxiety. If you can't accept your looks, you most likely assume others don't like your looks either. As a result, you feel self-conscious and inadequate in some of your social interactions.

- If your physical self-consciousness spills into your sexually intimate relationships, it can jeopardize your sexual fulfillment. If you believe your naked body is ugly or unacceptable, sex becomes anxiety producing. Sex researchers and therapists know that one cause of sexual difficulties is spectatoring—a self-conscious scrutiny of one's own body during sex instead of immersion in the sensate experience itself. By dwelling on worries about your attractiveness or on maneuvers to hide your body from your partner's view or touch, sex becomes an act of apprehension and avoidance. If you switch off the lights to cloak your body in darkness, you may be switching off your pleasure as well!

- *Depression* and a negative body image are often intertwined. Depression can lead people to detest their looks and vice versa. Self-disparagement and thoughts of hopelessness and helplessness about what you look like are depressing. In turn, this despondency, like quicksand, can further trap you in self-criticisms of your body. It's a vicious cycle of despair.

- A negative body image can bring about *eating disturbances*, such as anorexia nervosa or bulimia nervosa. These are problems that gradually build over time. If you worry that you look fat, you may diet and exercise to excess. Scientific studies reveal that chronic dieting may lead to binge eating, which can precipitate purging (vomiting). Not only does having a negative, "fat phobic" body image predispose disturbed patterns of eating, but having an eating disorder undermines body image. Changing a negative body image is as important to preventing eating disorders as it is to conquering them.

Origins of a Negative Body Image

People don't just wake up one day to the conviction that they cannot stand their looks. They've usually felt this way for quite some time. Body image forms gradually, beginning in childhood. Here is a diagram of the origins of a negative body image:

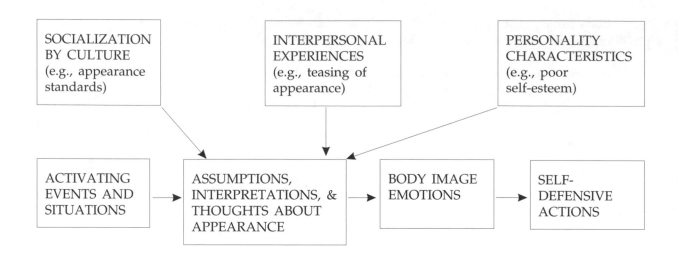

Socialization by Culture

Your basic sense of identity is rooted in your experience of being embodied. The body is a boundary between you and everything that is not you. By the age of two years, most children have self-awareness and can recognize their physical self as a reflection in the mirror. More and more, their bodily being comes to represent who they are in their own eyes. And they begin to reflect upon how other people view their appearance.

Preschool children have already started to learn how society views various physical characteristics. Little kids know that lovely Cinderella wins the handsome prince; her ugly and mean stepsisters lose out. They know that Barbie and Ken have the good life, with bodies to match. Body image takes shape as children absorb conceptions of what is valued as attractive—how they should look. Kids also form images of what is not attractive—how they should not look. Most importantly, they judge their own bodily appearance—how well does it live up to the shoulds? The answer affects feelings of self-worth.

From the word go, society dictates social values and the meanings of physical appearance. For example, it teaches that well-toned thinness for women and tallness and muscularity for men are desirable. Let's briefly take a closer look at the lessons we are taught by our culture.

My Fair Lady

The worship of thinness hasn't occurred in some cultures to the extent that it has in Western society. Societies in which food is scarce, for example, view a heavier body as evidence of successful survival. In earlier times, a full-figured physique was the epitome of feminine beauty. Rounded hips and thighs of prehistoric goddesses symbolized feminine fertility. In the art of the fifteenth to eighteenth centuries, full-bodied women were the standard of beauty. In the ancient Orient, a fat wife was such a symbol of honor for her husband that some men force-fed their wives to enhance their own social standing.

In the twentieth century, however, a thinner and less curvaceous body type has increasingly been promoted as the standard of feminine attractiveness. Fashion models, film stars, and beauty pageant contestants have become thinner, even as the female population has gotten heavier. As rates of anorexia nervosa and bulimia nervosa have steadily increased, emaciated "waif" models appear on magazine covers and in television ads. The broadcasted messages are not only "thin is in and feminine," but also that today's woman needs to look fit and strong as well. And as reflected in the prevalence of breast augmentation surgery and the record sales of the Wonder Bra, shapely breasts have become more important to the cultural ideal.

For the sake of beauty, women in our society are told to shave or wax their legs and arm-pits, pluck their eyebrows, dye and either curl or straighten their hair, pierce their ears, paint their faces and all twenty nails, and walk around in uncomfortable high heels. Women are also told that they should worry about unsightly age spots, split ends, the sprouting of a single gray hair, a chipped nail, and a visible panty line. Who can wonder why so many girls and women find so many things faulty about their looks!

The Handsome Prince

Though less demanding than women's appearance standards, societal norms and expecta-tions definitely exist for men. Guys are supposed to be tall, have broad shoulders, a muscular chest and biceps, a small rear, strong facial features, and a full head of hair. Most "manly heroes" and "leading men" are handsome hunks—Arnold Schwarzenegger, Denzel Washington, Tom Cruise, Kevin Costner, Richard Gere, Brad Pitt, Michael Jordan, Sylvester Stallone, Superman. John "Duke" Wayne protected his masculine, "stand tall" image by refusing to appear "topless" in public—that is, without his hairpiece.

These masculine body image prescriptions lead some boys and men to jeopardize their health with steroid abuse and excessive exercise. Now more than ever before, men seek cosmetic surgery, including hair transplants, pectoral implants, face lifts, and liposuction. Men, too, feel growing pressures to be physically attractive, believing that good looks are a prerequisite for suc-ceeding in relationships and life in general.

In various cultures at various times, attractiveness has required decorative scars on the face, a shaved head, tattoos fully covering the body, jewels placed in holes drilled in the teeth, large disks inserted in the lips, stacked rings to elongate the neck, and the maiming of women's feet to make them petite. All these things have been done, and most still are, in service of societal stan-dards of attractiveness.

Just as you may dismiss foreign appearance standards as "really crazy," I urge you to begin to question the mandates of our own culture. Who are the appearance masters that you feel obliged to serve? To defend yourself against these unhealthy messages, think about these two crucial facts:

- *Societal standards can't harm you unless you buy into them.* You don't have to adopt these ideals and pressure yourself to live up to them. You don't have to allow your sense of self-worth to be determined by voices not of your choosing.

- *Other people don't judge you as harshly as you judge yourself.* Many people demand more physical "perfection" of themselves than they think others expect of them, and even more than others truly expect. People are often out of touch with reality. Men are often more appreciative of a heavier female body type than women believe men are. Guys don't ide-alize blonde beauty to the degree women assume. Likewise, lots of women don't worship the same narrow images of "macho" male attractiveness that men assume women do.

Interpersonal Experiences

In the development of an unhappy body image, the media aren't the only messengers. There are other voices as well—those of peers, parents, and other loved ones.

Your family has most likely taught you about your own body. How many times have you heard this: "You're not really going to leave the house looking like that, are you?" Parents remind you to brush your hair, put on clean clothes with patterns and colors that don't clash, and stay trim. Families also communicate expectations by what psychologists call modeling. For example, if you grow up with a parent or sibling who constantly complains about his or her appearance, you learn that looks can be something to worry about. If you have a brother or sister doted on for being attractive, you may come to feel shortchanged by your looks. You may feel resentful and envious that you aren't as nice-looking.

Being repeatedly criticized, taunted, or teased about your appearance during the childhood or teen years can leave a lasting effect on body image development. Many adults who dislike their appearance can recall experiences of being teased or criticized as children because of their looks. Deeply etched in their memories are episodes of rebuke or ridicule for being too chubby or too skinny, too tall or too short, for having a large nose or big ears, or for how they dressed or wore their hair.

The human body changes dramatically at puberty. This time can also bring intense preoccupation with these changes and with physical appearance in general. Having the "right" body type, clothes, or hairstyle becomes far more important than algebra or geography. The relative timing of physical maturation can be pivotal in body image development. Girls whose hips and breasts develop earlier than those of their classmates may feel self-conscious. They don't appreciate their new shape as a sign of approaching womanhood. Many girls can only see it as grotesque fat. Boys whose spurt in height and muscularity is slower than that of their peers may privately worry that their body will never catch up.

The teen years are a tough time for body image. Teenagers' feelings of social adequacy depend in part on how they think their appearance is perceived by peers and how that will affect their chances in the dating game. One common occurrence during adolescence is facial acne. Acne can have a profound effect on body image and social adjustment.

Bodies don't stand still. They change naturally over time. You are able to control some aspects of your appearance—for example, you can get a new hairstyle or choose what clothes to wear. But other changes are beyond your complete control. For better or worse, heredity and life events influence your looks. Take hereditary pattern hair loss for instance. My own scientific research indicates that some folks—men and women—feel helplessly unhappy about their progressively thinning locks, while others just take it in stride—"hair today, gone tomorrow."

People also struggle to cope with their altered appearance following traumas, such as a mastectomy or severe facial burns. These unwanted changes certainly challenge one's body image. But the inspiring fact is that many of these people come to accept such drastic changes, incorporate them in a healthy body image, and move forward in their lives.

I want you to appreciate the important point I'm conveying here: How your body appears on the outside does not have to determine how you feel on the inside. Among people born with a disfiguring condition, some agonize that they don't look "normal," yet many others have little difficulty "looking different." Some folks whose appearance you envy are more unhappy with their looks than you would assume. Your appearance doesn't mandate how you must feel. If you're faced with unwelcome changes in your appearance, understand that it is possible to accept and accommodate the changes. This program will teach you how to accept your body—no matter what.

Personality Characteristics

The arrows of adversity aimed at us by our culture, family, or peers do not affect everyone's body image identically. Some of us have been able to transcend ill effects of our culture's prescriptions, our peers' teasing, our pimples on prom night, and even disfiguring conditions. Who are these resilient people?

They are people with solid self-esteem—they believe in themselves. Self-esteem is a powerful ally in facing and defeating life's challenges. The child, adolescent, or adult who has a secure sense of self—as being competent, lovable, and invested in hope and in living—doesn't so easily fall prey to societal shoulds or assaults on his or her physical worth. Self-fulfillment doesn't rely on aspirations for a perfect appearance.

On the other hand, people whose nature and nurture have handed them a basic sense of inadequacy are all too eager to find fault with themselves. Their infection of inner insecurity easily spreads to their "outer" self.

Although poor self-esteem can pave the way for developing a negative body image, it's only a predisposition—it's not a predestination. Learning to improve body image is possible for everyone. If your self-esteem is as negative as your body image, working on improving your self-esteem can benefit your body image as well. In fact, a colleague and I recently tested this proposition by studying the body image changes among people who completed a self-help program for enhancing self-esteem, without ever focusing on body image per se. Guess what? Their body images got better!

Current Causes

Social conditioning, past experiences, and personality traits can certainly program you to develop a negative body image. But history isn't everything. Even more important are the current causes—the here-and-now factors that affect your body image experiences in everyday life. These influences can propagate and reinforce your personal body image distress, or they can extricate you from your past programming. If past conditioning was omnipotent, a positive body image would be practically impossible. Yet, as you've learned, most people find ways to transcend the lessons of the past and accept their overall appearance, despite physical imperfections.

Inherently, human beings are "explainers." Moving beyond the past, however, requires that you relinquish explaining your complaining. Perhaps nothing is more upsetting than to be upset and not understand why. So, you search for the reasons you do what you do and feel what you feel. You explain your misery to yourself. You point the finger of blame at your dysfunctional family, tactless friends, lousy genes, hormonal fluctuations, bad luck, or astrological sign. Blaming your past or forces outside of your control may help you justify having a problem, but it doesn't help you solve it. Instead you conclude you are a helpless victim and you try to change nothing.

Change can only occur if you take responsibility for the choices you make today. After all, today is tomorrow's history, and that's history you can do something about. Taking responsibility for change starts with a simple realization: You feel what you think. Your judgments and interpretations of events, not the events themselves, govern your emotional reactions. You feel what you think. Your body image emotions also are driven by your thoughts, not by your actual appearance directly. Change how you *think* about your body and you change how you *feel* about it.

Learning Your Body Image ABCs

You probably have some episodes that repeat themselves like a broken record. Take some time now to recollect several recent episodes of body image distress, ones that you expect to recur. You will identify the following three elements of each episode and record them in your Body Image Diary. These three elements make up the ABC Sequence, as depicted in the diagram below.

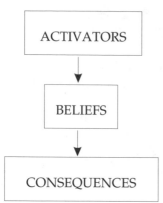

ACTIVATORS — What specific events and situations trigger your thoughts and feelings about your body?

BELIEFS — What thoughts, perceptions, and interpretations are occurring in your mind?

CONSEQUENCES — How are you reacting emotionally? How are you reacting behaviorally?

- *A* stands for the *Activators*. What events activated or triggered your negative feelings about your looks? In your diary, you'll write down a brief description of the particular situation and occurrences that immediately preceded your distress. Be specific.

- *B* stands for your *Beliefs*—your perceptions and interpretations of the activating event. What thoughts were running through your mind at the time? Try to replay the tape—the mental conversation you were having with yourself. How were you viewing the situation? What were you saying to yourself about the events? Recalling your thoughts out of their actual context can be difficult. Remind yourself by filling in the blank: "I was thinking _____ ," or "I was probably thinking _____ ."

- *C* stands for the *Consequences* of your thoughts and perceptions. How did you react emotionally? How did you react behaviorally?

In your diary, you will describe the Consequences in terms of the TIDE of the episode. I use TIDE as an acronym that will help you analyze the four essential aspects of consequences that occur.

- *T* stands for the *Types* of emotions you felt in the situation. Anxiety? Anger? Depression? Shame? Disgust? Envy? Embarrassment? Identify the feeling or feelings that you had.

- *I* stands for the *Intensity* of your emotions. Rate their strength at their peak, from 0 for "not at all intense" to 10 for "extremely intense."

- *D* stands for the episode's *Duration*. How long did your distress last? About how many minutes or hours did it take before you felt noticeably better?

- Finally, the *E* stands for the *Effects* of the episode on your behavior. Your actions at this point are often reflexive efforts to cope with or defend yourself against your unwanted emotions. Did you try to get out of the situation? Did you become sullen and withdraw? Did you attempt to fix or conceal the part of your body that you were bothered about? Did you take your feelings out on others? Did you take them out on yourself?

The more types of emotions you feel with greater intensity for a longer duration and with more behavioral effects, the more powerful the episode—like being caught up in a turbulent TIDE.

The Body Image Diary

Date _____

ABC Sequence

ACTIVATORS (Triggering events and situations):

_____

_____

_____

_____

BELIEFS (Thoughts and interpretations of the situation):

_____

_____

_____

_____

CONSEQUENCES (Emotional TIDE):

Types of Emotions: _____

_____

Intensity of Emotions (0 to 10): _____

Duration of the Episode: _____

Effects of the episode on your behavior: _____

_____

_____

_____

How to Keep Your Body Image Diary

A personal Body Image Diary is an essential tool for learning to like your looks. It helps you in monitoring, dissecting, and recording the ABC Sequences of your negative body image episodes.

Complete a Body Image Diary for as many different recent episodes of distress as possible. To become more skilled in identifying your body image ABCs, over the next several days, analyze and enter ten or more recent episodes. For each, mentally recreate the experience. Close your eyes and picture the situation. Replay your "tape" of the episode—the triggering events, your thoughts, your emotions, and your actions.

After analyzing the ABC Sequence and Emotional TIDE of past episodes, you'll be ready for current self-monitoring. For four or five days, monitor any episode as it occurs. Don't try to change the episode; just mentally monitor its ABCs as they unfold. Afterward, as soon as possible, make a diary entry.

Where to Go from Here

The next step is to challenge and change the negative beliefs you uncover in your diary. For detailed instructions in cognitive techniques, see the chapter on Changing Patterns of Limited Thinking in part V.

Excerpted and adapted with permission from *The Body Image Workbook: An 8-Step Program for Learning to Like Your Looks* by Thomas F. Cash, Ph.D. For more information on this and related books, see the "Further Reading" section in the back of the book.

CHAPTER 17

Alcohol and Drugs

When we have problems with alcohol and/or drug use, it can have a devastating impact on those around us, as well as ourselves. This chapter can help you assess whether or not you have a drug or alcohol problem, as well as guide you through the first steps of combating any substance abuse issues.

Do You Have a Problem?

Has anybody ever told you that you drink or drug too much?

☐ Yes

☐ No

Do others have a different opinion about your drinking or drugging behavior than you do?

☐ Yes

☐ No

If you answered *Yes* to either question, you may very well have a problem. Others can usually see harmful alcohol or drug use before you do.

Do you yourself sometimes think that alcohol, cocaine, marijuana, pain pills, or some other drug is causing problems in your life?

☐ Yes

☐ No

A *Yes* here is even stronger evidence that you have a problem, and that it's time to take action. Since alcohol and drugs tend to make you ignore or minimize danger signs, the mere suspicion that you might have a problem means that a very real problem has probably existed for some time.

If you answered *Yes* to any of these three questions, you should read on to explore in greater detail.

What Exactly Is Your Problem?

There are many names for problems with alcohol and other drugs: alcoholism, addiction, problem drinking, dipsomania, chemical dependency, drug abuse, substance dependence, and so on. Many terms and definitions have been proposed by medical doctors, psychologists, social workers, researchers, hospitals, insurance companies, the courts, and other interested parties.

Regardless of what you call your problem, you can safely assume that it's serious, and that you need to quit, if you demonstrate any one of these danger signs:

- You drink or drug too much or too often

- You can't keep promises to yourself about your use of alcohol or drugs

- Your use has endangered your life, job, relationships, or freedom

- You've developed a tolerance for alcohol or your drug of choice

- You have withdrawal symptoms when you stop using

The Crucial Difference Between Abuse and Dependence

Recent research shows that there are actually two distinct kinds of drug or alcohol problems: abuse and dependence. The crucial difference between them is whether you retain control over your drinking or drugging.

For example, George liked to party, especially on the weekends. From early Friday night to the wee hours of Sunday morning, he was on a tear. Monday mornings he often called in sick, or dragged in very late. His boss put him on probation. He was arrested for drunk driving one Saturday night, and lost his driver's license. His girlfriend moved out.

As bad as all this was, George's tolerance for alcohol remained about the same as it had been in high school—he didn't drink much more than he had in his earliest drinking years. He got a killer hangover every Monday morning; but, when it passed, he felt pretty good. He didn't get the shakes or the DTs, or need the hair of the dog the morning after.

George abused alcohol, but he did not develop the primary symptom of alcohol dependence—an inability to control his use. He had the problem of alcohol abuse, but not the disease of alcohol dependence. His drinking was a matter of choice and long habit, learned over the years; but he retained the ability to modify his drinking with willpower and reason. His path to recovery required him to make behavioral changes based on increased awareness, more accurate information, the lessons of adverse consequences, positive peer pressure, and just growing older and wiser.

On the other side of the coin, there was Jill, a part-time data processor and the devoted mother of two small children. Jill always showed up to work on time, kept a neat, clean house, and reliably picked her kids up at the day-care center every afternoon. Being a good mother was important to her, and she tried very hard to be patient, loving, and nurturing. She got along pretty well with her husband Frank.

Jill started smoking pot and drinking wine at night after the kids were in bed. At first this was just a way of relaxing. After a while, the one glass of wine with her husband became three or four, whether or not Frank had anything to drink. Instead of a toke or two, Jill usually finished off a whole joint.

When she noticed how much wine she was buying every week, Jill promised herself to cut down to two glasses a night. But more often than not she found herself unable to keep her promise. As things got worse, Jill tried to quit cold turkey, and was successful for a few days or even weeks at a time. Then she would convince herself that it was safe to start drinking again. Sometimes she was able to stick to her commitment and have only one or two drinks and half a joint. But before long, she would once again find herself losing control, sometimes passing out as a result. She still managed to get to work and the day-care center on time every day, and to be a good housekeeper and a conscientious mother.

Jill was suffering from the disease of chemical dependence—a pathological inability to control her intake of mood-altering chemicals. The giveaway symptom was her impaired control—she could no longer reliably predict the consequences when she took the first sip of her drink or drag on her joint.

Jill eventually found that it took more and more alcohol and marijuana to get the same results that small quantities used to produce. As her disease progressed, she found that without her nightly joint and glasses of wine, she felt agitated and anxious, and had trouble getting to sleep. As she lay in bed, her legs would twitch, and she felt hot and sweaty. Sometimes during the day, her hands shook.

Jill's increased tolerance and withdrawal symptoms showed that she was in the later stages of dependence on alcohol and marijuana. But she still managed to keep her house and family going. She didn't drive drunk, act noticeably odd in public, or endanger anybody. Nobody apart from her and her husband knew how much she drank and smoked.

Jill's disease of dependence was not as blatantly obvious as George's problem of abuse. Yet, unlike George, Jill couldn't correct her problem with willpower and reason. She couldn't "just say no," because her impaired control was not due to a lack of willpower, but was a matter of her biological affinity for alcohol and pot. Where George had the physiological capability to overcome his problem of abuse through choice and behavioral change, Jill needed outside help to overcome her disease of dependency. Her path to recovery involved medication that cut down her biochemical cravings, and a program of behavioral modification to help her avoid the first drink or drag.

Exercises

Complete the following two exercises to determine whether your problem is primarily substance abuse or substance dependence.

DSM-IV Substance Abuse Test

This test is based on the *Diagnostic and Statistical Manual, Edition IV*, published by the American Psychiatric Association to guide psychiatrists and others in diagnosing mental and emotional problems. This questionnaire tests for the behavioral danger signs of substance abuse.

Answer the following questions quickly and honestly, without stopping to rationalize or split hairs. For each question, go with your first, most spontaneous response.

1. In the last twelve months, has using alcohol or other drugs occasionally caused you to miss work or school, perform poorly at work or school, neglect your children, or fail to perform household duties?

   ❑ Yes

   ❑ No

2. In the last twelve months, while under the influence of alcohol or some other drug, have you occasionally driven a car, operated dangerous machinery (such as a power mower), or participated in potentially hazardous sports (such as swimming or rock climbing)?

   ❑ Yes

   ❑ No

3. In the last twelve months, have you been arrested for driving while intoxicated, disorderly conduct, or any other substance-related offense?

   ❑ Yes

   ❑ No

4. In the last twelve months, have you continued drinking or using drugs despite fights or arguments with people close to you expressing concern about your drug or alcohol use?

   ❑ Yes

   ❑ No

If you answered *Yes* to one or more of these questions, you are abusing alcohol or drugs and need to make immediate changes.

When George took this test, he felt scared and cornered, because he saw himself in every item. He went straight to the Employee Assistance Program counselor at work, who spoke to him frankly and gave him some literature to take home. This dose of reality helped George realize the harm that alcohol and drugs were doing to his body, and he decided to change his lifestyle. Eventually, with a lot of determination on his part, and support from a few close friends, George found new activities to replace his partying, made new friends, and put his drinking and drugging years behind him for good.

When Jill took the test, she felt relieved. Apparently, curling up with her wine and weed each night hadn't gotten her into the kind of trouble that could officially be called substance abuse. But Jill wasn't off the hook.

DSM-IV Substance Dependence Test

Substance dependence, as opposed to abuse, doesn't necessarily involve extreme behavior problems. And yet dependence is more serious and life-threatening, because it acts like a progressive disease. If Jill continues her alcohol and pot use, she will eventually experience the array of pain and sorrow that characterize later stage alcohol and drug dependence.

Take this next test to look for the danger signs of chemical dependence. Answer the questions quickly and honestly. Don't give yourself time to rationalize—just give the first answer that comes to you off the top of your head.

1. In the last twelve months, have you been consuming more alcohol or drugs than you originally intended to at a given time, or does your drinking and drugging go on longer than you originally intended?

   ❑ Yes

   ❑ No

2. In the last twelve months, have you been wanting to cut down, or have you tried to stop or cut down, and not been able to?

    ❑ Yes

    ❑ No

3. In the last twelve months, has your tolerance increased—does it take more alcohol or drugs than it used to take to get you high, or achieve the desired effect? Or does a given amount have less effect than it used to?

    ❑ Yes

    ❑ No

4. In the last twelve months, have you had any withdrawal symptoms? For instance, have you felt shaky the morning after drinking, or thick-headed after smoking marijuana, or paranoid after using cocaine?

    ❑ Yes

    ❑ No

5. In the last twelve months, have you spent a significant amount of time procuring alcohol or drugs, using alcohol or drugs, or recovering from their effects?

    ❑ Yes

    ❑ No

6. In the last twelve months, have you been spending more time drinking or drugging and less time with friends and family, in work or school-related activities, or pursuing hobbies, sports, or other interests?

    ❑ Yes

    ❑ No

7. In the last twelve months, have you experienced any emotional or physical side effects—such as depression, anxiety, liver damage, or stomach trouble—but continued to use drugs or alcohol anyway?

    ❑ Yes

    ❑ No

If you answered *Yes* to three or more of these questions, you would be considered by a physician, psychiatrist, psychologist, social worker, or alcohol and drug counselor to be "substance dependent." Especially revealing are the first two questions regarding using more and more of your drug of choice, and not being able to cut down when you want to.

Jill flunked this test. Here is how she responded:

1. Greater quantity and duration than intended. Jill answered *Yes*, because, from the beginning, and on every subsequent occasion, she intended to just have a drink or two to relax.

2. Desire for change. Jill had tried to cut down several times and failed. Her *Yes* answer to this question was her main clue that she had a life-threatening problem. Social drinkers can quit or slow down anytime they want. Abusers, with a bit of encouragement and motivation, can do the same. Jill's inability to consistently control her use was what defined her unmistakably as substance dependent.

3. Tolerance. Although Jill hadn't noticed any increased tolerance for marijuana, she had noticed that it now took three glasses of wine to make her feel the way two glasses used to. So she answered *Yes* to this question.

4. Withdrawal. Jill hadn't been having the shakes or DTs. But she did have hangovers on many mornings, and she suspected that the pot was eroding her powers of concentration. Nonetheless, she gave herself a break and answered *No*.

5. Time spent acquiring, using, or recovering. Jill answered *Yes*. She didn't have to spend much time acquiring pot—a cousin of hers had her own plants, and was happy to sell to Jill. But she wasted two or three hours nearly every night drinking and smoking.

6. Less time for other people and activities. Jill had to admit that she used to spend more time seeing friends, taking dance classes, helping her kids with art projects, and playing the guitar. Her habit of drinking and drug use at night also made her reluctant to accept invitations from the parents of her children's friends to get together and socialize.

7. Emotional and physical side effects. Jill checked *No* on this one, but in all honesty to herself, had to say "not yet." Her husband pointed out that she was unhappy and worried about her substance use. "That's an emotional side effect right there," he said.

Denial Checklist

Whether you have decided that your problem is abuse, dependence, a little of each, or neither, you should do this exercise. It will give you a clearer picture of what you think and say to yourself about alcohol and other drugs. It will also remind you that you are not that unique or alone—the phrases in the denial checklist are things that millions of people have told themselves and others for hundreds of years.

There are many kinds of denial besides saying outright, "I don't have a problem." The exercise breaks denial down into categories: stonewalling, minimizing, blaming, excusing, rationalizing, distracting, and attacking. Check off any of the statements you have made to others, or thought to yourself. Add your own favorites. Take your time, over several days or weeks if necessary, to fully explore all the creative ways in which you deny chemical dependency or abuse.

Stonewalling

☐ I don't have a problem.

☐ I can handle it.

☐ I'm not hooked—I can quit any time I want.

☐ Leave me alone—it's my business.

☐ I'm not hurting anyone but myself.

☐ So what?

☐ (Other) _____

Minimizing

☐ Sure I drink (smoke, snort, etc.), but it's not a problem.

☐ It was just a little dent in the car. At least I didn't hit anyone.

☐ It's no big deal.

☐ At least I didn't behave as badly as _____ .

☐ I made it home all right. Everything must have been okay.

☐ It will be all right if I just apologize and cool it for a while.

☐ (Other) _____

Blaming

☐ It's not the booze (coke, pills, etc.), it's the stress (coffee, cigarettes, allergies, medication, etc.).

☐ It wasn't my fault—it was (_____'s) fault for getting me drunk.

☐ I need it because of my bad back (nerves, rotten childhood, etc.).

☐ My wife (husband, mom, kid, etc.) drives me to it.

☐ I would have been all right if I hadn't mixed drinks (drank on an empty stomach, been sold coke cut with speed, etc.).

☐ I need it to deal with _____ (a person or situation).

☐ (Other) _____

Excusing

☐ I'm self-medicating. It helps me relax (cope with pain, digest, etc.).

☐ It's been a day that would drive anyone to drink.

☐ I got carried away because I was so happy (sad, mad, upset, nervous, etc.).

☐ Everybody makes mistakes once in a while.

☐ I'll have just one drink (hit, etc.) to steady my nerves.

☐ I must be doing okay—I always get to work on time (manage to cook dinner, finish assignments, pick up the kids, etc.).

☐ I'm not hung over. I have a touch of flu (food poisoning, etc.).

☐ My mom and dad and all my aunts and uncles and cousins drink. It's practically a family tradition.

☐ I'm under an incredible amount of stress right now.

☐ We're Irish—what do you expect?

☐ (Other) _____

Rationalizing

□ A nightcap will help me sleep; and, if I get a good night's sleep, I won't feel such a strong need to drink tomorrow.

□ I need the hair of the dog that bit me.

□ It's hot (cold, rainy, nice, etc.), let's have one.

□ I'm already loaded. One more won't make any difference.

□ I'll quit tomorrow.

□ I deserve a reward.

□ I need one for the road.

□ As long as you're buying . . .

□ I deserve to blow off steam once in a while.

□ It's a social lubricant.

□ Okay, I blew it this time. But I'll never do it again.

□ Life is short. Live it up!

□ I need a little lift when I'm down.

□ Drink is my only friend.

□ Let's celebrate.

□ Many leaders, artists, and intellectuals were big drinkers or druggies. For instance, Churchill drank excessive amounts of brandy, Coleridge ate opium, and everyone knows about Edgar Allen Poe. Half the great poets in the world were falling-down drunks at one time or another in their lives.

□ I broke my pledge and had one. I might as well have another.

□ For Christ's sake, you have to toast the bride!

□ I'm just a rebel.

□ I like living on the edge.

□ (Other) _____

Distracting

□ Alcohol and drugs aren't the cause of my problems. They're just a symptom of my crazy life.

□ I don't know why I have this strange pain (when you know it's probably an ulcer or liver damage caused by alcohol . . .).

□ We need more fiber in our diet (when you know your diarrhea and/or constipation are caused by drinking . . .).

□ My allergies are awful today (when you have the coke sniffles . . .).

□ You'd drink too if you had my life. Let me tell you about . . .

□ (Other) _____

Attacking

□ You've got a lot of nerve talking about my drinking!

□ Get off my back!

□ As soon as I unwind a little, you're breathing down my neck.

□ You're just like my mother—nag, nag, nag.

□ I'll stop doping (drinking, smoking, etc.) when you stop throwing money away (get a job, stop crying all the time, stop cheating on me, etc.).

□ Why don't you clean up this dump instead of counting my drinks?

□ Oh yeah? And who wrecked the car (ran over his own dog, set the mattress on fire, etc.)?

□ (Other) _____

Do any of these phrases sound familiar? Admitting to yourself that you have a problem with drugs or alcohol is very difficult. But it's the first step toward quitting for good, and reclaiming a better life.

When Jill went through the above exercise, she recognized many of her own ways of denying, excusing, and rationalizing her problem. It started her thinking about the many ways in which her family history and social isolation allowed her to keep drinking and smoking pot without having to fully count the costs or admit the toll it was taking on her health, relationships, and self-esteem.

When George completed the denial checklist, he had to confront his own rationalizations for over-the-edge behavior: "It's just wild oats," "I deserve to unwind," "I can stop any time I want," "I'm basically a party animal. Why not enjoy life while I'm young?"

Where Do You Go From Here?

What conclusion have you come to after working carefully through this section? Can you fill in these blanks?

I _____
  (your name)

□ *abuse* _____
         (substance)

□ *am dependent on* _____
                   (substance)

If you felt able to do so, congratulations on your courage in facing difficult truths about yourself. You can go on to the next step in your recovery.

If your exploration of your problem has shown you to be significantly dependent on alcohol or other drugs, you need help—a twelve-step program and possibly one of the new craving-blocking drugs. You also need to optimize your physical health by improving your nutrition, getting plenty of exercise, and practicing regular relaxation.

If this chapter has shown you to have an abuse or habit-based problem, you may benefit from a twelve-step program or self-help training in expressing feelings, exploring spirituality, improving communication skills, making amends, and preventing relapse by avoiding high-risk situations.

Concerned Group Intervention: A Proven Formula

Concerned intervention is a meeting of concerned persons with a chemically dependent person at which specific nonjudgmental examples of drinking or drugging-related behavior—which was in conflict with his or her own values—is presented in an atmosphere of concern, after which help options are offered that the chemically dependent person can accept with dignity.

Over the years we have modified and refined our particular formula for the concerned group intervention into a rather rigid series of steps which, when followed, produced a very high record of success. To the extent that it becomes necessary to change or depart from this proven approach, the likelihood of the chemically dependent person accepting help will be lessened. The intervention process, as we define it, involves three phases of activity: planning and coordinating, training and preparation, and intervention and follow-through. Accordingly, we will describe each of these phases and pass on suggestions learned from our experiences in real-life interventions.

Phase One: Planning and Coordinating

Find a Competent Counselor

You'll need trained help in dealing with a chemically dependent family member, friend, employee, or co-worker. Act. Do it now! Call a local alcohol or drug program or agency and ask about intervention counselors and programs. If that's too scary, right now call someone to whom you've turned in the past: physician, counselor, attorney, clergy person, etc. Don't ask them to help you intervene; if they could have, they already would have. Just ask them to steer you to someone or someplace that might understand intervention. When you do make contact with a potential intervention counselor, ask whether he or she is trained and experienced with the Johnson Institute model of intervention. Professionals with the proper training will be familiar with this term. Take the time to find an intervention counselor experienced with this model. It works.

The best and most successful intervention counselors have a unique combination of skills and background. First of all, they have current knowledge about chemical dependency and how it affects individuals and families. The intervention counselor must be able to penetrate the manipulation, controlling, and intimidation and see instead a diseased person full of emotional pain and desperately in need of help. At the same time, the counselor must be aware that the wall of defensive behavior, delusion, and denial surrounding the C.D. person must be breached or he may die—certainly spiritually and often physically.

Beyond just understanding this illness and the plight of its victims, the intervention counselor must possess the charisma and leadership skills required to corral as many as a dozen or more concerned people, all of whom are to some extent suffering co-dependency symptoms. To mold such a confluence of frequently opposed agendas into a unified, trained, and motivated intervention group is a high-order challenge. So the intervention counselor must be educator, therapist, coach, and, to a large extent, salesperson—salesperson because a high level of persuasive communication skills on the part of the counselor can be of great value during the closing moments of an intervention. Sometimes, when the data presented don't quite break through the C.D. person's delusion, a respectful, nonantagonistic, win/win dialogue between the counselor and the C.D. person can overcome objections and save the day. When you seek out professional intervention assistance, look for experience, emotional maturity, and a track record of successful interventions.

Arrange a Professional Intervention Planning Conference

Before involving many others in the process, one or two of the primary concerned persons should meet with the intervention counselor to sort out the problem, decide on courses of action, identify potential interveners, and plan the intervention effort. At this meeting one of the interveners is usually appointed as the single point of contact for all future communications and coordination concerning the intervention. Keep attendance at this gathering down to two or three key players—usually the person who initiated the idea and one other trusted concerned person. The purpose is to break the no-talk rules, gain an accurate picture of the situation, identify all potential interveners, develop the strategies and schedules needed to get everyone trained and prepared, decide on a treatment program, and select at least a tentative time and place for the actual intervention.

Recruit and Motivate Interveners

Under the guidance of the counselor, potential interveners are contacted and enlisted to participate in the intervention process. The core of this group is usually family members and close friends, but may include ex-spouses, disliked in-laws, "fragile" family members, young children, distant relatives, long-lost friends, and others who may be difficult to recruit but nonetheless represent potent interveners. This step is not easy. Chemically dependent families are often geographically and emotionally separated. Because of their own co-dependency, some family members or friends may be unwilling or unable to participate. So frequently it is necessary to "intervene on the interveners"—that is, design strategies to gain the support of key persons who are resistant. Some may just need a bit of reassurance and encouragement from the intervention counselor. Others will respond after receiving more current information. But some may require tough confrontation to break through their own denial. Such challenges in pulling together an intervention are the rule, not the exception. Families seldom march into the counselor's office arm in arm, possessed with unity of purpose and high motivation saying, "Murphy family reporting for intervention duty." In reality, most families considering intervention are divided, scared, confused, and full of doubt. Assistance will be needed to meld them into a cohesive and effective intervention team. Experienced intervention counselors know how to do this.

What About the Kids?

Consistently, we've observed children to have strong impact in an intervention. Yet the natural and understandable desire of older family members is to protect the kids. But that is much like trying to protect them from a storm by pretending it isn't out there. The children have heard the thunder and seen the lightning of this family disturbance and know much more about what is going on than adults suspect or wish to admit. More importantly, kids are feeling the emotional pain and need help as much as anyone in the family system. They need to talk about these sights and sounds, and the intervention is a good place to start. Follow the advice on this matter of the professional with whom you are working. But we have seen young children powerfully impact the C.D. person with a therapeutic result for the youngsters as well. For example, a six-year-old daughter revealed how her alcoholic father kept a pan next to his chair in which to throw up. After doing so, he would make her empty it. Kids need to talk about these awful realities. When unable to, they will turn them painfully inward and carry the damage into adulthood.

Phase Two: Training and Preparation

Attend an Education Program

The identified and recruited intervention participants need to attend an education program that provides an update on chemical dependency, its impact on families, and the principles of intervention. Public education about intervention is now found in almost any major community. Often these programs are presented as a free service by agencies such as the local council on alcoholism and drug abuse. Many treatment centers also sponsor community education on these subjects. Programs that present mock interventions or include films or video tapes portraying intervention scenes are especially valuable. Check the public service announcements in the local newspaper, call the council on alcoholism and drug abuse, or query the treatment centers usually listed in the Yellow Pages under "Alcoholism Information and Treatment Centers."

Get Help for Co-Dependency

Intervention training often gets interveners in touch with their own co-dependency. Participants suffering from the pains of co-dependency are strongly encouraged, at the very least, to seek help from a support group such as Al-anon, Adult Children of Alcoholics, Tough Love Parents, etc. Since just about everyone who has an emotional bond with a C.D. person suffers from some co-dependency, it's a good idea for all participants to get an evaluation from the counselor as to the propriety of seeking therapy for co-dependency.

Untreated co-dependent people can sabotage the intervention. They bring with them defensive behaviors; the controlling, the attention-getting tactics, the inappropriate humor, or the silence of fear. If these issues are not being dealt with in venues separate from the intervention, then valuable time and energy will be wasted during intervention preparation. Intervention facilitators must help participants break through their own delusion and denial in order to recall the C.D.'s unacceptable behavior. That is more easily accomplished if the participants are already in a "safe" system and getting the help they need for their own pain and defenses. If you have lived around a C.D. person for any length of time at any time in your life, you will benefit from help and you deserve it.

Break the No-Talk Rules

It is essential to create an atmosphere of openness, trust, and honesty within the intervention group. This may require free discussion of previously taboo events and subjects and the putting aside of long-standing differences. C.D. people, by virtue of chemically induced behavior and sophisticated defense systems, will often perpetrate an array of intrigues, secret alliances, triangles (sexual and otherwise), bizarre incidents, and other "delicate" situations. Not surfacing and processing such data early can lead to unexpected surprises that may sabotage the intervention effort and/or the concealment of valuable information. Family members are often reluctant to discuss these sensitive matters, believing they are the only ones who know. This is seldom the case, but these extreme examples of behavior-in-conflict-with-values make for the most powerful kinds of intervention statements.

For the C.D. person to see the severity of his condition, he must experience the emotional consequences of his worst drinking and/or drugging behaviors. To touch that pain demands breaking the no-talk rules and presenting the truth, no matter how uncomfortable that may be.

Write Intervention Statements

The concerned group will be coached on how to compose two or three very specific, hard-hitting but nonjudgmental written statements that point out powerful examples of the C.D. person's unacceptable drinking and/or drugging behavior. The use of written rather than extemporaneous intervention statements is strongly recommended. Unscripted interventions tend to quickly degenerate into win-lose, antagonistic, argumentative battles. It takes a while to come up with effective intervention statements. One older woman came to our information program several times. She told us that her drinking husband never did anything "bad." She couldn't grasp the notion that it was what he wasn't doing that was "bad." He was no longer husband, father, lover, friend; he just quietly drank. We ran into her months later. She told us through tear-filled eyes, "He finally did something bad. One night he died."

If you have trouble recalling incidents, think about ruined holidays, birthdays, anniversaries, kid's important school or sports functions, dangerous driving behavior, broken promises, blackouts, sexual impotency, physical and emotional abuse, missed work, passing out, throwing up, staying out all night, losing the car, or failure to perform as a spouse, parent, citizen, friend, worker. In other words, things the C.D. person did in ways he really didn't want to or things he really wanted to do but failed to do. At first such incidents may be difficult to remember. Talk with the others about your history with the C.D. person. Break the no-talk rules, and eventually hard-hitting statements will emerge. Write them down in the following format:

Intervention Statement Outline

1. Concern: State your love and/or concern for the C.D. person.

2. Incident: Describe in specific detail an incident in which the C.D. person did something under the influence that seriously violated his own values. Give dates, times, places, graphic portrayals, sounds, smells, expressions—exactly what happened.

3. Evidence: Provide proof that chemicals were involved in the incident, such as "I saw you drink three double scotches before we left the house. You then had a double martini before dinner and two glasses of wine with your meal, followed by two brandies."

4. Feelings: Describe how being a witness or participant in the incident made you feel—sad, terrified, sick to your stomach, angry, hurt, discounted, unloved, disappointed.

5. Concern: Close with another statement of concern.

The following statements have been used in various actual interventions:

I love you, John. Last Friday at 4 P.M. you called from the office and said you wanted to take me out for dinner and to be ready at 6 P.M. I dressed in the blue suit you said you liked so much and looked forward to the evening as I waited for you to arrive. I waited and waited, and finally at 11 P.M. I went to bed, not knowing what had happened and feeling disappointed, angry, and very scared. At 3 A.M. I heard banging on the front door and someone rattling the doorknob. I got up just in time to see you fall into the living room and grab at the couch for support. You stared at me with your eyes like slits and your jaw clenched, and thundered through slurred speech, "What the hell are you staring at?" I could smell the alcohol across the room and saw the red, glazed eyes. You pushed past me and sprawled onto the bed, fully clothed. I felt frightened, angry, and very alone.

When I approached you the next morning about what had happened, you did not recall anything and said, "You made that up. It wasn't that bad." I am very scared and feel so powerless. I am so concerned.

Mom, I love you a lot. Last month my friends came over for my birthday. We were in my room listening to records when you walked into the room dressed in your slip. You started dancing around the room to the music and slurred, "Aren't we having fun, fun, fun?" I could smell the alcohol on your breath and watched with dread as you whirled unsteadily around the room. I was so embarrassed. I didn't know what to do. My feet seemed glued to the floor. My friends scampered out of the house, laughing as they ran. I wanted to die. I wish I had my sober mom back.

Mom, I love you. Last Wednesday you said you would pick me up from school and I waited and waited for over an hour and you didn't come. I decided I had better walk home, and when I got there I found you on your bed, eyes half open, smelling of alcohol, clothes disheveled. I tried to wake you but you didn't wake up. You had threatened to kill yourself before, and this time I was afraid you had. I kept crying, "Mom, I love you. Mom, I love you," till your eyes opened wide and I knew you were alive. Please get help, Mom. I love you.

Jack, I care about you. We have no physical relationship anymore. Friday night I tried to set up a romantic evening. I fixed a candlelight dinner and arranged for the children to be at the movie. You came home in a good mood, smiling and happy, and held me as though you really cared. We had dinner and I played some of our favorite music. You insisted on having more and more wine, and as you drank, you changed. You talked over and over about what a son of a bitch your boss was and stopped paying any attention to me. I tried to get you to dance with me and you said, "You're too old to dance. You don't know any of the new dances like the girls at the club do." I was so hurt. I went into the kitchen and cried. Later on, you said you wanted me to make love to you. By then you smelled bad and were slurring your words and staggering. When we went to bed, you couldn't make love, Jack. You were unable to. You were impotent, Jack. I care about you so much.

Note the absence of judgment, moralizing, labeling, and generalities. The idea is to create a win/win, nonantagonistic, concerned, and loving atmosphere. If the intervention effort feels conspiratorial, accusative, or otherwise negative, the statements should be refined and revised until the net impact of listening to all the statements seems loving and nonjudgmental.

Concerned Group Work Sessions

Preparing for a formal intervention will require attendance at working meetings conducted by the intervention counselor(s) during which participants refine their draft statements, coordinate schedules, assign responsibilities, and rehearse. Get together as many times as needed to be certain each participant's statements are as potent and well composed as possible. It is helpful to view the situation this way: If all the statements were put in a hat and the C.D. person were to draw just one, would that single statement have the power to intervene? Such is an impossible goal, but it is a good target.

Follow the suggestions of the intervention counselor for edits, changes, and word choices; his or her experience is the best guide. Keep working on and refining the statements, but don't waste time and money arguing with the counselor. Intervention is not an exact science nor entirely an intuitive art, and you'll find that the counselor's professional experience is usually the best guide. Considerable time and effort is required to write, revise, edit, and fine-tune intervention statements. But once this work is done, leave well enough alone. Excessive revision and rehearsing will bring on staleness and rob the process of emotional power.

Gather for a Final Preparation Meeting

In this final session the intervention statements are critiqued one last time. The group then role-plays the intervention. This gives the participants an opportunity to feel the power of their combined statements, which removes some of the fear and apprehension. The practice session also assists the intervention counselor(s) in determining the sequence in which participants should read their statements, where they should sit in relation to each other and to the C.D. person, and other logistics. Subjects to be discussed at this meeting might include making treatment arrangements, escorting the C.D. person to the treatment facility, packing his bag, arranging for time off work, caring for the cats and dogs, or any other obstacles that might surface. The date, time, and place of the intervention attempt are determined along with logistics such as where participants will park and who will invite—and perhaps escort—the C.D. person to the meeting. Any remaining doubts, concerns, and "what ifs" are resolved. It is our custom to end this final gathering by having all join hands in a circle and then praying or meditating—whatever is your preference—in order to instill a sense of closure and unity.

Once we encountered a rather cynical power-broker type during an intervention on a very powerful political figure. Upon completion of the final preparation meeting, we led this joining of hands. From the look on his face, he obviously viewed this ritual as foolish and unnecessary. The touch-and-go but eventually successful intervention involved a group of fifteen family members, friends, and political allies and one very tough and highly resistant C.D. politician. Afterward, the cynic came to us and said, "When you had us join hands together last night I felt silly and questioned the need for such a device with mature people. But today, when it looked as if things were going badly, I remembered the feeling of being all together in this effort and it gave me great strength." Moral: Trust the counselor. He or she may know you and the situation better than you think.

Deal With the What Ifs

Last-minute doubts, apprehensions, and fears of those preparing for a formal intervention attempt need to be resolved. What if . . . he won't show up . . . arrives under the influence . . . flees after seeing the group . . . gets angry or violent . . . breaks down in tears . . . argues . . . refuses help . . . cuts them off financially? Won't he lose his job . . . be embarrassed publicly . . . hate us for doing this . . . feel that we ganged up and conspired . . . seek revenge? Isn't this disloyal, unfair, downright sneaky? The answers to these concerns and many other such "what ifs" could fill a book. In general, the response to all these questions is contained in the key words of the definition for a concerned group intervention: *A meeting of concerned persons with a chemically dependent person at which specific nonjudgmental examples of drinking—or drugging-related behavior—which was in conflict with his own values—is presented in an atmosphere of concern, after which help options are offered that the C.D. person can accept with dignity.* Such a confrontation is a loving act. By its very nature a professionally facilitated concerned group intervention should produce a calm, nonthreatening, businesslike scene. It is an "everybody wins" proposition in which the C.D. person receives a great deal of love and concern—only his behavior is attacked.

The data presented simply prove how an otherwise good, intelligent, sane human being is doing a lot of self-defeating things that cause an enormous amount of pain in himself and those he professes to love. There is no judging, labeling, personal attacking, anger, or other provocative behavior. Throughout a properly conducted intervention, the C.D. person's dignity is respected and his worth affirmed. If properly trained, participants will realize they are part of a life-saving endeavor. Furthermore, if the participants have joined a support group or sought other help for their co-dependency issues, they will have heard many of these "what if" situations discussed by fellow recovering family members who have already been involved in an intervention.

Trust the Professional(s)

Intervention counselors should have reassuring answers to most of these concerns. If the one you employ doesn't, get somebody else. Trained professionals will have strategies for getting the C.D. person to come to the meeting. They will know how to arrange the room, seat the people, engender a willingness on the part of the C.D. person to listen, determine the sequence in which statements are presented, handle objections raised by the C.D., prevent or deal with violence, and so on. Find a good intervention counselor and then trust the one you find.

What If He Won't Come to the Meeting?

He always does, but just about everyone preparing for an intervention worries about this possibility. A proven approach is as follows: Identify the person within the intervention group who has the most positive or least antagonistic relationship with the C.D. person. Have that designated messenger call the C.D. person and issue an invitation that sounds something like, "I need to talk to you about matters involving you that concern the entire family. Would you please meet with me at (intervention location/ date/ time)?" If the C.D. person asks for details, the messenger remains vague but does not lie. The response might be: "It's a confidential matter that I'd rather not discuss on the phone, but it is something very important and I really need your participation. Please come!" Of course, the C.D. person will suspect something is up, especially if many of those concerned have recently accelerated and strengthened their mini-intervention attempts. And that's okay. It is not necessary for the intervention to come as a total surprise in order to be effective. What those who have been intervened upon tell us later is that, yes, they knew something was going on but realized it would be difficult to avoid the meeting. Besides, they were curious and, in addition, felt confident of being able to handle whatever it was all about. After all, they had been manipulating and controlling this bunch for years. Why should this be any different?

What If He Flees?

Won't the C.D. person turn around and leave when he sees the concerned group? It's only happened to us twice. Once the C.D. person walked out and went into treatment on his own a few days later. Another time we went after the person and convinced her to return. However, to head off this contingency, we now designate someone in the group to go after the C.D. person should he attempt to leave. The person explains that this is a gathering of people who love him and simply want to discuss some matters of concern. Having such a contingency plan is reassuring to those involved, but there is no absolute guarantee that the C.D. person will return and listen.

Phase Three: The Intervention Phase

This Is It!

This is the actual meeting with the C.D. person at which the statements are read and help is offered. If the C.D. person accepts, he is taken directly from the intervention site to the treatment facility where arrangements have been made. Here is what it is like.

Typical Intervention Scene

The C.D. person is escorted into the room. The concerned persons are seated in a loose circle, with empty seats available for the C.D. person and the escort. Everybody is scared stiff, including any rational intervention counselor. As they enter the circle, a respected member of the group, who may be the escort, introduces the C.D. person to the intervention counselor, who shows the C.D. person a prearranged seat.

As the escort takes a seat, he or she closes the circle, thus psychologically bringing the C.D. person into the group and symbolically but not physically blocking his exit. The C.D. person looks surprised and usually snaps an angry comment such as, "What's this all about?" The lead intervention counselor responds with a preamble sounding something like this: "Hello, Charlie (or Shirley or whoever). My name is John O'Neill. This is my associate (if there is one). We work with families, and your family and friends came to us a while back because they were concerned about things that were happening in their lives that involve you. Our suggestion was to write down those concerns on a piece of paper so they can express them precisely and with love. They've done that, and so I'd like to ask that you listen to what they have to say. Then you can respond however you see fit. Would you be willing to listen to what they have to say?"

In the vast majority of cases the C.D. person agrees to listen, although sometimes with some snide remark for good measure. The counselor then points to the first intervener, who loudly, clearly, sincerely, and with feeling reads all of his or her statements. Anger is discouraged at the intervention. It should be temporarily put on hold to be dealt with later in treatment. But expressing all other feelings is strongly encouraged. There appears to be a correlation between the amount of tears shed and the impact of the statements. If the C.D. person starts to argue, the intervener stops reading. It takes two to argue, so everyone just remains silent. When the C.D. person quiets down, the intervener continues.

One by one, each person reads all of his or her statements. In some cases, the C.D. person has argued with the first few statements, but realizing no one was willing to fight, sat back and listened. Occasionally, a C.D. person has tried to confront others in the group about their own drinking or drugging. We quickly reemphasized that the purpose of the gathering was to share concerns about him, the chemical use of others could be discussed at another time. Sooner or later one of the statements really hits hard emotionally. Perhaps it described a serious event during a blackout or an act that grossly violated his values. The statements of young children in particular often have a very powerful impact. Unless the C.D. person has lost the capacity to feel, this specific but nonjudgmental data will begin to evoke an emotional response. At first it may take a trained observer to discern the impact; a change in breathing rate, downward eye movements, dry-throated swallowing, but often these minimal reactions will build into tears and even sobbing. It is important not to rescue the C.D. person from his pain at this critical moment. Grant him the privilege of, at least on this occasion, paying the emotional price for his drinking or other drugging behavior. It is this pain that fuels the willingness to accept help, so let it work.

When all the participants have presented their statements, the intervention counselor will probably allow a brief period of silence to let the power of the moment run its course. Then he or she will close with a statement such as this: "(Name of C.D. person), your family and friends believe that none of the things they have told you about would have ever happened had it not been for alcohol (or other drugs). They have cared enough about you to learn more about how this chemical affects individuals and families. They know now that some people are so constituted genetically that, if they experiment very long with mood-altering chemicals, episodes of loss of control—such as have been described here—will occur. They also know now that this loss of control happened not because they were bad, stupid, or crazy but because they have an illness. Part of this illness is that those who have it can't see that they've got it. That's why they held this meeting—to tell you as lovingly as possible just how serious your situation has become and how much pain it is causing you and those who love you. They wanted you to see what they have seen. They have found a program here in town (or wherever) that treats this illness and have made reservations for you to enter that program. Would you accept that help?"

Where Do We Go From Here?

From here the intervention can go in several directions. In over half of those that we have facilitated, the C.D. person's response was a variation of "I had no idea things were so bad, that I was hurting so many people so much, and really didn't believe anybody still cared. What do you want me to do?" It is noteworthy that in most of these cases, the family of the C.D. person had predicted that the C.D. person would be angry and negative and refuse help. Many C.D. persons, of course, do not immediately leap at the opportunity for help. Very often the denial will still be extreme and quite vocal. That is why it is important to retain a counselor with the courage, maturity, and skills needed to deal with any emotional barrage from the C.D. person—be it anger, tears, or fears—and then calmly, one by one, put to rest the C.D. person's objections and arguments.

What If He Says No?

During the course of intervention training, the concerned persons will be asked to ponder the question: "What will you do if the C.D. person says no? Will you continue to enable as you have in the past? Are you going to seek or continue to participate in help for yourself? Are you going to set any limits as to how much, if any, drinking- or drugging-related behavior you will accept? Will a 'no' affect your future dealings about sex, driving, socializing, or even the continuance of your relationship to him as parent, child, spouse, boss, friend, or neighbor?"

Each participant is asked to be prepared to "recontract" his relationship with the C.D. person if he turns down the offer of help. This step has seldom been necessary in our intervention work. But it has been a very important step for the concerned persons in order to remove the fear of a negative response. At the same time, this "recontracting" requirement helps the concerned persons become more aware of ways in which they are enabling and identifies behaviors they will no longer tolerate. The content of the recontracting statement must be based on what you honestly will or will not do. The counselor can suggest options, but only you can decide. Avoid empty threats. You have probably been threatening throughout this disease and taken no follow-up action. As a consequence, you may have become unbelievable. Now is the time to say what you mean and mean what you say. Here are some examples:

"Mom, Dad says I don't have to ride in the car with you from school when you've been drinking. I'll have my teacher call a cab for me. And if she asks why, I'll tell her the truth."

"Son, if you can't find it in your heart to accept the help offered, I want you to move out of the house before this weekend. There will be no more money. You are on your own. Remember we love you and the help is always there."

"Honey, I'm sorry you won't go to treatment. I intend to get the help that I need to recover from the way your disease has harmed me. From now on I will not call the boss and make excuses for you. If you don't do the chores around the house, they will be left undone. And I insist that there be no physical contact between us when you are under the influence."

"Since you will not accept help, I am leaving with the children and filing for divorce."

Remember, these recontracting statements will rarely if ever have to be employed. But it is important that each participant answer for himself or herself this question: "What will I do if he says no?"

Will It Work?

Emphatically yes! The odds are favorably high provided proven methods are followed. If your counselor is competent, if all the significant others in the C.D. person's life participate, if each of them is properly trained and prepared, if the statements they present are specific and powerful yet packaged in love and concern, and if the help options offered can be accepted with dignity, then there is more than an 80 percent probability that the C.D. person will agree to the help suggested. More importantly, when the above conditions are present, the system of family, friends, and co-workers surrounding the C.D. person has changed in many positive ways. The C.D. person will have to make changes to fit into this healthier system. This is another reason for saying that intervention is a process and not an event. The C.D. person may refuse help in the immediate moment of the intervention. But if those who love him have gotten help for their own co-dependency, broken the no-talk rules, and stopped the enabling, then the process keeps pressuring the C.D. person to see what's really happening and eventually opt for help.

The "What If" Commitment

Not to be confused with the "what if" concerns discussed earlier, the "what if" commitment is a last-ditch effort to achieve some positive results when the C.D. person adamantly refuses treatment. The C.D. person may take the position that "Yes, there is a problem, but I can handle it—I'll quit drinking/drugging on my own (or with the help of A.A., N.A., or other self-help programs)." The intervention counselor will, of course, try to show him how difficult it is to quit without help and even may advise against withdrawal from alcohol or other drugs without close medical supervision. But when every effort to coax the C.D. person into accepting treatment fails and it seems fruitless to go on, the counselor will close out the proceedings by saying something like the following: "I know you mean what you say about quitting (or cutting back), but most people who have experienced the kind of consequences of their drinking/drugging that have been described here find it impossible to return to controlled use or to quit without help." To which the C.D. person will predictably reply, "Well, I know that I can!" At which time the counselor will counter with, "What if you can't? Would you then accept treatment?" The idea is to get the C.D. person to agree that, if he cannot quit on his own, he will immediately enter treatment. Because the C.D. person is so sure that he can stop, he will usually agree. The counselor will then attempt to reinforce and elevate the strength of the commitment: "So you are making this commitment to your family and friends—that if you return to (or can't control) your drinking/drugging, you give your solemn word to immediately enter treatment. Is that correct?" The idea here is to effect another intervention in advance. If the C.D. person does experience further problems—and without a recovery program they just about always do—those who participated in the intervention remind him of his promise and hold him to it.

When the Attempt Fails

Sometimes there is not a happy ending. Usually when the C.D. person's feeling life, or "affect" as the psychologists call it, is shut down. Touching the pain is what powers the concerned-person intervention. When he can't get in touch with his own pain or the pain suffered by others, what is said has little impact. We recall the case of a five-year-old in tears climbing onto the lap of her father and begging him to "go get well at the hospital" and receiving not a twinge of emotional response. Even when such letdowns occur, it's not the end of the world. Whatever happens it is certainly the beginning of a new life. No more no-talk rules or pretending everything is all right or accepting the unacceptable. You're getting the help to recover, whatever the C.D. person chooses to do. And it isn't over. This is a process and not just a single event. The forces set loose at the intervention will continue to put pressure on the C.D. person to accept help. The ball is now in his court to stay. Even when intervention doesn't work—it sticks . . . it keeps working.

Loose Ends

Although chemical dependency is a universal disease, it unfolds uniquely in each victim's family. So, too, each intervention will have its own special challenges that may demand innovation and improvisation to overcome. In addition to the two more common outcomes just described, there are infinite variations: the C.D. person might agree to go if someone else in the group who also has a problem will enter treatment as well. (That happened to us once.) Some of the supposed "concerned persons" may turn out to be selling drugs to the C.D. person. (That has happened a couple of times.) The C.D. person whom everyone described as a pussycat will become violently angry, while another, thought to be awesomely threatening, will break down in tears and leap for the help offered. (Those kinds of unexpected reactions happen frequently.) One of the interveners who never shows emotion will break down, and this will have a profoundly penetrating effect on the C.D. person's delusion. (This is also a frequent occurrence, usually involving either a very tough guy or a child who never felt safe enough before to really speak of his or her pain.) C.D. persons have interrupted part way through the gathering and agreed to accept help. Others have refused vigorously, become very angry, and stayed that way for several days following, spouting all manner of windy threats, and then quietly entered the recommended treatment center unassisted.

In summary, the concerned group intervention process is highly effective when the group is properly educated and prepared and the counselor is experienced and skilled. Each effort is unique and exciting with potential for both failure and joy. But none of them we have observed has ever failed to produce more positive results than negative consequences. At the very least, the intervention experience gives the concerned persons a taste of wellness and from that there is no turning back.

Excerpted and adapted with permission from *The Addiction Workbook: A Step-by-Step Guide to Quitting Alcohol and Drugs* by Patrick Fanning and John O'Neill, L.C.D.C.; and *Concerned Intervention: When Your Loved One Won't Quit Alcohol and Drugs* by John O'Neill, L.C.D.C., and Patricia O'Neill, L.C.D.C. For more information on these and related books, see the "Further Reading" section in the back of the book.

CHAPTER 18

Smoking

If you've ever thought about quitting smoking or have tried unsuccessfully, this chapter can help you lay the groundwork for successful quitting.

Laying the Foundation for Successful Quitting

Who would you predict to be most successful in their efforts to quit smoking? Mark your predictions on the scale following each example.

Tom begins each morning by rolling over in bed and reaching for the pack of cigarettes on the night table. He proceeds to smoke two cigarettes, one right after the other, before getting out of bed. He then begins his morning routine (teeth brushing, shaving, etc.). Each activity is performed with a cigarette. Throughout the day Tom continues to light up a cigarette with every activity, both rest and work. Tom generally smokes at least two cigarettes when he is in the car, on the phone, or drinking coffee.

Extremely Successful   *Moderately Successful*   *Unable to Quit Smoking*
4   3   2   1

Jane is a physician at a large metropolitan hospital. She describes herself as a nervous person who tends to experience a lot of stress throughout her working day. Although she intellectually understands the dangers associated with smoking she finds herself reaching for a cigarette to calm and relax her. She rationalizes this behavior by saying to herself that this will be her last one.

Extremely Successful   *Moderately Successful*   *Unable to Quit Smoking*
4   3   2   1

Sam, a retired auto worker, complains of too much spare time. He reports an increase in his desire for a cigarette when he feels bored. He notices himself reaching for cigarettes to pass the time.

Extremely Successful		Moderately Successful		Unable to Quit Smoking
4		3	2	1

Sue has always had a "hot temper." She describes herself as "quick to anger." When she feels her anger increasing she automatically reaches for a cigarette to provide herself with "distance and cooling off time." This behavior occurs not only at work but at home as well.

Extremely Successful		Moderately Successful		Unable to Quit Smoking
4		3	2	1

Although you may have your own bias about who would be more successful in the process of quitting smoking, the reality is that each of these people could successfully quit if their motivation was strong enough. The key factor identified both clinically and through research is motivation. Only motivation separates those who successfully quit smoking from those who do not. Therefore, it is important to understand what motivation is and is not, and how you can strengthen your own motivation for quitting.

Motivation

You may have impulsively decided to quit smoking in the past and just thrown your cigarettes away. However, what you may have discovered after a few hours, days, weeks, or even months is that you returned to smoking. Quitting should not be an impulsive decision but rather a process that requires adequate preparation in order to lay the foundation for successful cessation. Without good preparation you may set yourself up for personal failure and subsequently may become reluctant to attempt quitting again, or even believe that you are not capable of quitting.

The first step in preparing yourself to quit smoking is to examine your motivation more directly. Motivation forms the basis of your commitment to stop smoking. Willpower, guts, strength, intestinal fortitude—these are all words that have been used by smokers when describing what it takes to quit smoking. Although quitting smoking for a lifetime does require strength and commitment, understanding the source of one's "willpower" or motivating reasons for quitting is an important first step. Recently, smokers have been bombarded by messages to quit smoking. Cigarette costs continue to rise, places where smoking is allowed have been limited, and socially smoking has become less acceptable. However, these reasons alone are often not enough to motivate smokers to quit. It is necessary to identify your own personal reasons for wanting to quit smoking, and to evaluate the importance of these reasons. Use the following exercise to begin identifying your personal reasons for needing to quit. If your reasons for needing to quit smoking equal your desire to continue smoking, your chances of successfully quitting are lower. But the more weight you can truthfully put on the "quitting" side, the more the scale tips toward a smoke-free life that's right for you.

Reaffirming Motivation

On a separate index card or sheet of paper rewrite your reasons for needing to quit. Carry this list with you in your pocket. Place it on your refrigerator. Display it in any area that will serve to remind and motivate you throughout the process of quitting smoking. Just as reaching for matches or a lighter has become a habit, make a new habit of checking your list as soon as the

Exercise

1. Begin by listing on the left side of the scale all your reasons for wanting to smoke. Be as specific as you can be. (See example.) On the right side of the scale list all the reasons why you need to quit smoking. Be specific.

2. Now compare each side of your scale. If your reasons for wanting to quit outweigh your reasons for why you continue to smoke, you are ready to begin the process of cessation. If your scale is fairly balanced, you need to re-examine your desire and commitment to the quitting process. As you work your way through this book, continue to add reasons to quit to the right side of the scale. Don't worry if the scale threatens to tip over!

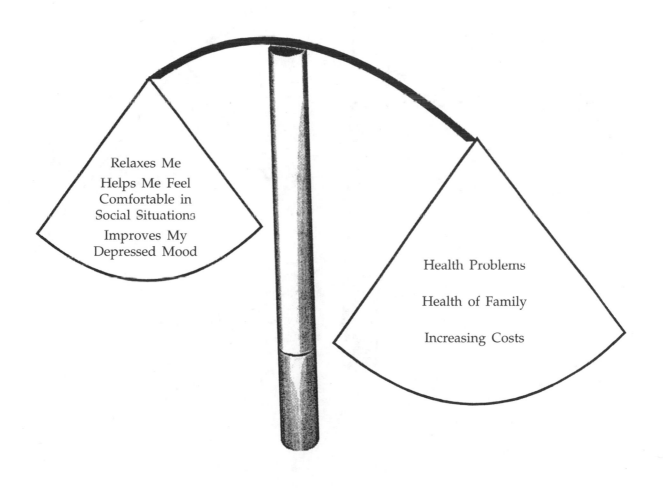

Relaxes Me

Helps Me Feel Comfortable in Social Situations

Improves My Depressed Mood

Health Problems

Health of Family

Increasing Costs

Your Balance Scale

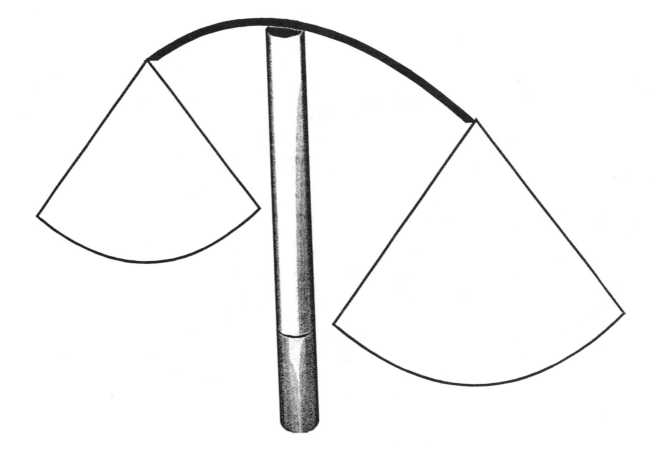

urge to smoke hits. Write your reasons as persuasively as you can. For instance, write your children's names, or note a specific goal you can reach if you save $25 a week.

Sample Index Card

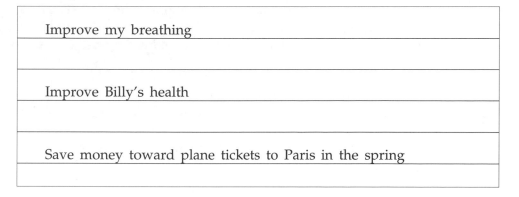

Improve my breathing
Improve Billy's health
Save money toward plane tickets to Paris in the spring

Don't worry if this step alone doesn't lead you to quit. It helps chip away at the unconsciousness of your smoking habit, and prepares you for the steps that follow.

Personal Excuses

Now that you have examined your personal reasons for wanting to quit, it's time to face something that many smokers do to undermine their own motivation to quit: make excuses. Every smoker at one time or another has used excuses to put off quitting. Excuses provide you with reasons to self-medicate with nicotine when quitting seems hard to bear. If you know and understand your own excuses, you will be empowered to alter those excuses with more healthy statements to yourself. Positive messages to yourself will help tremendously in keeping your motivation up. The following section offers samples of such messages. Try to find alternative statements that make sense to you.

How many of these excuses have you used?

Excuse: This is a bad time to quit because I have too many stressors in my life.
Alternative Statement: There will always be stressors in my life. This is a good opportunity to learn how to cope in a more healthy way while experiencing this stress.

Excuse: Quitting isn't worth the suffering.
Alternative Statement: The short-term discomfort that I may experience will only last up to a week and then my body will begin to heal. Quitting smoking now will minimize my risk for long-term suffering with other smoking-related diseases.

Excuse: I'm too young to have any real damage to my body. I'll quit in a couple of years.
Alternative Statement: I may not be physically experiencing the effects of my smoking, but with each cigarette I deposit thousands of cancer-causing agents in my bloodstream. I am setting myself up for future physical problems.

Excuse: If I do quit I will gain a lot of weight.
Alternative Statement: Weight gain caused by changes in the body after quitting smoking averages three to seven pounds. I can control weight gain through exercise

and snacking on healthy foods. Quitting smoking is the best thing I can do for my health and my appearance.

Excuse: It is probably too late for me to quit because too much damage has already occurred.
Alternative Statement: It is never too late to quit smoking. Immediately after I quit smoking my body will begin to heal. My breathing should improve, I'll cough less, my sense of taste and smell will return to normal, and I will reduce my risk for developing further medical problems.

Excuse: I've tried to quit before but I always fail.
Alternative Statement: It often takes smokers several attempts before they actually quit smoking. With each attempt I will learn what my "high risk" situations are and what causes me to reach for a cigarette. I will then know more about my habit for the next attempt at quitting.

Excuse: I need to smoke to calm my nerves.
Alternative Statement: Nicotine is actually a stimulant, which means it arouses the nervous system. There are other things I can learn to use to calm my nerves. For example, I can take a walk or use relaxation exercises.

Excuse: I need to smoke to feel comfortable in social situations.
Alternative Statement: There are other techniques I can use to make myself feel more comfortable such as carrying my keys to occupy my hands.

Excuse: I can't quit now because I get very irritable and I don't want to get into trouble at home or at work.
Alternative Statement: This irritability is short term. People frequently get irritable or crabby and they don't reach for a cigarette. I will elicit my co-workers' support in my efforts to quit.

Excuse: It hasn't really been proven that cigarette smoking is a cause of cancer.
Alternative Statement: This is not true. Cigarette smoking is the leading cause of preventable cancer.

Excuse: I enjoy smoking too much to give it up.
Alternative Statement: The temporary enjoyment that I get is leading me closer and closer to potential long-term suffering.

Review these excuses and add others that may be more personal to you. Write your alternative statements as persuasively and accurately as you can. Remember these excuses only serve to undermine your motivation and ability to quit smoking.

Excuse:
Alternative Statement:

Excuse:
Alternative Statement:

Excuse:
Alternative Statement:

Self-Efficacy

When thinking about quitting smoking, many people make the mistake of assuming that all it will take to stay off cigarettes is willpower or motivation. How many times have you said to yourself something like, "I just need to be strong to beat the urge to smoke"? The problem with this demand is that it implies that strength of will or motivation is all that is necessary to be smoke-free. But as you may know, many people have quit for a short period of time only to find themselves smoking again. Does this mean that they have lost their willpower or motivation? Not exactly. As you saw in the previous section, being motivated to quit and making a strong commitment to change are extremely important. But people also need to believe that they can or know how to cope with situations that will tempt them to smoke. A researcher named Albert Bandura referred to this belief as self-efficacy.

Consider self-efficacy as it relates to your preparation to quit smoking. You can think of self-efficacy as your judgment of your ability to cope with a specific "high risk" situation. How much confidence do you have in your ability to resist smoking in the situations that you find most tempting? This is not to be confused with self-esteem (what you think of yourself overall). People can feel very positive about themselves but still judge themselves as not able to do a certain thing like quit smoking. Someone with a low sense of self-efficacy, who has doubts about his or her abilities in particular situations, may tend to give up more easily when faced with situations that are really tempting. Simply exerting your willpower to resist smoking in such cases isn't enough; you must believe that you can do something to resist, and that you know how to do it. As you work through this book, you will learn several techniques to help you resist the urge to smoke.

Your sense of self-efficacy is influenced by a few factors. The first is how many successes or failures you may have had when trying to quit. If you have quit smoking in the past but gave in early because you were faced with stressful situations, you may feel less able to quit again. You may feel less confident, saying "I can't handle this." You may feel overcome with a craving to reach for a cigarette. As a smoker you may have come to believe that cigarettes help you cope.

People often rely on how they feel physically to determine whether they can cope with a stressful situation. The more tense or nervous you are, the more out of control you may feel and therefore less able to resist the urge to smoke. This book will present you with other options to cope with these feelings.

Self-Efficacy Evaluation

How strongly do you believe in your ability to quit smoking and to manage high risk smoking situations? Circle the number corresponding to how you feel about each statement.

- My last attempt at quitting smoking failed therefore I am afraid to try again.

Strongly Agree	Agree	Disagree	Strongly Disagree
1	2	3	4

- I believe that I am unable to tolerate any discomfort related to quitting.

Strongly Agree	Agree	Disagree	Strongly Disagree
1	2	3	4

- I believe that my smoking is more powerful than I am.

Strongly Agree	Agree	Disagree	Strongly Disagree
1	2	3	4

- I worry that nervousness or stress will overcome me and make it impossible to quit.

Strongly Agree	*Agree*	*Disagree*	*Strongly Disagree*
1	2	3	4

- I don't believe that I personally have what it takes to quit smoking.

Strongly Agree	*Agree*	*Disagree*	*Strongly Disagree*
1	2	3	4

- I am not strong enough to use alternative strategies to cope.

Strongly Agree	*Agree*	*Disagree*	*Strongly Disagree*
1	2	3	4

- I doubt my ability to manage my life without cigarettes.

Strongly Agree	*Agree*	*Disagree*	*Strongly Disagree*
1	2	3	4

- The next time I get really angry or upset, I will definitely need a cigarette.

Strongly Agree	*Agree*	*Disagree*	*Strongly Disagree*
1	2	3	4

If you answered mostly 3's and 4's, you have a strong belief in your ability to cope with situations without smoking. This will help you when you are faced with a particularly challenging situation. Remind yourself that you are capable. If you answered mostly 1's and 2's, you may be doubting your abilities to manage your life without cigarettes. The following are things you can do to improve your belief in your ability to quit smoking.

1. Learn new coping strategies, one of the end results of having worked through this chapter. Once you arm yourself with new ways of coping instead of smoking, you will increase your confidence in your ability to quit smoking.

2. Observe your friends and family members' attempts in order to develop your confidence. Follow the example of someone who has quit to maintain faith and to learn how to cope more effectively with the urge to smoke. You may be motivated to stop smoking from constant pressure from others, but this in itself won't help you as much as a successful role model to remain smoke-free.

3. Review your healthy alternative statements to yourself. If any fail to convince you, rewrite them when you're at your most disgusted with smoking.

4. Focus on being successful. Imagine yourself as a non-smoker, in control of your ability to use healthy coping strategies.

5. Remember that quitting smoking is a process and as such may take several attempts. Don't interpret past attempts as failures, but rather as learning opportunities.

6. Quitting smoking may seem like one of the most difficult things that you will do but remember that with practice you will succeed. The challenge will let you feel that much better about your ability to remain a non-smoker.

Nicotine Substitution Therapy

Have you ever used a nicotine substitution product (e.g., gum or patch) in your past attempts at quitting? _____

_____

What products have you tried? _____

_____

How did these products work for you? _____

_____

In order for these products to be most effective, they have to be right for you and used in the proper way. This chapter is designed to help you understand these products more fully and how they should be used.

Nicotine substituting products include a chewing gum, Nicorette (nicotine polacrilex), and nicotine skin patches, Nicoderm, Habitrol, Nicotrol, and Prostep. These products are designed to gradually reduce the amount of nicotine in your bloodstream to minimize the discomfort of physical withdrawal symptoms. However, before you can make a decision about using these products you must first be able to differentiate between your physical withdrawal symptoms and your psychological desire associated with smoking. Smokers often confuse psychological "urges" for physical "urges." It is important to understand that the physical urges are related to the nicotine withdrawal process. The psychological urge is really more the desire to smoke and is associated with multiple social triggers and emotional states (such as nervousness or boredom). This distinction is important because these products are designed only to help with the physical withdrawal symptoms and if used inappropriately may serve to actually strengthen the smoking habit. It is also recommended by each of the manufacturers that these products be used in conjunction with other self-help materials or formalized behavioral programs. Although the purpose of this section is to help you distinguish between the physical withdrawal symptoms and the psychological triggers to your smoking habit, it is important to understand that both can exist at the same time and both are important to address in the quitting process.

Physical Addiction

Nicotine is the addicting substance found in tobacco. The 1988 Surgeon General's report states that nicotine is as addicting as alcohol, cocaine, or heroin. This addiction process begins after repeated use of nicotine. Your body then develops a tolerance to the drug. That is, your body becomes more efficient at eliminating the drug and/or the receptor cells in your body become less sensitive to the drug. In turn, you need to smoke more to experience the same effects from your cigarettes. When you smoke, nicotine accumulates in your bloodstream. After a period of time without a cigarette the level of nicotine drops and your body "craves" more of the drug. Smoking another cigarette will immediately satisfy the craving, bring your blood levels back up, and reinforce the addiction.

For most smokers nicotine concentration levels show distinct patterns over a twenty-four to forty-eight hour period.

With each cigarette that you smoke, nicotine begins to accumulate in your bloodstream. The amount of nicotine in your blood reaches a plateau approximately six to eight hours after you begin smoking for the day.

When you have finished your last cigarette in the evening and throughout the time that you are sleeping, the amount of nicotine in your blood begins to gradually drop. As a result, in the morning the amount of nicotine in your blood is at its lowest and your body "craves" a cigarette to bring this blood level back up. This is why for most smokers that first cigarette in the morning is the "most important." Then as you continue to smoke throughout the day you keep your blood levels high and your "cravings" low.

This cycle of physical addiction begins when you experience "withdrawal symptoms" and you smoke to reduce these symptoms. This improvement in symptoms is a temporary "fix." Your body then becomes adjusted to the nicotine dose and you develop a tolerance to the drug. With the passage of time your nicotine levels will drop again and your body will require more nicotine to prevent withdrawal symptoms from recurring. The cycle continues.

Physical Withdrawal Symptoms

When you decide to stop giving your body nicotine and break the cycle, it may respond through "withdrawal symptoms." These physical symptoms may include:

- Restlessness

- Irritability

- Difficulty concentrating

- Sleep disturbances

- Increased appetite

- Headache

- Constipation

- Dry mouth or sore throat

- Fatigue

- Coughing

- Nicotine "craving"

It is important to understand that these symptoms are short-lived, lasting anywhere from one to two weeks. Almost all of the nicotine will be out of your system in two to three days. The amount and type of symptoms that smokers experience is very individual. Some smokers experience no physical symptoms while others report several symptoms. Understanding that these symptoms are temporary and are the body's way of healing itself can help turn these negative symptoms into a positive reminder that you are on the path of improving your health. It may be helpful to tell yourself that it is like you are getting the "flu" or a "cold." You know that you may feel bad for a while but with the passage of time each day brings you closer to feeling better. View these symptoms as "important discomforts" in the healing process.

The Symptoms of Healing list that follows will provide you with information about this healing process. As you move through the initial stages of quitting, use the information below as a motivator to remind you that there is a benefit to the short-term discomfort, either physical or psychological, that you may be experiencing. This will serve to strengthen your motivation and commitment to the quitting process.

Psychological Desire

You may feel a compulsive desire to continue using the drug nicotine in order to cope with certain emotional states or situations (such as to decrease anxiety or deal with boredom and social discomfort). By continuing to use nicotine as a dysfunctional way to cope you reinforce the habit and undermine your own more adaptive means of coping. This cycle of reinforcement begins when you experience a "difficult" situation or emotion and you reach for a cigarette to deal with it. After you smoke the cigarette you may feel temporarily better or more in control. This feeling serves to reinforce your reaching for a cigarette the next time that you experience the same feeling or situation.

This cycle can be broken when you recognize that you are using cigarettes to deal with emotions and you learn alternatives to cope more efficiently. As you practice using these skills you will become reinforced by experiencing more self-control and belief in yourself without the cigarettes.

Symptoms of Healing

As this healing process begins, noticeable physical changes occur. The American Cancer Society has reported that twenty minutes after your last cigarette your blood pressure, heart rate, and pulse return to normal. By staying off the cigarettes you decrease your risk factors for serious medical complications.

Carbon monoxide and nicotine levels begin to decrease rapidly. Also, the oxygen supply in your blood increases. As this occurs, you may experience an increase in "cravings." This is temporary and will decrease with time.

Your ability to smell and taste will dramatically improve. You may still be experiencing some coughing as your lungs begin to clear themselves from the poisons. This cough will subside over time.

Your bronchial tubes, which bring air to and from the lungs, begin to regain their elasticity and therefore can more efficiently bring in air. You may notice an improvement in your ability to breathe and subsequently you will become less "winded" or "out of breath" when performing activities. Also, while your body is working hard at removing toxin such as tar from the lungs and repairing nerve endings, you may feel tired or easily fatigued. This will not only improve with time but you will notice that you have more energy than you did when you were smoking.

The functioning of your lungs may improve by as much as 30 percent in the next two to three months. You may feel younger because of the increased energy and ability to exercise and do more physical activities.

Your chance for developing infections in the lungs is significantly reduced because the cilia in your lungs have begun to regrow and heal from the damage that smoking has caused. It is the job of these cilia to sweep out poisons and substances that can lead to infection.

Your risk for heart disease has been cut dramatically in half. You have also significantly reduced your risk of dying from a stroke, lung disease, heart disease, and other types of cancers including bladder, kidney, pancreas, larynx, and esophagus. These health improvements only continue to increase with the number of years that you remain a non-smoker.

Cold Turkey vs. Cutting Down

The question is often asked, "What is the advantage and disadvantage of quitting 'cold turkey' vs. cutting down, especially as it relates to my decision to use nicotine gum or a nicotine patch?" Consider first the difference between quitting cold turkey and cutting down in terms of what physically happens to the nicotine in your body.

Cold Turkey

Frequently you will hear smokers talk about quitting cold turkey vs. cutting down. What does this mean from a physical perspective? When a smoker quits cold turkey this means that he or she has gone from smoking his or her normal amount of cigarettes to abruptly stopping completely. The amount of nicotine in the bloodstream quickly drops off. As a result, the body may experience some withdrawal symptoms. The benefit to quitting this way is that it is quick and your body immediately begins to heal itself.

Cutting Down or Tapering

Some smokers decide to cut down the number of cigarettes that they are smoking and thereby to reduce the amount of nicotine in the body. The benefit to this process is the potential reduction in the physical withdrawal symptoms. However, some smokers find that it is difficult for them to maintain themselves at a lower level of nicotine because the body begins to "crave" the original amount that the smoker was consuming. Therefore, they often find themselves going up and down with the number of cigarettes in response to this craving, causing the body to experience "mini" withdrawal symptoms. To prevent this from happening nicotine substitution products were developed. Nicotine substitution products were designed to lower the amount of nicotine in the body gradually to minimize withdrawal symptoms.

With the aid of a nicotine substitute the cotine in your blood drops off more gradually. This gradual decrease over time *may* reduce the amount of withdrawal symptoms that some individuals experience.

Is Nicotine Replacement Right for You?

Now that you are able to differentiate between physical addiction and psychological urges, and understand the process of quitting cold turkey vs. tapering with a nicotine substitute, it is time to determine what is right for you.

The following questionnaire is designed to help identify the degree of your physical addiction.

Physical Nicotine Dependence Questionnaire

1. Do you wake up during the night to smoke?

2. Do you smoke immediately after awakening?

3. In the morning, do you smoke several cigarettes in a short period of time?

4. If you go more than 72 hours without a cigarette, do you feel physically ill?

5. Following past attempts to quit have you relapsed during the first two weeks after quitting?

6. Do you smoke when you are physically ill?

If you answered yes to the majority of these questions, you probably are physically dependent on nicotine. The higher your number of yes responses, the greater the degree of your physical dependence.

The Nicotine Replacement Decision Chart outlines choices for you based on your past quit attempts. Remember that nicotine replacement will only assist you with potential problematic withdrawal symptoms that you may experience. Information from past attempts will be useful in guiding you through your current quit attempt. Begin by answering the question in the top box and following your response to the next appropriate box.

If your answers in the flow chart suggest that nicotine replacement therapy may be a useful addition in your quitting attempt and you answered yes to the majority of questions on the Physical Nicotine Dependence Questionnaire, you may consider discussing with your physician the possibility of using a nicotine product. Remember, these products are by prescription only and as such will need to be dispensed and monitored by your physician.

Nicorette Chewing Gum

Nicorette is a sugar-free chewing gum which contains nicotine. Each piece of the gum contains the equivalent of about 2 mg. of nicotine. By comparison, each cigarette contains approximately 1 mg. of nicotine. However, it is important to understand that the actual amount of nicotine that you are getting depends on how you inhale your cigarette and similarly how you chew your nicotine gum. In controlled studies looking at how people chew nicotine gum it was found that smokers extracted anywhere from 10 percent to 90 percent of the 2 mg. of nicotine found in the gum. This variability was related to how efficiently the smokers chewed the gum. This is because the nicotine is attached to the gum, therefore you must chew it properly in order to release it from the gum. Instructions for using the gum include:

1. **Stop smoking.** The purpose of using a nicotine replacement product is to bring the amount of nicotine in your bloodstream down slowly to minimize potential withdrawal symptoms and to eliminate exposure to the other substances found in cigarettes (tar, formaldehyde, etc.). Smoking while you chew the gum would dramatically increase your levels of nicotine (and other harmful substances.)

2. Use approximately **10 to 20** pieces per day and do not exceed 30 pieces.

3. When you feel a **physical** urge to smoke, place a piece of gum in your mouth.

4. Chew the gum **slowly** and **intermittently** as this will provide even and slow release of the nicotine into the saliva for absorption into the lining of the mouth. **Chewing the gum too fast may result in hiccups, nausea, or a sore throat.**

5. Chew the gum slowly only until you taste a peppery sensation or tingling. Then **stop** chewing the gum and **park** it between your cheek and gum.

6. When the tingling sensation is **gone** begin slowly chewing the gum again.

7. Keep chewing the gum on and off for approximately **20 to 30 minutes** to continue releasing the nicotine.

Nicotine Replacement Decision Chart

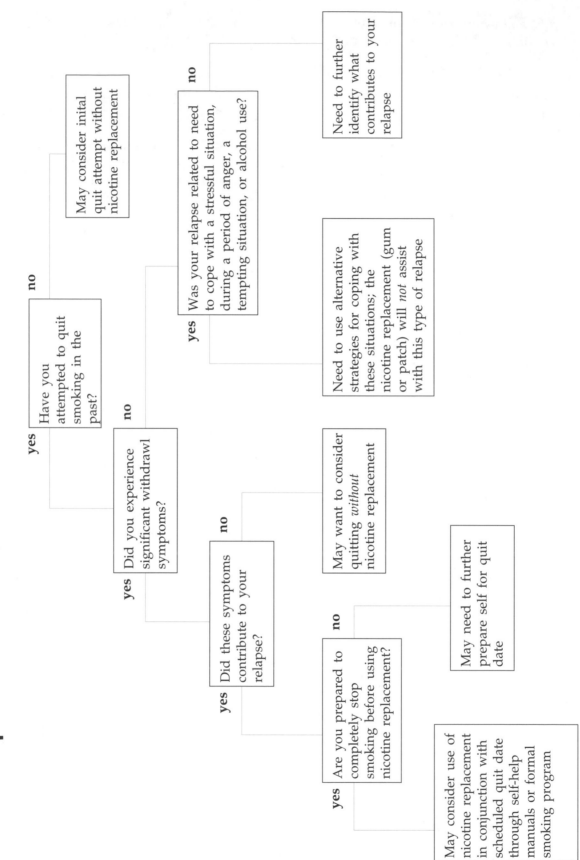

Have you attempted to quit smoking in the past?

yes →

no → May consider inital quit attempt without nicotine replacement

Did you experience significant withdrawl symptoms?

no →

yes → **Was your relapse related to need to cope with a stressful situation, during a period of anger, a tempting situation, or alcohol use?**

no → Need to further identify what contributes to your relapse

yes → Need to use alternative strategies for coping with these situations; the nicotine replacement (gum or patch) will *not* assist with this type of relapse

Did these symptoms contribute to your relapse?

no → May want to consider quitting *without* nicotine replacement

yes → **Are you prepared to completely stop smoking before using nicotine replacement?**

no → May need to further prepare self for quit date

yes → May consider use of nicotine replacement in conjunction with scheduled quit date through self-help manuals or formal smoking program

8. If you have **dentures** or problems with temporal mandibular joint disease **(TMJ)**, discuss potential problems in using this product with your physician.

9. **Avoid drinking alcohol, fruit juices (particularly orange juice), coffee, or cola drinks** during the first 15 minutes of using the nicotine gum. Using these products may interfere with the absorption of the nicotine by changing the acid content of your mouth.

10. Gradually reduce the number of pieces of gum that you are using. **Do not use the gum as a substitute for times associated with psychological desire or habit** (for instance, when talking on the phone, when depressed, after a meal, etc.). The gum is designed to assist **only** with physical urges and withdrawal.

11. It is time to discontinue use of the product when you can get yourself down to approximately **two to three pieces of gum per day.** Do not use the gum beyond three to six months.

Nicotine Patches

Nicotine patches are a transdermal system that provides nicotine to the body through the skin. There are four major patches available on the market today. Each patch consists of a different schedule for the delivery of nicotine including dosage and duration of use. The graphs that follow outline the similarities and differences among the patches.

The usual dosage and schedule for the Nicoderm and Habitrol patches are similar. When using these products, you begin by wearing a 21 mg. patch of nicotine for six weeks. This is then removed and replaced with a 14 mg. patch to be worn for two weeks. Finally, this patch is removed, and you will wear a 7 mg. patch for another two weeks.

The schedule for Nicotrol patches begins with wearing a 21 mg. patch for four to twelve weeks depending on the advice of your physician. This patch is then removed and replaced with a 14 mg. patch to be worn between two and four weeks. The last patch used is 7 mg. and is worn between two and four weeks.

The Prostep patch is 22 mg. of nicotine and is usually worn for approximately twelve weeks.

General instructions for using these products include:

1. **Stop smoking.** Similar to the nicotine gum these products are designed to assist with physical withdrawal symptoms by gradually reducing the nicotine content in your bloodstream. By smoking and using these products you defeat the purpose that they were designed for—compensating for withdrawal—and you increase your risk of developing medical complications.

2. Apply the nicotine patch to a clean, non-hairy area on your front or back area above the waist or to the upper, outer area of the arm.

3. Apply a **new patch daily** at the same time to a different area of the body.

4. You can continue to **swim, bathe, or use a hot tub** while wearing the patch.

5. The **nicotine patch should be used with self-help materials or a formalized smoking cessation program** designed to assist with the psychological desire and use of cigarettes for coping. Use of the patch alone will not address these issues.

Typical Dosage and Schedule for Nicotine Patches

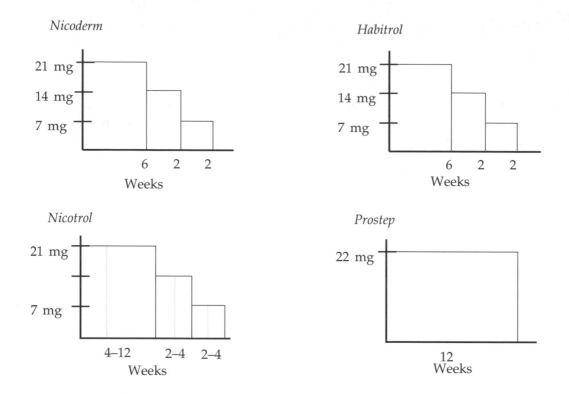

Quit Date

Quitting smoking is an act that requires preparation. If you've worked methodically up to this point in the chapter, you may be ready to choose your own personal quit date within the next two weeks. Mark this date on a visible calendar. This will serve as a reminder to you that the act of quitting smoking is not something that you are doing on a whim but rather something that you are preparing for and planning to accomplish.

As you approach the date marked on your calendar, you'll need to prepare yourself for the actual quitting process. Since smoking has been part of your whole existence including your physical self, your emotional self, and part of your general surroundings, each of these areas needs preparation for the quitting process.

Preparation of Surroundings

Cigarette smoking has been part of your life and as such has probably left its mark all around you. In your efforts to quit smoking it is important for you to remove the evidence and reminders of your smoking habit. This will serve to decrease temptation from these reminders as well as to strengthen your commitment to the quitting process through visible reminders.

1. **Two weeks prior to quit date, limit your smoking to one room in your home.** This room should be the least comfortable place. For example, choose the laundry room, the basement, or the porch. Move all of your smoking paraphernalia, such as ashtray and lighter, to that room. Limiting where you smoke will help you to cut down on the quan-

tity of cigarettes that you smoke by making the process more inconvenient. A pack of cigarettes that is next to the couch and in front of the television set will probably be smoked. Further, by limiting where you smoke you also eliminate many cues and triggers. If you tend to smoke when watching television or finishing a meal, you will begin to break that association by learning to smoke without engaging in either activity. Smoking should become merely an act of inhaling and putting out your cigarette and not a part of your daily routines.

2. **Clean out your car.** Remove all evidence that your car was that of a smoker. Vacuum out the carpet, remove the ashtray and lighter, and discard any remaining cigarettes. After your car is clean, make this a non-smoking area for yourself and other guests who ride in your car. By preparing your car, you will begin to break any associations that you may have between driving your car and smoking a cigarette. For example, if somebody cuts you off when you are driving and normally you would reach for a cigarette, you will now be forced to adopt an alternative strategy to manage this frustration. Also, as a non-smoking area your car will become a safe haven for you when you are tempted to smoke. Now you have eliminated one more trigger or cue for your smoking.

3. **Clean and deodorize your home.** Since you have now limited your smoking to only one room in your home, you can begin to clean and prepare the remaining rooms for your actual quit date. Get your carpets and draperies cleaned. Remove the odor of cigarettes from your furniture and clothing. Discover and remove those hidden cigarettes that may be lurking in the couch cushion, under the bed, or in the back of the refrigerator. During those initial days after your quit date, you may be tempted by any stray cigarette that you can find. Remove the temptation now before your quit date.

Preparation of Your Physical Self

Once your surroundings are prepared it is time to get yourself physically in shape for the quitting process. As you've seen in the preceding chapters, nicotine is a physically addicting chemical and as such your body may experience some withdrawal symptoms after you quit smoking. To make the process a little more comfortable, it is important to get yourself physically prepared for these changes.

1. **Visit your dentist.** Get your teeth cleaned. This will serve to remind you that you are about to begin life as a non-smoker. With the tar and nicotine removed from your teeth you are literally starting fresh without cigarettes.

2. **Monitor your alcohol consumption prior to and immediately after quitting.** The effects of alcohol are intensified when used in conjunction with cigarettes. That is, when alcohol and cigarettes are used together they each bring out the most harmful physical effects of the other. Further, when you drink alcohol your inhibitions are decreased and you are therefore more likely to relapse into smoking. For many smokers alcohol is also paired or associated with smoking. Therefore, when you have a drink you may automatically begin thinking about a cigarette, which puts you more at risk for relapsing into smoking. It may be important for you to avoid alcohol during the first couple of months after quitting until you are beyond the most difficult phase of quitting. Then you can slowly reintroduce alcohol consumption back into your life.

3. **Reduce your caffeine consumption prior to quitting.** Nicotine acts on the body by changing your metabolism. If you are used to consuming a fair amount of caffeine as a

smoker, your body may not be able to tolerate the same amount after you quit smoking. If this is the case, you may experience a jittery/nervous sensation which may not be related to tobacco withdrawal but rather caffeine intoxication. Several weeks before your quit date begin to reduce your caffeine consumption. Remember, caffeine is not just found in coffee but also in chocolate, soda pop, etc. Once you have quit smoking you will then be in a better position to re-establish an appropriate amount of caffeine for you.

4. **Get plenty of rest.** During your first smoke-free week it is important to get plenty of rest. You probably have been bombarding your body with the drug nicotine for many years. Once you stop the drug your body needs time to readjust without the drug. This healing process can be difficult and exhausting for the first couple of weeks. Plenty of rest will help move you physically through this process with greater ease. Think about this phase as a time for recovery.

5. **Drink plenty of fluids.** The healing process requires good nutrition and plenty of fluids. Try to drink fruit juices, which tend to cut down on the craving for nicotine for many people.

6. **Use healthy oral substitutes.** During the initial few weeks after quitting it is important to have healthy foods prepared for snacking. For example, keep celery, carrots, raisins, apples, pickles, sunflower seeds, etc., readily available for snacking. These snacks will help you when a craving strikes and you need something oral to satisfy you. However, make sure that the snacks you are choosing are low in calories and high in bulk. This will help with the craving but minimize the weight gain.

7. **Chew sugarless gum and hard candy.** During the first few weeks after you quit smoking your throat may feel dry or you may have a "tickle" cough; sucking on ice chips, hard candy, or chewing gum can help. Also, you can use the candy or gum as a substitute when you have a craving.

Preparation of Your Emotional Self

One of the biggest challenges to quitting smoking is preparing yourself emotionally. Many smokers talk about feeling a sense of loss when thinking about quitting smoking. You may find yourself thinking about quitting smoking as losing a friend or at the very least losing your coping strategy. Either way you describe it you may sense the loss of security and control when you quit smoking. To overcome these feelings you need to prepare yourself emotionally for the process of quitting smoking, and for life after cigarettes.

1. **Repeat to yourself your reasons for needing to quit smoking.** Your reasons for needing to quit smoking will provide you with the strength and willpower to get through the quitting process. Review these reasons. Reinforce them to yourself several times a day. Write them down and carry them with you. Place them in a visible area for yourself.

2. **Plan activities for your first smoke-free week.** The worst thing that can happen on your quit date or the weeks that follow is to find yourself in a situation where you are craving a cigarette and you have no alternative strategy available to you other than reaching for a cigarette. Plan activities that are inconsistent with smoking such as doing crossword puzzles, jogging, swimming, washing dishes, going to the grocery store, visiting the library or church, etc. Idle or empty time can be dangerous during the initial quitting process. Stay active and busy.

3. **Occupy your hands with other objects.** Use pencils, toothpicks, paper clips, rubber bands, etc., to occupy your hands when you feel something is missing without a cigarette.

4. **Beware of cigarette advertisements.** As a smoker you have probably been bombarded with literature on cigarettes, offered many coupons and rebates on cigarettes, and tempted by magazine and billboard ads. Don't be tempted. It may be helpful for you to analyze and seriously consider what these ads are really saying to you. For example, ask yourself how companies have been able to sell you a product that causes serious medical diseases that can lead to death. Why is it that the individuals who are portrayed in these ads always have smooth skin and white teeth? Nicotine alters the elasticity in the skin and yellows your teeth. Is your health really only worth that fifty cent coupon? Why do cigarette ads always show healthy, young, attractive individuals who are very happy? Most smokers tend to suffer from some effects of their smoking habit such as coughing and more frequent episodes of colds, bronchitis, and pneumonia. Many smokers continue to smoke as a way of dealing with depression and stress. What is so cool and refreshing about tar sticking to your lungs, and 4,000-plus substances being deposited in your lungs (including arsenic, formaldehyde, and carbon monoxide)? After years of smoking many smokers would not be able to participate in the vigorous activities that are shown in cigarette ads, nor are they able to breathe in and smell the fresh mountain air that is shown. Cigarette advertisements are successful in luring individuals into smoking and continuing to smoke by appealing to your perceived vulnerabilities. Everyone wants to be seen as attractive, successful, sexy, and fun. The reality is that by being pulled in by these ads you are risking your life to help the tobacco company make money. If you remind yourself of these realities you will be less likely to be tempted and intrigued by these ads. Rather you should be angry that they are making money at your expense.

5. **Never allow yourself to think that one cigarette won't hurt.** Many smokers relapse because they fall into the trap of believing that they can control their smoking and one cigarette won't hurt. This is harmful thinking because the majority of smokers may be able to have one for a while but eventually this will lead to two and before you realize it you will be back smoking the same quantity of cigarettes. Further, in order for your body to begin healing itself and to complete the withdrawal process you need to have all nicotine out of your system. By smoking one cigarette you re-introduce nicotine back into your system, which delays healing.

6. **"Smoking is no longer an option for me."** Immediately after quitting you may find yourself looking for excuses to justify smoking. Excuses are easy to find when you are looking for them. However, if you have told yourself that smoking is not an option for you anymore you will need to find another option when you feel stressed or nervous, or when you are finishing a meal or waiting for a friend. On your quit date remind yourself that smoking is no longer an option for you and therefore you must handle whatever situation presents itself to you. This statement will empower you to find and use alternative coping strategies.

Fear of "Losing a Friend"

As your quit date approaches, you may find yourself feeling sad—as if you were about to lose a friend. Frequently, smokers will describe their cigarettes as a good "friend." Smoking may have helped them deal with periods of stress in their life, been a source of comfort when they felt lonely and depressed, and in some ways proved a companion when they felt socially awkward, angry, or isolated. If you share these feelings you may be fearful of what life will be like without this "friend." The following exercise is one developed in workshops. Smokers have reported that when they put this "friend" in a different context they could let go with a little more ease. By following the instructions below you, too, will be able to see your "friend" in a new way.

Close your eyes and picture your cigarette. Imagine that the cigarette is as tall as you are and you are standing side by side. Put your arm around the cigarette. You are now feeling comfort and support from your "friend." You believe that this "friend" will support you, will help you to feel in control, will take away your worry and stress, and will provide companionship for you when you are lonely. Imagine that the two of you are walking arm in arm. You believe in this "friend" and you trust this "friend." You are now approaching a grassy knoll. As you get closer to the hill, you see a hole in the ground with dirt piled around it. Your "friend" brings you closer to the hole. You feel the cold air and see that it is a grave site. Your name is on the gravestone. Arm in arm your "friend" walks you around the hole. You continue to get closer and closer to the edge of the hole. You begin to lose your footing and you reach for your "friend." You are afraid. You keep reaching and reaching and reaching for your "friend" but your friend keeps walking you closer and closer to the dark hole. Is this your "friend"?

The above exercise can be frightening and sobering. However, it is important for you to focus on the reality of your smoking. A friend would not want you to be in harm's way. A friend wants what is best for you. Although you may not find yourself using the word "friend" when you think about your cigarettes, you may be using and relying on them as such. Remember, a true friend does not just put a bandage on a situation but rather helps to guide you toward long-term coping. Cigarettes may make you feel better for the moment but in the end they lead you closer and closer to years of suffering. Cigarettes are not your friend.

Enlisting Social Support for Your Quit Date

1. **Use your support systems.** Remind your friends and family that you are going through the quitting process and that it is important to you that they support you. Smokers who have more social support have more success in quitting. Avoid friends or family members who may be jealous of your attempt and success at quitting smoking, particularly if they themselves have failed in the past to quit smoking. Rely on individuals who really want to see you succeed, including those who have successfully quit smoking or who are non-smokers.

2. **Be assertive and direct when asking for support.** Be assertive when asking that others not smoke around you or place you in high risk situations. Be specific in your request for support or help. For example, you may ask that others be tolerant of irritable behavior during the first couple of weeks, suggest that others not smoke around you, and seek out rewards and praise from others for your efforts. Everyone needs encouragement and praise for persevering through the difficult process of quitting smoking. Don't view this as a sign of weakness.

3. **Negotiating with a live-in smoker.** Living with a smoker may make your efforts to quit smoking more difficult. Therefore, it is important to work out an agreement prior to your quit date that you can both feel comfortable with. For example, you may request that the smoker not leave cigarettes lying around the house. It may be a good idea to have the smoker smoke in only one room in the house or at least not smoke in your presence during the first couple of weeks after your quit date. Reinforce to the smoker how important

quitting smoking is to you and how you value his or her support. Request that the smoker not do things or say things to undermine your efforts to quit smoking. If the smoker really cares about you and your health he or she will want to support your efforts in improving your overall well-being. Sometimes it is difficult for current smokers (even those with good intentions) to really support someone else's efforts to quit smoking. This can occur for several reasons. The smoker may be jealous that you are succeeding at quitting while he or she is not and therefore feel weak by comparison. The smoker may feel abandoned for having lost his or her "smoking partner." This may take some of the social pleasure of smoking away from him or her. Prior to your quit date, it will be helpful for you to discuss these feelings with the smoker in order to prevent any potential sabotage of your efforts and to increase all-around support of you.

4. **Working with a smoker.** What do you do if a co-worker smokes and is not interested in quitting? It is much easier to negotiate with a family member or friend than it is with a co-worker because loved ones presumably have your best interest at heart. However, this may not be the case with fellow employees. It is important to make a request for support or at the very least for respect of your efforts to quit smoking. Your co-workers may feel that you do not have a right to impose on them or they may share feelings such as jealousy. This is all right. You still have a right to make the request and to work out an equitable arrangement regarding smoking in the workplace. For example, you may ask for a transfer to a work area that is smoke-free. You may find your co-workers commenting on your attitude and saying, "You are so crabby you're driving us crazy—just smoke a cigarette." Remind yourself and them that part of your irritability is related to nicotine withdrawal and therefore it is short-term. This short-term irritability is probably related to physical changes in your body. However, it is important that you not use this as an opportunity to intentionally treat others poorly. Monitor your own behavior and mood. Get distance from a situation if you feel yourself getting irritated. This will help reduce any potential conflict in the workplace. Finally, you may also need to discuss the office smoking policy with your employer. Be aware of your rights.

Your Quit Date and the Weeks That Follow

1. **Visualize and reinterpret your physical symptoms as "symptoms of recovery."** Earlier in this chapter you saw a list of physical withdrawal symptoms that you may experience during the initial phase of quitting. Keep in mind that these symptoms are short-term and necessary to the healing process. Try to think about them as "symptoms of recovery." This means that when you are feeling irritable and restless or are having a "craving" you will remind yourself that although these symptoms may not feel good they remind you that your body is healing. If your body were transparent you would be able to see positive changes occurring. However, since you cannot see the changes you need to use these "physical symptoms" as a reminder or cue that your body is healing. "The pain is healing pain." Each time you feel "uncomfortable" think about what is happening in your body. Use the following imagery exercise to guide you through this healing process.

Close your eyes and imagine your lungs. See the black tar sitting on the tiny little air sacs that makes it hard for you to breathe at times. Each time you feel "uncomfortable" imagine this tar gradually being lifted off your lungs. Each breath that you take feels easier. You feel the clean air healing the wounded lung tissue. You see the four thousand-plus particles that are floating in your bloodstream being washed away. You feel your arteries relaxing and allowing blood to pass more readily through, cutting your risk for strokes and heart attacks. With each passing day you see more and more healing occurring inside your body. With each "discomfort" that you feel you see healing occurring in your body. You remind yourself that these symptoms are short-term.

2. **Pay attention to your "high risk" situations.** These are times, such as when you are stressed at work or finishing a meal, when you are most likely to desire a cigarette. During the initial weeks after quitting smoking it is important that you pay close attention to these situations or feelings. Prepare for them and have alternative strategies available. You are most at risk for automatically falling back into your routine of smoking during the first couple of weeks after quitting smoking if you are not vigilant about these "high risk" areas. Try either to avoid these situations or at the very least to have alternative strategies available.

3. **Use distraction techniques.** When you find yourself tempted to smoke a cigarette get some distance from the thought or situation. Distraction is a wonderful technique for preventing impulsive smoking. Distraction could include physically removing yourself from the situation, shifting your thought to something other than smoking, or engaging in an activity that makes smoking difficult (such as washing dishes, exercising, or visiting a non-smoking friend). It is important to remember that the "desire" to smoke is generally very brief, lasting only seconds. Initially after quitting you may find that the "desire" for a cigarette feels fairly strong and you may "desire" a cigarette quite frequently. However, with time you will notice that the strength and frequency of the desire will decrease. This is why distraction can be very helpful. If you distract yourself for a brief period of time, the "desire" will fade and over time you will not experience the desire as often. Say to yourself, "This desire will only last for a short period of time and if I give into it and smoke I will have to start the healing process all over again. If I can distract myself the desire will pass and I will be one step closer to reducing the frequency of this desire." Reward yourself each time you successfully distract yourself away from the "desire."

4. **Reinforce your reasons for needing to quit smoking.** During the initial weeks after quitting smoking you will need to continue to reinforce for yourself your reasons for needing to quit smoking. Remember, these reasons need to be specific and personal to you. These reasons will help get you through the periods of temptation.

5. **Repeat to yourself the benefits of quitting smoking.** You need to remind yourself that good will come of the discomfort, inconvenience, lifestyle changes, and general effort that you are making during this quitting process. Repeat the following list of benefits to yourself several times a day.

   1. Circulation improves
   2. Decreases or cures allergies (smokers have three times more allergies than non-smokers)
   3. Eliminates chronic bronchitis (which decreases energy level, resistance to infection, and predisposes one to emphysema) in a few months after cessation
   4. Reduces number of cavities and increases chance of keeping your own teeth (smokers have three times more cavities and gum disease than non-smokers)
   5. Decreases risk of esophageal cancer by 500 percent
   6. Decreases risk of kidney cancer by 50 percent
   7. Decreases frequency and intensity of headaches
   8. Non-smoking women have less discomfort and less problems with menopause

9. Decreases risk of osteoporosis

10. Increases lung and breathing capacity

11. Increases female fertility by 50 percent

12. Significantly decreases your risk for lung cancer and emphysema

Excerpted and adapted with permission from *The Stop Smoking Workbook: Your Guide to Healthy Quitting* by Lori Stevic-Rust, Ph.D., and Anita Maximin, Psy.D. For more information on this and related books, see the "Further Reading" section in the back of the book.

CHAPTER 19

Gambling

Problem gambling can affect your entire family emotionally, financially, socially, and even physically. Many of these effects are subtle and hidden from view. Even when family members recognize the effects, they may not immediately think of gambling as the source of the difficulties. Taking into account how the entire family responds to the problem gambler helps to cope with these strains. Ignoring the family's role may make it easier for members to unintentionally contribute to the problem gambler's behavior.

We often take family life for granted as part of our everyday reality. It is a little like the air we breathe; most of the time we don't pay much attention to it. Only when we grow short of breath do we become alert to the atmosphere around us. By doing so, we prepare ourselves to take steps to improve our situation. In the same way, with your family facing a possible crisis in the form of problem gambling, you can reap big dividends from assessing your family's current circumstances.

In this chapter, you will learn to understand and address problem gambling as a family matter. The specific ways in which the gambler's behavior may be having a negative impact on each family member are discussed. We also point out some of the less as well as the more effective ways your family can respond to the presence of problem gambling.

Understanding Problem Gambling in Your Family

Problem gambling affects the family as a whole, as well as each and every member. In some families, problem gambling becomes a central organizing factor. Anything that happens to one member inevitably affects every other member. Like the body, the family is composed of individual parts, each of which affects the others. In the body, for example, a broken leg will lead to lack of activity, resulting in decreased muscle tone and decreased cardiovascular functioning. The family works the same way. The changes in one individual brought about by the presence of problem gambling triggers changes in other family members.

For example, if a woman becomes depressed about the family's financial troubles resulting from her husband's problem gambling, the children in the family may become depressed as well, not because the family is facing difficult financial conditions, but because their mother has become withdrawn and inattentive to their needs for affection. It is important to remember, however, that to respond effectively to the situation it is not necessary to track every possible effect of problem gambling on the family. A general appreciation of problem gambling as a familywide problem and an understanding of the major ways it may be currently impacting your family should help you to manage the situation.

Roles and Responsibilities

Most family roles and responsibilities are divided among family members. Parents are primarily responsible for caring for the younger members of the family and teaching them how to speak and act in various situations. Children may be responsible for learning, performing daily chores, and providing emotional support to other family members. The effects of problem gambling will vary depending on the roles and responsibilities of the problem gambler within the family and the relationship of other family members to that individual. The effects of a parent's gambling problem on the family will be quite different than that of a teenager's gambling problem, because their roles and responsibilities are different. Similarly, parents and children will be affected in quite different ways by a grandparent's problem gambling because parents' and children's relationships to that grandparent are different.

Family Life Cycles

Families go through predictable periods of change as individual family members age and families evolve. The general characteristics of the family life cycle are similar for most families. Typical stages include marriage, settling down, becoming parents, child raising, mid-life, and retirement, each with its own role expectations and tasks. In the early years of marriage, couples typically establish their own family identity separate from their families-of-origin. With the arrival of children, the emphasis shifts to caring for the young and transmitting cultural values to the next generation. During mid-life, the family may be focused on redefining the relationship between parents and their adult children and accommodating itself to new family members brought in by the marriages of their children and the arrival of grandchildren. Furthermore, toward the end of the family life cycle, parents typically become increasingly reliant on their adult children for practical and emotional support. Within this broad cycle, each family establishes its own unique course, depending on the particular events experienced by that family (e.g., adjusting to a divorce, an illness, or death, or a sudden change in social or economic status).

As families move through these stages of growth and change, the roles and responsibilities of individual family members change as well. Thus, a woman at mid-life who has spent two decades raising her children, now in their early twenties, may suddenly face an empty nest in which her maternal responsibilities are dramatically diminished. During such times of transition, family members go through periods of adjustment and perhaps conflict as they learn to renegotiate their relationships. This is a normal and expected development for all families.

Problem gambling usually disrupts the ability of the whole family and its members to perform the particular tasks appropriate to their stage in the life cycle. For example, one of the primary tasks for a recently married couple is to develop an identity independent of their families-of-origin. The loss of a well-paying job and several thousand dollars of debt forced one gambling client and his wife to borrow money from the wife's in-laws. But the money came attached with unwelcome strings: phone calls several times a week from the wife's parents, showering advice on the husband and private recriminations on the daughter for her poor choice of a marital partner. Both the client and his wife felt trapped in this new relationship with the wife's parents. In another example, an eighty-year-old retired postal worker, living alone, began running up sizeable debts with a local bookie. He bitterly resented the alarmed intervention of his adult children, viewing it as meddling with his independence, which, in any case, he had been gradually losing in recent years as his health had declined.

How Problem Gambling Affects the Family

Problem gambling disrupts family life through its negative financial consequences, the deterioration of basic trust between the gambler and other family members, and the loss of the problem gambler's ability to carry out his or her normal family roles and responsibilities. These developments in turn produce social, emotional, and even physical changes in the family's well-being.

Family members often respond to these effects long before they become aware of problem gambling in their family, making subtle changes in their routine behaviors, shifting family roles and responsibilities, alternating everyday patterns of interaction and communication, and reducing their contacts with the outside world. Because these changes occur gradually, family members may be unaware of them. As the problem gambling grows more severe and disruptive, however, the family's adjustments will necessarily become more dramatic, eventually forcing their way into the family's consciousness.

Financial and Social Effects

The obvious financial consequences of problem gambling include loss of income, depletion of savings, incurring large debts, damage to the family's credit rating, and decline in overall standard of living. Additionally, there are many other indirect effects that arise from such changes in the family's financial status. A lowered standard of living can produce a sense of deprivation, depressed feelings, and anger toward the gambler as the cause of the change in the family's fortunes. Family members may be involuntarily cut off from important social relationships when the problem gambler herself alienates extended family, friends, neighbors, or co-workers by borrowing money and not repaying it.

Families of problem gamblers often choose voluntarily to withdraw from social contacts with extended family, friends, neighbors, and co-workers. They do so partly to focus their energies on addressing the increased stresses within the family, but largely to avoid situations where they might reveal details of the problem gambler's behavior and the family's current financial troubles. For example, an adolescent son of a client revealed in a family session how he had been avoiding close friends at school for months because he was ashamed that his father's gambling debts had forced the family to sell their house and move to a small apartment in a neighborhood several miles away.

Family members often reinforce and add to their depressed feelings after they pull back from regular contact with extended family, friends, and neighbors. These contacts are essential for emotional health; without them, some families turn inward, become overly involved in each others' lives and adopt an "us versus them" attitude.

Loss of Trust

The psychologist Erik Erikson observed that the formation and nurturing of basic trust is the first fundamental task in human development. Trust is essential in family relationships. It extends to nearly every aspect of family life. When we say we trust a family member, we mean not only that we trust them to be honest in their words, but honest in their deeds. In other words, we know we can depend on them in large and small ways, from providing child care, to emotional support, to handling money responsibly, to taking a phone message. A violation of trust—betrayal—is considered one of the worst transgressions any relationship can endure.

When a family member conceals and lies about his problem gambling, he introduces distrust into family relationships. Although this distrust is most evident between the gambler and family members, the problem gambler's deception also may create subtle doubts in the minds of other family members about their ability to trust each other. If children, for example, learn that one parent has lied to them about gambling, they may wonder how much they can depend on the honesty and reliability of the other parent. Betrayal of trust can produce profound feelings of depression, anxiety, sadness, and anger among family members. It can also make it more difficult for the family to organize effectively to address the problem and can inhibit family members from reaching out for social support outside the family.

We often think of trust as an all-or-nothing phenomenon. However, viewing trust in this manner makes the restoration of trust in family life very difficult. Any significant betrayal appears to leave little in the way of foundations on which to begin rebuilding trusting relationships. In reality, most families will find they can still rely on an individual who has betrayed them—to some degree and in some areas. Adopting this more flexible view can be an important first step toward recovering trust within the family.

Impairment in Roles and Responsibilities

The problem gambler's ability to perform her normal roles and responsibilities in the family declines as she becomes more preoccupied with winning back her losses and erasing the negative consequences of her gambling. This often leaves other family members feeling they cannot depend on the gambler to act responsibly and live up to family commitments and expectations. A young mother who repeatedly fails in her promise to pick up her children at the end of the school day may use excuses to conceal the real reason for her tardiness—playing the slot machines at a local club. Her young children may grow increasingly anxious and angry, without truly understanding why their mother is late.

Family members are often forced to take over many of the roles and responsibilities at which the gambler has failed. Taking over new roles may leave them feeling anxious and resentful toward the gambler for having forced them into a new and uncomfortable role in the family. In one family, a wife who had developed a gambling problem brought in a critical second paycheck which helped cover the family's monthly expenses. Distraught over her gambling problem, she grew seriously depressed and lost her job. Her husband had to moonlight at a local convenience store in the evening in addition to his day job. On weekends, he spent most of his time looking after their two young children. Within three months, he desperately needed counseling, explaining he felt exhausted, angry, and depressed.

Paradoxically, for some individuals, taking over new roles may have a positive effect, at least initially. An adult daughter with a cognitively impaired mother who had always dominated her was placed in charge of her mother's financial affairs after a judge declared her mother legally incompetent for having gambled away her life savings on the state lottery and magazine contests. In therapy, the daughter confessed that she had mixed emotions about this new arrangement. On the one hand, she was secretly enjoying the reversal in roles, but, on the other, she felt guilty about her pleasure in such a sad and destructive situation. Her ambivalence disappeared quickly, however. Within a matter of weeks, she became thoroughly irritated by her mother's constant complaints and the time required each week to go over her mother's accounts.

Pessimistic Beliefs

The longer problem gambling goes on, the more likely family members come to believe they are helpless to change the situation. If the problem gambler is concealing the problem from the family, family members will fail to understand the source of their difficulties. No matter what the family does to try and improve conditions, things will stay the same or get worse, because the true source of the problem remains hidden. Even after the family suspects the truth, or the problem gambler has confessed her situation, the problems may seem insurmountable, particularly when the gambling family member continues his gambling or returns to gambling after having stopped for some weeks or months. Thoughts of helplessness may give rise to feelings of intense sadness and despair, frustration, and anger. These beliefs can spill over into other areas of family life, making it harder for family members to take on new roles and responsibilities to keep the family functioning.

The Impact on Physical Health

Family members are often unaware of the indirect effects that problem gambling can have on physical health, but those effects are often significant. Physical difficulties result from negative changes in emotional functioning, reinforced by social isolation. Chronic anxiety, anger, and sadness can impair the healthy functioning of the immune system, interrupt normal routines, and make it more difficult to obtain adequate sleep, nutrition, and exercise. Family members may respond to added stress with increased vulnerability to infectious disease and a variety of symptoms including headaches, gastrointestinal difficulties, backaches, asthmatic symptoms, cardiovascular difficulties, allergies, and skin problems.

Disruptions in physical health can compound disruptions in other areas. One client developed debilitating headaches around the time his wife's problem gambling became increasingly severe. He was forced to take time off from work and lost a promotion that would have eased the financial pressures on the family considerably. Of course, nongambling factors also may contribute to family stress and to physical ailments. Whatever the cause, if your health or that of other family members is suffering, we advise you to seek appropriate medical care and to discuss your family situation with your regular physician.

Position of the Gambler in the Family

The position of the problem gambler in the family—whether parent, spouse, child, or older relative—will influence how problem gambling affects the family, how the problem gambler relates to other family members, and how other family members respond to the problem gambler.

If Your Partner Has a Gambling Problem

If your partner has a gambling problem, the effects on your family are pervasive because of his or her central role in the family's life. In a well-functioning family, adult partners play multiple roles, including breadwinner, nurturing parent, marital partner, and social representative of the family to the outside world. Problem gambling behavior disrupts your partner's ability to perform each of these roles. As these disruptions become obvious (e.g., overdue bills piling up, friends and neighbors avoiding family members, loss of interest by the gambling spouse in sexual activity, lack of attention to the children), your stress will grow, likely resulting in feelings of depression, anxiety, anger, and perhaps a sense of betrayal. One woman in treatment spoke of feeling "alone and abandoned" by her problem gambling husband. She was angry that her husband had let her wonder for more than two years why things had gone wrong in their relationship. When he finally admitted to gambling, she was tempted to retaliate by starting an affair with an attractive co-worker.

Partners of problem gamblers often compensate by taking over the responsibilities abdicated by the gambler. They may feel the need to become a "super parent" for the children or a surrogate parent for the gambling partner. For example, a husband whose partner has a gambling problem may run himself ragged leaving work early each weekday to be home when the children arrive at the end of the day, cooking dinner, putting the kids to bed, and attending school sports events on the weekend. Similarly, the wife of a problem gambler may need to get a second job and take over managing the family finances, traditionally handled by her problem gambling husband. This approach may buy her a sense of control but it will likely result in more stress on her and the rest of the family at a time when the problem gambler is less available to meet any of the family's needs.

If you have children, any increased stress on you will likely affect the lives of your children too. Children are particularly vulnerable to the effects of stress, because they are less well equipped intellectually and emotionally to deal with disruptions in family life. Moreover, children are intensely dependent on their parents for emotional as well as practical support.

Young children are less able to reflect on their feelings and more likely to act on them. Children's distress often shows up as declining performance in school, neglect of household chores, or misbehavior. Younger children often have idealized images of their parents that they try to preserve in the face of evidence to the contrary. They may resist acknowledging any problem associated with the gambling parent and may, instead, offer explanations and rationalizations for their parent's erratic behavior, both to other family members and to friends and neighbors.

Older children may feel subtle pressures to take on some of the roles and responsibilities neglected by their gambling parent, becoming a little "Mom" or "Dad" to younger children in the family or a surrogate spouse for the nongambling parent. Older children in particular may feel intense embarrassment and shame about their gambling parent's behavior and the consequences for their families. They may avoid social contacts with friends or relatives, where such contacts might lead to questions about Dad's being laid off from work, or the repossessing of one of the family cars, or the angry arguments between their parents.

If Your Child Has a Gambling Problem

Discovering that your adolescent or college-age child has a gambling problem can be a devastating experience. Adolescents and many young adults continue to play a central role in the emotional life of the family, and to a lesser degree in the social life of the family—even if they have physically left the household to attend school or to work. In many families, children may also remain integrated to some degree in the economic life of the family. They may be living at home, working, and contributing financially to family expenses or receiving financial support from parents for school or living arrangements elsewhere. Consequently, an adolescent or college-age child with a gambling problem can disrupt both the emotional and financial life of the family.

Adolescent children are in a transitional stage between childhood and adulthood. Although they seek increasing independence from family life, they still require parental support and guidance. Parents are involved in a transition of their own: from full-time parents to independent adults free of parental responsibilities. Problem gambling may play a central role in a child/parent struggle over redefining the adolescent or college-age child's relationship to parents and other members of the family. A desperate adolescent may turn to parents for emotional support or to be "bailed out" of debt. Alternatively, parents may intervene on their own initiative if they suspect their child is in serious trouble. Either way, parents may take on increasing responsibility for the child's psychological and financial welfare just when the child is expected to be doing more for himself or herself.

Both parents and child may feel strong ambivalence. Parents will be concerned for their child's welfare, yet irritated and frustrated by the adolescent's irresponsibility. While some parents will be tempted to rescue their children, and release the child from all financial responsibility, others may blame the child for not heeding past advice and guidance. They may angrily decide to let the child suffer the consequences of his or her actions. They may also harbor secret doubts about their adequacy as parents, feeling guilty and self-reproachful, wondering where they went wrong and what they could have done differently. The child, on the other hand, may openly resent the intervention of his parents, even as he covertly feels grateful for it. Parental intervention may arouse simultaneous feelings in the child of shame, guilt, and relief. If the adolescent or young adult had left home and now returns, both parents and other children must adjust to the child's reentry into the daily life of the family. In situations where the gambling child has accumulated significant debts, the financial impact on the family can be significant. Depending on the financial status of the family, all family members may be affected by the financial burden.

If Your Parent or Older Relative Has a Gambling Problem

The effects of problem gambling on your family members will vary depending on the degree to which an older parent or relative is physically and socially integrated into your family's affairs and everyday family life. If an older parent is living in the same household with you, the effects of problem gambling on the household will be immediate and unavoidable. But even when older adults are living at some physical distance from the family, the development of a gambling problem still can affect your family's emotional, social, and financial functioning significantly.

Helping an older relative with a gambling problem can take many different forms, from simply offering advice all the way to petitioning a court of law for control of the elderly family member's financial affairs. Such interventions may re-ignite old struggles between you and your parent over power and control of finances, daily living conditions, and discretionary life choices, which you may have thought resolved decades earlier. Aging relatives want to maintain their capacity for independent living as long as possible, including decision-making control over their personal and financial affairs. Your parent is likely to experience your concerned efforts as a direct challenge to his or her autonomy and competency.

Such struggles can be emotionally volatile and stressful for both you and your older relative. Your parent may feel angry at you, guilty and ashamed about his gambling problem, and anxious about losing control over personal matters. You may feel frustrated and irritated that your relative is not more appreciative of your concerned efforts. You also may find yourself anxious about challenging your parent's authority—an emotional holdover from earlier struggles when you were an adolescent. These battles and their attendant emotions can be exacerbated in those situations where your family has a direct financial stake in the affairs of your older parent. This can happen if you feel financially responsible for the older individual or if you are counting on receiving a share of your older relative's inheritance—an inheritance which you may see dwindling from gambling losses.

If you have other siblings, you may have difficulty coordinating your actions vis-à-vis your elderly parent. Siblings may have different emotional reactions to an elderly parent's problem gambling, depending on their relationship with the parent. They may also have different ideas about what should be done. Siblings often live at varying distances from the parent; the burden of taking care of the situation may fall on those siblings who are geographically closest. You may feel resentment if you end up more involved with your parent and you may feel guilty if others take on the lion's share of the effort. Working with siblings may bring up old conflicts and rivalries, particularly those involving competition as children for the attention and favor of your parents.

If there are younger children in the family, they can be affected in a number of ways by the uncontrolled gambling of a grandparent or other older relative. As adults become stressed and preoccupied dealing with the behavior of their elderly relatives, this stress and inattention will be passed on to their own children. Just as they idealize their parents to some degree, children may idealize their grandparents as well. Grandparents and parents may vie for the loyalties of grandchildren, trying to convert the child to their point of view about the gambling of the grandparent. This may be the case especially when grandparents live in the same household or nearby. Being placed in this position represents a no-win situation for younger children, since, in effect, they are asked to take sides in a struggle that they may understand only vaguely and have no way of resolving. If parents continue to be preoccupied over an extended period of time with a grandparent's gambling problem, younger children may be asked to become more self-sufficient and to take over new tasks for the family unit, such as helping in the preparation of meals or caring for the youngest members of the family. If attempted interventions result in the alienation of the grandparent from the adults in the family, then children may be deprived of the emotional presence and support they previously enjoyed from a close relationship with the older relative.

Ineffective Family Responses

Every family has a unique pattern of response to problem gambling. All families respond effectively in some ways and less effectively in others. Knowing how to recognize and address ineffective family responses will help you to develop a sound and effective approach to dealing with problem gambling.

1. Denial: Almost all families respond to changing conditions with some degree of denial, particularly in the early stages of a gambling problem. Denial refers to the tendency to neither notice nor acknowledge the behavior of the problem gambler and the effects of that behavior on the family. It can take many forms. Some family members simply may act as if the problem doesn't exist. Some may refuse to talk about it. Some may become openly angry if you bring up the subject and assert that your family member needs to seek help. Other family members may fail to notice any changes in their emotions or their behavior attributable to the problem gambling. Even when the gambler's behavior and its impacts on the family can no longer be ignored, family members may persist in denial by downplaying the severity of the situation.

In the short run, denial may be an effective response, insofar as it allows family members to maintain smooth family relations, continue functioning in their daily lives, and avoid disruptive feelings of depression, anxiety, anger, guilt, or shame. In the long run, however, denial becomes ineffective, because it allows all family members (including the problem gambler) to pretend that the gambling behavior does not exist or pose any significant problem for the family, or to persist in the belief that it will eventually "fix itself."

2. Co-dependence: A co-dependent family member unintentionally supports or reinforces the problem gambler's dysfunctional behavior. Co-dependent responses develop slowly over time as well-meaning family members take steps that seem appropriate, logical, and even necessary without recognizing that their behavior generates unintended consequences.

   Co-dependent responses include enabling and rescuing. Enabling is generally done to keep the family functioning but also makes it easier for the gambler to gamble. For example, a wife may step in and start taking her son to his weekend Little League games because "Dad is just too busy at work these days and we don't want to bother him." Rescuing is done to minimize short-term damage to the gambler but often carries more severe negative long-term consequences. For example, children may bail out an elderly father from his frequent losses at the casino because allowing him to continue gambling seems to help him cope with the recent loss of his lifelong spouse. After all, they reason, he's on a fixed income and he always seems excited and upbeat the day after his weekly trip to the casino, doesn't he?

   Co-dependent responses can include decision making, ways of thinking, and emotional responses. A wife may share her husband's excitement when he comes home with $500 in lottery ticket winnings while ignoring the $3,000 he lost over the previous four weeks. A co-dependent partner may blame herself for "causing" her husband to play poker five nights a week. A father may feel secret enjoyment from hearing his son's stories of nights of big wins and big losses. Family members may avoid social contacts with friends or relatives who might challenge the problem gambler's behavior. In these cases, the family member's co-dependent behavior may be driven by the emotional benefits that he or she derives, while the larger context of the gambling's impact on the family is ignored.

   Sometimes, as gambling dominates the family landscape, a family member's life may be increasingly devoted to keeping the family functioning, minimizing short-term pain to the gambler while enjoying the few emotional benefits available in this environment. In this case, with her life revolving around gambling, a family member may understandably find her very sense of self defined only in relation to the gambling behavior.

3. Blaming: Blaming responses are common in families dealing with problem gambling. It is often easier to blame the problem gambler than to take the initiative to improve the situation. Divided and upset, family members may also blame each other for acting in ways that fail to relieve the crisis. In the family of one elderly problem gambling client, two sons and a daughter fell into repeated bickering about the best way to intervene to "protect" their father—and what was left of their potential inheritance—from his addiction to lotto scratch tickets. When one of the sons finally petitioned a judge for legal guardianship of the father's affairs, the other two siblings were outraged and testified that their brother was violating their father's rights as a competent adult.

   Blame is a natural response when we perceive someone has fallen short of our expectations, violated our rights, or failed to meet social obligations or responsibilities. It involves a thought—in which we designate someone as responsible for some action—and an emotional component—usually anger. Blame shifts the burden of responsibility onto the other person for some perceived failure. It relieves the blamer of anxiety from any concerns about failing in his or her responsibilities. It allows the blamer to feel self-righteous about his or her own actions.

Although blame may make the blamer feel better in the short run, it usually results in the blamed person feeling anger, resentment, and/or shame. Often those who are blamed respond with defensiveness or denial. Blame does little to promote dialogue or collaborative problem solving.

As previously noted, sometimes family members end up blaming themselves for the gambler's problem, a form of co-dependency. Family members may also blame themselves for ineffective responses or for failing to make things right in the family in spite of the gambler's behavior. This is also ineffective, as it may result in depressed mood, shame, and sadness, immobilizing family members instead of motivating them to take effective action.

4. Withdrawal and isolation: As stated previously, many families respond to problem gambling by withdrawing from social contact and isolating themselves from their friends, neighbors, and others who could be of assistance. But family members may also withdraw and isolate themselves from the problem gambler and each other. This is a natural response when emotional resources are overtaxed. It is designed to protect an individual from exposure to stressful encounters, anxiety, and conflict and the demands of other family members to do something to meet their needs or rectify the situation. Isolation also occurs when family members have been taught they must solve their problems "on their own," or they are too anxious or ashamed to seek support from others. Family members may also find themselves isolated if the family disagrees about the reality of the situation or the best course of action to address the problem. For example, you may have a sense of isolation if you are alone in suspecting or acknowledging problem gambling in the family.

There are three forms of isolation: physical, interpersonal, and emotional. Although it's possible to be physically isolated from your friends and neighbors, you're likely to be surrounded by your family. In spite of this, if family members communicate poorly with each other, you can be interpersonally isolated. And if no one talks openly about their feelings in the family, you will be emotionally isolated.

Withdrawal and isolation are ineffective ways to deal with problem gambling because they divide family members and prevent them from openly acknowledging the problem, discussing the issues, providing each other emotional support, and seeking support and information from outside the family. It also prevents the family from adopting a unified approach to dealing with the problem gambler and denies the problem gambler access to family support. Isolation also can make it easier to adopt co-dependent behaviors that actually reinforce the problem.

Putting It All Together

The important thing to remember about denial, codependency, blaming and shaming, and withdrawal and isolation is that almost no family confronting a gambling problem will escape them entirely, for these types of responses often appear to yield short-run benefits for individual family members and the family as a whole. But the persistence of these responses is counterproductive. Early understanding and recognition of these ineffective responses will help you to develop an effective set of family responses.

Effective Family Responses

1. Work together as a family: Since each family member is affected by problem gambling, each should be involved in a way that is consistent with their age, ability to understand, and appropriate responsibility for family affairs. Even the youngest family members can be offered explanations that they can understand. Older children can be enlisted to support measures the family chooses to take to address the problem.

   How the family works together to resolve the situation will depend on which family member is the problem gambler. When the gambler is a spouse, much of the effort will be confined to discussions and activities involving the married couple, particularly where younger children are involved. When older adolescent children form part of the family, they can be brought into general discussions and planning—and should certainly be informed of major decisions affecting their lives—but the decisions should remain in the hands of the adults.

   In the case of an older relative with a gambling problem, coordination between adult siblings who may be living in separate households will be critical to ensure that all agree on the nature of the problem and on the appropriate measures for resolving it. When an adolescent or college-age child is the gambler, both parents and the gambling child need to work closely together to coordinate their activities.

2. Openly acknowledge the existence of a problem: Families who successfully deal with problem gambling overcome their initial denial. Often, speaking candidly will make a gambling problem seem less formidable. Families who address a gambling problem openly are better equipped to take realistic stock of their situation and to develop adequate measures in response. Open discussion promotes involvement of all family members in developing solutions, including the problem gambler. Candor reduces the pressures on the family to maintain the gambling problem as a secret from the extended family and the outside world. Once problem gambling is no longer a secret, family members' sense of shame is often dissipated, and they are able to reach out to others beyond the family for emotional and practical support.

3. Restore basic trust: Family trust involves honesty in communication and dependency in roles and relationships. Trust must be restored between the problem gambler and family members and, if necessary, among other family members. The tendency to think of trust as completely undermining a relationship is often most pronounced in our closest relationships. If someone violates our complete trust, it is easy to conclude that the absence of complete trust is no trust. We often hear people say when they have been lied to by someone close to them, "I'll never trust him again."

   The key to restoring trust is recognizing that it is not an all-or-nothing phenomenon. Close examination will usually indicate that family members continue to trust each other to varying degrees in many family roles and relationships.

   Although trust can be disrupted overnight, it neither develops nor is rebuilt overnight. As your family struggles to rebuild this essential foundation of family life, you must understand that a successful effort often takes as long as a year. In the early stages, you will want to focus on those areas of trust that are most critical for addressing problem gambling and beginning the healing process.

4. Communicate clearly and caringly: Active listening strengthens the emotional bonds between family members and reassures them that others in the family care about them, respect them, and are interested in what they have to say. Speaking clearly and openly ensures that others fully understand the meaning behind your words. You can draw on

many techniques to improve communication within your family—see the chapters on Communication and Couple Skills in part I.

5. Provide emotional and practical support to each family member: Because each member of the family will be affected by the presence of problem gambling in different ways, support for each family member may take widely differing forms. Each family member should try to identify the kinds of support he or she needs and not be hesitant to ask for it. For children, emotional support might be as simple as offering reassurance that the family will successfully work through the current crisis, or it might involve a parent or an older sibling devoting extra time to reading, playing, or talking with the young child. For adults, it might take the form of a husband listening to his wife's fears about the well-being of their college-age daughter who has become involved in frequent sports betting. For a couple coping with the problem gambling of one of the partner's elderly parents, it might involve the other partner planning a surprise weekend away—just for fun and relaxation. Similarly, practical support may take many forms. For example, an older child might offer to relieve his mother from having to prepare dinner on those nights when she attends Gamblers Anonymous meetings.

6. Seek support from others outside the immediate family: Support from others may come from relatives, friends, work colleagues, spiritual counselors, members of Gamblers Anonymous, and professional counseling. Try to make use of a wide variety of these resources, for information, advice, emotional backing, and practical aid. Initially, many families feel isolated when forced to deal with a gambling problem. Overcoming that initial isolation is key to solving the problem successfully in the long term. Among friends and relatives—and even among many clerical and mental health professionals—this may require educating them about the nature of problem gambling and its effects before they are able to adequately provide needed forms of support.

Excerpted and adapted with permission from *Don't Leave It to Chance: A Guide for Families of Problem Gamblers* by Edward J. Federman, Ph.D., Charles E. Drebing, Ph.D., and Christopher Krebs, M.A. For more information on this and related books, see the "Further Reading" section in the back of the book.

CHAPTER 20

Internet Addiction

While surfing the Internet can be a fun, informative way to spend time, some of us may find that the future begins taking over too much of our time and negatively impacting our life. This chapter will help you assess whether or not you have an unhealthy relationship with the Internet, and possibly help others whom you are concerned about.

Are You Getting High on the Internet?

The fact that substances, such as alcohol and other mood-altering drugs, can create a physical and/or psychological dependence is well known and accepted. Not simply an interest, but rather a *driven pattern of use* that can produce a negative effect in your life.

More recently, however, there has been an acknowledgement that the compulsive performance of certain *behaviors* may mimic the addictive process found with drugs, alcohol, and other substances. The addition of behaviors, such as gambling, food, sex, work, TV, exercise, and shopping, to the definitions of addiction and compulsion represents a big change in the psychology and addictionology fields. Previously it was believed that a substance was necessary to evoke the symptoms of tolerance and withdrawal. We now know this is not true. I've seen many people in my practice who are addicted to a variety of behaviors. And some of these people are reporting serious consequences to their excessive Internet use.

Mike's story is fairly typical of the many stories that are reported to me. Mike is a fifteen-year-old high school student. He is a typical kid from a multimedia savvy generation. He found my Web site under Internet addiction and took my research survey. Mike e-mailed me asking if I had any suggestions for him as he thought he might have a problem. He was spending numerous hours online daily and it was beginning to affect his schoolwork. He was starting to feel that he had a problem with his Internet use and didn't know how to deal with it. When I asked him if he had seen a psychologist or therapist about this, he indicated that his psychologist didn't know about the Internet and was completely unfamiliar with the concept of compulsive Internet use.

This is not an unusual situation, as most mental health professionals know little about Internet addiction.

Although Internet addiction isn't an epidemic by any means, Mike's case is not unique. Cases like his are most probably under-reported and under-recognized by mental health and addictions professionals. Many professionals in the medical or psychological community are only now starting to recognize numerous cases in their own practice that appear to involve problems with use or abuse of the Internet.

Is the Internet Your Repeated Pleasure?

Whether or not we label this new phenomenon as a compulsion or as an addiction is of little relevance to those whose lives are being negatively affected. Labels will not help you decide if you're engaging in any behavior compulsively. You must first ask yourself if you've ever felt compelled to do something, especially something that started off as pleasurable, repeatedly? Have you ever done so, even when you knew that the consequences might be negative? The answer for most of us is probably yes to both questions. The Internet can be *your* repeated pleasure, and it is a pleasure that you may begin to repeat, irrespective of any consequences. In some cases you may not even notice any consequences rather they will be noticed by others.

Twenty years ago it was believed you couldn't become addicted to gambling. Now we accept compulsive gambling as fact. What gamblers always knew, took the mental health community decades to accept and integrate into popular acceptance. It seems that any new application or idea is rarely accepted as truth until the idea is no longer new. For those who suffer with any addiction, this delay in professional acceptance can slow down treatment or intervention. The Internet is probably where gambling was twenty years ago, as we're only now becoming aware of the dark side of this exciting technology.

What happens when you do something regularly that is pleasurable? The answer is, you do it more, and the more you do it, the greater the likelihood that your behavior can become habitual. You might also be surprised to discover that there are neurochemical changes in the brain that occur during the addiction process which give you a "hit" just like a drug. If this "chemical high" were pleasurable enough, wouldn't this induce you to repeat this behavior? The answer is probably "yes" for certain people, under the right circumstances. In order to answer this question specifically about the Internet, a broader definition of addiction becomes necessary.

Defining Addiction

Do you find yourself spending virtually all your time alone with your computer? Has your life begun to become *unmanageable* because of your Internet use? Do you feel *powerless* to stop or cut down your use? If you can answer yes to these questions, you may meet the criteria for Internet abuse or addiction. Use the following questions to evaluate whether or not you may be experiencing a problem in your life:

- Does a substance or behavior elicit a clear change in your mood? And is that substance or behavior later sought and utilized to achieve its mood-altering effects?

- Does ingesting the substance or performing the behaviors interfere with your life in any way, shape, or form? That is, does it have a negative impact on your work, school, family, friends, relationships, etc.?

Not only are these definitions of addiction very practical, but they also serve as clues on how behavior may at times become addictive (often without our being aware of it). Sometimes it's easier for people who know you best to see changes in your behavior even before you do. This is true because we tend to adjust over time to the gradual changes in our lives and often don't notice as the negative behavior pattern take effect.

Although there may be a problem (as recognized by others), it is not until *you* recognize how the problem is affecting you that recovery begins. If you can answer affirmatively to one or both of the previous questions (on p. 302), then you probably fit this practical definition of addiction. These definitions are similar to the definitions used by the twelve-step, Alcoholics Anonymous program (AA). They may not seem very scientific, but they work in everyday life. I credit AA's phenomenal success to these simple and practical definitions that most people can relate to. The chief components that are reflective of an addiction are feelings of powerlessness and unmanageability of one's life, and the negative effect this can produce.

Assessing Your Behavior

Let me give you an example. I perform a fair number of court-ordered alcohol and substance abuse evaluations. In many cases they have been pulled over for drunk driving (DWI/ DUI), and as a condition of their arrest, they're to be evaluated in order to determine the need for treatment. Many of the people I evaluate have had two or three previous arrests for DWI/DUI, yet most of the time they're not aware that their behavior may reflect a problem in their life. Most often, they don't consider themselves to be alcoholics. More often than not, until I point out the fact that getting arrested may actually represent an interference with their life, they simply don't see it.

I recently saw a man who had two DWIs as well as a drug arrest, but could not see that *he had a problem with drugs or alcohol*! This is probably due to his not having felt negative effects of his behavior (even if it's obvious to others) while in the midst of an addictive cycle. Often it's the *consequences* and *problems* in life from addictive behavior that will lead us to examine our behavior patterns. No consequences often equals little motivation to change. The trick is to try to begin to change before there are very serious consequences.

A Road to Recovery

Changing an addictive pattern always involves examining your behavior, motivations, insight, and judgments. However, when you begin a recovery process, the reasons why you became addicted to begin with aren't initially addressed. Instead, the main focus in the early stages of treatment is on *changing patterns of behavior* to begin the healing process. The remainder of this chapter will address general themes of addiction and help you determine whether you are addicted.

The term *addiction* is actually not used in the diagnostic manuals of psychology and psychiatry. Typically the terms *abuse*, *dependency*, *impulse problem*, and *compulsion* are used to describe most types of addiction. For the purposes of this book, the terminology is unimportant and I prefer more pragmatic methods of diagnosing addiction, which are as follows:

When you can't stop doing something that is bad for you, others notice it before you do.

It is hard to see your own negative behavior. And addiction can include the development of tolerance and/or withdrawal, which can only be noticed from within. For practical purposes, addiction and abuse could then be defined as follows:

Addiction involves a behavior or substance on which you are dependent and that is painfully difficult to stop. Abuse, on the other hand, may simply be a repeated pattern of use without tolerance or pain (withdrawal) as a result of trying to stop.

What Can I Become Addicted To?

Again, the unfortunate truth is probably everything, or more specifically, *everything fun* and *pleasurable*. The Internet, just as gambling, is simply another stimulating form of pleasurable entertainment that can produce an addictive potential similar to drugs or alcohol. Remember, we are pleasure-seeking creatures, and pleasurable behaviors are almost always repeated (or we give it a good try at attempting to do so!). We're still animals, where the basic biological principle of increasing pleasure and minimizing pain is part of our daily behavior. If you ever doubt this, just watch an infant or toddler trying to gain something they want and you'll see a less sophisticated version of yourself. We are in part motivated by this pleasure principle all the time, but we typically attempt to use adult compromises to counterbalance our innate hedonism.

This is not to say that we don't have other, more mature thoughts, feelings, and choices. Indeed we do have the ability to choose. However, while in an addiction cycle, our *ability to choose becomes significantly impaired*. This is the essence of addiction.

What all addictive behaviors have in common is the ability to impact neurochemical changes in brain chemistry. It is often these indirect neurochemical changes that make you feel so good. The chief neurotransmitters responsible for this brain "high" are most likely to be dopamine and norepinephrine. They produce a pleasurable sensation in the brain, which we experience as a "good feeling," which therefore increases the stimulating behavior. Just as in drug and alcohol use, these brain chemicals are, in part, responsible for improving our mood after exercise, sex, shopping, and Net surfing. The initial choice to use either a drug, alcohol, or the Internet is yours. However, once an addictive cycle begins, the choice is soon replaced by a less voluntary and more compulsive pattern of use. We develop a pleasurable habit, with unpleasurable consequences.

Logging On—How Does It Start?

Suppose you've worked all week and you're tired and stressed. You just got paid and you find yourself bored, edgy, perhaps a bit lonely, and a little down in the dumps. Perhaps you didn't take enough time for yourself? Maybe, like many people, you ignored your deeper psychological needs while just trying to get through daily routines. Add some children to the equation, and it only becomes more difficult. You resign yourself to an evening of TV and high-fat ice cream, but those don't quite do the trick.

So you decide to head for your computer to see what's happening in cyberspace. Sound familiar yet? Suddenly, you find yourself more excited, and perhaps a bit more energetic. You notice a pleasant combination of arousal and anticipation. You find yourself in a chat room and see who's online. After an hour of surfing around, you get an IM (*instant message*) from someone who wishes to talk to you. You don't know this person, but they seem interested in you. You strike up a conversation and hit it off.

This pattern continues night after night. Soon you're scheduling more frequent rendezvous, and spending more and more time online. You may even schedule time with an online correspondent in an *electronic bedroom*, which is a private chat room where you can be virtually alone. Other cybernuts may likely join you as you begin to develop a virtual social life online.

Initially you may have felt a sense of euphoria, excitement, and exhilaration. For a short period of time, during and just after your Internet adventures, there was a sense of peace. People often report a sense of "endless boundaries" and "feeling connected to the whole world," which are pretty powerful feelings. This "high" is directly related to the changes in brain chemistry that we discussed previously, and sets the groundwork for the addictive cycle to begin. The actual addiction cycle starts when you begin to seek this relief and pleasure on a consistent basis in order to regain that sense of excitement. This also acts to medicate the shame and guilt that comes from the negative consequences of your extended time online. Soon the high is replaced by a simple reduction of discomfort; a familiar habit that just keeps you on an even keel. This provides additional fuel for the addiction cycle to maintain itself. When this pattern is continued on a repeated basis you can develop an Internet addiction.

In my practice and research, I have seen people spend up to sixteen hours, or more, a day online. At times, I have seen them neglect their spouse, children, friends, family, jobs, and school. In the earlier days of the Internet (only a few short years ago), people would run up huge telephone and ISP (Internet Service Provider) bills in the thousands of dollars. The consequences might even require them to file bankruptcy or to make significant sacrifices in lifestyle. Perhaps even more devastating than the financial consequences are the disruptions to your marriage, family, or job. Often, it's the emotional impact and consequences on loved ones that are the most devastating. All addictive behavior patterns, including Internet and the computer, can create this negative impact on our relationships. In fact, if you go into many homes today there is a good likelihood that you may find some form of compulsive behavior or addiction. The type and degree will vary, but the basic themes are similar.

These are typical occurrences dealt with in most mental health practices today. Often, however, the psychologist or therapist may not ask the right questions about addictions in your life, and this is especially so with regard to the Internet.

If It Gets You High, It's All the Same

Often people separate the consumption of substances, such as alcohol, drugs, or food, from compulsive behaviors, creating an artificial distinction between them. This is probably because of the drug's obvious and immediate chemical effects. What I'm proposing is that on a neurochemical level, the act of creating *any* pleasurable sensation also creates a chemical change in the brain. Whether that chemical sensation is caused by a behavior, such as gambling, sex, eating, shopping, or the Internet, or by the ingestion of a drug, is largely irrelevant. How you get to that out-of-control place doesn't really matter. The fact that you *are* there makes all the difference in the world. But it only makes a difference if you're conscious of *your addictive pattern*.

Why Me?

The reasons that some people develop a problem while others do not are not clearly understood. Addictions research suggests that addiction comes from a combination of factors, including heredity, family history, diet/nutrition, levels of stress, general health, psychological functioning, along with the potency of the source addiction. All of these factors combined contribute to the likelihood that an individual will find that they're addicted to a certain behavior or mood-altering drug.

There is no such thing as an "addictive personality." Addiction is a human problem or illness that affects many people (there are estimates that as many as fifty million people are affected in the United States by drugs and alcohol alone). There are millions more living addicted lifestyles involving a variety of behaviors including, sex, gambling, Internet, food, shopping, and TV. It's yet another example of our imperfect humanity.

It is *not* a character weakness that determines your susceptibility to addiction. Many of the patients whom I've treated for addiction were successful, intelligent, and insightful people. They often report that the "one" (and sometimes only) problem they couldn't solve on their own was their addiction. And it took them some time to come to this conclusion. It didn't seem to matter what they were addicted to. The only thing that mattered was that they felt helpless in controlling it themselves, often with years of unsuccessful attempts at cutting back or discontinuing use!

The Internet Abuse Test

If you or a family member are worried that you may be too involved with the Internet, then taking this simple self-test may help you determine if you have a problem with your Internet use. Here are twelve warning signs that may indicate that you are getting lost in cyberspace. If you can answer yes to between three and five, then consider taking a look at the time and energy you spend online.

You might consider examining your Internet use pattern and attempt to cut down. If you answer positively to six or more, then you may have a more serious problem and should take the eleven-question Virtual Addiction Test (VAT).

Internet Abuse Test (IAT)

1. You spend an excessive amount of time in online chat rooms, particularly in the rooms having to do with sex or sexuality, or in private rooms engaged in sexual conversations and/or cybersex.

2. You find yourself gravitating toward one or more individuals with whom you have regularly scheduled, or unscheduled but desired, contacts.

3. You find yourself becoming depressed or lonely as you spend more time online.

4. You have made numerous attempts to have other contact with individuals on the Net, either by phone, in writing, or meeting in person.

5. You find yourself hiding information from your spouse, significant other, friends, or family regarding the amount of time and/or your activities on the Internet. In other words, you find yourself being secretive about the nature and the extent of your use.

6. You were initially excited when you came upon a stimulating situation accidentally on the Internet, but now actively seek it out each time you log on to the Net.

7. You constantly have thoughts about using the Internet for purposes of making sexual connections and/or fulfilling your social and interpersonal needs.

8. You find the anonymity of online interactions to be more stimulating and satisfying than your real-time relationships.

9. You find it difficult to stop logging on to the Internet and feel compelled to do so on a daily basis.

10. You experience guilt or shame about your use of the Internet.

11. You engage in active fantasy or masturbation while online, perhaps to the exclusion of sex with your partner or spouse.

12. You find that significant individuals in your life, including your significant other, spouse, friends, or family, are becoming troubled with the amount of time and/or energy you're devoting to the Internet. For example, someone significant in your life is complaining about your absence due to the excessive amount of time you're spending on the Net.

Your IAT score: _____
3–5 = warning; 6+ = probable Internet abuse problem

Sometimes there are more serious results of your compulsive use of the Internet. This occurs when excessive use or abuse escalates into an addiction. The addiction criteria that follow address a more advanced state of compulsive Internet use. The following tentative criteria for Internet addiction roughly parallel the psychiatric diagnosis for compulsive or pathological gambling, as it seems there is a similarity between the two problems.

It's not only the amount of time spent online that determines compulsive Internet use, but rather the combination of various negative behaviors that can produce significant problems in your life.

The Virtual Addiction Test (VAT)

If you believe you have a more serious problem, and you have six or more warning signs of Internet abuse as measured by the Internet Abuse Test (IAT), you should take the Virtual Addiction Test (VAT) below. If you answer yes to five or more of the questions on this test than you may have an Internet addiction problem.

1. Do you feel "out of control" when using the Internet; e.g., feel "carried away"?

2. When not on the Internet, do you find that you're preoccupied with the Internet or computers (e.g., thinking about or reliving past experiences on the Internet, planning your next experience on the Internet, or thinking of ways to gain access to the Internet in the future)?

3. Do you find that you need to spend greater amounts of time on the Internet to achieve satisfaction similar to previous events?

4. Do you find yourself seeking more sexually stimulating material in order to achieve the same result as previously? (Tolerance symptoms.)

5. Have you repeated unsuccessful efforts to control, cut back, or stop using the Internet?

6. Do you feel restless or irritable when attempting to cut down or stop using the Internet? (Withdrawl symptoms.)

7. Are you using the Internet as a way of escaping from problems or relieving a bad mood (e.g., feelings of helplessness, guilt, anxiety, or depression)?

8. After spending what you consider an excessive amount of time on the Internet and vowing not to do so the next day, do you find yourself back on the next day or soon after?

9. Do you find yourself lying to family members, therapists, or others to conceal the extent of your involvement with the Internet?

10. Do you find yourself committing illegal acts related to your use of the Internet?

11. Have you jeopardized or lost a significant relationship, educational, or career opportunity because of your Internet use?

Your IAT score: _____

If you score *five* or more, there is a reasonable probability that you are addicted to the Internet.

Whether or not you have to give up using the Internet permanently in order to deal with an Internet addiction problem will depend on your particular behavior pattern. Although we can safely say that one must be abstinent from gambling in order to maintain recovery, this may not be the case with the Internet. The best assumption at this point would probably be that it depends upon the degree and pattern of Internet abuse, along with one's personal circumstances in determining whether controlled or moderate use is possible.

My best plan for dealing with Internet abuse or addiction would at the very least include a significant reduction in use, and/or limiting how, when, and why you use the Net. Changing your pattern of use can go a long way in transforming a compulsive behavior to a more manageable one. For some people, however, abstinence will be necessary (at least for a while) in order to break the addictive cycle. After the addiction cycle is broken, you may be able to resume moderate use.

Excerpted and adapted with permission from *Virtual Addiction: Help for Netheads, Cyberfreaks, and Those Who Love Them* by David Greenfield, Ph.D. For more information on this and related books, see the "Further Reading" section in the back of the book. Dr. Greenfield can be reached through the Center for Internet Studies, www.virtual-addiction.com.

PART IV

COPING WITH PHYSICAL PROBLEMS

In Western culture, the mind and body are often treated as separate. This belief has persisted for hundreds of years, despite many attempts by healers, spiritual leaders, and some scientists to refute it. Recent research in neurophysiology may someday settle the question once and for all. Until then, we are stuck with an automatic assumption that some problems, such as depression, anxiety, and anger, are mind problems, and some problems, such as pain, cancer, and asthma are body problems.

In fact, many emotional problems manifest themselves in the body, causing symptoms that seem purely physical. And many body problems also cause considerable emotional distress, causing you to feel that you are not only sick, but "going crazy" too. This section covers some of the most common physical problems or changes that you can experience strongly on the emotional level:

Self-Care and Nurturing explores the psychology of taking care or not taking care of yourself.

Premenstrual Syndrome explains the causes and symptoms of PMS and how to begin a personalized coping plan.

Perimenopause covers the normal and subtle changes in a woman's body after age thirty-five.

Menopause explains what happens as mentruation gradually ceases in older women and how to cope with the physical and emotional changes.

Testicular and Prostate Cancer guides men in early detection of these common problems.

Chronic Illness and Pain explains the nature of pain and outlines the most common and effective treatment strategies.

Preparing for Surgery helps those contemplating elective surgery assess their readiness, gather information, make crucial decisions, and assertively obtain the best care.

CHAPTER 21

Self-Care and Nurturing

One of the best ways to prevent physical problems or cope with the ones you currently have is to regularly do nurturing things for yourself. This chapter will help you assess your current measures of self-care, as well as provide suggestions for optimal wellness.

Ask yourself these questions:

How long since you had a physical exam?

When did you last get your teeth cleaned?

Do you get enough sleep every night?

Do you take breaks to relax during the day?

Do you eat regular meals?

Do you eat a balanced diet?

Can you list the four basic food groups?

Do you get regular exercise?

How much do you weigh?

Are you reasonably fit for your age?

Do you smoke or drink or do drugs?

How much?

Do you drive drunk or drugged?

What are your chronic physical problems?

What should you be doing about them?

Do you need glasses but don't have any?

Do you drive fast or leave your seat belt off?

Do you use goggles, respirators, or other safety measures when appropriate?

Do you have a first aid kit in your home?

Do you practice safe sex?

The point of all these questions is not to induce guilt. The point is to uncover your attitude toward your body. You may feel that taking care of your body isn't very important.

Wrong. It's the only body you have. It deserves care. You deserve to take care of yourself, to make your one and only body as healthy, fit, and comfortable as you can.

This chapter will get you started. To begin, make an appointment for a physical exam if:

- You have some nagging symptoms that you were just hoping would go away.

- You are under forty and haven't had a checkup in three years.

- You are over forty and haven't had a checkup in over a year. (Men, make sure the checkup includes a rectal exam for prostate cancer. Women, make sure to get a mamogram and pap smear.)

Relaxation and Stress Reduction

Learning to relax is the single most important skill you can acquire to take care of your body. It's more crucial than even diet and exercise. It's so important that full Progressive Muscle Relaxation instructions have been put in the chapter on Stress in part V.

Self-Nurturing

The capacity to self-nurture is a major antidote for stress. Many people aren't taught how to nurture either others or themselves. As a result they are not aware of how to give themselves experiences that are healing and calming.

Self-nurturing activities have the defining characteristic of leaving you feeling good when they're over. You're not exhausted, irritable, disappointed, empty, or strung out afterward. Self-nurturing activities are intrinsically pleasurable, *regardless of outcome.* An example is a sports activity that is really nurturing and feels good whether you win or lose. Self-nurturing activities leave you able to function more effectively rather than less effectively. You're better equipped to cope, relate, and take care of business.

Self-nurturing activities generally are not:

- Frenetic diversions. They don't take you for a ride and leave you flat.

- Numbing. They don't shut off or mask your feelings.

- Indulgent. They are not compulsive pleasures that help you evade family and work responsibilities.

Self-nurturing is an opportunity to give to yourself, to take some control in your life by doing the things that calm and relax you. It is a healthy discipline that leads to feelings of replenishment. The following are sixteen examples of self-nurturing activities. There are literally hundreds of ways to replenish yourself, but these will give you some ideas that might lead you to identify the kind of self-nurturing that will work for you.

1. **Aerobics.** This includes running, working out, swimming, speed walking, biking, and so forth. Many people experience aerobics as a high that melts away stress and replaces it with feelings of well-being.

2. **Athletics.** Tennis, golf, handball, racquetball; anything you really enjoy regardless of the score at the end of the game. Athletic activities that are nurturing rarely are highly competitive. To consistently enjoy a sport, you have to do it for the muscle joy, not as a confirmation of prowess or a bolster for your self-esteem.

3. **Reading.** It's lovely sometimes to enter the world of a book and take time off from ordinary existence.

4. **Journal writing.** Some use a journal as a path to self-exploration and a way to increase awareness as they review the experiences of a day. Creative writing in any form can serve the same purpose. You can use material from your own experience as the foundation for a creative process. It's an opportunity to tune in to what you feel.

5. **Listening to or playing music.**

6. **Taking time out for contemplation and quiet.** This is the act of being your own companion, of drifting with your own thoughts, noticing your own feelings, and giving yourself a time to live in the here-and-now.

7. **Meditation.** Some find meditation to be of tremendous value for replenishing. The act of focusing and refocusing on your breath, a sound, or an image has a cleansing effect. You are literally washing your mind of stress.

8. **Creating an aesthetic, calming environment.** Make your living environment into something that pleases the eye and soothes the psyche. This may require nothing more than having a comfortable chair and reading lamp. Or it may involve creating an elaborate Japanese garden. Literally anything you do to enhance the sense of order and attractiveness in your surroundings may have a nurturing effect.

9. **Eating.** For many people, food is a reliable way of feeling good. Whether you carefully prepare your own meal or eat out where all that is done for you, eating is a good way of giving to yourself.

10. **Taking walks.** The evening stroll is an underrated pleasure. Many people build walking into their daily schedule as a way of relieving stress and slowing their pace.

11. **Hot baths or showers.** Heat is relaxing. Giving yourself time to enjoy hot water is a way of calming and replenishing yourself.

12. **Calling someone.** For this to be genuinely nourishing, the call can't be a task or obligation. The person you call has to be someone you feel good conversing with.

13. **Getting a massage.**

14. **Pursuing a hobby.** Whether it's darkroom photography, stamp collecting, or rebuilding musical instruments, a hobby has a way of focusing your energies onto a physical task. You forget everything, and live very much in the moment as you become absorbed in the process.

15. **Gardening.** The connection with the earth and the process of growing living things is very calming and life-affirming.

16. **Finding projects.** It could be building a sandbox for your kids, a bookshelf for your girl-friend, or a flower box for the bedroom window.

In the space provided, write three self-nurturing activities that you'd be willing to schedule into your life.

Consider this a commitment. Self-nurturing is something you may have gotten little training in, but it is a basic skill for living a satisfying life. Schedule one of your listed self-nurturing activities for each of the next seven days. Write it into your appointment calendar. Commit yourself to doing it, whether you feel like making the effort or not when the time comes. At the end of the week evaluate which activities were most satisfying, most relaxing. Keep scheduling those, but also add new items to your list so that you can expand your repertoire of self-giving.

Diet and Exercise

Diet and exercise are particularly important because:

- The way to prevent heart attack and stroke is to keep your blood pressure and your blood cholesterol levels low.

- The best way to keep blood pressure and cholesterol down is *to eat right and stay active.*

Blood Pressure. When you go for that physical exam, write down your blood pressure before you forget it:

Date _____   Blood pressure _____
_____

The top number is your systolic pressure. This is the highest pressure reached each time your heart beats, the maximum force exerted by your heart on the walls of your arteries. Systolic pressure varies greatly throughout the day and night, going down when you sleep or rest and going up when you exercise or experience strong emotions like anger or fear. Systolic pressure tends to increase with age. When this top number consistently measures above 140, it's time to start worrying and taking measures to decrease your blood pressure.

The bottom number is your diastolic pressure. Your circulatory system is under pressure at all times, even between heartbeats. At the point when your heart is its most relaxed, a baseline amount of pressure is still present. This is the diastolic pressure. It tends to increase slightly with age, but it is much more stable than the systolic pressure from moment to moment. In terms of health, the diastolic pressure is the most important, since it represents the constant, inescapable pressure that your circulatory system must withstand all the time. When your diastolic pressure gets much over 80, it's time to make some changes in your diet and exercise.

Cholesterol. When you get your physical exam, make sure they take blood and test it for cholesterol levels. Cholesterol is a substance contained in animal fat and certain other foods. If there is too much in your blood, it is deposited on the walls of your blood vessels, narrowing them, increasing your blood pressure, and putting you in higher danger of heart attack.

There are different kinds of cholesterol reported on blood tests. The crucial measurement is your serum cholesterol level (measured in milligrams per decaliter). Your doctor is sure to point out which number that is. Write the number down here:

Date _____   Serum cholesterol _____ mpd

If your cholesterol count is over 200 mpd, it's too high, and again you need to make changes in your diet and get more exercise.

Diet. There are hundreds of books and magazine articles about nutrition. You could easily make a life study about it. If you're interested you can read up on nutrition, buy cookbooks, browse in health food stores, and become an expert on what you should and shouldn't eat.

But if a poor diet has got you into trouble, you're probably not very interested in nutrition and unlikely to devote a lot of time to study. Ask your doctor for some dietary guidelines to follow. Doctors usually have photocopied food lists and menus to hand out. If not, here are the basics:

- Eat a variety of foods, including something every day from the basic food groups: vegetables and fruits—four servings; bread, cereals, grains—four servings; meat, poultry, fish, beans, peas—two servings; milk, cheese, yogurt—two servings.

- Reduce fat, especially animal fat in red meat, gravy, eggs.

- Reduce sodium (salt), especially hidden salt in processed foods.

- Reduce sugar.

- Increase whole foods instead of highly processed foods.

- Avoid alcohol.

Exercise. Again, you can buy books, subscribe to magazines, join a health club, and become an expert on exercise. But if lack of exercise is a long-term problem, you also probably have long-term lack of interest. So here are the basics:

- The only kind of exercise that will strengthen your heart and lower your blood pressure is aerobic exercise.

- For an activity to be aerobic, it must get your heart and breathing going fast and keep it elevated for at least twenty minutes.

- Very fast walking, jogging, and swimming are the best aerobic exercises. Stationary bikes, treadmills, stair-steppers, and rowing machines are possible substitutes.

- Whatever you choose to do, do it at least three times a week and keep your heart rate up for twenty minutes each time.

- Start slowly. You don't want to bring on the heart attack you are supposed to be preventing. If you can't carry on a conversation while exercising, you are going at it too hard.

Excerpted and adapted with permission from *Being a Man: A Guide to the New Masculinity* by Patrick Fanning and Matthew McKay, Ph.D. For more information on this and related books, see the "Further Reading" section in the back of the book.

CHAPTER 22

Premenstrual Syndrome

What Is Premenstrual Syndrome?: Answers to Common Questions

Sheila's Story

For several months in a row, I had to cancel my board meetings. I'd get a headache, it would take over, and I'd have to go to bed. I would call my husband, and he would come home and watch the kids for a day or two, because I just couldn't.

I went to a general practitioner for help, and he referred me to a neurologist. I was put on several medications. Sometimes these medications helped my headache, but they always knocked me out! So my husband still had to come home to help with the children. I also went to a pain-control center, and the doctor at the pain-control center prescribed a different drug.

After a while, I would actually plan and make special preparations for the time when I would have this debilitating headache. I would put down a plastic tablecloth in the living room and set out snacks for the kids—things that were easy to fix and eat. Then I would bring out my pillow and lie on the couch. I taped the emergency phone number to the wall. I wrote it in big numbers so the kids could read it and call their father if necessary.

One day I was on the phone explaining that I couldn't attend the board meeting and that perhaps I should resign from the board, and one of my friends overheard me. When I hung up, we started chatting. I mentioned that it was too bad that the board meetings were not in the middle of the month, because I always felt fine at that time.

My friend said, "Isn't it interesting that your headaches are always at a certain time of the month . . . the same time as the board meetings? Is this around the time of your period?"

It was two days before my period. So we discussed the possibility that it was cyclical.

We started piecing things together. My friend had a lot more information about PMS than I did.

After the discussion, I decided that I had to explore every avenue. I started charting myself and verified that my headaches were occurring only before my period. A consultation with my doctor confirmed that I was suffering from PMS.

So, it took a board meeting to find out about PMS! The board meeting was like a monthly barometer.

PMS: A Medical Disorder

What is PMS? "The world's commonest, and probably the oldest, disease" is the way that one of the world's leading pioneers in the study of PMS, Dr. Katharina Dalton of the University College Hospital, in London, describes this medical disorder. PMS affects a large segment of the female population of the world. It is a physical disorder that is attributed to hormonal fluctuations that take place in a woman's body. PMS often manifests itself as disturbed mood, sleep, and appetite.

The fact that PMS is a physical disorder is what makes it so difficult to understand. Why? Because the psychological symptoms are the most problematic and hard to treat. It is difficult to believe that what a woman is going through is physical in origin. PMS can cause such mental stress that it shakes the foundation of her identity—who she perceives herself to be.

The *American Journal of Psychiatry* describes premenstrual syndrome as a menstrually related physical/psychological disorder that can be defined as "the cyclic occurrence of symptoms that are of sufficient severity to interfere with some aspects of life, and which appear with a consistent and predictable relationship to menses."

The two aspects that are crucial to the correct definition of PMS are:

- It occurs regularly in the same phase of the menstrual cycle (between ovulation and onset of menstruation), followed by a symptom-free phase each cycle.

- The symptoms are of sufficient severity to interfere with some aspect of living.

How Does PMS Affect a Woman?

PMS affects a woman as a cyclical emotional, behavioral, and physical disturbance. Dr. Dalton has described how the numerous symptoms associated with PMS can affect every aspect of a woman's life. Understandably, when a woman suffers from emotional and psychological distress for a significant portion of the time, it is going to affect her interpersonal relationships. In fact, at the beginning of their definitive article on PMS, in the *American Journal of Obstetrics and Gynecology*, Drs. Reid and Yen state that a temporary deterioration in a woman's interpersonal relationships frequently develops in the premenstrual week.

What Are the Symptoms?

The premenstrual syndrome is a biobehavioral phenomenon made up diverse and interacting physical, psychological, emotional, cognitive, and behavioral symptoms. Medical books list more than 150 symptoms associated with PMS. Here are the major symptoms:

Psychological Symptoms

anger

loss of control

sudden mood swings

emotional over-responsiveness

unexplained crying

irritability

anxiety

forgetfulness

decreased concentration

confusion

withdrawal

rejection-sensitive

depression

nightmares

suicidal thoughts

Physical Symptoms

bloating

weight gain

acne

migraine headaches

breast tenderness

joint and muscle pain

backaches

changes in sex drive

food cravings

constipation

diarrhea

sweating

shakiness

seizures

Who Gets PMS?

Most medical researchers estimate that 40 percent of all women suffer from PMS *during some time in their lives*. Other researchers report that 85 percent to 90 percent of women experience symptoms of PMS in their menstruating years. Using the smaller percentage, premenstrual syndrome affects at least 45 million women in the United States alone.

Although PMS affects so many women, it is not a well-known or well-understood medical disorder. Thus, many women have suffered from PMS without realizing it. Many women are relieved to find out that PMS is an identifiable problem that can be treated.

It is important to note that I am not saying that every woman's problems are caused by PMS. Many people say that PMS is a convenient excuse for unacceptable behavior or a catchall for problems. Indeed, the symptoms of PMS can appear very similar to other problems, but the symptoms of PMS are not present all month.

Many women do not suffer from PMS. Many women—especially younger women—experience the time before their period as a creative time when they feel very sensitive to the world around them.

Should I Expect to Get PMS?

If your mother or other women in your immediate family suffered from cyclical mood swings, irritability, and depression, you may develop similar problems.

If you are going to develop PMS, it is most likely to affect you at specific times in your life, not during your entire lifetime. The time when you are most likely to be significantly affected by PMS is during your thirties. This is so common that PMS is often called "the mid-thirties syndrome."

Can I Have PMS If . . .

. . . I'm nursing?
. . . I'm going through the change of life?
. . . I'm having erratic periods?
. . . I've had a hysterectomy?

The answer to all these questions is "yes." PMS is a cyclically related disorder, and a cyclical disorder can occur at any time during your life. Thus, contrary to popular ideas, the symptoms of PMS can be experienced by women who are not menstruating.

Are There Tests That Determine If I Have PMS?

No. Contrary to what you might have read or what someone might have told you, the most current medical research clearly indicates that hormonal tests are inconclusive. There are no medical tests that can tell you if you have PMS.

How Can I Tell If I Have PMS?

Charting is the only method that can tell you if you have PMS. Charting your symptoms shows you if there is a pattern to the changes occurring in your body.

Is PMS the Same Every Month?

No, variation is the rule rather than the exception. If you have PMS, it is impossible to say that you will have the same set of symptoms every month and that your symptoms will last the same length of time.

The symptoms may start earlier than expected in some months and later in others. There are many variables that come into play: stress in your personal life or on the job, exercise, diet, and so forth. These can speed up, delay, or intensify PMS symptoms.

Some months are definitely worse than others. You may notice that one month is particularly difficult, and the next month is not nearly so bad. This can create a lot of confusion in your mind. Often, women report that about every third month is a particularly bad one.

Can I Have PMS and Still Get Menstrual Cramps?

Yes. Many women have heard that if they experience cramps with their periods, they cannot have PMS. This is because of conflicting information about the relationship of menstrual cramps to PMS. However, my data, as well as the most recent medical research, clearly indicate that if you have menstrual cramps you have a greater tendency to suffer from PMS.

Can PMS Affect Chronic Physical Disorders?

PMS can exacerbate several types of chronic disorders, including: sinusitis, vaginal yeast infections, seizures, herpes, allergies, and asthma attacks. In other words, if you have asthma attacks, you may have more asthma attacks when you are premenstrual. If you have seizures, you might notice an increase in the number of seizures before your periods. Dr. Dalton notes that no tissue in the body seems to be exempt from cyclical changes of the menstrual cycle, and all tissues can be affected by cyclical premenstrual symptoms or exacerbations of chronic disorders.

Your doctor will not necessarily make the association between intensification of your chronic disorder and the fact that you are premenstrual. You can help your doctor make this connection by keeping track of your chronic illnesses in your charts.

If There's Something Physically Wrong with Me, Why Do I Feel So Bad Emotionally?

We are used to separating mind and body. We think that if something is physical, it is not going to affect our mental attitude. But the mind and body are dynamically interrelated.

PMS is a physically based disorder that manifests itself physically, psychologically, and behaviorally. The importance of understanding how PMS affects your attitudes and emotions cannot be overstated.

How Do I Know That the Problems I'm Having Are Related to PMS and Not Something Else?

When a woman asks me this question (and almost every woman does), the problems to which she is referring are typically relationship problems: problems with her boyfriend, husband, children, or friends.

This is the best way I have found to explain how PMS can both mix up (disrupt) and become mixed up with other things going on in your life. Look at a clear glass of water. This represents the relationship. Throw in a handful of sand. This represents PMS. What you get is murky water. Until you let the sand settle to the bottom, you will not see clearly which problems belong to the relationship and which belong to PMS.

Other problems or stresses that you might be experiencing should not be downplayed or scoffed at—either by you or your therapist. These might include other medical problems, financial problems, or problems at work. These problems can intensify PMS symptoms. If you are suffering from PMS, you will probably be less able to cope with these problems when you are premenstrual. They will seem more intense and less manageable during your PMS time. Conversely, once you begin to treat PMS symptoms, you will probably find that you are clearer about which problems are being caused by PMS and which ones are there for other reasons—but are intensified as a result of PMS.

Does It Get Worse as I Get Older?

Women whom I have counseled report that the symptoms seem to get worse as time goes by. They usually notice that the symptoms last longer and become more intense as they get older.

Does It Ever Go Away or Do I Have to Live with This for the Rest of My Life?

In many cases the symptoms can increase in intensity and duration until you go through menopause. However, treatments are available that include self-help measures and, if necessary, professional help.

Your Daily Chart

The most positive method to determine if you have PMS is the simple and inexpensive method of charting. Through charting, you can determine if there is a relationship between mood changes and the menstrual cycle.

The daily chart is a day-to-day record of how you are feeling—both physically and psychologically. The pattern of changes in your state of mind and how you feel will become apparent after two to three months of daily charting.

Don't forget to chart on days when you feel great and are not experiencing any problems. In order for a pattern to be clearly established, the *good days must be charted along with the bad.*

Because the daily chart needs to be filled out over a 2- or 3-month period, you should make three copies of the following chart:

Symptom #1 _____   Symptom #3 _____

Symptom #2 _____   Symptom #4 _____

Ratings: 0 (no symptoms), 1, 2, 3, 4, 5, 6, 7, 8, 9, 10 (most severe)

Month #1

Day 1   Symptom #1 _____   Comments: _____

_____   Symptom #2 _____   Comments: _____

(date)   Symptom #3 _____   Comments: _____

Symptom #4 _____   Comments: _____

Food and beverage intake: _____

_____

_____

Exercise: _____

_____

_____

Comment on the day: _____

_____

Overall rating for the day: _____

Day 2   Symptom #1 _____   Comments: _____

_____   Symptom #2 _____   Comments: _____

(date)   Symptom #3 _____   Comments: _____

Symptom #4 _____   Comments: _____

Food and beverage intake: _____

_____

_____

Exercise: _____

_____

_____

Comment on the day: _____

_____

Overall rating for the day: _____

Day 3   Symptom #1 _____   Comments: _____

_____   Symptom #2 _____   Comments: _____

(date)   Symptom #3 _____   Comments: _____

Symptom #4 _____   Comments: _____

Food and beverage intake: _____

_____

_____

Exercise: _____

_____

_____

Comment on the day: _____

_____

Overall rating for the day: _____

Day 4   Symptom #1 _____   Comments: _____

_____   Symptom #2 _____   Comments: _____

(date)   Symptom #3 _____   Comments: _____

Symptom #4 _____   Comments: _____

Food and beverage intake: _____

_____

_____

Exercise: _____

_____

_____

Comment on the day: _____

_____

Overall rating for the day: _____

Day 5   Symptom #1 _____   Comments: _____

_____   Symptom #2 _____   Comments: _____

(date)   Symptom #3 _____   Comments: _____

Symptom #4 _____   Comments: _____

Food and beverage intake: _____

_____

_____

Exercise: _____

_____

_____

Comment on the day: _____

_____

Overall rating for the day: _____

Day 6 Symptom #1 _____ Comments: _____

_____ Symptom #2 _____ Comments: _____

(date) Symptom #3 _____ Comments: _____

Symptom #4 _____ Comments: _____

Food and beverage intake: _____

_____

_____

Exercise: _____

_____

_____

Comment on the day: _____

_____

Overall rating for the day: _____

Day 7 Symptom #1 _____ Comments: _____

_____ Symptom #2 _____ Comments: _____

(date) Symptom #3 _____ Comments: _____

Symptom #4 _____ Comments: _____

Food and beverage intake: _____

_____

_____

Exercise: _____

_____

Comment on the day: _____

Overall rating for the day: _____

Day 8 Symptom #1 _____ Comments: _____

_____ Symptom #2 _____ Comments: _____

(date) Symptom #3 _____ Comments: _____

Symptom #4 _____ Comments: _____

Food and beverage intake: _____

_____

_____

Exercise: _____

_____

_____

Comment on the day: _____

_____

Overall rating for the day: _____

Day 9 Symptom #1 _____ Comments: _____

_____ Symptom #2 _____ Comments: _____

(date) Symptom #3 _____ Comments: _____

Symptom #4 _____ Comments: _____

Food and beverage intake: _____

_____

_____

Exercise: _____

_____

_____

Comment on the day: _____

_____

Overall rating for the day: _____

Day 10 Symptom #1 _____ Comments: _____

_____ Symptom #2 _____ Comments: _____

(date) Symptom #3 _____ Comments: _____

Symptom #4 _____ Comments: _____

Food and beverage intake: _____

_____

_____

Exercise: _____

_____

_____

Comment on the day: _____

_____

Overall rating for the day: _____

Day 11 Symptom #1 _____ Comments: _____

_____ Symptom #2 _____ Comments: _____

(date) Symptom #3 _____ Comments: _____

Symptom #4 _____ Comments: _____

Food and beverage intake: _____

_____

_____

Exercise: _____

_____

_____

Comment on the day: _____

_____

Overall rating for the day: _____

Day 12 Symptom #1 _____ Comments: _____

_____ Symptom #2 _____ Comments: _____

(date) Symptom #3 _____ Comments: _____

Symptom #4 _____ Comments: _____

Food and beverage intake: _____

_____

_____

Exercise: _____

_____

_____

Comment on the day: _____

_____

Overall rating for the day: _____

Day 13 Symptom #1 _____ Comments: _____

_____ Symptom #2 _____ Comments: _____

(date)   Symptom #3 _____ Comments: _____

Symptom #4 _____ Comments: _____

Food and beverage intake: _____

_____

_____

_____

Exercise: _____

_____

_____

Comment on the day: _____

_____

Overall rating for the day: _____

Day 14 Symptom #1 _____ Comments: _____

_____ Symptom #2 _____ Comments: _____

(date)   Symptom #3 _____ Comments: _____

Symptom #4 _____ Comments: _____

Food and beverage intake: _____

_____

_____

Exercise: _____

_____

Comment on the day: _____

Overall rating for the day: _____

Day 15 Symptom #1 _____ Comments: _____

_____ Symptom #2 _____ Comments: _____

(date) Symptom #3 _____ Comments: _____

Symptom #4 _____ Comments: _____

Food and beverage intake: _____

_____

_____

Exercise: _____

_____

Comment on the day: _____

Overall rating for the day: _____

Day 16 Symptom #1 _____ Comments: _____

_____ Symptom #2 _____ Comments: _____

(date) Symptom #3 _____ Comments: _____

Symptom #4 _____ Comments: _____

Food and beverage intake: _____

_____

_____

Exercise: _____

_____

Comment on the day: _____

_____

Overall rating for the day: _____

Day 17 Symptom #1 _____ Comments: _____

_____ Symptom #2 _____ Comments: _____

(date) Symptom #3 _____ Comments: _____

Symptom #4 _____ Comments: _____

Food and beverage intake: _____

_____

_____

Exercise: _____

_____

_____

Comment on the day: _____

_____

Overall rating for the day: _____

Day 18 Symptom #1 _____ Comments: _____

_____ Symptom #2 _____ Comments: _____

(date) Symptom #3 _____ Comments: _____

Symptom #4 _____ Comments: _____

Food and beverage intake: _____

_____

_____

Exercise: _____

_____

_____

Comment on the day: _____

_____

Overall rating for the day: _____

Day 19 Symptom #1 _____ Comments: _____

_____ Symptom #2 _____ Comments: _____

(date) Symptom #3 _____ Comments: _____

Symptom #4 _____ Comments: _____

Food and beverage intake: _____

_____

_____

Exercise: _____

_____

_____

Comment on the day: _____

_____

Overall rating for the day: _____

Day 20 Symptom #1 _____ Comments: _____

_____ Symptom #2 _____ Comments: _____

(date) Symptom #3 _____ Comments: _____

Symptom #4 _____ Comments: _____

Food and beverage intake: _____

_____

_____

Exercise: _____

_____

_____

Comment on the day: _____

_____

Overall rating for the day: _____

Day 21 Symptom #1 _____ Comments: _____

_____ Symptom #2 _____ Comments: _____

(date) Symptom #3 _____ Comments: _____

Symptom #4 _____ Comments: _____

Food and beverage intake: _____

_____

_____

Exercise: _____

_____

Comment on the day: _____

Overall rating for the day: _____

Day 22 Symptom #1 _____ Comments: _____

_____ Symptom #2 _____ Comments: _____

(date) Symptom #3 _____ Comments: _____

Symptom #4 _____ Comments: _____

Food and beverage intake: _____

_____

_____

Exercise: _____

_____

_____

Comment on the day: _____

_____

Overall rating for the day: _____

Day 23 Symptom #1 _____ Comments: _____

_____ Symptom #2 _____ Comments: _____

(date) Symptom #3 _____ Comments: _____

Symptom #4 _____ Comments: _____

Food and beverage intake: _____

_____

_____

Exercise: _____

_____

_____

Comment on the day: _____

_____

Overall rating for the day: _____

Day 24 Symptom #1 _____ Comments: _____

_____ Symptom #2 _____ Comments: _____

(date) Symptom #3 _____ Comments: _____

_____ Symptom #4 _____ Comments: _____

Food and beverage intake: _____

_____

_____

Exercise: _____

_____

_____

Comment on the day: _____

_____

Overall rating for the day: _____

Day 25 Symptom #1 _____ Comments: _____

_____ Symptom #2 _____ Comments: _____

(date) Symptom #3 _____ Comments: _____

_____ Symptom #4 _____ Comments: _____

Food and beverage intake: _____

_____

_____

Exercise: _____

_____

_____

Comment on the day: _____

_____

Overall rating for the day: _____

Day 26 Symptom #1 _____ Comments: _____

_____ Symptom #2 _____ Comments: _____

(date) Symptom #3 _____ Comments: _____

_____ Symptom #4 _____ Comments: _____

Food and beverage intake: _____

_____

Exercise: _____

Comment on the day: _____

Overall rating for the day: _____

Day 27 Symptom #1 _____ Comments: _____

_____ Symptom #2 _____ Comments: _____

(date)   Symptom #3 _____ Comments: _____

Symptom #4 _____ Comments: _____

Food and beverage intake: _____

_____

Exercise: _____

Comment on the day: _____

Overall rating for the day: _____

Day 28 Symptom #1 _____ Comments: _____

_____ Symptom #2 _____ Comments: _____

(date)   Symptom #3 _____ Comments: _____

Symptom #4 _____ Comments: _____

Food and beverage intake: _____

_____

Exercise: _____

Comment on the day: _____

Overall rating for the day: _____

Day 29 Symptom #1 _____ Comments: _____

_____ Symptom #2 _____ Comments: _____

(date) Symptom #3 _____ Comments: _____

Symptom #4 _____ Comments: _____

Food and beverage intake: _____

_____

_____

Exercise: _____

_____

Comment on the day: _____

Overall rating for the day: _____

Day 30 Symptom #1 _____ Comments: _____

_____ Symptom #2 _____ Comments: _____

(date) Symptom #3 _____ Comments: _____

Symptom #4 _____ Comments: _____

Food and beverage intake: _____

_____

_____

Exercise: _____

_____

Comment on the day: _____

Overall rating for the day: _____

Day 31 Symptom #1 _____ Comments: _____

_____   Symptom #2 _____ Comments: _____

(date)   Symptom #3 _____ Comments: _____

Symptom #4 _____ Comments: _____

Food and beverage intake: _____

_____

_____

Exercise: _____

_____

_____

Comment on the day: _____

_____

Overall rating for the day: _____

Fill in the actual date after the first day, second day, etc., of your charting. It doesn't matter what day of your cycle you begin charting. What is most important is that you begin charting as soon as possible.

Target Your Symptoms

Focus on the most problematic symptoms that you are experiencing. Target four of these symptoms to chart daily. These should include two physical and two psychological symptoms. For example, two psychological symptoms that you might chart are irritability and depression. Two physical symptoms that you might chart are headaches and bloating.

Fill in the symptoms that you are going to chart:

Symptom #1 (Psychological) _____

Symptom #2 (Psychological) _____

Symptom #3 (Physical) _____

Symptom #4 (Physical) _____

Note Intensity of Symptoms

Your symptoms should be rated on a scale of 0 to 10, with 0 representing least intensity of symptoms and 10 representing severest intensity. The number indicating the daily intensity of each symptom should be entered in the chart in the space provided after Symptom # 1, Symptom #2, and so forth.

Note Menstruation/Ovulation

The day that you start menstruating should be indicated by a circled "M." For each day that you have your period, indicate an "M." Also note the day that you ovulate with an "O". The day that you ovulate is usually the halfway point in your cycle. If you have a 28-day cycle, the halfway point is from the 13th to 15th days. You can tell when you ovulate because you will feel a little bit of cramping or pain in your lower abdomen, and your vaginal discharge will be heavier and have more mucus.

Watch What You Eat

When you are charting, it is a good idea to record your intake of salt, sugar, caffeine, and alcohol. If on a particular day you craved sweets or ate extra-salty foods, for instance, this should be noted in the "Food Intake" section for that day.

Exercise

Note what exercise you got for each day.

Comment on the Day

The evening is the best time to reflect on the day's events. How did your symptoms affect your behavior? Were you less productive? Were you less able to cope with your children? Did you start an argument with your partner? If this was a good day, note the ways in which it was pleasant, productive, and so forth.

Rate Each Day

Finally, on a scale of 0 to 40, rate your overall mood for each day. In this rating, 0 represents a perfect day and 40 represents the worst possible day. A rating of 20 would represent an average day, neither very good nor very bad. (Note that if you were having a really bad day and each of your symptoms was rated at 10, this would add up to 40 for the day.)

Sample Daily Chart

Symptom #1 __Irritability__   Symptom #3 __Depression__

Symptom #2 __Food cravings__   Symptom #4 __Breast soreness__

Ratings: 0 (no symptoms), 1, 2, 3, 4, 5, 6, 7, 8, 9, 10 (most severe)

Month #1

Day 1   Symptom #1 ___0___ Comments: _____

Oct 1   Symptom #2 ___0___ Comments: _____

(date)   Symptom #3   0   Comments: _____

            Symptom #4   0   Comments: _____

Food and beverage intake: __Breakfast—good_____

Lunch—small _____

Dinner—good _____

Exercise: __Jogged 2 miles_____

Comment on the day: __Great_____

Overall rating for the day: _____

Day 2   Symptom #1   2   Comments: __On edge with kids_____

Oct 2   Symptom #2   1   Comments: _____

(date)   Symptom #3   1   Comments: _____

            Symptom #4   2   Comments: __minor_____

Food and beverage intake: __Breakfast—small_____

Lunch—good _____

Dinner—good _____

Exercise: __none_____

Comment on the day: __Some irritability in morning—mild. All in all, a good day.__

Overall rating for the day: __6_____

Day 3   Symptom #1   2   Comments: __Short fuse_____

Oct 3   Symptom #2   2   Comments: _____

(date)   Symptom #3   2   Comments: __Hungry for sweets_____

            Symptom #4   2   Comments: __Fairly noticeable_____

Food and beverage intake: __Breakfast—small_____

Lunch—skipped _____

Dinner—good _____

Exercise: __none_____

Comment on the day: __I've had better days_____

Overall rating for the day: __10_____

Day 4   Symptom #1   4   Comments: _____

Oct 4   Symptom #2   2   Comments: __Grey sky feeling_____

(date)   Symptom #3   2   Comments: __Worked hard not to binge_____

Symptom #4 _____4_____ Comments: _____

Food and beverage intake: __Breakfast—small_____

Lunch—good _____

Dinner—good _____

Exercise: __Tried to go jogging, but breasts hurt_____

Comment on the day: __Forgot a dental appointment. Not a great day_____

Overall rating for the day: __12_____

Your On-Sight Chart

This chart (see the following sample) is to help you identify the pattern of changes in your monthly cycle. It contains the daily ratings you assign your symptoms on your daily charts. After three months of charting, the result is that "on sight" you will be able to identify clearly if you have a pattern of good times and bad times. The intensity of these times will also be apparent, as the rise and fall in the numbers refers to the rising and falling intensity of your symptoms. If you find that your symptoms do not have a clear pattern related to your menstrual cycle, you should consider discussing your symptoms with your doctor or a counselor.

Indicate Menstruation/Ovulation

An On-Sight Chart is provided for you. To fill it in, refer back to your daily charts. Which day did you start your period? Transfer to the correct day on the on-sight chart the circled "M" that shows when your period started. What day did you ovulate? Transfer to the correct day on the on-sight chart the circled "O" that shows when you ovulated.

Indicate Intensity of Symptoms

The coded numbers used in the daily chart that refer to the intensity of your symptoms should be entered into the on-sight chart. Add them up for each day, as indicated on the sample chart.

Sample On-Sight Chart

Day #	Month #1	Month #2	Month #3
1	0000 = 0	0010 = 1	
2	2112 = 6	2110 = 4	
3	2224 = 10	3121 = 7	
4	4224 = 12	4232 = 11	
5	2224 = 10	4354 = 16	
6	4426 = 16	5576 = 23	
7	4446 = 18	5687 = 26	
8	6446 = 20	5698 = 28	
9	8666 = 26	7898 = 32	
10	6866 = 26	9889 = 34	
11	8886 = 30	10101010 = 40	
12	8888 = 32	910910 = 38	
13	9899 = 35	8621 = 17^M	
14	6444 = 18	1001 = 2^M	
15	2112 = 6 ^{M}	1001 = 2^M	
16	0000 = 0^M	0000 = 0^M	
17	0000 = 0^M	0000 = 0	
18	0000 = 0	0000 = 0	
19	0000 = 0	0000 = 0	
20	0000 = 0	0000 = 0	
21	0000 = 0	1000 = 1	
22	1000 = 1	0000 = 0	
23	0000 = 0	0000 = 0	
24	0000 = 0	0102 = 3	
25	0000 = 0	0101 = 2	
26	0000 = 0	5653 = 19	
27	1000 = 1	6662 = 20°	
28	6642 = 18	3412 = 10	
29	4642 = 16°	3212 = 8	
30	2412 = 9	1011 = 3	

Your On-Sight Chart

Day #	Month #1	Month #2	Month #3	Month #4
1				
2				
3				
4				
5				
6				
7				
8				
9				
10				
11				
12				
13				
14				
15				
16				
17				
18				
19				
20				
21				
22				
23				
24				
25				
26				
27				
28				
29				
30				

Your Mood Chart

This chart (sample shown below) gives you a clear picture of your mood swings. It is a graph on which you record your daily ratings, allowing you to see the pattern of emotional ups and downs that are associated with your menstrual cycle.

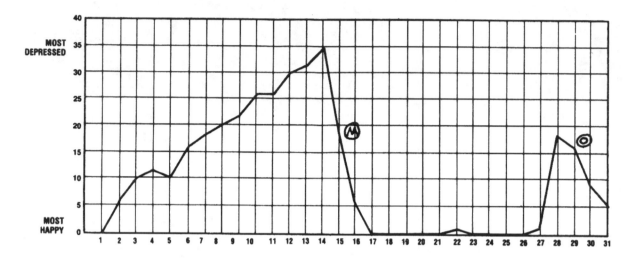

To make your mood chart, take your overall rating for each day from your daily chart and plot it on the blank graph provided. For each day, plot the overall rating and then connect the points. If you feel ambitious, you can rate your moods for both the morning and the evening. This way you can see how much your mood fluctuates within each day.

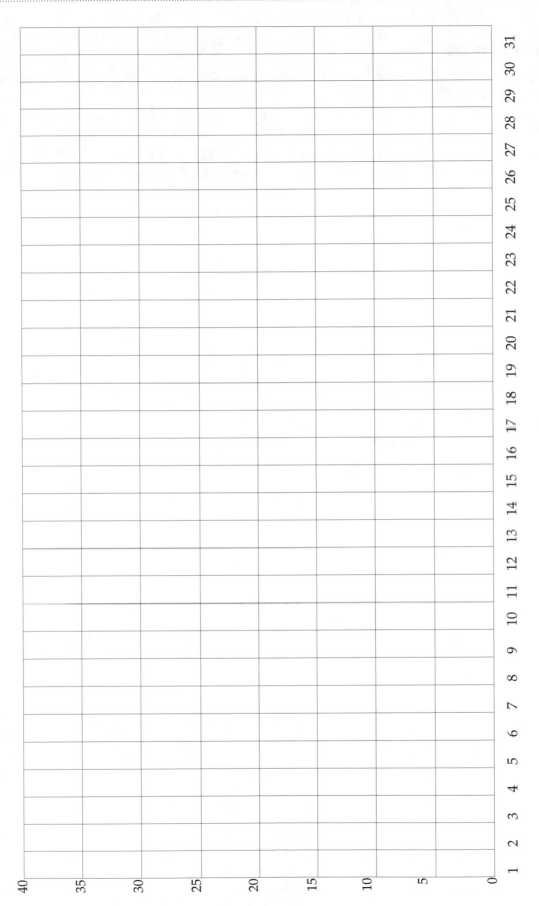

Your Mood Chart

References

Reid, R. L. and S. C. C. Yen, M. D. 1981. "Premenstrual Syndrome." *American Journal of Obstetrics and Gynecology* 139:85–104.

Rubinow, David R., and Peter Roy-Byrne. 1984. "Premenstrual Syndromes: Overview from a Methodological Perspective." *American Journal of Psychiatry* 141,2:163.

Steege, John F., Anna L. Stout, and Sharon L. Rupp. 1985. "Relationships Among Premenstrual Symptoms and Menstrual Cycle Characteristics." *Obstetrics and Gynecology* 65, 3:398–402. March.

Excerpted and adapted with permission from *PMS: Women Tell Women How to Control Premenstrual Syndrome* by Stephanie DeGraff Bender and Kathleen Kelleher. For more information on this and related books, see the "Further Reading" section in the back of the book.

CHAPTER 23

Perimenopause

Perimenopause—Changes in Women's Health after Thirty-Five

We can almost hear what you're thinking: "Changes? You mean I'm already changing, and I'm only thirty-seven?" Yes, it's true. "Is this the Change of Life?" No, it's not menopause. It's peri-menopause—what comes before and just after menopause. "What's causing it?" Your female hormones are declining. "I can stop it though, right?" Not a chance.

Change is what life is about. Whether for good or for ill, all of us continually change as time passes. As for hormonal change, there is a gender difference. Males change in a steady, slow fashion. Females are rhythmic. The difference is mediated by hormones. Every month your uterus builds a new lining and then, if a pregnancy is not begun, sheds it. Every month your breasts change in concert with this rhythm. Think of the other patterns of change you experience on a rhythmic basis: in appetite, skin, mood, sexual desire, and energy, among many others.

Then there are the macro-hormone changes of puberty, pregnancy, and menopause. The engine of the rhythmic pattern of change is female hormone production. It follows, then, that a change in hormone output will alter your rhythms. In this book you will learn about the changes that occur in your body and in your life as a result of decreasing hormone levels. A transition is gradually taking place that you can prepare for and influence in a positive fashion. This book is a guide to maintaining good health during these transition years. It will teach you how to prepare for the best half of your life.

Let's Talk Hormones

Estrogen and progesterone are the female hormones that regulate many of the changes we've mentioned. Of the two, estrogen is the most influential in causing the changes we will be discussing. The life peak of estrogen production is reached at age twenty-seven to twenty-eight. Then a faintly declining plateau is maintained until about thirty-five. Although there is a slight decline in the plateau years, there is always sufficient estrogen to fully support your body. After age thirty-five, though, the average amount of estrogen production per cycle begins to decline sufficiently to produce subtle changes in your body. This marks the earliest beginning of perimenopause. The following figure demonstrates your estrogen level at various ages. Dr. Bernard Eskin reported in 1995 that the decline is in the amount of estrogen you produce in the second half of your cycle after ovulation. Estrogen output in the first half of your cycle remains sufficient to cause ovulation for many more years. Most people, including many health care professionals, don't know this. The decline is not a landslide. You will not suddenly (nor need you ever) become the stereotypic "little old lady." In your forties the decline accelerates, and by age fifty-one to fifty-two, female hormone output is minimal. This section is about those fifteen years from age thirty-five to fifty, and a few years beyond.

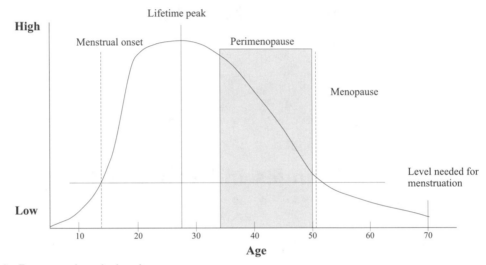

Figure 23.1. Estrogen Levels by Age

It provides you with a general description of what happens during these years, how it happens, and the role of hormone diminution in causing changes. This is a normal process in every woman—no exceptions. There is plenty you can do, however, to control these changes. The medical term for these transitional years is perimenopause, which means the period of time leading up to, and the short period of time just after, menopause. Menopause itself refers to the point in time right after your last menstrual period has happened. Postmenopause refers to the years of life following menopause.

In the past two decades, perimenopause has been regarded as those four to six years after the mid-forties when the symptoms and effects of hormone decrease begin to become quite noticeable. The changes include irregular menstrual cycles, menstrual flow variability, hot flashes, fragmented sleep, mood swings, short-term memory loss, unexplained fatigue, and diminished sexual desire. The reality is that these changes begin a decade earlier than the mid-forties, but they are not signaled by dramatic symptoms—they don't suddenly grab you one morning as you step out of the shower. If you are attuned to your body rhythms, you may be able to detect the subtle changes that are taking place.

What is the significance of these changed body rhythms and feelings, and what should you do about them? Your initial response might be to ignore them or to deny the possibility that they are a result of hormone decline. If you do seek advice, you may find that your doctor knows little more than you about these changes and, if you are still having menstrual periods, may not recognize that your hot flashes, fatigue, and sleep disruptions might be from hormone depletion. You might hear statements like, "You're just tense; you need to relax" or "You're too young for hormonal decline." In this case, it might be time to change doctors; and the more you educate yourself about the transitional years and the biological markers you may experience, the easier it will be to find a health-care advisor who can help you during this phase of your life. Then, you and your doctor can work together to smooth the way for your own transitional years.

Biological Markers

Let's take a look at the changes in body function and behavior, as well as the cognitive changes, that may arise for you in the transitional years. There is enormous variation among women in terms of which of these symptoms they experience, and to what degree. Some of them may seem unpleasant, and some of them can even be threatening to your health. Throughout this book, you'll find ways of managing the troublesome changes.

- **Ovarian slowdown:** At birth, a female infant has all the eggs (ova) she will ever have. (This is in contrast to males, who manufacture new sperm throughout life. Each egg in the ovary is contained in a structure called a follicle. Female sex hormones, estrogen and progesterone, are produced by the cells of the follicle walls. As egg release (ovulation) takes place on a monthly basis, your follicles gradually diminish in number. This reduction begins to be noticeable after age thirty-five in a measurable decrease in average monthly hormone production (Eskin 1995). The reduction proceeds over about fifteen years to an eventual point at which not enough hormones are produced to cause menstrual periods; they cease entirely (menopause). Menopause doesn't just pop up at age fifty-one or fifty-two. It is a process that has its beginnings in the mid-thirties as the result of the natural aging of the reproductive system. The reduced estrogen availability has an enormous influence on your body and the way it functions. For example, a woman forty years old may have difficulty becoming pregnant because the eggs her ovaries supply are also forty years old and may have lost some of their reproductive efficiency.

- **Menstrual cycle and menstrual period changes:** Changes in your menstrual cycle and menstrual period can vary tremendously. Cycles may become longer or shorter or fall into a "no-pattern" pattern. Menstrual bleeding may be heavier or lighter, more prolonged or shorter, or entirely absent. Variable and declining hormone production is the cause.

- **Hot flashes:** Decreased estrogen availability changes the heat release and conservation mechanisms in your body. This results in flushing of the upper body, head, and neck. Hot flashes most commonly begin in the mid-forties, but they can also affect women in their thirties.

- **Reduced stamina:** It is most commonly women who are not fit to begin with who experience reduced stamina in the transitional years. A decrease in muscle tone and strength bears a direct relationship to a woman's diet and how much she exercises.

- **Changes in the skin, vagina, and hair:** The most common time for changes in the skin, vagina, and hair is after the mid-forties. With lessened estrogen, natural secretions diminish, and tissues become thinner and drier than they had been. Atrophy is the medical term for these changes; it refers to the loss of tissue in any part of the body as a result of diminished tissue nutrition. In the transitional years, the tissues most likely to show atrophic change are the skin and mucous membranes, including the face, neck, chest, hair, vagina, and bladder. Diminished natural secretions result in thinning and drying of these tissues, resulting in wrinkles, loss of luster in hair, lessened vaginal lubrication, and urinary tract infections. Skin damage and wrinkling can be accelerated by ultraviolet sunlight exposure and by smoking.

- **Premenstrual Syndrome (PMS) may worsen:** If PMS symptoms worsen, it is usually in the late thirties and early forties. Some women develop PMS for the first time in their late forties. PMS usually disappears about the time of menopause.

- **Cognitive changes:** Brain cells have what are known as estrogen receptors. If these receptors don't get their regular supply of estrogen they can cause wide swings in emotional responses, including transitory episodes of moodiness, short-term memory loss, unexplained sadness, decreased sexual desire, and lessened ability to concentrate.

- **Osteoporosis:** Loss of bone mass, and therefore bone strength, is a well-proven result of estrogen loss. Other factors, such as a poor diet, lack of exercise, and smoking, also contribute to a deteriorating skeleton, but the fundamental causative agent and the cornerstone for prevention is estrogen. Osteoporosis tends to be a postmenopausal event. Nonetheless, be aware that a major deterrent to this crippling and potentially life-threatening problem is to develop a sturdy skeleton before you reach mid-life.

- **Cardiovascular disease (CVD):** It is important to point out that heart disease is the number one cause of death for women between the ages of fifty to seventy-five (in other words, after menopause). It may surprise you to learn that heart attack deaths are twelve times more common than breast cancer deaths (American Heart Association 1997). A major goal for you in the transitional years of life is to find out how to maintain cardiovascular fitness.

- **Thyroid problems:** The thyroid requires estrogen to function normally. A lack of estrogen can lead to underactive thyroid hormone production (hypothyroidism). This condition can leave you feeling weak and lethargic, depressed and moody. If your thyroid is found to be sluggish and you are transitional, your estrogen production may be at the root of it.

- **Decreased sexual desire:** Decreased sexual desire can (but not necessarily does) occur during the transitional years. This is a complex issue, and when it does occur, the symptom may have its roots in a number of areas, including relationship problems, lifestyle excesses, and self-esteem issues, as well as hormone loss.

The Ovary Connection

To help you better understand the topics covered in this section, let's take a look at some anatomy and a little physiology.

The Anatomy

By the time a female fetus is twenty weeks old, her ovaries contain about seven million egg follicles. Over the remainder of intrauterine life, the growing ovaries gradually push the surface follicles out of the ovaries into the abdominal cavity, and they disintegrate. At birth, a baby girl has about two million follicles left. This number continues to diminish so that at puberty, about 400,000 remain. Does it worry you that this may not be enough? Turns out that it's plenty. The rate of loss slows from an average of 250,000 follicles per week during fetal life to about 2,500 per week in childhood, and after puberty it is less than 1,000 per month. A woman ovulates only 400 to 500 times during the childbearing years, so the numbers work out okay.

Each month several hundred follicles are readied for release of an egg. Usually only one is released at ovulation, and the rest of the follicles shrink away. Occasionally, of course, multiple ovulations take place, producing a multiple pregnancy. Humans are not well designed for litters, however, and single egg release is the usual result. By the mid-thirties and beyond, the number of follicles will have diminished sufficiently to result in a decreased blood level of estrogen and progesterone, the female sex hormones. As this process continues, perimenopausal changes begin and the ability to achieve a successful pregnancy declines.

Menopause is ultimately reached by about age fifty-one, at which time the childbearing years of life are concluded. Clearly, it is not a sudden process. In fact, in light of the inexorable decrease of ovarian follicles culminating in menopause, one might make the case that the process of menopause begins in fetal life!

The Physiology

Alphabet Soup	
GnRH	Gonadotropin releasing hormone
FSH	Follicle stimulating hormone
LH	Leuteinizing hormone (LH)

To understand the changes of perimenopause, it is important to know how the ovarian cycle, or menstrual cycle, works. Then it becomes easier to understand what happens when it doesn't work.

The cycle is really sort of a daisy chain, as you can see in the following figure. (Don't worry—we'll explain the fine print in a moment.) The chain involves three hormone-producing glands:

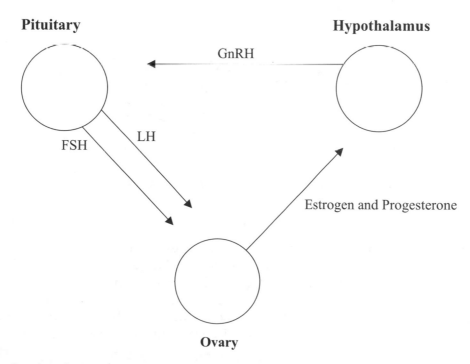

Figure 23.2. Ovarian Cycle

- The *hypothalamus*, in the brain

- The *pituitary*, in the brain

- The *ovaries*, in the pelvis

These glands work in concert with each other. Each produces hormones that are recognized by the other two, acting as chemical messengers that are carried to their targets by your bloodstream. Some of these hormones influence the ovarian cycle.

We need to start our discussion somewhere in the cycle, so let's enter it at the end of a menstrual period, after the uterine lining has been shed. At this point, your ovaries are producing low levels of estrogen and progesterone, as the chart shown in the following figure demonstrates. The hypothalamus detects this and sends a hormone called gonadotropin releasing hormone (GnRH) to the pituitary. In response, the pituitary releases two hormones that target the ovaries: follicle stimulating hormone (FSH) and leuteinizing hormone (LH). FSH stimulates the ovaries to do two things: start producing more estrogen (which, among other things, rebuilds the lining of the uterus) and get a follicle ready for ovulation. At mid-cycle, estrogen reaches a critical level, which triggers a sudden surge of LH from the pituitary; this causes ovulation.

After the follicle has released its egg, it turns into a structure called the corpus luteum, which manufactures progesterone. Progesterone increases the blood supply in the uterine lining and fills the glands of the lining with glycogen (a sugar). This prepares the lining of the uterus for receiving and nourishing a fertilized egg.

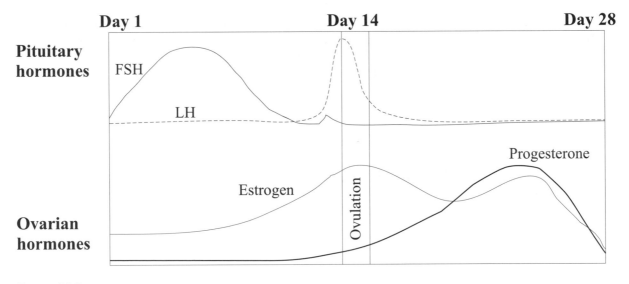

Figure 23.3

At this point the bloodstream contains high levels of estrogen, progesterone, and inhibin. In response, the hypothalamus reduces the GnRH level, signaling the pituitary to cut back on FSH and LH. This in turn causes the ovaries to decrease estrogen and progesterone production. The net result is that, once again, the bloodstream contains a low level of female hormones. The lining of the uterus is no longer supported by hormones, and it is shed—in other words, a menstrual period occurs. Then the cycle, which usually takes about four weeks, begins again.

Diagnosis of Perimenopause

As we mentioned earlier in this chapter, if you are still having menstrual periods, you may find it hard to believe that hormone depletion may be causing the symptoms you've been having—and equally hard to have this confirmed by a doctor. There are steps you can take, though, to ensure proper diagnosis and treatment of the symptoms you experience during the transitional years.

Get Smart: Educate Yourself

Health care in the U.S. today is less personalized than it used to be, and it has become increasingly important for people to become more personally involved in maintaining their own wellness. The responsibility for initiating certain procedures, such as screening exams, falls more and more into the individual's own hands.

Diagnosing perimenopause (or any other altered body state, for that matter) is a process that you can actually initiate by becoming aware that a change has taken place in your body. We're not talking about an occasional change in menstrual flow or timing or occasionally tender breasts, excess fluid retention, or an increase in skin blemishes; variations of this type are normal. What we are talking about is an awareness of a persistent and recurring change—you can look back over recent cycles and realize that they are different from those in prior years. The more you know about your body, the better able you are to observe these changes.

An important aspect of educating yourself is becoming aware of your personal risk factors for particular health problems. How you live your life, what foods you eat, how well you exercise, the toxins to which you are exposed, preexisting conditions, and in some cases, inheritance, can play major roles in your current and future health. For example, if you are a smoker, then cancer, heart disease, and osteoporosis may all be part of your future. Also, try to find out as much as you can about your family's health history, which can provide further clues to your own risk factors. The risk factors you identify for yourself can help decide the kinds of screening tests you might need, and their frequency. The goal, of course, is to avoid illness or to treat it early.

Once you have chosen a doctor, you can arrange for a complete physical exam, which is also important to your understanding of your body. The exam should include your height, weight, blood pressure, head (including eyes, mouth, throat, ears), neck (including thyroid, lymph glands, blood vessels), chest, breasts, armpits with lymph glands, heart, abdomen, pelvic with rectal, extremities, pulses, skin, and neurological. A complete exam is a must for your first visit to the doctor you choose; but if you are in good health in your transitional years, it isn't necessary to have a complete exam every year.

Choosing Your Health Care Advisor

You need a competent and compassionate professional to work with you in maintaining good health during your transitional years. Unfortunately, many talented physicians and alternative medical professionals are not yet well informed about the health concerns of women in transition or the hormonal changes that can occur, so be sure the person you choose is familiar with these issues. Good candidates are gynecologists, internists, family practitioners, and endocrinologists (hormone specialists). In addition, many clinics specialize in women's health care, and others limit their services to menopause and perimenopause. Be alert to whether your consultant is truly listening to you; skillful health professionals know that taking a careful medical history can help pinpoint a problem.

Testing Hormone Levels

Until recently, doctors often tested women for follicle stimulating hormone (FSH) to determine whether their ovaries were producing enough estrogen. The FSH testing was based on the knowledge that in menopausal women, the FSH level is high because of low production of estrogen. The pituitary gland is sending out high levels of FSH in an effort to get the failing ovaries to produce more estrogen. The problem with FSH testing in perimenopausal women, however, is that estrogen production may wax and wane from one month to the next, so consistent results are not possible. For this reason, most doctors no longer rely on FSH blood levels to diagnose perimenopause. What other options are there?

One option, advocated by leading experts in the field, is to do a clinical test: give you a trial dose of a hormone supplement. If your perimenopausal symptoms are improved, you are on the right track. (If not, you and your doctor need to look elsewhere for a cause of the changes you are experiencing such as thyroid abnormalities, ovarian disease, or perhaps stressful events in your life.) Some women are now opting to use low-dose birth control pills during their entire perimenopause. They can control perimenopausal symptoms, help prevent long-term problems such as heart disease and osteoporosis, and prevent pregnancy.

CAUTION! If you have abnormal uterine bleeding, it must not be treated with hormones unless it is clearly established that you do not have uterine disease.

Your Hormones Are Down a Little—Should You Worry?

You may be wondering why generations of women before yours didn't worry about perimenopausal symptoms. One reason was that relatively little was known about menopause, and the term perimenopause was not even used until the late 1970s or early 1980s. Menopause was neither a topic of conversation nor a subject of research.

Another reason is that prior to the twentieth century, women often did not live many years after the childbearing years. In the last hundred years or so, though, women have been living longer, thanks to improvements in areas like nutrition, sanitation, medical care, housing, clothing, work savers, and accident prevention. The current life expectancy for American women is just over eighty years.

What hasn't changed, however, is the age at which female hormones decline. It has been happening in a woman's forties for many centuries, and it still is. For American women, the average age of menopause is fifty-one. (The age differs in other cultures.) The simple arithmetic is that many women now live more than one third of their lives after their childbearing role is completed. Staying healthy during these years takes some advance planning and preparation.

Planning and Preparation

During the transitional years of perimenopause, you have a good shot at keeping the balance of your life healthy and enjoyable. If you don't have to have hot flashes, moodiness, and short-term memory loss, why put up with them? Granted, these symptoms are not life threats, and they will subside in a few years even if you do nothing. Still, controlling or eliminating these symptoms can improve your quality of life. In addition, you now have an opportunity to prevent or modify your risk for a few more ominous problems that can plague significant portions of the last half of your life.

With the help of your health consultant, you can follow a proactive program of prevention ranging from hormone replacement, to lifestyle changes, to use of alternative medical remedies, to more aggressive preventive care, including screening techniques and a fitness program. Life is a journey, so why not enjoy the trip?

Hormone Replacement—The Easy Part

If the primary cause of perimenopausal change is decreased estrogen production, *hormone replacement therapy* (HRT) is a logical option for dealing with it. There has been much debate in recent years on the appropriateness of this form of management. Certainly, there are risks in using HRT, but there are also risks in failing to do so. Take a look at the following table, which lists the changes caused by estrogen loss through the transitional years and beyond. This is a daunting list of potential problems, but you may experience few or none of them. The point of the following table is to demonstrate that estrogen is widely utilized throughout your body, and that HRT is not recommended solely for the relief of relatively minor symptoms. Estrogen levels affect your entire body; and reduction of this hormone changes the way your body looks and operates.

Table 1.1 Symptoms and Signs of Estrogen Loss

Irregular periods	Vaginal dryness
Hot flashes	Decreased sexual desire
Mood swings	Reduced muscle tone
Fragmented sleep	Reduced stamina
Short-term memory loss	Constipation
Difficulty concentrating	Recurrent urinary tract infection
Irritability	Breast sag
Anxiety	Eye dryness
Minor depression	Underactive thyroid
Skin dryness	Osteoporosis
Wrinkling	Rise in cholesterol
Reduced sexual lubrication	Beginning risk of heart disease

Be aware that a variety of not as yet mainstream alternative treatment modalities other than HRT are available for perimenopausal changes. Some, like Chinese herbal medicine, predate Western medicine by many centuries. Many perimenopausal changes are considerably helped by these alternative remedies, but unfortunately, there is a scarcity of information from the medical community as to the safety and effectiveness of such treatments as homeopathy, Chinese herbal medicine, acupuncture, holistic medicine, and mind/body medicine.

Lifestyle Changes—The Hard Part

You might think at this point that all you need is to load up on hormone replacement and go merrily on with your life. Alas, there is much more to maintaining good health and vitality than HRT. These are the major issues:

- **Fitness:** has been embraced by boomers as by no other generation of Americans. Improving your diet and increasing your exercise are the two major components of fitness.

- **Stress management:** In our culture of busy, striving-to-keep-afloat individuals and two-income families, stress management is of signal importance to us all. Stress may be magnified during your perimenopausal transition, so it is helpful for you to know how to deal with it. When poorly controlled, stress takes a serious toll on relationships important to you—those with your partner, children, co-workers, relatives, and friends—and it takes its toll on your body as well. See also the chapter on Stress in part V.

- **Alcohol, tobacco, and other deleterious drugs:** Lifestyle choices that include use of harmful drugs may contribute to many of the adverse perimenopausal changes.

References

American Heart Association. 1997. *Heart and Stroke Statistical Update.* Dallas, TX.

Eskin, B., and L. Dumas. 1995. *Midlife Can Wait: How to Stay Young and Healthy After 35.* New York: Ballantine Books.

Excerpted and adapted with permission from *Perimenopause: Changes in Women's Health After 35* by James E. Huston, M.D. and L. Darlene Lanka, M.D. For more information on this and related books, see the "Further Reading" section in the back of the book.

CHAPTER 24

Menopause

Historical Review

From the time when the term was first used, up to the 1960s, menopause was perceived as a disease and thought to cause a multitude of symptoms and illnesses, ranging from diarrhea to diabetes. Well into the 1900s, thousands of women were committed to mental institutions, diagnosed as having a mental disease called "involutional melancholia," which was thought to be related to menopause. Some physicians characterized menopausal women as "peevish," or "quarrelsome and obstinate."

It is understandable then why women have anticipated menopause with fear and apprehension. One of the challenges facing women today is to change this negative image of menopause. Instead of associating it with old age, sickness, and loss of sexuality and attractiveness, women are beginning to look at menopause as a positive natural event. They are dispelling the myth of it being a deficiency disease, or a medical or psychological crisis.

Cross-Cultural Studies

Cross-cultural studies support the idea that menopause can be a positive life event. There are cultures in the world where menopause is viewed favorably. In such cultures there are often fewer physical complaints associated with the cessation of menstruation when compared to those cultures in which menopause is viewed negatively.

For example, a study of Indian women of the Rajput caste found no evidence of the depression or other negative changes associated with menopause that have frequently been reported elsewhere. The researchers felt that this was because, after menopause, previously veiled and secluded women in that caste are given access to many of the activities formerly reserved only for men. Thus, for them menopause means greater status and freedom. This is also the case in other non-Western cultures where postmenopausal women encounter culturally sanctioned role changes that either increase their status or decrease their burdens.

Even in the West there are groups that are more accepting of menopause. For example, Amish women often view menopause as a natural part of life, and therefore, stay active, confront changes positively, and even maintain a sense of humor about it.

Most cross-cultural studies reveal that the status of postmenopausal women is increased in cultures where there are

- Strong ties to the extended family system

- Social systems that extol strong mother-child relationships and reproduction

- Well-defined grandmother and mother-in-law roles

- Extensive menstrual taboos

- Respect and reverence for age

In contrast, having a youth-oriented culture increases the potential for problems during menopause. What you can learn from other cultures is that the presence of a clearly defined role, positive status for postmenopausal women, and important life tasks beyond child-rearing years are significant factors determining the way women react to menopause.

Politics of Menopause and Women's Health

Another reason for the negative images and messages surrounding menopause has been women's limited political power within the medical and research communities, as well as within society as a whole. Until fairly recently, most physicians were men. Women who consulted physicians about physical complaints or symptoms occurring during menopause were often patronized by male doctors, or dismissed as "hysterical."

Also until recently, studies about diseases and their treatments often did not include women. Much of the information about the causes, treatments, and prevention of illness comes from studies conducted primarily with men and therefore may not be applicable for specific health problems as they affect women.

Thanks to efforts to correct these factors, women now have greater representation within medical research, experience more responsiveness from the medical profession, and have their concerns taken more seriously by society at large. Consequently, they are becoming more active participants in their own health care management.

The Biology of Menopause

Menopause occurs as the ovaries run out of eggs. Estrogen production falls and menstrual periods become irregular. The average age of menopause is 51.2 years. Early menopause can occur due to surgical removal of or radiation to the ovaries or chromosomal abnormalities.

Some women menstruate well into their fifties. This is a normal variant. However, if you are in your fifties and are still menstruating, your risk for breast and uterine cancer increases. It is important to notify your physician and get a comprehensive annual physical exam. Measuring FSH level is the most useful way to determine whether you are menopausal.

Short-Term Effects of Menopause

There are a number of changes that you may experience as a result of menopause. Some of them begin during perimenopause, while others occur later and are the result of being without estrogen for a longer period of time.

Changes in Your Menstrual Cycle

Approximately 80 percent of all women will experience some kind of change in their cycle about seven years prior to menopause, with cycles becoming either more frequent or infrequent and periods becoming shorter or longer. These differences reflect the changes in hormonal production by your ovaries. If no follicles develop within the ovary, no estrogen is produced, and you will miss a cycle. If ovulation does not occur, estrogen production continues with a resultant thickening of the uterine lining, and when the lining sloughs off, heavy bleeding results. Alternatively, your cycle may be shorter because estrogen is not being made in the preovulatory phase, so the follicular phase of your cycle is shorter and your period comes prematurely.

What It Means

Symptom	Reason
Short cycles	Preovulatory estrogen is not being made. The follicular phase of your cycle will be less than 14 days. You still ovulate and have your period 2 weeks later, but your cycle is shorter.
Light bleeding	You are not producing as much estrogen. Your uterine lining will be thinner. When menstruation occurs, there will be less flow.
Heavy bleeding	You are not ovulating. Estrogen continues to stimulate the growth of the uterine lining with no progesterone to oppose it. Your lining will be thicker than usual, so when it is shed, blood flow will be heavier.
Missed period	No follicle develops so no estrogen is produced. The uterine lining does not thicken and is not sloughed off.

You may find it helpful to keep track of your menstrual periods as you approach menopause. This will allow you to record any irregularities in your period and highlight potential problems. The simplest thing to do is get a calendar and mark the day your period begins and ends. Note whether bleeding was light, moderate, or heavy. Note any other symptoms if appropriate; for example, cramps, breast soreness, bloating, or moodiness. If you have had spotting at another time of the month, note this and indicate the type of flow. If possible, estimate when ovulation occurred.

When to See Your Doctor

The following is a list of potential danger signs. While heavy bleeding or irregular cycles are frequently normal during the perimenopause, you should check with your physician if you have any of the following symptoms:

- Extremely heavy, frequent, prolonged bleeding

- Bleeding between periods

- Bleeding during intercourse

- Bleeding that begins after you have not menstruated for about one year. **This is extremely important because it may be an early sign of cancer.**

Hot Flashes

The hot flash, the most common menopausal sign, is an episode of intense warmth in the upper body or a drenching sweat followed by chills. It may be preceded by a sense of anxiety, tension, dizziness, nausea, tingling in the fingers, and palpitations. Sometimes, it can manifest itself as a vague sense of "not feeling right."

Eighty percent of menopausal women have hot flashes. Frequency and individual experiences vary considerably. Hot flashes usually stop one to two years after the last period but may continue for up to ten years past that point. They may last from a few seconds to a few minutes, and tend to occur more frequently during the night. For most women, hot flashes are uncomfortable but bearable. For 10 to 15 percent, however, they can be quite debilitating.

What causes hot flashes?

During a hot flash, epinephrine (adrenaline) levels rise. It is unclear why this happens, but scientists believe that it may be caused by changes in the hypothalamus, which regulates body temperature along with the menstrual cycle. As a result, heart rate rises, and there is an increase in blood flow and body temperature.

Tips for Managing Your Hot Flashes

- Watch your diet. Try to avoid alcohol, caffeine, and spicy foods. Too much sugar, hot soups or drinks, and very large meals can also set off hot flashes.

- Stop smoking. Nicotine is known to increase and intensify hot flashes.

- Keep cool. Wear natural fibers that "breathe." At night, sleep with a sheet or light covers. Keep room temperatures at a comfortable level. Drink cool drinks and take cold showers. Cooling yourself with a fan or splashing your face with water can help.

- Exercise. Being physically active can decrease the severity of hot flashes. Exercise improves circulation and makes your body better able to tolerate temperature extremes and cool down quickly. It also increases the amount of estrogen and other hormones that are circulating, which will diminish the severity of the hot flash.

- Reduce your stress level. Stress can make hot flashes worse. See the chapter on Stress in part V.

- Get medical help. Replacing the estrogen that is lost during menopause is the most effective way of eliminating hot flashes. Because of potential side effects of estrogen use, however, this decision should be made carefully. For a more detailed discussion of hormone replacement therapy, see chapter 6.

The changes in the hypothalamus are brought about by declining estrogen levels. The more abrupt the drop in your estrogen level, the more severe your hot flashes. Further, thin women often have a more difficult time with hot flashes than heavy women. Researchers believe that heavier women continue to produce estrogen in their fat cells and thus have a more gradual decline in estrogen during menopause.

Managing your hot flashes

Keep track of when, under what circumstances (stress, certain foods), and how often your hot flashes occur. Often, it will become evident that there is a pattern.

Sleep Changes

Women can experience restless, fragmented sleep five to seven years before menopause. Changes in your sleeping patterns may be the earliest indicators of hormonal change. Sleep loss affects people in different ways and can lead to problems such as lack of concentration, memory loss, irritability, fatigue, and muscle aches and pains.

Tips for Dealing with Sleep Deprivation

- Maintain a regular schedule. Wake up and go to sleep at around the same time each day.
- Avoid caffeine and alcohol, which affect sleep.
- Avoid over-the-counter drugs such as nasal decongestants, antihistamines, and diet aids, which can affect sleep.
- Stop smoking. Nicotine acts as a stimulant.
- Exercise on a regular basis. However, do not exercise too close to bedtime, as it can be overly stimulating.
- Take a hot bath before you go to bed. Raising your body temperature is a way to induce deeper, longer lasting sleep. However, hot baths may also trigger hot flashes in some women.
- Drink milk at bedtime.
- Adjust the temperature of your bedroom.
- Sleep in light cotton clothing with a minimal amount of bedding. Avoid polyester and nylon, either in nightclothes or sheets, as they hold the perspiration next to your body and can intensify your discomfort.

Mood Changes

Recent studies suggest that estrogen enhances mood in healthy, nondepressed adult women, even before menopause. In addition, changes in mood are often reported as women reach menopause and estrogen levels drop. Besides the decrease in estrogen, there may be other possible causes for the mood changes. If you have already been diagnosed as having PMS, clinical depression, or have ongoing emotional problems, you may find that your symptoms become exacerbated during perimenopause. For more information about mood changes, see chapter 10.

Changes in the Vagina and Urethra

As your estrogen level drops, the tissues of the vagina and urethra become thinner and drier. Sexual intercourse may become painful and uncomfortable and sexual arousal can take longer with less lubrication. Vaginal infections and a decrease or loss of sexual drive may occur.

Tips for Dealing with Vaginal Dryness

- Regular sex is one of the best cures for vaginal dryness. This entails achieving orgasm once or twice a week with a partner or by masturbation. Sex increases the blood flow to your vagina, stimulates the mucous membrane, and exercises the surrounding tissue.
- Use lubricants. There are several over-the-counter lubricants such as Astroglide, K-Y Jelly, or Replens. You can also have your physician prescribe estrogen cream.
- Wear the right underclothes. Vaginal dryness can lead to itching and the growth of bacteria, which can lead to infection. Wear panties and panty hose with cotton crotches to allow the air to circulate.

Other Short-Term Effects

There are other miscellaneous changes that can occur with low estrogen levels that are generally less frequent and less severe than those mentioned above. These changes include crawling skin (formication), headaches, memory loss, and fatigue. They affect a smaller percentage of women and may disappear after menopause.

Crawling Skin (Formication)

This symptom can occur during perimenopause. It feels like an itchy, crawling sensation and will respond to estrogen. It usually disappears during menopause.

Headaches

After menopause, some women with menstrual migraines will stop having headaches while others will report an increase in the frequency of their headaches. You can keep a record of your headaches on your hot flash chart. Identify any potential triggers including food, alcohol, stress levels, and amount of sleep. By doing this, you may be able to identify what sets off your headaches.

In addition to cutting out triggers, it is helpful to know that exercise and sexual activity diminish migraines. If you are on hormone replacement therapy (HRT) and you are having headaches, you might want to try a different brand of hormones.

Memory Loss

It is not uncommon for women to experience short-term memory loss around the time of perimenopause. This appears to be temporary and is helped by HRT. It is probably related to lack of sleep, stress, or the normal aging process.

Whenever anyone experiences memory problems it is quite disconcerting, and many people will become concerned about Alzheimer's disease or related problems. It helps to know that age does not affect intelligence. If you were smart when you were younger, you will maintain this into old age. Older people remember almost as much as younger people, with the main difference being that it often takes them longer to retrieve the information. Only 5 to 7 percent of women show serious intellectual impairment after the age of sixty-five.

If memory loss persists after menopause or is disabling, you should seek medical advice. High blood pressure, some medications, vitamin deficiencies, anemia, sleep loss, or stress can affect memory.

Tips for Dealing with Memory Loss

- Use notes, lists, and day planners.

- Use bright color-coded tabs and highlighters. Bright colors grab your attention and are remembered more easily (for example, use purple ink on green notepaper).

- Use or create acronyms by combining the first letters of key words to be remembered. For example, an acronym for the names of the Great Lakes would be HOMES—Huron, Ontario, Michigan, Erie, Superior.

- Create a mnemonic device by using the first letter of each word to be remembered to make a sentence or rhyme. For example, a common mnemonic for the lines in the treble clef music staff of E, G, B, D, F, is "Every Good Boy Does Fine."

- Associate information to be remembered with knowledge and life experiences you already have. For example, associate a phone number with someone's birthday or anniversary (228-1954 could be your son's birthday on 2/28/54).

- Use input from a variety of senses to reinforce learning. For example, read the information to be remembered, write it down, and repeat it out loud.

- Create mental images or a series of pictures for the information to be remembered. The pictures should be absurd or unusual to enhance recall. For example, to remember Dr. Steinman's name, associate it with a man holding an enormous beer stein).

- Rehearse (recite/repeat) the material to be remembered.

- Review new information immediately, since research suggests that most forgetting occurs in the first few minutes after the information is taken in. For example, as soon as someone is introduced to you, use their name in your next sentence.

Long-Term Effects of Menopause

Coronary Heart Disease

Coronary heart disease (CHD) is one of the most serious developments that can occur after menopause. Unusual in women before menopause, CHD is a leading cause of death in women after menopause, exceeding that of all cancers. A fifty-year-old woman has a one in two chance of developing coronary heart disease in her lifetime. Almost one in three women will die from it.

Coronary heart disease develops when there is narrowing of one or more of the blood vessels carrying blood to the heart. As you age, there is a slow accumulation of cholesterol material within the walls of the blood vessels that supply the heart. These vessels become narrower as the cholesterol plaque continues to grow (see the following sketch). Consequently, there is a decrease in blood flow to the heart muscle itself. The heart cannot pump the blood in a normal fashion and is therefore more prone to irregular heartbeats (arrhythmias).

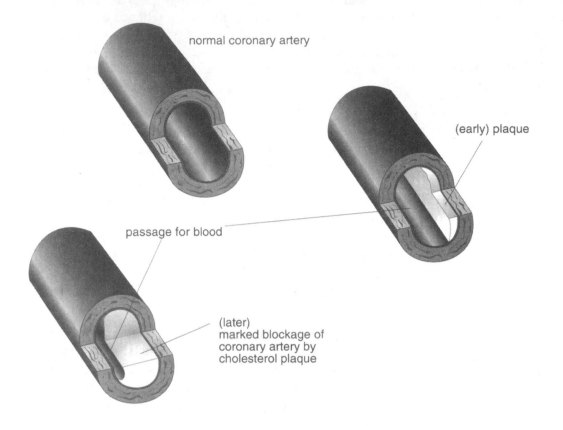

As the blood flow to the heart decreases, and under physical exertion, women (and men) can experience a particular type of chest pain called angina pectoris. This is a crushing midchest pain that can radiate to the left arm or neck. Prolonged episodes of angina pectoris can cause some of the heart muscle to die. This is called a heart attack, or a myocardial infarction. As the heart muscle continues to deteriorate, the heart can no longer pump blood efficiently, and blood pools in the lungs. When this happens, it is called congestive heart failure. CHD is still considered to be a disease generally afflicting men. Reflecting the gender bias of most health studies, much of the research on heart disease has been done only on men. Often, however, women will not have classic symptoms and their heart attacks may go unnoticed. Women's symptoms may include being nauseated, tired, or just not feeling well. Women tend to develop coronary heart disease some ten years later than men and have their first heart attack in their sixties, some years after menopause. They also tend to die at a higher rate from the initial heart attack than men, because their heart attacks occur later and their symptoms can be atypical and thus misdiagnosed.

Biological risk factors

Some women are at greater risk of developing heart disease than others. The following table lists the biological risk factors for the development of coronary heart disease:

Biological Risk Factors for Coronary Heart Disease (CHD)

Check all risk factors that apply to you. Discuss any "yes" or "don't know" answers with your physician and develop a plan to minimize or treat the conditions.

	Yes	No	Don't Know
Cigarette smoking			
High blood pressure			
Diabetes			
Obesity			
Oophorectomy			
Postmenopausal and not using HRT			
Family history of first heart attack before age 60			
Elevated cholesterol			
Elevated triglycerides			
Advanced age (71 to 80)			
African-American			

Prevention of heart disease

On a positive note, you can reduce your chances of developing heart disease by reducing the risk factors you have. All of the following can help:

- Eliminating cigarette smoking

- Aggressively treating high blood pressure, if it exists

- Controlling diabetes

- Maintaining a normal body weight for your age and height

- Treating elevated cholesterol and triglyceride levels through diet, exercise, and, if indicated, medication

- Using hormone replacement therapy (this may reduce heart disease by as much as 50 percent, though there is conflicting research on this matter)

In addition, there are other things that you can do to prevent or slow down the development of heart disease. Among these are good nutrition and exercise.

Osteoporosis

Osteoporosis, or "porous bones," is another of the most serious health problems related to menopause. Bone is constantly being broken down and replaced. Osteoporosis occurs when more bone is broken down than is built, causing bone loss to occur. Bones then break more easily, resulting in broken hips and wrists, and compression fractures of the vertebra (which are responsible for the loss of height and curvature of the spine). Estrogen protects bones from calcium loss. However, at menopause, when the levels of estrogen are dropping, there is a loss of bone density. This loss occurs most rapidly in the first five years of menopause, when bone loss can reach 3 to 4 percent of the total bone mass.

About one out of every three postmenopausal women has, or is in the process of developing, osteoporosis. Over a million women will develop fractures due to osteoporosis, and 25 to 30 percent of these will be hip fractures. The total medical cost of treating this disorder and its complications is around $10 billion per year. That does not take into account the human toll in pain and suffering. In 25 percent of Caucasian and Asian women, compression fractures of the vertebra and wrists begin at age sixty. Consequently, these women will become shorter and, as they age, will develop the classic "dowager's hump."

Fractures can have serious consequences. Around 20 percent of women undergoing hip replacement surgery after a hip fracture will die within one year of their injuries, a death rate that is greater than that of cancer of the breast and uterus combined. (The death is usually due to blood and fat clots released from the fracture site.) Approximately half of these women will require constant nursing care as a result of the hip fracture.

The main risk for developing osteoporosis is related to bone mass. If you have more bone mass, your chances of developing osteoporosis are reduced. The following table lists some other risk factors.

Risk Factors for Osteoporosis

Check all risk factors that apply to you. Discuss any "yes" answers with your physician and develop a plan to minimize or treat.

	Yes	No
Caucasian or Asian		
Very thin		
Early menopause (before age 40)		
Surgical menopause		
Family history of osteoporosis		
Low calcium intake (<1500 mg/day)		
Low vitamin D intake		
High caffeine intake		
High alcohol intake		
High protein intake		
Cigarette smoking		
Sedentary lifestyle		
Endocrine disorder		
Diabetes		
Hyperthyroidism		
Cushing's disease		
Hyperparathyroidism		
Steroid therapy for more than 6 months		
Postmenopausal and not on HRT		

Evaluation of osteoporosis

Osteoporosis is usually asymptomatic and not recognized until a fracture occurs. At least 25 percent of bone has to be lost before osteoporosis can be diagnosed from a routine X ray. There are a variety of tests other than routine X rays for measuring bone mineral content. DEXA (Duo Energy X-ray Absorptiometry) is currently felt to be the best test available. It is a painless procedure that scans an image of your hip and spine. A computer compares your bone density with the bone density of a young adult and of someone your age. Once performed only at major medical centers, bone density tests are now widely available. Many doctors will recommend this test if you have a number of the risk factors for osteoporosis. Make sure you go to a facility that has a lot of experience in performing these tests. Biochemical markers, such as Osteomark, are now being used to test for bone turnover.

Prevention of osteoporosis

Getting an adequate amount of calcium as an adolescent is one of the most important factors in preventing osteoporosis because it is in adolescence that the greatest amount of bone mass is laid down. However, most studies show that adolescent girls get far less than their minimum daily requirement (800–1200 mg) of calcium per day, placing them at risk for the development of osteoporosis.

Exercise may also play a part in the prevention of osteoporosis. This is especially true if you have been sedentary. However, no one has quantified the intensity of exercise required to have a positive effect on the skeletal system. While exercise can increase bone density, it will not, by itself, prevent osteoporosis. The beneficial effects of exercise will last only as long as it is continued.

Many studies have shown that hormone replacement therapy reduces the amount of postmenopausal bone loss, as well as the incidence of fractures, and is considered to be the best prevention for osteoporosis. Five years of estrogen therapy will reduce the risk of developing fractures by half. The minimum daily dosage of estrogen needed to prevent osteoporosis is 0.625 mg of Premarin, 0.625 mg of estrone sulfate, or .5 mg of estradiol. Transdermal patches may also decrease the loss of bone mass.

A Prescription for the Prevention of Osteoporosis

- 1000 mg calcium per day for premenopausal women
- 1500 mg of calcium per day for postmenopausal women
- Exercise
- Decrease risk factors (see the previous table)
- The use of HRT early in menopause

New treatments for osteoporosis

These medications help increase bone density and stop bone loss before fractures occur. They are intended for postmenopausal women who already have low bone density.

- *Fossamax* (alendronate) decreases bone loss and increases bone density. It is more potent than *Didronel* (etidronate), which is also used to treat osteoporosis. It also has fewer side effects, such as diarrhea and nausea. Fossamax is available by prescription.

- *Miacalcin* (calcitonin) has been offered for sale as a nasal spray. It decreases bone loss, like Fossamax and Didronel, but it doesn't increase bone density.

- *Slow release fluoride* stimulates new bone formation. If calcium citrate is added, stronger bone is produced. Slow release fluoride is not widely recommended because it is associated with a higher incidence of vertebral fractures and has not yet received FDA approval.

Genitourinary Systems

Some changes in the vagina and urethra have already been discussed in chapter 3. In addition to these, the vulva (the lips surrounding the vaginal opening) become thinner. The vulva may also shrink, making the vaginal opening too tight for comfortable sexual intercourse. When this happens, intercourse can cause pain and irritation of the urethra.

Bladder problems

Stress Urinary Incontinence (SUI) refers to the involuntary loss of urine when you laugh, cough, or sneeze. Stress Urinary Incontinence occurs because the urethra begins to stretch away from the pubic bone. This can occur prior to menopause, but is most disturbing after age sixty. Vaginal births and years of standing and straining can make this condition more likely.

Fifty percent of women with SUI can avoid surgery if they have good pelvic muscle tone and practice the Kegel exercise (see box below). If you do these exercises for approximately two minutes four times a day, it will take about two to three months before incontinence stops. If the exercises are discontinued, the incontinence will return. For the remaining women, collagen injections around the urethra can build support or surgery can be done. About 75 percent of women with SUI will no longer have symptoms after surgery.

The Kegel Exercise

Dr. Arnold Kegel invented this exercise in the 1950s. It helps to strengthen the pubococcygeal muscle, which helps you stop the flow of urine and prevent a bowel movement. It also is the muscle that contracts during orgasm.

1. Locate your pelvic floor muscles by pretending to stop the flow of urine while urinating. Alternatively, you can contract the anal sphincter as you would to prevent a bowel movement. You will feel a distinct tightening of your muscles.

2. Tighten these muscles again, hold for 10 seconds, and then release. Repeat this 10 times.

3. Repeat 5 to 10 times each day.

Since no one will be aware that you are doing this exercise, you can do it anywhere—while watching television, in the car at a stoplight, or at your desk during the day. The important thing is to make it a daily habit.

Skin Changes

Skin thickness declines at the same rate as bone density. Thirty percent of skin collagen (connective tissue) is lost in the first ten years after the onset of menopause. The skin bruises easily, and may have either increased pigmentation—called "liver spots"—or decreased pigmentation. Facial acne can also appear. The breasts can lose fatty tissue and elasticity, which leads to smaller, sagging breasts. Wrinkles, another common age-related skin change, are caused primarily by sun damage and years of facial expressions.

Tips to Minimize Wrinkles

- Wear sunscreen daily and minimize your exposure to the sun.
- There is some evidence that HRT can be helpful.
- Don't drink or smoke. Alcohol and smoking are both associated with an increase in wrinkles.
- Maintain a healthy diet and lifestyle including plenty of water, exercise, and adequate rest.
- Some antioxidant vitamins (A, C, and E) seem to benefit the skin.
- Retin-A is used by many dermatologists for wrinkles caused by sun damage and for brown "age" spots.
- Alpha-hydroxy acids, such as lactic acid and glycolic acid, can be purchased over the counter, frequently in moisturizers. They act in a manner similar to Retin-A, but with less effectiveness, as well as fewer side effects.
- Dermabrasion, chemical peels, laser techniques, and cosmetic surgery are more invasive ways of treating wrinkles.

Hair Changes

As a result of the hormonal changes of menopause and aging, you are likely to notice changes in your hair that may include

- Thinning of scalp and pubic hair

- Loss of luster

Complete baldness is unlikely, but if your hair loss persists, you may want to consult a dermatologist. There is no treatment to restore the luster of the hair, unless it is due to hairstyling products and techniques. Graying of hair is hereditary, and is not reversed by HRT.

Hirsutism is the growth of dark, thick hair on the chin, lip, or neck, or around the nipples due to excessive androgenic hormones. You will want to consult with your physician if it develops since there are other causes of hirsutism that should be evaluated. For benign excessive hair growth, treatment alternatives include HRT, shaving, tweezing, waxing, bleaching, electrolysis, and depilatories. If you use a depilatory, make sure it is specifically developed for facial use and that you are not allergic to it.

Excerpted and adapted with permission from *The Taking Charge of Menopause Workbook* by Robert M. Dosh, Ph.D., Susan N. Fukushima, M.D., Jane E. Lewis, Ph.D., Robert L. Ross, M.D., and Lynne A. Steinman, Ph.D. For more information on this and related books, see the "Further Reading" section in the back of the book.

CHAPTER 25

Testicular and Prostate Cancer

For men over forty, an annual physical checkup should include a rectal prostate exam. You lie on your side with your knees pulled up to your chest. The doctor inserts a gloved, lubricated finger about an inch and a half into your rectum and feels the base of the prostate gland. The illustration shows where the prostate lies at the base of the bladder.

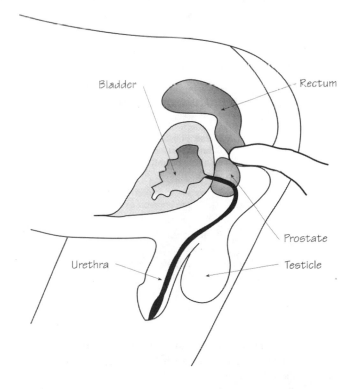

If your prostate feels enlarged, irregular, or abnormally firm, it could be a sign of trouble. Prostate trouble can be a cancerous tumor, an infection, or a relatively harmless enlargement known as *benign prostatic hypertrophy*. Only the rectal exam can detect a tumor early. In the early stages of prostate cancer, you feel no symptoms. By the time prostate cancer becomes painful or starts to interfere with urination, it is well established and your chances of cure are worse. Given the way your body is constructed, you can't check your own prostate, so you have to have the doctor do it for you.

If you do have symptoms—it's hard to urinate, it's hard to stop urinating, you have to urinate frequently, it burns, or there's blood in your urine—don't panic. It's probably a benign enlargement of your prostate and not a tumor. But get examined right away and find out for sure.

Prostate cancer occurs most often around age 55. It kills about 30,000 men each year. By comparison, breast cancer kills about 50,000 women each year.

Testicular Cancer

Testicular cancer is one of the few cancers that affects younger men more than older men. It occurs most often between the ages of fifteen and thirty-five. It almost always affects one testicle, not both. The symptoms are a heavy feeling in the testicle, sometimes pain, and a small, pea-sized lump on the surface of the testicle. Treatment consists of surgery to remove the affected testicle, with chemotherapy and radiation if the cancer has spread to other parts of the body. Removal of one testicle still leaves you with enough sperm and hormones for a normal sex life.

Discovered early, the cure rate for testicular cancer is nearly 100 percent. Discovered late, your chances of cure drop to 70 percent. So it's wise to check yourself regularly, at least every month or two. It's very easy: after a shower or bath, when the skin on your scrotum is loose and soft, roll each testicle gently between thumb and forefinger. You're looking for anything that feels different from last time—a lump on the surface, an enlarged testicle, or any unusual hard spots. You can expect to find a small firm area near the rear of each testicle, and a cord leading up from the top. Those features are normal.

If you find any lumps or hard spots, or if one testicle gets bigger, you should see a doctor. It doesn't automatically mean that you have cancer. There are three or four kinds of relatively harmless infections or benign masses that can cause similar changes in your testicles—but only a doctor's exam and an ultrasound test can rule out cancer.

Excerpted and adapted with permission from *Being a Man: A Guide to the New Masculinity* by Patrick Fanning and Matthew McKay, Ph.D. For more information on this and related books, see part IV of the "Further Reading" section in the back of the book.

CHAPTER 26

Chronic Illness and Pain

Theories of Pain

Pain is an extremely complex interaction of the mind and body. Among the many theories and suggested treatments for chronic pain, one basic rule stands out:

When you have chronic pain, your mind as well as your body is involved.

First, understand the following five basic concepts:

1. Acute pain is a signal to the body that it has been or is being damaged in some way. It is an alarm that requests immediate attention. The sensation of acute pain protects you from getting too close to a flame or from walking on a fractured foot. Burns and broken bones are examples of acute pain. The word *acute* comes from the Latin word meaning "needle" and basically means "sharp." When acute pain occurs as a result of a wound, a broken bone, or a bite, it requires immediate attention because of the tissue damage. When treated with the appropriate medical care, the wound heals, the bone mends, and usually the pain goes away.

2. The word *chronic* is derived from a Greek word for "time." Chronic pain is persistent pain that tends to be constant rather than intermittent and can become a pattern of painful sensations that persist long after the initial injury. A chronic illness hangs around for months or years. You can usually get decisive medical care for your acute pain, but treating chronic pain can become a maze of misunderstanding and misdiagnosis.

3. Chronic pain is real. Your pain may not be obvious to someone else, but you know when you hurt.

4. Pain is a subjective experience. Everyone is a unique individual, and everyone handles pain in different ways. You have probably seen some people cry out loudly at what seems to be a minor injury, while others are stoic and keep a "stiff upper lip."

5. Chronic pain is influenced by your environment. Because it involves far more than tissue damage and a physical disability, chronic pain is not a simple problem. Chronic pain can be affected adversely or positively by your family, your job, and your world in general. The environmental and emotional factors in the diagram below can frustrate the treatment efforts and confuse and depress not only the sufferer, but his or her family and the health care professional as well.

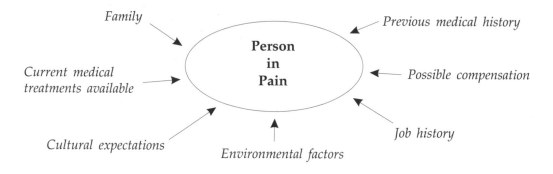

Diagram 26.1.

Beyond the Physiology Of Pain

Pain has been the subject of study and controversy for centuries, but only in the last several decades has careful research revealed illuminating new concepts about our perception of and reaction to pain. In 1956, a researcher named Beecher compared the reactions to pain of soldiers in battle with the reactions of a comparable number of civilians about to undergo an operation. Amazingly, he found that soldiers who had severe wounds complained less of pain and required less medication than did the civilians. To the soldiers, their severe wounds meant an end to battle and a return to the safety of the hospital. To the civilians, their wounds meant removal from the safety of home to the anxiety of being in the hospital and facing surgery. According to Dr. Beecher, the soldiers perceived less pain because they had reduced anxiety. This classic study showed that there is more to pain than mere sensation. A painful war wound means an end to battle and a quick ticket home. The pain of surgery means disease and an uncertain future. The meaning of pain affects the experience of pain.

Specificity Theory

Until recently, pain has been regarded as a straightforward mechanism—an individual gets hurt and that message is relayed directly to the brain. This simple stimulus-response concept, known as the specificity theory, is still taught in some medical schools. The theory assumes that the intensity of the pain is directly proportional to the amount of damage. In other words, if you have an obvious injury, you are expected to hurt; an unseen injury cannot hurt as much. This theory supposes that if surgery or medication can eliminate the cause of the pain, the pain should disappear. But when the pain drags on and there seems to be no obvious medical answer for it, this stimulus-response concept of pain is clearly an inadequate explanation.

A Broader Approach

More recent theories have shown that the experience of pain is not a simple cause-and-effect relationship between the body and the brain. Rather, it is a complex web of pain signals, chemical messengers, emotions, and thoughts involving several different pathways of pain. These pathways can transmit the pain signal either at lightning speed or slowly and continuously. Often, the pathways can continue to transmit a pain signal after the injury has supposedly healed, or even when an injured site has been entirely removed (as in the case of phantom limb pain). Imprinting, a fairly recent concept, may serve as the explanation here. The nervous system gets "conditioned" to transmit certain pain messages. In other words, for some reason the pain gets "stamped" onto the pain pathways, inducing the central nervous system to retain the memory of the pain for a while. The theory supposes that one way the nervous system gets stamped or stays turned on to the pain may be through a disruption in the balance of neurochemical transmitters relaying the pain messages. As a result of the imprinting theory, researchers have become absorbed in spinal cord research for the treatment of both acute and chronic pain.

Sometimes the pain sensation is transformed along its pathway so that when it reaches the brain it is perceived as something other than pain, or the brain sends messages back to the injured area to stop the pain sensation. In other words, there is continuous feedback motion from pain to brain and back again.

This fluid and constantly changing motion can be prevented or relieved by surgery and medications. You can have a surgeon sever a nerve in hope of cutting off the transmission of pain, or you can take drugs to try to block the pain. But more often than not, the pain is somehow regenerated even after surgery. As the drug effect wears off, you find you have to take higher and higher drug dosages. Since drugs and surgery are costly, in most cases you are left with what is usually offered as the last, but is actually the best, alternative—internally changing that fluid motion of pain to brain by changing your attitude toward the pain. You can change the way your pain feels by changing how your body and your brain feel. In order to do this, you will find it helpful to know specifically what happens to those pain sensations from a physiological viewpoint so that you know why pain sensations can be changed internally. The following simplified descriptions of pathways for pain transmission show how your attitudes can make a difference and explain how such therapies as nerve blocks, acupuncture, and nerve stimulators can work. To understand the phenomena of pain in your body, we'll look more closely at the physiology of pain.

Pain Pathways—Going Up and Down

Going up: fast and slow pain. Pain starts with a physical event—a cut, burn, tear, or bump. Nerve endings, or pain receptors, in the periphery of your body (limbs and organs) pick up the pain. The receptors send the pain information from one bunch of nerve fibers to another to cells in the spinal cord, where the message is then relayed to the brain. This pathway is called the ascending tract.

This process can happen at different rates of speed because the nerve fibers that transmit the pain messages come in different sizes. Large diameter A-beta nerve fibers transmit pain quickly along the cable network. This is commonly known as "fast pain." You know it as the kind of pain that feels like pressure. Two smaller diameter A-delta and C nerve fibers transmit pain information at a slower rate of speed. You know the A-delta pain as a sharp and stabbing pain you feel from a cut or burn. The C fiber pain is dull and aching and is typically called "slow pain" or secondary pain. As someone with chronic pain, you are all too familiar with C fiber slow pain—the dull aching sensation usually associated with chronic problems.

The spinal cord is the central concourse along which all pain messages travel to and from the brain. When you stub your toe and your peripheral nerves register alarm, the pain is immediately relayed along the nerve fibers of your foot and leg to a special area within the dorsal horn of the spinal cord called the substantia gelatinosa. The cells within the substantia gelatinosa relay this "fast pain" message along the pain tract, or the neospinothalamic pathway. The trip ends at specific locations in the brain, namely the thalamus and the cortex. The cortex is the portion of the brain where most of your thought processes take place. A pain message arrives and the cortex prompts you to say "ouch!" and begin rubbing the afflicted area.

By contrast, chronic pain tends to move along a different, slower tract called the *paleospinothalamic* pathway. This "slow pain" tends to be dull, aching, burning, and cramping. Initially it travels the same route as the fast pain through the dorsal horn of the spinal cord. Once there, however, the slow pain message separates in the brain stem area to turn toward final destinations in a different portion of the brain, the *hypothalamus* and *limbic structures*. The hypothalamus is the gland responsible for instructing the pituitary gland to release certain stress hormones. It is sometimes referred to as the central clearinghouse of the brain. The limbic structures are the place where your emotions are processed. Their involvement in the process helps to explain how your feelings can influence your pain.

Going down. Just as there is a "pain to brain" motion, there is also a "brain to pain" motion that attempts to counteract the pain message trying to make its way up. You have probably heard about athletes who sprain or strain something during a game but continue to play seemingly unaffected until the game is over. Or recall the study mentioned earlier about soldiers wounded in battle who did not complain of pain because they were so relieved to be off the battlefield. In both of these cases, the brain instructs the body not to register, or pay attention to, the pain until later, if at all.

This downward pathway from the brain is called a descending tract; the brain uses it to send chemical substances and nerve impulses back down to the cells in the spinal cord to act against the pain message sent up by the pain receptors. Dr. John Rowlingson, Director of the University of Virginia Department of Anesthesiology Pain Management Center, notes that although not as much is known about these descending systems, they are largely chemical in nature and can be described as acting centrally to modify the pain messages coming into the spinal cord and brain. This might explain why therapies that act primarily in the brain, such as hypnosis, biofeedback, and brain stimulation, work so well to control pain.

Neurotransmitters

Another essential link needed to forge the chain of pain events is the presence of chemical substances within each cell of the nerve tract. These substances are called neurotransmitters; they can either pass the pain message on its way or make sure that the pain message is stopped. Neurotransmitters can act as painkillers or pain producers. A commonly known neurotransmitter is serotonin, one of the most important chemicals involved in pain relief.

A group of neurotransmitters believed to be the body's own natural painkillers are called endorphins and enkephalins. These substances are produced in the brain and can have the same powerful effect as morphine or heroin. New research indicates that different people produce different amounts of these natural painkillers, which may explain why some people experience pain more than others do. For example, when an athlete is performing with an injury, he or she may be producing enough endorphins to override the pain message.

The Gate Control Theory

Have you ever bumped your shin and then instinctively rubbed it to make it feel better? You probably noticed that when you did, the shin seemed to ache a little less. Why is this so?

In 1965, Drs. Melzack and Wall proposed that there were "gates" on the bundles of nerve fibers on the spinal cord that can either open to allow pain impulses through to your brain or close to cut them off. The Gate Control Theory proposes that a sufficient amount of stimuli can close the gate to the pain sensation. Specifically, the large diameter nerve fibers close the gate to the small diameter fibers, so that A-beta pain supersedes the pain of the A-delta and C fibers. This gating mechanism can also be influenced by other factors, such as messages sent from the brain instructing certain gates to close to the pain sensation.

The rubbing that you do after you bump your shin is a fast pain sensation transmitted quickly over the large fibers; it cancels out the sharp pain of hitting your shin, slowly transmitted by the small fibers. The result is that you feel the rubbing rather than the sharp pain. This mechanism explains why stimulators and acupuncture can be so effective in managing pain—they operate on the gating mechanism to close out slower pain sensations.

Many studies have attempted to prove the Gate Control Theory, but none have shown conclusively that all facets of the theory are valid. Still, the importance of this theory should not be underrated, since it has served to stimulate much thinking on the subject of pain and helped us come to the conclusions we have today about effective treatment of chronic pain.

Pain Treatment Strategies

Every day you can read in newspapers and magazines about some new technique for managing chronic pain. Some of these techniques have just appeared on the scene, while others have been around for centuries. Some are conservative in nature, while others strain your imagination as to their connection to pain control. You can be massaged by a masseuse, whirlpooled in a jacuzzi, operated on by a surgeon, medicated by a medical doctor, exercised by a physical therapist or exercise physiologist, manipulated by a myotherapist, hypnotized by a hypnotherapist, analyzed by a psychiatrist, behaviorally modified by a psychologist, or rehabbed by a social worker. The possibilities are mind-numbing, and explanations are so confusing and conflicting, that you may feel like giving up before you start.

Take time to discuss with your doctor any of the techniques that you would like to use. Try to educate yourself as much as possible about each technique, so that you know what you are getting into. Don't be afraid to ask questions! If your doctor is too rushed to explain, or doesn't know something, go get another opinion. You need to become better informed, and to motivate yourself to take charge of your healing process.

Also, be aware that not all techniques work for everyone. What works for your best friend may not be the key to your recovery. You may know instinctively that a certain technique is not for you, while you can adapt to others quite readily. Or you may need to try everything once to get a feel for it. In any case, this process of pain management takes time. Explore all your options and decide which works best for you. Most importantly, keep an open mind, be patient, and be persistent.

Electrical Stimulators

If you have gone to a pain clinic you may have been prescribed an electrical stimulator for pain relief. One common type of stimulator is a small box-shaped device known as a transcutaneous (across the skin) electrical nerve stimulator (TENS). The small box is a transmitter which can be carried in the pocket or worn around the waist hanging on your belt. It transmits electrical impulses through wires to electrodes that are taped to the skin surrounding the painful area. When the unit is turned on, most people feel an electrical buzzing or tingling sensation, the intensity of which can be controlled by a dial on the transmitting box.

The device is designed to work on the principle of the Gate Control Theory, discussed earlier. An electrical impulse is transmitted over the large nerve fiber tracts, which in turn inhibit the small nerve fiber tracts from transmitting pain. In other words, you feel a tingling sensation rather than a pain sensation. You can increase or decrease the intensity of the tingling sensation as your pain increases or decreases.

TENS also works in two other ways. First, in addition to inhibiting the pain sensation, the tingling sensation also helps to distract you from it. Second, some researchers feel that TENS stimulates the release of endorphins in the brain and spinal cord. As noted above, endorphins are your body's own natural painkiller.

Some people find that brief periods of stimulation can provide hours, days, or weeks of pain relief. Others find that they need to wear the device regularly in order to feel some relief. Daily stimulation sometimes provides gradually increasing pain relief over periods of weeks or months. A great advantage of a TENS unit is that once you locate the point on your body that provides you with the greatest amount of pain relief, you can use this method at home or work as needed, giving you a significant measure of control over your own pain therapy.

TENS units are simple and easy to use and can be purchased through most medical supply offices. Some people may find that they develop a skin irritation from the unit's electrode paste or tape. Check with your doctor for types of nonallergenic paste and nonabrasive tape. These devices are safe and are found to have virtually no significant side effects even with continuous use. Although, be aware that you may want to provide periodic, rather than continuous, daily stimulation so that your body will not adapt to the message. Discuss this issue with your doctor.

TENS units are found to be most useful as an adjunct to other forms of therapy commonly found in multimodal pain clinics, such as exercise, physical therapy, appropriate medication use, and relaxation techniques.

A further development in the concept of TENS is spinal cord and brain stimulation to hyperstimulate the nervous system from different locations. This can be provided with implanted, permanent electrodes, much like a pacemaker for regulating cardiac rhythms.

Acupuncture

Acupuncture is an ancient and time-tested method of pain and disease control discovered in China as early as 3000 B.C. Chinese folklore says that a warrior discovered the principle of acupuncture during a battle. He was pierced by an arrow in his leg, and found that the wound from the arrow made another wound in his shoulder feel better.

Acupuncture works on the principal of meridians, or imaginary lines, drawn on the body that represent internal organs and the torso. Points on these lines are thought to connect different parts of the body. For example, a point on the skin between the thumb and index finger connects to various parts of the head for control of headaches; a point on the leg is specified for control of gastric disorders. When one of these points is stimulated by an acupuncture needle or deeply massaged (acupressure), a headache or stomachache can be relieved. In practice, a thin metal or gold needle is inserted at the acupuncture point and gently twirled. The round tipped needle simply spreads the skin rather than puncturing it, thereby reducing the chance of infection. Some needles are twirled for brief periods of ten to twenty minutes and then removed; others are left in over a longer period of time.

Remember the Gate Control Theory? Here is another direct application of it. The stimulation of the needles is thought to set off a series of electrical impulses that travel the large nerve fiber tracts, cutting off the more painful sensations sent along the small fiber tracts. With acupuncture you feel a pleasant, tingling, warm sensation, much like the sensation you get from a TENS unit.

There are three other explanations for the effectiveness of acupuncture. First, acupuncture has been shown to stimulate better circulation to tissues; often the effects of poor circulation to an injured area can increase pain and retard the healing process. Second, acupuncture can release tension in the muscle surrounding the acupuncture point. Third, recent research suggests that acupuncture stimulates the production of endorphins, the natural painkiller, in the brain and spinal cord.

A related acupuncture method has served to further awaken Western interest in the field. Electroacupuncture involves stimulation of body tissues through needles hooked up to battery-driven stimulators. In modern China, this method is used to produce intense analgesia during surgery. "Films of such operations are extremely dramatic, and the feeling arose that if acupuncture could produce sufficient analgesia for surgery, it must surely be effective for chronic pain of all kinds" (Melzack and Wall 1991).

Consult your doctor for help in contacting trained and licensed acupuncture specialists.

Trigger Points

When a trigger point is pressed, it causes a great deal of pain, sometimes reproducing an exact chronic pain sensation. Trigger points in muscles or ligaments can also be identified by muscle spasms or contractions. They are known to lie above or near the point in the muscle where the motor nerves are firing most intensely (thereby producing pain).

Although the exact mechanism of trigger points is unknown, they are probably caused by a direct stress to your muscle such as trauma (tear during an injury), chronic tension, abnormal posture, or muscle fatigue. Sometimes trigger points lay dormant for many years after recovery from an injury. You may not have chronic pain complaints, but instead are accumulating unsuspected latent trigger points. These can be activated by chronic strain from sedentary living habits, minor stresses from daily living, anxiety, or overstretching or fatigue of your muscles.

Trigger points are thought to be similar to acupuncture points in location. Every trigger point has a corresponding acupuncture point and that there is a close correlation between the pain syndromes associated with each point. In other words, the Western medical world labels these points differently from the Eastern medical world, but they represent the same underlying nerve mechanisms. However, acupuncture points aren't supposed to produce pain when pressed, so they are dissimilar to trigger points in that respect.

Trigger points are often injected for pain relief. These trigger point injections are a form of nerve block.

Nerve Blocks

When you have chronic pain, you are tempted to tense your muscles in an attempt to brace yourself against the pain. This common and automatic response can lead to a pain-spasm-pain cycle. As a result of this response, your muscles remain in a tense or contracted state, blood flow is decreased to the muscle, and your posture can become abnormal. In other words, your muscles become immobile and inflexible, which further contributes to your pain.

Local anesthetic nerve blocks and trigger point injections can interrupt this cycle. An anesthesiologist specially trained in the area of pain management injects a local anesthetic solution into the painful area, causing the nerve fibers to become numb or anesthetized and to stop sending pain signals. You should feel an alleviation of your pain immediately following each injection. This is a good time to do gentle stretching exercises to improve your mobility and relax your muscles and to return to normal posture. Sometimes the mere insertion of the doctor's needle can aid in pain relief, as an acupuncture needle would do.

If you have acute pain, the effect of the nerve block will often outlast the duration of the painful stimulus from your injury or surgical incision. However, local anesthetic blocks for chronic pain often do not produce long-term benefits. An exception to this is the repeated use of blocks for causalgia (burning pain) or causalgia-like symptoms such as in complex regional pain syndrome, where permanent pain relief can often be achieved, if treated early.

Heat and Cold Therapy

Getting you back to full or at least freer movement is an important goal of chronic pain management. The pain-spasm-pain cycle discussed in the previous section reinforces immobility—you brace yourself against the pain and hold your muscles stiffly for long periods of time, which further contributes to your pain and makes even menial activity a chore. A physical therapist or an exercise physiologist can help you reverse this process by gradually increasing your mobility through strength and flexibility exercises.

Other forms of physical therapy can be useful as adjuncts to a multimodal approach to pain management. Both heat and cold therapy reduce muscle tension or spasm. If you try heat, the physical therapist will usually apply hot packs for twenty minutes under six to eight layers of towels. Cold packs are also applied for twenty minutes, but under two layers of towels. An ice block massage involves lightly rubbing the painful area with a cake of ice for at least ten minutes or until numbness occurs. In one study, the ice block massage was considered more effective than the cold pack because it provided more intense stimulation to the painful area; the cold pack cooled tissues more slowly.

Both heat and cold therapy reduce muscle spasms and swelling from an injury or inflammation. Both also decrease the number of nerve impulses from the painful area to the spinal cord, which means that less small fiber input (carrying the pain message) is available to open the pain gate.

You can decide for yourself which temperature provides more relief. Both are considered equally effective methods of pain reduction.

Massage

Massage can be a relaxing and revitalizing experience and an excellent addition to a pain management program. Its therapeutic effects include soothing aching muscles and benefitting emotional well-being.

Its benefits are gaining widespread acceptance in the medical community as growing research reveals the healing power of massage for both acute and chronic pain. Martha Brown Menard combines her Ph.D. in educational research with a practice in massage. Her study of the effects of massage on postsurgical hysterectomy patients produced several significant findings: First, after four days of a daily forty-five minute massage, patients in the massage group produced not quite half the level of urinary cortisol of patients in the nonmassage group. Cortisol, produced by the adrenal glands, is one of the hormones your body produces in response to stress. The massage group patients also reported reduced pain and stress. Equally important, for the four weeks following their discharge, the massage group patients had no additional physician visits.

Massage can stimulate blood flow and release toxins from muscles and tissues. It can also help to break the pain-spasm-pain cycle by relaxing muscles that are tight or in spasm, increasing circulation, improving oxygen and nutrition flow to the painful area, increasing range of motion, and finding and relaxing trigger points. Systematically working with each muscle in your body, your massage therapist may use a light stroke or deep kneading action, depending on what he or she thinks is right for you and your comfort level. Trigger points, which often recur in the same places, are relieved through sustained pressure. As you find out which ones contribute to your pain you can learn to massage them yourself to help decrease your pain.

Often, you start to lose muscle tone in as little as three weeks after an injury. For people who have to be inactive due to injury, illness, or age, massage can help compensate for lack of exercise and muscular contraction. In other words, massage is not intended as a substitute for exercise, but can help prevent or reduce muscular atrophy in the interim.

Perhaps most important, however, is that massage acts on an emotional level. As Dr. Menard sees in her practice and research, people who are in pain often have significant feelings of loneliness and isolation. Massage can become a way to help a person vent about what has been going on in their lives and feel that they are being cared for. Massage helps to create feelings of acceptance, safety, nurturing, and trust.

A well-trained therapist will take a medical history from you to determine the acute or chronic nature of your problem, extent of medication use, and other pertinent information. A massage is usually contraindicated (not recommended) in cases of inflammation, edema (swelling), herniated discs, fever, and other conditions that require you to wait until the acute nature of those conditions has subsided.

You can do massage for yourself, especially for neck and headache pain. This will help when you're feeling tense; but for a more relaxing and effective experience, try letting your partner, trusted friend, or massage therapist give you a massage. Make sure, however, that they listen to your feedback and do not massage spasms or painful areas too heavily when they hurt. You want your massage to be a pleasant experience.

References

Melzack, R., and P. Wall. 1991. *The Challenge of Pain*. Rev. ed. New York: Penguin Books.

Excerpted and adapted with permission from *The Chronic Pain Control Workbook* by Ellen Mohr Catalano, M.A., and Kimeron N. Hardin, Ph.D. For more information on this and related books, see the "Further Reading" section in the back of the book.

CHAPTER 27

Preparing for Surgery

In the United States, approximately fifty million operations are performed each year. Of these, 20 percent are in response to an emergency, whereas 80 percent are considered "elective." An elective surgery is one in which the patient and/or the doctor can choose when and where to have the operation. Our preparation for surgery program is appropriate for any elective surgery done on an inpatient or outpatient basis.

When helping people to prepare for surgery, we are often asked, "Why do I need to prepare for surgery? I think I know what will happen. I'll go into the hospital, they'll put me to sleep, they'll fix the problem, I'll wake up, and then I'll go home. Who needs to prepare for that?"

Many people, including some surgeons, take a very matter-of-fact view of surgery such as that above. We term this the "auto-mechanic" view, which likens surgery to fixing a car. Given the fact that you are a human being, which is much more than a collection of bone and tissue, this notion of how surgery works could not be further from the truth. The fact is that surgery is stressful and it can have a significant impact on your mind, body, and emotions.

Using mind-body techniques to prepare for surgery, and to cope with the postsurgical recovery period, can have very positive benefits, such as the following:

- Less anxiety both before and after surgery

- Fewer complications related to the surgery and recovery

- Less pain and less need for postoperative pain medication

- Quicker return to health

- Shorter stay in the hospital

Hospital Stress

Going to the hospital, either as an inpatient or outpatient, can be stressful in different ways to different people. Dr. Beverly Volicer (1977) investigated the types of events related to hospitalization that surgical patients have found to be stressful. She categorized these stressors as:

- Unfamiliarity of surroundings
- Loss of independence
- Separation from spouse or significant other
- Financial problems
- Isolation from other people
- Lack of information
- Threat of severe illness
- Separation from family
- Problems with medications

To become aware of those aspects of the entire process that might be stressful for you is an important step in preparing for surgery and hospitalization. The hospital stress rating scale (HSRS) was originally developed by Dr. Volicer to evaluate the stress associated with various aspects of hospitalization. In Dr. Volicer's research, the HSRS was completed by patients after they had been admitted to the hospital. For the purposes of preparing for surgery we have patients complete the HSRS before hospitalization.

Please complete and score the following HSRS to determine your areas of stress associated with hospitalization:

Hospital Stress Rating Scale*

Instructions. Think about each hospitalization-related event below and decide if it would be stressful for you. If it would be stressful for you, or has been in the past, check the line next to it. The "mean value" column will be completed later.

Unfamiliarity of Surroundings	Check here if stressful	Mean Value
1. Having strangers sleep in the same room with you		
2. Having to sleep in a strange bed		
3. Having strange machines around		
4. Being awakened in the night by the nurse		
5. Being aware of unusual smells around you		
6. Being in a room that is too cold or too hot		
7. Having to eat cold or tasteless food		
8. Being cared for by an unfamiliar doctor		

Loss of Independence

9. Having to eat at different times than you usually do

10. Having to wear a hospital gown

11. Having to be assisted with bathing

12. Not being able to get newspapers, radio, or TV when you want them

13. Having a roommate who has too many visitors

14. Having to stay in bed or the same room all day

15. Having to be assisted with a bedpan

16. Not having your call light answered

17. Being fed through tubes

18. Thinking you may lose your sight

Separation from Spouse or Significant Other

19. Worrying about your spouse being away from you

20. Missing your spouse

Financial Problems

21. Thinking about losing income because of your illness

22. Not having enough insurance to pay for your hospitalization

Isolation from Other People

23. Having a roommate who is seriously ill or cannot talk with you

24. Having a roommate who is unfriendly

25. Not having friends visit you

26. Not being able to call family or friends on the phone

27. Having the staff be in too much of a hurry

28. Thinking you might lose your hearing

Lack of Information

29. Thinking you might have pain because of surgery or test procedures

30. Not knowing when to expect things will be done to you

31. Having nurses or doctors talk too fast or use words you can't understand

32. Not having your questions answered by staff

33. Not knowing the results or reasons for your treatments

34. Not knowing for sure what illnesses you have

35. Not being told what your diagnosis is

	Check here if stressful	Mean Value
Threat of Severe Illness		
36. Thinking your appearance might be changed after your hospitalization		
37. Being put in the hospital because of an accident		
38. Knowing you have to have an operation		
39. Having a sudden hospitalization you weren't planning to have		
40. Knowing you have a serious illness		
41. Thinking you might lose a kidney or some other organ		
42. Thinking you might have cancer		
Separation from Family		
43. Being in the hospital during holidays or special occasions		
44. Not having family visit you		
45. Being hospitalized far away from home		
Problems with Medications		
46. Having medications cause you discomfort		
47. Feeling you are becoming dependent on medications		
48. Not getting relief from pain medications		
49. Not getting pain medication when you need it		

Scoring the HSRS

The mean values for each hospital event are listed below. Write in the mean values for those events that you checked as being of significant concern or stressful.

Event	Value	Event	Value	Event	Value
1	14	11	17	21	26
2	16	12	18	22	27
3	17	13	18	23	21
4	17	14	19	24	22
5	19	15	22	25	22
6	22	16	27	26	23
7	23	17	29	27	25
8	23	18	41	28	35
9	15	19	23	29	22
10	16	20	28	30	24

31	26	37	27	43	22
32	28	38	27	44	27
33	32	39	27	45	27
34	34	40	35	46	26
35	34	41	36	47	26
36	22	42	39	48	31
				49	31

Your overall level of "hospital stress" can be determined by adding all mean values for the events that you checked. After adding all of the mean values, record your total hospital stress score on the HSRS scoring table that follows. You also can determine your level of stress for each of the separate hospital-related factors by adding the mean values of the items you checked in each section separately. For example, if you checked number 1, 4, and 5 listed under the Unfamiliarity of Surroundings section, then your score for that section would be 50 (14+17+19). For each of the nine sections, add up your mean value scores and record the results in the HSRS scoring table.

The average score column will help you interpret your score as compared to other surgery patients. The average scores in the chart below are from the 250 surgical patients in Dr. Volicer's research study.

HSRS Scoring Table

	Average Score	Your Score
Total Hospital Stress	290	_____
Unfamiliarity of Surroundings	55	_____
Loss of Independence	68	_____
Separation from Spouse or Significant Other	23	_____
Financial Problems	8	_____
Isolation from Other People	11	_____
Lack of Information	40	_____
Threat of Severe Illness	62	_____
Separation from Family	9	_____
Problems with Medications	14	_____

*   Hospital Stress Rating Scale. Reprinted from *Journal of Human Stress*, June 1977, B. J. Volicer, M. A. Isenberg, and M. W. Burns, "Medical-Surgical Differences in Hospital Stress Factors," page 7, copyright 1977, with permission from Heldref Publications, Washington, D.C.

Hospital Stress

The results of the hospital stress rating scale, as shown in the summary sheet, can help you prepare to cope with those aspects of the hospital environment that may be stressful for you. Of course, this is different for everyone. For instance, if your scores are above average in the categories of Loss of Independence and Separation from Family, you might focus on these issues when developing your coping strategies and relaxation exercises. You might also plan ahead by determining what the hospital visiting hours are, and how your family members will schedule their time with you. Your concern over the loss of your independence might be addressed by practicing assertiveness and communication techniques. See the chapter on Communication in part I. If lack of information is a high concern, you might consider more detailed answers to the questions presented in the next section. These are just a few examples of how to use the results of the HSRS in designing your program.

Coping

People respond to stress in individual ways by using different types of "coping strategies." Your coping strategies are elicited when you appraise a situation as stressful or threatening. They are your attempt to decrease the stress associated with the threatening situation. Examples of coping strategies might include such responses as trying to focus on positive aspects of the situation, expressing emotions, gaining support from family and friends, or denying the stress altogether. The particular type of coping strategies that you use will depend upon your personality characteristics, your social and family situation, and the nature of the stress you experience.

The following questionnaire helps you to assess the coping strategies you are most likely to use. This information is an essential part of the preparation for surgery program and helps you to choose healthy rather than unhealthy coping strategies.

Ways of Coping Scale-Revised*

Instructions: Please read the following list of things people do in reaction to their medical condition and/or undergoing surgery and hospitalization. Please indicate whether you have ever done any of these things in reaction to your medical condition or a previous surgery, hospitalization, or stressful medical procedure. Rate each item according to the following scale.

0 = Never have done it
1 = Done it on an infrequent basis
2 = Done it sometimes

3 = Done it often
4 = Do it most of the time

Changing Thoughts

1. Concentrated on something good that could come out of the whole thing   0   1   2   3   4

2. Rediscover what is important in life   0   1   2   3   4

3. Felt like you changed or grew as a person in a good way   0   1   2   3   4

4. Found new faith or some truth about life   0   1   2   3   4

5. Remembered times when your life was more difficult   0   1   2   3   4

6. Religion became more important	0	1	2	3	4
7. Thought about people who were worse off than you	0	1	2	3	4
8. Reminded yourself that things could be worse	0	1	2	3	4
9. Looked for the silver lining, so to speak; tried to look on the bright side of things	0	1	2	3	4
10. Did something totally new that you never would have done if this hadn't happened	0	1	2	3	4
11. Changed the way you did things so that the illness was less of a problem	0	1	2	3	4
12. Got away from it for a while; tried to rest or take a vacation	0	1	2	3	4

Emotional Expression

1. Took it out on other people	0	1	2	3	4
2. Got help with day-to-day chores or travel	0	1	2	3	4
3. Joked about it	0	1	2	3	4
4. Let your feelings out somehow	0	1	2	3	4
5. Avoided being with people in general	0	1	2	3	4
6. Recalled past successes	0	1	2	3	4
7. Daydreamed or imagined a better time or place than the one you were in	0	1	2	3	4
8. Slept more than usual	0	1	2	3	4

Fantasizing

1. Wished that you could change what happened	0	1	2	3	4
2. Wished that you could change the way you felt	0	1	2	3	4
3. Felt bad that you couldn't avoid the problem	0	1	2	3	4
4. Wished that the situation would go away or somehow be over with	0	1	2	3	4
5. Hoped a miracle would happen	0	1	2	3	4
6. Wished you were a stronger person	0	1	2	3	4
7. Had fantasies or wishes about how things might turn out	0	1	2	3	4

Self-Blame

1. Blamed yourself	0	1	2	3	4
2. Thought about fantastic or unreal things that made you feel better	0	1	2	3	4
3. Saw the doctor and did what he or she recommended	0	1	2	3	4

4. Got mad at the people or things that caused the problem	0	1	2	3	4
5. Criticized or took it out on yourself	0	1	2	3	4
6. Realized you brought the problem on yourself	0	1	2	3	4
7. Refused to believe it had happened	0	1	2	3	4

Seeking Information

1. Looked up medical information	0	1	2	3	4
2. Read books or magazine articles (or watched TV) about your medical condition or surgery	0	1	2	3	4
3. Came up with some different solutions to the problem	0	1	2	3	4
4. Asked someone other than your doctor you respected for advice and followed it	0	1	2	3	4
5. Made a plan of action and followed it	0	1	2	3	4

Minimizing the Threat

1. Kept your feelings to yourself	0	1	2	3	4
2. Went on as if nothing had happened	0	1	2	3	4
3. Talked to someone about how you were feeling	0	1	2	3	4
4. Didn't let it get to you; refused to think too much about it	0	1	2	3	4
5. Kept others from knowing how bad things were	0	1	2	3	4
6. Tried to forget the whole thing	0	1	2	3	4
7. Talked to someone other than a doctor who could do something about the problem for you	0	1	2	3	4
8. Tried to work it out by yourself	0	1	2	3	4
9. Accepted sympathy and understanding from someone	0	1	2	3	4
10. Made light of the situation; refused to get too serious about it	0	1	2	3	4
11. Went along with fate; sometimes you just have bad luck	0	1	2	3	4

Scoring the Ways of Coping Scale

The six sections of the Ways of Coping Scale can be scored separately. First, add the total for each section and record the number in the Ways of Coping Scoring Table under the heading "Total Score." Next, divide that number by the number of items in the section (this is the number under the heading "Divide by"). This will give an average score for that type of coping strategy. Record this number under the heading "Average."

Ways of Coping Scoring Table

Section	Total Score	Divide by:	Average
Changing Thoughts	_____	12	_____
Emotional Expression	_____	8	_____
Fantasizing	_____	7	_____
Self-Blame	_____	7	_____
Seeking Information	_____	5	_____
Minimizing the Threat	_____	11	_____

* Ways of Coping Scale. Reprinted from *Social Science and Medicine*, Volume 18, B. J. Felton, T. A. Revenson, and G. A. Hinrichsen, "Stress and Coping in the Explanation of Psychological Adjustment Among Chronically Ill Adults," pages 892–893, copyright 1984, with kind permission from Elsevier Science, Ltd., The Boulevard, Langford Lane, Kidlington OX5 1GB, UK.

Your Coping Style

The Ways of Coping Scale Summary provides information about how you tend to cope with stressful situations. If you scored high in the Changing Thoughts section, then you may be very comfortable with the cognitive techniques in the chapter on Changing Patterns of Limited Thinking in part V. On the other hand, if your score was very low in this section, then these cognitive techniques may initially seem difficult. In any case, it is important that you learn these strategies as they are essential to the surgical coping and recovery process.

A high score on the Emotional Expression section might indicate that you are prone to "take it out on others" or to withdraw. Awareness of this pattern can help you avoid it through use of cognitive, relaxation, and assertiveness techniques.

Excessive fantasizing or a tendency toward self-blame can be destructive, especially under stress. Using specific guided imagery can help you to develop "healthy" fantasies. You may employ affirmations and challenge negative thoughts to decrease self-blame.

If you scored high in the area of Seeking Information, you may be likely to cope with a stressful situation by collecting as much detailed information as possible. Pay particular attention to the questions in the next section.

If you tend to minimize the threat, collecting detailed information may not benefit you. If you scored high in this area, collect only as much information as you feel comfortable with. Also, the strategies of distraction and focusing on other aspects of your life may be effective.

Gathering Information About Your Surgery: Taking an Active Role

After completing the assessments in the previous section, you will have a lot of good information about your emotional state and the issues that need to be addressed as part of your preparation for surgery program. This section is another exercise in gathering important information about your surgery and recovery to ensure that you have adequate information about:

• Surgical decision making

• The details of your surgery

• What to do before the surgery

• What to expect and do after the surgery

• What to expect during your hospitalization

Understanding and Remembering Medical Information

When helping to prepare patients for surgery, we often find that they actually know little about the nature and purpose of the operation being planned. Research consistently shows that patients are often dissatisfied with the medical information they receive, and so have poor understanding and recall of that information.

How Well Do People Understand and Remember What They Are Told by Their Doctor?

Many patients have a poor understanding of the medical information presented to them and remember little of what they are told. Medical forms are often complex. Many surgical consent forms are written at the level of scientific journals, beyond the comprehension of most people. Not surprisingly, only about 40 percent or less of patients read them carefully.

Patients can become frustrated in their attempts to get understandable information from their doctors. As a result, they have questions they don't ask and desire more information than they are given.

Retention of information about surgery is another problem. Patients remember 30 percent to 50 percent of the simple verbal information they are given about surgery and only slightly more when it is written.

Inadequate comprehension and memory of information about surgery frequently leads to patient dissatisfaction with communication and can compromise overall treatment.

Bernard was scheduled to undergo hip replacement surgery and was referred for a brief mind-body preparation for surgery program. In the initial evaluation, we asked him about his understanding of the surgery (questions similar to those contained in this chapter). Bernard's case was dramatic in that he could answer virtually none of the questions even though his surgery was only two weeks away. He wasn't sure which hospital was scheduled for the surgery and couldn't relate any details about the surgery or the postoperative rehabilitation. It became evident that his lack of information was due to two factors. He was afraid to question his doctors and he was too nervous to remember what he was told. The preparation for surgery program helped Bernard learn how to acquire, understand, and remember the information he needed.

A good understanding of the surgery and related procedures can improve your outcome and make surgery a less stressful experience. Information can be obtained from several sources including your surgeon, family doctor, patient education brochures, the hospital, and your insurance company. Some other suggested sources of information will be provided throughout this chapter.

Ask your surgeon, doctor, or other healthcare professional these questions, get clear answers, and write them down in the spaces provided. You may want to take someone with you on your presurgical doctor visits.

Surgical Decision Making

What is wrong with me? What is my diagnosis?

You should have a sufficient understanding of your diagnosis to be able to express it in your own words. Also, knowing your exact diagnosis is important when you talk with different doctors who don't know you well and who may not have previous medical records readily available. It is a good idea to write down your diagnosis.

_____

_____

_____

_____

Why do I need the surgery?

_____

_____

_____

_____

How will the surgery improve my condition?

Surgery is done with the goal of curing a medical condition (e.g., gallbladder, tonsil, or appendix removal), improving the quality of life (e.g., joint replacement, back surgery to relieve pain), or extending life (e.g., removing a cancerous tumor). You should find out exactly how your surgery is expected to help you.

_____

_____

_____

_____

What other treatment options are available and have they been successful?

You should feel sure that appropriate nonsurgical treatment methods have been attempted and that surgery is the best choice for your condition.

_____

_____

_____

_____

What will happen if I decline the surgery or delay it until a later date? How long can I safely delay the surgery?

Most surgeries are elective and the scheduling of the operation is somewhat flexible. Therefore, when you schedule your surgery you may want to consider job and family commitments, the surgeon's schedule, and time to prepare for the operation, among other matters.

_____

_____

_____

_____

What are the risks of the surgery? Do the benefits of the surgery outweigh the risks?

All the possible risks of a surgical procedure will usually be presented to you in written form on an informed consent sheet. You will be required to sign this prior to the surgery. This information is often presented in a legal format which can be intimidating and difficult to understand. You should discuss risks and benefits with your surgeon as you make decisions about your surgery.

_____

_____

_____

_____

If the surgery is successful, what results can I expect? If it is unsuccessful (or only partially successful), what remaining symptoms can I expect and what are my treatment options?

Many patients have unrealistic expectations and are disappointed about the outcome of their surgery even though it was a "technical" success. Some surgeries are designed to reduce pain or improve functioning but not to "cure" the problem. If the patient expects a "cure" but is only somewhat improved, the postoperative recovery may be made more difficult by unmet expectations.

We once worked with a woman who, one month after her operation, was very distressed about her ongoing "strange" physical symptoms, including numbness in her arms, heaviness in her legs and feet, and "feeling big all over." She had had extensive surgery to remove a spinal tumor in the area of her neck. Even though it was a very serious medical condition, the tumor was discovered before the patient had any real physical symptoms. The surgery was a technical success. Removal of the tumor left her physical abilities almost completely intact. Still, she expressed great distress and depression because she had experienced no symptoms prior to surgery, but after surgery had symptoms she neither understood nor expected. Had she been given realistic expectations prior to surgery about these possible symptoms, her postoperative coping could have been greatly enhanced.

The Details of Your Surgery

Can you describe the surgery to me in simple language?

   You should have a general understanding of the nature of your surgical procedure, although detailed knowledge may not be helpful to you. It is important that you be able to explain, in your own words, what the surgery will entail. Consider your answers to these questions depending on whether you are an information-seeker or information-avoider.

Do you have a brochure or information sheet that describes the surgery?   YES   NO

If not, do you know where I can obtain a brochure, written for laypeople, that describes the procedure?   YES   NO

How will I feel immediately after the surgery in the recovery room?

   Research has shown that patients who are well-informed about the physical sensations they may expect following surgery adjust better to the recovery period. You should be told what you will feel, hear, smell, taste, and see before, during, and after the procedure. Many questions in this section address this issue. Record the answer to the question above on the lines below.

How long can I expect to be hospitalized? How can I expect to feel, what will I be able to do, and what should I try and do, each day in the hospital after the surgery?

It is important to know beforehand what kind of physical sensations you can expect as your body heals from the surgery. These may include pain, nausea, numbness, tingling, itching, etc., in certain areas of your body (especially with specific movements); shortness of breath or dizziness; or difficulty in urinating or walking.

The specific symptoms you might experience after surgery will depend on your condition and the nature of your surgery. If you know what kind of sensations to expect after your surgery, you will not be worried or fearful when they occur. This will help to decrease your overall suffering and increase your sense of control. It is also helpful to know what will be expected from you as you recover. For instance, you may be required to get out of bed and walk fairly soon after surgery or to do certain exercises. Record below how you will be expected to feel and what you will be expected to do as part of your recovery.

Day One

Day Two

Day Three

Day Four

Day Five

Day Six

Day Seven

(Make any necessary additions on a separate piece of paper.)

What complications might arise after surgery or after being discharged from the hospital? What is the best way to manage these complications if they arise? With whom should I discuss these issues?

During your surgery and recovery, several professionals may take care of you, including doctors, nurses, physician's assistants, respiratory therapists, physical therapists, and others. This can be quite confusing and overwhelming if you have questions to ask. Consider that the answers to some questions may not be known prior to surgery.

_____

_____

_____

_____

Will I need assistance at home after I am discharged from the hospital? Should I arrange for that now? Will I go directly home after discharge or is it possible that I may go to a rehabilitation or transitional care facility? Will I need any medical supplies at home?

Depending on your medical condition and the type of surgery you are undergoing, you may need a period of professional assistance at home (home nursing) or to be transferred to another type of treatment setting (transitional unit or hospital) for extended postoperative care. However, this is more often the case for the elderly or those with medical complications. It is very helpful to know about this possibility beforehand.

_____

_____

_____

_____

Once I go home, how will my level of functioning be limited and for how long?

It is useful to know how much bed rest you will need and the extent and duration of any physical limitations you may experience. If there is an extended postoperative phase with significant physical limitations, you can plan ahead by doing such things as getting materials together for your diversion (videotapes, books, etc.), arranging for food and other necessary items, and organizing help and visitation from family and friends.

_____

_____

_____

_____

Is it possible that I may need a blood transfusion during the surgery?   YES   NO

Can I give blood in advance in case I need it during the surgery?   YES   NO

Where should I go to give blood before my operation?

Record below the address, phone number, and contact person at the blood collection center.

_____

_____

_____

_____

Is there enough time before surgery to give the blood that I may need?

As discussed above, there is a limit to how quickly you can give your own blood for surgery. Should you decide to use your own blood, be sure there is enough time before your surgery to provide an adequate supply. List below the dates for your own blood donations.

_____

_____

_____

_____

What to Do Before the Surgery

What presurgical tests or evaluations are necessary? Who will be doing these and when should they be done?

You may need a presurgical/preadmission medical evaluation, especially if you are undergoing general anesthesia. This includes evaluation of your heart (electrocardiogram), lungs (chest X rays), and kidneys (urinalysis). Your presurgical medical evaluation might also include blood tests to assess for infection, clotting time, and other things. This evaluation might be done by your family doctor or another physician. Find out from your surgeon which doctor will be responsible for this presurgical/preadmission evaluation.

_____

_____

_____

_____

Should I make sure my family physician knows about the surgery?

Yes   Not Necessary   Notified on: _____

Will my family doctor be involved in my postoperative care? Does he or she need any special medical records?

In this age of managed care, you must assume more responsibility to see that you get good care. This responsibility includes helping to coordinate the roles of the various doctors involved. If they need medical records, it may be most efficient to get them yourself. Many doctors' offices and hospitals are slow in sending records to outside sources. We highly recommend that your family physician should be provided with copies of all your medical records.

_____

_____

_____

_____

_____

Do I need to be on a special diet before or after the surgery? If so, can you explain it in detail?

_____

_____

_____

_____

_____

Questions About the Hospitalization

Will this operation be done on an outpatient or inpatient basis?

Outpatient   Inpatient

In what hospital will the operation be done?
    Record the address, general directions, and phone number below.

_____

_____

_____

Are the surgery and hospitalization preapproved by the insurance company?
    The answer to this question will come from several sources including your doctor's office, the hospital admitting department, and your insurance company.

Exact Procedure Approved: _____

_____

Date of Approval: _____

_____

Have you received a copy of the hospitalization approval letter from your insurance company?   YES   NO

Number of hospitalization days preapproved by the insurance company: _____

What if my surgeon recommends a longer hospitalization than has been approved? How do I get approval and who can assist me?

We often hear horror stories from patients about insurance coverage issues. Usually the patient believes a procedure or charge is covered only to find, after the fact, that it is not. Dr. Deardorff experienced this when his wife underwent a cesarean section with a three-day "preapproved" hospital stay. Due to a high fever, her doctor kept her in the hospital for a fourth day with clearly documented medical reasons. The insurance company denied coverage for the fourth day retroactively and attempted to collect the entire charge for that day (a very significant amount). After two years of correspondence and phone conversation with the insurance company and hospital, the charges were finally covered.

Get very specific information on this issue prior to the surgery. Do not rely on your doctor's office or the hospital to see that coverage is adequate.

_____

_____

_____

_____

Phone contact log with the hospital and insurance company about coverage:

Since you are ultimately financially responsible for your medical bills, we have found that it is very important to document discussions about insurance coverage and reimbursement issues. A phone contact log provides a means of keeping track of conversations in case problems arise at a later date.

Name of Person	Date and Time	Topic

What doctors can I expect to see in the hospital and what are their roles?

Many doctors may be involved in your treatment depending on the nature of your surgery and other medical problems. It can be helpful to know what specialists may assist in your care and whether you should see a particular doctor again after you are discharged. Prior to surgery you may not know all the doctors who will be involved in your care, so don't be afraid to ask for each doctor's business card. We have found that by keeping the cards in an inexpensive, plastic business-card notebook you will be able to find them when you need them.

Doctor	Office Phone	Specialty/Purpose	Follow-up After Discharge	
			YES	NO
			YES	NO

		YES	NO
		YES	NO
		YES	NO

When will I first see my surgeon in the hospital after the surgery?
   Ask about this in advance.

_____

_____

_____

Will my surgeon be in town and managing my case the entire time I am in the hospital?
   Your surgeon may plan to be out of town or on vacation immediately following your surgery. It can be distressing to have another doctor manage your postoperative recovery if you are not expecting it. Ask about this and make contact with the backup physician prior to the surgery if necessary.

_____

_____

_____

Hospital Checklist

1. Scheduling and Approvals

____ Do you have your insurance preapproval letter?

____ Has your insurance deductible been met?

____ Do you know how much your copayment will be?

____ Does your employer know about the time you will need off from work?

2. Preoperative procedures

____ Are all of the preoperative procedures completed (lab and blood tests, internal medicine evaluation, etc.)?

____ Does your surgeon have all of your necessary records?

____ Do you have copies of important records (or the completed medical fact sheet)?

____ Do you need a sedative for the night before?

____ Do you need to rent any special equipment for recovery at home?

____ Are "advanced directives" (living will or durable power of attorney for health care) completed if you desire them?

____ Are presurgical instructions understood and completed (e.g., no food or liquid twenty-four hours before, bowel preparation, etc.)?

____ Is an interpreter service arranged if necessary?

3. Bring to the hospital

____ Your insurance card

____ Pajamas or nightgown, robe, slippers, appropriate clothes, toiletries

____ List of medications

____ Completed medical fact sheet (3 copies)

____ Your plastic business-card notebook

____ Reading/inspirational materials (if desired)

____ Notepad and pencil

4. Do not bring valuables to the hospital

5. Other

_____

_____

_____

_____

References

Volicer, B. J., M. A. Isenberg, and M. W. Burns. 1977. Medica-surgical differences in hospital stress factors. *Journal of Human Stress* 3:1–13.

Excerpted and adapted with permission from *Preparing for Surgery* by William W. Deardorff, Ph.D., and John L. Reeves II, Ph.D. For more information on this and related books, see the "Further Reading" section in the back of the book.

PART V

COPING WITH BAD MOODS AND PAINFUL FEELINGS

This section is the heart of this book, since coping with bad moods and painful feelings is at the heart of emotional wellness. Stress, low self-esteem, anxiety, depression, and grief make life seem hardly worth living for millions of people. You may have been referred to this section from some other part of the book. That's because this section contains the most powerful techniques for dealing with a wide range of problems. Over the last twenty years psychologists have adapted many proven cognitive-behavioral treatments to the self-help formats presented here:

Stress teaches the two most important and frequently prescribed self-regulation skills you can learn—Controlled Breathing and Progressive Muscle Relaxation.

Self-Esteem shows how to raise self-esteem by detecting, analyzing, and talking back to your pathological critic—the internal critical voice we all have.

Uncovering Automatic Thoughts introduces the startling notion that only thoughts cause feelings and gives you practice in monitoring your automatic thoughts in a thought journal.

Changing Patterns of Limited Thinking outlines the eight most common patterns of limited thinking and shows how changing your interpretation of yourself, others, and the world can profoundly change how you feel.

Changing Hot Thoughts teaches you how to dispassionately consider the evidence for and against the "hot thoughts" that habitually make you unhappy or hold you back.

Anxiety—Overview of the Disorders explains important diagnostic differences among various anxiety disorders such as panic attacks, phobias, social phobia, obsessions and compulsions, and post-traumatic stress disorder.

Panic Attacks teaches simple breathing techniques to stop panic when it occurs, as well as how to prevent it from happening.

Phobias shows you how to practice systematic desensitization so that you can approach feared objects, situations, and experiences that are keeping you from a full enjoyment of and participation in life.

Social Phobia shows how to analyze, understand, and overcome the embarrassment and shyness that may keep you isolated and make you avoid social situations.

Obsessions and Compulsions explains the nature and treatment of obsessions such as a preoccupation with germs or danger, and compulsions such as excessive hand washing, checking, or hoarding.

Traumatic Experiences helps you determine whether your symptoms, such as flashbacks, anxiety, emotional numbness, and so on, meet the criteria for a diagnosis of post-traumatic stress disorder (PTSD), a common syndrome affecting those who have survived traumatic experiences such as combat, violence, accidents, abuse, or natural disasters.

Grief helps you understand the normal stages of sadness, anger, numbness, guilt, and so on that accompany the loss of a loved one.

Preparing for a Parent's Death provides counsel for those dealing with a dying parent.

Depression summarizes the causes, symptoms, and treatments for depression and bipolar disorder. The chapter also gets you started on making lifestyle changes to cope with depression, such as scheduling pleasant activities, increasing exposure to natural light, and relying on supportive relationships.

Suicide Prevention covers the warning signs and crisis intervention actions to take if you or someone you know is having suicidal thoughts.

CHAPTER 28

Stress

Stress is a part of everyday life. It affects all of us at different times. However, left unchecked, stress can accumulate and take a toll on our emotional and physical well-being. This chapter provides stress-reducing techniques that are simple and effective.

Breathing

Breathing is a necessity of life that most people take for granted. With each breath of air, you obtain oxygen and release the waste product carbon dioxide. Poor breathing habits diminish the flow of these gases to and from your body, making it harder for you to cope with stressful situations. Improper breathing contributes to anxiety, panic attacks, depression, muscle tension, headaches, and fatigue. As you learn to be aware of your breathing and practice slowing and normalizing your breaths, your mind will quiet and your body will relax. Breathing awareness and good breathing habits will enhance your psychological and physical well-being, whether you practice them alone or in combination with other relaxation techniques.

Let's examine a breath. When you inhale, air is drawn in through your nose, where it is warmed to body temperature, humidified, and partially cleansed. Your diaphragm, a sheet-like muscle separating the lungs and the abdomen, facilitates your breathing by expanding and contracting as you breathe in and out.

Your lungs are like a tree with many branches (bronchial tubes) that carry air to elastic air sacs (alveoli). The alveoli have the balloon-like ability to expand when air is taken into the lungs and contract when air is let out. Small blood vessels (capillaries) surrounding the alveoli receive oxygen and transport it to your heart.

The blood that your heart pumps carries oxygen to all parts of your body. An exchange occurs in which blood cells receive oxygen and release carbon dioxide, a waste product that is carried back to your heart and lungs and exhaled. This efficient method of transporting and exchanging oxygen is vital to sustain life.

When you breathe, you typically use one of two patterns: (1) chest or thoracic breathing and (2) abdominal or diaphragmatic breathing.

Chest or thoracic breathing is often associated with anxiety or other emotional distress. It is also common in people who wear restricted clothing or lead sedentary or stressful lives. Chest breathing is shallow and often irregular and rapid. When air is inhaled, the chest expands and the shoulders rise to take in the air. Anxious people may experience breathholding, hyperventilation or constricted breathing, shortness of breath, or fear of passing out. If an insufficient amount of air reaches your lungs, your blood is not properly oxygenated, your heart rate and muscle tension increase, and your stress response is turned on.

Abdominal or diaphragmatic breathing is the natural breathing of newborn babies and sleeping adults. Inhaled air is drawn deep into the lungs and exhaled as the diaphragm contracts and expands. Breathing is even and nonconstricting. The respiratory system is able to do its job of producing energy from oxygen and removing waste products.

By increasing your awareness of your own breathing patterns and shifting to more abdominal breathing, you can reduce the muscle tension and anxiety present with stress-related symptoms or thoughts. Diaphragmatic breathing is the easiest way of eliciting the relaxation response.

Breathing exercises have been found to be effective in reducing generalized anxiety disorders, panic attacks and agoraphobia, depression, irritability, muscle tension, headaches, and fatigue. They are used in the treatment and prevention of breathholding, hyperventilation, shallow breathing, and cold hands and feet.

While a breathing exercise can be learned in a matter of minutes and some benefits experienced immediately, the profound effects of the exercise may not be fully appreciated until after months of persistent practice. After you have tried the exercises presented in this chapter, develop a breathing program incorporating those exercises you find most beneficial and follow your program with patience and persistence.

Breathing for Awareness and Relaxation

Your first step is to increase your awareness of your breathing habits and to learn how to use breathing as a relaxation skill.

Breathing Awareness

Close your eyes. Put your right hand on your abdomen, right at the waistline, and put your left hand on your chest, right in the center.

Without trying to change your breathing, simply notice how you are breathing. Which hand rises the most as you inhale—the hand on your chest or the hand on your belly?

If your abdomen expands, then you are breathing from your abdomen or diaphragm. If your belly doesn't move or moves less than your chest, then you are breathing from your chest.

The trick to shifting from chest to abdominal breathing is to make one or two full exhalations that push out the air from the bottom of your lungs. This will create a vacuum that will pull in a deep, diaphragmatic breath on your next inhalation.

Diaphragmatic or Abdominal Breathing

1. Lie down on a rug or blanket on the floor in a "dead body" pose—your legs straight and slightly apart, your toes pointed comfortably outward, your arms at your sides and not touching your body, your palms up, and your eyes closed.

2. Bring your attention to your breathing and place your hand on the spot that seems to rise and fall the most as you inhale and exhale.

3. Gently place both of your hands or a book on your abdomen and follow your breathing. Notice how your abdomen rises with each inhalation and falls with each exhalation.

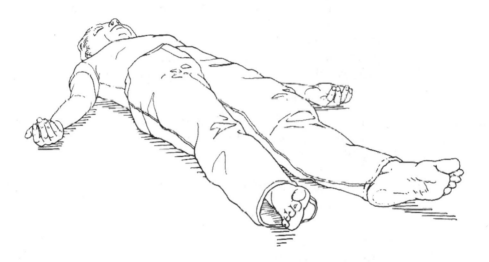

4. Breathe through your nose. (If possible, always clear your nasal passages before doing breathing exercises.)

5. If you experience difficulty breathing into your abdomen, press your hand down on your abdomen as you exhale and let your abdomen push your hand back up as you inhale deeply.

6. Is your chest moving in harmony with your abdomen or is it rigid? Spend a minute or two letting your chest follow the movement of your abdomen.

7. If you continue to experience difficulty breathing into your abdomen, an alternative is to lie on your stomach, with your head rested on your folded hands. Take deep abdominal breaths so you can feel your abdomen pushing against the floor.

Deep Breathing

1. Although this exercise can be practiced in a variety of poses, the following is recommended: lie down on a blanket or rug on the floor. Bend your knees and move your feet

about eight inches apart, with your toes turned slightly outward. Make sure that your spine is straight.

2. Scan your body for tension.

3. Place one hand on your abdomen and one hand on your chest.

4. Inhale slowly and deeply through your nose into your abdomen to push up your hand as much as feels comfortable. Your chest should move only a little and only with your abdomen.

5. When you feel at ease with step 4, smile slightly and inhale through your nose and exhale through your mouth, making a quiet, relaxing, whooshing sound like the wind as you blow gently out. Your mouth, tongue, and jaw will be relaxed. Take long, slow, deep breaths that raise and lower your abdomen. Focus on the sound and feeling of breathing as you become more and more relaxed.

6. Continue deep breathing for about five or ten minutes at a time, once or twice a day, for a couple of weeks. Then, if you like, extend this period to twenty minutes.

7. At the end of each deep breathing session, take a little time to once more scan your body for tension. Compare the tension you feel at the conclusion of the exercise with that which you experienced when you began.

8. When you become at ease with breathing into your abdomen, practice it any time during the day when you feel like it and you are sitting down or standing still. Concentrate on your abdomen moving up and down, the air moving in and out of your lungs, and the feeling of relaxation that deep breathing gives you.

9. When you have learned to relax yourself using deep breathing, practice it whenever you feel yourself getting tense.

Complete Natural Breathing

1. Begin by sitting or standing up straight in a good posture.

2. Breathe through your nose.

3. As you inhale, first fill the lower section of your lungs. (Your diaphragm will push your abdomen outward to make room for the air.) Second, fill the middle part of your lungs as your lower ribs and chest move forward slightly to accommodate the air. Third, fill the upper part of your lungs as your raise your chest slightly and draw in your abdomen a little to support your lungs. (You might imagine you're blowing up a balloon.) These three steps can be performed in one smooth, continuous inhalation, which with practice can be completed in a couple of seconds.

4. Now hold your breath for a few seconds to experience your full lungs.

5. As you slowly exhale, pull your abdomen in slightly and slowly lift it up as your lungs empty. When you have completely exhaled, relax your abdomen and chest.

6. Now and then at the end of the inhalation phase, raise your shoulders and collarbone slightly so that the very top of your lungs are sure to be replenished with fresh air.

Breathing to Release Tension

Use the following exercises to enhance relaxation and release tension.

Breath Counting

1. Sit or lie in a comfortable position with your arms and legs uncrossed and your spine straight.

2. Breathe in deeply into your abdomen. Let yourself pause before you exhale.

3. As you exhale, count "One" to yourself. As you continue to inhale and exhale, count each exhalation by saying "Two . . . three . . . four."

4. Continue counting your exhalations in sets of four for five to ten minutes.

5. Notice your breathing gradually slowing, your body relaxing, and your mind calming as you practice this breathing meditation.

The Relaxing Sigh

1. During the day, you probably catch yourself sighing or yawning. This is generally a sign that you are not getting enough oxygen. Sighing and yawning are your body's way of remedying the situation. A sigh is often accompanied by a sense that things are not quite as they should be and a feeling of tension. Since a sigh actually does release a bit of this tension, you can practice sighing at will as a means of relaxing.

2. Sit or stand up straight.

3. Sigh deeply, letting out a sound of deep relief as the air rushes out of your lungs.

4. Don't think about inhaling—just let the air come in naturally.

5. Take eight to twelve of these relaxing sighs and let yourself experience the feeling of relaxation. Repeat whenever you feel the need for it.

Letting Go of Tension

1. Sit comfortably in a chair with your feet on the floor.

2. Breathe in deeply into your abdomen and say to yourself, "Breathe in relaxation." Let yourself pause before you exhale.

3. Breathe out from your abdomen and say to yourself, "Breathe out tension." Pause before you inhale.

4. Use each inhalation as a moment to become aware of any tension in your body.

5. Use each exhalation as an opportunity to let go of tension.

6. You may find it helpful to use your imagination to picture or feel the relaxation entering and the tension leaving your body.

Progressive Relaxation

You cannot have the feeling of warm well-being in your body and at the same time experience psychological stress. Progressive relaxation of your muscles reduces pulse rate and blood pressure as well as decreasing perspiration and respiration rates. Deep muscle relaxation, when successfully mastered, can be used as an anti-anxiety pill.

Edmund Jacobson, a Chicago physician, published the book *Progressive Relaxation* in 1929. In this book he described his deep muscle relaxation technique, which he asserted required no imagination, willpower, or suggestion. His technique is based on the premise that the body responds to anxiety-provoking thoughts and events with muscle tension. This physiological tension, in turn, increases the subjective experience of anxiety. Deep muscle relaxation reduces physiological tension and is incompatible with anxiety: The habit of responding with one blocks the habit of responding with the other.

Progressive relaxation is used in the treatment of muscular tension, anxiety, insomnia, depression, fatigue, irritable bowel, muscle spasms, neck and back pain, high blood pressure, mild phobias, and stuttering.

Most people do not realize which of their muscles are chronically tense. Progressive relaxation provides a way of identifying particular muscles and muscle groups and distinguishing between sensations of tension and deep relaxation. Four major muscle groups will be covered:

1. Hands, forearms, and biceps.

2. Head, face, throat, and shoulders, including concentration on forehead, cheeks, nose, eyes, jaws, lips, tongue, and neck. Considerable attention is devoted to your head, because from the emotional point of view, the most important muscles in your body are situated in and around this region.

3. Chest, stomach, and lower back.

4. Thighs, buttocks, calves, and feet.

Progressive relaxation can be practiced lying down or in a chair with your head supported. Each muscle or muscle grouping is tensed from five to seven seconds and then relaxed for twenty to thirty seconds. This procedure is repeated at least once. If an area remains tense, you can practice up to five times. You may also find it useful to use the following relaxing expressions when untensing:

Let go of the tension.

Throw away the tension—I am feeling calm and rested.

Relax and smooth out the muscles.

Let the tension dissolve away.

Once the procedure is familiar enough to be remembered, keep your eyes closed and focus attention on just one muscle group at a time. The instructions for progressive relaxation are divided into two sections. The first part, which you may wish to tape and replay when practicing, will familiarize you with the muscles in your body which are most commonly tense. The second section shortens the procedure by simultaneously tensing and relaxing many muscles at one time so that deep muscle relaxation can be achieved in a very brief period.

Basic Procedure

Get in a comfortable position and relax. Now clench your right fist, tighter and tighter, studying the tension as you do so. Keep it clenched and notice the tension in your fist, hand, and forearm. Now relax. Feel the looseness in your right hand, and notice the contrast with the tension. Repeat this procedure with your right fist again, always noticing as you relax that this is the opposite of tension—relax and feel the difference. Repeat the entire procedure with your left fist, then both fists at once.

Now bend your elbows and tense your biceps. Tense them as hard as you can and observe the feeling of tautness. Relax, straighten out your arms. Let the relaxation develop and feel that difference. Repeat this, and all succeeding procedures at least once.

Turning attention to your head, wrinkle your forehead as tight as you can. Now relax and smooth it out. Let yourself imagine your entire forehead and scalp becoming smooth and at rest. Now frown and notice the strain spreading throughout your forehead. Let go. Allow your brow to become smooth again. Close your eyes now, squint them tighter. Look for the tension. Relax your eyes. Let them remain closed gently and comfortably. Now clench your jaw, bite hard, notice the tension throughout your jaw. Relax your jaw. When the jaw is relaxed, your lips will be slightly parted. Let yourself really appreciate the contrast between tension and relaxation. Now press your tongue against the roof of your mouth. Feel the ache in the back of your mouth. Relax. Press your lips now, purse them into an "O." Relax your lips. Notice that your forehead, scalp, eyes, jaw, tongue, and lips are all relaxed.

Press your head back as far as it can comfortably go and observe the tension in your neck. Roll it to the right and feel the changing locus of stress, roll it to the left. Straighten your head and bring it forward, press your chin against your chest. Feel the tension in your throat, the back of your neck. Relax, allowing your head to return to a comfortable position. Let the relaxation deepen. Now shrug your shoulders. Keep the tension as you hunch your head down between your shoulders. Relax your shoulders. Drop them back and feel the relaxation spreading through your neck, throat, and shoulders, pure relaxation, deeper and deeper.

Give your entire body a chance to relax. Feel the comfort and the heaviness. Now breathe in and fill your lungs completely. Hold your breath. Notice the tension. Now exhale, let your chest become loose, let the air hiss out. Continue relaxing, letting your breath come freely and gently. Repeat this several times, noticing the tension draining from your body as you exhale. Next, tighten your stomach and hold. Note the tension, then relax. Now place your hand on your stomach. Breathe deeply into your stomach, pushing your hand up. Hold, and relax. Feel the contrast of relaxation as the air rushes out. Now arch your back, without straining. Keep the rest of your body as relaxed as possible. Focus on the tension in your lower back. Now relax, deeper and deeper.

Tighten your buttocks and thighs. Flex your thighs by pressing down your heels as hard as you can. Relax and feel the difference. Now curl your toes downward, making your calves tense. Study the tension. Relax. Now bend your toes toward your face, creating tension in your shins. Relax again.

Feel the heaviness throughout your lower body as the relaxation deepens. Relax your feet, ankles, calves, shins, knees, thighs, and buttocks. Now let the relaxation spread to your stomach, lower back, and chest. Let go more and more. Experience the relaxation deepening in your shoulders, arms, and hands. Deeper and deeper. Notice the feeling of looseness and relaxation in your neck, jaws, and all your facial muscles.

Shorthand Procedure

The following is a procedure for achieving deep muscle relaxation quickly. Whole muscle groups are simultaneously tensed and then relaxed. As before, repeat each procedure at least once, tensing each muscle group from five to seven seconds and then relaxing from fifteen to thirty seconds. Remember to notice the contrast between the sensations of tension and relaxation.

1. Curl both fists, tightening biceps and forearms (Charles Atlas pose). Relax.

2. Wrinkle up forehead. At the same time, press your head as far back as possible, roll it clockwise in a complete circle, reverse. Now wrinkle up the muscles of your face like a walnut: frowning, eyes squinted, lips pursed, tongue pressing the roof of the mouth, and shoulders hunched. Relax.

3. Arch back as you take a deep breath into the chest. Hold. Relax. Take a deep breath, pressing out the stomach. Hold. Relax.

4. Pull feet and toes back toward face, tightening shins. Hold. Relax. Curl toes, simultaneously tightening calves, thighs, and buttocks. Relax.

Special Considerations

1. If you make a tape of the basic procedure to facilitate your relaxation program, remember to space each procedure so that time is allowed to experience the tension and relaxation before going on to the next muscle or muscle group.

2. Most people have somewhat limited success when they begin deep muscle relaxation, but it is only a matter of practice. Whereas twenty minutes of work might initially bring only partial relaxation, it will eventually be possible to relax your whole body in a few moments.

3. Sometimes in the beginning, it may seem to you as though relaxation is complete. But although the muscle or muscle group may well be partially relaxed, a certain number of muscle fibers will still be contracted. It is the act of relaxing these additional fibers that will bring about the emotional effects you want. It is helpful to say to yourself during the relaxation phase, "Let go more and more."

4. Caution should be taken in tensing the neck and back. Excessive tightening can result in muscle or spinal damage. It is also commonly observed that overtightening the toes or feet results in muscle cramping.

5. People new to this technique sometimes make the error of relaxing tension gradually. This slow-motion release of tension may look relaxed, but it actually requires sustained tension. When you release the tension in a particular muscle, let it go instantly, as though you had just turned off an electrical current. Let your muscles become suddenly limp.

Excerpted and adapted with permission from *The Relaxation & Stress Reduction Workbook*, fourth edition, by Martha Davis, Ph.D., Elizabeth Robbins Eshelman, M.S.W., and Matthew McKay, Ph.D. For more information on this and related books, see the "Further Reading" section in the back of the book.

CHAPTER 29

Self-Esteem

When our self-esteem is compromised, our self-identity, our relationships with others, and our feelings about our place in the world are all impacted. This chapter will provide exercises that everyone can use to boost their feelings of self-worth.

The Pathological Critic

The pathological critic is a term coined by psychologist Eugene Sagan to describe the negative inner voice that attacks and judges you. Everyone has a critical inner voice. But people with low self-esteem tend to have a more vicious and vocal pathological critic.

The critic blames you for things that go wrong. The critic compares you to others—to their achievements and abilities—and finds you wanting. The critic sets impossible standards of perfection and then beats you up for the smallest mistake. The critic keeps an album of your failures, but never once reminds you of your strengths or accomplishments. The critic has a script describing how you ought to live and screams that you are wrong and bad if your needs drive you to violate his rules. The critic tells you to be the best—and if you're not the best, you're nothing. He calls you names—stupid, incompetent, ugly, selfish, weak—and makes you believe that all of them are true. The critic reads your friends' minds and convinces you that they are bored, turned off, disappointed, or disgusted by you. The critic exaggerates your weaknesses by insisting that you "*always* say stupid things," or "*always* screw up a relationship," or "*never* finish anything on time."

The pathological critic is busy undermining your self-worth every day of your life. Yet his voice is so insidious, so woven into the fabric of your thought that you never notice its devastating effect. The self-attacks always seem reasonable and justified. The carping, judging inner voice seems natural, a familiar part of you. In truth, the critic is a kind of psychological jackal who, with every attack, weakens and breaks down any good feelings you have about yourself.

Although we refer to the critic as "he" for convenience, your critic's voice may sound female. Your critic's voice may sound like your mother, your father, or your own speaking voice.

The first and most important thing you need to know about your critic is that no matter how distorted and false his attacks may be, he is almost always believed. When your critic says, "God, I'm dumb," this judgment seems just as true to you as the awareness that you're tired this morning, or that you have brown eyes, or that you don't understand word processors. It feels normal to judge yourself because you are so intimately aware of what you feel and do. But the attacks of the critic aren't part of the normal process of noticing what you feel and do. For example, when you examine how you felt on a first date, the critic drowns out any normal, reasonable reflections by shouting through a bullhorn that you were a callow bore, a fumbler, a nervous phony, and that your date won't ever want to see you again. The critic takes your self-esteem and puts it through a Cuisinart.

A loud, voluble critic is enormously toxic. He is more poisonous to your psychological health than almost any trauma or loss. That's because grief and pain wash away with time. But the critic is always with you—judging, blaming, finding fault. You have no defense against him. "There you go again," he says, "being an idiot." And you automatically feel wrong and bad, like a child who's been slapped for saying something naughty.

Consider the case of a twenty-nine-year-old entomologist, recently graduated with a Ph.D., who was applying for a faculty position. During interviews he would observe the dress and manner of the interview committee and make guesses about the sort of people they were and how they were responding to him. He would handle questions by weighing the best possible answer, given what the committee seemed to expect. And while he was doing all that, he was also listening to a continuous monologue in which his critic said, "You're a fraud, you don't know anything. You won't fool these people. Wait till they read that mediocre piece of hogwash you call your dissertation . . . That was a stupid answer. Can't you crack a joke? Do something! They'll see how boring you are. Even if you get the job, you'll only lose it when your incompetence starts to show. You're not fooling anybody."

The entomologist believed every word. It all seemed to make sense. Because he'd heard it for years, the steady stream of poison felt normal, reasonable, and true. During the interview he became more and more stiff, his answers more vague. His voice slipped into a monotone while he perspired and developed a little stammer. He was listening to the critic, and the critic was turning him into the very thing he feared.

Another important thing you need to know about the critic is that he speaks in a kind of shorthand. He might only scream the word "lazy." But those two syllables contain the memory of the hundreds of times your father complained about laziness, attacked your laziness, said how he hated laziness. It's all there, and you feel the entire weight of his disgust as the critic says the word.

Sometimes the critic uses images or pictures from the past to undermine your sense of worth. He shows a rerun of some awkward moment on a date; he pulls out snapshots of a dressing-down you got from your boss, images of a failed relationship, and scenes of the times you blew up at your kids.

A legal secretary found that her critic often used the word "screwup." When she thought about it, she realized that "screwup" stood for a list of negative qualities. It meant someone who was incompetent, unliked, a taker of foolish risks, a person (like her father) who would run away from problems. When the critic said "screwup," she firmly believed that she was all of these things.

One of the strange things about the critic is that he often seems to have more control of your mind than you do. He will suddenly start to sound off, launching one attack after another or dragging you over and over through a painful scene. Through a process called *chaining*, he may show you a past failure, which reminds you of another and another in a long string of painful associations. And though you try to turn him off, you keep being reminded of yet another mistake, another rejection, another embarrassment.

Although the critic seems to have a will of his own, his independence is really an illusion. The truth is that you are so used to listening to him, so used to believing him, that you have not yet learned how to turn him off. With practice, however, you can learn to analyze and refute what the critic says. You can tune him out *before* he has a chance to poison your feelings of self-worth.

An Arsenal of Shoulds

The critic has many weapons. Among the most effective are the values and rules of living you grew up with. The critic has a way of turning your "shoulds" against you. He compares the way you are with the way you ought to be and judges you inadequate or wrong. He calls you stupid if the A you should have had slips to a B. He says, "A marriage should last forever," and calls you a failure after your divorce. He says, "A real man supports his family," and calls you a loser when you're laid off from work. He says, "The kids come first," and calls you selfish when you crave some nights off.

A thirty-five-year-old bartender described how his critic used old "shoulds" he'd learned as a child. "My father was a lawyer, so the critic says that I should be a professional and that anything else is a waste. I feel like I should have forced myself to go to school. I feel like I should read real books instead of the sports page. I feel like I should be *doing* something in the world instead of mixing drinks and heading over to my girlfriend's house." This man's self-esteem was severely damaged by a critic who insisted that he be something other than himself. The fact was that he liked the comradery of the bar and wasn't the least bit intellectual. But he continually rejected himself for not living up to his family's expectations.

The Origin of the Critic

The critic is born during your earliest experience of socialization by your parents. All through childhood, your parents are teaching you which behaviors are acceptable, which are dangerous, which are morally wrong, which are lovable, and which are annoying. They do this by hugging and praising you for appropriate behavior and punishing you for dangerous, wrong, or annoying behavior. It's impossible to grow up without having experienced a great number of punishing events. Personality theorist Harry Stack Sullivan called these punishing events *forbidding gestures*.

By design, forbidding gestures are frightening and rejecting. A child who is spanked or scolded feels the withdrawal of parental approval very acutely. He or she is, for a while, a bad person. Either consciously or unconsciously, a child knows that his or her parents are the source of all physical and emotional nourishment. If he or she were to be rejected, cast out by the family, he or she would die. So parental approval is a matter of life or death to a child. The experience of being bad can be very deeply felt, because being bad carries with it the terrible risk of losing all support.

All children grow up with emotional residues from the forbidding gestures. They retain conscious and unconscious memories of all those times when they felt wrong or bad. These are the unavoidable scars that growing up inflicts on your self-esteem. This experience is also where the critic gets his start, feeding on these early "not-okay" feelings. There is still a part of you willing to believe you're bad just as soon as someone gets angry at you, or you make a mistake, or you fall short of a goal. That early feeling of being not-okay is why the critic's attacks seem to fit in so well with what you already believe about yourself. His voice is the voice of a disapproving parent, the punishing, forbidding voice that shaped your behavior as a child.

The volume and viciousness of a critic's attacks are directly related to the strength of your not-okay feelings. If the early forbidding gestures were relatively mild, the adult critic may only rarely attack. But if you were given very strong messages about your wrongness or badness as a child, then the adult critic will come gunning for you every chance he gets.

There are five main factors that determine the strength of your early not-okay feelings:

1. *The degree to which issues of taste, personal needs, safety, or good judgment were mislabeled as moral imperatives.* In some families, when dad wants things quiet, a child is made to feel morally wrong if he or she is noisy. Other families make a low grade into a sin. Some children are made to feel wrong for needing time with friends or for having sexual feelings. Some children are *bad* if they forget their chores, *bad* if they prefer a certain haircut, or *bad* if they ride their skateboard in the street. When the issue is really a matter of taste, failure to perform tasks, or poor judgment, but parents make a child feel morally wrong, they are laying the foundation for low self-esteem. It's important to recognize that certain words and phrases carry heavy moral messages. If a child hears that he or she is lazy, or selfish, or looks like a bum, or acts like a screwball, the specific situations are very soon forgotten. But he or she is left with an enduring sense of wrongness.

2. *The degree to which parents failed to differentiate between behavior and identity.* A child who hears a stern warning about the dangers of running in the street will have better self-esteem than a child who only hears that he's a "bad boy" when he runs into the street. The child who's a "bad boy" is getting the message that he and his behavior are not okay. He doesn't learn the difference between what he does and what he is. As an adult, his critic will attack both his behavior and his worth. Parents who carefully distinguish between *inappropriate behavior* and the basic *goodness of the child* raise children who feel better about themselves and have a far gentler inner critic.

3. *The frequency of the forbidding gestures.* The frequency of negative messages from parents has an impact on early feelings of worth. Hitler's minister of propaganda once observed that the secret to having any lie believed was merely to repeat it often enough. The lie that you are not okay wasn't learned with your parents' first rebuke. It was learned through repeated criticism. You have to hear "What's the matter with you?" and "Stop screwing around" a good many times before the message sinks in. But after a while you get the point—you're not okay.

4. *The consistency of the forbidding gestures.* Suppose your parents didn't like you to use the word "shit." You may have thought that prohibition rather stuffy, but if they were consistent, you managed to get along without that admittedly versatile word. Suppose, however, that they let you say "shit" sometimes and blew up when you said it at other times. And suppose they were equally inconsistent about other rules. At first you would be confused, but the randomness of the attacks would eventually lead you to a very painful conclusion. It wasn't what you *did*—sometimes that was okay, sometimes it wasn't—it was *you*. There was something wrong with you. Children who have experienced inconsistent parenting often feel an ineffable feeling of guilt. They feel as if they've done something wrong, but because they can never get the rules straight, they have no idea what.

5. *The frequency with which forbidding gestures were tied to parental anger or withdrawal.* Children can tolerate a fair amount of criticism without experiencing much damage to their

sense of worth. But if the criticism is accompanied by parental anger or withdrawal (threatened or actual), it has enormous potency. Anger and withdrawal give an unmistakable message: "You're bad, and I'm rejecting you." Since this is the most terrifying thing that a child can hear, he or she is very certain to remember it. Long after the incident has blown over, the child retains the strong impression of his or her wrongness. And the critic will use that sense of wrongness to psychologically beat and kick you as an adult.

Why You Listen to the Critic

You listen to the critic because it is very rewarding to do so. Incredible as it seems, the critic helps you to meet certain basic needs, and listening to his vicious attacks can be reinforcing. But how can so much pain be reinforcing? How can attacking yourself be the least bit pleasurable or help to satisfy your needs?

The first step to understanding the function of your critic is to recognize that everyone has certain basic needs. Everyone needs to feel:

1. Secure and unafraid

2. Effective and competent in the world

3. Accepted by parents and significant others

4. A sense of worth and okayness in most situations

People with adequate self-esteem tend to have very different strategies for meeting these needs than people with low self-esteem. If you have adequate self-esteem, you also have a degree of confidence in yourself. You keep yourself secure by confronting or eliminating things that frighten you. You solve problems instead of worrying about them, and you find ways to make people respond positively to you. You cope directly with interpersonal conflicts rather than wait for them to pass. Conversely, low self-esteem robs you of confidence. You don't feel as able to cope with anxiety, interpersonal problems, or challenging risks. Life is more painful because you don't feel as effective, and it's hard to face the anxiety involved in making things change.

This is where the critic comes in. People with low self-esteem often rely on the critic to help them cope with feelings of anxiety, helplessness, rejection, and inadequacy. Paradoxically, while the critic is beating you up, he is also making you feel better. This is why it's so hard to get rid of the critic. He can play a crucial role in making you more safe and comfortable in the world. Unfortunately, the price you pay for the critic's support is very high and further undermines your sense of worth. But you are reinforced to keep listening because every time the critic pipes up you feel a little less anxious, less incompetent, less powerless, or less vulnerable to others.

The Role of Reinforcement

To understand how the critic's painful attacks can be reinforcing, it's necessary first to examine how reinforcement shapes your behavior and your thinking.

Positive reinforcement occurs when a rewarding event follows a particular behavior and results in an increase in the future likelihood of that behavior. If your wife gives you a warm hug and a thank-you after you've cut the lawn, she is positively reinforcing your gardening activities. If the boss praises the clean, spare writing style in your last report, she is positively reinforcing the writing behavior she prefers. Because affection and praise are such powerful rewards, you are likely to repeat your gardening and writing behaviors in the future.

Just as with physical behavior, the frequency of cognitive behavior (thoughts) can also be increased through positive reinforcement. If you feel aroused following a particular sexual fantasy, you are quite likely to conjure up that fantasy again. Thinking critically of others can be reinforced by increased feelings of worth. Daydreams of an upcoming vacation, if they are followed by a sense of excitement and anticipation, will be repeated. The increased feeling of worth that follows your memories of success and achievement makes you more likely to return to them. Obsessing about the misfortunes of someone you dislike can be reinforced by feelings of pleasure or vindication.

Negative reinforcement can only occur when you are in physical or psychological pain. Any behavior that succeeds in stopping the pain is reinforced, and is therefore more likely to occur when you feel similar pain in the future. For example, when students are preparing for final exams, they often find that the most boring, mundane activities have become irresistibly interesting. Activities like doodling or scoring baskets in the trash can are being reinforced because they provide relief from high-stress studying. As a general rule, anything that relieves stress and anxiety will be reinforced. Anger is often reinforced by the immediate drop in tension following a blowup. TV watching, eating, hot baths, withdrawal, complaining, hobbies, and sports activities may all at times be reinforced by tension or anxiety reduction. Blaming others relieves anxiety over your mistakes and can be reinforced until it becomes very high-frequency behavior. Macho behavior has the effect of relieving social anxiety for some men, and the decrease in anxiety is so rewarding that the macho style becomes a heavy armor in which they become trapped.

As with positive reinforcement, negative reinforcement shapes how you think. Any thought that relieves feelings of anxiety, guilt, hopelessness, or inadequacy will be reinforced. Suppose, for example, that you feel anxious every time you visit your crusty, judgmental father-in-law. Driving over to his house one day, you begin thinking about what a narrow bigot he really is, how few of his opinions are supported by anything resembling a fact, how tyrannical he is when crossed. Suddenly you feel more angry than anxious, and you experience a strange sense of relief. Since your critical thoughts are reinforced by reduced anxiety, you notice on subsequent visits an increasingly judgmental attitude toward the old man.

A person who feels anxious about mistakes at work may find that devaluing the job ("it's idiot's work") and the boss ("a nitpicking, anal type") reduced anxiety. It's likely that the devaluing thoughts will be entertained again if anxiety should once more increase. Feelings of hopelessness can sometimes be relieved by romantic fantasies, grandiose success fantasies, rescue or escape dreams, or simple problem-solving thoughts. In every case, the particular cognition that succeeds in reducing the sense of hopelessness will be remembered. When the same feelings recur, the same recognition has a high probability of being used again.

The mourning process is a classic example of the power of negative reinforcement. What makes people keep dredging up painful memories of the lost person or object? Why keep thinking and thinking about those sweet days that can never come again? Paradoxically, these obsessive ruminations about the loss have the power of relieving pain. The awareness of a loss creates high levels of physical and emotional tension. The frustration and helplessness build until they must be discharged. Calling up specific images and memories of the lost person or object helps discharge that tension in the form of tears and then a brief sort of numbness. The stage in mourning of obsessive remembering is therefore reinforced by tension reduction and a few moments of relative peace.

In summary, negative reinforcement is basically a problem-solving process. You're in pain. You want to feel better. You keep searching for some action or thought that is analgesic. When you find a thought or behavior that works to decrease your pain, you file it away as a successful solution to a particular problem. When the problem recurs, you will return again and again to your proven coping strategy.

The variable ratio reinforcement schedule. So far, only continuous reinforcement schedules have been discussed. Continuous reinforcement means that a particular thought or behavior is *always* reinforced. Every time you engage in the behavior, you are rewarded by pleasure or relief. An important aspect of continuous reinforcement schedules is that they lead very quickly to *extinction* if the thought or behavior stops being reinforced. Shortly after you cease getting rewarded for a previously reinforced thought or behavior, you simply stop doing it.

The situation is very different with a variable ratio reinforcement schedule. Here reinforcement is not continuous. You may be rewarded after emitting the behavior five times, then after twenty times, then after forty-three times, then twelve times, and so on. The schedule isn't predictable. Sometimes you might have to engage in the behavior hundreds or even thousands of times before being reinforced. The result of the unpredictability is that you will keep doing a previously reinforced behavior for a long time *without* reinforcement before extinction. It takes a long time to give up.

Slot machines operate on the variable ratio reinforcement schedule, which is why people become addicted and play them to the point of exhaustion. Sometimes it takes only one quarter for a jackpot, sometimes hundreds. People tend to play a long time before giving up because reinforcement *could* occur on any given quarter.

Here are two examples of how the variable ratio reinforcement schedule can have a powerful influence on your thoughts.

1. Obsessive worries are occasionally reinforced when the worry leads to a workable solution that reduces anxiety. This might happen once or twice a year, or even a few times in a lifetime. But the worrier keeps at it, moving from worry to worry, like the gambler who plays quarter after quarter, hoping this one or the next one will finally pay off.

2. The obsessive reliving of an awkward social exchange is sometimes reinforced by those wonderful moments when you suddenly see it differently and don't feel so rejected or incompetent after all. You remember something you did or said that seems, in memory, to save the situation. Your shame melts away, and you feel accepting of yourself again. The sad fact is that your obsessive reliving is hardly ever rewarded by such a reprieve. Usually you suffer, hour after hour, the mental videotapes of an embarrassing exchange, waiting to put in the quarter that makes you feel adequate once more.

How the Critic Gets Reinforced

Your self-critical statements can be both positively and negatively reinforced. Ironically, while the critic is tearing you down, he is also helping you solve problems and meet, in limited ways, certain basic needs. The following are specific examples of how the critic helps meet some of your needs.

Positive Reinforcement for the Critic

The need to do right. Everyone has a rather large inner list of rules and values that regulate behavior. These rules are often useful because they control dangerous impulses and provide a sense of structure and order in your life. The rules create an ethical framework by defining what is moral and immoral. They prescribe how to act with authority figures and friends, how to be sexual, how to handle money, and so on. When you violate these inner rules, life becomes chaotic and you lose your sense of worth. So the critic helps you follow the rules. He tells you how wrong and bad you are whenever you break a rule or feel tempted to break one. He harangues you so much that you try to "do right." As one man put it, "My critic gives me the backbone not to go around lying, cheating, and being lazy. I need that."

The need to feel right. Even while he's telling you that you're no good, the critic can paradoxically help you feel a greater sense of worth and acceptance. The catch is that it's only temporary.

1. *Self-worth.* There are two ways the critic helps you temporarily to feel more worth: by comparing you to others and by setting high, perfectionistic standards.

Here's how comparing works: The critic continually evaluates how you stack up in terms of intelligence, achievements, earning capacity, sexual attractiveness, likability, social competence, openness—virtually any trait or quality you value. Many times you find yourself less adequate than the other person in one or more dimensions, and your self-esteem takes a blow. But once in a while you decide that you are more attractive, smarter, or warmer, and you feel a moment's satisfaction at being higher on the totem pole. Though it comes only occasionally, that moment's satisfaction is reinforcing. The comparing your critic does is being reinforced on a variable ratio schedule. Most efforts to compare yourself to others leave you feeling less adequate, but those times when it pays off—when you look good by comparison—keep you caught in the comparing habit.

The second way the critic boosts your worth is by setting incredibly high standards for how you must perform at work, as a lover, as a parent, as a conversationalist, as a housekeeper, or as a first baseman on the softball team. Most of the time you will fail to live up to the critic's demands, and you'll feel inadequate. But once in a great while, everything comes together in a miraculous perfection. You achieve a milestone at work, you have a deep and lovely conversation with your son, you hit two home runs for your team, and tell six entertaining stories at the pizza parlor afterwards. And that's how you reinforce the critic—with a variable ratio schedule. Every so often you do live up to his lofty standards and, for a brief time, feel at peace with yourself. So the critic keeps insisting on perfection, because it feels so good when you are, for that little while, perfect.

2. *Feeling accepted by critical parents.* To meet this need, your own critic joins your parents in attacking you. If your parents disparaged you for selfishness, your critic will do likewise. If your parents rejected your sexual behavior, the inner critic will also call you immoral. If your parents labeled you stupid or fat or a failure, then your critic will join them by calling you the same names. Every time you use a critical self-statement that agrees with your parents' negative judgments, you are reinforced by feeling close to them. By identifying with their point of view, you may paradoxically feel safer, more accepted, more loved. You are seeing things their way, and in joining them you experience a sense of belonging and emotional security that strongly reinforces your own critical voice.

The need to achieve. The critic helps you achieve goals by whipping you like an old dray horse. He drives you with vicious attacks on your worth. If you don't make three sales this week, you're lazy, you're incompetent, you're a lousy breadwinner. If you don't get a 3.5 average, you're stupid and talentless and will prove to everyone you aren't graduate school material. What reinforces the critic is that you do achieve things when driven. You do make sales, you do hit the books. And every time the critic drives you to complete a task, his caustic battering is reinforced.

Negative Reinforcement for the Critic

The need to control painful feelings. When the critic helps you to diminish or entirely stop painful feelings, his voice is highly reinforced. Even though the long-term effect is to destroy your self-esteem, the short-term effect of critical self-talk may be a reduction in painful affect. Here are some examples of how the critic can help you feel less guilty, afraid, depressed, and angry.

1. *Feeling not okay or bad or valueless.* On a very deep level, everyone has doubts about his or her worth. But if you have low self-esteem, those doubts can be magnified so that a good part of your inner life is dominated by feelings of inadequacy and hopelessness. That sense of inadequacy is so incredibly painful that you'll do almost anything to escape it. Enter the critic. The critic helps you cope by creating impossible standards of perfection. You have to get promoted every six months, cook gourmet meals, spend three hours a night helping your kid with his homework, be a total turn-on to your mate, and make nonstop, spicy conversation straight from the pages of *The New York Times Book Review.* The standard is impossible, but while the critic is driving you to be perfect, you no longer feel so inadequate, so hopeless. You feel instead a kind of omnipotence—if you just worked hard enough, kicked yourself hard enough, fought hard enough to transform yourself, all things would be possible.

2. *Fear of failure.* A woman who was contemplating a job search for a more creative kind of work began feeling very nervous at the thought of leaving the safety of her old job. Her critic came to the rescue. The critic said, "You can't do it. You'll be fired. You haven't got enough artistic talent. They'll see right through you." Under this barrage of self-rejecting statements, she decided to wait for a year before doing anything. Immediately her anxiety level decreased. And the critic was reinforced because his attack led directly to a reduction in her level of distress. The critic is very useful in protecting you against the anxiety inherent in change and risk taking. As soon as he undermines your confidence to the point where you abandon your plan for change, he's reinforced by your feeling of relief.

3. *Fear of rejection.* One way to control the fear of rejection is to constantly predict it so that you're never caught by surprise. The critic does a lot of mind reading: "She won't like you. He's bored to tears. They don't really want you on the committee. He doesn't like your work. Your lover's frown says he is losing interest." The mind reading helps to protect you against being caught by surprise. If you anticipate rejection, failure, or defeat, it won't hurt quite so badly when it comes. The critic's mind reading is reinforced on a variable ratio schedule. Once in a while, the critic does accurately predict some hurt or rejection. And since the anticipation helps desensitize you to the worst of the pain, the critic is reinforced to keep on mind reading.

   Another way to cope with the fear of rejection is to reject yourself first. When the critic attacks you for all your flaws and shortcomings, no one else can say anything you haven't already heard. A 38-year-old loan officer described it this way: "After my divorce, I kept calling myself a loser. I think that saying that protected me. It felt like if I kept saying it, nobody else would. They wouldn't have to call me a loser because I was doing it already." A well-known poet described the same feeling: "I always had a sense that if I kept putting my work down it would magically keep other people from doing it." Attacking yourself is very reinforcing if it helps relieve your anxiety about being attacked by others.

4. *Anger.* Feelings of anger toward people you love can be very frightening. As the anger begins to enter awareness, you may feel a huge surge of anxiety. One way of coping is to turn the anger around and attack yourself. You're the one who's failed, who hasn't understood, whose mistakes caused the problem in the first place. As the critic goes on the attack, your anxiety decreases. Now you won't have to risk hurting someone. Or worse, getting them so angry that they hurt you.

5. *Guilt.* The critic obligingly helps you deal with guilt by providing punishment. You have sinned, and the critic will make you pay. As the critic attacks you over and over for your selfishness, your greed, or your insensitivity, you gradually feel a sense of atonement, sometimes even a sense of undoing, as if the sin never happened. While you sit in the critic's screening room reviewing again and again videos of your transgressions, the feeling of guilt dissipates. The critic is reinforced once more because the violence he does to your sense of worth helps you to conquer for a while that awful feeling of wrongness.

6. *Frustration.* "I've nursed seven sick people all day, I've shopped, I've cooked, I've listened to some blaring lead guitar riffs from my son's room, I've got the bills spread out on the kitchen table. Those are the times I get down on myself. I think of all the stupid decisions I've made, and I get really angry. Like I'm the one who made this life, I lost the marriage, I'm the one who's so afraid I can't change anything. After a while I feel a little calmer and just go to bed" (thirty-six-year-old Intensive Care Unit nurse). Notice how the critic's attacks are reinforced by a drop in arousal levels. The self-directed anger has the effect of discharging tension from a tiring day, a noisy house, and anxiety over bills. When you use the critic to get angry at yourself, your covert goal may actually be an attempt to blow off high levels of frustration and negative arousal. The extent to which this strategy works and your tension is reduced is the extent to which the critic is reinforced for beating you up.

These examples of how the critic helps you meet basic needs are not exhaustive. They are designed to get you thinking about your critic and how his attacks get reinforced. It's extremely important that you learn to identify the function of your self-attacks, how they help as well as hurt you. Right now, go back over the list of positive and negative reinforcements for the critic. Put an asterisk by each one that applies to you. When you have determined which needs your critic is helping you to meet, and some of the ways his attacks get reinforced, you can go on to the next step: catching your critic.

Catching Your Critic

To gain control of the critic, you have to first be able to hear him. Every conscious moment of your life, you are engaging in an inner monologue. You are interpreting experience, problem solving, speculating about the future, reviewing past events. Most of this continuous self-talk is helpful, or at worst innocuous. But somewhere hidden in the monologue are your critic's indictments. Catching the critic in the act of putting you down requires a special vigilance. You have to keep listening in on the intercom of your inner monologue. You have to notice the critic when he says, "Stupid . . . another dumb mistake . . . you're weak . . . you'll never get a job because something's wrong with you . . . you're bad at conversation . . . you're turning her off."

Sometimes the critic hits you with images of past mistakes or failures. Sometimes he doesn't use words or images. The thought arrives as an awareness, a knowledge, an impression. The criticism is so lightning quick that it seems beyond the scope of language. A salesman put it this way: "There are times I just *know* I'm wasting my life. I can feel this sense of emptiness. It's like a heavy feeling in my stomach."

Catching the critic will take a real commitment. You'll need to be especially aware of your inner monologue in problematic situations:

- Meeting strangers

- Contact with people you find sexually attractive

- Situations in which you have made a mistake

- Situations in which you feel criticized and defensive

- Interactions with authority figures

- Situations in which you feel hurt or someone has been angry at you

- Situations in which you risk rejection or failure

- Conversations with parents or anyone who might be disapproving

Exercise

Monitor your critic. For one day, stay as vigilant as possible for self-attacks. Count the number of critical statements you make to yourself. You may be surprised at how frequently your internal monologue turns to negative self-appraisal. On days two and three, take a further step. Instead of just counting the critic's attacks, keep a notebook handy and write them down. Here's a sample taken from the notebook of a twenty-four-year-old first grade teacher:

Thought Number	Time	Critical Statement
1	8:15	The principal must be sick of my getting here late.
2	8:40	Skimpy lesson plan. God I'm lazy.
3	9:30	These kids are slow and I'm not helping them much.
4	9:45	Stupid to send Sheila with the lunch list, she'll fool around in the halls.
5	10:00	What kind of teacher are you? These kids are moving ahead so slow.
6	12:15	Stupid remark in the lunchroom.
7	12:20	Why am I so inane?
8	2:20	It was a madhouse today. When will I learn to control the class?
9	2:35	Why don't I get some of the kids' drawings on the wall boards? I'm so disorganized.
10	3:10	Parked like an idiot—look at the angle of the car.
11	3:40	Look at the mess. Nice housekeeping.

The more of these self-attacks you write down the better. Congratulate yourself if you catch at least ten of the critic's barbs each day.

At night you will have one more task. On a piece of typing or binder paper, draw a line down the middle. On one side put the heading, *Helps Me Avoid Feeling.* On the other put the heading, *Helps Me Feel or Do.* Now for each critical thought in your notebook, write down the function of that thought—how it is reinforced either positively or negatively, how it either allows you to feel or do something good or avoid feeling something unpleasant. Here's what the school teacher wrote:

Thought Number	Helps Me Feel or Do	Helps Me Avoid Feeling
1		Surprised and hurt if she calls me on my tardiness.
2	Motivated to be more careful with my work.	
3	Motivated to develop a more creative lesson plan, maybe get some consultation.	
4	Motivated to pay more attention to whom I send.	
5	Motivated to work harder at my lesson plan.	
6		Social anxiety. I already know I'm stupid so they can't hurt me.
7		Social anxiety.
8	Motivated to consult with other teachers on discipline techniques.	Surprised and hurt if the principal criticizes me.
9		Surprised and hurt if the principal criticizes me. Guilt at breaking my commitment to being more organized.
10	Motivated to pay more attention to how I park.	Guilt at parking unsafely.
11	Motivated to be more neat.	

As she went over her work, she realized, as you will when you do this exercise, that there were certain basic themes. Many of the critic's attacks were reinforced because the attacks drove her to higher levels of achievement and self-improvement. When she thought about it, she realized that the critic was setting very high standards of performance for her. On the few occasions when she actually met those standards, she had a wonderful feeling of self-acceptance. This feeling was intoxicating, and she knew it reinforced her perfectionism. She also noticed themes of avoiding social anxiety and fear of being surprised by a rejection. Armed with this new knowledge, the teacher was ready for the most important step: disarming the critic.

Disarming the Critic

By now you should be getting better acquainted with your critic. Hopefully you've improved at separating the critic's voice from the continuous stream of self-talk that goes on throughout the day. This task is a little bit like tapping the family phone of a suspected Mafioso. You have to sift through a lot of innocuous conversation in order to hear him betray himself. You can't stop listening, because at any moment he could say something incriminating.

Before you can disarm the critic, you have to know him. Secrecy is his greatest strength. So if you can get really good at hearing and identifying his voice, you will have won a major victory. Remember that every time the critic attacks he is doing you real psychological harm. He is further wounding your sense of worth and making it harder to feel competent and happy in the world. You can't afford what he is doing to you. It's costing you too much.

Since it's not really possible to stay on total alert every moment of your waking life, you need to know when you should be especially vigilant. In the last chapter, you were given a list of problematic situations—times when you have made a mistake, been criticized, or dealt with people who might be disapproving. But there's another time when you need to watch for the critic. That's when you are feeling depressed or down on yourself. These emotions are usually triggered by the critic, and their presence indicates that he is at work. In order to catch the critic in the act of making you depressed, you need to do four things:

1. Close your eyes and take some deep breaths. Draw the air deep into your abdomen so that your diaphragm can stretch and relax.

2. Relax your body. Notice and eliminate any tension in your legs and arms, your face, jaw, neck, and shoulders.

3. Notice where you feel depression in your body. Focus on that place and really get to know the feeling there.

4. Listen to the thoughts that go with the feeling in that part of your body. Notice everything that you're saying to yourself. Now try to remember how the feeling began and what the critic was saying then.

If you follow these four steps each time you feel depressed or down on yourself, you'll become much clearer about the specific content of the critic's attacks.

If you did the exercises in the last chapter, you are now more aware of the basic themes of your critical voice. As you analyze your critical thoughts, determining what they help you feel or help you avoid feeling, you'll begin to see a pattern to the attacks. One person may find that his critic's primary function is to help him atone for guilt. Someone else may experience a critic whose main effort is to provide achievement motivation. Another person's critic may help desensitize her to the fear of rejection. Or a critic may harangue you to stay on the straight and narrow path. When you become aware of the theme or themes your critic uses, you are ready to fight back.

Beginning to disarm the critic involves two steps: (1) unmasking his purpose, and (2) talking back.

Unmasking His Purpose

There are few things more effective for winning arguments than to suddenly unmask your opponent's ulterior motives. A classic example is tobacco company "research" that finds no link between cigarette smoking and heart disease. Since the ulterior motives of the tobacco industry are clear, few people take their arguments seriously.

When you unmask the critic, you expose his true purpose and functions. Here are some examples of ways you might unmask your critic:

• You're kicking me right now to force me to live by the rules I grew up with.

• You're comparing me to everyone so that once in a while I'll find someone lower on the totem pole than me.

• You're slapping me around like my parents used to do, and I believe you because I believed them.

- You're beating me so that I'll achieve more and more and maybe feel better about myself.

- You're insisting that I be perfect because if I did everything exactly right, I might finally feel okay about myself.

- You're saying I can't do it so that I won't bother trying and won't have to worry about screwing up.

- You're telling me they won't like me so that I won't be so hurt if I'm rejected.

- You're saying she's disgusted by me so that no matter what the truth is, I'll be prepared for the worst.

- You're telling me to be perfect so that I'll stupidly think that maybe I could be perfect and for a few minutes feel better about myself.

- You're kicking me around so that I can atone for divorcing Jill.

Getting clear about the critic's function makes everything he says less believable. You know his ulterior motive. No matter how he rants and raves, you've exposed his secret agenda and therefore feel less vulnerable to him. Remember that the critic attacks you because his voice is in some way being reinforced. When you are able to identify the role your critic plays in your psychological life, when you are able to call his game, you are beginning to seriously undermine the credibility of his message.

Talking Back

The idea of talking back to your own critical voice may seem strange to you. But in truth much of this book is about talking back: learning to refute and reject the old negative programming you received as a child. While growing up, Wanda received literally thousands of devaluing messages—first from her father, and then from her own critical voice. Whenever her father was angry, he would call her stupid. In particular, he ridiculed her for doing things "the hard way" and for getting only C's in high school. All of her life, Wanda has believed her father's judgment. These days, her critic constantly berates her for doing things "the stupid way." Wanda's self-esteem can't improve until she stops these messages by learning to talk back to the critic. She needs a psychological cannon to blow the critic away so that he finally shuts up.

What follows are three methods for talking back. Properly delivered, they will render the critic speechless for a few minutes. Experiment with each of them; try them singly and in combination. Find out which ones work best for you.

The Howitzer Mantras

These are selected words and phrases that are designed to hit the critic like a cannon blast. Here are some examples:

This is poison. Stop it!

These are lies.

These are lies my father told me.

Stop this shit!

No more put-downs.

Shut up!

Screw you, asshole.

To hell with these put-downs!

Get off my back!

Stop this garbage!

Choose a mantra that helps you feel angry. It's good to get mad. Profanity is a perfectly healthy response to the critic. When using the Howitzer Mantras, shout them inside. Mentally scream at the critic so that you can drown him out with your anger and indignation.

If the critic continues his assault despite your telling him to "shut up" or "stop this nonsense," it's time for stronger measures. Put a rubber band around your wrist and snap it while subvocalizing your mantra. Let's say, for example, that the critic is kicking you about some aspect of your appearance. One of your mantras is "Stop this shit!" You scream it internally and simultaneously snap the rubber band. By snapping the rubber band, you are emphasizing your "stop" commands and making successful thought-interruption more likely. The sharp stinging sensation breaks the chain of negative cognitions and acts as a punisher so that the critic is less likely to attack in the near future. The important thing is to catch the critic just as he starts, before he is allowed to do much damage. If you snap the rubber band and internally scream your mantra whenever you hear the critic's voice, the frequency of his attacks will greatly diminish.

Asking the price

One of the best ways to disarm the critic is to think about the price you pay for his attacks. What does listening to the critic cost you? A thirty-two-year-old sales representative for a printing firm made the following list as he evaluated the toll the critic took on his work, relationships, and level of well-being.

- Defensive with my wife about any criticism.

- Blow up at my daughter when she doesn't mind.

- Lost friendship with Al because I got hostile.

- Dump on my mother when I detect the slightest criticism.

- Afraid to be assertive with potential clients because they might reject me. (This probably costs me ten thousand a year in commissions.)

- Tend to be cold and distant with bosses and authorities because I am afraid of them.

- Feel anxious and on guard with people.

- Constantly thinking that people don't like me.

- Afraid to try new things for fear that I'll screw them up.

Poor self-esteem was costing the sales representative a great deal in every area of his life. When the critic attacked, he could now talk back by saying, "You make me defensive and afraid of people, you cut my income, you lose me friends, you make me harsh with my little girl."

It's time for you to evaluate the cost of your own critic. Make a list of ways in which your self-esteem has affected you in terms of your relationships, work, and level of well-being. When you've completed the list, combine the most important items into a summary statement that you can use when the critic attacks. Fight back by telling the critic, "I can't afford this, you've cost me . . ."

Affirmation of worth

This method is very hard to practice—especially if you have a deeply held belief that there is something wrong with you, that you are not okay. But you must learn to affirm yourself if you are to fully disarm the critic. The first two methods of talking back are important, but they aren't enough. You can't *permanently* turn off the critic's vitriol by calling him names, telling him to shut up, and insisting that he costs too much. That helps for a while. But you're creating a vacuum by silencing the critic without putting anything in his place. And soon enough his voice will be back, filling that vacuum with more attacks. When the critic has been silenced, you need to replace his voice with a positive awareness of your own worth.

Affirming your worth is no easy task. Right now you believe that your worth depends on your behavior. Metaphorically, you see yourself as an empty vessel that must be filled, drop by drop, with your achievements. You start out essentially worthless, a body that moves and talks. The critic would have you believe that there is no *intrinsic* value in a life, only a *potential for* doing something worthwhile, something important.

The truth is that your value is your consciousness, your ability to perceive and experience. The value of a human life is that it exists. You are a complex miracle of creation. You are a person who is trying to live, and that makes you as worthwhile as every other person who is doing the very same thing. Achievement has nothing to do with it. Whatever you do, whatever you contribute should come not from the need to prove your value, but from the natural flow of your aliveness. What you do should come from the drive to fully live, rather than the fight to justify yourself.

Whether you're a researcher unlocking the cure for cancer or a guy sweeping the street, you have known hope and fear, affection and loss, wanting and disappointment. You have looked out at the world and tried to make sense of it, you have coped with the unique set of problems you were born into, you have endured pain. Over the years you've tried many strategies to help you feel better in the face of pain. Some of your strategies have worked, some haven't. Some have worked short-term, but in the long run brought greater distress. It doesn't matter. You are just trying to live. And in spite of all that is hard in life, you are still trying. This is your worth, you humanness.

The following affirmations are examples of things you might say to yourself to keep the critic at bay.

- I am worthwhile because I breathe and feel and am aware.

- Why do I hurt myself? I am trying to survive, I do the best I can.

- I feel pain, I love, I try to survive. I am a good person.

- My pain, my hope, my struggle to survive links me to every other human being. We are all just trying to live and we are doing the best we can.

One of these may feel right to you. Or none of them. What's important is that you arrive at a statement that you do believe and that you can use to replace your critical voice.

For additional training in talking back to your critic, see the chapters in this part on Uncovering Automatic Thoughts, Changing Patterns of Limited Thinking, and Changing Hot Thoughts.

Excerpted and adapted with permission from *Self-Esteem* by Matthew McKay, Ph.D., and Patrick Fanning. For more information on this and related books, see the "Further Reading" section in the back of the book.

CHAPTER 30

Uncovering Automatic Thoughts

Our automatic thoughts and beliefs about ourselves, others, and particular circumstances have an enormous impact on how we see the world. Often, our automatic thoughts negatively influence our perspective—without our even realizing it. This chapter will help you identify some of your own automatic thoughts and observe how they are affecting your life.

Uncovering Automatic Thoughts

Thoughts cause feelings. This is the essential insight of cognitive therapy. All of the cognitive techniques that have been developed and refined in the last half of the twentieth century flow out of this one simple idea: that thoughts cause feelings, and many emotions you feel are preceded and caused by a thought, however abbreviated, fleeting, or unnoticed that thought may be.

In other words, events by themselves have no emotional content. It is your interpretation of an event that causes your emotions. This is often represented as the "ABC" model of emotions:

A. Event ──────▶ B. Thought ──────▶ C. Feeling

For example:

A. Event: You get into your car, turn the key, and nothing happens.

B. Thought: You interpret the event by saying to yourself, "Oh no, my battery's dead. This is awful; I'm stuck—I'll be late."

C. Feeling: You experience an emotion appropriate to your thoughts. In this case, you feel depressed and anxious about being late.

Change the thought and you change the feeling. If you had thought, "My son must have left the lights on all night again," you might have felt anger. If you had thought, "I'll have an extra cup of coffee, relax, and wait for a jump from the tow truck," you would have felt mild annoyance at most.

In this chapter you will learn how to uncover the automatic thoughts in this cycle. This is the basic skill you need to master in order to use cognitive therapy to reduce painful feelings.

Symptom Effectiveness

By itself, uncovering automatic thoughts is not considered a full-scale treatment. It is the first step in many different cognitive behavioral treatments. However, you may feel some immediate reduction in anxiety, depression, or anger as a result of exploring how you react to upsetting situations. This is a good sign that cognitive therapy is likely to help you quickly. On the other hand, it is more likely that you will not experience any improvement in symptoms by the end of this chapter. In fact, some feelings may actually intensify as a result of exploring them. Don't worry. Remember that this is an early step along the way.

Time for Mastery

Most people make significant progress during the first week of faithfully keeping a Thought Journal. The longer you practice tuning into your automatic thoughts, the better you get at it. It's a skill like knitting, skiing, writing, or singing on key—practice makes perfect.

Instructions

Negative Feedback Loop

The Event ————→ Thought ————→ Feeling sequence is the basic building block of emotional life. But the building blocks can become very jumbled and confusing. The emotional life of real people is not always a simple series of ABC reactions, each with its discrete starting event, thought, and resultant feeling. More often a series of ABC reactions join in a feedback loop. The ending feeling from one sequence becomes the starting event for another sequence.

In the case of painful feelings, a negative feedback loop can be set up in which an uncomfortable feeling itself becomes an "event," the subject of further thoughts, which produce more painful feelings, which become a larger event inspiring more negative thoughts, and so on. The loop continues until you work yourself into a rage, an anxiety attack, or a deep depression.

Feelings have physiological components. When you experience emotions such as fear, anger, or joy, your heart speeds up, you breathe faster and less deeply, you sweat more, and your blood vessels contract and dilate in different parts of your body. "Quiet" emotions such as depression, sadness, or grief involve a slowing down of some of your physiological systems. Both your emotion and the accompanying bodily sensations trigger an evaluation process—you start trying to interpret and label what you feel.

Feedback Loop

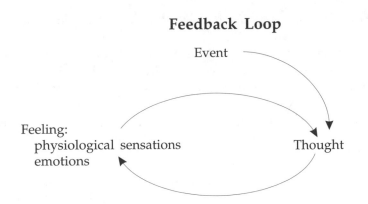

For example, if your car wouldn't start late at night when you were in a bad neighborhood, the negative feedback loop might go like this:

A. Event: Car doesn't start.

B. Thought: "Oh no, this is awful. I'll be late—and this is a dangerous street."

C. Heart beating fast, feeling hot and sweaty, irritation, anxiety.

B. Thought: "I'm scared . . . I could get mugged—this is really bad!"

C. Stomach clenching, hard to breathe, dizzy, fear.

B. Thought: "I'm freaking out . . . I'll lose control. . . . Can't move . . . can't get safe."

C. Strong adrenaline rush, panic.

The Nature of Automatic Thoughts

You are constantly describing the world to yourself, giving each event or experience some label. You automatically make interpretations of everything you see, hear, touch, and feel. You judge events as good or bad, pleasurable or painful, safe or dangerous. This process colors all of your experiences, labeling them with private meanings.

These labels and judgments are fashioned from the unending dialog you have with yourself, a waterfall of thoughts cascading down the back of your mind. These thoughts are constant and rarely noticed, but they are powerful enough to create your most intense emotions. The internal dialog is called self-talk by rational-emotive therapist Albert Ellis, and automatic thoughts by cognitive theorist Aaron Beck. Beck prefers the term automatic thoughts "because it more accurately describes the way thoughts are experienced. The person perceives these thoughts as though they are by reflex—without any prior reflection or reasoning; and they impress him as plausible and valid" (Beck 1976)

Automatic thoughts usually have the following characteristics:

1. **They often appear in shorthand,** composed of just a few essential words phrased in telegraphic style: "lonely . . . getting sick . . . can't stand it . . . cancer . . . no good." One word or a short phrase functions as a label for a group of painful memories, fears, or self-reproaches.

   An automatic thought needn't be expressed in words at all. It can be a brief visual image, an imagined sound or smell, or any physical sensation. A woman who was afraid of heights had a half-second image of the floor tilting and felt herself sliding down toward the window. This momentary fantasy triggered acute anxiety whenever she ascended above the third floor.

Sometimes the automatic thought is a brief reconstruction of some event in the past. A depressed woman kept seeing the stairway in Macy's where her husband had first announced his plan to leave her. The image of the stairway was enough to unleash all the feelings associated with that loss.

Occasionally an automatic thought can take the form of intuitive knowledge, without words, images, or sense impressions. For example, a chef who was plagued with self-doubt "just knew" that it was useless to try to get promoted to head chef.

2. **Automatic thoughts are almost always believed**, no matter how illogical they appear upon analysis. For example, a man who reacted with rage to the death of his best friend actually believed for a time that his friend deliberately died to punish him.

Automatic thoughts have the same believable quality as direct sense impressions. You attach the same truth value to automatic thoughts as you do to sights and sounds in the real world. If you see a man getting into a Porsche and have the thought, "He's rich; he doesn't care for anyone but himself," the judgment is as real to you as the color of the car.

3. **Automatic thoughts are experienced as spontaneous.** You believe automatic thoughts because they are automatic. They seem to arise spontaneously out of ongoing events. They just pop into your mind and you hardly notice them, let alone subject them to logical analysis.

4. **Automatic thoughts are often couched in terms of should, ought, or must**. A woman who's husband had recently died thought, "You ought to go it alone. You shouldn't burden your friends." Each time the thought popped into her mind, she felt a wave of hopelessness. People torture themselves with "shoulds" such as "I should be happy. I should be more energetic, creative, responsible, loving, generous. . . ." Each ironclad "should" precipitates a sense of guilt or a loss of self-esteem.

"Shoulds" are hard to eradicate, since their origin and function is actually adaptive. They are simple rules to live by that have worked in the past. They are templates for survival that you can access quickly in times of stress. The problem is that they become so automatic that you don't have time to analyze them, and so rigid that you can't modify them to fit changing situations.

5. **Automatic thoughts tend to "awfulize."** These thoughts predict catastrophe, see danger in everything, and always expect the worst. A stomachache is a symptom of cancer, the look of distraction in a lover's face is the first sign of withdrawal. "Awfulizers" are the major source of anxiety.

Awfulizers are also hard to eradicate because of their adaptive function. They help you predict the future and prepare for the worst-case scenario.

6. **Automatic thoughts are relatively idiosyncratic.** In a crowded theater a woman suddenly stood up, slapped the face of the man next to her, and hurried up the aisle and out the exit. The witnesses to this event reacted in different ways.

One woman was frightened because she thought, "She's really going to get it when they get home." She imagined the details of a brutal beating and recalled times when she had been physically abused. A teenager was angry because he thought, "That poor guy. He probably just wanted a kiss and she humiliated him. What a bitch." A middle-aged man became depressed when he told himself, "Now he's lost her and he'll never get her back." He could see his ex-wife's face set in angry lines. A social worker felt a pleasurable excitement as she thought, "Serves him right. I wish some timid women I know had seen that."

Each response was based on a unique way of viewing the stimulus event and resulted in a different strong emotion.

7. **Automatic thoughts are persistent and self-perpetuating.** They are hard to turn off or change because they are reflexive and plausible. They weave unnoticed through the fabric of your internal dialog and seem to come and go with a will of their own. One automatic thought tends to act as a cue for another and another and another. You may have experienced this chaining effect as one depressing thought triggers a long chain of associated depressing thoughts.

8. **Automatic thoughts often differ from your public statements.** Most people talk to others very differently from the way they talk to themselves. To others they usually describe events in their lives as logical sequences of cause and effect. But to themselves they may describe the same events with self-deprecating venom or dire predictions.

One executive calmly explained aloud, "Since I got laid off, I've been a little depressed." This matter-of-fact statement differed sharply from the actual thoughts that unemployment triggered in him: "I'm a failure . . . I'll never work again . . . My family will starve . . . I can't make it in this world." He had an image of himself spiraling down into a bottomless black pit.

9. **Automatic thoughts repeat habitual themes.** Chronic anger, anxiety, or depression results from a focus on one particular group of automatic thoughts to the exclusion of all contrary thoughts. The theme of anxious people is danger. They are preoccupied with the anticipation of dangerous situations, forever scanning the horizon for future pain. Depressed individuals often focus on the past and obsess about the theme of loss. They also focus on their own feelings and flaws. Chronically angry people repeat automatic thoughts about the hurtful and deliberate behavior of others.

Preoccupation with these habitual themes creates a kind of tunnel vision in which you think only one kind of thought and notice only one aspect of your environment. The result is one predominant and usually quite painful emotion. Beck has used the term selective abstraction to describe this tunnel vision. Selective abstraction means looking at one set of cues in your environment to the exclusion of all others.

10. **Automatic thoughts are learned.** Since childhood people have been telling you what to think. You have been conditioned by family, friends, and the media to interpret events a certain way. Over the years you have learned and practiced habitual patterns of automatic thoughts that are difficult to detect, let alone change. That's the bad news. The good news is that what has been learned can be unlearned and changed.

Listening to Your Automatic Thoughts

Hearing your automatic thoughts is the first step in gaining control of unpleasant emotions. Most of your internal dialog is harmless. The automatic thoughts that cause harm can be identified because they almost always precede a continuing painful feeling.

To identify the automatic thoughts that are causing a continued painful feeling, try to recall the thoughts you had just prior to the start of the emotion and those that go along with the sustained emotion. You can think of it as listening in on an intercom. The intercom is always on, even while you are conversing with others and going about your life. You are functioning in the world and you are also talking to yourself at the same time. Listen in on the intercom of your internal dialog, and hear what you are telling yourself. Your automatic thoughts are assigning private, idiosyncratic meanings to many external events and internal sensations. They are making judgments and interpretations of your experience.

Automatic thoughts are often lightning fast and very difficult to catch. They flash on as a brief mental image, or are telegraphed in a single word. Here are two methods for coping with the swiftness of your thoughts:

1. Reconstruct a problem situation, going over it again and again in your imagination until the painful emotion begins to emerge. What are you thinking as the emotion comes up? Regard your thoughts as a slow-motion film. Look at your internal dialog, frame by frame. Notice the millisecond it takes to say, "I can't stand it," or the half-second image of a terrifying event. Notice how you are internally describing and interpreting the actions of others: "She's bored. . . . He's putting me down."

2. Stretch out the shorthand statement into the original sentence from which it was extracted. "Feeling sick" is really "I'm feeling sick and I know I'm going to get worse . . . I can't stand it." "Crazy" means "I feel like I'm losing control, and that must mean I'm going crazy. . . . My friends will reject me."

Hearing the shorthand isn't enough. It is necessary to listen to your entire interior argument in order to understand the distorted logic from which your painful emotions bloom.

Recording Your Thoughts

To appreciate the power of your automatic thoughts and the part they play in your emotional life, keep a Thought Journal. As soon as possible after you experience an unpleasant feeling, record it on the form that follows.

The form is self-explanatory, except for how to rate your feelings. The Thought Journal allows you to assess your distress level with a scale running from 0 (the feeling causes no distress) to 100 (the most distressing emotion you have ever felt).

Make several copies of this journal and carry one with you at all times. You will use the material you generate in your Thought Journal in the next two chapters.

Use your Thought Journal for one week, making an entry only when you feel a painful emotion. You may find that concentrating on your automatic thoughts makes the feelings worse for a while. Keep working on it—it's normal to feel worse before you start to feel better.

The process of uncovering automatic thoughts may also make you begin to distrust these thoughts and begin questioning and disputing them as they pop up. The next chapter, on changing patterns of limited thinking, will give you specific tools for disputing automatic thoughts.

At this point it is important for you to recognize that thoughts create and sustain emotions. To reduce the frequency of painful emotions, you will first need to listen to what you think, then ask how true it is. What you think will ultimately create what you feel.

Thought Counting

Sometimes thoughts come so quickly and in such abbreviated form that you can't identify them, even though you know you just had some. In that case, you can simply count automatic thoughts.

Thought Journal

Situation	Feelings	Automatic Thoughts
When? Where? Who? What happened?	*One-word summaries Rate 0–100*	*What you were thinking just before and during the unpleasant feeling*

Thought Journal

Situation *When? Where? Who? What happened?*	Feelings *One-word summaries Rate 0–100*	Automatic Thoughts *What you were thinking just before and during the unpleasant feeling*
Stuck on freeway	anger **80**	Late Boss angry Last one in Have to rush all day
Given extra work	anxiety **90**	I'll be here all night Can't stand it Jenny will be mad if I'm late
Given extra work	resentment **75**	They always dump on me It's not fair
Have to work through lunch	anxiety **85**	I'm hungry, I'm tired I can't stand this
Have to work through lunch	anger **65**	Why don't they get enough staff to help? This is ridiculous
Working late, have to call wife	anxiety **75**	She's really going to blow up
Driving home	depression **80**	This is my whole life There's no way out of this
Watching TV with kids	depression **90**	They never talk to me They hardly know me They don't care
Wife goes to bed early	depression **75**	She's really mad She's disgusted with me

Each time you notice that you've had an automatic thought, make a mark on a three-by-five card you carry with you. You can also keep track of the number of your automatic thoughts on a golf wrist-counter or a knitting stitch-counter.

Counting your automatic thoughts helps get some distance from them and a feeling of control. Rather than assuming that your automatic thoughts are an accurate assessment of events, you are noting them and letting them go. Once you've counted a thought, you needn't dwell on it.

This process will eventually slow your thoughts and sharpen your attention so that the actual content of the thoughts starts to become clear. When that happens, you may want to continue counting, this time categorizing your thoughts and counting how many you have of various types: catastrophic thoughts, loss thoughts, insecure thoughts, and so on.

If you forget to count your thoughts, set your watch alarm or a timer to go off every twenty minutes. When the alarm or timer goes off, stop what you're doing and look inside yourself. Count any negative thoughts you notice.

References

Beck, A. T. 1976. *Cognitive Therapy and the Emotional Disorders.* New York: International Universities Press.

Excerpted and adapted with permission from *Thoughts and Feelings: Taking Control of Your Moods and Your Life* by Matthew McKay, Ph.D., Martha Davis, Ph.D., and Patrick Fanning. For more information on this and related books, see the "Further Reading" section in the back of the book.

CHAPTER 31

Changing Patterns of Limited Thinking

A man walks up to a drugstore counter and asks for a particular brand of dental floss. The clerk says it's out of stock. The man concludes that the clerk has the dental floss, but just wants to get rid of him because she doesn't like his looks. This logic seems obviously irrational and paranoid.

But consider the case of the woman whose husband comes home with a cloudy look on his face. She immediately concludes that he is angry because she was too tired to make love the previous night. She expects to be hurt by some sort of retaliation and responds quickly by becoming peevish and defensive. This logic makes perfect sense to her and she does not question her conclusion until she learns that her husband had a minor auto accident on the way home.

The progression of logic she used goes like this:

1. My husband looks upset.

2. My husband often gets upset when I disappoint him.

3. Therefore, he's upset with me for disappointing him.

The problem with this logic lies in her assumptions that her husband's moods must all relate to her and that she is the prime cause of his ups and downs. This pattern of limited thinking is called personalization, the tendency to relate all the objects and events around you to yourself. Personalization limits you and causes pain because you consistently misinterpret what you see and then act on that misinterpretation.

This chapter will examine eight limited thinking patterns and give you practice in identifying them. The chapter continues by teaching you to analyze the automatic thoughts you recorded in the chapter on Uncovering Automatic Thoughts, noticing which of the limited thinking patterns you habitually employ in difficult situations. You'll learn how to compose balanced, alternative self-statements that will become more believable than your painful automatic thoughts.

Symptom Effectiveness

Challenging automatic thoughts is a powerful way to counter perfectionism, curb procrastination, and relieve depression and anxiety.

The techniques in this chapter are based on the cognitive therapy of Aaron Beck (1976), who pioneered the method of analyzing automatic thoughts for cognitive distortions and to compose rational comebacks to refute and replace distorted thinking. This approach works well for abstract thinkers—people who can analyze their automatic thoughts to find thematic patterns of limited thinking.

Time for Mastery

You should begin to get results in one to four weeks of analyzing your automatic thoughts.

If you try all of the exercises in this chapter and still have difficulty picking out your limited-thinking patterns, don't give up hope. Go on to the chapter on Changing Hot Thoughts, which will help you accomplish the same result by compiling the evidence for and against the thoughts that trigger your painful emotions.

Instructions

Eight Patterns of Limited Thinking

1. **Filtering** This pattern is characterized by a sort of tunnel vision—looking at only one element of a situation to the exclusion of everything else. A single detail is picked out and the whole event or situation is colored by this detail. For example, a computer draftsman who was uncomfortable with criticism was praised for the quality of his recent detail drawings and asked if he could get the next job out a little more quickly. He went home depressed, having decided that his employer thought he was dawdling. He filtered out the praise and focused only on the criticism.

    Each person looks through his or her own particular tunnel. Depressed people are hypersensitive to loss and blind to gain. For anxious people, the slightest possibility of danger sticks out like a barb in a scene that is otherwise safe and secure. People who experience chronic anger look through a tunnel that highlights evidence of injustice and screens out fairness and equity.

    Memory can also be very selective. You may remember only certain kinds of events from your entire history and stock of experience. When you filter your memories, you often pass over positive experiences and dwell only on the memories that characteristically leave you angry, anxious, or depressed.

    The filtering pattern "awfulizes" your thoughts by pulling negative events out of context and magnifying them, while ignoring all your good experiences. Your fears, losses, and irritations become exaggerated in importance because they fill your awareness to the exclusion of everything else. Key words for the filtering pattern are terrible, awful, disgusting, scary, horrendous, and so on. A key phrase is "I can't stand it."

2. **Polarized Thinking** This is black-and-white thinking, with no shades of gray allowed. You insist on "either/or" choices, perceiving everything at the extremes with very little room for a middle ground. People and things are good or bad, wonderful or horrible, delightful or intolerable. Since your interpretations are extreme, your emotional reactions are extreme, fluctuating from despair to elation to rage to ecstasy to terror.

The greatest danger in polarized thinking is its impact on how you judge yourself. You could believe that if you aren't successful or brilliant, then you must be a failure or an imbecile. There's no room for mistakes or mediocrity. For example, a charter bus driver told himself he was a real loser when he took the wrong freeway exit and had to drive two miles out of his way. One mistake meant that he was incompetent and worthless. A single mother with three children was determined to be strong and "in charge." The moment she felt tired or nervous, she began thinking of herself as weak and disgusting, and she often criticized herself in conversations with friends.

3. **Overgeneralization** In this pattern you make a broad, general conclusion based on a single incident or piece of evidence. One dropped stitch leads you to conclude: "I'll never learn how to knit." You interpret a rejection on the dance floor as: "Nobody would ever want to dance with me."

This pattern can lead to an increasingly restricted life. If you got sick on a train once, you decide never to take a train again. If you got dizzy on a sixth floor balcony, you never go out there again. If you felt anxious the last time your husband took a business trip, you'll be a wreck every time he leaves town. One bad experience means that whenever you're in a similar situation you will repeat the bad experience.

Overgeneralizations are often couched in the form of absolute statements, as if there were some immutable law that governs and limits your chances for happiness. Some of the cue words that indicate you may be overgeneralizing are all, every, none, never, always, everybody, and nobody. For example, you are overgeneralizing when you absolutely conclude: "Nobody loves me," "I'll never be able to trust anyone again," "I will always be sad," "I could never get a better job," "No one would stay friends with me if they really knew me."

Another hallmark of overgeneralization is the global label for persons, places, and things you don't like: Somebody who refused to give you a ride home is labeled a "total jerk." A quiet guy on a date is a "dull clam." Republicans are "greedy corporate toadies." New York City is "hell on earth." Television is an "evil, corrupting influence." You're "stupid" and "totally wasting your life."

Each of these labels may contain a grain of truth, but it generalizes that grain into a global judgment. The overgeneralized label ignores all contrary evidence, making your view of the world stereotyped and one-dimensional.

4. **Mind Reading** When you mind read, you make snap judgments about others. You assume you know how others are feeling and what motivates them: "He's just acting that way because he's jealous" "She's only interested in your money" "He's afraid to show he cares."

If your brother visits a new woman acquaintance three times in one week, you might conclude that he is (a) in love, (b) angry at his old girlfriend and hoping she'll find out, (c) depressed and on the rebound, or (d) afraid of being alone again. Without asking, you have no way of knowing which is true. Mind reading makes one conclusion seem so obviously correct that you assume it's true, act on it in some inappropriate way, and get into trouble.

As a mind reader, you also make assumptions about how people are reacting to you. You might assume what your boyfriend is thinking and say to yourself, "This close he sees how unattractive I am." If he is mind reading too, he may be saying to himself, "She thinks I'm really immature." You may have a casual encounter with your supervisor at work and come away thinking, "They're getting ready to fire me." These assumptions are born of intuition, hunches, vague misgivings, or a couple of past experiences. They are untested and unprovable, but you believe them nonetheless.

Mind reading depends on a process called projection. You imagine that people feel the same way you do and react to things the same way you do. Therefore you don't watch or listen closely enough to notice that they are actually different. If you get angry when someone is late, you imagine everyone feels that way. If you feel excruciatingly sensitive to rejection, you expect that most people are the same. If you are very judgmental about particular habits and traits, you assume others share your beliefs.

5. **Catastrophizing** If you "catastrophize," a small leak in the sailboat means it will surely sink. A contractor whose estimate gets underbid concludes he'll never get another job. A headache suggests that brain cancer is looming. Catastrophic thoughts often start with the words what if. You read a newspaper article describing a tragedy or hear gossip about some disaster befalling an acquaintance, and you start wondering, "What if it happens to me? What if I break my leg skiing? What if they hijack my plane? What if I get sick and have to go on disability? What if my son starts taking drugs?" The list is endless. There are no limits to a really fertile catastrophic imagination.

6. **Magnifying** When you magnify, you emphasize things out of proportion to their actual importance. Small mistakes become tragic failures. Minor suggestions become scathing criticism. A slight backache becomes a ruptured disk. Minor setbacks become cause for despair. Slight obstacles become overwhelming barriers.

Words like huge, impossible, and overwhelming are magnifying terms. This pattern creates a tone of doom and hysterical pessimism.

The flip side of magnifying is minimizing. When you magnify, you view everything negative and difficult in your life through a telescope that magnifies your problems. But when you view your assets, such as your ability to cope and find solutions, you look through the wrong end of the telescope so that everything positive is minimized.

7. **Personalization** There are two kinds of personalization. The first kind involves directly comparing yourself with other people: "He plays piano so much better than I," "I'm not smart enough to go with this crowd," "She knows herself a lot better than I do," "He feels things so deeply while I'm dead inside," "I'm the slowest person in the office." Sometimes the comparison is actually favorable to you: "He's dumb (and I'm smart)," "I'm better looking than she." The opportunities for comparison never end. And, even when the comparison is favorable, the underlying assumption is that your worth is questionable. Consequently you must continue to test your value, constantly measuring yourself against others. If you come out better, you have a moment's relief. If you come up short, you feel diminished.

This chapter began with an example of the other kind of personalization—the tendency to relate everything around you to yourself. A depressed mother blames herself when she sees any sadness in her children. A businessman thinks that every time his partner complains of being tired he means he's tired, of him. A man whose wife complains of rising prices hears the complaints as attacks on his ability as a breadwinner.

8. **Shoulds** In this pattern, you operate from a list of inflexible rules about how you and other people should act. The rules are right and indisputable. Any deviation from your particular values or standards is bad. As a result, you are often judging others and finding fault. People irritate you. They don't act correctly and they don't think correctly. They have unacceptable traits, habits, and opinions that make them hard to tolerate. They should know the rules, and they should follow them.

One woman felt that her husband should want to take her on Sunday drives. She decided that a man who loves his wife ought to take her to the country and then out to eat in a nice place. The fact that he didn't want to meant that he "only thought about himself." Cue words indicating the presence of this pattern are should, ought, or must. In fact, Albert Ellis (1961) has dubbed this thinking pattern "musterbation."

Your shoulds are just as hard on you as they are on other people. You feel compelled to be or act a certain way, but you never bother to ask objectively if it really makes sense. Psychiatrist Karen Horney (1939) called this the "tyranny of shoulds."

Here is a list of some of the most common and unreasonable shoulds:

- I should be the epitome of generosity, consideration, dignity, courage, and unselfishness.
- I should be the perfect lover, friend, parent, teacher, student, or spouse.
- I should be able to endure any hardship with equanimity.
- I should be able to find a quick solution to every problem.
- I should never feel hurt; I should always be happy and serene.
- I should know, understand, and foresee everything.
- I should always be spontaneous, but also always control my feelings.
- I should never feel certain emotions, such as anger or jealousy.
- I should love my children equally.
- I should never make mistakes.
- My emotions should be constant. Once I feel love, I should always feel love.
- I should be totally self-reliant.
- I should assert myself but I should never hurt anybody else.
- I should never be tired or get sick.
- I should always be at peak efficiency.

Summary

Eight Limited-Thinking Patterns

1. **Filtering:** You focus on the negative details while ignoring all the positive aspects of a situation.

2. **Polarized Thinking:** Things are black or white, good or bad. You have to be perfect or you're a failure. There's no middle ground, no room for mistakes.

3. **Overgeneralization:** You reach a general conclusion based on a single incident or piece of evidence. You exaggerate the frequency of problems and use negative global labels.

4. **Mind Reading:** Without their saying so, you know what people are feeling and why they act the way they do. In particular, you have certain knowledge of how people think and feel about you.

5. **Catastrophizing:** You expect, even visualize disaster. You notice or hear about a problem and start asking, "What if?": What if tragedy strikes? What if it happens to you?

6. **Magnifying:** You exaggerate the degree or intensity of a problem. You turn up the volume on anything bad, making it loud, large, and overwhelming.

7. **Personalization:** You assume that everything people do or say is some kind of reaction to you. You also compare yourself to others, trying to determine who is smarter, more competent, better looking, and so on.

8. **Shoulds:** You have a list of ironclad rules about how you and other people should act. People who break the rules anger you, and you feel guilty when you violate the rules.

Exercises

The following exercises are designed to help you notice and identify limited-thinking patterns. Work through the exercises one after another. Refer back to the above summary and carefully analyze how each statement or situation is based on one or more limited-thinking patterns.

Matching Exercise

Draw a line connecting the sentence in the first column and the pattern it exemplifies in the second column.

Statement	Pattern
1. Ever since Lisa, I've never trusted a redhead.	Filtering
2. Quite a few people here seem smarter than me.	Polarized Thinking
3. You're either for me or against me.	Overgeneralization
4. I could have enjoyed the picnic, but the chicken was burnt.	Mind Reading
5. He's always smiling, but I know he doesn't like me.	Catastrophizing
6. I'm afraid the relationship's over because he hasn't called for two days.	Magnifying
7. You should never ask people personal questions.	Personalization
8. These tax forms are impossible—I'll never get finished.	Shoulds

Answer Key
1. Overgeneralization
2. Personalization
3. Polarized Thinking
4. Filtering
5. Mind Reading
6. Catastrophizing
7. Shoulds
8. Magnifying

Multiple Choice

In this exercise, circle the limited-thinking pattern(s) present in each example. There may be more than one right answer.

1. The washing machine breaks down. A mother with twins in diapers says to herself, "This always happens. I can't stand it. The whole day's ruined."

    a. Overgeneralization   c. Shoulds   e. Filtering
    b. Polarized Thinking   d. Mind Reading

2. "He looked up from across the table and said, 'That's interesting.' I knew he was dying for breakfast to be over so he could get away from me."

    a. Magnifying   c. Shoulds   e. Personalization
    b. Polarized Thinking   d. Mind Reading

3. A man was trying to get his girlfriend to be warmer and more supportive. He got irritated every night when she didn't ask him how his day was or failed to give him the attention he expected.

a. Shoulds   c. Overgeneralization   e. Magnifying
b. Personalization d. Catastrophizing

4. A driver feels nervous on long trips, afraid of having car trouble or getting sick and being stranded far from home. Faced with having to drive 500 miles to Chicago and back, he tells himself, "It's too far. My car has over 60,000 miles on it—it'll never make it."

a. Overgeneralization c. Filtering   e. Mind Reading
b. Catastrophizing   d. Magnifying

5. Getting ready for the prom, a high school student thinks, "I've got the worst hips in my homeroom, and the second-worst hair. . . . If this French twist comes undone, I'll just die. I'll never get it back together and the evening will be ruined. . . . I hope Ron gets his dad's car. If only he does, everything will be perfect."

a. Personalization   c. Filtering   e. Catastrophizing
b. Polarized Thinking d. Mind Reading

Answer Key
1. a, e
2. d.
3. a.
4. b, d
5. a, b, e

Circle the Pattern and Quote the Phrase

The following exercises require a little more work on your part. Read the statement and circle the applicable patterns in the list following the statement. Next to each pattern, write the phrase that contains it.

1. "Jim's so easily upset, you just can't talk to him. He blows up at everything. He just doesn't have my patience. What if he blows up at work? He'll lose his job and we'll be homeless in about two weeks."

Pattern	Phrase Containing the Pattern
Filtering	
Polarized Thinking	
Overgeneralization	
Mind Reading	
Catastrophizing	
Magnifying	
Personalization	
Shoulds	

2. "One time she came up to me and said, 'This nursing station looks like a cyclone hit it. Better clean up the mess before the shift is over.' Well, I said, 'This was a mess when I got here. It's not my fault. The night shift shouldn't be allowed to punch out unless all the charts are filed.' She knew it wasn't my mess. She wants to fire me and she's just looking for an excuse."

Pattern	Phrase Containing the Pattern
Filtering	_____
Polarized Thinking	_____
Overgeneralization	_____
Mind Reading	_____
Catastrophizing	_____
Magnifying	_____
Personalization	_____
Shoulds	_____

3. "A lot of the time I feel nervous when I'm out with Ed. I keep thinking how smart he is, how sophisticated, and that I'm just a hayseed by comparison. He cocks his head and he looks at me and I know he's thinking how dumb I am. He's really sweet and we have a good time talking. But when he cocks his head, I feel like I'll be dumped. One time he kind of wrinkled up his face when I said something a little critical about his jacket. Now I'm afraid to say anything for fear of hurting him.

"Usually I think Ed is completely wonderful. But last week he made me take the bus to his house instead of picking me up. I suddenly felt he didn't give a damn, that he was just another jerk. That was a passing thing, and now he's wonderful again. My only problem is this business of being nervous when he cocks his head."

Pattern	Phrase Containing the Pattern
Filtering	_____
Polarized Thinking	_____
Overgeneralization	_____
Mind Reading	_____
Catastrophizing	_____
Magnifying	_____
Personalization	_____
Shoulds	_____

4. "There are three ways to make a magazine go: work, work, and more work. If you have to work sixteen hours a day to get it out, then that's what you have to do. These kids today want to go home at five o'clock. If they're too lazy to work, I say get rid of them.

Profits get slimmer every year because of total laziness. It's the way they're raised—the way the whole damn country is falling apart. In five years it'll drive me under. There are just two kinds of editors: the ones who get the job done and the nine-to-fivers. It's the nine-to-fivers who will put me under. I can't fight the whole world."

Pattern	Phrase Containing the Pattern
Filtering	
Polarized Thinking	
Overgeneralization	
Mind Reading	
Catastrophizing	
Magnifying	
Personalization	
Shoulds	

Answer Key

Overgeneralization: "He blows up at everything."
Catastrophizing: "He'll lose his job and we'll be homeless."
Mind Reading: "She knew . . . She wants . . . she's just looking . . ."
Shoulds: "The night shift shouldn't . . ."
Mind Reading: "I know he's thinking how dumb I am."
Personalization: "I feel nervous when I'm out with Ed." (Assuming all Ed's behavior relates to her)
Polarized Thinking: "he was just another jerk . . . now he's wonderful again."
Shoulds: "that's what you have to do."
Filtering: "Profits get slimmer . . . total laziness" (sees laziness only)
Polarized Thinking: "There are just two kinds of editors."
Magnifying: "I can't fight the whole world."

Thought Journal

Now that you have learned to identify limited-thinking patterns, it's time to apply your new skill to the Thought Journal you started in the previous chapter. Three new columns have been added to the blank form that follows. You now have space to fill in your limited-thinking patterns, balanced or alternative thoughts, and a re-rating of your feelings.

Start by analyzing your most distressing automatic thoughts to see which limited-thinking pattern each one fits best. You may find evidence of more than one limited-thinking pattern, so write down all that apply.

In the next column, rewrite your automatic thoughts in a more balanced way, or compose an alternative thought that refutes the automatic thought. You can refer back to the section on rational comebacks for help in countering the limited-thinking patterns. In the last column, re-rate your bad feeling now that you have worked on your automatic thoughts. The feeling should be less intense after this work.

Thought Journal

Situation *When? Where?* *Who? What* *happened?*	Feelings *One-word* *summaries.* *Rate 0–100.*	Automatic Thoughts *What you were thinking just* *before and during the unpleasant* *feeling.*	Limited-Thinking Pattern	Balancing or Alternative Thoughts *Circle possible action plans.*	Re-rate Feelings *0–100.*

Composing Balancing or Alternative Thoughts

Listed below are rational, complete alternatives to the eight limited-thinking patterns. It isn't necessary to read through the list from beginning to end. Use it as a reference when you are having problems with a particular pattern.

1. Filtering

Pattern Summary	**Key Balancing Statement**
• Focusing on the negative	• Shift focus
• Filtering out the positive	

You have been stuck in a mental groove, focusing on things from your environment that typically frighten, sadden, or anger you. In order to conquer filtering you will have to deliberately shift focus. You can shift focus in two ways: First, place your attention on coping strategies for dealing with the problem rather than obsessing about the problem itself. Second, focus on the opposite of your primary mental theme. For example, if you tend to focus on the theme of loss, instead focus on what you still have that is of value. If your theme is danger, focus instead on things in your environment that represent comfort and safety. If your theme is injustice or stupidity or incompetence, shift focus to what people do that does meet with your approval.

2. Polarized thinking

Pattern Summary	**Key Balancing Statement**
• Seeing everything as awful or great, with no middle ground.	• No black and white judgments
	• Think in percentages

The key to overcoming polarized thinking is to stop making black or white judgments. People are not either happy or sad, loving or rejecting, brave or cowardly, smart or stupid. They fall somewhere along a continuum. They are a little bit of each. Human beings are just too complex to be reduced to either/or judgments.

If you have to make these kinds of ratings, think in terms of percentages: "About 30 percent of me is scared to death, and 70 percent is holding on and coping"; "About 60 percent of the time he seems terribly preoccupied with himself, but there's the 40 percent when he can be really generous"; "5 percent of the time I'm an ignoramus; the rest of the time I do all right."

3. Overgeneralization

Pattern Summary	**Key Balancing Statement**
• Making sweeping statements based on scanty evidence	• Quantify
	• What's the evidence?
	• There are no absolutes
	• No negative labels

Overgeneralization is exaggeration—the tendency to take a button and sew a vest on it. Fight it by quantifying instead of using words like huge, awful, massive, minuscule, and so on. For example, if you catch yourself thinking, "We're buried under massive debt," rephrase with a quantity: "We owe $27,000."

Another way to avoid overgeneralization is to examine how much evidence you really have for your conclusion. If the conclusion is based on one or two cases, a single mistake, or one small symptom, then throw it out until you have more convincing proof. This is such a powerful technique that most of the next chapter is devoted to amassing evidence for and against your hot thoughts.

Stop thinking in absolutes by avoiding words such as every, all, always, none, never, everybody, and nobody. Statements that include these words ignore the exceptions and shades of gray. Replace absolutes with words such as may, sometimes, and often. Be particularly sensitive to absolute predictions about the future such as "No one will ever love me." They are extremely dangerous because they can become self-fulfilling prophecies.

Pay close attention to the words you use to describe yourself and others. Replace frequently used negative labels with more neutral terms. For example, if you call your habitual caution cowardice, replace it with care. Think of your excitable mother as vivacious instead of ditzy. Instead of blaming yourself for being lazy, call yourself laid-back.

4. Mind Reading

Pattern Summary	Key Balancing Statement
• Assuming you know what others are thinking and feeling	• Check it out
	• Evidence for conclusions?
	• Alternative interpretations?

In the long run, you are probably better off making no inferences about people at all. Either believe what they tell you or hold no belief at all until some conclusive evidence comes your way. Treat all of your notions about people as hypotheses to be tested and checked out by asking them.

Sometimes you can't check out your interpretations. For instance, you may not be ready to ask your daughter if her withdrawal from family life means she's pregnant or taking drugs. But you can allay your anxiety by generating alternative interpretations of her behavior. Perhaps she's in love. Or premenstrual. Or studying hard. Or depressed about something. Or deeply engrossed in a project. Or worrying about her future. By generating a string of possibilities, you may find a more neutral interpretation that is more likely to be true than your direst suspicions. This process also underlines the fact that you really can't know accurately what others are thinking and feeling unless they tell you.

5. Catastrophizing

Pattern Summary	Key Balancing Statement
• Assuming the worst will happen	• What are the odds?

Catastrophizing is the royal road to anxiety. As soon as you catch yourself catastrophizing, ask yourself, "What are the odds?" Make an honest assessment of the situation in terms of odds or percent of probability. Are the chances of disaster one in 100,000 (.001 percent)? One in a thousand (.1 percent)? One in twenty (5 percent)? Looking at the odds helps you realistically evaluate whatever is frightening you.

6. Magnifying

Pattern Summary	Key Balancing Statement
• Enlarging difficulties	• Get things in proportion
• Minimizing the positive	• No need to magnify

To combat magnifying, stop using words like terrible, awful, disgusting, horrendous, etc. In particular, banish phrases like: "I can't stand it," "It's impossible," "It's unbearable." You can stand it, because history shows that human beings can survive almost any psychological blow and can endure incredible physical pain. You can get used to and cope with almost anything. Try saying to yourself phrases such as "I can cope" and "I can survive this."

7. Personalization

Pattern Summary	Key Balancing Statement
• Assuming the reactions of others always relate to you	• Check it out
• Comparing yourself to others	• We all have strong and weak points
	• Comparison is meaningless

When you catch yourself comparing yourself to others, remind yourself that everyone has strong and weak points. By matching your weak points to others with corresponding strong points, you are just looking for ways to demoralize yourself.

The fact is, human beings are too complex for casual comparisons to have any meaning. It would take you months to catalog and compare all the thousands of traits and abilities of two people.

If you assume that the reactions of others are often about you, force yourself to check it out. Maybe the boss isn't frowning because you're late. Make no conclusion unless you are satisfied that you have reasonable evidence and proof.

8. Shoulds

Pattern Summary	Key Balancing Statement
• Holding arbitrary rules for behavior of self and others	• Flexible rules
	• Values are personal

Reexamine and question any personal rules or expectations that include the words should, ought, or must. Flexible rules and expectations don't use these words because there are always exceptions and special circumstances. Think of at least three exceptions to your rule, and then imagine all the exceptions there must be that you can't think of.

You may get irritated when people don't act according to your values. But your personal values are just that—personal. They may work for you, but, as missionaries have discovered all over the world, they don't always work for others. People aren't all the same.

The key is to focus on each person's uniqueness—his or her particular needs, limitations, fears, and pleasures. Because it is impossible to know all of these complex interrelations even with intimates, you can't be certain whether your values apply to another. You are entitled to an opinion, but allow for the possibility of being wrong. Also, allow for other people to find different things important.

Example

On the next page is a portion of the Thought Journal from the previous chapter, showing how the bookkeeper completed it.

The bookkeeper felt better after identifying his limited-thinking patterns and composing his alternate thoughts. He realized that he had magnified the workload to the point that he had collapsed emotionally and was working inefficiently at low-priority tasks. He circled "I can prioritize the work" as an action plan for any time he felt overwhelmed at work.

He went on to examine the depression he felt at home.

Action Plans

Your balancing or alternative thoughts may suggest new directions you can take, such as checking out assumptions, gathering information, making an assertive request, clearing up misunderstandings, making plans, changing your schedule, resolving unfinished business, or making commitments. Circle those items and plan when you will put them into action.

In the example of the bookkeeper, he circled "I can prioritize the work" as an action plan to reduce anxiety on the job. He also circled "I should check it out" as an action plan to relieve the depression he felt when he assumed his wife was mad at him. It took him several days to work up the courage to ask his wife how she felt. It turned out she was angry, but she was mostly worried about him turning into a workaholic and getting an ulcer or having a heart attack.

It may be difficult, time consuming, or embarrassing to follow your action plan. You may have to break your plan down into a series of easier steps and schedule each step. But it's worth doing. Behavior that is inspired by your balancing or alternative thoughts will greatly reduce the frequency and power of your negative automatic thoughts.

For more action plans, see the next chapter.

Continue for a week keeping your Thought Journal, identifying your automatic thoughts and analyzing them for limited-thinking patterns. After a week you should be adept at recognizing your habitual patterns of limited thinking. You will begin to notice your automatic thoughts popping up in stressful situations. Eventually you will recognize limited-thinking patterns in real life, and correct them with balancing or alternative thoughts as you go.

If you still have trouble spotting the limited-thinking patterns after a week of practice, go on to the next chapter and try the "evidence for/evidence against" approach. It may be a better alternative for you.

References

Beck, A. T. 1976. *Cognitive Therapy and the Emotional Disorders*. New York: International Universities Press.

Ellis, A., and R. Harper. 1961. *A Guide to Rational Living*. N. Hollywood, Calif.: Wilshire Books.

Horney, K. 1939. *New Ways of Psychoanalysis*. New York: Norton.

Thought Journal

Situation When? Where? Who? What happened?	Feelings One-word summaries. Rate 0–100.	Automatic Thoughts What you were thinking just before and during the unpleasant feeling.	Limited-Thinking Pattern	Balancing or Alternative Thoughts Circle possible action plans.	Re-rate Feelings 0–100.
Given extra work.	Anxiety, 90	I'll be here all night. Can't stand it. Jenny will be mad if I'm late.	Magnifying	Of course I can stand it. I've been standing it for twelve years. Jenny knows what's going on. She expects long hours this time of the year.	50
"	Resentment, 75	They always dump on me. It's not fair.		I can prioritize the work and con-centrate on one thing at a time.	50
Have to work through lunch.	Anxiety, 85	I'm hungry, I'm tired. I can't stand this.	Catastrophizing	It's always this way at tax time. It will be better in May.	30
Watch TV with kids.	Depression, 75	They never talk to me. They hardly know me. They don't care.	Filtering Overgeneralizing	They talk to me about baseball and trading cards and school stuff. It's the TV—they're engrossed in it and I'm not, so I sit there obsessing.	25
Wife goes to bed early	Depression, 85	She's really mad. She's disgusted with me.	Mind reading	I have no evidence that she's mad or disgusted. I shoudl check it out.	30

CHAPTER 32

Changing Hot Thoughts

If the techniques in the previous chapter, Changing Patterns Limited Thinking, worked well for you, this chapter may not even be necessary. This chapter presents an alternative approach based on evidence gathering and analysis that provides a powerful weapon against automatic thoughts.

This chapter is to be used in conjunction with the chapter on Uncovering Automatic Thoughts. It will give you skills to do three things: (1) identify the evidence that supports your hot (or trigger) thoughts, (2) uncover evidence that contradicts your hot thoughts, and (3) synthesize what you have learned into a healthier, more realistic perspective.

Gathering evidence on both sides of the question is crucial to reaching a clearer, more objective understanding of your experience. Albert Ellis (Ellis and Harper 1961) was the first to develop a method (rational emotive therapy) to evaluate evidence for and against key beliefs. But by assuming that hot thoughts are always irrational, and focusing mostly on the evidence against them, his approach may not always feel objective. It also may alienate people who have solid evidence to support certain hot thoughts.

Christine Padesky (Greenberger and Padesky 1995), building on Beck's (1976) and Ellis's work, developed the strategies for gathering and analyzing evidence used in this chapter. Padesky doesn't assume that hot thoughts are totally irrational. She focuses instead on looking at all the evidence and working toward a balanced position.

Symptom Effectiveness

Thought journals have been used effectively to treat depression, anxiety, and related problems. Numerous studies over the past twenty years demonstrate the usefulness of this technique.

Thought and Evidence Journal

Situation When? Where? Who? What happened?	Feelings One-word summaries. Rate 0–100.	Automatic Thoughts What you were thinking just before and during the unpleasant feeling.	Evidence For	Evidence Against	Balanced or Alternative Thoughts Circle possible action plans.	Re-rate Feelings 0–100.

Time for Mastery

Using the Thought and Evidence Journal described in this chapter, you can make significant changes in your moods in as little as one week. However, it will take from two to twelve weeks to consolidate some of these changes, allowing your new, more balanced thoughts to gain strength through repetition.

Instructions

In this chapter you'll be working on an extension of the Thought Journal you began in the chapter on Uncovering Automatic Thoughts. Photocopy the blank Thought and Evidence Journal so you can have a supply of pages to use whenever you need one.

Step 1: Select a Hot Thought.

Return to the Thought Journal that you began keeping in the chapter on Uncovering Automatic Thoughts to select a hot thought from your record of automatic thoughts. Choose a thought that impacted your mood either because of its power or frequency. Rate each thought on a scale (0–100) that measures how strongly it contributed to your painful feelings. Circle the thought with the highest score—that's the hot one you'll work on now.

In Len's Thought Journal there is a section that contains one of his most upsetting hot thoughts. Len is a rep for a large printing company. His customers are mostly publishers and advertising companies.

When Len rated all of his automatic thoughts on a scale measuring their impact on his mood, "I'm a first-class failure" turned out to be his hottest thought by far. By itself, the thought could hit Len hard enough to stir up strong feelings of inadequacy and depression.

Len's Thought Journal

Situation *When? Where? Who? What happened?*	Feelings *One-word summaries. Rate 0–100.*	Automatic Thoughts *What you were thinking just before and during the unpleasant feeling.*
Sales figures for December were posted. I'm second from the bottom in sales out of nine reps.	Depression. **85**	I'm a stinko salesman. **70.** They all think something's wrong with me. **40** Print buyers probably don't like me. **40.** I'm a first-class failure. **95.** Commissions will be way down—it's going to hurt. **65.** I'm not working hard enough. **20.**

Step 2: Identify Evidence That Supports Your Hot Thought.

Now is your chance to write down the experiences and the facts that would appear to support your hot thought. This is not the place to put your feelings, impressions, assumptions about the reactions of others, or unsupported beliefs. In the column marked "Evidence For," stay with the objective facts. Confine yourself to exactly what was said, what was done, how many times, and so on.

While it's important to stick with the facts, it's also important to acknowledge all the past and present evidence that supports and verifies your hot thought.

Len identified five pieces of evidence that seemed to support the hot thought: "I'm a first-class failure." Here is what he wrote in his "Evidence For" column:

1. Only $24,000 in sales for December.

2. Couldn't close the Silex Corp. when they seemed almost ready to give me the contract.

3. Boss asked if I had any problems.

4. This is the third time in twelve months I've been below $30,000 in sales.

5. Had a disagreement with Randolph and he pulled his job.

Notice that Len doesn't talk about conjectures, assumptions, or a "feeling" that he's doing a bad job. He confines himself to the facts and an objective description of events.

Step 3: Uncover Evidence against Your Hot Thought.

You'll probably find this to be the hardest part of the technique. It's easy to think of things that support your hot thought, but you'll often draw a blank when it's time to explore evidence against it. You'll most likely need some help.

To assist you in the search for evidence against your hot thought, there are ten key questions you need to ask. Go through all ten questions for every hot thought you are analyzing—each of them will help you explore new ways of thinking.

Ten Key Questions

1. Is there an alternative interpretation of the situation, other than your hot thought?

2. Is the hot thought really accurate, or is it an overgeneralization? Is it true that (the situation) means (your hot thought)? In Len's case, for example, do low sales figures in December mean that he's a failure?

3. Are there exceptions to the generalizations made by your hot thought?

4. Are there balancing realities that might soften negative aspects of the situation? In Len's case, for example, are there other things besides sales that he can feel good about in his job?

5. What are the likely consequences and outcomes of the situation? This question helps you differentiate what you fear might happen from what you can reasonably expect will happen.

6. Are there experiences from your past that would lead you to a conclusion other than your hot thought?

7. Are there objective facts that would contradict items in the "Evidence For" column? Is it really true, for example, that Len lost the Silex contract because he was a failure as a salesman? Are there facts at odds with this interpretation?

8. What are the real odds that what you fear happening in the situation will actually occur? Think like a bookmaker. Are the odds 1 in 2, 1 in 50, 1 in 1,000, 1 in 500,000? Think of all the people right now in this same situation; how many of them end up facing the catastrophic outcome you fear?

9. Do you have the social or problem-solving skills to handle the situation differently?

10. Could you create a plan to change the situation? Is there someone you know who might deal with this differently? What would that person do?

Write on a separate piece of paper your answers to all of the questions relevant to your hot thought. It may take some thinking: to find exceptions to the generalization created by your hot thought; to think objectively about the odds of something catastrophic happening; or to recall balancing realities that give you confidence and hope in the face of problems. The work you put into this step in the evidence gathering process will directly impact your ability to challenge hot thoughts.

Len spent more than half an hour trying to answer the ten questions. Here's what they helped him develop in the "Evidence Against" column:

1. December's normally a low month. That might explain most of my drop-off in sales. (Question #1)

2. To be accurate: For the year I ranked fourth of the nine reps. That's not great, but it's not being a failure. (Question #2)

3. Some months have been good. I did $68,000 in August, and $64,000 in March. (Question #3)

4. I have many good relationships with customers; in some cases I have really helped them with major decisions. Most know they can trust me as an advisor. (Question #4)

5. My sales are good enough at number four in the company that they wouldn't fire me. (Question #5)

6. Five years ago I was ranked number two, and I'm always in the top half of the pack. There have been a lot of individual months over the years when I got the best-salesman award. (Question #6)

7. I was just outbid on Silex—it wasn't my fault. (Question #7)

8. Randolph said he wanted recycled paper and pulled the job when he didn't like the price. Not my fault. (Question #7)

9. I need to think about my relationship to each customer and less about the dollar worth of each contract. I know that works better for me. (Question #10)

Len found it particularly useful to look for objective facts that either counterbalanced or contradicted each item in the "Evidence For" column. He kept asking himself, "What in my experience balances out this piece of evidence?" and "What objective facts contradict this piece of evidence?" Len was surprised how much he discovered in the "Evidence Against" column, and he realized there were a lot of things he shut out of his awareness when he was feeling depressed.

Step 4: Write Your Balanced or Alternative Thoughts.

Now it's time to synthesize everything you've learned in both the "Evidence For" and "Evidence Against" columns. Read over both columns slowly and carefully. Don't try to deny or ignore evidence on either side. Now write new, balanced thoughts that incorporate what you've learned as you gathered the evidence. In your balanced thoughts it's okay to acknowledge important items in the "Evidence For" column, but it's equally important to summarize the main things you learned in the "Evidence Against" column.

Here's what Len wrote in the "Balanced or Alternative Thoughts" column in his Thought and Evidence Journal:

My sales are down, and I've lost two deals, but I have a solid sales record over the years, and I've had a lot of good months. I just need to focus on my customer relationships, and not the money.

Notice that Len didn't ignore or deny that sales were down, but he was able to use items from his "Evidence Against" column to develop a clear, balanced statement that acknowledged his track record as a competent salesman.

Synthesizing statements don't have to be long. But they do need to summarize the main points on both sides of the question. Don't be afraid to rewrite your "Balanced or Alternative Thoughts" several times until the statement feels strong and convincing.

When you're satisfied with the accuracy of what you've written, rate your belief in this new balanced thought as a percentage ranging from 0 to 100. Len, for example, rated his belief in his new balanced thought as 85 percent. If you don't believe your new thought more than 60 percent, you should revise it further—perhaps detailing more items from the "Evidence Against" column. It's also possible that the evidence you've gathered isn't yet convincing enough, and you need to work further on developing ideas for your "Evidence Against" column.

Step 5: Re-rate Your Mood.

It's time to find out where all this work has gotten you. As part of your Thought and Evidence Journal, you identified a painful feeling and rated its intensity on a 0–100 scale. Now it's time to rate the intensity of that same feeling again to see if anything has changed now that you've gathered evidence and developed a new balanced thought.

Len found that his depression had changed substantially following his efforts to gather evidence. His depression rating was now 30 on the 100-point scale. Most of the remaining depression seemed based on a realistic concern about reduced income from his low December sales.

Seeing your mood change can be a strong reinforcement for doing the Evidence work in your Thought and Evidence Journal. In the space of just a few minutes you can successfully confront powerful hot thoughts and make positive changes in how you feel.

Step 6: Record and Save Alternative Thoughts.

We encourage you to record what you've learned each time you complete the process of examining evidence and developing balanced or alternative thoughts. It's helpful to put this information on three-by-five file cards that you can keep with you and read whenever you wish. On one side of the file card write a description of the problem situation and your hot thought. On the opposite side of the card write your alternative or balanced thought. Over time, you will create a number of these cards. They can be a resource to remind you of your new, healthier thoughts when upsetting circumstances might induce you to forget them.

Step 7: Practice Your Balanced Thoughts.

You can use your completed file cards in a simple exercise that will give you practice with your balanced thoughts. Start by reading the side of the card that describes the trigger situation and your hot thought. Work at forming a clear visualization of the situation: Picture the scene, see the shapes and colors, be aware of who is there and what they look like. Hear the voices and other sounds that are part of the trigger scene. Notice the temperature. Notice if you're touching anything, and what it feels like.

When the image of the scene is very clear, read your hot thought. Try to focus on it to the point of having an emotional reaction. When you can picture the scene clearly and feel some of the emotions that go with it, it's time to turn the card over and read your balanced thoughts. Think of the balanced thoughts while continuing to visualize the scene, and continue to pair the balanced thoughts and the scene until your emotional reaction subsides.

Len did this exercise by picturing the monthly sales notice while thinking his hot thought, "I'm a first-class failure." After feeling a small surge in depression, he paired the image of the sales report with the balanced thoughts described earlier. It took several minutes of focusing on the balanced thoughts before his depression started to subside. One of the important things Len learned from this exercise was that he could both increase and decrease his depression by focusing on key thoughts.

Your Action Plan

Return your attention to the "Evidence Against" column in your Thought and Evidence Journal. Look for an item that involves using coping skills or implementing a plan to handle the situation differently. Circle the item(s) that suggest a plan of action. In the space below, write three specific steps you could take to implement your action plan in the problem situation.

1. _____

2. _____

3. _____

Len's action plan focused on his decision to think about customer relationships rather than the dollar value of each contract. He decided to:

1. Send New Year's greetings to all of his regular customers.

2. Call each customer with a request for feedback about how he and his company could improve service.

3. Focus on enjoying his customers as people—for example, taking the time to chat instead of pushing quickly to business.

Example

Here is an example of the whole process in action. Take a look at how Holly implements the techniques in this chapter, paying special attention to the Thought and Evidence Journal and resulting action plan.

Holly was a modern-dance teacher. Her classes were offered on a drop-in basis, and she was paid per pupil. One of her seven classes had recently shown a sharp decline in attendance. To make matters worse, after class one night one of the remaining students had criticized Holly for giving little attention or feedback to individual dancers.

Holly felt like she'd been slapped. She went home wondering if she should—or would be allowed to—continue teaching. Here's how she started her Thought and Evidence Journal:

Notice that Holly had two strong feelings: depression and anxiety. That's because thoughts such as "I'm a fraud" and "I'm no good at this" tended to make her feel bad about herself and depressed. On the other hand, a thought such as "I'll lose my job" was scary and anxiety provoking. Under "Automatic Thoughts" Holly really had two hot thoughts. "I'm a fraud" and "I'll lose my job" were both rated 85—major contributors to her bad feelings. Holly decided to work on "I'll lose my job" for the remainder of the journal because she was more anxious than depressed. Later, Holly went back and repeated her evidence gathering for the hot thought "I'm a fraud."

Notice under "Evidence For" that Holly focused on facts. She included evidence only for what had actually happened or what had actually been said. She didn't include any feelings, opinions, or assumptions as evidence—only the facts.

In the "Evidence Against" column Holly used the ten key questions to uncover evidence contrary to her hot thought. A few of the questions weren't relevant, but others helped her remember past and present experiences that made losing her job seem unlikely.

Because Holly's "Evidence Against" column was so substantial, she went through it carefully and circled the items that seemed salient and convincing. To write her balanced thoughts, Holly acknowledged the truth of several problems in the "Evidence For" column but counterweighted it with strong evidence against. When Holly reevaluated her feelings, anxiety was down substantially—from 85 to 20. But depression had improved only slightly. That's why Holly elected to do the Thought and Evidence Journal again, using "I'm a fraud" as her hot thought.

Holly's Thought and Evidence Journal

Situation *When?* *Where? Who?* *What* *happened?*	Feelings *One-word* *summaries.* *Rate 0–100.*	Automatic Thoughts *What you were thinking* *just before and during* *the unpleasant feeling.*	Evidence For	Evidence Against	Balanced or Alternative Thoughts *Circle possible* *action plans.*	Re-rate Feelings *0–100.*
Class dwindling. Criticized for not giving individual attention.	Depressed, **65.** Anxious, **80.**	I'm turning off the class. **30** I'm not good at this. **50** I'm a fraud. **85** I'll lose my job. **85** Stupid me—I never notice what's happening until it's too late. **50** I'll have to cancel the class. **20**	Class size dropped from 11 to 5. Complaint from dancer in class. Lost a few dancers from one or two of my other classes. Someone also complained a few months ago about my not giving feedback	A popular Afro-Haitian instructor just started a class at the same time as mine. (Q-1) Classes fluctuate a lot, sometimes dwindle and get canceled. No one gets fired for it. (Q-2) Two of my classes are actually growing, the 6 p.m. on Tuesday had 23 dancers last week. (Q-3) Jill said I put together some lovely sequences, and several dancers standing around agreed. I'm good at choreographing teaching exercises. (Q-4) Most likely the class will stabilize at this number. At the worst I'll lose one of seven classes. (Q-5) Only one person has actually been fired—and that was for encouraging movements that risk injury. I doubt I'll be fired for a class with low attendance. (Q-6) The odds of being fired are less than 1 in 500. (Q-8) I can individually ask other dancers about their reactions to the class. Also I can focus on giving feedback to dancers in the back row, whom I often miss. (Q-10)	One class has dwindled, and I'm not great at giving feedback. But fluctuations are normal. No one gets fired except for risking injuries. Many dancers like my class, and I have a plan for improving feedback. **90%**	depressed, **50** anxious, **25**

Recording Alternative Thoughts

Holly put a description of the situation and the hot thought "I'll lose my job" on one side of a file card. On the other side she wrote her balanced thoughts. Holly began by visualizing the problem situation and focusing on her hot thought. When she felt the first tinglings of anxiety, she turned the file card over and visualized the problem situation in conjunction with her new, balanced thoughts.

The exercise showed Holly that she could change her feelings by shifting from hot to balanced thoughts.

Holly's Action Plan

There were two parts to Holly's plan: (1) ask for feedback from certain dancers she knew in class, and (2) give more attention to the dancers in the back row. Holly decided to implement her plan with three specific steps:

1. Ask Maria, Eleanor, Michelle, and Farrin about my class in general and specifically, find out what they've observed about the feedback I give dancers.

2. Bring the back row to the front row halfway through every class.

3. Try to find something to praise about each dancer.

Special Considerations

1. If you have more than one main hot thought, do a separate Thought and Evidence Journal for each hot thought.

2. If you have difficulty developing alternative interpretations to the hot thought, imagine how a friend or some objective observer might look at the situation.

3. If you have difficulty identifying exceptions, think of times you've been in the target situation without anything negative happening. Or perhaps when you experienced something positive: Was there a time when you handled the situation particularly well? Were you ever praised in the situation?

4. If you have difficulty remembering objective facts contrary to items in the "Evidence For" column, you might enlist a friend or family member to help you.

5. If you have difficulty assessing odds of a dangerous outcome, make an estimate of all the times in the last year someone in the United States has been in this same situation. How many times has the feared catastrophe occurred?

6. If you have difficulty making an action plan, imagine how a very competent friend or acquaintance would handle the same situation. What would he or she do, say, or try that might create a different outcome?

References

Beck, A. T. 1976. *Cognitive Therapy and the Emotional Disorders*. New York: International Universities Press.

Ellis, A., and R. Harper. 1961. *A Guide to Rational Living*. N. Hollywood, Calif.: Wilshire Books.

Greenberger, D., and C. Padesky. 1995. *Mind Over Mood*. New York: Guilford Press.

CHAPTER 33

Anxiety—Overview of the Disorders

This chapter provides an overview of the different manifestations of anxiety, as well as a self-diagnosis questionnaire. It can help you determine which of the following chapters will be most helpful in addressing your anxiety.

Susan awakens suddenly almost every night, a couple of hours after going to sleep, with a tightness in her throat, a racing heart, dizziness, and a fear that she's going to die. Although she's shaking all over, she hasn't a clue why. After many nights of getting up and pacing her living room floor in an attempt to get a grip on herself, she decides to go see her doctor to find out whether something is wrong with her heart.

Cindy, a medical secretary, has been having attacks like Susan's whenever she's in a confined public situation. Not only does she fear losing control over herself, but she dreads what others might think of her if this were to happen. Recently she has been avoiding going into any kind of store other than the local 7-Eleven, unless her boyfriend is with her. She has also needed to leave restaurants and movie theaters during dates with her boyfriend. Now she is beginning to wonder whether she can cope with her job. She has been forcing herself to go into work, yet after a few minutes among her office mates she starts to fear that she's losing control of herself. Suddenly she feels as though she has to leave.

Steve has a responsible position as a software engineer, but feels he is unable to advance because of his inability to contribute in group meetings. It's almost more than he can bear just to sit in on meetings, let alone offer his opinions. Yesterday his boss asked him whether he would be available to make a presentation on his segment of a large project. At that point Steve became extremely nervous and tongue-tied. He walked out of the room, stammering that he would let his boss know by the next day about the presentation. Privately, he thought about resigning.

Mike is so embarrassed about a peculiar fear he's had over the past few months that he can't tell anyone, not even his wife. While driving he is frequently gripped by the fear that he has run over someone or perhaps an animal. Even though there is no "thud" suggesting that anything like this has happened, he feels compelled to make a U-turn and retrace the route he's just driven to make absolutely sure. In fact, recently, his paranoia about having hit someone has grown so strong that he has to retrace his route three or four times to assure himself that nothing has happened. Mike is a bright, successful professional and feels utterly humiliated about his compulsion to check. He's beginning to wonder if he's going crazy.

Susan, Cindy, Steve, and Mike are all confronted by anxiety. Yet it is not ordinary anxiety. Their experiences differ in two fundamental respects from the "normal" anxiety people experience in response to everyday life. First, their anxiety has gone out of control. In each case, the individual feels powerless to direct what's happening. This sense of powerlessness in turn creates even more anxiety. Second, the anxiety is interfering with the normal functioning of their lives. Susan's sleep is disrupted. Cindy and Steve may lose their jobs. And Mike has lost the ability to drive in an efficient and timely manner.

The examples of Susan, Cindy, Steve, and Mike illustrate four types of anxiety disorder: panic disorder, agoraphobia, social phobia, and obsessive-compulsive disorder. Later in this chapter, you can find detailed descriptions of the characteristics of each specific anxiety disorder. But I would first like you to consider the common theme that runs through them all. What is the nature of anxiety itself?

What Is Anxiety?

You can better understand the nature of anxiety by looking both at what it is and what it is not. For example, anxiety can be distinguished from fear in several ways. When you are afraid, your fear is usually directed toward some concrete, external object or situation. The event that you fear usually is within the bounds of possibility. You might fear not meeting a deadline, failing an exam, being unable to pay your bills, or being rejected by someone you want to please. When you experience anxiety, on the other hand, you often can't specify what it is you're anxious about. The focus of anxiety is more internal than external. It seems to be a response to a vague, distant, or even unrecognized danger. You might be anxious about "losing control" of yourself or some situation. Or you might feel a vague anxiety about "something bad happening."

Anxiety affects your whole being. It is a physiological, behavioral, and psychological reaction all at once. On a physiological level, anxiety may include bodily reactions such as rapid heartbeat, muscle tension, queasiness, dry mouth, or sweating. On a behavioral level, it can sabotage your ability to act, express yourself, or deal with certain everyday situations.

Psychologically, anxiety is a subjective state of apprehension and uneasiness. In its most extreme form, it can cause you to feel detached from yourself and even fearful of dying or going crazy.

The fact that anxiety can affect you on a physiological, behavioral, and psychological level has important implications for your attempts to recover. A complete program of recovery from an anxiety disorder must intervene at all three levels to

1. Reduce physiological reactivity

2. Eliminate avoidance behavior

3. Change subjective interpretations (or "self-talk") which perpetuate a state of apprehension and worry

Anxiety Versus Anxiety Disorders

Anxiety is an inevitable part of life in contemporary society. It's important to realize that there are many situations that come up in everyday life in which it is appropriate and reasonable to react with some anxiety. If you didn't feel any anxiety in response to everyday challenges involving potential loss or failure, something would be wrong.

Anxiety disorders are distinguished from everyday, normal anxiety in that they involve anxiety that 1) is more intense (for example, panic attacks), 2) lasts longer (anxiety that may persist for months instead of going away after a stressful situation has passed), or 3) leads to phobias that interfere with your life.

Criteria for diagnosing specific anxiety disorders have been established by the American Psychiatric Association and are listed in a well-known diagnostic manual used by mental health professionals. This manual is called *DSM-IV* (*Diagnostic and Statistical Manual of Mental Disorders*—Fourth Edition). The following descriptions of various anxiety disorders are based on the criteria in *DSM-IV*, as is the self-diagnosis questionnaire at the end of this chapter. This workbook can help you even if your specific anxiety disorder or reaction doesn't fit any of the *DSM-IV's* diagnostic categories. On the other hand, don't be unduly concerned if your reaction is perfectly described by one of the diagnostic categories. Approximately 13 percent of the people in the United States would find themselves in your company.

Panic Disorder

Panic disorder is characterized by sudden episodes of acute apprehension or intense fear that occur "out of the blue" without any apparent cause. Intense panic usually lasts no more than a few minutes, but, in rare instances, can return in "waves" for a period of up to two hours. During the panic itself, any of the following symptoms can occur:

- Shortness of breath or a feeling of being smothered

- Heart palpitations—pounding heart or accelerated heart rate

- Dizziness, unsteadiness, or faintness

- Trembling or shaking

- Feeling of choking

- Sweating

- Nausea or abdominal distress

- Feeling of unreality—as if you're "not all there" (depersonalization)

- Numbness or tingling in hands and feet

- Hot and cold flashes

- Chest pain or discomfort

- Fears of going crazy or losing control

- Fears of dying

At least four of these symptoms are present in a full-blown panic attack, while having two or three of them is referred to as a limited-symptom attack.

Your symptoms would be diagnosed as panic disorder if you: 1) have had two or more panic attacks, and 2) at least one of these attacks has been followed by one month (or more) of persistent concern about having another panic attack, or worry about the possible implications of having another panic attack. It's important to recognize that panic disorder, by itself, does not involve any phobias. The panic doesn't occur because you are thinking about, approaching, or actually entering a phobic situation. Instead, it occurs spontaneously and unexpectedly for no apparent reason. Also, the panic attacks are not due to the physiological effects of a drug (prescription or recreational) or a medical condition.

You may have two or three panic attacks without ever having another one again or without having another one for years. Or you may have several panic attacks followed by a panic-free period, only to have the panic return a month or two later. Sometimes an initial panic attack may be followed by recurring attacks three or more times per week unremittingly until you seek treatment. In all of these cases, there is a tendency to develop anticipatory anxiety or apprehension between panic attacks focusing on fear of having another one.

If you are suffering from panic disorder, you may be very frightened by your symptoms and consult with doctors to find a medical cause. Heart palpitations and an irregular heartbeat may lead to EKG and other cardiac tests, which, in most cases, turn out normal. (Sometimes mitral valve prolapse, a benign arrhythmia of the heart, may coexist with panic disorder.) Fortunately, an increasing number of physicians have some knowledge of panic disorder and are able to distinguish it from purely physical complaints.

A diagnosis of panic disorder is made only after possible medical causes—including hypoglycemia, hyperthyroidism, reaction to excess caffeine, or withdrawal from alcohol, tranquilizers, or sedatives—have been ruled out. The causes of panic disorder involve a combination of heredity, chemical imbalances in the brain, and personal stress. Sudden losses or major life changes may trigger the onset of panic attacks.

People tend to develop panic disorder during late adolescence or their twenties. In a majority of cases, panic is complicated by the development of agoraphobia (as described in the following section). Between one and two percent of the population has "pure" panic disorder, while about five percent, or one in every twenty people, suffer from panic attacks complicated by agoraphobia.

Of all the anxiety disorders, panic disorder is the one for which prescription medications are most frequently given. Panic attacks can be reduced or even blocked by two different types of medications: antidepressants such as imipramine (Tofranil) or paroxetine (Paxil), or minor tranquilizers such as alprazolam (Xanax) or clonazepam (Klonopin). The problem with medications is that when they are withdrawn, even after having been taken for six months to a year, panic attacks often return. This is more often the case with tranquilizers than with antidepressant medications. Milder cases of panic disorder may be helped without medication. By reducing stress and improving your physical health, you can increase your resistance to panic attacks. A personal wellness program that includes 1) regular exercise, 2) daily practice of deep relaxation, 3) good nutrition, and 4) a shift in attitude to a calmer, more easygoing approach to life may enable you to reduce panic without relying on prescription medications.

The most effective nondrug therapy for panic disorder is panic-control therapy combined with interoceptive desensitization. For complete instructions, see the chapter on Panic Attacks in this part.

Agoraphobia

Of all the anxiety disorders, agoraphobia is the most prevalent. It is estimated that one in twenty, or about five percent of the general population, suffers from varying degrees of agoraphobia. The only disorder that affects a greater number of people in the United States is alcoholism.

The word agoraphobia means fear of open spaces; however, the essence of agoraphobia is a fear of panic attacks. If you suffer from agoraphobia, you are afraid of being in situations from which escape might be difficult—or in which help might be unavailable—if you suddenly had a panic attack. You may avoid grocery stores or freeways, for example, not so much because of their inherent characteristics, but because these are situations from which escape might be difficult or embarrassing in the event of panic. Fear of embarrassment plays a key role. Most agoraphobics fear not only having panic attacks but what other people will think should they be seen having a panic attack.

It is common for the agoraphobic to avoid a variety of situations. Some of the more common ones include

- Crowded public places such as grocery stores, department stores, restaurants

- Enclosed or confined places such as tunnels, bridges, or the hairdresser's chair

- Public transportation such as trains, buses, subways, planes

- Being at home alone

Perhaps the most common feature of agoraphobia is anxiety about being far away from home or far from a "safe person" (usually your spouse, partner, a parent, or anyone to whom you have a primary attachment). You may completely avoid driving alone or may be afraid of driving alone beyond a certain short distance from home. In more severe cases, you might be able to walk alone only a few yards from home or you might be housebound altogether. I know of one agoraphobic who was unable to leave her bedroom without being accompanied.

If you have agoraphobia, you are not only phobic about a variety of situations but tend to be anxious much of the time. This anxiety arises from anticipating that you might be stuck in a situation in which you would panic. What would happen, for example, if you were asked to go somewhere you ordinarily avoid and had to explain your way out of it? Or what would happen if you suddenly were left alone? Because of the severe restrictions in your activities and life, you may also be depressed. Depression arises from feeling in the grip of a condition over which you have no control or that you are powerless to change.

Agoraphobia appears to be engendered by panic disorder. At first you simply have panic attacks that occur for no apparent reason (panic disorder). After a while, though, you become aware that your attacks occur more frequently in confined situations away from home or when you are by yourself. You begin to be afraid of these situations. At the point where you actually start to avoid these situations for fear of panicking, you've started to develop agoraphobia. From that point you might go on to develop a mild, moderate, or severe problem. In a mild case, you might feel uncomfortable in confined situations but not actually avoid them. You continue to work or shop on your own, but do not want to go far from home otherwise. In a moderate case, you might start to avoid some situations, such as public transportation, elevators, driving far from home, or being in restaurants. However, your restriction is only partial, and there are certain situations away from home or your safe person that you can handle on your own, even with some discomfort. Severe agoraphobia is marked by an all-inclusive restriction of activities to the point where you are unable to leave your house without being accompanied.

Just why some people with panic attacks develop agoraphobia and others do not is unknown at this time. Nor is it understood why some people develop much more severe cases than others. What is known is that agoraphobia is caused by a combination of heredity and environment. Agoraphobics may have a parent, sibling, or other relative who also has the problem. When one identical twin is agoraphobic, the other has a high likelihood of being agoraphobic, too. On the environmental side, there are certain types of childhood circumstances that predispose a child to agoraphobia. These include growing up with parents who are 1) perfectionist and overcritical, 2) overprotective, and/or 3) overly anxious to the point of communicating to their child that the world is a "dangerous place."

Agoraphobia affects people in all walks of life and at all levels of the socioeconomic scale. Approximately 80 percent of agoraphobics are women, although this percentage has been dropping recently. It is possible to speculate that as women are increasingly expected to hold down full-time jobs (making a housebound lifestyle less socially acceptable), the percentage of women and men with agoraphobia may tend to equalize.

Agoraphobia can occur without a history of panic disorder. It has all of the same features—such as avoidance of a variety of situations—but there is no history of having had full-blown panic attacks. Instead, the focus of your fear is on only one or two symptoms among all those listed for panic disorder. For example, you might be afraid only of having heart palpitations if you venture too far from home or go to a crowded public place. Sometimes the fear is of an incapacitating symptom not on the list of panic attack symptoms. For example, you might be afraid to drive long distances and/or to be far from a town because of a fear of losing bladder control or having a bout of diarrhea.

The good news about agoraphobia is that it is a very treatable condition. The first step in treatment is to learn to relax and to cope with panic attacks. In some cases, medication may be necessary. As a second step, situations that have been avoided are gradually confronted through a process of graded exposure. Such exposure is conducted first in imagination and then in real life. Third, constructive ways of thinking are learned and substituted in place of worrisome, fearful thinking. Finally, because agoraphobics often have difficulty standing up for themselves and their rights, assertiveness training is frequently a part of the treatment. With adequate treatment, approximately 80–90 percent of agoraphobics can achieve a lasting recovery. For treatment instructions, see the chapter on Phobias in this part.

Social Phobia

Social phobia is one of the more common anxiety disorders. It involves fear of embarrassment or humiliation in situations where you are exposed to the scrutiny of others or must perform. This fear is much stronger than the normal anxiety most nonphobic people experience in social or performance situations. Usually it's so strong that it causes you to avoid the situation altogether, although some people with social phobia endure social situations, albeit with considerable anxiety. Typically, your concern is that you will say or do something that will cause others to judge you as being anxious, weak, "crazy," or stupid. Your concern is generally out of proportion to the situation, and you recognize that it's excessive (children with social phobia, however, do not recognize the excessiveness of their fear).

The most common social phobia is fear of public speaking. In fact, this is the most common of all phobias and affects performers, speakers, people whose jobs require them to make presentations, and students who have to speak before their class. Public speaking phobia affects a large percentage of the population and is equally prevalent among men and women.

Other common social phobias include:

- Fear of blushing in public

- Fear of choking on or spilling food while eating in public

- Fear of being watched at work

- Fear of using public toilets

- Fear of writing or signing documents in the presence of others

- Fear of crowds

- Fear of taking examinations

Sometimes social phobia is less specific and involves a generalized fear of any social or group situation where you feel that you might be watched or evaluated. When your fear is of a wide range of social situations (for example, initiating conversations, participating in small groups, speaking to authority figures, dating, attending parties, and so on), the condition is referred to as generalized social phobia.

While social anxieties are common, you would be given a formal diagnosis of social phobia only if your avoidance interferes with work, social activities, or important relationships, and/or it causes you considerable distress. As with agoraphobia, panic attacks can accompany social phobia, although your panic is related more to being embarrassed or humiliated than to being confined or trapped. Also the panic arises only in connection with a specific type of social situation.

Social phobias tend to develop earlier than agoraphobia and can begin in late childhood or adolescence. They often develop in shy children around the time they are faced with increased peer pressure at school. Typically these phobias persist (without treatment) through adolescence and young adulthood, but have a tendency to decrease in severity later in life. Recent studies suggest that social phobia affects 1.8 to 3.2 percent of the U.S. population and is three times more prevalent among men than women.

You can recover from social phobias by gradually exposing yourself to the situation you have been avoiding, first in imagination and then in real life. Working on assertiveness and self-esteem is also critical for developing the confidence you need to be more comfortable in social and performance situations.

Treatment for social phobia is often best carried out in a group setting. The best treatment combines exposure to social settings along with restructuring of mistaken beliefs associated with embarrassment and fear of rejection.

Sometimes medications have been used to treat social phobia. Beta-blocker medications, such as Inderal and Tenormin, can reduce physiological reactions associated with social anxiety, such as rapid heart beat, blushing, and sweating. Minor tranquilizers (such as Xanax and Klonopin) or MAO-inhibitor antidepressants (such as Nardil and Parnate), although not without certain risks, have been helpful in treating particular cases of social phobia. See the chapter on Social Phobia later in part V.

Specific Phobia

Specific phobia typically involves a strong fear and avoidance of one particular type of object or situation. There are no spontaneous panic attacks, and there is no fear of panic attacks, as in agoraphobia. There is also no fear of humiliation or embarrassment in social situations, as in social phobia. Direct exposure to the feared object or situation may elicit a panic reaction, however. The fear and avoidance are strong enough to interfere with your normal routines, work, or relationships, and to cause you significant distress. Even though you recognize its irrationalities, a specific phobia can cause you considerable anxiety.

Among the most common specific phobias are the following:

Animal Phobias. These can include fear and avoidance of snakes, bats, rats, spiders, bees, dogs, and other creatures. Often these phobias begin in childhood, where they are considered as normal fears. Only when they persist into adulthood and disrupt your life or cause significant distress do they come to be classified as specific phobias.

Acrophobia (fear of heights). With acrophobia, you tend to be afraid of high floors of buildings or of finding yourself atop mountains, hills, or high-level bridges. In such situations you may experience 1) vertigo (dizziness) or 2) an urge to jump, usually experienced as some external force drawing you to the edge.

Elevator Phobia. This phobia may involve a fear that the cables will break and the elevator will crash, or a fear that the elevator will get stuck and you will be trapped inside. You may have panic reactions, but you have no history of panic disorder or agoraphobia.

Airplane Phobia. This most often involves a fear that the plane will crash. Alternatively, it can involve a fear that the cabin will depressurize, causing you to asphyxiate. More recently, phobias about planes being hijacked or bombed have become common. When flying, you may have a panic attack. Otherwise you have no history of panic disorder or agoraphobia. Fear of flying is a very common phobia. Approximately 10 percent of the population will not fly at all, while an additional 20 percent experience considerable anxiety while flying.

Doctor or Dentist Phobias. This can begin as a fear of painful procedures (injections, having teeth filled) conducted in a doctor's or dentist's office. Later it can generalize to anything having to do with doctors or dentists. The danger is that you may avoid needed medical treatment.

Phobias of Thunder and/or Lightning. Almost invariably phobias of thunder and lightning begin in childhood. When they persist beyond adolescence they are classified as specific phobias.

Blood-Injury Phobia. This is a unique phobia in that you have a tendency to faint (rather than panic) if exposed to blood or your own pain through injections or inadvertent injury. People with blood-injury phobia tend to be both physically and psychologically healthy in other regards.

Illness Phobia. Usually this phobia involves a fear of contracting and/or ultimately succumbing to a specific illness, such as a heart attack or cancer. With illness phobias you tend to seek constant reassurance from doctors and will avoid any situation that reminds you of the dreaded disease. Illness phobia is different from hypochondria, where you tend to imagine many different types of disease rather than focusing on one.

Specific phobias are common and affect approximately 10 percent of the population. However, since they do not always result in severe impairment, only a minority of people with specific phobias actually seek treatment. These types of phobias occur in men and women about equally. Animal phobias tend to be more common in women, while illness phobias are more common in men.

As previously mentioned, specific phobias are often childhood fears that were never outgrown. In other instances they may develop after a traumatic event, such as an accident, natural disaster, illness, or visit to the dentist—in other words, as a result of conditioning. A final cause is childhood modeling. Repeated observation of a parent with a specific phobia can lead a child to develop it as well.

Specific phobias tend to be easier to treat than agoraphobia or social phobia since they do not involve panic attacks or multiple phobias. The treatment of choice for specific phobias is imagery desensitization and/or real-life exposure, which often succeeds in alleviating the problem.

To sum up, specific phobia is usually a benign disorder, particularly if it begins as a common childhood fear. Though it may last for years, it rarely gets worse and often diminishes over time. Typically it is not associated with other psychiatric disturbances. People with specific phobias are usually functioning at a high level in all other respects. See the chapter on Phobia in part V.

Generalized Anxiety Disorder

Generalized anxiety disorder is characterized by chronic anxiety that persists for at least six months but is unaccompanied by panic attacks, phobias, or obsessions. You simply experience persistent anxiety and worry without the complicating features of other anxiety disorders. To be given a diagnosis of generalized anxiety disorder, your anxiety and worry must focus on two or more stressful life circumstances (such as finances, relationships, health, or school performance) a majority of days during a six-month period. It's common, if you're dealing with generalized anxiety disorder, to have a large number of worries, and to spend a lot of your time worrying. Yet you find it difficult to exercise much control over your worrying. Moreover, the intensity and frequency of the worry are always out of proportion to the actual likelihood of the feared events happening.

In addition to frequent worry, generalized anxiety disorder involves having at least three of the following six symptoms (with some symptoms present more days than not over the past six months):

- Restlessness—feeling keyed up

- Being easily fatigued

- Difficulty concentrating

- Irritability

- Muscle tension

- Difficulties with sleep

Finally, you're likely to receive a diagnosis of generalized anxiety disorder if your worry and associated symptoms cause you significant distress and/or interfere with your ability to function occupationally, socially, or in other important areas.

If a doctor tells you that you suffer from generalized anxiety disorder, he or she has probably ruled out possible medical causes of chronic anxiety, such as hyperventilation, thyroid problems, or drug-induced anxiety. Generalized anxiety disorder often occurs together with depression: a competent therapist can usually determine which disorder is primary and which is secondary. In some cases, though, it is difficult to say which came first.

Generalized anxiety disorder can develop at any age. In children and adolescents, the focus of worry often tends to be on performance in school or sports events. In adults, the focus can vary. This disorder affects approximately four percent of the American population, and may be slightly more common in females than males (55–60 percent of those diagnosed with the disorder are female).

Although there are no specific phobias associated with generalized anxiety disorder, one view suggests that the disorder is sustained by "basic fears" of a broader nature than specific phobias, such as

- Fear of losing control

- Fear of not being able to cope

- Fear of failure

- Fear of rejection or abandonment

- Fear of death and disease

Generalized anxiety disorder can be aggravated by any stressful situation that elicits these fears, such as increased demands for performance, intensified marital conflict, physical illness, or any situation that heightens your perception of danger or threat.

The underlying causes of generalized anxiety disorder are unknown. It is likely to involve a combination of heredity and predisposing childhood experiences, such as excessive parental expectations or parental abandonment and rejection.

Generalized anxiety disorder may be alleviated by using a full range of strategies. Reducing muscle tension and improving your physical wellness through a program of regular exercise, relaxation, and good nutrition are a good beginning. See the chapter on Stress in this part. Modifying self-talk and the basic belief systems that perpetuate your anxiety is crucial to developing a more relaxed approach to life. See the chapters on Uncovering Automatic Thoughts, Changing Patterns of Limited Thinking, and Changing Hot Thoughts in this part. Learning to express your feelings and act assertively can help; see the chapter on Communication in part I. Finally, working on your self-esteem will help you overcome any deep-seated feelings of insecurity or inadequacy which may underlie your anxiety, regardless of the type of anxiety disorder you happen to be facing. See the chapter on Self-Esteem in part V.

Obsessive-Compulsive Disorder

Some people naturally tend to be more neat, tidy, and orderly than others. These traits can in fact be useful in many situations, both at work and at home. In obsessive-compulsive disorder, however, they are carried to an extreme and disruptive degree. Obsessive-compulsive people can spend many hours cleaning, tidying, checking, or ordering, to the point where these activities interfere with the rest of the business of their lives.

Obsessions are recurring ideas, thoughts, images, or impulses that seem senseless but nonetheless continue to intrude into your mind. Examples include images of violence, thoughts of doing violence to someone else, or fears of leaving on lights or the stove or leaving your door unlocked. You recognize that these thoughts or fears are irrational and try to suppress them, but they continue to intrude into your mind for hours, days, weeks, or longer. These thoughts or images are not merely excessive worries about real-life problems and are usually unrelated to a real-life problem.

Compulsions are behaviors or rituals that you perform to dispel the anxiety brought on by obsessions. For example, you may wash your hands numerous times to dispel a fear of being contaminated, check the stove again and again to see if it is turned off, or look continually in your rearview mirror while driving to assuage anxiety about having hit somebody. You realize that these rituals are unreasonable. Yet you feel compelled to perform them to ward off the anxiety associated with your particular obsession. The conflict between your wish to be free of the compulsive ritual and the irresistible desire to perform it is a source of anxiety, shame, and even despair. Eventually you may cease struggling with your compulsions and give over to them entirely.

Obsessions may occur by themselves, without necessarily being accompanied by compulsions. In fact, about 25 percent of the people who suffer from obsessive-compulsive disorder only have obsessions, and these often center around fears of causing harm to a loved one.

The most common compulsions include washing, checking, and counting. If you are a washer, you are constantly concerned about avoiding contamination. You avoid touching door-knobs, shaking hands, or coming into contact with any object you associate with germs, filth, or a toxic substance. You can spend literally hours washing hands or showering to reduce anxiety about being contaminated. Women more often have this compulsion than men. Men outnumber women as checkers, however. Doors have to be repeatedly checked to dispel obsessions about being robbed; stoves are repeatedly checked to dispel obsessions about starting a fire; or roads repeatedly checked to dispel obsessions about having hit someone. In the counting compulsion, you must count up to a certain number or repeat a word a certain number of times to dispel anxiety about harm befalling you or someone else.

Obsessive-compulsive disorder is often accompanied by depression. Preoccupation with obsessions, in fact, tends to wax and wane with depression. This disorder may also be accompanied by phobic avoidance—such as when a person with an obsession about dirt avoids public rest rooms or touching doorknobs.

It is very important to realize that as bizarre as obsessive-compulsive behavior may sound, it has nothing to do with "being crazy." You always recognize the irrationality and senselessness of your thoughts and behavior and you are very frustrated (as well as depressed) about your inability to control them.

Obsessive-compulsive disorder used to be considered a rare behavior disturbance. However, recent studies have shown that as many as two to three percent of the general population may suffer, to varying degrees, from obsessive-compulsive disorder. The reason prevalence rates have been underestimated up to now is that most sufferers have been very reluctant to tell anyone about their problem. This disorder appears to affect men and women in equal numbers. Although many cases of obsessive-compulsive disorder begin in adolescence and young adulthood, about half begin in childhood. The age of onset tends to be earlier in males than females.

The causes of obsessive-compulsive disorder are unclear. There is some evidence that a deficiency of a neurotransmitter substance in the brain known as serotonin, or a disturbance in serotonin metabolism, is associated with the disorder. This is borne out by the fact that many sufferers improve when they take medications that increase brain serotonin levels, such as clomipramine (Anafranil) or specific serotonin-enhancing antidepressants such as fluoxetine (Prozac), sertraline (Zoloft), and paroxetine (Paxil). Further research needs to be done.

Two treatment strategies have been helpful in relieving obsessions and compulsions. The first is a behavior modification strategy called exposure and response prevention. This involves systematically being exposed to situations that arouse obsessive thoughts and then being prevented from engaging in any compulsive behaviors. For example, if you are obsessive about contamination and wash your hands compulsively, you would be required to expose yourself to something you considered dirty, such as a doorknob, and then to reduce the number of times you wash your hands or refrain from washing at all. Similarly, if you check the door five times whenever you leave your house, you would be required to gradually reduce the number of checks down to one. Most likely, someone would work with you in those situations in which you tend to be compulsive to enforce this "response prevention."

The other form of treatment that has been helpful involves medication. Of all the medications that have been tried, Anafranil and SSRI (selective serotonin reuptake inhibitor) antidepressants such as Prozac, Zoloft, and Paxil have been most effective, resulting in improvement or elimination of symptoms in 50–60 percent of the people treated. When medication and behavioral methods are combined, the improvement rate approaches 80 percent.

Self-help strategies can be helpful if you are affected by obsessive-compulsive disorder. Yet the primary mode of treatment I would suggest is to consult a professional who is well versed in the use of behavioral methods, such as exposure and response prevention, as well as in the use of appropriate medications. Self-help can complement behavioral and pharmacological treatment approaches. See the chapter on Obsessions and Compulsions later in part V.

Post-Traumatic Stress Disorder

The essential feature of post-traumatic stress disorder is the development of disabling psychological symptoms following a traumatic event. It was first identified during World War I, when soldiers were observed to suffer chronic anxiety, nightmares, and flashbacks for weeks, months, or even years following combat. This condition came to be known as shell shock.

Post-traumatic stress disorder can occur in anyone in the wake of a severe trauma outside the normal range of human experience. These are traumas that would produce intense fear, terror, and feelings of helplessness in anyone and include natural disasters such as earthquakes or tornadoes, car or plane crashes, rape, assault, or other violent crimes against yourself or your immediate family. It appears that the symptoms are more intense and longer lasting when the trauma is personal, as in rape or other violent crimes.

Among the variety of symptoms that can occur with post-traumatic stress disorder, the following nine are particularly common:

- Repetitive, distressing thoughts about the event

- Nightmares related to the event

- Flashbacks so intense that you feel or act as though the trauma were occurring all over again

- An attempt to avoid thoughts or feelings associated with the trauma

- An attempt to avoid activities or external situations associated with the trauma—such as a phobia about driving developing after you have been in an auto accident

- Emotional numbness—being out of touch with your feelings

- Feelings of detachment or estrangement from others

- Losing interest in activities that used to give you pleasure

- Persistent symptoms of increased anxiety, such as difficulty falling or staying asleep, difficulty concentrating, startling easily, or irritability and outbursts of anger

For you to receive a diagnosis or post-traumatic stress disorder, these symptoms need to have persisted for at least one month (with less than one month's duration, the appropriate diagnosis is "acute stress disorder"—see below). In addition, the disturbance must be causing you significant distress, interfering with social, vocational, or other important areas of your life.

If you suffer from post-traumatic stress disorder, you tend to be anxious and depressed. Sometimes you will find yourself acting impulsively, suddenly changing residence or going on a trip with hardly any plans. If you have been through a trauma where others around you died, you may suffer from guilt about having survived.

Post-traumatic stress disorder can affect people at any age. Children with the disorder tend not to relive the trauma consciously but continually reenact it in their play or in distressing dreams.

While many self-help strategies are helpful if you're dealing with post-traumatic stress disorder, the principal treatment is psychotherapy that enables you to work through intense feelings of fear, loss, and/or guilt surrounding the original traumatic event. Insight-oriented therapy focused on expressing feelings and integrating the original experience can help reduce symptoms and increase your sense of mastery over your life. Sometimes hypnosis may be used to assist you in going back and "walking through" the original trauma. See the chapter on Traumatic Experiences in part V.

Self-Diagnosis Questionnaire

The following questionnaire is designed to help you identify which particular anxiety disorder you may be dealing with. It is based on the official classification of anxiety disorders used by all mental health professionals and known as *DSM-IV* (*Diagnostic and Statistical Manual of Mental Disorders—Fourth Edition*).

1. Do you have spontaneous anxiety attacks that come out of the blue? (Only answer "yes" if you do not have any phobias.) Yes _____ No _____

2. Have you had at least one such attack in the last month? Yes _____ No _____

3. If you had an anxiety attack in the last month, did you worry about having another one? Or did you worry about the implications of your attack for your physical or mental health? Yes _____ No _____

4. In your worst experience with anxiety, did you have more than three of the following symptoms?

   ❑ shortness of breath or smothering sensation

   ❑ dizziness or unsteady feeling

   ❑ heart palpitations or rapid heartbeat

   ❑ trembling or shaking

   ❑ sweating

   ❑ choking

   ❑ nausea or abdominal distress

   ❑ feelings of being detached or out of touch with your body

   ❑ numbness or tingling sensations

   ❑ flushes or chills

   ❑ chest pain or discomfort

   ❑ fear of dying

   ❑ fear of going crazy or doing something out of control

   If your answers to 1, 2, 3, and 4 were Yes, stop. You've met the conditions for panic disorder.

   If your answer to 1 was Yes, but your anxiety reaction involved three or fewer of the symptoms listed under 4, you're experiencing what are called limited-symptom attacks, but do not have full-blown panic disorder.

   If you have panic attacks and phobias, go on.

5. Does fear of having panic attacks cause you to avoid going into certain situations? Yes _____ No _____

   If your answer to 5 was Yes, stop. It is likely that you are dealing with agoraphobia. See question 6 to determine the extent of your agoraphobia.

6. Which of the following situations do you avoid because you are afraid of panicking?

- ❑ going far away from home
- ❑ shopping in a grocery store
- ❑ standing in a grocery store line
- ❑ going to department stores
- ❑ going to shopping malls
- ❑ driving on freeways
- ❑ driving on surface streets far from home
- ❑ driving anywhere by yourself
- ❑ using public transportation (buses, trains, etc.)
- ❑ going over bridges (whether you're the driver or passenger)
- ❑ going through tunnels (as driver or passenger)
- ❑ flying in planes
- ❑ riding in elevators
- ❑ being in high places
- ❑ going to a dentist's or doctor's office
- ❑ sitting in a barber's or beautician's chair
- ❑ eating in restaurants
- ❑ going to work
- ❑ being too far from a safe person or safe place
- ❑ being alone
- ❑ going outside your house
- ❑ other _____

The number of situations you checked above indicates the extent of your agoraphobia and the degree to which it limits your activity.

If your answer to 5 was No, but you do have phobias, go on.

7. Do you avoid certain situations not primarily because you are afraid of panicking but because you're afraid of being embarrassed or negatively evaluated by other people (your embarrassment could subsequently lead you to panic)? Yes ____ No ____

If your answer to 7 was Yes, stop. It's likely that you are dealing with social phobia. See question 8 to determine the extent of your social phobia.

8. Which of the following situations do you avoid because of a fear of embarrassing or humiliating yourself?
- ❑ sitting in any kind of group (for example, at work, in school classrooms, social organizations, self-help groups)
- ❑ giving a talk or presentation before a small group of people
- ❑ giving a talk or presentation before a large group of people
- ❑ parties and social functions
- ❑ using public rest rooms
- ❑ eating in front of others
- ❑ writing or signing your name in the presence of others
- ❑ dating

❑ any situation where you might say something foolish

❑ other _____

The number of situations you checked indicates the extent to which social phobia limits your activities.

If your answers to questions 5 and 7 were No, but you have other phobias, continue.

9. Do you fear and avoid any one (or more than one) of the following?

    ❑ insects or animals, such as spiders, bees, snakes, rats, bats, or dogs

    ❑ heights (high floors in buildings, tops of hills or mountains, high-level bridges)

    ❑ driving

    ❑ tunnels

    ❑ bridges

    ❑ elevators

    ❑ airplanes (flying)

    ❑ doctors or dentists

    ❑ thunder or lightning

    ❑ water

    ❑ blood

    ❑ injections or medical procedures

    ❑ illness such as heart attacks or cancer

    ❑ darkness

    ❑ other _____

10. Do you have high degrees of anxiety usually only when you have to face one of these situations? Yes _____ No _____

    If you checked one or more items in 9 and answered Yes to 10, stop. It's likely that you're dealing with a specific phobia. If not, proceed.

11. Do you feel quite anxious much of the time but do not have distinct panic attacks, do not have phobias, and do not have specific obsessions or compulsions? Yes _____ No _____

12. Have you been prone to excessive worry for at least the last six months? Yes _____ No _____

13. Has your anxiety and worry been associated with at least three of the following six symptoms?

    ❑ restlessness or feeling keyed up or on edge

    ❑ being easily fatigued

    ❑ difficulty concentrating or mind going blank

    ❑ irritability

    ❑ muscle tension

    ❑ sleep disturbance (difficulty falling or staying asleep, or restless unsatisfying sleep)

If your answers to 11, 12, and 13 were Yes, stop. It's likely that you're dealing with generalized anxiety disorder. If you answered Yes to 11 but No to 12 or 13, you're dealing with an anxiety condition that is not severe enough to qualify as generalized anxiety disorder.

14. Do you have recurring intrusive thoughts such as hurting or harming a close relative, being contaminated with dirt or a toxic substance, fearing you forgot to lock your door or turn off an appliance, or an unpleasant fantasy of catastrophe? (You recognize that these thoughts are irrational but you can't keep them from coming into your mind.) Yes ____ No ____

15. Do you perform ritualistic actions such as washing your hands, checking, or counting to relieve anxiety over irrational fears that enter your mind? Yes ____ No ____

If you answered Yes to 14 but No to 15, you are probably dealing with obsessive-compulsive disorder, but have obsessions only.

If you answered Yes to 14 and 15, you're probably dealing with obsessive-compulsive disorder, with both obsessions and compulsions.

If you answered No to 14 and 15 and most or all of the preceding questions, but still have anxiety or anxiety-related symptoms, you may be dealing with post-traumatic stress disorder or a nonspecific anxiety condition. Use the section in this chapter on post-traumatic stress disorder to determine whether your symptoms fit this category.

Co-Occurrence of Anxiety Disorders

Many people have more than one anxiety disorder. For example, one survey of people with panic disorder found that 15–30 percent of them also have social phobia, 10–20 percent have a specific phobia, 25 percent have generalized anxiety disorder, and 8–10 percent have obsessive-compulsive disorder. People with agoraphobia quite often have social phobias and/or obsessive-compulsive difficulties. If you find that your particular condition fits the description for more than one anxiety disorder, you are not alone.

Causes of Anxiety Disorders

Here is an outline summarizing the many complex causes of anxiety disorders:

Causes of Anxiety Disorders

I. *Long-Term, Predisposing Causes*
   A. Heredity
   B. Childhood Circumstances
      1. Your Parents Communicate an Overly Cautious View of the World
      2. Your Parents Are Overly Critical and Set Excessively High Standards
      3. Emotional Insecurity and Dependence
      4. Your Parents Suppress Your Self-Assertiveness
   C. Cumulative Stress Over Time

II. *Biological Causes*
   A. Physiology of Panic
   B. Panic Attacks and the Noradrenergic Hypothesis
   C. Generalized Anxiety and the GABA/Benzodiazepine Hypothesis
   D. Obsessive-Compulsive Disorder and the Serotonin Hypothesis
   E. Medical Conditions That Can Cause Panic Attacks or Anxiety

III. Short-Term, Triggering Causes
   A. Stressors That Precipitate Panic Attacks
      1. Significant Personal Loss
      2. Significant Life Change
      3. Stimulants and Recreational Drugs
   B. Conditioning and the Origin of Phobias
   C. Trauma, Simple Phobias, and Post-Traumatic Stress Disorder

IV. Maintaining Causes
   A. Avoidance of Phobic Situations
   B. Anxious Self-Talk
   C. Mistaken Beliefs
   D. Withheld Feelings
   E. Lack of Assertiveness
   F. Lack of Self-Nurturing Skills
   G. Muscle Tension
   H. Stimulants and Other Dietary Factors
   I. High-Stress Lifestyle
   J. Lack of Meaning or Sense of Purpose

Excerpted and adapted with permission from *The Anxiety and Phobia Workbook* by Edmund J. Bourne, Ph.D. For more information on this and related books, see the "Further Reading" section in the back of the book.

CHAPTER 34

Panic Attacks

If you could only run away from these sudden, terrifying attacks: Your heart is pounding heavily or fluttering a mile a minute, you can't seem to get enough air, your hands are numb, your chest is tight, and you feel dizzy and unreal. You fear doing the everyday things that other people normally do: Going to the supermarket, or to a movie, driving a car or crossing a bridge. You are scared. Even if you realize that there is no realistic basis for your fear, you feel that you can't handle it; you just can't cope. You think that you may lose your mind, totally lose control, collapse, or die. Except that . . . you cannot run away from your body.

If this description sounds familiar, you may be one of the many who suffer from panic disorder. And, like so many who have this condition, you may unwittingly hold to certain beliefs that help to maintain the disorder. Some of these beliefs are that anxiety should be avoided at all cost; that anxiety and panic symptoms can last forever and even get worse and worse; and that such symptoms can escalate to physical disaster (heart attack or stroke) or psychological (going crazy) and/or behavioral (losing control) harm. These beliefs, the emotional fear, and the physical symptoms feed on each other. The anxious, chronic apprehension that you develop over the possibility of another attack ensures that the cycle will continue.

Must you remain totally trapped in the fear that your disorder creates? Is there no way out? I know there is. I have seen many people overcome panic disorder. It took a great deal of courage and the willingness to persist in the work that they needed to do. But they did it, and I believe you can, too. I strongly encourage you not to settle for a life with the limitations that panic disorder imposes.

Fear of panic lies at the core of panic disorder. The goal is to eliminate the fear of anxiety symptoms that is at the heart of panic disorder. If you no longer fear the bodily sensations and learn to cope with them, you can master panic attacks and overcome panic disorder. Cognitive-behavioral methods can help alter your thoughts about the catastrophic nature of panics, help you realize in your experiential mind that physical or psychological discomfort does not necessarily equal danger, and that panic sensations do not lead to disaster. Finally, these cognitive-behavioral methods can produce changes in brain chemistry that facilitate further improvement.

Recognizing Panic Attacks

A panic attack is identified by the presence of at least four of the following physical sensations and psychological reactions (reprinted with permission from the *Diagnositc and Statistical Manual of Mental Disorders*, Fourth ed. Washington, D.C.: American Psychiatric Association, 1994.):

1. Palpitations, pounding heart, or accelerated heart rate

2. Sweating

3. Trembling or shaking

4. Sensations of shortness of breath or smothering

5. Feeling of choking

6. Chest pain or discomfort

7. Nausea or abdominal distress

8. Feeling dizzy, unsteady, lightheaded, or faint

9. Derealization (feelings of unreality) or depersonalization (being detached from oneself)

10. Fear of losing control or going crazy

11. Fear of dying

12. Paresthesias (numbness or tingling sensations)

13. Chills or hot flushes

A sudden surge of anxiety, with fewer than four of these symptoms, is called a "limited symptom attack." It can be very uncomfortable and it is often experienced periodically by people on their way to recovery from panic attacks. Some people experience other sensations such as sudden diarrhea, instant headaches, intense weakness or stiffness in the legs, or blurred vision. Research on panic symptoms suggests that three symptoms are particularly common: palpitations, dizziness, and suffocation sensations. As the disorder continues over time, and no physical catastrophe occurs, the fear of going crazy or losing control often becomes the chief fear.

It is important to keep the definition of a panic attack clearly in mind. The expression "I panicked" is often used as synonymous for "I got extremely upset," which is clearly not the same as having a panic attack. Remember, high anxiety with several physical symptoms is not a panic attack unless it has a clear, sudden, intense onset.

Can the Symptoms Mean Anything Other than Panic Attacks?

Experiencing a surge of these symptoms does not necessarily mean that you are having a panic attack. Some diseases or physical dysfunctions produce sensations similar to those of panic. Hypoglycemia, hyperthyroidism, Cushing's syndrome, pheochromocytoma, caffeine or amphetamine intoxication, temporal lobe epilepsy, cardiac arrhythmias, audiovestibular system dysfunction, and mitral valve prolapse all produce sensations similar to panic. Sometimes a physical ailment can precipitate a panic attack. If you have not had a physical check-up in the last year or since the panics started, you may wish to do so to rule out a medical condition. Remember, sometimes physical ailments mimic panic, and they can also trigger or interact with panic.

Recording Your Panic Attacks

Clinical research has shown that the mere act of recording each panic helps in the mastery of and recovery from panic disorder. Look at the following worksheet. It allows you to make recordings for one month at a time. Make your recordings at the end of the day, but keep a tab during the day to recall your "SUDS" score as accurately as possible. "SUDS" stands for "Subjective Units of Distress." 0 SUDS equals no anxiety, 50 equals moderate anxiety, and 100 equals an intolerably high level of anxiety.

How to Use Worksheet 1 to Record Your Panic Attacks

Record the number of panics (zero, one, two, three, four, or five or more) for each date in the upper graph. Place an X where the two lines intersect (do not place the X in the white, empty space).

If you had no (zero) panic that day, there will also be no SUDS marking for that day. If you had one or more panics, rate the highest SUDS. That is, use the number from 0 to 100 that best describes your highest level of anxiety/fear during the panic(s). As with the upper graph, place an X where the lines intersect (not in the white empty space).

Remember—record only true panic attacks—sudden, intense surges of fear that occur and peak within ten minutes. Don't record longer stretches of prolonged anxiety. You may be surprised to find that your actual number of panic attacks is fewer than you think.

The Physiology of Fear and Panic

For survival, all organisms able to sense and move are able to anticipate threats and react quickly when threatened. This reaction is variously called the stress response, alarm response, or fight/flight response. Although this response is an ancient survival strategy, it is just as relevant today. If I were attacked while walking down the street, my body would very quickly mobilize a great amount of energy to save my life. Or if I were in a building that caught fire, I would need to assess the situation very quickly and determine how to save myself. These are the kinds of threats that mobilize the fight/flight response.

When the threat registers in the brain, fear activates the hypothalamus, and a signal is sent to the autonomic nervous system. (This is the part of the nervous system that usually functions "automatically" or outside of awareness. It is responsible for the regulation of respiration, circulation, digestion, body temperature, etc.) The autonomic nervous system consists of two main parts: the sympathetic nervous system (SNS) and the parasympathetic nervous system (PNS). In essence, the SNS is responsible for mobilizing the body and preparing it for the fight/flight response. The PNS relaxes the body and brings it back to normal. The two systems help to maintain the body's balance.

In the fight/flight response, many changes take place in the body. Fear activates the SNS as an entire unit producing a mass discharge. The ensuing reaction, the SNS-adrenal-medullary arousal (so named because of the SNS stimulation and the release of the adrenaline and noradrenaline hormones from the adrenal medulla), results in the following changes:

- *Cardiovascular*: The heart's output is increased with the heart beating faster and harder, to redistribute the blood volume to help deliver oxygen and glucose where it is needed. There is increased blood flow to the big muscles and decreased flow to the skin, hands and feet, gastrointestinal tract, and kidneys. The increased blood flow with added

Graphing Panic Frequency and Intensity

Name: _____ Month & Year: _____

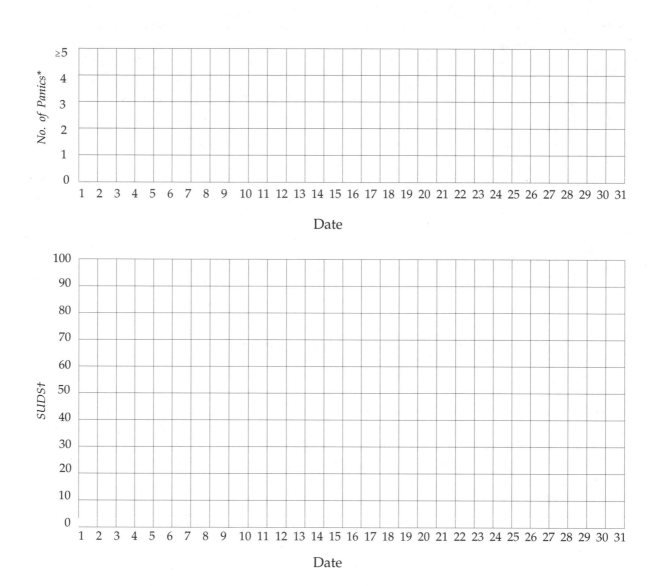

---

*   Panic is defined here as a very sudden, intense surge of fear.

†   If one or more panics, rate highest SUDS. SUDS: Subjective Units of Distress Scale. 0 = Totally calm, no anxiety or fear. 50 = Moderate level of anxiety/fear. 100 = Intolerable leves of anxiety/fear.

amounts of oxygen and glucose going to the arms and legs results in the greater muscle strength needed to fight or flee. The resulting symptoms include tachycardia (rapid heart beat) and numbness and tingling in the extremities (because of decreased blood flow). Think of the symptoms you experience in a panic and you will begin to see the connections between panic attacks and the physiology of the fight/flight response.

- *Pulmonary:* The lungs respond to the danger signals by greatly increased breathing (heavier and faster) to bring in the extra oxygen needed for the muscle tissues (as explained above).

- *Skin and Sweat Glands:* Because of decreased blood volume from the skin, there is vascular constriction in and under the skin, which produces symptoms such as numbness and tingling. Sweating helps regulate the body temperature and prevents it from rising to dangerous levels.

- *Mental/Behavioral:* Adrenaline increases concentration. When you are extremely alert to threat signals, you do not worry about irrelevant matters, such as whether you left dirty dishes in the sink. Your behavior will require either aggression to fight off the attacker, or fleeing for fear of your life.

- *Other effects include:* Dilation of the pupils to increase the visual field, accelerated blood coagulation to protect against hemorrhage, and increased blood pressure to improve circulation. The hypothalamus helps to coordinate the SNS effects with those of other neuroendocrine systems. Thus, certain hormones (catecholamine and corticotropic hormones) are secreted in larger amounts and are responsible for some of the physiological changes occurring in the fight/flight response. You may wonder what would happen if the SNS maintained this arousal state indefinitely. This would be very dangerous, indeed, but in fact, it does not happen. The reason it does not happen is that before adrenaline and noradrenaline can reach potentially harmful levels, they are destroyed by other chemicals; and the PNS automatically "kicks in" to restore balance in the body.

For a number of years, researchers have been aware of the connection between the physiology of the fight/flight response and panic attacks. The first panic can be seen as a misfiring of the fight/flight response, or a "false alarm." In 1988, Dr. David Barlow, in his book *Anxiety and Its Disorders: The Nature and Treatment of Anxiety and Panic*, emphasized this connection in the treatment of panic disorder. Since then, many panic disorder sufferers have found this information invaluable in their struggle to understand their panics.

The SNS is stimulated in a number of situations. Stressors other than fear can also activate the SNS. Physical stresses might include surgery, injury, or certain illnesses. Mental stresses might include rage, facing dilemmas with no easy solutions, or other emotional upheavals. A variety of different situations can all elicit the same stress reaction. Emotional stressors are among the more common precipitants of the stress response.

Panic disorder seems to occur more in people with a psychological vulnerability and/or a biological predisposition. The first panic attack often occurs in a stressful context. When asked about conditions preceding their first panic, people often describe stressful circumstances such as divorce, death, illness within self or family, bankruptcy, interpersonal conflict, and illegal drug usage. Frequently, the stresses involve new, demanding situations and experiences. But often people do not make the connection, because the panic doesn't necessarily take place right in the middle of a particularly stressful event but when things have calmed down. Stressful life experiences activate the SNS, sometimes in its entirety, producing the fight/flight or alarm response.

In panic, the physical reactions are the same as in true danger—but there is no outlet. If you panic when you are in a traffic jam on a bridge, you do not have someone to fight and you cannot very well leave your car and flee. Yet your body prepared itself for such action. There is now too much oxygen coming in compared to your body's need. This leads to diminished oxygen release to the tissues. As a result of less oxygen to the tissues, including the brain, you may have feelings of lightheadedness or dizziness, or feelings of unreality, or blurred vision. You may try to compensate by breathing harder, perhaps causing yourself discomfort and chest pains. So here is the paradox: You may feel as if you are not breathing enough air, when in fact you are *taking in more oxygen than you need*! When experiencing the above-described sensations, intervening by slowing your breathing is very helpful.

Breathing Retraining: Severing the Connection between Panic and Hyperventilation

Let's begin by describing a situation in which you might experience a variety of physical symptoms. Imagine yourself in a very crowded store or sitting in the back seat of a two-door car. You start to feel weak in the knees, lightheaded, and dizzy; your hands tingle or they are numb; you have heart palpitations and a lump in your throat; and you feel that the ground beneath you is shifting. More than feeling breathless, you have this need to take a deep, satisfying breath. But no matter how hard you strain for air, you can't seem to get enough. You are hungry for air, but there's just not enough. Now you fear that you may embarrass yourself, faint, or die, and you want to scream out loud, "Let me out of here!" Yet there does not seem to be enough air for even those few words, and you're now desperate to step outside and get fresh air. Once outside, you finally feel that you can breathe again.

What caused these symptoms? Anxiety, panic, or hyperventilation, or any combination of the three can produce those sensations.

Overbreathing Test

Before proceeding further, let us do a test that may help determine how much you can benefit from breathing retraining. The overbreathing test is not dangerous and it is very unlikely to trigger a panic. Nevertheless, people with certain conditions should not take this test, unless permitted by their physicians.

CAUTION: You can do this test unless you fall in any of the following categories: If you have epilepsy or a history of seizures, serious asthma, chronic arrhythmia, heart or lung problems, a history of fainting and/or very low blood pressure, or are pregnant. (If you have any doubts, consult your physician.) If you cannot do this test for any of the reasons above, proceed to the section "Recognizing Hyperventilation."

What You Need

1. A timer or a watch or clock with a second hand.

2. Pad and pen.

3. A brown 6"x 10" paper bag (lunch-size bag). (Do NOT use a plastic bag.)

Practicing Before Taking the Real Test

The overbreathing test is sort of like panting, but a little slower. You need to breathe deeply, in and out through your mouth. Make your breath audible, i.e., produce a sound as you exhale, loud enough so that it can be heard across the room. Now, stand up and while standing, practice by taking four to six breaths like that. When you have finished, return to this page.

PLEASE PRACTICE NOW.

Did you feel strong symptoms? Then it was probably done correctly. For the real test, below, make sure that you blow out a lot of air each time you breathe out.

Test Instructions

1. Overbreathe as described for 1.5 minutes while standing.

2. While doing the exercise, pay attention to any sensations that you feel and remember them.

3. If you find the sensations intolerable, naturally, you can stop, but if at all possible, try to complete the 1.5 minutes.

4. After the test, place the paper bag over your mouth and nose, not allowing much air to escape from the edge of the bag. Now breathe normally in and out. See how quickly you can stop the symptoms that were activated by the overbreathing.

5. Write down all the sensations that you had during the test.

PLEASE DO THE TEST NOW (before continuing reading).

Did the symptoms produced in this test resemble some of the symptoms you have in a panic?

If you felt just a little lightheaded but nothing like the sensations in a panic.

I'm glad that you tried! It is possible that hyperventilation does not play a major part in your panics. However, we know that about 60 percent of all panic attacks are accompanied by acute hyperventilation. Possibly you have not given it your best shot. You may have been apprehensive and not done it quite right, or you may not have done it long enough. Review the instructions carefully and try the test at least one more time to make sure.

If you were too scared to do the test.

It is good that you are honest with yourself and with me. Let us review. If you do not fall into any of the medical-exclusion categories, there should not be any risk involved in doing this exercise, but I can understand that being very sensitive to panic symptoms, this test might scare you.

At this point, a coach may be essential to you. (I always take this test along with my clients, so they will feel more comfortable. You can imagine how many times I have done this!) If you are too frightened, you may ask your coach to do it alone first. Then the coach can share with you what it was like. You will know better what to expect and will be able to discuss your apprehensions. A truly helpful coach will encourage you and be there for you. Then you can do it along with your coach. Remember, the more you understand what contributes to your panic, the easier it will be to learn the skills necessary to overcome them. Understanding increases hope and motivation.

If the symptoms were very similar to those in panic.

This is good news! You are moving closer to understanding your panic symptoms and how they are produced. This is not to say that hyperventilation alone causes panics. Panic attacks are quite complex. Yet open your mind to the possibility of a connection.

If you found many similarities between the hyperventilation and your panic symptoms, you stand to gain a great deal from breathing retraining. Often, the symptoms can be effectively and directly diminished, which will lower the intensity of your anxiety and fear.

Recognizing Hyperventilation

Symptoms of Hyperventilation

The major components of this syndrome are as follows:

- Lightheadedness

- Giddiness

- Dizziness

- Shortness of breath with a sense of impending suffocation (called dyspnea)

- Heart palpitations

Other common symptoms are:

- Numbness and/or tingling sensations (paresthesias)

- Chest pain

- Dry mouth and throat

- Clammy hands

- Swallowing difficulty

- Tremors

- Sweating

- Weakness and fatigue

As mentioned earlier, hyperventilation can be brought on by some organic causes due to injury or disease. It is more often brought on by drug effects and withdrawal from drugs, emotional reactions to stress, and just plain faulty breathing habits. Breathing retraining is then the preferred course to bring hyperventilation under control.

Breathing Retraining

If you are a chronic hyperventilator, this retraining is crucial to normalize the chemistry in your body and to make you less vulnerable to minor changes in breathing. Whether or not you hyperventilate acutely in a panic, diaphragmatic breathing can be an extremely useful coping skill for you.

Take a Deep Breath

Before proceeding, let us check your current breathing.

What you need:

1. A mirror.

2. Pad and pen.

Instructions:

1. Watch yourself in the mirror, and immediately afterward write down in detail what you did.

2. Take one or two deep breaths in and out.

PLEASE DO THE TEST NOW (before continuing reading).

- Now that your responses have been written down, look for the following:

- What did your chest do?

- What did your mouth do?

- What did your shoulders do?

- Was there a pause anywhere?

- How fast did you breathe?

Keep your notes for later reference.

Stage 1: Compare Your Regular Breathing with Diaphragmatic Breathing

The goal of breathing retraining is to bring about balance in the oxygen/carbon dioxide levels. This is accomplished by slow, diaphragmatic breathing through the nose. It can help reduce the severity of symptoms during acute panic. The more you can slow down the physical sensations during periods of high anxiety, the more you can use your rational mind to assess what is going on.

Why is it important to breathe in and out through the nose? The nose's primary function is to control our breathing. It reduces the volume of air going in and out. You are much less likely to hyperventilate while breathing in and out only through your nose.

Of course, if you have a bad cold, allergies, or something else blocking the passage of air through your nose you will not be able to do this. In that case, keep your mouth open just a little and try to let the same amount of air go slowly in and out through your mouth. Other autonomic (involuntary) functions are very difficult to control directly, but breathing—which is also automatic—can be brought under voluntary control. You can learn to control your breathing under relaxed and stressful conditions, even in the midst of a panic.

What you need:

1. Your notes from "Take a Deep Breath" to compare what you did previously with what we will do now.

2. A mirror.

Instructions:

1. Standing up, place one hand on your diaphragm/stomach area so that at least your little finger (and maybe your ring finger) is positioned over your navel.

2. Take in a deep breath through your nose while pushing the diaphragm/stomach out against your hand. When you slowly exhale through your nose, the diaphragm/stomach area should be pulled back in. Here is an easy way to remember it: When you take a deep breath you need to make room for the extra air that you are inhaling. You don't want to direct that air just to your chest (you remember why) but to take it all the way down to your diaphragm, so naturally, your diaphragm must expand. With that expansion your lungs get pushed downward and can utilize the oxygen to the fullest. Conversely, when you exhale and release the used air, your diaphragm should naturally pull back in.

3. Try not to lift your chest or shoulders. Your shoulders should not move. Keep your mouth closed throughout the breathing cycle. Breathe as slowly as you can without making it feel artificial.

PLEASE PRACTICE NOW. Try it several times.

It may not feel natural at all, especially if you have been a chronic chest (thoracic) breather. It may be exactly the opposite of what you are used to doing. Get feedback from the mirror. Is it difficult? If yes, then you are conforming to the norm. Take heart: There is an almost foolproof way of learning to breathe diaphragmatically.

Stage 2: Learning Diaphragmatic Breathing

I will provide very detailed instructions for you to learn this well.

What you need:

• One or two bed pillows.

Instructions:

1. We will proceed from the easiest to the more difficult steps. Practice all the steps. Practice without fail at least five minutes, twice a day, every day, until you master all the steps. Do not proceed to the next step until you have mastered the previous one. Remember to breathe in and out through your nose, keeping your mouth closed at all times. Breathe slowly rather than quickly. Take about one week to practice before proceeding.

2. Lie down on your stomach on a bed or carpeted floor. Bend your arms so that your hands are resting alongside your head. Breathe diaphragmatically in and out through your nose slowly and deeply. Feel what is happening. It is very difficult to expand your chest in this position. Since your stomach is flat against a surface, you will feel your back (around the waist) expand upward. Do this until you have a good feel for it, for as long as you need.

3. With your arms at your sides, lie down on your back on a bed or carpeted floor, without a pillow under your head. Instead, place one or two pillows on your diaphragm/stomach. You should be able to observe the top of the pillow from the corner of your eyes. (If it strains your neck, make sure you use two pillows.) When you breathe in, expand your diaphragm/stomach so the pillow moves up. When you breathe out,

the pillow should go down again. I want you to exaggerate the movements, so the pillow clearly moves up and down. Inhale slowly, and when ready, exhale slowly.

If you have studied yoga, do not follow the instructions that suggest you should take in a deep breath, hold for a few seconds, and breathe out. Instead, pause only at the end of the breathing cycle. Either breathe out slower than you breathe in (e.g., 1, 2, 3 seconds breathing in; 1, 2, 3, 4, 5 seconds breathing out) or breathe in and out at the same rate and hold after the exhalation (e.g., 1, 2, 3, 4 seconds in; 1, 2, 3, 4 seconds out—and then hold). Hold only for as long as is comfortable before you take in your next breath. Practice this for as long as you need until you have a good feel for it. I usually do not instruct people to count seconds, but you may do so if you find it helpful. The ideal rate of breathing at rest is 8 to 10 breaths per minute. The exact number of breaths per minute is not crucial, however. What is important is to practice breathing increasingly slowly.

4. Once you can do the exercise above with a pillow, put it aside and practice the same way, only with your hand resting on your diaphragm/stomach rather than the pillow.

5. When you can do the exercise well with your hand, lie with your arms at your sides while looking at the ceiling. Or close your eyes. Now put your mind in your diaphragm/stomach and feel it. The way I view this, it is like "becoming one with my breathing," as if my mind were not located in my head but in my diaphragm/stomach area. The goal is to feel your diaphragm/stomach area without looking at or touching it.

6. Lie on your side on a bed or carpeted floor. Place a pillow under your head and your hands somewhere near your head or holding the pillow. Breathe diaphragmatically. Feel your diaphragm/stomach area move out (breathing in) and move in (breathing out).

7. Sit on a sofa leaning back and watch your stomach move out and in. Your shoulders should be perfectly still.

8. Sit erect in a straight-backed chair and practice the same exercise as in number 7, above.

9. Stand and practice as we did in Stage 1, earlier in this chapter.

10. Remember, breathe as slowly as you can.

Overcoming the Fear of Physical Symptoms in Panic

Think of a high-anxiety situation that you experienced some time before you had your first panic attack. I'm talking about situations such as your first job interview or a final exam in school. What happened when you got anxious? Do you recall your heart beating faster or starting to sweat more than usual? Were you afraid of those sensations back then? Most likely not. Yet they revealed your anxiety, and you may then have tried to calm yourself down. But now it's different, isn't it? Not only do you suffer from anxiety, but from fear of the anxiety, and as mentioned frequently in this book, fear intensifies your physical sensations.

The more you fear the physical sensations of panic, the more you develop hypervigilance, even to normal bodily sensations. In other words, you start to monitor normal changes in your body. Even "harmless" (i.e., nonpanic) sensations can then elicit panic, because to you the sensations signal danger. Viewing panics as dangerous has become a part of your experiential mind, which is that part of your mind rooted in emotionally important experiences. The best way to change this view of panics is to have "corrective" experiences.

In sum, panic disorder is like being phobic about your own internal sensations, except that, unlike other phobic fears, you cannot run away from your body or the symptoms it produces. It is a learned fear of your own physical sensations. You need to relearn that they are not dangerous. In the past you used distraction and other means to minimize or avoid the sensations. In this section you will do the opposite; you will learn through direct experience that they are harmless. If you then respond differently to the sensations, the sensations will no longer produce anxiety.

The type of practice you will learn from is called interoceptive exposure, which means to expose oneself directly to one's internal sensations. The conditioned (learned) fear of panics will diminish, becoming weaker and weaker. As you keep practicing, you will slowly decondition yourself. This is a proven, highly effective method for overcoming fear in panic disorder.

Desensitization to the physical sensations of panic is achieved by eliciting sensations similar to those in panic. This work will allow you to test your thoughts about the uncontrollability and catastrophic nature of panic.

The sensations that we want to bring on include rapid heart beat, dizziness, lightheadedness, tingling, heat, stomach discomfort, suffocation, shortness of breath, chest tension, choking sensations, throat tightness, and feelings of unreality. These are among the primary panic sensations. To keep things in perspective, let me remind you that these symptoms are not scary for everyone. Some people seek them out: Children like to spin like tops to make themselves dizzy, people of all ages go on amusement park rides, watch horror movies and sports events, and sometimes even engage in such potentially destructive ways as taking illegal drugs to feel some of those sensations! The personal interpretations of these symptoms can be either excitement or fear and can be viewed as either comfortable or uncomfortable. As you learn that the symptoms are not dangerous, your anxiety sensitivity (i.e., fear of the symptoms) should decrease.

Exclusions

You are **cautioned not to do these exercises** if you have epilepsy or a history of seizures, serious asthma, chronic arrhythmia, heart or lung problems, a history of fainting and/or very low blood pressure, or if you are pregnant. If you have any doubts, consult your physician. Describe the specific exercises to your physician, who will easily tell whether any of the exercises are contraindicated for you.

Actually, you have already done one of the interoceptive exercises. The overbreathing test is here referred to as "Hyperventilation." You can do the exercises in any order. It is recommended that you start with the ones that seem easiest for you. You can modify the times, especially when starting. If you cannot tolerate the sensations, stop earlier. However, keep in mind that eventually you want to feel the sensations to their fullest. If you are too fearful to do the exercises alone, use a coach. Do not ask an anxious person to be your coach. You want someone calm. Ask your coach to be a cheerleader for you. If you wish, you can follow this plan: (a) Have the coach do the exercise first. (b) Do it with the coach. (c) Do it while your coach watches you. (d) Do it alone. All exercises eventually should be done alone.

Instructions

Use SUDS = Subjective Units of Distress Scale. 0 = Totally calm, no anxiety or fear. 50 = Moderate level of anxiety/fear. 100 = Intolerable level of anxiety/fear. Use the number from 0 to 100 that best describes your anxiety/fear level.

Some exercises have (a) and (b) versions. Follow the first time limit given for each exercise in version (a), and keep repeating it, till your SUDS is less than 20. Then follow with version (b), and keep repeating the exercise, till your SUDS is less than 20.

It is extremely important that you distinguish between sensation intensity and anxiety/fear. You can feel very strong sensations and they may be very uncomfortable, but do they produce fear? For instance, one of my clients always got extremely strong sensations while hyperventilating, but his SUDS level decreased from a 75 to a 10.

The intensity of the sensations themselves (aside from anxiety/fear) may decline in strength as they lose their novelty or they may remain high. It is perfectly normal to continue to experience strong sensations, as long as your anxiety (SUDS) diminishes to less than 20.

If some exercises produce strong anxiety, this is actually very good, since you then have something concrete to work with to help reduce your fear. If the anxiety level is high when you start with an exercise, and you keep working on it, the effect of watching the anxiety decrease is very powerful.

If the sensations produced are very similar to those in panic, this is excellent. But even if the sensations are different, it is good practice for decreasing your general vulnerability. As I mentioned before, beyond diminishing fear of panics, the goal is also to lower your general anxiety sensitivity. Also, some day you may have a panic with different sensations than you have experienced, and this could help you in such an event.

If an exercise produces a SUDS below 20 the first time, try version (b). If it remains less than 20, go to another exercise.

MAKE A SCHEDULE FOR PRACTICE. Plan on doing these exercises five days a week. Do the exposures several times in a row, either the same or different exercises. Remember, the more diligently you work, the faster your progress. If you find yourself avoiding doing them or doing them less well, get support from your coach.

Plan rewards that you really look forward to, especially if you find yourself putting off doing the exercises.

Interoceptive Exercises

Exercise	Length of Time*	Instructions
1. Shake head side to side	30 sec.	Lower your head a bit and shake it loosely from side to side with your eyes open. When the timer goes off, suddenly lift your head and stare straight ahead for a little while.
2. Head between legs	1 min.	Sit in a straight chair. Bend your head down between your legs, trying to keep it lower than your heart level. When the timer goes off, suddenly lift your head and stare straight ahead for a little while.
3. Run in place	1 min.	Jog in place. Jog vigorously. (Or run up stairs.)
4. Complete body tension	1 min.	While sitting, make fists with your hands, tense your feet, bring your shoulders forward and tense your chest and entire body. Breathe deeply throughout.

Exercise	Length of Time*	Instructions
5. Hold breath	30 sec.	Just as you begin timing, take a deep breath and try to hold it for 30 sec. If you cannot hold for that length of time, stop earlier.
6. Spin	(a) 1 min. (b) 1 min. and walk	Spin around yourself at a good pace. Give yourself room and have a wall nearby to put your hand against if you lose your balance. Or use an office chair that spins and push against the floor as you spin.
7. Straw breathing	(a) 2 min. (b) 2 min. (pinching nose)	Place the thin straw in your mouth and breathe in and out through it. Do (b) while also slightly pinching your nose with your other hand.
8. Hyperventilate	1 min.	While standing, breathe deeply in and out through your mouth (like panting, but slower, and breathing out more than breathing in). Make it audible, i.e., make a sound that can be heard across the room.

* Do (a) first and keep repeating it until your SUDS level is less than 20. Then do (b), and keep repeating until your SUDS level is less than 20.

Worksheet: Interoceptive Exposure Record

Name: _____ Date _____

SUDS: Subjective Units of Distress Scale

0 = Totally calm, no anxiety/fear
50 = Moderate level of anxiety/fear
100 = Intolerable level of anxiety/fear

Exercise	Describe Any Sensations Felt	SUDS	Check if SUDS >20
Shake head, 30 sec.			
Head down, 1.5 min.			
Run in place, 1 min.			
Body tension, 1 min.			
Hold breath, 30 sec.			
Spin, 1 min.			
Straw breathing, 2 min.			
Hyperventilation, 1.5 min.			

You may ask, "Is this really necessary?"

Your apprehension is very understandable. In the past, the emphasis was on slowing down the physical reactions with relaxation. However, research has shown increasingly that one has to confront fears, face them, and deal with them. This is partly because fear grows in the absence of the fearful sensation or situation. By now, you have acquired a lot of knowledge about panics, and appreciate how important it is to overcome the fear of the symptoms of panics. There is no way around this.

If this task seems too difficult for you, take two approaches, already mentioned. The first is: Do the exercises with a coach. Ask your coach to do them while you watch before you try them yourself. This is not a sign of weakness. Most of my clients would not do them either, if they did not do them first with me and/or the group. The other is to start with whichever exercise seems easiest to you.

References

Barlow, D. H. 1988. *Anxiety and Its Disorders: The Nature and Treatment of Anxiety and Panic.* New York: Basic Books.

Beck, A. T. 1976. *Cognitive Therapy and the Emotional Disorders.* New York: International Universities Press.

Excerpted and adapted with permission from *An End to Panic: Breakthrough Techniques for Overcoming Panic Disorder* by Elke Zuercher-White, Ph.D. For more information on this and related books, see the "Further Reading" section in the back of the book.

CHAPTER 35

Phobias

Help for Phobias: Imagery Desensitization

The most effective way to overcome a phobia is simply to face it. Continuing to avoid a situation that frightens you is, more than anything else, what keeps the phobia alive.

Having to face a particular situation you have been avoiding for years may at the outset seem an impossible task. Yet this task can be made manageable by breaking it down into sufficiently small steps. Instead of entering a situation all at once, you can do it very gradually in small or even minute increments. And instead of confronting the situation directly in real life, you can face it first in your imagination. This is where imagery desensitization comes in.

Sensitization is a process of becoming sensitized to a particular stimulus. In the case of phobias, it involves learning to associate anxiety with a particular situation. Perhaps you once panicked while sitting in a restaurant or by yourself at home. If your anxiety level was high, it's likely that you acquired a strong association between being in that particular situation and being anxious. Thereafter, being in, near, or perhaps just thinking about the situation automatically triggered your anxiety: a connection between the situation and a strong anxiety response was established. Because this connection was automatic and seemingly beyond your control, you probably did all you could to avoid putting yourself in the situation again. Your avoidance was rewarded because it saved you from reexperiencing your anxiety. At the point where you began to always avoid the situation, you developed a full-fledged phobia.

Desensitization is the process of unlearning the connection between anxiety and a particular situation. For desensitization to occur, you need to enter a phobic situation while you're in a relaxed or relatively relaxed state. With imagery desensitization, you visualize being in a phobic situation while you're relaxed. If you begin to feel anxious, you retreat from your imagined phobic situation and imagine yourself instead in a very peaceful scene. With real-life desensitization, you confront a phobic situation directly, but physically retreat to a safe place if your anxiety reaches a certain level. In both cases the point is to 1) unlearn a connection between a phobic situation (such as driving on the freeway) and an anxiety response and 2) reassociate feelings of relaxation and calmness with that particular situation. Repeatedly visualizing a phobic situation while relaxed—or actually entering it while relaxed—will eventually allow you to overcome your tendency to respond with anxiety. If you can train yourself to relax in response to something, you will no longer feel anxious about it. Relaxation and anxiety are incompatible responses, so the goal of desensitization is to learn to remain in the phobic situation and be relaxed at the same time.

You may be asking why it's necessary to go through the desensitization process initially in your imagination. Why not just face the dreaded object or situation in real life? More than 30 years ago, the behavioral psychologist Joseph Wolpe discovered the efficacy of desensitization through imagery. In some cases it is so effective that it supplants the need for real-life desensitization. In other cases, imagery desensitization reduces anxiety sufficiently to make the task of real-life desensitization possible.

Much of the anxiety you have, say, about flying, driving, or being in an elevator is connected with your thoughts and fantasies about these situations. Becoming desensitized first to anxious thoughts and scenes experienced in fantasy can pave the way toward handling the phobic situation in real life. Even if the real-life situation continues to evoke some anxiety, this anxiety may be considerably reduced after having practiced imagery desensitization. This transfer effect from imagery to real life was discovered in the early sixties and has been confirmed by research and practice in desensitization techniques over the past 30 years. I strongly recommend that you use the guidelines in this chapter and practice desensitizing yourself to your phobia through imagery before attempting real-life desensitization.

Practicing imagery desensitization before confronting a phobia in real life also helps to overcome anticipatory anxiety. As the term implies, this is the anxiety you experience in anticipation of having to deal with a phobic situation. Hours or days before making a speech or your first flight, for example, you may experience numerous anxious thoughts and images about the upcoming situation. Dwelling on these anxious thoughts and images only creates more and more anxiety, long before you ever deal with the actual situation. By systematically training youself to relax as you imagine scenes of a future phobic situation, you can reduce your anticipatory anxiety substantially.

A final important reason for practicing desensitization through imagery is that there are many situations in which it is inconvenient if not impossible to expose yourself to your phobic situation in real life. This is particularly a problem if your phobia has to do with natural disasters such as earthquakes or hurricanes. It will also certainly be inconvenient and expensive to undergo a series of real-life exposures if you're phobic about the bar exam or transcontinental flights. Much of the fear and anticipatory anxiety around these phobias can be removed through a systematic program that never strays from the realm of your imagination.

Success with imagery desensitization depends on four things:

1. Your capacity to attain a deep state of relaxation. See the chapter on Stress earlier in part V

2. Constructing an appropriate hierarchy: a series of scenes or situations relating to your phobia which are ranked from mildly anxiety-provoking to very anxiety-provoking

3. The vividness and detail with which you can visualize each scene in the hierarchy, as well as your peaceful scene

4. Your patience and perseverance in practicing desensitization on a regular basis

Constructing an Appropriate Hierarchy

A well-constructed hierarchy allows you to approach a phobic situation gradually through a sequence of steps. You can use the following guidelines and sample hierarchies to develop your own:

1. Choose a particular phobic situation you want to work on, whether this involves going to the grocery store, driving on the freeway, or giving a talk before a group.

2. Imagine having to deal with this situation in a very limited way—one that hardly bothers you at all. You can create this scenario by imagining yourself somewhat removed in space or time from full exposure to the situation—such as parking in front of the grocery store without going in, or imagining your feelings one month before you have to give a presentation. Or you can diminish the difficulty of the situation by visualizing yourself with a supportive person at your side. Try in these ways to create a very mild instance of your phobia and designate it as the first step in your hierarchy.

3. Now imagine what would be the strongest or most challenging scene relating to your phobia, and place it at the opposite extreme as the highest step in your hierarchy. For example, if you're phobic about grocery stores, your highest step might be waiting in a long line at the checkout counter by yourself. For flying, such a step might involve taking off on a transcontinental flight, or encountering severe air turbulence midflight. For public speaking, you might imagine either presenting to a large crowd, giving a long presentation, or speaking on a very demanding topic. See if you can identify what specific parameters of your phobia make you more or less anxious and use them to develop scenes of varying intensity. The scenes in the first example below become progressively more challenging in terms of three distinct parameters: 1) distance driven, 2) degree of traffic congestion, and 3) driving alone.

4. Now take some time to imagine six or more scenes of graduated intensity related to your phobia and rank them according to their anxiety-provoking potential. It is desirable to have these scenes correspond to things you will actually do later in real-life exposure. Place your scenes in ascending order between the two extremes you've already defined. Use the sample hierarchies below to assist you. Then write down your list of scenes on the Hierarchy Worksheet.

Phobia About Driving on Freeways

Visualize:

1. Watching from a distance as cars drive past on the freeway

2. Riding in a car on the freeway with someone else driving (this could be broken down into several steps, varying the distance traveled or time spent on the freeway)

3. Driving on the freeway the distance of one exit with a friend sitting next to you at a time when there is little traffic

4. Driving the distance of one exit with a friend when the freeway is busier (but not at rush hour)

5. Repeat step 3 alone

6. Repeat step 4 alone

7. Driving the distance of two exits with a friend sitting next to you at a time when there is little traffic

8. Driving the distance of two exits with a friend sitting next to you at a time when there is moderate traffic

9. Repeat step 7 alone

10. Repeat step 8 alone

11. In steps above this level you would increase the distance you drive and also include driving during rush-hour conditions.

Phobia About Giving Presentations at Work

Visualize:

1. Preparing a talk which you don't give

2. Preparing a talk and delivering it in front of one friend

3. Preparing a talk and delivering it in front of three friends

4. Giving a brief presentation to three or four people at work who you know well

5. Same as step 4 but a longer presentation

6. Giving a brief presentation to ten to fifteen acquaintances at work

7. Same as step 6 but a longer presentation

8. Giving a brief presentation to three or four strangers

9. Same as step 8 but a longer presentation

10. Giving a brief presentation to ten to fifteen strangers

11. Giving a brief presentation to 50 strangers

Phobia About Getting Injections

Visualize:

1. Watching a movie in which a minor character gets a shot

2. A friend talking about her flu shot

3. Making a routine doctor's appointment

4. Driving to a medical center

5. Parking your car in the medical center parking lot

6. Thinking about shots in the doctor's waiting room

7. A woman coming out of the treatment room rubbing her arm

8. A nurse with a tray of syringes walking past

9. Entering an examination room

10. A doctor entering the room and asking you about your symptoms

11. The doctor saying you need an injection

12. A nurse entering the room with injection materials

13. The nurse filling a syringe

14. The smell of alcohol being applied to a cotton ball

15. A hypodermic needle poised in the doctor's hand

16. Receiving a penicillin shot in the buttocks

17. Receiving a flu shot in the arm

18. Having a large blood sample taken

Note that in all three examples, increments from one step to the next are very small. One of the keys to success with imagery desensitization is creating a hierarchy with sufficiently small steps so that it is relatively easy to progress from one level to the next.

5. Generally, eight to twelve steps in a hierarchy are sufficient, although in some cases you may want to include as many as twenty. Fewer than eight steps is usually an insufficient number to make the hierarchy meaningful.

6. Sometimes you may find it difficult to go from one step to the next in your hierarchy. You may be able to relax in the context of the scene you've created in step 9, but become very anxious when you visualize step 10. In this instance you need to construct an intermediate scene (at "9½") that can serve as a bridge between the two original scenes.

7. If you have difficulty feeling comfortable with the initial scene in your hierarchy, you need to create a still-less-threatening scene to start out with.

How to Practice Imagery Desensitization

Desensitization through imagery is a two-step process. First, you need to take the time to get very relaxed. Second, you go through the desensitization process itself, which involves alternating back and forth between visualizing a particular step in your hierarchy and recapturing your feelings of deep relaxation. Be sure to follow all of the steps outlined below.

1. Relax. Spend ten to fifteen minutes getting relaxed. Use progressive muscle relaxation or any other relaxation technique that works well for you. See the chapter on Stress earlier in part V.

2. Visualize yourself in a peaceful scene. This is a relaxing place you can vividly picture in your mind. It can be a scene outdoors (such as a beach, a meadow, or the mountains), indoors (curling up by a fireplace), or can come completely from your imagination. Above all it is a place where you feel safe. Spend about one minute there.

3. Visualize yourself in the first scene of your phobia hierarchy. Stay there for thirty seconds to one minute, trying to picture everything with as much vividness and detail as possible, as if you were "right there." Do not picture yourself as being anxious. If you see yourself in the scene at all, imagine yourself acting and feeling calm and confident—dealing with the situation in the way you would most like to. If you feel little or no anxiety (below level 2 on a ten-step Anxiety Scale), proceed to the next scene up in your hierarchy.

4. If you experience mild to moderate anxiety (level 2 or 3 on a ten-step Anxiety Scale), spend thirty seconds to one minute in the scene, allowing yourself to relax to it. You can do this by breathing away any anxious sensations in your body or by repeating a calming affirmation such as, "I am calm and at ease." Picture yourself handling the situation in a calm and confident manner.

5. After up to a minute of exposure, retreat from the phobic scene to your peaceful scene. Spend about 1 minute in your peaceful scene or long enough to get fully relaxed. Then repeat your visualization of the same phobic scene as in step 4 for thirty seconds to one minute. Keep alternating between a given phobic scene and your peaceful scene (about one minute each) until the phobic scene loses its capacity to elicit any (or more than very mild) anxiety. Then you are ready to proceed to the next step up in your hierarchy.

6. If visualizing a particular scene causes you strong anxiety (level 4 or above on the Anxiety Scale), do not spend more than ten seconds there. Retreat immediately to your peaceful scene and stay there until you're fully relaxed. Expose yourself gradually to the more difficult scenes, alternating short intervals of exposure with retreat to your peaceful scenes. If a particular scene in your hierarchy continues to cause difficulty, you probably need to add another step—one that is intermediate in difficulty between the last step you completed successfully and the one that is troublesome.

7. Continue progressing up your hierarchy step by step in imagination. Generally it will take a minimum of two exposures to a scene to reduce your anxiety to it. Keep in mind that it's important not to proceed to a more advanced step until you're fully comfortable with the preceding step. Practice imagery desensitization for fifteen to twenty minutes each day and begin your practice not with a new step but with the last step you successfully negotiated. (Then proceed to a new step.)

To sum up, imagery desensitization involves four steps that you apply to each scene in your hierarchy:

1. *Visualize* the phobic scene as vividly as possible.

2. *React to the scene*, allowing yourself to relax with it for thirty seconds to one minute if your anxiety stays below level 4. Picture yourself handling the scene in a calm and confident manner. If your anxiety to the scene reaches level 4 or above, retreat to your peaceful scene after five to ten seconds of exposure.

3. *Relax* in your peaceful scene for up to a minute, until you're fully calm.

4. *Repeat* the process of alternating between a phobic scene and your peaceful scene until the phobic scene loses its power to elicit anxiety. At this point proceed to the next scene up in your hierarchy.

How to Get the Most Out of Imagery Desensitization

The process of desensitization will work best if you adhere to the following guidelines:

1. Spend about fifteen to twenty minutes the first time you practice imagery desensitization. As you gain skill in relaxation and visualization, you can lengthen your sessions to thirty minutes. In this time period (on a good day), you can expect to master two or three scenes in your hierarchy.

Hierarchy for _____

(specify phobia)

Instructions: Start with a relatively easy or mild instance of facing your phobia. Develop at least eight steps which involve progressively more challenging exposures. The final step should be your goal or even a step beyond what you've designated as your goal.

Step   *Scene*

1. _____

2. _____

3. _____

4. _____

5. _____

6. _____

7. _____

8. _____

9. _____

10. _____

11. _____

12. _____

13. _____

14. _____

15. _____

16. _____

17. _____

18. _____

19. _____

20. _____

Note: Make copies of this sheet and use one copy for each of your phobias.

2. You need to be very relaxed for this sort of desensitization to be effective. If you feel that you aren't deeply relaxed, then you might spend more time—twenty to thirty minutes—relaxing at the outset, and spend more time relaxing in your peaceful scene after each exposure to a particular phobic scene. Make sure that you fully recover from any anxiety after each exposure.

3. If you have difficulty developing a peaceful scene of your own, refer to the chapter on Visualization in part VII.

4. You need to be able to visualize each phobic scene as well as your peaceful scene in detail, as if you were really there. If you are having difficulty with visualizing effectively, you might ask yourself the following questions about each scene to heighten its vividness and detail:

   • What objects or people are in the scene?

   • What colors do you see in the scene?

   • Is the light bright or dim?

   • What sounds can you hear in the scene?

   • Can you hear the wind or a breeze?

   • What is the temperature of the air?

   • What are you wearing?

   • Can you smell or taste anything?

   • What other physical sensations are you aware of?

   • What are your emotions within the scene?

5. Stop a particular session if you feel tired, bored, or overly upset.

6. Try to practice every day if possible. Desensitization through imagery will be most effective following your regular period of relaxation.

7. Even if the first few scenes in your hierarchy don't elicit any anxiety at all, it's important to expose yourself to each of them at least once. (You can proceed from one to the next without retreating to your peaceful scene if your anxiety stays below level 2.) Imagery desensitization is at work even when you're not feeling any anxiety in response to a given scene because you are still associating relaxation with your phobia.

Putting Imagery Desensitization on Tape

You might find it helpful to put instructions for desensitization on tape to reduce any distractions while going through the process. Use the guidelines below for making your own tape.

   • Begin your tape with ten to fifteen minutes of instructions for deep relaxation. Use the instructions for progressive muscle relaxation given in the chapter on Stress earlier in part V. Or any visualization that can induce a state of deep relaxation (see the chapters on Relaxation and Visualization in part VII).

   • Following the relaxation phase, visualize yourself in your peaceful scene. Use the instructions given in chapter 4 to introduce your scene. Spend at least one minute there.

   • After going to your peaceful scene, record your own instructions for desensitization, according to the guidelines below.

Picture yourself in the first scene of your phobia hierarchy . . . Imagine what it would be like if you were actually there.

(Pause fifteen to twenty seconds.)

Now allow yourself to relax in this scene . . . do whatever you need to do to relax.

(Pause fifteen to twenty seconds.)

Picture yourself handling the situation in just the way you would like to . . . Imagine that you are feeling relaxed, calm, and confident. You might also wish to take in a deep breath . . . and as you exhale, let out any tense or uncomfortable feelings.

(Pause fifteen to twenty seconds.)

Now let go of this scene and go back to your peaceful scene. Remain there until you feel fully relaxed. Put your recorder on pause if you need to until all your anxiety is gone.

(Let one minute elapse on the tape, then continue recording.)

If you felt any anxiety imagining the previous scene in your hierarchy, go back and imagine yourself there again . . . Take a minute to let go and relax in the context of that scene, and then return to your peaceful scene until you are fully relaxed . . . You can place your cassette player on pause to do this . . . If you felt little or no anxiety within the previous scene, you're ready to go on.

(Leave a ten-second pause on the tape, then continue recording.)

Now, if you were fully relaxed in the previous scene, go on to the next scene in your hierarchy . . . Imagine what it would be like if you were actually there.

(Pause fifteen to twenty seconds.)

(Repeat the above instructions a second time, starting from the phrase: "Now allow yourself to relax in this scene . . .")

Your tape should consist of 1) ten to fifteen minutes of instructions for deep relaxation, 2) instructions for going to your peaceful scene, with a minute of silence for being there, and 3) the above instructions for systematic desensitization repeated twice.

In general, it is best not to work on more than two new scenes in your hierarchy at a given time if they are triggering any anxiety. You can work through more than two scenes in your hierarchy only if they are not causing you any discomfort. Please note that it is important not to move up to a new scene in your hierarchy until you've completely desensitized to the preceding scene. This means that you can visualize it in detail and feel little or no anxiety. When you begin your practice session, it's a good idea to go back and practice on the scene you most recently desensitized to before proceeding to a new scene. You can then allow yourself to progress to new scenes further up in your hierarchy.

Excerpted and adapted with permission from *The Anxiety and Phobia Workbook* by Edmund J. Bourne, Ph.D. For more information on this and related books, see the "Further Reading" section in the back of the book.

CHAPTER 36

Social Phobia

Social phobia is a *disorder* characterized by a persistent fear of criticism or rejection by others. People with social phobias fear they may behave in a way that will be embarrassing or humiliating. Take George, for example. He has a social phobia. He is so afraid of making a mistake in front of co-workers that he frequently stays late to finish his work after others have gone home. His anticipation of being judged as incompetent or stupid is so frightening for George that he tries to avoid situations where there is any potential for embarrassment.

There are many situations in which social fears can crop up, but several are particularly common:

- Public speaking

- Entertaining an audience

- Taking tests

- Eating in restaurants

- Writing in public

- Using public restrooms

- Dating

When people become afraid of one of these situations they are said to have a specific social phobia. Specific social phobias involve a focused area of fear, discomfort, and avoidance. People with this kind of social phobia dread one or a limited number of particular situations, although they may be relatively comfortable in other social settings. Specific social phobias usually involve performance anxiety—concern that some task or behavior will be executed in an incorrect or unacceptable way. Let's look at the most common situations in which social phobias develop.

Public Speaking

Public speaking is consistently ranked as the most frequently feared social situation in the United States. If you are terrified to speak to a group of people, you may have this type of specific social phobia. Fear of public speaking can seriously interfere with your life. This was certainly the case for José, a 38-year-old salesperson. He did fine making the sale when it was a one-on-one presentation. However, if he had to give a sales pitch to a group of people, he was in trouble. Speaking even to a gathering of three people was sure to make him extremely nervous. He complained of sweating, rapid heart rate, and shortness of breath. He was sure others would notice that there was something wrong with him. He worried that he would sound stupid and that people would think that he didn't know his product line. José even worried that someone would report him to his supervisor as being incompetent. He tried to avoid these group sales presentations whenever possible. José was trying to save up for his children's college education and was sure he'd lost a lot of money because of his fear of public speaking.

If you are one of the many with this particular fear, your worries may be very similar to José's. You may have additional concerns as well, which may sound something like this: "What if others notice I'm anxious?"; "What if they can see my hands trembling?"; "What if I stumble on my words?"; "Worse yet, what if I totally forget what I'm supposed to say?"; "What if someone asks me a question I can't answer?"; "What if I sound stupid?"; "What if my voice quivers?" You can probably add several other anxieties to this list.

Entertaining an Audience

Commonly referred to as "stage fright," entertaining an audience is another social situation that is often feared. If you have this phobia, you may be able to perform a task requiring great skill, as long as you are alone. However, performing in front of others—well, that's another matter!

This type of phobia is common even among professional athletes. For example, Los Angeles Dodger second baseman Steve Sax was named Rookie-of-the-Year in 1982. However, during the following season he suddenly found it difficult to make even routine throws to first base. More recently, New York Mets catcher Mackey Sasser developed a problem with throwing the ball back to the pitcher—something that most catchers never even think about. What do you think could have happened to cause such a drastic turnaround in these players' performance? Sax had made a few bad throws early in the season and became increasingly focused on not making another mistake. The more he concentrated on not making another bad throw, the more anxious he became. The more anxious he became, the worse he actually performed. The situation was similar for Sasser.

Taking Tests and Writing

Two common terms, test anxiety and writer's block, actually refer to the social fears of taking tests and writing. A bright seventh-grader, Anne, experienced both of these. She studied hard, but her grades were only average. Anne didn't think it was fair that she could work so hard and get only Cs. The typical scenario for Anne went something like this. The night before she had an exam, her mother quizzed her on the material, which Anne almost always knew well. However, the morning of the test, Anne woke up feeling nervous. She worried that she might not know the material well enough or that her mind would go blank, which had happened in the past. Despite her mother's reassurance, Anne became so tense that she could barely eat any breakfast. Sometimes she was even in tears before she got to school. When she sat down to actually take the test, she couldn't concentrate. The words looked blurry to her and she noticed her heart beating rapidly. In fulfillment of her worst fear, she felt her mind go completely blank.

One of Anne's teachers required her students to write essays in class. This presented another problem situation for Anne. Although she could write fluently at home, her ideas came to a standstill under the pressure of writing in class.

You don't have to be a student to experience writer's block. It's quite common for people whose job depends on writing—for example, journalists—to experience writer's block from time to time. The common fear is that whatever you produce, whether it's test answers or a newspaper article, will be inadequate and unacceptable to others.

Eating in Restaurants

Eating anyplace where others might be watching is yet another specific situation in which social phobias can develop. If you have this fear, you may worry that you will do something embarrassing, such as spill your drink all over yourself or your companions. You may also have a vague sense that others are watching you, which makes you feel even clumsier with your food. These kinds of worries often become self-fulfilling prophecies. The more you worry about the possibility of doing something embarrassing, the more anxious you become. The more anxious you become, the more likely you are to actually begin trembling or make abrupt, clumsy movements. This problem can build to the point where it becomes difficult to get food or a beverage to your mouth without dropping or spilling it.

This was the situation for Angela. She was close to her family and wanted to be a part of family celebrations and get-togethers. And yet the family gatherings had become unbearable ordeals for her. She began to shake when the family assembled around the table. Angela tried to hide her anxiety; but the more she tried to hide it, the worse it got. She became a master at scooting her food around on the plate to make it look as if she was eating. When she got home from one of these family functions, she was famished. Much to her confusion, she had no difficulty eating in the privacy of her own home.

Writing in Public

Writing in public is another situation that can cause a great deal of anxiety for people. Imagine being unable to sign your name in front of a sales clerk! Imagine not being able to take out a loan because you would be unable to get through all of the signatures and paperwork required! If you have this type of phobia, your concerns may have evolved something like this. At one point, you may have worried that your handwriting was sloppy. Or perhaps you were sensitive about the possibility of misspelling a word, or that your hand would shake as you wrote. Whatever the case, your worries escalated to the point where your hand may have actually become a little shaky and you did, in fact, have difficulty writing. Your handwriting may be beautiful as long as no one is watching you. Or you may have become so sensitive, that even if no one else is around, just the thought that someone may see your handwriting is enough to make you worry.

Doreen, a twenty-year-old education major, had this phobia. She was doing her student teaching at a local junior high school. She had always been a little self-conscious about her handwriting; now she was worried about having to write on the blackboard. What if her new students noticed she was nervous? What if her arm shook? What if the students didn't take her seriously because of her poor writing? Doreen did everything she could to avoid writing on the board. She stayed up until late at night planning every detail of her lessons for the next day. She went to school early every morning to make copies of typed handouts and assignments, arriving at her classroom with armloads of materials.

Using Public Restrooms

Another social phobia is the fear of using public restrooms. If you have this problem, you may have been too embarrassed to tell anyone about it.

This was the case for Amy, who had never told anyone that she had enormous anxieties about using public restrooms. She could go into the toilet stall, but if anyone else was in the restroom, her muscles became so tense that she was unable to urinate. Amy wondered if something was wrong with her. Maybe she was crazy. Maybe she had a physical problem. Finally, when Amy went for a yearly routine physical, she resolved to tell her physician about her problem urinating. She felt terribly anxious about broaching the subject—what if the doctor laughed at her? She worried about this for days prior to the examination.

When Amy presented her problem, the doctor assured her that it was unlikely to have a physical origin: she just had a "bashful bladder." The technical name for this problem is "psychogenic urinary retention." Amy felt somewhat relieved to have a name for it. But what was she to do about it? She was quite active with volunteer work, and it was becoming more and more difficult to plan breaks in her schedule so she could go home to use the bathroom.

Fear of using public restrooms is one fear that may present itself somewhat differently in men and women, largely due to the differences in the way men's and women's public restrooms are set up. If you are a woman with this phobia, you may worry that you have to hurry to urinate, especially if there is a line of people waiting. For Amy, busy airport restrooms were the worst. She worried that she would take too long and that the other women would become angry. She also worried what others might think of her. "Why is she taking so long?" "What could she possibly be doing in there?" In addition, some people may also be sensitive to the sounds they make. Although Amy knew that everyone urinates and that everyone makes noise, this still bothered her. It always helped her if a fan was on to block out the other sounds. Some people with this type of phobia also worry about passing gas ("farting") or defecating in a public restroom.

If you are a man with this phobia, your fears are likely to take on a slightly different form due to the fact that most men's restrooms do not have private stalls for urinating. Dave had this particular problem. If other men were around when he went to use a urinal, he became anxious that he would not be able to urinate right away. As he stood there, waiting to urinate, his thoughts would run wild. "What if the other men think I'm some kind of pervert?" "They might think I'm masturbating because I'm taking so long." "What if they think I'm gay?" In fact, his anxiety made things worse by making it even more difficult for him to urinate.

Dating

Dating is another situation that provokes social fears. You may be able to speak to a group of one hundred people with little anxiety, and yet be terrified at the prospect of going out on a date. Take Michael, for example. As a new college professor, he frequently gave lectures to large groups of students. During his free time, he enjoyed going to movies and sporting events with several male friends. Despite Michael's ease in most social situations, he was fearful of asking a woman out for a date. He was afraid that she'd say no, and of his subsequent feeling of rejection. He was also afraid that she might say yes—once on a date, Michael worried that he would do something to embarrass himself. Consequently, he didn't date.

Although some social anxiety is common on dates, a dating phobia can be quite debilitating, sometimes preventing people from having any intimate relationships.

Some sexual dysfunctions can be a form of social phobia and can also wreak havoc with relationships. Bruce, for example, a medical school student in his early twenties, was very unsure of himself when it came to women, even though women found him attractive. Bruce had one girlfriend during his senior year of college. He thought everything was going well, until their relationship moved in a more intimate direction. He was so anxious about whether or not he would be able to perform sexually that he was unable to achieve an erection when he was with his girlfriend. However, he was perfectly capable of getting an erection when alone. When Bruce moved away to attend medical school, he and his girlfriend broke up. Now he is reluctant to develop another relationship, for fear that the pattern will repeat itself.

When You're Afraid of Many (or All) Social Situations

In contrast to people with specific social phobias, you may dread many, if not all, situations in which there is a chance of experiencing disapproval. People with these widespread social fears are said to have a *generalized* social phobia. In addition to fearing a variety of social situations, people with generalized social phobias are also more likely to lack certain skills, such as how to be assertive or how to communicate effectively, that are important ingredients for feeling comfortable with other people. As you'll see below in the case of Rebecca, having a generalized social phobia can be extremely pervasive and debilitating, affecting virtually every area of your life.

Rebecca was always a quiet child. She never spoke up in class, and dreaded the inevitable times when teachers would call on her to answer a question. She was teased by the other children for being so quiet and mouse-like. Despite her discomfort, Rebecca managed to get by until she reached college. No, she was never involved in any extracurricular activities. No, she never dated. And, no, she didn't have many friends. But, according to Rebecca, this time in her life was easy compared to what lay ahead.

Rebecca decided to go to a community college. Although she was bright, she didn't make very good grades in high school; community college seemed her only option. The year got off to a bad start. Rebecca came down with mononucleosis. She had to miss a month of school and fell behind in her work. As if that weren't enough to deal with, Rebecca was still weak when she first began attending classes, and her hands were a bit unsteady and shaky. By now you've probably learned enough to guess what happened next. Rebecca started worrying that others would notice her hands trembling. Well, to make a long story short, Rebecca became paralyzed with fear, and was unable to keep her grades up. She soon dropped out of college.

Things went from bad to worse. Rebecca got a job working at a children's home. She was mostly to do paperwork, which she didn't mind too much, because she could work by herself. However, she was also supposed to assist at mealtimes, making sure that the children ate and behaved properly. Although Rebecca liked children, this part of the job was terrifying for her. When some of the children misbehaved, she was unable to deal with the situation. She was afraid to say anything. She soon quit this job. In fact, Rebecca tried out several different jobs, but ended up quitting, or getting fired from, each position.

Rebecca gave up on working and spent up to half of her day in bed. She felt it was the only place she could be safe from the scrutiny and evaluation of other people. When she was dressed and moving about her house, she worried that the phone might ring at any minute or that someone would knock at her door. Rebecca felt terribly guilty about her behavior. Here she was home all day long while her parents were away at work. She wished she could at least go to the grocery store so she could have dinner ready in the evening. Even what seemed to be everyday situations involving other people (such as handing the cashier her money) had become overwhelming for Rebecca. Although her parents tried to be understanding, they wished their daughter would try to get another job, maybe find a little apartment for herself, and find a nice young man to date. Sometimes they became so frustrated that they said things to Rebecca that they later regretted.

If you find yourself in a similar situation to Rebecca's, dreading almost all social contact, don't despair. Although overcoming a generalized social phobia of this magnitude will take time and hard work, it can be done.

What Are the Symptoms of Social Phobia?

The symptoms of social phobia can generally be grouped into three major categories. The first category includes the bodily symptoms of anxiety, which you experience when you are in, or when you are anticipating, the social situations you fear. The second category includes your cognitions (thoughts) and expectations about these social situations. The third category includes your actions or behaviors related to these situations. Let's go over the bodily symptoms first.

Bodily Symptoms

You are likely to experience a number of unpleasant bodily reactions when you fear social disapproval. These may include any one or combination of the following symptoms:

- Rapid heart rate, or heart palpitations

- Trembling or shaking

- Shortness of breath

- Sweating

- Blushing

- Abdominal distress

- Dizziness

Sometimes these symptoms come on rapidly, become quite intense, and then diminish with time. This experience is called a *panic attack*. Panic is an apt word to describe the intense fear you may feel when confronted with certain social situations. In addition to these intense, panic-like experiences, you may also experience chronic tension from continually being "on your guard" around others. This chronic tension may result in headaches, fatigue, stomachaches, and other stress-related symptoms.

Cognitive Symptoms

In addition to experiencing a number of bodily symptoms of anxiety, you are likely to have certain thoughts about what you *should* be like in social situations. Notice that the word "should" is emphasized. Before you've finished working your way through this book, you'll learn that certain should words can be dangerous to your mental health!

When you're in a social situation and experiencing intense anxiety, you probably have a number of thoughts running through your mind. You may have these thoughts so often that they feel quite automatic, almost beyond your control. Imagine yourself in the last social situation that caused you anxiety. What kinds of thoughts were going through your mind? If you don't remember, that's okay. Often these thoughts are so quick that you may not be able to keep track of them at first. Some examples of the kinds of thoughts you may have include:

- *I look out of place.*

- *I sound stupid.*

- *I don't fit in.*

- *I'm blowing it.*

Many psychologists call these kinds of thoughts irrational. "Irrational" is defined in Webster's dictionary as "not based on reason" or "defective in mental power." Well, we don't think you're either defective in mental power or unreasonable. Rather, we prefer to label these thoughts as maladaptive. "Maladaptive" is defined as "poorly suited to a particular use, purpose, or situation." In other words, thinking this way does not serve you well in social situations. In fact, such thinking makes it much more likely that you'll become anxious and, as a consequence, perform poorly or uncomfortably. This is one of the most paradoxical features of anxiety—by thinking that the worst will happen, you may unwittingly bring this about.

Behavioral Symptoms

The behavioral symptoms of social phobia are a response to your experience of intense discomfort in social situations. Like physical pain, anxiety is a warning signal that you need to take action. However, for people with social phobias, common responses to this warning signal are typically unhelpful.

The first of these responses—freezing—may not seem properly classifiable as an action at all. In fact, it's the absence of action. Freezing (or the more technical term, *atonic immobility*) is a largely involuntary, physiological response that can occur when you perceive danger. Initially, this response served to help our species evolve and survive, although currently it is largely maladaptive. In prehistoric times, the freezing response typically occurred in times of mortal danger, such as in the presence of a threatening animal. The freezing response provided time to assess the danger of the situation, and prevented impulsive actions that might provoke an attack. Immobility also provided the greatest chance of camouflage in cases where escape or aggression was impossible.

When human beings experience this freezing response, it inhibits or prevents voluntary actions, such as movement, speech, or recall. That's why when you are scared in a situation involving other people, you may be literally unable to talk. You might even find it difficult to remember your name or phone number! In essence, you feel paralyzed. What's important to remember is that this response is usually of very brief duration, and will pass if you remain in the situation a little longer.

Another behavioral symptom you're likely to experience is avoidance. We have already noted that because many social situations are uncomfortable for you, you are likely to avoid them altogether. Your avoidance is not unlike that of the person who is afraid of elevators and consequently chooses to take the stairs. However, not everyone avoids feared situations completely. Some people are unable or unwilling to avoid, and will suffer through, some of the situations they dread. Even they, however, may engage in subtle forms of avoidance. For example, you may enter a situation but then leave too soon. This is called escape behavior. Or, while in a social situation, you may attempt to distract yourself from acknowledging your surroundings: for example, your mind may wander, or you may fidget with a pen in your hand. You may also disengage yourself from the situation, perhaps by staring off into the corner, or somehow going into your own private world. Daydreaming is a common way in which people disengage. Both distraction and disengagement are forms of avoidance.

Setting Your Goals and Objectives

Before you set out to overcome a social phobia, you first need to develop your goals and objectives. Without them, your efforts will lack focus and direction. Goals and objectives are, in essence, your map to help you navigate the road to recovery. Goals tell you where you're generally headed, while objectives let you know exactly when you've arrived.

Defining Your Goal

The first step you need to complete is to define a goal. Having a goal answers the question, "What do I want to accomplish?" You might be surprised at how often people jump into action without first having carefully considered this question. You might feel that the answer is obvious. "I want to get rid of my social phobia." Of course, this is a desirable goal, but it is far too general to be a useful goal. A useful goal must be specific.

To help you determine your specific goal, ask yourself these questions:

- What type of social situation do I want to stop avoiding?

- How do I want to feel in that social situation?

As you can see from these questions, a specific goal will contain two components: 1) the situation you want to learn to handle better, and 2) how you want to feel in that situation. Here are some common examples of specific goals:

- I want to give public presentations comfortably.

- I want to go on dates with minimal anxiety.

- I want to eat in restaurants with relative ease.

- I want to use public restrooms without fear of embarrassment.

Now that you have some examples, think about what goal you want to work on and jot it down in the space below. Again, make sure it contains both the type of situation you want to master and how you want to feel in the situation.

My goal: _____

One important note about your goal before we move on: It's important that your goal be realistic and achievable. Tackling a social phobia with unrealistic expectations will only lead to frustration and disappointment. For example, it is not realistic to expect to eliminate all anxiety in all situations. You may be able to become more comfortable in social situations, but everyone experiences some anxiety. It is equally unhelpful to set too high a standard for your performance. A realistic goal does not demand that you behave perfectly. Human beings are not perfect. Striving to give a flawless speech or to always say the right thing is a setup for failure because you have set a goal that is impossible to achieve. Sure it's nice to do your best, but it's even more important to become comfortable with the fact that we're all imperfect by nature. Okay, look back at your goal again. Make sure you've worded it in such a way that it's realistic.

What if I Have More Than One Goal?

Granted, many of you may have more than one goal. Perhaps you want to learn to be more comfortable in dating situations, but you also want to learn to give public presentations with ease. Although it would be nice if you could achieve all of your goals simultaneously, it usually doesn't work this way. Typically, it makes more sense to work on certain goals first, and others later on. Working on more than one goal at once can dilute your efforts, making it difficult to see progress. In contrast, when you work on one goal at a time, you can focus all your energy on one area. You may even be surprised that by achieving one goal, your other goals will be much easier to accomplish later on.

So if you have more than one goal, how do you decide where to begin? Putting your goals in order of importance is one approach, but this is not the only issue to consider. Also consider which of your goals might be more realistic to tackle first. Some people may prefer to tackle an easy goal first, thus getting off to a good, smooth start, and getting their feet wet slowly. Others may want to work on a more challenging goal first, to get it out of the way early on. Still others may have less latitude in making a choice. If your job requires you to give a speech in a month, it's obviously going to be more important for you to work on that goal first, even though you may also want to learn to ask someone out for a date.

Ultimately, the priority you give each of your goals is up to you. Keep in mind that there's really no right or wrong order. If you start working on one goal and later realize that you need to work on a different goal first, you can easily make the switch. The purpose of establishing priorities for your goals is to have a game plan, but game plans can always change. We suggest that you work using one goal (switching to another goal only if necessary). Later, you can work on achieving your other goals as well.

Defining Your Objectives

After you've set the goal you want to work toward, the next step is to define your objectives. Sometimes in everyday speech the words "goal" and "objective" are used interchangeably, but we're giving them two distinct meanings in this context. Defining your goal answers the question, "What do I want to accomplish?" Defining your objective answers the question, "How will I know when I have accomplished my goal?" or "What will be different once I reach my goal?" Objectives are important because they are the signals that will tell you when you have been successful. Objectives also help personalize your goal and give more direction to your recovery plan.

Typically, objectives involve changes in specific behaviors, thoughts, and feelings that will occur when you accomplish your goal. You may have several different objectives for a single goal. For example, if your goal is to be able to eat in public, your objectives might include accepting invitations to go out to eat, sitting through an entire dinner in the middle of a crowded restaurant, and becoming comfortable eating lunch at the company cafeteria with business colleagues. As you can see, when you have reached your objectives, you will have achieved your goal.

Let's look at another example of developing objectives for a specific goal.

Goal:

I want to be more outgoing and comfortable at social gatherings.

Objectives:

- I will feel less anxious when I am introduced to a stranger.
- I will be able to make eye contact.
- I won't turn down invitations to family gatherings.
- I will feel like I can hold my own in a conversation.
- I will stop assuming that I am saying the wrong thing all the time.
- I will make new friends.

Can you see how objectives help define and personalize a goal? Can you also see how objectives guide you, letting you know what kinds of things you need to do to begin your recovery?

Before you set out to write your own objectives, take a look at the goal and objectives set out by Ginny, a twenty-eight-year-old mother of two elementary-school-age children.

Goal:

I want to be more outgoing and confident in my work as a parent and in my role in the community.

Objectives:

- I will be less afraid to sit up front at church.
- I will return to my volunteer activities.
- I will talk to the other parents when carpooling.
- I will be able to introduce myself at meetings.

Now that you've seen how Ginny defined her goal and objectives, try a hand at writing your own.

My Goal and Objectives

Goal:

_____

Objectives:

- _____
- _____
- _____
- _____
- _____

Assessing Your Fears and Developing Your Recovery Plan

The next step in developing your personalized recovery plan is to thoroughly assess yourself and your fears. Only by taking a thorough look at your particular symptoms can you hope to overcome your fears. Otherwise, your recovery efforts may result in frustration and disappointment.

1. *How Does My Body React To Disapproval?* Most people experience physical symptoms when they are afraid or anxious. What symptoms do you experience? The following checklist is designed to help you answer this question. If you are unsure of your symptoms, try entering one of the situations you fear and notice what bodily reactions you have. Read the list of symptoms below and check those that you experience when you are socially anxious.

Bodily Symptoms of Social Phobia

☐ Rapid heart rate

☐ Dry mouth

☐ Shortness of breath

☐ Urinary urgency

☐ Abdominal distress

☐ Tingling sensations

☐ Sweating

☐ Muscle twitching

☐ Blushing

☐ Chest pain

☐ Trembling or shaking

☐ Numbness

☐ Dizziness or feeling faint

☐ Hot flashes or chills

☐ Tense muscles

☐ Choking or lump in throat

☐ Other: _____

☐ Other: _____

Most people with social phobias experience at least some of these physical symptoms when they are anticipating, or actually entering, a feared social situation. If you checked a number (or all) of these physical symptoms, don't despair. You can learn to handle your body's reactions to fear effectively. See the chapter on Stress earlier in part V.

One important word of caution: Sometimes physical symptoms mask a medical problem. If you have not had a recent physical examination, please make an appointment with your doctor to make sure that this is not the case for you.

2. *How Does My Mind React To Disapproval?* Your mind, as well as your body, can react strongly when fear is present. Most noticeably, you begin to experience fearful thoughts or cognitions. Below is a list of some of the cognitive symptoms of social phobia you may experience. Place a checkmark next to any of these thoughts you experience when you're socially anxious.

Cognitive Symptoms of Social Phobia

- ☐ I look out of place.
- ☐ I'm unlovable.
- ☐ I sound stupid.
- ☐ I look nervous.
- ☐ I don't fit in.
- ☐ I'm so embarrassed.
- ☐ I'm blowing it.
- ☐ I'm too quiet.
- ☐ I know they hate me.
- ☐ I sound boring.
- ☐ I look ugly.
- ☐ I'm such a klutz.
- ☐ I look fat.
- ☐ I'm unattractive.
- ☐ I'll be rejected.
- ☐ No one likes me.
- ☐ I appear incompetent.
- ☐ Others are talking about me.
- ☐ Other: _____
- ☐ Other: _____

You may experience other fearful thoughts besides these. Feel free to add to the list any other thoughts that pop into your head when you become anxious in social situations. Now look back over your list. Are these thoughts disturbing to you? Do they keep coming back and bothering you? At the time you experience them, do you believe they might be true? If you answered yes to any of these questions, you'll want to learn more about handling your mind's reaction to the fear of disapproval. See the chapters on Uncovering Automatic Thoughts, Changing Patterns of Limited Thinking, and Changing Hot Thoughts earlier in part V.

3. *How Do I Try To Avoid Disapproval?* You've already assessed how your body and mind react to disapproval. Now you'll examine how you behave when you're scared. Typically, people attempt to avoid the things they fear. It's natural for you to avoid situations that make you uncomfortable. However, as you've already learned, avoidance only prolongs the life of a social phobia.

It's easy to see how avoiding a situation altogether can keep you from becoming less afraid of it. There are less obvious forms of avoidance, though. Consider the various ways in which you engage in what's called *partial avoidance*. Partial avoidance refers to limiting what you will or will not do in certain social situations. Let's take Wayman's case by way of illustration.

Wayman attended lots of parties and dinners with his wife, despite a strong social phobia. Although he never refused to attend these activities, Wayman avoided introducing himself to strangers, would only agree to stay for a maximum of two hours, and insisted that his wife never leave his side for more than a few moments. As you can see, this kind of partial avoidance can be quite disabling. Other examples of partial avoidance are having to restrict yourself to a certain safe location, refusing work promotions that would require additional social demands, drinking alcohol, refraining from eye contact with others, and mentally distracting yourself from anxiety or the social situation creating it. Carefully consider the checklist below and mark all the behavioral symptoms of partial avoidance that apply to your social phobia.

Behavioral Symptoms of Social Phobia

I engage in partial avoidance of my feared social situation by . . .

☐ Turning up the radio

☐ Daydreaming

☐ Thinking about other things

☐ Staying close to a safe person

☐ Limiting my opportunities

☐ Only going to safe places

☐ Using other distractions

☐ Not making eye contact

☐ Staying only a certain length of time

☐ Setting other special conditions

☐ Using alcohol or drugs

☐ Other: _____

For more techniques to conquer avoidance, see the chapter on Phobias earlier in part V.

Excerpted and adapted with permission from *Dying of Embarrassment: Help for Social Anxiety and Social Phobia* by Barbara G. Markway, Ph.D., Cheryl N. Carmin, Ph.D., Alec Pollard, Ph.D., and Teresa Flynn, Ph.D. For more information on this and related books, see the "Further Reading" section in the back of the book.

CHAPTER 37

Obsessions and Compulsions

Obsessive Compulsive Disorder (OCD) is an illness. It is also a psychiatric diagnosis. One thing to realize right away is that these two things—the illness and the diagnosis—are not necessarily the same.

If this confuses you, consider the fact that the official definitions of psychiatric diagnoses have changed repeatedly over the years. Probably, the illnesses have not changed—much, at least—but mental health professionals have changed the way they look at these illnesses and define them. The hope is that the definitions of diagnoses come closer to matching the illnesses themselves as more is learned.

Essentially, the current definition of OCD is simple, but read it carefully:

The essential features of Obsessive Compulsive Disorder are repeated obsessions or compulsions (not necessarily both) that are significantly distressing or time-consuming or that cause significant interference with social or occupational functioning.

Note that either obsessions or compulsions are enough to make a diagnosis of OCD. Most OCD sufferers have both, but some have only one or the other. Note, too, the important requirement that these symptoms be *significantly* distressing or time-consuming or interfere *significantly* with your functioning. "Normal" people may occasionally, even repeatedly, have unwanted thoughts (such as an urge to hurt someone) or behaviors (such as superstitious habits) that do not cause enough distress or impairment to warrant any treatment or diagnosis.

Next, you need to be clear on the meaning of the two words that both name and define OCD: obsessions and compulsions.

Obsessions are persistent ideas, thoughts, impulses, or images that are experienced, at least initially, as intrusive or senseless.

Note that both this definition and the definition of compulsions given later emphasize repetitive, persistent experiences—experiences that happen over and over again in a fairly consistent way. A single thought that happens once would not qualify, however upsetting it may be. In the most typical OCD sufferer, a given obsession may occur hundreds or thousands of times.

Note also the requirement that the obsession be experienced—at least at first—as intrusive or senseless. This means that you do not want the thought and would like to be rid of it. As a result, you might try to push it out of your mind, only to have it come back again and again.

In contrast, a depressed person without OCD might brood on something that seems to him or her quite important to think about, like financial troubles. This does not fit the definition of an obsession used here. If unproductive worrying of this sort takes up a lot of time and becomes a problem in itself, you might call this *rumination* instead.

A different example of a preoccupation that is not an obsession would be someone who firmly believes his food to be poisoned even though there is no real evidence to support this. You would call this a *delusion*.

Yet another example would be a person who devotes an excessive amount of time and attention to something—a project, a romantic attachment—that is neither obviously crazy nor particularly bothersome to the person himself, although it may be bothersome to other people because it is extreme. Coloquially, some may say the person is "obsessed" with the project or person. But this is not an obsession as found in OCD. Rather, this is a preoccupation or *overvalued ideation*. None of these phenomena are true obsessions, although they may be related in some cases to OCD. True obsessions are thoughts or ideas that you can see don't make sense, even though you worry about them.

There may come times in the course of OCD when you lose sight of the fact that your obsessions don't make sense, when you do start to believe in them. But much of the time, especially early in the illness, most OCD sufferers have a different perspective. Obsessions feel like *symptoms*. Sometimes these thoughts and experiences can be confused with "worries." But if the worries seem ridiculous, they are probably obsessions. For example, someone who is having trouble paying bills might worry about this excessively, to the point of rumination; but someone who has enough money and knows it, but still spends hours he doesn't want to spend imagining financial catastrophes that don't seem likely even to him, may be obsessive.

Note that obsessions don't have to be thoughts. The definition allows for obsessive *impulses* and *images*. Perhaps obsessive *feelings* should be allowed as well. Obsessions can take many forms. Among the most common obsessions are thoughts of doing harm to others—to someone you are *not* angry with and don't really wish to harm, even to someone you love. These obsessions may take the form of a *fear that* you might harm that person, or of a mental *picture* of violence. Another common obsession is a sense of *doubt* that you really did something properly—"Did I really lock the door (turn off the gas, shut off the faucet, unplug the iron, etc.)?" There may be associated obsessive fears that burglars will break in, the house will burn down, and so forth. Also common is the obsessive fear that something is contaminated—with dirt, germs, broken glass, chemical toxins, etc. Sometimes there is an obsessive sense that something is just not "right"—not correctly arranged or ordered or not done in the right way or sequence. An obsession may be as simple as a single meaningless word that keeps repeating itself in your mind, or as complex as a vast array of different "worries" with complicated mental explanations behind them.

One way for people to think about obsessions (and how much of a problem they can be) is to consider the common experience of having a jingle in your head that keeps replaying itself in an annoying way. This can be an example of a "normal" obsession that doesn't last long enough or cause enough trouble to qualify for a diagnosis of OCD. In some cases though, it could represent a real symptom of OCD. The question is how much it interferes with normal functioning, and how long it lasts or how much energy it consumes. Suppose that jingle ran through your head all day, every day?

An important characteristic of most obsessions is that they cause anxiety or tension. In fact, some experts prefer to define obsessions in this way, as "anxiety-provoking mental experiences." On the other hand, it is possible that obsessions can provoke other kinds of unpleasant feelings besides anxiety—for example, guilt or disgust.

Finally, OCD sufferers can usually recognize obsessions as products of their own minds, even if unwanted. If words that plague you seem to come from outside your head, like external voices, they are more likely auditory hallucinations or illusions than obsessions. Similarly, if a distressing image is not a *mental* picture but appears in space before your eyes and seems quite real, it is more likely a visual hallucination or illusion. Usually this distinction is clear, but sometimes it can be difficult to make. Some obsessive-compulsive people may refer to their obsessive thoughts as "inner voices," which can confuse even a psychiatrist into thinking they are hallucinations!

> Compulsions are repetitive, purposeful, and intentional behaviors that are performed in response to an obsession, according to certain rules, or in a stereotyped fashion. They may be designed to neutralize or to prevent discomfort or some dreaded event or situation.

Compulsions are often considered the hallmark of OCD, maybe because they are often observable to others in a way that obsessions are not. However, perhaps 20 percent of OCD sufferers have only obsessions without any apparent compulsions. One way of classifying types of OCD separates this group of "pure obsessionals" and categorizes the rest by their specific compulsive behaviors: washers, checkers, repeaters, and so forth.

The classic case is the handwasher. Whether or not you have this specific problem, you may find it useful to consider this as an example to better understand the meaning of obsessions and compulsions.

The handwasher usually has obsessive fears of contamination—for example, by germs (one of many possible contaminants). The washer may feel that various objects and surfaces—for example, doorknobs—are contaminated with germs, which get on his hands when he touches them. He then fears spreading these germs by his hands to other parts of his body or other objects, where they might make him or others sick. Feeling anxious about this contamination on his hands, he washes them, which generally makes him feel better, at least temporarily. However, the handwashing may not seem to him good enough unless he does it for an especially long time, or repeats it a certain number of times, or uses especially hot water, or takes care not to touch the faucet in the process. In any case, he usually finds himself recontaminated again soon after he has gotten clean, so that the handwashing process needs to be repeated many times a day. This may leave his hands red and raw. It may also take up a lot of time, causing delays in getting other things done.

Think about how this handwashing meets the definition for a compulsion. It is a behavior that is repetitive. It is purposeful—the purpose being to remove contaminants. It is intentional—the washer knows what he is doing or about to do and "intends" to do it, even though at the same time he may consider it "sick" behavior and try to fight it. It does not take him by surprise, in an involuntary way, like a tic. The washing is performed in response to the obsessive fear or feeling of contamination. It is often performed in a very specific way—for a certain length of time or with just so many rinses and washes before it is done. It is designed to neutralize the distress of feeling contaminated and to prevent the feared result of contaminating others or getting sick oneself.

As you can see, the example of compulsive handwashing fits the definition of compulsion very well. Of course, this is a classic example on which the definition is based. Another classic example is checking. A checker may repeatedly go back to check a lock, in response to the obsessive fear or doubt that she has really locked the door. Each time she checks the lock, it reassures her, at least a little, but often not for long. As she leaves the door, she wonders if she really got it right; she may have to go back and recheck it many times before she can let it be. The purpose of the behavior is to reduce the possibility of someone breaking in, and it would make sense except that it has to be repeated so many times that you know it is a waste of time. Most people might check something like this, but only once.

In contrast, other OCD sufferers who repeat certain actions may do so out of a "magical" or "superstitious" sense that, unless they do so, some disaster will happen that is not at all logically connected to their actions. For example, one woman may spend a lot of time repeating a certain phrase—until she feels she has "gotten it just right"—out of the obsessive fear that if she does not do so, her mother may die. She "knows" this makes no sense at all, just as you "know" a black cat won't bring bad luck, but she feels anxious anyway. The variety of such "repeating" or "ordering" behaviors is potentially limitless, but commonly it includes walking through doorways in a certain manner, arranging objects in specific ways, and repeating actions such as touching an object a certain number of times.

Some of this repetitive, superstitious behavior may be done mentally—for example, by counting or praying silently. This brings up the idea of "cognitive compulsions" mentioned earlier. Some people believe that thinking about something in a certain way is necessary to avert danger. These cognitive compulsions (such as making a mental list to prevent forgetting, or forming a "good" thought to counteract a "bad" one) are important to distinguish from obsessions because their treatment in behavior therapy is different. Their hallmark is that they *reduce* anxiety, rather than increase it as obsessions do.

Compulsive behaviors may take other, subtler forms. For example, one common response to obsessive fears is to seek reassurance from others. You might look to your doctor to reassure you that you don't have cancer or AIDS for instance. This reassurance, once obtained, may give temporary relief but often leads to further reassurance-seeking, which can exasperate others. It may take the form of repetitive questioning, telephoning, arguing, etc. It is important to recognize a compulsive ritual for what it is because it may call for a very different response from therapists, friends, and family than what most people are inclined to do—that is, they should probably *not* provide the reassurance the OCD sufferer demands.

Yet another form that compulsive behavior may take is *hoarding,* often of worthless objects or even garbage. Sometimes this is motivated by the obsessive fear that the person might throw out something of eventual use or of great importance. Usually such people do *not* have such a clear understanding that their saving is senseless.

Finally, *slowness* is a common problem in OCD. This may be the result of having to do many rituals in the course of ordinary activities, or may represent a type of compulsive behavior in itself. For example, a person may become so meticulous in doing ordinary things like eating or dressing "just right" that these activities take hours and allow little time for anything else during the day.

In addition to the many different types of obsessive and compulsive behaviors that are the essential features of the *diagnosis* of OCD, OCD usually involves other symptoms that are not so necessary to the diagnosis. That is to say, these symptoms can often occur in other illnesses as well. The following section describes some of these symptoms.

Other Symptoms of OCD

OCD is grouped together with certain other diagnoses—generalized anxiety disorder, agoraphobia, social phobia, simple phobia, panic disorder, post-traumatic stress disorder—as all belonging to the class of "anxiety disorders." This is the most common type of mental disorder in the general population. Other *classes* of disorders include affective disorders (for example, depression and mania), impulse control disorders (for example, trichotillomania), organic mental disorders (for example, Alzheimer's disease), and substance abuse disorders (for example, alcoholism).

It is still not completely clear whether OCD "belongs" more with the anxiety disorders than with another class, such as affective disorders or impulse control disorders. However, anxiety—the feeling of fear in the absence of any logical danger—is very common in OCD. Also, anxiety plays a key role in behavioral theory as to how obsessive-compulsive symptoms come about.

When the anxiety seems clearly related to the obsessions, as when the washer becomes nervous after touching a doorknob, it is considered part of the OCD. But if anxiety, especially when associated with *physical* symptoms of tension (such as racing heartbeat, shortness of breath, etc.), occurs in other situations or unpredictably, it may mean the presence of still another anxiety disorder, such as panic disorder or generalized anxiety disorder, in addition to the OCD.

Another common characteristic of OCD that links it to the other anxiety disorders is *avoidance* behavior. Avoidance is especially typical of phobic patients. Compulsive washers have sometimes been described as "germ phobics." One difference is that the obsessive-compulsive patient, even the washer, often cannot avoid what he fears as completely as, say, a phobic patient may avoid heights. But sometimes the obsessive-compulsive patient succeeds in avoiding contamination so thoroughly that there is little need for compulsive washing. In such cases, the avoidance behavior itself is often the biggest problem. The person may simply isolate himself in his house, or in his room, and greatly limit his contacts with the outside world. The famous case of Howard Hughes was one example of this; at the end of his life he lived like a hermit, avoiding germs by secluding himself.

Depression is also very common in OCD. In contrast to OCD itself, which tends to persist in varying degrees for years and years in most sufferers, depression tends to come and go in "episodes." When a depressive episode is severe enough to disrupt functioning—to affect sleeping, eating, energy, concentration—it may deserve an additional diagnosis, such as major depression.

At one time, such a diagnosis as major depression would have excluded the diagnosis of OCD, which would have been considered "secondary" to the depression. The same "exclusionary" principle would have applied to other "primary" diagnoses, such as schizophrenia, bipolar disorder (manic-depressive illness), or Tourette's syndrome (characterized by tics). Now the diagnostic practice is different: when you meet the criteria for more than one disorder, you get more than one diagnosis. This new practice may be helping to increase the frequency with which people are diagnosed as having OCD; no longer do other diagnoses get "priority."

Nevertheless, there are still some disorders that may take the place of OCD in diagnostic terms. Some of these disorders may really be different types of OCD, but we currently call them by different names (see below). Others may be distinct illnesses in themselves, but in some way also close "relatives" of OCD. This is one area where the diagnostic system may change as more is learned about how these different illnesses relate to each other.

Do You Have Something "Like" OCD?

"Compulsive" hair-pulling (trichotillomania) is one common example of such a condition. Some people pull out their hair, usually from the head, because it eases tension. Nevertheless, they also make efforts to stop themselves, even tying up their own hands at night! Hair-pulling may result in unsightly bald spots that require a wig. This is a lot like OCD in many ways, except that there is rarely an obsession behind the compulsive pulling of hair, unless it is the urge to pull itself.

Also, hair-pullers sometimes report that it "feels good," unlike compulsive washing or checking. Others just find themselves unconsciously doing it, like a habit. For such reasons, trichotillomania is classified with "impulse control disorders." These include also nail-biting and compulsive stealing (kleptomania). Kleptomania may also closely resemble OCD, particularly when the object stolen is of no value or use to the kleptomaniac, who may simply throw it away. But again, there is often no obsessive thought behind the stealing, which sometimes causes pleasure as well as release of tension.

Hypochondriacs often seem "obsessed" with physical illnesses. If a hypochondriac is absolutely *convinced* he has an illness despite contrary evidence from laboratory tests and doctors, he is not obsessive but *delusional*. However, many hypochondriacs are not *sure* they have a certain illness, but worry that they *might*. These people find the doctors' reassurances at least temporarily a relief. If the hypochondriac keeps going to doctor after doctor in search of more and more reassurance, this begins to look a lot like the compulsive reassurance-seeking common to OCD.

Yet another type of person is preoccupied with an imagined or exaggerated defect in his or her physical body This is sometimes called "dysmorphophobia" or body dysmorphic disorder. For example, such a person may be concerned that his nose is too large, even though it looks all right to most observers, and may seek plastic surgery to correct it.

Another type of person who may become "obsessed" with imagined defects in physical appearance is the person with an eating disorder, such as anorexia nervosa or bulimia (binge-eating). Such people often feel themselves to be fat, even when thin or of normal weight for their height. Or they may have *fears* of getting fat. Often they have rituals around eating. Eating, especially binge-eating, may cause great anxiety, which is relieved by purging—for example, causing oneself to throw up. The fears of being overweight and the purging have characteristics of obsessive and of compulsive behavior: the former increase anxiety and the latter relieves it. The binge-eating also may have "compulsive" characteristics, with surprisingly little pleasure involved; some bulimic patients binge on such unappetizing objects as melon rinds or bread flour.

All of these disorders—trichotillomania, kleptomania, hypochondriasis, body dysmorphic disorder, anorexia, bulimia—have certain obsessive-compulsive characteristics but are currently given different diagnostic labels. If you have such a disorder, you may also receive a diagnosis of OCD, but only if you have other symptoms of an obsessive-compulsive nature that fall *outside* the first diagnosis. For example, if you are an anorexic with cleaning rituals, you may have both anorexia nervosa and OCD; but if all your rituals have to do with food, you do not qualify for a diagnosis of OCD, just anorexia. The fact that such combinations of illnesses occur quite commonly in the same people adds to the suspicion that they may be related.

Still other illnesses may bear a similar relationship to OCD. Morbid jealousy and infatuation (as in the well-known movie *Fatal Attraction)* and some sexual disorders, such as exhibitionism, are examples.

A case that deserves special consideration is Gilles de la Tourette's syndrome, often called simply Tourette's syndrome. This illness is characterized by tics. Tics are repetitive behaviors distinguished from compulsions by the lack of a sense of purpose or intention; they come on "involuntarily." They are often simple movements, such as squinting of the eye, but may be quite complicated, such as spoken words. Sometimes in practice it is difficult to tell whether a given behavior is better called a tic or a compulsion. But often a patient with tics from Tourette's syndrome may also have clear obsessive-compulsive symptoms as well. Furthermore, relatives of Tourette's patients have an increased risk of having either Tourette's themselves-or OCD. This suggests a special relationship between Tourette's syndrome and OCD, which has yet to be understood.

Be careful to keep in mind that not all repetitive behaviors are "compulsive" in the sense of OCD. In OCD, rituals are usually driven by anxiety, not pleasure or gain, and the ritualizer has a sense that the ritual is irrational and makes efforts to fight it. Autistic people (such as in the movie *Rain Man)* may have rituals without any sense of their being senseless, or any impulse to fight them. This may also happen with psychotic individuals. Such behaviors are sometimes called "stereotypic," not compulsive. Alcoholics, drug abusers, gamblers, and many sexual deviants may refer to their behavior as "compulsive" and even fight it, but they also get a lot of pleasure out of it. This element of pleasure is not present for obsessive-compulsives.

Reducing Obsessions and Compulsions: The Planning Stage

Getting Up the Courage

It requires a great deal of motivation and courage for a person with obsessive compulsive disorder (OCD) to begin an exposure treatment program. After all, the treatment is based on confronting one's obsessive fears and preventing the compulsive acts that ease those fears. Researchers in behavioral treatment for OCD have noted that as many as 25 to 30 percent of those who consider entering such psychological treatment programs decide not to attempt it. In many cases, these people seek medication treatment despite the fact that behavioral treatment has been shown to be quite effective with OCD and possibly more helpful than drug therapy.

Their reluctance is understandable, if unfortunate. Behavioral treatment involves deciding to expose oneself to the very situations that gave rise to so much avoidance and compulsive effort to neutralize the fear. It is perhaps akin to a height phobic person electing to go up in a hot air balloon or a speech phobic agreeing to give a talk to 200 people. Neither of these actions is actually dangerous, but it can feel terrifying at the time. Of course, exposure treatment is nearly always done in a gradual fashion. Nonetheless, the experience of fear is an inevitable part of the exposure treatment process.

How do you muster the courage to begin? There is no simple answer. For most obsessive-compulsives, it is a matter of weighing the discomfort of treatment against the burden of their daily struggle with obsessions and rituals. Most OCD sufferers find themselves anxious, depressed, and frustrated at their limited functioning before undertaking treatment. Particularly if the OCD symptoms have lasted for some years and/or have not responded adequately to medication, exposure treatment usually proves easier in the long run than living with such restricting and upsetting symptoms. Mustering the courage to begin confronting those fears is never easy. But regular reminders of the potential benefits and the very probability that you will benefit from exposure may help you keep your goals in mind.

Do You Need Professional Help?

The decision to seek professional help from a behaviorally trained therapist rests on several factors. People with very severe obsessive and compulsive symptoms—fears and rituals that consume many hours per day—are likely to require professional help, since the problem can seem too overwhelming to face alone. Professional therapy may also be needed when OCD symptoms are very complex and therefore difficult for the person to describe or record on paper. Especially when cognitive compulsions alternate in close association with obsessive ideas, an experienced therapist may offer crucial help in determining when to apply exposure and when to block or avoid the obsessive thoughts. Finally, some people feel more motivated and work harder and more consistently toward their goals when they have to report to another person or group of people. If you are the sort of person who prefers to diet or give up a bad habit by joining a support group or teaming up with a friend, then regular contact with a therapist may be a good strategy for achieving your aims.

Once you decide you need professional help, how do you select a therapist? Although many mental health professionals believe they can treat OCD, many are inadequately trained or experienced in the specific treatment of this disorder. The person you choose for treatment should have both 1) *direct experience* in applying exposure and response prevention with several cases of OCD (or be immediately supervised by a professional with such experience) and 2) *behavioral training* in this method from another professional experienced in treatment of OCD (preferably, though not necessarily, someone who has published professional papers in this area).

Do not hesitate to ask a prospective therapist questions about his or her training (what type and by whom) and experience, including how many people with OCD he or she has treated and what the results have been. A good therapist will not resent the questions, but rather assume that you are appropriately concerned about obtaining high quality treatment for your problem.

To obtain the names of prospective therapists in your area, you can contact the OCD Foundation at P.O. Box 9573, New Haven, CT 06535. Their referrals may include behavior therapists, as well as physicians expert in the drug treatment of OCD but not in behavior therapy. Or you may contact the Association for the Advancement of Behavior Therapy (AABT) at 15 West 36th St., New York, NY 10018 for a listing of their behaviorally trained members (usually these are psychologists). Members of the latter organization will have training in behavior therapy, but may not be trained or experienced in the treatment of OCD. You will have to investigate this for yourself.

Another strategy is to contact people who have published research papers in this area: often they can refer you to someone nearby who is well-trained, perhaps even someone they have trained themselves. Again, bear in mind the distinction between pharmacotherapists (psychiatrists expert in prescribing drugs for OCD) and behavior therapists; both may have something valuable to offer you, but they won't be the same things. A pharmacotherapist with experience in OCD may also be able to refer you to a good behavior therapist.

Of course, once you locate a suitable therapist, you'll want to be sure you feel comfortable with this person and able to work well together. Therapy should be a positive learning experience for you. You should feel that your therapist asks helpful questions in trying to clarify the nature of your difficulties. You'll want to be given useful information about the nature of your OCD symptoms and about the treatment plan. A good therapist will be supportive and encouraging, but very firm in urging you to expose yourself to fearful situations and to stop your rituals.

Remember, however, that you must carry out the therapy instructions yourself, to the best of your ability. The more involved the OCD sufferer is in his or her treatment, the more effective treatment is likely to be, especially over the long term. It is important that you learn and understand the treatment methods. Even with the therapist's guidance you'll need to take much of the initiative yourself.

The key, then, to successful professional treatment involves a balanced combination of factors: a therapist with adequate behavioral training, specific experience in treating OCD, and a manner that you feel comfortable with, as well as your own motivation and commitment to the process. Keep in mind that in behavior therapy of OCD, the technique may be as important as the personality and manner of the therapist. A very likeable and sympathetic therapist who does not employ the right techniques may be quite unable to help you, but may be hard for you to give up. You may wish to keep periodic contact with a therapist who has been treating you for other problems, while you see a behavior therapist for your OCD symptoms. It is important that the two therapists consult with each other at the beginning of such an arrangement so you do not receive conflicting suggestions during treatment.

Treatment for OCD, whether you undertake it on your own or with professional help, will consist of:

- Defining your symptoms and goals
- Direct exposure to obsessive fears
- Imaginal exposure to obsessive fears
- Stopping rituals
- Possible medication

Excerpted and adapted with permission from *When Once Is Not Enough: Help for Obsessive Compulsives* by Gail Steketee, Ph.D., and Kerrin White, Ph.D. For more information on this and related books, see the "Further Reading" section in the back of the book.

CHAPTER 38

Traumatic Experiences

Under different names, post-traumatic stress disorder (PTSD) has been documented by doctors, historians, and poets as far back as the days of the ancient Greeks. For example, the historian Herodotus wrote that during the battle of Marathon in 490 B.C. an Athenian soldier who had suffered no wounds became permanently blind after witnessing the death of the soldier standing next to him. In the 17th century, Samuel Pepys wrote of the panic and distress of those who survived the great fire of London in 1666: "A most horrid, malicious, blood fire . . . So great was our fear . . . it was enough to put us out of our wits." For weeks after the fire, Pepys, like many other survivors of the fire, suffered from insomnia, anger, and depression, all common symptoms of PTSD.

In the 19th century, the French neurologist Jean-Martin Charcot diagnosed women who reported having been sexually abused as children and battered wives as suffering from hysteria. Freud and his followers perpetuated this view into the 20th century. In reality, however, the symptoms of these women were those of PTSD. Earlier, during the middle ages, abused girls and women with severe PTSD symptoms were often assumed to be witches or possessed by demons, and were subsequently put away, burned at the stake, or hung.

The Uniqueness of the PTSD Diagnosis

At some time in your life you have probably cut your finger with a knife. If the blade was dull, you may have suffered only a little nick. If the blade was sharp, you may have bled all over. If the blade was very sharp and the force behind it was great enough, you might even have lost part of your finger.

The extent of your injury depended more on the sharpness of the blade and the power behind it than on the toughness of your skin. Given enough force, even extremely tough skin would not protect you from the knife, and anyone else in the same situation would also be injured, even if he or she had the toughest skin in the world.

The same holds true on a psychological level. There are events in life that would make almost anyone "bleed all over." It is such events that make people susceptible to developing PTSD.

In the past, many medical and mental health professionals believed that people suffered from depression, anxiety, and certain other symptoms primarily because of internal psychological conflicts and problems, rather than in response to external events. In the case of nontraumatized persons, this belief is not necessarily false. It is, however, incomplete, in that it fails to take into account the effect of social and economic pressures, as well as other outside stresses, on the individual.

In the case of trauma survivors, trauma alone, regardless of any previous psychological problems, can lead to the development of a variety of symptoms. These symptoms are reactions to a single, overwhelming external event, or series of such events, far more than they are to any internal psychological problem.

Ample research shows that, given sufficient stress, other factors, such as an individual's previous mental stability and psychological state, are irrelevant in predicting the development of PTSD. During World War II, for example, some soldiers with sterling records of mental health and family stability developed PTSD. In contrast, other soldiers who had preexisting social or psychological problems, did not develop PTSD. The critical variable in the development of PTSD was the degree of exposure to combat—the amount of stress to which the soldier had been exposed.

Similarly, a large-scale study of crime victims found that a victim's race, sex, educational status, or income level did not predict whether he or she would develop PTSD. Neither did a history of previous psychiatric illness—for example, panic disorder, agoraphobia, or depression—predict PTSD. The determining factor was instead the stressfulness of the crime. PTSD rates were lower among individuals who had been the victim of a relatively low-stress crime, such as a burglary that occurred when no one was home.

In contrast, PTSD rates were higher among individuals who had endured high-stress crimes: those in which the individual or others were injured, a weapon was involved, or there otherwise was or appeared to be a threat to life.

Over and over it has been found that the development of PTSD symptoms, and the severity of those symptoms, has more to do with the intensity and duration of the stressful event than any preexisting personality pattern.

In the *Diagnostic and Statistical Manual of Mental Disorders—Fourth Edition* (DSM-IV), the official handbook of psychiatric problems, the listing for post-traumatic stress disorder is the only diagnosis that places the origin of the symptoms on external events rather than on the individual personality. The PTSD diagnosis is also the only one that recognizes that, subject to enough stress, any human being has the potential for developing PTSD or PTSD symptoms.

What this means to you is that, although your pretrauma personality, belief system, and values certainly affected your reaction to and interpretation of the traumatic event, you did not develop PTSD because of some inherent inferiority or weakness in your personality. Trauma changes personalities, not the other way around.

The Criteria for Post-Traumatic Stress Disorder

According to the official definition of PTSD, to qualify as having PTSD you must meet the following criteria:

- Criterion A: You have been exposed to a traumatic event involving actual or threatened death or injury, during which you respond with panic, horror, and feelings of helplessness.

- Criterion B: You reexperience the trauma in the form of dreams, flashbacks, intrusive memories, or unrest at being in situations that remind you of the original trauma.

- Criterion C: You show evidence of avoidance behavior—a numbing of emotions and reduced interest in others and the outside world.

- Criterion D: You experience physiological hyperarousal, as evidenced by insomnia, agitation, irritability, or outbursts of rage.

- Criterion E: The symptoms in Criteria B, C, and D persist for at least one month.

- Criterion F: The symptoms have significantly affected your social or vocational abilities or other important areas of your life.

PTSD can be either acute or delayed-onset. Acute PTSD occurs within six months after a traumatic event. In delayed-onset PTSD, the symptoms occur anytime later than six months after the traumatic event. This can be one year, twenty years, or even forty years after the traumatic event. For example, previously asymptomatic sixty-year-old people can develop PTSD in response to having been sexually or physically abused as children.

Criterion A: A Traumatic Event

In life, we all face crises, large and small, ranging from the loss of a wallet to the death of a loved one. Yet these events, although stressful and often called traumatic, are not considered true trauma. *Trauma*, in the technical sense of the word, refers to situations in which you are rendered powerless and great danger is involved. Trauma in this sense refers to events involving death and injury or the possibility of death and injury. These events must be unusual and out of the ordinary, not events that are part of the normal course of life. They are events that evoke a state of extreme horror, helplessness, and fear, events of such intensity and magnitude that they would overtax any human being's ability to cope.

For example, although the loss of a job or a parent may change your life forever, these events are not considered traumas because they are expected life losses. However, if instead of losing one family member, you lost several family members or friends in an accident or natural disaster, you would be considered a trauma survivor. Such simultaneous multiple losses are clearly out of the ordinary and overwhelming.

In general, the word *trauma* is reserved for natural catastrophes (hurricanes, floods, fires, earthquakes, and so on) and man-made catastrophes (war, concentration camp experiences, physical assault, sexual assault, and other forms of victimization involving a threat to life and limb).

Victims of vehicular accidents and crimes other than those listed can also develop PTSD, as can individuals injured on the job, if they sustain severe injuries. Depending on the situation, witnessing death or injury or its aftermath can also lead to PTSD, as can the loss of a child.

You are in a traumatic situation when you either know or believe that you may be injured or killed or that others about you may be. For example, if a mugger says he will shoot you, you have every reason to believe you are in danger; such a situation would definitely be classified as a trauma. If the mugger says nothing but you sense from the look on his face or certain gestures that he is capable of murder—or for any other reason you believe you may die or be seriously injured during the mugging—you are also being traumatized.

PTSD can also develop in persons who witness trauma on a daily basis or are subject to nearly constant and unabated stress as part of their job. This statement holds true even for individuals who are carefully screened for mental health problems prior to admission to their field. For example, PTSD has been found among rescue workers, firefighters, health care professionals, and police officers, as well as in nurses and doctors who served in Vietnam and other wars.

Trauma Means Wounding

Perhaps you have heard a doctor talk about head trauma, bone trauma, or trauma to some other part of the body. On a physical level, trauma has two meanings. The first is that some part or particular organ of the body has been suddenly damaged by a force so great that the body's natural protections (the skin, skull, and so on) were unable to prevent injury. The second meaning refers to injuries in which the body's natural healing abilities are inadequate to mend the wound without medical assistance.

Just as the body can be traumatized, so can the psyche. On the psychological and mental levels, trauma refers to the wounding of your emotions, your spirit, your will to live, your beliefs about yourself and the world, your dignity, and your sense of security. The assault on your psyche is so great that your normal ways of thinking and feeling and the usual ways you have handled stress in the past are now inadequate.

Being traumatized is not like being offended or rejected in a work or a love relationship. Such events can injure your emotions, your pride, and perhaps your sense of fairness, but they are not of the order of magnitude of trauma. During trauma, you touch your own death or the deaths of others. At the same time, you feel, or are, helpless to prevent death or injury.

As human beings, we must all confront the fact of our mortality. We and our loved ones will die some day, no matter who we are or what we do. Usually this awareness becomes most powerful in our middle or later years, when we see parents and their contemporaries dying or when we ourselves acquire an illness. However, if you have survived a rape, aggravated assault, flood, or war, or if you are a rescue worker or a nurse in an emergency room in an area with a high rate of violent crime, you will confront the existential reality of death sooner, and more vividly, than most.

Depersonalization and Trauma

During trauma you are subject to a process called *depersonalization*. Depersonalization refers to the stripping away of your personhood—your individuality and your humanity. The sense of being depersonalized or dehumanized is especially strong when the injuries sustained or the wounding and death witnessed seem senseless or preventable.

At the moment of attack, whether the assailant is a mugger, rapist, enemy soldier, or a hurricane, you do not feel like a valuable person with the right to safety, happiness, and health. At that moment, you feel more like a thing, a vulnerable object subject to the will of a power or force greater than yourself (Haley 1984).

When the assailant is a natural force, such as a tornado, the catastrophe can be explained away as an accident of fate (provided human error was not involved). However, when the assailant is another person, your trust in other human beings and in society in general can be severely shaken or shattered entirely.

Questionnaire for Criterion A

This questionnaire and those that follow will help you determine whether you suffer from PTSD. They are based on the official definition of PTSD in *DSM-IV*, the handbook used by all mental health professionals.

Using this questionnaire, describe in your journal the traumatic event or events that happened to you and your feelings during and after the event. Be as specific and detailed as you can. This process may bring up memories you would rather forget. It may also give rise to pain, anger, sadness, or remorse. However, your purpose in reading this book is to better understand what happened and how what happened has affected your life. Through this understanding, you will be able to exert greater control over your present and future life experiences.

As you read this questionnaire and those that follow, you may begin to hyperventilate or gag, feel faint or dizzy, or begin to experience hallucinations, flashbacks, or out-of-body experiences. If so, stop immediately, touch a physical object, talk to someone right away, or use another technique to orient and calm yourself.

According to the *DSM-IV*, you must have experienced a traumatic event or series of events in order to qualify as having PTSD. In your life you may have experienced several frightening, sad, or unhappy events, and many major losses. However, only certain events can be categorized as traumatic. By answering the following questions in detail, you can determine whether or not you have been traumatized.

1. Have you ever been in a natural catastrophe, such as an earthquake, fire, flood, hurricane, tornado, volcano, landslide, or a dangerous dust storm or windstorm? Have you experienced a community or work-related disaster, such as an explosion or chemical spill?

2. Have you ever lived in a refugee or concentration camp or been tortured?

3. Were you ever sexually or physically assaulted, either by a stranger, a group of strangers, a family member, or anyone else?

   Sexual assault includes fondling and molestation; oral, anal, or vaginal sex; or any other forced sexual activity. Physical assault includes any form of physical contact intended to intimidate or cause pain. Being hit, slapped, thrown down stairs, beaten with fists or a weapon—stick, belt, billy club, gun—or being threatened or attacked with a weapon, are all considered forms of assault.

4. As a child, were you physically maltreated with excessive beatings or spankings? Were a parent's or caretaker's disciplinary measures sadistic?

   For example, were you ever forced to eat worms or insects, to stand nude in the cold or in front of others, or to injure a pet, sibling, or another person? Were you ever confined in a cage, a closet, or tied up? Were you deprived of adequate nutrition and medical care you needed?

5. Have you ever witnessed the death, torture, rape, or beating of another person as part of war or crime? Have you ever seen someone die or be badly injured in a car, airplane, or other such accident?

6. Has anyone in your family or a close friend been murdered or committed suicide?

7. As a child, did you ever witness the beating, rape, murder, torture, or suicide of a parent, caretaker, or friend?

8. Have you ever been in a war, either as a combatant, a medic, a prisoner of war, or a member of a support team or grave registration unit? Were you ever, in any way, exposed to combat, enemy or friendly fire, or atrocities?

9. Have you ever been kidnapped, abducted, raped, burglarized, robbed, or mugged?

10. Were you ever injured in a burglary, robbery, mugging, or other criminal episode, or in a car, boat, bicycle, airplane, or other vehicular accident?

11. Have you ever been involved in a situation in which you felt that you or a member of your family would be harmed or killed? Even if your life or the lives of your family members were not directly threatened, did you distinctly fear that you or they were in serious danger?

    It does not matter if, in retrospect, you realize your fears were unfounded. Neither does it matter if, later on, you decided you were "overreacting" or "foolish" for your fears. The critical issue is whether at the time of the trauma, you perceived the situation as life threatening to yourself or others.

12. Were you ever a member of a medical team, a firefighting team, a police force, a rescue squad, or a rescue operation that involved at least one of the following conditions?

    • Danger to your safety and life
    • Witnessing death and injury
    • Making life-and-death decisions
    • High-stress working conditions—long hours, unsafe conditions

If the answer to any one of these questions is yes, then you have experienced a traumatic event. However, to meet the first *DSM-IV* criterion for PTSD, you must also have responded to the traumatic event with either fear, helplessness, or horror.

Even if you meet criterion A, you do no necessarily have PTSD, but it does place you at risk for suffering from or developing either partial or full-blown PTSD or some PTSD symptoms. To have PTSD, you also must meet five other criteria: You must reexperience the trauma, show evidence of numbing or other avoidance behavior, exhibit signs of hyperarousal, have all of these symptoms for at least one month, and have experienced difficulties at work, or home, or in other important areas of your life as a result of these symptoms.

Criterion B: Reexperiencing the Trauma

The fundamental dynamic underlying PTSD is a cycle of reexperiencing the trauma, followed by avoidance or repression of the traumatic memories and a numbing of emotions. This cycle of intrusive recall, followed by avoidance and numbing, also has a strong biological component.

During the recall stage of the PTSD cycle, your memories and the emotions associated with them will emerge, in conscious or unconscious awareness, over and over again in a variety of forms. You may have intrusive thoughts or images, dreams and nightmares, even flashbacks about the event. You may suddenly find yourself thinking or feeling as if you were back in the original trauma situation, or you may experience physical pain or medical problems for no apparent reason. All these phenomena are part of the process of reexperiencing the trauma.

According to Freud, reexperiencing the trauma, including repeating it in present-day life, are ways of dissipating the intense psychic energy generated by the trauma and of trying to gain mastery over it. It is as if you were watching a movie that ended sadly. You replay the movie, hoping that perhaps this time the ending will be a happy one. It isn't, of course, but you keep watching the movie again and again anyway. The unresolved trauma can absorb so much psychic energy in some trauma survivors that they have less psychic energy to devote to work, friends, and family, and most importantly to themselves, in the present.

Dreams, Nightmares, and Insomnia

You may have dreams or nightmares about the traumatic event. During these dreams you may shake, shout, and thrash about. You may or may not remember the dream upon awakening. However, the feelings of terror and fear you experience in the dream may persist for quite some time.

Some dreams or nightmares may be almost exact replays of the traumatic event, or they may be very similar. Other dreams, however, may simply incorporate the feelings you had during the trauma—helplessness, fear, anger, and grief.

Partially as a result of these dreams, falling asleep and staying asleep may be major problems for you. Or it may be that at night, without the distraction of the activities of the day, thoughts of the traumatic event begin to surface. You might start thinking about the event itself or about other events involving losses and threats to safety, or you might experience vague anxiety, nameless fears, or a generalized irritability. Alternatively, sleep problems may indicate that you are suffering from a biochemical depression, as well as PTSD. Alcohol and drug use can also affect sleep patterns. Insomnia is also associated with hyperarousal—another symptom of PTSD (see criterion D, below).

Flashbacks

A flashback is a sudden, vivid recollection of the traumatic event accompanied by a strong emotion. During a flashback you do not black out or lose consciousness, but you do, temporarily, leave the present and find yourself back in the original traumatic situation. You may see the scene of the trauma, smell it, and hear its sounds. You may or may not lose your awareness of present reality. You may find yourself acting as if you were actually in the original traumatic situation, or you may not. You may alternate between the current reality and experiencing the past. A flashback can last anywhere from a few seconds to several hours.

In an auditory flashback, you hear sounds associated with the trauma. Such sounds include human voices, such as screaming or sobbing, or other sounds, such as banging or explosions. Auditory flashbacks differ from the voices associated with schizophrenia and other psychoses in that the sounds are almost direct replicas of those heard during the traumatic event.

For example, when Mr. Gregg walks by ditches, sometimes he hears the screams and sobs of the soldiers he saw die in ditches during World War II. These are considered auditory flashbacks. Sometimes flashbacks include only one of the senses, sometimes more. For example, some flashbacks are only visual; others are visual and auditory.

You don't have to be a combat veteran to have flashbacks. Flashbacks have been documented among survivors of Nazi concentration camps, crime victims, victims of occupational and technological disasters, and rape and incest survivors. Flashbacks tend to occur among persons who have had to endure situations where there was an "intense, chronic, or pervasive loss of security" and lack of safety.

You may be reluctant to acknowledge or tell anyone that you are having a flashback for fear of sounding "crazy." Flashbacks are not a sign that you are losing your mind, but rather that some traumatic material is breaking forth into your consciousness. The more you deal with the trauma on a conscious level—by talking about it, writing about it, or otherwise getting it out into the open—the less need there will be for it to appear in flashbacks or nightmares.

Other Forms of Reexperiencing the Trauma

Somatic flashbacks are an additional form of reexperiencing the trauma. During somatic flashbacks, a physical pain or medical condition emerges as a means of expressing the feelings and bodily states associated with trauma.

For example, Lewis usually develops a short-lived medical condition around the anniversary of a deadly attack on his squad. Georgia lost her parents in a murder-suicide in the month of June. The first June after their deaths, she broke out in hives. The second June, she developed a urinary tract infection. The third June, she contracted bronchitis; the fourth June, severe headaches.

The hives, infections, and headaches were real and needed medical care. And while it could be argued that Georgia might have developed these conditions even if she had not been traumatized, the fact that she never had these conditions before and that they manifested themselves only in June suggests that they are trauma related.

Another form of reexperiencing the trauma, which may be a kind of unconscious flashback, consists of suddenly feeling painful or angry feelings that do not seem clearly related to any particular memory of the traumatic event. For example, you may experience irritability, panic attacks, rage reactions, or intense psychic pain, without any conscious thought of the traumatic event.

"I can understand why I sulk or explode when I hear about another cop being killed in the line of duty. But many times I get moody or angry for no reason at all," explains a police officer. What this man, and his family, may not fully appreciate is that often there is a reason for the emotional upset, even though that reason may not be obvious. The reason may lie in the intensity of his repressed feelings about the deaths or injuries of other police officers, or in the very real possibility that someday he will be injured or killed on the job.

Questionnaire for Criterion B

According to the official definition of PTSD in *DSM-IV* you must be able to answer yes to at least one of the following questions. In your journal, write about the ways you reexperience the trauma. Again, try to be as specific as possible; include information on frequency, duration, and so on. Also note the date you first began to reexperience the trauma (as closely as possible).

1. Do you, on a persistent or recurring basis, find yourself having intrusive or involuntary thoughts of the traumatic event? Do you find yourself thinking about the trauma when you don't mean to or when you are trying hard not to think about it? Do visions or pictures of the trauma pop into your mind?

2. Do you have dreams or nightmares about the event?

3. Do you have dreams or nightmares that are not replays of the actual event, but that take place in the location where the event occurred, contain some of the actions involved in the event, or include some of the feelings you felt during the event?

    For instance, if you were raped in a parking lot, you may dream about the parking lot without any vision of the rape. Or you may dream about being attacked in some other way or about drowning, suffocating, falling into a well, or watching your house catch on fire. These are not rape dreams, but they capture the feelings of helplessness, fear, anger, and anxiety you most likely experienced during the rape. PTSD-related dreams also include those about a life-threatening event happening to a member of your family or someone you love.

4. Do you find yourself suddenly acting or feeling as if you were back in the original trauma situation? For example, do you have flashbacks, see visions, or hear sounds of the event? Do you have waves of strong feelings about the trauma or otherwise feel as if you have just lived through the trauma again, even without having a flashback or a vision?

5. Do you have physical reactions when exposed to events that are similar to or symbolize the traumatic event?

   Such physical reactions include hyperventilation, sweating, vomiting, dizziness, muscle or stomach cramping, shaking, or physical pain not related to any medical condition. For example, someone raped in a green car might feel faint when she sees a green car. A medical staff person who served in a combat zone might start sweating when he sees pictures of wounded soldiers or articles on treating war casualties. If the traumatic event occurred in May, you might start having stomach cramps around that time of year.

6. Do you become extremely upset (angry, teary, confused, frightened, anxious, or panicky) at people, places, or events that resemble an aspect of the original trauma?

7. Do you become distressed around the anniversary date of the trauma?

How many of the above questions were you able to write about? If you had an affirmative response to at least one of these questions, then you have met the reexperiencing criterion for PTSD.

Even if you answered no to all these questions, continue on with the questionnaires in this chapter. Quite possibly you do not suffer from full-blown PTSD, but from partial PTSD, and even partial PTSD requires healing.

Criterion C: Numbing and Avoidance

Reexperiencing the trauma can be cyclical or it can be sporadic. You may be symptom free for many weeks or months, but then begin to suffer as anniversaries of events associated with the trauma approach. A personal loss or other current-life stress or change—even positive changes such as the birth of a baby or a wedding—can call up memories or flashbacks. In addition, sometimes "triggers" in the environment—people, places, and things that remind you of the trauma— can set off a memory.

Whenever or however you reexperience the trauma, it is usually pure agony. As a result, both emotionally and physically you alternate between being "hyper" (discussed later) and being "numb" or "shut down."

Emotional Shutdown or Psychic Numbing

What happens when you shut down is similar to something that happens when the human body is injured. Have you ever cut yourself and not felt the pain immediately, or been whiplashed in a car accident but not felt the soreness until several days later? The body often emits a natural anesthetic that permits us some time to take care of our wounds and do whatever is necessary to protect ourselves from further injury.

For example, due to this natural anesthetic, severely wounded soldiers have walked miles to safety. Similarly, abused women and battered children sometimes report experiencing minimal pain from their injuries during or immediately after being attacked.

In a similar way the psyche, in self-protection, can numb itself against onslaughts of unbearable emotional pain. During whatever traumatic event you endured, it was probably essential for you to put aside your feelings. Feeling those emotions at the time could have been life threatening.

For example, if a rape victim began to connect with her feelings while being assaulted, she would be less able to assess the dangerousness of her assailant or figure out how to escape or otherwise minimize the threat of injury. Similarly, in the midst of a hurricane or tornado, you would most likely be preoccupied with how to stay safe, not with your emotional reactions.

This deadening, or shutting off, of emotions is called psychic or emotional numbing. It is a central feature of PTSD and has been found among survivors of all forms of assault, survivors of natural catastrophes, survivors of the bombing of Hiroshima and the Nazi holocaust, and other war-related situations. Many researchers believe that, like the body's natural anesthetic, emotional numbing may be partially biological.

Avoidance and Triggers

During the times you reexperience the trauma, you may experience some of the feelings associated with the trauma that you did not feel, or felt only partially, due to the psychic numbing that attends trauma. These feelings of fear, anger, sadness, and guilt may shake you to the core. In response to the power of these feelings, you may shut down, just as you did during the traumatic event. Shutting down serves as a means of reducing the intensity of these feelings, so that the mood swings and variations in your energy levels don't make you feel "crazy" or out of control. Otherwise, if you don't understand what is going on inside you, you might start berating yourself and want to lash out at others—or simply hide.

Having flashbacks, being hyper, and shutting down are not only personally painful but are states that can be easily misunderstood and misinterpreted by others. Hence you may find yourself, to avoid the pain, avoiding situations that you have found bring forth (or that you fear might bring forth) either hyper or numbing symptoms. As a result, you, like so many other trauma survivors, may find yourself retreating—mentally, socially, and physically.

For example, just as rape survivors may stay inside their homes at night, hurricane survivors may stay inside when only a minor thunderstorm is predicted. Flood survivors may avoid water-related activities, and car- or airplane-accident survivors may drastically limit their travel. Medics, nurses, and doctors who have worked in high-stress environments may seek work in nonmedical fields. Similarly, people who have suffered massive injuries on the job may change their line of work.

Crime victims may avoid the site of the crime or places that remind them of the crime; if the crime occurred in a restaurant, they may have great difficulty dining out for quite some time. War veterans may avoid the sound of popcorn popping because it reminds them of airplanes or helicopters. Or they might avoid plastic trash bags or fires because they are reminded of body bags or burning villages.

Every trauma survivor has his or her own set of triggers that can touch off memories of the trauma. Avoiding trigger situations makes utter sense—you are trying to prevent a resurgence of your PTSD symptoms. However, the avoidance can generate yet another set of problems, again particularly in relationships.

Questionnaire for Criterion C

The following questions concern psychic numbing and avoidance behavior. Answer yes to the following questions only if the symptoms described presented themselves after the traumatic event. If any of the numbing or avoidance behaviors listed below were present prior to the traumatic event, they are not a symptom of PTSD. Describe your yes answers in detail in your journal, and note the date the symptoms began, as accurately as possible.

1. Since the traumatic event, have you ever had periods of time when you felt emotionally numb or dead inside? Have you ever had periods when you have had great difficulty feeling tender, loving feelings, or any feelings at all, except perhaps for anger, resentment, and hatred?

2. Have you tried not to talk about the event or avoided thoughts or feelings associated with it?

3. Since the traumatic event, have you felt alienated and apart from others?

4. Have you had a sense of doom or foreboding since the event? Do you feel that you will die young or never experience the rewards of living? For example, do you feel you will never have a family, a career, the love of others, financial security?

5. Have you lost interest in activities that used to involve you or give you pleasure? These might include sports, hobbies, and other recreational activities, participation in a group, activities involving socializing with others, and eating, dancing, sex, and other sensual activities.

6. Are you unable to remember certain aspects of the trauma? For example, do you have difficult remembering when it began or how long it lasted? Are there certain details or entire episodes you can't recall? Are there hours, days, weeks, months, or years you can't remember at all? Do you have difficulty remembering the names, faces, or fates of any of the other people involved in the trauma?

To how many of the above questions did you answer yes? If you have answered yes to at least three of the above questions, then you have met criterion C for PTSD. Remember, only those avoidance or numbing symptoms that appeared *after* the traumatic event count. If you had one of these symptoms prior to the traumatic event, do not include it as a yes response.

Even if you answered yes to less than three of the above questions, continue reading this chapter and completing the following questionnaires. It may well be that even if you don't suffer from full-blown PTSD, you have partial PTSD or troublesome PTSD symptoms that need attention.

Criterion D: Hyperarousal Symptoms

The fourth PTSD criterion concerns symptoms of increased physical alertness or, in psychological terms, hyperalertness or hyperarousal.

Fight-or-Flight and Freeze Reactions

Trauma involves life-threatening situations. The possibility that you might die or be injured gives rise to feelings of terror and anxiety. Or, if you are not threatened yourself, you may feel horror and grief at seeing others die or be injured. You may also be angry at the circumstances that are causing the devastation. All of these trauma-generated emotions—the fear, anxiety, and anger—are emotions that have a strong physiological component. They cause your body to react and change your body chemistry.

In a dangerous situation, your adrenal glands may begin to pump either adrenaline or noradrenaline into your system. Adrenaline places your body into a state of biological hyperalertness. Your heart rate, blood pressure, muscle tension, and blood-sugar level increase. Your pupils dilate. The blood flow to your arms and legs decreases, while the flow to your head and trunk increases so that you can think and move better and more quickly. This is called the fight-or-flight reaction.

Alternatively, if your adrenals pump noradrenaline into your system, you may have a freeze reaction, during which moving or acting is difficult, if not impossible. Some PTSD sufferers have described their freeze reaction as "moving or thinking in slow motion." Others find themselves temporarily unable to move at all. However, even if you freeze, you will most likely be experiencing some of the other symptoms of hyperarousal.

If you experience hyperarousal symptoms, you are experiencing an adrenaline surge like that you may have experienced during the trauma.

Questionnaire for Criterion D

According to *DSM-IV*, PTSD sufferers must have at least two of the following symptoms of increased arousal:

- Difficulty falling or staying asleep

- Irritability or outbursts of anger

- Difficulty concentrating

- Hypervigilance or overprotectiveness toward oneself and others

- Exaggerated startle response (jumping or otherwise overreacting to noises or the sudden appearance of a person)

Answer yes to the following questions only if you experience the symptoms relatively frequently and you came to experience these symptoms persistently after, not before, the traumatic event. Record and describe any yes answers in your journal along with the date you first experienced the symptom.

1. Do you have difficulty falling or staying asleep? Is your sleep fitful and disturbed in any other ways?

   Insomnia may be a particular problem for you if you were traumatized or abused while in bed, reclining, or asleep. Due to your experience, an association has been made in your mind between being asleep or lying down and being in danger. Therefore, you may feel you have to be on alert at bedtime. Insomnia tends to be a special problem for war veterans, incest survivors, crime victims, and anyone else who has been physically or sexually attacked while sleeping.

2. Do you suffer from periods of irritability that are not directly associated with any present stress or problem in your life? Do you feel tense much of the time? Does your high tension level ever lead to outbursts of anger, such as smashing plates, punching holes in the wall, throwing objects around the house, yelling at other drivers, shouting at family

members, friends, or co-workers? Do you frequently have to restrain yourself from lashing out at others?

3. Do you have difficulty concentrating? Can you concentrate enough to read an entire magazine article or book, or can you read only a few paragraphs or pages at a time? Are you easily distracted when trying to complete a job or listen to someone talk?

4. Are you overprotective, or in psychological terms, hypervigilant? Are you extremely concerned with your safety and the safety of your loved ones?

   For example, when you enter a room, do you stand by the door or some other exit for a while to scan the room for potential danger? Do you examine people to see if they might be carrying a weapon or could be dangerous in some other way? Do you identify places where it would be safe to hide in case of trouble? Whether with others or alone in your home, do you situate yourself so that you can keep surveillance over your environment or make a quick escape in case of danger? Do you carry or sleep with a weapon?

   Do you try to restrict the comings and goings of people you care about for fear they will be injured? Do you have an "anxiety attack" if a family member is late coming home? Do you insist that family members and friends call you when they arrive at their destination or if they plan to be even five or ten minutes late?

   Do crowds make you anxious? Do you avoid shopping malls, parades, movie theaters, concerts, circuses, or large parties? Do you avoid situations where it is difficult to control your level of safety? Do you drive in an excessively cautious manner, even by the most conservative standards? Do you double- or triple check seatbelts before setting out?

5. Are you easily startled? Do you jump at loud or sudden noises or at noises that resemble some aspect of the trauma?

   For example, if you are a combat veteran, do you dive to the floor if you hear an airplane overhead? Do you jump if someone touches you from behind or wakes you from your sleep? If you were a victim of a crime committed by an intruder in your home, do you startle when someone unexpectedly comes into the room?

To how many questions did you answer yes? If you have answered yes to at least two of the above questions, and the symptom did not exist before the trauma, then you have met the hyperarousal criteria for full-blown PTSD. Whether or not you have met the hyperarousal requirement, continue on to the next sections to determine the severity of your PTSD symptoms.

Criterion E: Duration

After undergoing any experience that is dangerous, frightening, or distressing, it is normal to experience shock, fear, confusion, helplessness, anxiety, and depression. PTSD, however, is something more. PTSD includes these reactions, but on a deeper, more complex, and more enduring level, as indicated by the *DSM-IV* criteria you have read about above.

According to *DSM-IV*, PTSD symptoms must persist for at least 30 days in order to be considered PTSD. This is, of course, just a rule of thumb. There isn't much difference between 30 days and 31 or 32 days. However, if the symptoms persist much longer than five or six weeks, you should seek help. The sooner you seek help, the quicker you can enter the recovery stage.

Refer back to the answers you wrote in your journal in response to the questionnaires, and note when the symptoms began.

Criterion F: Degree of Impairment

PTSD cases are not all the same. PTSD takes different forms in different people, depending on their personality, their spiritual or religious beliefs, their culture, the amount and quality of their social support system, and the meaning they and their family and community ascribe to trauma.

Criterion F addresses the degree that your PTSD symptoms affect your life. You can have PTSD without it taking over your entire life. The crucial question in assessing the severity of your PTSD is, How much does it affect my ability to work, love, and play?

The answer to this question is highly subjective. No specific guidelines to what constitutes "impairment" exist, except in the most extreme cases. Obviously, if you can no longer work because you cannot tolerate crowds or commuting, because you cannot concentrate on the task at hand due to intrusive thoughts, or because you do not have the energy to complete your duties due to depression or insomnia, then your vocational abilities have been significantly affected.

Similarly, if you are unable to maintain friendships, family relationships, or intimate involvements due to your distrust, negative mood states, cynical or critical attitudes, or other aftereffects of the trauma, your personal life has suffered a great deal due to the trauma.

Man-Made vs. Natural Catastrophes

Two other important considerations in assessing the degree to which you suffer from PTSD are whether you are a survivor of a natural or a man-made disaster and whether you are a single-trauma or a multiple-trauma survivor.

According to *DSM-IV*, survivors of man-made catastrophes suffer from longer and more intense PTSD than survivors of natural catastrophes. Because, it is argued, natural catastrophes can be explained away as acts of God or bad luck, natural-catastrophe survivors are less likely to lose their trust in other human beings and in society than are survivors of man-made catastrophes.

However, in many cases the suffering caused by natural disasters involves one or more significant human errors or betrayals, either by individuals or institutions. For example, in the case of the 1972 Buffalo Creek Flood in West Virginia, survivors did not blame excess rain or the hand of God for causing the dam to break. Instead, many held the Pittston Coal Company's failure to build an adequate slag pile responsible.

Natural-catastrophe survivors may also feel betrayed or let down by rescue operations and other services. For example, they may have to face long lines, delays, and considerable red tape before they receive promised compensations for their losses. And in many cases, when the compensation appears, it is not adequate to cover the losses suffered. In sum, from the survivor's point of view, there are few purely natural disasters. Consequently, natural-trauma survivors may have more in common with survivors of man-made catastrophes than is often thought.

However, survivors of natural disasters do in fact differ from other survivors, especially abuse survivors, in that they tend to be less stigmatized. Natural-catastrophe survivors are in general spared the "blame-the-victim" attitudes that frequently afflict survivors of man-made catastrophes.

For example, in many cases victims of rape, incest, and other types of abuse are blamed for either provoking the abuse or for accepting it, as if it had been their choice. Furthermore, survivors of man-made catastrophes are much more likely to be seen by others as lacking in strength, caution, intelligence, or moral integrity. The message they are given is, What happened to you is your own fault. If you had been more careful, less stupid, more righteous, it wouldn't have happened to you.

Single-Trauma vs. Multiple-Trauma Survivors

The extent of your PTSD will also be influenced by whether you have been exposed to one or more than one traumatic incident. Rape is traumatic; however, incest, which typically involves multiple rapes or molestations over an extended period, is more traumatic. Similarly, seeing people die in a car accident, although traumatic, is generally not as traumatic as being in combat or being a policeman in a deteriorating neighborhood and seeing death and violence day in and day out.

Several prominent researchers and therapists who have worked with trauma survivors have noticed differences between individuals subject to one-time assaults to their psyche and life and those subject to repeated threats. For example, Lenore Terr (1991), who has extensively studied PTSD in traumatized children, suggests that individuals who have endured a one-time or "Type 1" trauma suffer from different effects than those who undergo repeated or "Type 2" traumas. People who have experienced Type 2 traumas are more likely to exhibit dissociation and other forms of self-hypnosis as well as extreme mood swings. Psychologist Judith Herman (1992), who has studied abused children and incest survivors, suggests that the syndromes resulting from such abuse and other forms of severe, repeated trauma be called "complex post-traumatic stress disorder."

One of the differences between Type 1 and Type 2 survivors can be recovery time. For example, one-time rape survivors who get good help soon after the rape can recover in six months to a year. In contrast, incest survivors, depending on their age and the severity of their molestation, may require anywhere from two to three years or longer to heal.

Questionnaire for Criterion F

To determine the degree to which your PTSD has affected your life, answer the following questions in terms of your overall functioning over the last year. Although your symptoms may be more severe and troublesome around anniversaries of the trauma or during periods of external stress, answer the questions in terms of your behavior and mood for the year as a whole.

Part I: First, review the number of PTSD symptoms you recorded in your journal for each of the criteria. Make a note of your answers to the following questions:

1. Criterion A: How many traumas have you experienced?

2. Criterion B: Only one form of reexperiencing is necessary to meet the criteria for PTSD. In how many ways do you reexperience the trauma? How much is that in excess of the required number?

3. Criterion C: Two forms of numbing or avoidance behavior are necessary to meet the *DSM-IV* criteria. How many of the questions in the Criterion C questionnaire did you answer yes to? How much is that in excess of the required number?

4. Criterion D: Three hyperarousal symptoms are necessary to constitute PTSD. From how many hyperarousal symptoms do you suffer? How much is that in excess of the required number?

5. How long have you been experiencing PTSD symptoms?

6. Criterion F: In what ways have your PTSD symptoms or other reactions to the trauma affected your ability to work, relate to people, or to live your life?

Part II: Which of the following paragraphs (adapted from *DSM-IV*) best describes you now? Keep in mind the number of symptoms you have in excess of the *DSM-IV* criteria for PTSD.

1. I have few (if any) PTSD symptoms in excess of those required to meet the *DSM-IV* criteria for PTSD. My symptoms have not seriously interfered with my ability to work or study, to socialize, or to maintain healthy family and other relationships. Sometimes I become anxious before an exam or an evaluation at work. If I am under a great deal of stress, I may fall behind at work or school and have some trouble sleeping or concentrating. However, in general I am satisfied with life and am able to manage most situations. I have at least a few gratifying personal relationships.

2. I have just a few PTSD symptoms in excess of those required to meet the *DSM-IV* criteria for PTSD. My symptoms only moderately interfere with my social, occupational, and personal adjustments. Sometimes I have panic or anxiety attacks or periods of depression, but I get over them. I don't have a lot of friends and I wish I didn't clash so often with my co-workers and family members. However, I have been able to hold a job, stay in school, and maintain a few important relationships.

3. I have many symptoms in excess of those required to be diagnosed as having PTSD. My symptoms have severely affected either my work, my personal life, or both. I find it hard to work or concentrate and to get along with most others. I feel the traumatic event dominates my present life.

4. I am so depressed that I avoid other people, stay inside a lot, and am troubled by thoughts of suicide or homicide. Sometimes I cannot keep myself clean or take care of myself by making necessary medical or other appointments. At times I am a danger to others, as well as myself, and I have trouble in almost every area of life.

5. Prior to the traumatic event, I suffered from a mental or emotional disorder. The trauma only increased the severity of my previous problem.

6. Prior to the traumatic event, I suffered from a mental or emotional disorder that was under control and not severely affecting my life. However, the traumatic event led to a reemergence of my previous psychological problem.

7. The traumatic event has led to the development of new mental and emotional disorders.

8. At times I hallucinate or am delusional. I have trouble thinking clearly or rationally. I make poor financial and personal decisions and feel cut off from almost everyone.

If statement 1 describes you best, you are probably suffering from a mild case of PTSD. If statement 2 describes you best, your PTSD is probably in the moderate range. However, if any of statements 3 through 8 best describe your current level of functioning, you have a severe case of PTSD.

Now That I Know, What Comes Next?

Congratulations. You did it. You persisted in finishing this chapter—no matter how difficult it was to look at the trauma and its negative effects. As a result, you now know if you have PTSD or only some symptoms of PTSD, and you know whether it is partial or full PTSD.

Should future life stresses or trauma increase your partial PTSD to full PTSD, or intensify the degree to which your PTSD symptoms hinder your life, you will not need to panic and conclude that you are losing your mind. Since you are now aware of the symptoms of PTSD, you can take a more objective look at yourself and say, It's PTSD, not insanity, not psychosis, not some incurable mental cancer.

The more you learn about PTSD, the more in control of your life you will feel. Even if you only have a few PTSD symptoms, you will benefit from any information you can acquire about PTSD in all its aspects, because knowledge is the best antidote to fear. If you had a serious physical illness, you would want to know the severity of your condition. This way you could better plan your treatment and self-care program. A mild case of diabetes, for example, could necessitate limited life changes and minimal medical care. In contrast, a severe case could mean extensive life changes and intense medical attention. In a parallel manner, if your PTSD is mild, you may not need long-term intensive therapy. However, if your PTSD is severe, you may need to consider options such as inpatient care, psychiatric evaluation for medication, and a combination of individual counseling and group support.

References

DSM-IV. 1994. *Diagnostic and Statistical Manual of Mental Disorders—Fourth Edition*. Washington DC: American Psychiatric Association.

Haley, Sarah. 1984. I Feel a Little Sad: The application of object relations theory to hypnotherapy of post-traumatic stress disorder in Vietnam veterans. Paper presented at Society for Clinical and Experimental Hypnosis, October, San Antonio, TX.

Herman, Judith. 1992. *Trauma and Recovery: The Aftermath of Violence—from Domestic Abuse to Political Terror*. New York: Basic Books.

Terr, Lenore. 1991. Childhood traumas: An outline and overview. *American Journal of Psychiatry* 148, 10–20.

CHAPTER 39

Grief

Immediately upon being notified of your loved one's death you may have reacted with, "Oh no, this is a mistake. You have the wrong person." Even if you were expecting the death, you may have tried to delay its reality with questions. "How do you know? Are you certain? I just left his room at the hospital. I just spoke to him a few moments ago." You were really saying, "This horrible thing is not possible and it will not happen." You chose not to believe because disbelief made your life bearable. Within a few hours or days, you knew, intellectually and rationally, that your loved one was dead; however, you may have continued to resist accepting the fact. You may have found yourself feeling numb, moving as if in a dream.

Experiencing Disbelief and Numbness

Sometimes the disbelief and numbness you experience upon the death and at the funeral itself are so strong that you cannot accurately remember what happened. One grieving couple accused two of their boy's teenaged friends of missing their son's funeral. The teenagers had, in fact, attended. A week after her husband's memorial service, a middle-aged widow completely forgot that two of her cousins had stayed overnight in her home for two days and had taken care of responsibilities after the funeral.

If you can identify with this, if you have "shut off" for periods of time, what you have said is, "If I don't see, hear, taste, or touch, then nothing is really happening." It is as if you had chosen to become unaware or to disassociate yourself from events, to deaden your physical and mental self in order to avoid emotional death. Further, this kind of numbing allows you to suppress such uncomfortable emotions as rage or guilt which might otherwise be very prominent.

Besides avoiding the emotions which result from loss, there is another major motivation which may cause you to deny your loved one's death. This is the reluctance to admit your own mortality. Acknowledging and accepting the death of someone close to you means that you accept, also, your own inevitable death. You must say to yourself, "We are not permanent; we are temporary." Depending upon the beliefs you hold in regard to life after death or rebirth, this temporary condition on the earth will foster in you varying degrees of denial.

In the early stages of survival, belief and disbelief frequently operate simultaneously. Looking for a lost loved one is part of a common antithetical situation in which the bereaved often find themselves. While you may actively search for, or imagine seeing, the dead person, part of you knows that he or she is not alive. The disbelief you experience is produced by the part of your mind that helps you to endure the unendurable. You are protecting yourself.

Sensing the invisible presence. You may find yourself hearing the noises your son would make if he were coming up the back steps and into the kitchen. You may feel the touch of your husband's hand on your shoulder. Months after her death, you may catch the scent of your wife's perfume in the bathroom. These kinds of experiences are as normal as dreams. In dreams your subconscious allows things to happen which you fervently wish would actually occur. You are now experiencing this same phenomenon during your waking state.

Some bereaved people set up a method for communicating with their loved ones. A retired teacher created signals that indicated to her that her dead husband was in the room. A child talked to her pillow for years, pretending it was her father. A widower sat in the living room every night and told his deceased wife about his day, what he was feeling and doing.

The duration of disbelief. The period of time you remain in this mode, and the degree to which it occupies you, may vary greatly from those of other family members. Some bereaved people find that occasional bouts of disbelief continue to surface in their lives for a couple of years.

The Need for Ritual

In order to fully realize a death, it is imperative for you to see some evidence of it. For example, a mother who is notified by telephone of her son's death in a drowning accident in which the body was not recovered, will be less likely to accept death as readily as a mother who is summoned to the hospital to identify the body of her son who was killed in an automobile accident. However traumatic it may be, viewing the body of the deceased allows you to take the first step from disbelief to belief, particularly if the death has been unexpected or sudden.

You have heard bereaved people say such things as, "I want to remember my daughter *as she was* when she went out the door to the prom." "I want to remember my husband *the way he was* before his last business trip." "I want to remember grandma *as she used to be*, joking around with dad." It is desirable to have these kinds of loving memories because they provide emotional warmth, but they need to be viewed in the proper perspective. "As she was," and "the way he was," and "as she used to be," all have one factor in common: Those ways were as a *living* person and the person is *not living*. That distinction is assimilated more easily when you see that the person is not alive or when you attend some form of final service. You will be less likely to deny something you have seen or participated in.

The terms used in the mortuary industry often contribute to your wish to deny death. The dead person is placed in the "slumber room" where people file by, pretending they are viewing the person taking a "long rest." This delicacy can be appreciated at one level, but at another it makes absurd the finality of the person's bodily presence.

The funeral should begin the separation of those who are alive from the dead person. Its function is not to separate the sleeping from the waking.

Of course, the funeral does much more than validate your loved one's death. It serves also as an acceptable outlet for a physical show of emotion, and perhaps even more important, it provides a forum for sharing the person with others, sharing what the person loved, enjoyed, and gave. The funeral not only says, "good-bye," it also says, "I'm hurting," "I'm missing," "Thank you for having lived," and "Your life has left this effect upon your relatives and friends, your part of the world."

As the funeral publicly acknowledges the end of the person's life in the way that the family and friends knew it, it reunites those people whose lives touched because of the loved one. This final service or memorial puts together an immediate, though temporary, support group.

After the funeral is over and the members of your temporary support group have returned to "life as normal," you will experience a number of emotions. Just as there are no definite stages of the grieving process, there are seldom, if ever, any absolutely pure emotions. It would be rare to find a person who is feeling sadness and *only* sadness, or fear and *only* fear. Feelings arise from a provocative event or condition in your life. During the grieving process, you may feel a jumble of emotions. Some of them will be ones with which you are familiar because they are a part of your emotional history. You have felt them many times before under stressful conditions. Other feelings may come as a surprise to you and to those around you, and these unfamiliar feelings may be even more dominant than those which are familiar. Among these strong emotions is anger.

Experiencing Anger

Your loved one is supposed to live, to enjoy life, to have more time. Then what is supposed to happen doesn't happen. Your spouse, sister, child, or friend dies. When this death occurs, it seems to be an error of the greatest magnitude. You had your ideas and suppositions about your loved one's life. You were involved in it and now that person isn't even here. Your perception of the way things are has been changed to the way things really are. You have been proven wrong. Because your belief system has been damaged, it makes you angry.

As you confront this new reality with hostility, you are behaving quite normally as a bereaved person. Anger is not only a logical and natural part of *your* grieving, it is a part of the whole history of grieving.

The direction in which your anger is focused will vary depending on your situation, your personality and even your gender. You may be angry at God and religion, the unfairness of "the world," other people, yourself, or even the deceased. It helps to see how your anger works in each case.

Anger at God

"How could God do this?" is frequently asked by those suffering the affects of a loved one's death. If this is a question you have wrestled with, your thinking may follow these lines: "After all, God is supposed to do things right and suddenly the Almighty has been ruthless." To make matters worse, well-meaning friends and relatives try to placate you with, "It was God's will" . . . "The Lord needed him" . . . "She was such an angel, she was just too good to live" . . . "It is all in God's Plan."

If you are among those who do not find comfort in these words, "God's Plan" may seem to be synonymous with punishment and then you wonder what you did wrong; otherwise, why would you be punished? A woman who lost her fiance shortly before they were to be married asked, "How could God do this to me? Wasn't I a decent person? Why was this happening to me?"

Hearing that a death, particularly a premature death, is "God's Plan" only compounds your anger at God and religion. If God is supposed to be loving, how could this unloving act be committed?

Anger at the Unfairness of the World

Closely related to the anger directed toward God and religion is anger at some unknown force in the world, the force that is supposed to keep things *fair*.

This line of reasoning causes you to ask, "If a power exists that is *just*, how could this great injustice be levied against me?" "Where is all the morality of life I have been taught to believe exists?"

Death of a loved one feels extremely unfair; it is not something either you or the other person deserved. As you try in vain to answer the unanswerable questions regarding the timing or conditions of your loved one's death, anguish, bitterness, disillusionment, and occasional irrationality become part of your emotional and mental state.

Anger toward Others

The others who suffer chastisement, verbal abuse, and perhaps even physical violence, may be anyone who is *not dead*. That is, linked with your anger at the unfairness of death is a contempt for other people around you whose lives go on as usual. Because they have not been devastated as you have (or you *think* they haven't), you want to extract from them some kind of dues for your loss. You want to punish them for being alive, perhaps even for causing the death of your loved one. Often the routine involvement of ambulance drivers, paramedics, nurses, or doctors is viewed as *participation* in your loved one's death.

You may feel that your loved one's illness was misdiagnosed, that he or she had not been adequately tested. You conclude that if only the symptoms could have been recognized at an earlier stage, the death would not have occurred.

In case after case, the hospital staff seems to have taken the wrong action. They took away the clothes of your deceased before you had a chance to get them. They were unresponsive to your daughter's pain before she died. They forgot to give your brother his prescribed medication. They didn't tell the truth about your child's illness and they didn't answer your questions.

A woman who lost her fiance in a crash which also resulted in her own hospitalization recounted the following:

> Brian had been asking for me in his conscious moments. He had called my name. I always felt if the hospital staff had let me go to him and let me hold his hand it might have changed things.

Anger is also incited by the passiveness or avoidance exhibited by others when you most need support. Often, as soon as the funeral is over, or shortly thereafter, friends, relatives, or community members act as if nothing has happened. This is particularly true if the death was that of an infant or if the death occurred as a result of a suicide. Regardless of the cause or type of death, it is important to have your loss acknowledged. Recognition of a traumatic event is extremely important to you. You want the other person to recognize your sorrow, not to pretend that everything is as it always has been; because for you, the survivor, things will never be the same again.

Anger toward Yourself

Studies have shown that males more often direct their anger outward, while women direct it toward themselves. Women are less prone to telling someone off, initiating a lawsuit, or displaying violent anger. Instead of chopping down a tree or smashing up the car, they will find reasons to punish themselves.

Sometimes the anger is so severe and illogical that the bereaved person may feel mentally ill, particularly if the individual does not ordinarily feel anger, let alone express it. If your anger is of this type, you may worry that it will never dissipate. It is true that if your anger is self-directed and does not seek an outlet, it may ultimately produce another undesirable condition such as physical illness, severe depression, or self-destructive behavior. But if your anger has an outlet, it will eventually weaken.

Anger toward the Deceased

Anger doesn't respect any boundaries as far as its "target" is concerned. You can even be angry with your loved one who has died. Widows and widowers frequently feel they have been *deserted*. It is this feeling of being victimized by the deceased that causes the survivor additional anguish.

Typically, widows say, "He left me with this mess." Almost immediately they have to deal with insurance policies, social security, monthly payments with which they are not familiar, and death benefits. They have to begin sleuthing for their basic economic survival by identifying and making decisions regarding any available financial resources. Sometimes this means discovering that the resources are nonexistent and they have to create them.

The young widow may have to manage her preschoolers, find a baby-sitter and full-time employment. The forty- or fifty-year-old widow may have to return to school in mid-life to acquire new marketable skills.

Children and Anger

Children who lose siblings or parents not only feel anger, they often express it more easily than adults. In Jill Krementz' *How It Feels When a Parent Dies*, a fifteen-year-old boy talked about his feelings toward his mother who was killed in an auto accident.

> I was really mad at Mom. I never blamed the taxi drivers. I don't know why, but I didn't. I just took it for granted that accidents happen and it wasn't their faults, but Mom should have known better. She should have jumped back more quickly like Timmy did. Timmy was mad, too—mad that he hadn't been able to pull her back. He felt hopeless that he couldn't help her, and that was rough. I even asked Dad, "Do you think Mom knows she's ruined our lives?"

If a child's anger is not expressed at the time he or she first begins to feel it, this hostility may continue in one form or another for years.

From Rage to Recuperation

Regardless of where your anger is directed at the medical community, at yourself, your best friend, your mother, the neighbor, or the person who survived the accident in which your loved one was killed, you can experience relief. You do not have to feel stuck in this energy-depleting condition for months. There are numerous concrete ways in which you can vent, dilute, or otherwise weaken the anger that will ultimately weaken *you* if you don't get rid of it.

A mother whose young son was killed in an accident found that talking about her anger, expressing her rage, provided great relief.

> If something hurts me, I'm going to let it be known now. I'm not going to put it back inside. The death of Allan has taught me to bring out anger whether or not it seems appropriate. Whether or not it is even right.

Often, very deep feelings like these can be expiated by writing them out.

An activity that requires physical endurance, such as running, swimming, biking, or tennis, will also help. But your activity doesn't *have* to be sports oriented or even "socially acceptable." It is okay to hit inanimate objects as long as you don't cause harm to yourself or anyone else.

It is permissible to show anger in public, as long as you don't stop an airplane in midflight or hurl heads of lettuce all over the local supermarket. If you are provoked, avoided, or not listened to, you'll feel better if you express how you feel. In other words, you can be *human* when you're out in public.

It is also okay to go off alone and scream. An English woman who had been raised to be "proper" told of her experience in expressing her anger. As a child growing up, she had been admonished by her father whenever she began to display any emotion. "Remember dear," he would say, "after all, you ARE *English.*" When, in her mid-fifties, she was notified of her father's death, she found herself in an extremely emotional state. Her story is one of insight and humor.

> When daddy died I went down through the trees and walked along the riverbank yelling and screaming. I had never done that before. I ranted and raved for a very long time. Then, suddenly, I looked up at the clouds and I could hear daddy's voice admonishing me, "Quiet down, dear. After all, you ARE *English!*"

Feeling Powerless and Abandoned

In general, anger results from feeling abandoned and powerless. Ask yourself where your emotional pain is coming from. What information do you get? Talk about that information with a supportive friend, relative, or counselor. For example, a widowed teacher found that his anger stemmed from viewing his wife as a punisher. She had given him a bad time when she was alive and, by dying, had ruined the rest of his life. However, *at the same time,* he had been dependent on his wife. The two of them had shared a consistent closeness for seventeen years. In discussing his feelings with a close friend he uncovered his own ambivalence. He was able to accept that his wife was neither a saint nor a devil. He viewed her as a whole person with attributes as well as deficiencies. With his new perspective, his anger lessened and he began to progress through the grieving process.

Feeling powerless means you perceive yourself as a victim. The way to change your "victimization" is to give yourself some sense of power. This is not as difficult as it may sound. You gain power by exerting control, and there are numerous ways in which this can be done. An example of this on a national scale is the mother who founded MADD, Mothers Against Drunk Driving. Her devastating experience produced an organization which lobbies for stricter laws and enforcement in regard to driving under the influence of alcohol. Of course, you don't have to start a national organization to vindicate your anger. You can first look at your experience in dealing with your particular loss. Next, you can examine that experience and identify what could have possibly prevented it or made it less confusing or painful. It may be that you convince a local group, agency, or institution to make modifications or to develop new procedures.

Anger and Responsibility

You have been encouraged here to find ways to dissipate your anger, to vent your rage. For when anger is grounded, when it is focused and released, it will begin to slow, to lose energy, and you can begin to heal. However, it would be injudicious to suggest you can do anything and everything that serves to release your anger. Even though the majority of survivors are likely to err on the side of restraint, rather than on the side of overindulgence, it is necessary to mention some limitations.

The boundaries for safe and legitimate anger are simple. First, your anger should not be directed at someone who will predictably retaliate *with greater* anger and aggression. You will only escalate your own frustration and anger when you try to defend yourself. This does not mean pick on people who can't defend themselves. It means don't inflate *the cause* for your anger by antagonizing someone who you can't change and who may use verbal or physical tactics which will intensify your rage and anguish.

Second, your accusations or revelations should not be directed toward someone who could suffer unjustly from them. That is, it would not be appropriate to be accusatory toward your mate who was driving the car in which your child was killed. It would, however, be appropriate to focus and channel your anger toward a judicial system which allowed your daughter's assailant to be released from prison.

Feeling Guilty

Of the many conditions which occur during the grieving period, guilt seems to affect the broadest segment of the bereaved population and arises from the widest variety of sources. People can generate many reasons to make themselves feel guilty. A new reason for guilt can be adopted every day of the grieving period, and each new guilt will seem as valid as the one which preceded it.

Those who have no guilt about the death of a loved one are in the minority. Unless you belong to that minority, you are no doubt experiencing some debilitating feelings. Regardless of the cause of death, the age of the deceased, and the extent of your actual control over your loved one's life, *chances are you have decided you have done something wrong for which you should feel guilty.* These self-accusations arise from a variety of circumstances and a limited perspective.

Regardless of the blame with which you now burden yourself, what you are saying is this: You should be in charge of what happens in the world. Blaming yourself takes away the responsibility of others. It also says that the one who is dead had no control over his or her life situation. Usually, this is not the case.

Your Changed Lifestyle

Death may change your daily circumstances significantly, either by making your life materially easier or by allowing you more time for your own personal use. It may be the first time you have been able to leave the house for longer than an hour at a time. It may allow you to see old friends you have not been able to visit with during the long illness of your child, husband, or mother. You may take up a hobby or recreation, but you cannot enjoy one minute of it because you perceive the activity as being the outcome of your loved one's death. Each time you pick up a paintbrush or a golf club, go to a movie or have coffee with a friend, you may feel a pang of guilt. If the pangs become too intense, you stop doing whatever it is that you would otherwise enjoy.

Parental Guilt

The loss of a child almost always produces excessive guilt in the surviving parents or parent. The reasons for this guilt are endless. If your child died of an illness that is, or could be considered to be congenital, you may feel guilty about allowing the child to have been conceived. If your child died as the result of an accident, regardless of the *type* of accident, you may feel guilty about not preventing the tragedy. You can torment yourself for months, even years, with, "How could that have been avoided? What could I personally have done to eliminate any possibility of that accident occurring?"

If you somehow see yourself as an active participant in the tragedy which resulted in your loved one's death, your guilt will be even more profound. If you were driving the car, flying the plane, encouraging the sport, permitting the sailing, financing the mountain climbing trip, swimming in the same river, you may feel you could have prevented the loss of your child. When the results are tragic and you assume guilt for the death, you often experience guilt in relation to other family members as well.

Children's Guilt

Children can be just as critical of themselves as adults. When a parent dies a child may condemn himself for having caused the parent to worry over trivial things, for not being affectionate, for refusing to mind, or for failing to help around the house.

Surviving children will, at one time or another, ferret out reasons to see themselves as selfish, mean, or careless in regard to their dead brother or sister.

If the surviving sibling has longed to be the *only child* prior to the brother's or sister's death, the survivor will feel especially and profoundly guilty. The child thinks, "I wished her away. She died because I wanted it to happen or *thought* I wanted it to happen." In some cases, the child reflects, "I wished him away and now my life is better. But I don't deserve for my life to be better because I am a bad person."

It is not uncommon for a child to perceive of his or her life as having improved after the death of a brother or sister. This is especially true if the survivor gets more attention from the parents, gains a long-sought freedom or a new privilege, or is given more money, toys, clothes, trips, or other material things.

The child who sees his or her changed life situation as more pleasant and gratifying, may actually exhibit positive personality changes after the sibling's death. The surviving child may be happier, demonstrate increased confidence, be more talkative or more spontaneous without the presence of a brother or sister.

Survivor Guilt

War, accidents, and disasters such as train and airplane crashes, earthquakes, and floods produce a special form of remorse in those who were involved in the tragic event but did not die. This remorse is called survivor guilt.

The statements which follow illustrate both the circumstances as well as the thought processes which produce this type of guilt.

When we got on the plane, my husband offered me that seat next to the window, but I said for him to sit there. I wanted to be on the aisle.

Translation: By not sitting in the seat, I condemned my husband to death.

We had been together for a year in the same platoon. We were both making our way uphill under enemy fire. Before I knew it, there was a loud blast and Brad's body went flying through the air. He had been my best friend. One minute there we were, the two of us, the next minute he was gone.

Translation: We were both equal, but I was chosen to survive. I was given priority over him.

Survivor guilt emanates from the same belief, regardless of the specific details of the situation; the belief is that one death has somehow been exchanged for another, that one person was allowed to live *at the cost* of another's life.

Those who suffer the pain of survivor guilt may remain preoccupied with the deceased, and may go so far as to assume the characteristics of the one who has died.

The survivor may also exhibit any number of a wide variety of symptoms including, most commonly, depression, low self-esteem, poor physical health, or alcoholism.

Understanding and Dispelling Your Guilt

The Death Exchange

While you may genuinely wish your own life could have been substituted for that of your child, spouse, parent, or friend, it is important to recognize that death is not the result of an exchange or competition. You may readily agree, saying to yourself, "Of course, everyone knows that." Yet at a certain level of consciousness many survivors do *not* seem to know that. Along with other prominent feelings, these survivors undergo remorse based on the idea that the death was going to occur, but the wrong person was taken.

Cause and Effect Syndrome

You may suffer from the belief that perhaps you could have prevented the death. *If only* you had performed some specific act or had some specific conversation, your loved one would still be alive.

This type of thinking is not surprising, given the human need for harmony; that is, most people have an inherent need to believe that a kind of order exists in our universe. That order says that someone is responsible for things that happen. This belief produces this kind of thinking: "If someone had done something differently, then that would not have happened. If I had done *this*, then *that* would not have occurred. If you, as a survivor, are feeling guilty for what you think you did or did not do, you are burdening yourself with debilitating guilt, rather than admitting there is no cause and effect order at work in our universe and that *no one* is responsible.

Consider the guilt you are experiencing. Remember your guilt is a choice. Ask yourself if it helps you to generate and then magnify your own anguish. Think about the consequences you may have to endure as a result: physical illness, depression, unabating rage, extreme sadness, or disillusionment.

Not Being Good Enough

You may view yourself, after your loved one's death, as being inattentive, selfish, or cold, even cruel. Your husband was in a coma and you didn't go to the hospital every time you had an opportunity to do so. Your child wanted a new bicycle and you told her the old one was good enough. Your sister begged you to go on a trip with her and you opted to spend the weekend with your boyfriend instead. Your mother always wanted you to finish college and you dropped out to join the army. You could have helped your brother paint his house, but you stayed home to watch the Super Bowl game.

This line of thinking does its best to build a case for the prosecution, but if you examine the opposite side of your behavior, this self-blame will not survive. For example, consider trying this writing exercise: Get a blank notebook. Take some time to mentally review your relationship with your loved one. Try to recall every bad action, deed, or conversation you initiated. Screen out those on the borderline and include only those about which you have no doubt.

If you're a widower, you may start (as many do) with, "I didn't tell her I loved her enough." Or, "I got angry at her over every little thing." A widow may begin with, "I complained about him being too lethargic . . . or too overweight . . . or too serious . . . or too sexual." When your list is complete, read it over to yourself.

Now take another sheet of paper and follow the same procedure for every positive or kind action, for every enjoyable, supportive conversation you can vividly remember. Take your time. Your list might look something like this: "I nearly always shopped for her favorite food." "I supported his career change." Or, "I often complimented her on her sales skills . . . or cooking . . . or mechanical ability." "I encouraged her to return to school," or, "I bragged about him at the office." Instead of denying any good element of your behavior, go to the source. Pin down what you did. Be thorough.

You now have two lists. Before you is the evidence that nothing is all one way or the other. You were not completely terrible nor completely wonderful because unless you felt no closeness to the individual, your relationship was a blend of good and bad.

Feeling High

More than a few mourners confide that they experience guilt for having felt a kind of euphoria, a high, upon the death of their loved one. "How could I have been happy when my husband was dying before my eyes?" "How could I have floated out of the hospital with a smile on my face when my child just died?" these people ask. "It was as if I was on some kind of drug," they will tell you—and indeed they were. The "drug" was adrenaline. Though actually a hormone, adrenaline closely resembles an amphetamine in its effect. When under stress the body releases adrenaline (as well as other hormones) which may energize the person, produce a rush, and give a feeling of extreme well-being.

Inherited Guilt

If you were the recipient of material goods from your loved one, you may feel that receiving the car, money, house, or other possessions is the equivalent of *collaborating with death*. You may even feel that you are an unworthy recipient. These, then, are facts for you to consider:

You cannot cause or sanction a death by taking what has been willed to you. Further, you have no right to judge who would be a "worthy recipient." Your loved one's will is a validation of that person's personal priorities and affirmations in regard to all the individuals he or she knew. You should honor the validation.

Often, those who spend an inheritance in great haste are regarding their money as tainted, something to be gotten rid of as quickly as possible. If kept and used as normal income, the money would be a constant reminder of the dead loved one and, consequently, of the survivor's loneliness or sadness.

Changing Your Perspective

All of the guilts which have been considered here are those which arise from a limited and self-punishing perspective; that is, these guilts grew from thoughts that were either distorted or illogical. In direct contrast, you have been presented with a new perspective based on facts. In summary, these facts are as follows:

- Death is not the result of an exchange or competition.

- Death has no scoreboard and no quota.

- Death has no "selection" process.

- You are not collaborating with death by enjoying an inheritance.

- All human relationships have both good and bad components. The bad components in your relationship will not kill your loved one.

- Enchantment with the process of your loved one's death, or even euphoria at or after the death, are not abnormal nor necessarily undesirable reactions.

Guilt That Won't Go Away

If your guilt is terribly deep and immobilizing, or if it continues for a prolonged period during which you see practically no change, chances are you have some ambivalence, either recognized or unrecognized, in regard to your loved one. This is not to suggest that you did not genuinely love him or her, nor that you do not experience a deep sense of loss. It is to suggest, instead, that you may have some negative feelings in regard to your relationship with your loved one. These feelings are bringing you to an emotional halt.

It is not uncommon for a survivor to confide that he or she had, in a burst of frustration or outrage, wished the loved one dead. Having had this thought, even having voiced this wish to the loved one, did not cause the death. The message to a survivor grappling with this memory is this: You are not powerful enough to cause someone to die in this way. Your wish for the death, regardless of how intense it was at the time, and the actual deed of killing the person are two separate actions entirely. Your wish is not the deed.

Don't continue to try to coexist with the emotional pain your guilt causes. Consider discussing your feelings with a counselor. Counselors are accustomed to helping survivors deal with ambivalence or extreme remorse. Both can be resolved.

Experiencing Fear and Anxiety

Fear and anxiety are the source of much emotional pain and concern among survivors. Many experts make a distinction between fear and anxiety, and an even more definite distinction among the various types of anxiety. However, for purposes of discussion which will meet your needs as a survivor, only one general distinction is made here. Fear, within this context, refers to a feeling of extreme fright or alarm which is related to a definite object (act, event, person, or thing). You fear crying in public. You fear the dark. You fear failing at something—getting lost on your way to an appointment, talking to your children about your feelings, performing tasks your wife used to do. In contrast, anxiety refers to that state of extreme apprehension which cannot be directly related to any one thing, person, or event. This anxiety is described by the wife of an accident victim:

> I would go to bed at night and huddle to myself and shake. The thought of having to cope with anything, anything at all, was overwhelming. My heart beat fast. I ached, my body felt tense. I couldn't really explain why I felt the way I did or what was bothering me, but the feeling was horrible and immobilizing.

This woman's experience could be referred to as a "panic attack," or extreme anxiety. She seemed to sense that something horrible was going to happen, but she didn't know what it was. Many survivors confide that they have these same feelings and sensations:

- heart palpitations
- loss of appetite
- ringing in the ears
- digestive problems
- nausea
- dizziness
- nightmares
- constriction in the throat
- muscular pain
- impeded concentration
- poor memory
- damp hands
- dry mouth
- insomnia

You may be experiencing one or more of the above symptoms either on a regular basis, or occasionally. You may feel as if you are constantly traumatized and apprehensive. If so, you may, as a middle-aged attorney put it, be "annoyed at the idea that you are going through these feelings of panic and you don't know why." There is, however, a way to sort this out. Your anxiety, in fact, is a normal outcome of your experience. You have real reasons for feeling the way you do. You have recently been the victim of a circumstance beyond your control. This situation has caused you to be less sure of yourself and your environment than you once were. The uncertainty and fright are even more pronounced if you have lost someone unexpectedly, such as by sudden infant death syndrome, an automobile accident, an airplane crash, or by suicide or homicide.

Feeling victimized. You now feel as if you have little or no power over what happens or does not happen. The brother of a man who died suddenly of undetermined causes put it this way: "You are everything's victim. Anything can get you. You don't even have to know what it is." This feeling of powerlessness, of victimization, coupled with a subconscious belief that there is some mysterious zone in which anything can happen, will indeed produce an anxiety which seems to have no focal point.

Feeling disassociated. Your anxiety can be produced, too, simply by the separation of yourself from the other person. The two of you were close, then suddenly the other one is gone and only you remain.

It is as if your base has been knocked out from under you and you're supposed to build an instant foundation to support yourself. The separation you experience is twofold: You have been permanently separated from the person you love and, in addition, you are cut off from what you were together. It is frightening and you feel inadequate. At about this same time you may feel intense longing for the other person, a longing so strong that it is almost tangible.

Identifiable Fears

In contrast to experiencing anxiety whose origins may be impossible for you to identify, you may experience some very concrete fears. For example, a parent may be afraid of losing another child in an accident. A widow may be terrified of someone breaking into her house. A widower may be anxious and fearful about his domestic survival. A survivor of a loss due to illness may fear that he or she will also become fatally ill. Many survivors of all ages fear they will die soon after the death of a loved one.

All of these fears can be categorized as "fears of impending doom." For the most part, the anticipated situations are not likely to occur. It is unlikely that a parent would lose two children in separate accidents. A widow's house is not more likely to be robbed because there is one resident rather than two. It is unlikely that a widower would not be able to learn how to cook well enough to keep himself alive, or how to operate the washing machine. And unless an illness has been already transmitted or is genetic, it is not realistic for the surviving friend or relative to anticipate becoming ill. Further, this fear can be quickly put to rest by a physical examination.

For explicit information about reducing fear and anxiety, see the chapters on Stress and Anxiety earlier in part V.

Experiencing Sadness

I didn't know it was possible to feel such sadness. I have been unhappy before, but never like this. Sometimes the sadness is almost like physical pain. In fact, I wish it were. I think it might be easier to get rid of. Sometimes I think maybe I'm not going to feel that way any more. Then it comes back. (*Father of a nine-year-old son who died as the result of a burst blood vessel in his brain*)

You may have successfully pushed away thoughts of your loss for a few hours. You may even be able to go several consecutive days without "breaking down." Then, just when you think you are beginning to function without showing how you feel inside, something triggers all the emotion that has been waiting for an outlet. Perhaps you see a child who reminds you of your deceased son or daughter. You may hear your boyfriend's favorite song on the radio, see your wife's best friend driving down the street, or find a forgotten birthday card from your sister. Suddenly all that feeling that you had so successfully suppressed rushes to the surface. It is then that you are reminded of the deep sadness which you carry with you as a constant, but not always evident companion.

Unanticipated tears. Your feelings may spill forth at times when there seems to be no outside source to provoke such a reaction. For no obvious reason, you may begin to cry in the supermarket, while driving home from work, or while dining in a restuarant. During ordinary activities such as these you find yourself in tears so suddenly you are astonished. When this happens, you are at a loss to explain exactly what it is you are crying about.

> After my son died, many times when we went out to dinner at another couple's house, or to a party, I would go into the bathroom at the other people's houses and cry. (*Mother of an accident victim*)

> I would go to the bank, or to see the accountant, and I would start to cry. I would just stand there and cry and I knew people felt awkward, but I couldn't control it. (*Young widowed nurse*)

Bereaved people usually think they owe others an explanation for crying without giving "prior notice." However, there isn't any way a grieving person can convey the deep source from which personal sadness erupts. Each individual's emotions will be triggered by incidents that he or she least suspects would recall the loss.

There may be similar occasional incidences of spontaneous crying throughout your life. Generally, however, your bursts of unexpected tears should be less frequent after about the first eighteen months of your loss.

Releasing Your Sadness

If, during your grieving period, you are working hard at repressing your sadness, you are only delaying the necessary expiation which must precede healing. The more you allow yourself to cry, the more possible it will be for you to progress through the mourning period. Remember the statement of the young widowed nurse who was experiencing anxiety.

> I had to learn to cry. When I did, the anxiousness went away and the sadness took its place. . . . I even had to learn to sigh because I had been letting the anxious feeling lay in my stomach and it was causing stomach cramps.

Because grief has to show up somewhere, it will manifest itself in some way, even if you are determined (or someone else is determined) to keep it from being evident. Suppressed emotion can result in sleeplessness, heart palpitations, a choking sensation, irregular breathing, and weight loss as well as a number of other physical symptoms.

> I couldn't get the grief out in the hospital because when I started to cry and get it out they gave me medication. I had to wait until I got home, which was four months later. Then I went back to the house where we had been living and indulged myself thoroughly. I cried and ranted and raved. (*Young woman accident victim whose fiancé was killed*)

If you don't cry, chances are you are trying to protect those around you from any discomfort, you are taking medication, or you are making a concerted effort to be a "strong person."

The word "strong" is much distorted when discussing the actions of the bereaved. "He shows such strength through all of this," or "She is such a strong person," implies that if the survivor showed feelings, *honestly* showed them, he or she would be the opposite of strong, which is *weak*.

When a friend or relative whom you know well and trust, asks you how you are, you don't have to reply with, "Fine," if you're not fine. If you feel sad, talk about your feeling. Share your thoughts. Mention the experiences that are making you feel sad.

There are also benefits to be gained by joining a support group. In the company of others who have had a similar experience, you can say you feel sad and you don't need to tone down your sadness or apologize for it. The participants of the group will be aware of your needs and will not cause you to feel uncomfortable. They won't insist that you "get over that now," or that you "quit feeling sorry for yourself." They know you have every right in the world to feel sorry for yourself. You have been hurt. Your life has been altered. You miss the person who is gone.

If it is difficult to express your feelings aloud and you feel more at ease writing about them, then do that. Get a notebook and "talk it out" on paper. It should be pointed out that keeping a journal or writing a poem is not exclusively a female activity. Many men write poems which deal with the loss of a loved one. For some men, it seems safer to write about loss than talk about it. Unfortunately and historically, men have had—the pressure is lessening—to be overly concerned with appearing strong at all costs. Sometimes the cost is their health, job, or marriage.

Being "strong" (and silent) after death has been an unrealistic expectation of our particular culture. However, as professionals and human service agencies become more attuned to the psychological effects of death, this expectation diminishes. This attitudinal change, though gradual, reflects a more realistic view of mourning, one which is long overdue in our Western culture.

Experiencing Despair

Often, after a death, people feel that the human experience is an equation with zeroes on both sides. Life is perceived as being "as empty as death" and death as final as a void, a zero. During the first year or so of bereavement, people having this kind of reaction may feel as if they are drowning. They consider the smallest everyday task such as getting dressed, washing their hair, or answering the telephone to be nearly impossible. Merely getting out of bed can be a long and arduous process that requires not minutes, but hours.

Awareness of mortality. Along with the despair you feel, you also experience the psychic shock that accompanies the full realization of your own mortality. This realization is the inevitable outcome of losing someone close to you.

As you reflect upon this inevitability, you assess and evaluate many of your actions, desires, and goals. You ruminate about what you will do now, and what your limitations are in the future. It may seem as if you have to chop your way through an impenetrable forest in order to reach a clearing. And worse, you don't know what to expect when you get there. You think, "What is it all for?" You find yourself tired, dismayed, and feeling hopeless.

During this period, you may also reflect temporarily on the unknown aspects of death. You may ask, "Just what is death, anyway?" "What happens when you die?"

Trying to Make Sense of Death

Death often seems grossly "unfair." It certainly does not follow any accessible logic. Depending upon the content and degree of your religious or metaphysical beliefs, death may be viewed as anything from a completely mysterious state about which *nothing* is known, to a state which is only slightly perplexing because *most aspects* of it are intuitively understood. For most people, however, death represents a realm which has few, if any, definitive characteristics. Bereaved people commonly feel they have no answers to any of the major death-related questions: "What does death mean to the individual?" "What happens in terms of the separation of the spirit and body, or of the soul and body?" "What is the possibility of 'life' after death?" "What is the possibility of rebirth, punishment, or reward?" Trying to make sense of what happens would be easier if it were possible to answer the seven-year-old boy who, when told of his mother's sudden death, asked, "Where *is* death?"

If it were possible to give absolute answers to *what* death means and *where* it is, two of the biggest mysteries of all time would be solved. For those whose religious beliefs provide answers to these questions, any exploration may be seen as entirely unnecessary. However, research has shown that most bereaved people welcome any attempt at an investigation into the invisible realm of death.

People's beliefs about the meaning of death can be seen as quite distinct, one from another. In trying to make some sense of death, most people have adopted one of the following orientations:

- Death is being with God in heaven.

- Death is an invisible force that takes you when it is your time to go. Death is the Grim Reaper.

- Death is a time of judgment during which your life is evaluated and you are consigned to either a heaven or hell.

- Death is only non-living. It is the ultimate existential experience.

- Death is an elevation to another life, a continued existence in a realm without the consequences of human frailty—hostility, materialistic values, etc.

- Death is a rebirth. It is beginning again in a new and different life. (Voltaire wrote, "After all it is no more surprising to be born twice than it is to be born once.")

- Death is the state between two other states, as sleep is the state between two waking states.

You will be inclined to believe one of these more than the rest because the core content of one orientation diminishes or precludes belief in the content of another. In addition to holding a particular belief, there are several predispositional factors which may lessen your interest in boldly examining death. These factors stem from several lines of thinking: 1) If I do not fear death, then I do not completely respect its power. I must respect death because before it, I am helpless. 2) 1 am presumptuous to think I can fathom the unfathomable. We can never really *know* anything about death; we can only guess or fantasize. 3) If I can explain and define death, then I am reducing the magnitude of my loved one's death and am minimizing my own personal loss.

So if we think of death as the greatest of all dilemmas, to be feared, contended with, or used as a measurement for suffering, we can't observe or examine it.

Of course, we all "capitulate" to death as physical bodies. But this does not mean that we must also ignore death, mentally and emotionally. Beginning in the 1970s, studies were undertaken to examine the what and *where* of death. These scientific inquiries were conducted among subjects who had what are termed "near-death experiences."

The near-death experience. These subjects had been considered "clinically dead"; they lacked any respiration or pulse, or they were as close to death as you can get without being clinically dead. These men and women had come near to death, or had experienced apparent death as a result of a serious illness, an accident, or an attempted suicide. They were of various ages, incomes, and educational backgrounds. Some of the people were religious, others were not.

When interviewed privately these people described what they saw, felt, heard, and understood while they were in the near-death state.

The research disclosed a remarkable phenomenon. Individuals who had never met, and who had no access to one another's interviews, told of experiences which were so nearly identical that they could not be dismissed as coincidental, or having been suggested or imagined. This does not mean that this research is a definitive ultimate or that it will offer every one of us a glimpse of what death is and where it is. But we cannot completely ignore the common and similar experiences of people who are otherwise different in background, behavior, and belief.

The survivor's independent descriptions of the near-death experience provided researchers with sufficient material to advance many hypotheses regarding the pattern of dying as well as the quality of death. Following are several characteristics of near-death experience which may be of particular interest to those considering the what and where of death:

- The experience is positive, sometimes even euphoric, with a stabilizing calmness, sureness, and deep peace.

- There is no loneliness.

- There is no pain.

- The dying person often views, as if from a distance, the "end" of life; that is, the individual may witness others frantically trying to save his or her body.

The person who is entering the realm of death is so at peace there is no desire to return to physical life on earth. Many of the near-death subjects returned because they felt it was imperative for them to continue their lives. They were needed to take care of someone, to finish some work which they had begun, or to fulfill some other purpose. They had *decided* to come back, or they were sent back by an unspoken directive that issued from within the realm of death. Some people felt they had been *called back* to life by someone.

You are free, of course, to accept or reject these selected findings. They are presented here in the belief that they constitute a valid offering, one which permits a survivor to reflect with less sadness and despair on what he or she may previously have seen as the existential void or terror-filled "fate" of a loved one.

Experiencing Confusion and Disorientation

Sometime after the death you will realize that you cannot be as you were before. You may find yourself confused about your changed identity since your loved one's death. It takes more than a few months to gradually develop a different perspective on your life and, specifically, on *who you are now*.

A Changed Identity

Before you experienced this recent death, your life proceeded in a certain way; now that way has been altered. Your schedule, environment, and circumstances have changed. Because of this, you too are not exactly as you were. You have lost a person who was a part of your identity. You were Michael's mother, or John's uncle, or Ann's sister. Now that part of you no longer actively exists. Even though you continue to be John's uncle or Ann's sister in your heart and memory, the reality is that you are no longer interacting with John or Ann. *The loss of the person has subtracted from you part of your self-definition.*

To compound this confusion, a new and possibly even undesirable identity is thrust upon you as a result of death.

> I was this woman who had just lost this child. That is who I was. (*Mother of a young cancer victim*)

> I was the girl whose father had just died. People said it to each other and I overheard them. I heard people talking in the neighborhood, at school, everywhere I went. Only my mother seemed to treat me as a regular person. (*Teacher reflecting on her father's death when she was five years of age*)

> In our small community I was the young widow. I was aware of other people watching me to see if I behaved as a young widow should, but I didn't know what that behavior was. All I knew was that my life had drastically changed forever. (*Accountant widowed at twenty-eight years of age*)

In addition to your life circumstances being altered, and your activities changing as a result of your loved one's death, you have definite *feelings* about the role you played as the deceased's wife, husband, sibling, or friend. You had a place for this role in your emotional makeup. For example, you may have been *proud* to be the mother of a boy who played the violin in the youth symphony, or was awarded a college scholarship, or scored a touchdown. You got *satisfaction* from being your little brother's idol. You felt *important* when your niece preferred your company to that of the other relatives. You *enjoyed* the *respect* you received as the husband of an accomplished, popular wife. But these elements of gratification have been cancelled out by your loved one's death.

A psychologist working with the bereaved commented on this state, during which redefinition becomes necessary.

> So much of us is defined by what we do in the world and who we are in the world; losing a child or a partner changes that. Often, a lot of self-esteem is tied in with the other person.

A Changed Perspective

Almost without exception, the bereaved person changes his or her priorities in regard to social participation and personal goals. You may now find yourself taking a look at exactly how you have spent the precious years of your life. As you compare the past to the present, your perspective changes. What once seemed important, such as a party, your club, shopping, a golf game, possibly even your occupation, may no longer have the same importance. In fact, you may place no value on it whatsoever.

> What really matters is people, their relationships, love and caring. Nothing else really matters—money, power, and all that. It means nothing. (*Mother of an accident victim*)

> I'm not as social as I was. I don't want to do as much. I don't like big parties. I don't like small talk. I've always been a little bit that way but now I am more so. (*Mother of a teenaged accident victim*)

Working toward Clarification and Redefinition

After a period of assessing your life to date, you will likely adopt a revised set of values, or even a new set of values. This may mean that your life structure will be greatly altered. You may, for example, have no desire at all to relate to particular individuals with whom you once spent much of your time. You may not want to devote as many hours to domestic chores, church duties, or business dinners. You may think it a waste to expend as much energy participating in sports. You may not even want to continue the same career.

> I changed my job because I felt it wasn't relevant to my life anymore. That is why I went back to school. I wanted to be trained so I could do something in the helping, feeling field. (*Parent who left sales to get a degree in social work*)

Commonly, a survivor has less interest in social functions or materially oriented activities, and an increased interest in those areas of life concerned with human values, such as love, compassion, assistance to others, or political or social activism. Many people in the field of bereavement are those who have redirected their careers after being affected by the death of a loved one. Businessmen who have been through loss often spend less time with their associates and more time with their families. Homemakers return to school to undertake study in the field of psychology and sociology. Bereaved siblings become social activists or volunteers in human services organizations.

All priority changes are not major ones such as these. They come in various degrees. Your own changes may be extremely ambitious or quite modest. They may also be so instinctive that you don't notice them. For example, you may no longer accept invitations to large gatherings or spend as many weekends working on your boat, or watching television. Instead, you may devote more time to something that seems more valuable to you, such as helping your child with homework, pursuing your own education, or having "quality visits" with older family members. You may treat yourself and a companion to a picnic in the woods, a walk on the beach, or a lovely dinner. You may take time off for a leisurely trip.

What you do for yourself will change continually as your personal needs change. You will find your grief producing growth —a growth that is almost indiscernible at first, but as the days progress, redefinition and restructuring will become increasingly evident.

When you're healing successfully, your life embodies a purpose, a future, and an appreciation for those *components of your being* which make you the most human. The *same* components that produce deep grief after your loved one's death also serve to make life worthwhile and something to be treasured. To have a life free of grief, you would have to live without love. No one would willingly choose such an alternative.

Excerpted and adapted with permission from *Beyond Grief: A Guide for Recovering from the Loss of a Loved One* by Carol Staudacher. For more information on this and related books, see the "Further Reading" section in the back of the book.

CHAPTER 40

Preparing for a Parent's Death

"Don't mention death to your father" was the note my mother passed me as he lay dying in a rented hospital bed in their living room in San Diego.

She was taking care of my father now that he could no longer take care of himself. She knew that during the course of his fatal illness I had often tried to talk with him about death. She also knew his reaction most of the time when confronted with his dying: God forbid.

So we did not mention it, my mother and I, as we cared for my father the last nine days of his life. He died October 24th at 5:00 A.M., in his own apartment, surrounded by what he knew and loved.

I prepared for this home death in much the same way I had prepared for childbirth. People joked that I was becoming a death expert. I, who had spent a lifetime hiding from the idea of death, barely able to say the word without spitting over my shoulder and knocking on wood.

But I knew I had two choices: I could deny what was going to happen and refuse to accept my father's death, although he would die anyway. Or I could try to help. If I wasn't afraid, we could talk and say good-bye.

I began by reading every book on death and dying I could find. I was fortunate to come across Stephen Levine's *Who Dies,* a book filled with the kind of stories I needed to hear. By the time I finished reading it, I felt that I would be able to handle the fear, and that I would know how to deal with the pain.

That is how my mother and I came to be sitting in the dining room eating dinner while, eight feet away, my father lay in his bed, dying. "Did you ever imagine you would be able to do this?" I asked my mother, who couldn't even visit cemeteries, so unwilling is she to look at anything that has to do with death. She laughed, "Never."

My father had been in that bed for six days, unable to move or talk and, for the past day, unable even to swallow food or water. Hospice, our main source of support, had told us that we could stop feeding him and giving him medication. His body was shutting down. Food would only make him more uncomfortable.

Eating, in the last six months, had been his favorite activity. He was always hungry. Now he could not swallow and he could not eat. This was hard on my mother and me, as we equated caring for him well with feeding him.

He lay in his bed, his right arm paralyzed and stiff, his fist clenched against his chest, so frozen up I could barely move his arm to change his pajamas. Purple blotches appeared everywhere on his dry, lifeless skin, like internal stains; his muscles were weak but tight from inactivity. No longer able to speak, he would bang his left fist down on the bed or shake the side bars when he wanted to communicate.

I was watching my father's skin, muscles, and bone literally fade away. For comfort, I'd consult *Who Dies*, and was reminded that a mere five hundred years ago, people had as limited an understanding of the material world as we now have of the spiritual world. All people, *even the smart ones*, thought that the world was flat and you fell off at a certain point. People still fall off the earth, but now it's when they die. We see the body go but can't yet see what happens to the spirit.

Some friends have said, "Seeing your father become like a baby, having to wipe him, feed him, diaper him, hear him moan, must have taken its toll on you." And although this is true, it also helped me prepare for his death. It gave me something to do and allowed me to be of use instead of standing by helplessly.

The call from my father came early in April. "I've been in the hospital. I have brain cancer." Panic and despair were my initial reactions. I began to ask questions. What tests had been done? What was the prognosis? What were his choices for treatment? There were more calls back and forth, a search for hopeful information. Long-distance conversations with his oncologist, who, after giving me a lot of detail, said kindly, "I'm sorry."

On my first trip out to San Diego, my fear of flying was coupled with fear of my father's death. I could handle neither, but had to deal with both.

I arrived in the late afternoon and took a bus to my parents' apartment. My father was in the hospital with a high fever; my mother was with him. Unlike past visits, when they were both at the airport to greet me, I was on my own.

On the bus I sit next to a seventy-year-old man from Yonkers, New York. He is drunk and telling jokes to the Mexican lady next to him, getting everyone, including our Irish bus driver, to laugh. The old man's friendliness and humor draw all of us on the bus together, and it is a rich moment. Suddenly, he falls back against his seat, his eyes roll back, and it looks like he has passed out. But soon it becomes clear that he has suffered a stroke: part of his body is paralyzed. Now his illness connects all of us. We go into action like a well-prepared team. I become the diagnostician; the bus driver pulls off the highway and phones 911. A young woman comes forward to help make the old man more comfortable; everyone has a suggestion to offer. Finally the ambulance comes and takes him away. The bus continues on its way, and I have begun my visit with a spontaneous, on-the-bus training program for medical emergencies. I wonder how many medical emergencies I will be facing with my own father.

I visit my father in the hospital. They have discovered that he has pneumonia. They can treat that. But he is despondent and negative, angry that he is ill. He starts to cry when I talk about his grandchildren, describing how they are doing. I realize that he fears he may never see them again.

When my father regains strength, we walk the halls of the hospital, my mother on one side, me on the other, his I.V. trailing behind. There are many others walking the halls with their I.V.'s and tubes of blood who look far worse than my father, but they smile hellos to those they pass. I want to look away so I will not see the wasted flesh, the pallid faces; so I will not become frightened. But I am moved, despite my fear, by their ability to live in new ways in this new place with all that apparatus. They will not be crushed by their illness.

I meet my father's doctor. He is a caring person who relates information to me respectfully; but I have five minutes, that's all. His beeper rings and he is off. He can't afford to give more time, emotionally or financially. He is working on the medical line, a technician doing his part. I long for someone who is a healer, but all I find are doctors.

That night in my parents' apartment, my mother and I sleep together. We awaken at dawn and begin to talk. We hold each other. Boundaries disappear. This is a moment that will shape the months ahead, a time when my mother and I draw closer, tending to my father's needs, weaving a much stronger connection than we have ever had before.

I return home to Michigan. My father begins radiation therapy. The treatment makes him tired and he loses all his hair. He complains, but is glad for a chance to shrink the tumors, and he regains some hope. He believes in his doctor.

I suggest to my father that he take Vitamin C, do creative visualization, exercise a lot, and change his diet. He barely listens, feeling safe only on the route outlined by his physician. I stop making suggestions.

In June my parents come to Michigan to visit. For the first time, my father looks old and frail. Just three months ago he was president of his condominium association, a vital, energetic, young 74-year-old. Now he walks slowly, rests a lot, and is very demanding. My mother waits on him. I wish he would act differently, but I know that he is very frightened and angry.

I take my parents on an excursion to Windsor, Canada. My father is having more difficulty walking; he is shuffling his left leg. I help him sit down on a park bench overlooking the river while my mother and I go shopping. I am almost afraid to leave him alone. The paper he is reading blows away and he cannot retrieve it.

A few days later, he has a seizure while sitting on my living room couch. We telephone the emergency medical service and they quickly respond. The shaking and convulsing lasted at most one minute, but it seemed like half an hour. My husband, Jack, is the only one who knows what to do, which is basically to keep my father from hurting himself. I rush between the first-aid book and my father.

I ride with him in the ambulance to the hospital. It is a very sad moment. This seizure means that the radiation hasn't worked.

My father only wants to go home to see his doctor. The emergency room staff give him anti-seizure medication and release him. They assume that he will fly home the next day.

By morning he can barely walk. While brushing his teeth in the bathroom he falls into the tub. Jack and I have to carry my father down the stairs. I call his doctor in San Diego as we are about to leave for the airport and he insists that my father cannot fly in his present condition. He must first get a CAT scan. I am upset but realize that the doctor is right.

My father is easily persuaded to stay, since it's his doctor's advice. My neighbor Kim puts us in touch with his personal physician, who is willing to admit my father to Henry Ford Hospital through a local emergency room.

Once again we are alone in an emergency room waiting to be seen. We had spent part of the previous night talking about dying. Finally death has been mentioned. He wants to be cremated and laughs when I tell him I had been planning to ask my husband to build a casket for him. There is some acceptance in his voice. He is not crying. We talk about my grandparents, who died in their late eighties. I tell him I had hoped he would be around another decade—he had always been so healthy. I wonder if it was easier for him because his parents were so much older. He thinks it was.

Now in the emergency room of Henry Ford, we continue our dialogue. Maybe there will be something else *these* doctors can do. His mind is still clear. He thinks up a list of hopeful signs. We talk about my mother. I assure him that she will be able to rely on me as she had on him.

Later that night, he is transferred to the hospital. He goes by ambulance while I follow in my car, crying the whole way there. I go up to his room and lie on the bed with him until the resident arrives.

The hospital gives him a battery of tests. He is seen by radiology, oncology, neurology. Finally, after all the results are analyzed, his doctor tells me there is nothing more that can be done. My father is going to die. I feel like I am going to faint while at the same time I am asking questions. I am holding on to the counter of the nurses' station. I ask where my father will be going. At first the doctor and the resident don't understand, but then they catch on that I mean where is my father going *after* he dies. The doctor says that they don't know the answer. They don't teach *that* in medical school. I ask to be the one to tell my father.

We go into his room—the doctor, the resident, and myself. I tell my father what they have told me. They ask him about life support if he should get sick, and he answers that he doesn't want it. Then he starts to cry.

We bring him home a week later. That first evening is a disaster, but it is also when my mother shows her true colors, bright and strong.

My father cannot walk, and we have not yet gotten a wheelchair. My husband is away, so she, with a bad hip, and I must carry him. We are able to get him into bed, but then he has to go to the bathroom. We struggle to get him there in time, then find ourselves stuck in my back bathroom, too small really for three adults to fit into, trying to lift him from the toilet to wipe him and turn him enough to get him out the door.

It is a frustrating moment. We could easily have started to cry. Instead our eyes meet and we are struck with the utter absurdity of the situation. We both start to laugh and cannot stop. That laughter must have released some extra energy. We are finally able to get him up, wiped, and out the door. He does not laugh with us, but he doesn't seem embarrassed or upset.

This is another moment that will shape the months ahead. At other, equally frustrating times, my mother the comic reappears.

In fact, a minute later, we are in another difficult situation. My father has to urinate; but before we can walk him back to the bathroom he loses control, urinating on himself, the floor, and the couch. "Oh well, it won't take long to clean it up," my mother says. How easily we adapt by turning these moments into commonplace occurrences that can be handled. Our language shapes our responses: "Oh well," instead of "Oh no."

That first evening turns out to be the hardest. Afterwards, we get all the equipment and help we need. We make the downstairs playroom into a sickroom. There is a bed from upstairs so my parents can continue to sleep together, a portable toilet, a bedpan, and his wheelchair in a room that is already filled with toys and books.

We also get home health care, a visiting nurse, and a physical therapist, who come twice a week. They are more like healers than doctors; they take the time to talk with all of us and never seem rushed.

My father improves to the point where he can stand on his own, then walk on his own. He approaches his physical therapy energetically. Each time Dee, the therapist, comes, they go for a walk. Soon he is able to walk around the block. Dee encourages him to take three long walks a day, but he is afraid to go by himself.

Chip, my husband's partner who is working next door, offers to accompany my father on walks. Three times a day for three weeks, Chip is there, slowly walking alongside my father. These walks are more than physical therapy for him. They are visible signs that he is getting better. He does not know or want to know that it is the medication that has improved his condition.

For another couple of weeks, things go well. We return the wheelchair. My father shuffles carefully around on his own. We start to relax. Then he falls bending down to retrieve a piece of candy and hurts his arm. I am away at a meeting in Detroit when my mother calls to ask me to come home. My father is very upset.

The next day, I take him to be seen by a doctor—another emergency room visit. But this time I have no resources to call on. I feel drained. I can't bear the sounds of the room, babies crying, people moaning. I can't bear to see all these people who look sick and injured. Whenever I can do so unobtrusively, I put my hands over my ears to shut everything out and close my eyes.

An x-ray reveals that my father has broken his wrist. He feels this to be a tremendous setback for him. After the doctors put his arm in a cast, I take him home. He is now depressed, and I feel unable to be cheerful. We are silent on the ride home.

But by the time his 75th birthday arrives a week later, my father has adjusted to his cast and regained his optimism. Now he blames all problems of balance on his heavy cast. We have a big party to celebrate his birthday. My cousin flies in from California. My father's closest friend, Mildred, whom he has known since he was 16, flies in from New York City. My whole community of friends comes out for the party. I worry that it will be a very sad evening and that I will cry, but it turns out to be a lot of fun. My mother plays the piano; Mildred, who is an actress, dances and sings, and we all join in. People stay very late. My father looks well and has a great time.

A few days later, my father decides that he wants to go home. I feel guilty: he and my mother have been at my house for two months; I am ready for them to leave. But I think he is planning to go home because he believes he is going to live, and I know that he is going to die.

I want him to know that he doesn't have to leave. We talk. I ask him where he would prefer to die. He tells me at home. But he also feels that he will enjoy himself more there while he is alive. And if he becomes ill again, he can return to Michigan. *If* he becomes ill again: he is still hoping for the best.

I drive my parents to the airport. My children remain at home. I know that I will be feeling very sad. I want time to cry. We arrive early. My father immediately has to get to the bathroom. He is too frail and shaky to be left on his own, so I go with him into the men's bathroom, standing in the doorway watching him in his stall. If he falls, I can quickly move to his aid.

We then walk slowly to the plane. My mother keeps up the conversation and we all hide in talk from the feelings we are having. Everyone knows how sad this moment is, but none of us wants to say it out loud. We act as if this were just another trip home.

I get permission to accompany my father onto the plane. I am planning to help him into his seat. But I am overcome with sadness. Any moment now I will begin to sob. I quickly say goodbye to the frail, shaky old man my father has become and rush off. As soon as my back is turned, I start to cry and continue crying through the airport terminal, into the car, and for most of the ride home. In fact, I miss the right exit and end up lost, going home the long way.

That evening our house feels empty. We all move around slowly, fixing dinner, cleaning up, not trying to get away from our feelings, just letting them out to wander about the house.

Two months go by. My father has adjusted well to being back home. My Uncle Henry stops by regularly to take him out for walks. Relatives visit and take him to dinner. My mother cooks enormous meals. Then he falls getting into a chair. Two days later, he falls in the bathroom. He panics. He is afraid to be left alone.

On the phone he cries. Finally he tells me, "If you want to see your father alive, you better come now." I decide to fly out immediately. I am spending too much energy trying to decide what to do. I can handle a few extra trips across the country, but I can't handle my father's dying without seeing him again.

I arrive in San Diego two days later. My father is propped up with pillows in his bed. When I enter the room he starts to cry. We embrace and hold each other close for a very long time. When we pull apart I see how bad he looks. His face is swollen and puffy. He cannot sit up without support. Our few minutes together have already tired him out. He asks for help to lie down and take a nap.

From that moment on he starts to let go. Each day for the next nine days he drifts further and further away. He has seen me again and knows that I will be there.

By nighttime the hospital bed arrives. Hospice has been contacted and they begin their enormously helpful support work. They provide all the equipment we need. They come to our house regularly. They teach me to change my father and his bed with him in it. They help us to know what to expect, giving me their infamous blue paper which lists the signs of dying.

But aside from the equipment and their physical and emotional support, the hospice people give us something even more important. They give off an aura: their presence provides a spirit of caring and acceptance that seeps into our pores and remains after the hospice staff leaves. They are calm and peaceful in the face of dying.

My mother and I try to copy their style. We make up a schedule and routine. My father needs twenty-four-hour attention now, so she and I sleep in shifts.

The nights are definitely the hardest. My father wakes up a lot, needing help, and I am tired. But worst of all, when it grows dark, I start to feel afraid. As his death draws closer, I know that I don't want to be alone. And I want to spare my mother, who would have a difficult time watching my father in distress.

I call my cousin Joan in northern California and ask her to fly down that night. I am an only child, and she and I are very close. I know that my father will be dying soon. I have been checking that blue paper: I know by his symptoms that his body is preparing itself for death.

He has become incontinent. He sleeps most of the time. He often seems restless, pulling at his bed linen, constantly throwing off his covers. That was number seven on a list of ten. Number eight: "Your loved one will have decreased need for food and drink because the body will naturally begin to conserve energy which is expended on these tasks." Number nine: "You may notice a change in breathing patterns: breathing may become irregular for ten-to-thirty-second periods of no breathing."

My mother goes to bed at 7:00 P.M. My cousin arrives at 8:00. We embrace, then approach my father's bed. I can see her quickly move from discomfort and sadness to alertness.

My father has started exhibiting symptom number nine. It is very upsetting to hear. He gasps for breath, then sounds like he is choking, then doesn't breathe at all, then starts to gasp again. Over and over and over again. I call hospice. They explain that there is nothing we can do to help him. This is the Cheyne-Stokes syndrome. It could last 24 hours.

Joan and I sit close by my father's bed. We take turns brushing each other's hair and rubbing each other's back. We hold my father's hand and gently stroke his head. Wordlessly we find a common ground. To us it's as if my father were in labor. There is nothing we can do but keep him company. We stay next to him, occasionally lying down nearby to get some sleep.

Early in the morning, he stops gasping and choking. His breathing becomes almost imperceptible. Then he is still. At 5:00 A.M. as we stand next to him, he stops breathing. One breath and then no more. We wait and watch. No more breath. But even without breath he is still there. We stay by his side and watch him closely. After a while, I go into the bedroom and tell my mother. For the first time in six months, she starts to cry. I hold her and cry with her. "At least he wasn't in pain," she says.

Nervous, unsure of her reaction, she comes with me into the living room. Slowly she approaches my father's bed. She looks at him, then leans over and kisses his forehead to say good-bye. "I thought I'd be afraid seeing him this way, but I don't feel frightened," she says. "Let's keep him home a little while longer."

So we wait several hours before we call the mortuary. We brew a pot of hot steaming coffee which we have with almond croissants. The three of us sit at the dining room table having breakfast, waiting until we are ready to let my father go.

Hospice helps again. We are able to avoid police and coroners. By the time the mortuary men come, my father is gone from his body. My mother goes into the bedroom, but Joan and I watch as the two men take the body away. It seems as if they are taking away a pod, not a person. In fact, we giggle silently, for the two men wear dark sunglasses and look like seedy private detectives. We wonder to ourselves how it feels to do their job.

Afterwards we go downstairs to sit by the pool. The sun is shining and feels very hot. It is hard to understand this beautiful morning in terms of the last few hours we've shared. Both are real: the warm sun, watching my father die. We feel like proud veterans who have been given a chance to do something special. We are embarrassed about it, but admit that we feel like bragging. We swear then, we will only brag to each other.

Years have passed since my father's death. At times I want to renege on my acceptance. I don't want my father to be dead. But many of my friends are traveling the same territory. So at least I'm not alone.

My friend Chip composed a song for my father on the piano. He calls it "Sid's Minute." My husband and I took many of my father's clothes. We have his sweaters, jackets, and socks. We wear them a lot. I'm still collecting stories and reading—immersing myself in books about death. It's not that I'm stuck. I'm just not ready to move to a different place yet. My father is dead; he left me an invisible gift—a new connection to my ancestors' breath. And the experience of handling one of the hardest parts of life: death.

So Few Resources

After my father died, I couldn't stop talking about my experience. I wanted to share with others how we had lived through his dying. I began to realize that my friends and I needed a new tradition: we needed to trade stories of our parents' deaths as we had previously traded stories of our children's births.

It was not so long ago that birth was considered scary and secretive. There was little information available that explained what actually occurred. Men were left out of the experience entirely, told to stay outside in the waiting room. Only the doctors and nurses were prepared.

But I was fortunate to come of age during a special time, the sixties, and to be part of a generation that insisted on being involved in the decisions and events affecting our lives. We learned to discuss and explore subjects that other generations had kept closed, like sex, relationships, and childbirth.

Consequently, I was a veteran of childbirth education classes and the self-help movement. I was educated in the finest libraries and bookstores in the country; I developed a basic strategy to handle any new and potentially frightening situations. That strategy consisted of reading and talking—two things I do well.

The day after I found out I was pregnant, I was at the local bookstore sitting on a stool in front of the pregnancy and birth section, going through every book on the shelf. Nine months later I was an expert. When a fear arose, I comforted my self with statistics from one of the dozens of books I had. I learned the language, the details, the options of birth. And I developed a network of people I could call on with my questions and concerns: I surrounded myself with people who were involved in pregnancy and birth.

All the preparation and connection paid off. I had one very difficult birth, my first, which lasted three days, and one very easy birth, my second, which lasted three hours. I was prepared for both.

The day I learned of my father's terminal illness, I was back at the local bookstore, sitting on a stool in front of the three books they carried on death and dying. This time when I attempted. to educate myself, I found limited resources. That is why I have written this book. *We need to be helped to prepare for death as well as we have been helped to prepare for birth.* We need more stories, more information, and more details so that we no longer feel frightened and ignorant.

I never saw myself as someone who was capable of dealing with death. When one of my high school acquaintances died of leukemia during my junior year, I quickly tried to forget it. I had little to do with my grandparents when they were dying. If anyone had told me that I would be enjoying a steaming cup of coffee and an almond croissant in my parents' dining room while my father's body lay a few feet away from me, I would *not* have believed them.

As a psychotherapist, I had always seen myself as part of a profession that could deal with taboo subjects like incest, suicide, and sex. But I had not been trained to help people with their repressed and often invisible anxiety around death. In my two years of graduate school training, I do not recall attending any lectures on the psychological implications of our individual and collective terror of death. In the twenty-six years I've been practicing, death continues to be a heavily avoided subject in the profession. Odd, since it's not as if some of us die and some of us don't, some of us will lose parents and some of us won't.

Clients don't often come in and say, "I'm scared of dying"; and, until recently, it certainly wasn't a subject I was going to bring up.

However, after my own experience with my father's illness and death, I found that I was better able to help my clients deal with their own parents' aging, sickness, and dying.

Everyone seems to start out in denial. I remember my own contact with that stage, when my father told me he had brain cancer. I wondered what I would do if my father died. And then it struck me: it wasn't if—it was *when*.

I recall a client who told me about a terrible fight she had with her mother, who was grossly overweight and had begun to develop serious health problems. "I don't know what I would do if my mother died." I gently pointed out that her mother was going to die, sometime. She seemed shocked by this knowledge. "I can't bear to think about that. She's always been there for me. What would I do without her?"

An editor friend, reading a draft of *Last Touch,* the book from which this chapter was taken, told me that the book would help a lot of people. Luckily, he was not one of them: "My parents aren't going to die," he said jokingly.

My friends and my clients were all eager to hear about my experience with my father's death. They couldn't stop asking questions. What was it like? How did you feel? What did you do? How did you prepare? What made it easier? What made it harder? Where did you find help? What does a natural death look like?

Last Touch emerged from these conversations. At work, dinner parties, my college reunion, whenever people learned what I was writing about, they would volunteer their own stories, eager to have someone to talk to about their experiences.

The American Way of Death

Death is a part of life. However, in our society, death is hidden from most of us. Most of our choices that have to do with illness and death are made for us, not by us. But this has not always been so. One woman I interviewed was six when her grandfather died at home. She vividly remembers viewing his body, laid out in the parlor; it all seemed quite ordinary to her.

In traditional societies, and indeed for nearly all of human history, death has been an accepted, natural, and shared part of family and community life. It is only very recently, with the breakdown of community and the rise of complex and impersonal social institutions, that the duties of death have been delegated to professionals, to strangers.

Just one hundred years ago, most people built their own houses, made their own clothes, and raised their own food. Little was delegated to others (except among the very wealthy, who had servants or slaves). But as our society entered the age of specialization, we stopped trusting ourselves to handle our own lives; we lost the ability to distinguish what is good to do for ourselves, and what we need others to help us do.

We became mobile, moving long distances from our family, often to crowded, urban housing. Home funerals and home burials grew more logistically difficult; we could no longer bury our relatives on our land. Slowly, death moved from our homes to hospitals and funeral parlors. Embalming was developed to preserve the body so that relatives living at long distances could travel to the funeral. The benefits of this approach came with a price: we became ignorant of the natural process of death.

Then, in 1963, Jessica Mitford wrote an exposé of the funeral business, *The American Way of Death*. Shortly afterward came Elisabeth Kubler-Ross's book *On Death and Dying*. Both books got us thinking and talking about death. In 1967, hospice, a movement to provide a supportive environment for the dying, was founded in England by Cicely Saunders.

Still, death continues to be seen as an enemy in our culture. As Lewis Thomas wrote in *The Lives of a Cell*, "We will have to give up the notion that death is a catastrophe or detestable or avoidable or even strange. We will need to learn more about the cycling of life in the rest of the system and about our connection to the process. Everything that comes alive seems to be in trade for something that dies, cell for cell."

Not all cultures are the same. To Buddhists, life is seen as preparation for the moment of death. Ram Dass, one of the most influential leaders of the consciousness movement, recalls someone saying to an Indian guru who was dying, "Don't go." The guru responded, "Where could I go?" If you are more than your physical body, death is just a transformational experience. You aren't going anywhere, you are simply parting company with your body.

Some cultures actually encourage preparation for death. In childhood, members of some Native American tribes learn how to perform a death chant, an instant centering technique to use whenever they are in a difficult situation: to help with the dangerous, the unknown; with death.

In Mexico on the Day of the Dead, people celebrate the nature of change by having picnics in nearby cemeteries. Children eat candy skulls and get paper skeletons which they blow apart with firecrackers. There are similar festivals in Hungary and Japan.

In Hasidic teaching, there is a tradition that helps people prepare for whatever might happen to them. As Stephen Levine explains, in *Who Dies*, "That kind of presence for our life is the perfect preparation for death. It means being open to whatever happens. Because if everything is okay except death, then eventually you notice that everything's okay but death and loss. And then everything's okay except death and loss and a bad pastrami sandwich. Then everything's okay but death, loss, a bad pastrami sandwich, and the plumber coming."

Back a generation or two in most families, decisions about death and dying were dictated largely by cultural and religious customs, not by personal choice. For many of us, this is still true. For others, the traditions have been obscured as our families have assimilated into secular society. For instance, a Jewish friend knew vaguely that after a death mourners are supposed to sit on stools, and mirrors are covered—but she was not sure why.

Our families are also becoming more and more religiously complex. Take my family. My grandparents were practicing Orthodox Jews. My parents were Jewish but not religious. My husband was raised a Catholic. His parents are practicing Catholics. Our children attend a Jewish temple and a Catholic church.

What death customs will prevail? Should we follow cultural traditions, our own values and spiritual beliefs, or our parents' wishes? It would be equally appropriate for my family to sit *shiva* (have a wake), depending on which side we wanted to please.

Since most of us in American society have been, to one degree or another, sheltered from death, the prospect of dealing with a parent's death can seem overwhelming. It certainly felt that way to me. With other difficult tasks in life, if what you are planning seems too hard, you can simply change your mind—decide not to build your house yourself or learn to run 10 miles a day. But your parent's death is not something you can simply choose to avoid or postpone.

Necessary Choices

Over time I came to see that my father's dying presented our family, and me personally, with a series of choices:

- What kind of medical treatment would he seek?

- How would we relate to his doctors and other caregivers?

- How often, and for how long, would I visit him?

- How much care would my mother and I be able to offer my father?

- How much emotional support?

- How would we take care of each other?

- What kind of funeral would be appropriate?

There were many, many other choices, many of them painful. As I became more familiar with the options that were available, I was better able to think intelligently about them, and to balance my father's needs against my own and those of my husband and children.

Each person faces a different set of choices in dealing with a parent's illness and death. These choices will be affected by your economic situation, your commitments to work and children, your geographical distance from your parent, your relationships with your siblings, and your own and your family's cultural traditions and personal values.

Most significantly, your choices will be shaped by your emotional history and relationship with your parents. Many people don't have the kind of relationships they would like to have with their parents; this book is not just for those who have good relationships. Whether your relationship has been wonderful or miserable or somewhere in between, once your parent becomes terminally ill, there are better and worse ways to relate. There are things to know that will make you more helpful, choices to be made, options to be explored.

You and your parent may enter this stage with complicated histories, past resentments, and contradictory feelings. But these do not have to get in the way of helping your parent if you are clear about what you can and want to do.

The loss of your parent will be hard on you, whether you have a good relationship or a difficult one; and if you are not prepared for your parent's death—it will be even harder. It is not an easy path.

To be there for your parent, to get ready, you must do more than just collect information. You need to connect with others, and to get some sense of the different kinds of experiences that may await you. You need an armful of death and dying stories.

Of course we don't want our parents to die. We don't want anyone to die, including ourselves. But a parent's death is a powerful, significant, and universal experience. Sometimes it's a last chance at a relationship. How you experience those few hours, weeks, or months can affect the rest of your life.

Excerpted and adapted with permission from *Last Touch: Preparing for a Parent's Death* by Marilyn R. Becker, M.S.W. For more information on this and related books, see the "Further Reading" section in the back of the book.

CHAPTER 41

Depression

A mood is an emotion that temporarily colors all aspects of your life. Anxiety, elation, melancholy, anger, and peacefulness are only some of the moods within the great range of human emotion. For many people, moods are not problematic. For others, a mood may persist long after the circumstances that triggered it have passed.

When a mood outlives its context, it can become a serious liability to healthy emotional functioning. Individuals whose moods impair their work, relationships, and potential for happiness are said to have a mood disorder. If you are such an individual, this chapter has been designed to help you understand your moods and bring them under control.

Doctors recognize two main types of mood disorders: depressive disorders and bipolar disorders. Depressive disorders consist of one or more periods of major depression. Bipolar disorders involve a series of moods that include at least one manic period and one or more periods of major depression. A detailed definition of each of these conditions is given in the *Diagnostic and Statistical Manual of Mental Disorders—Fourth Edition (DSM-IV)*, which is prepared by the American Psychiatric Association and available in all public libraries.

Depression and bipolar illness are unnessarily costly in terms of human suffering, wasted potential, and strain on the health care system. Statistics compiled by the National Institute of Mental Health indicate that depression affects over ten million people per year in the United States. Over an average lifetime between 8 and 15 percent of the population experience serious depressive reactions. Two out of three of these people are women. Bipolar illness affects between 1 and 10 percent of the population, and occurs equally in men and women. Fifteen percent of people who are diagnosed as having a depressive disorder end their lives by suicide. This accounts for about half of all suicides in the United States.

The real tragedy, though, is that 80 percent of all depression and bipolar illness is highly responsive to treatment. Many medical, psychological, and lifestyle interventions are currently available. It is estimated that only one out of three seriously depressed people ever seeks treatment. There are no comparable figures for people with other treatable medical diseases, such as diabetes. The pain caused by this situation is needless. Depression and bipolar disorders are treatable and, in many cases, can be cured.

Symptoms of Major Depression

Most people have experienced depression at least once in their life. The predominant effect of depression is a loss of energy. Few things, if any, seem interesting; motivation drops off to zero. Although this feels terrible, people in the grips of such depressions are still able to do the things they need to do in order to survive. They go to work, pay the bills, cook their food, and relate to the people in their life who demand their attention. This normal type of depression feels rotten, but life continues in spite of it.

The line between normal and major depression is crossed when that down, rotten feeling invades every part of your life. Experiences that may seem objectively satisfying to others feel like failure and frustration to you. Eventually you may try to avoid having any experience at all. Communicating with people, even those you love, may seem difficult or intrusive. You may shrink from speaking with people entirely. And when you envision the future—whether it be tomorrow, two months, or two years down the road—you see no light at the end of the tunnel. You have no sense that your gloom and despair will ever lift. In short, a major depression differs from a normal depression in that its symptoms are much more severe, last much longer, and eventually impair a person's ability to function.

There are several criteria by which a major depression is clinically defined.

First, a condition must exhibit at least five of the following nine symptoms, and these symptoms must have been present for at least two weeks:

1. Depressed mood most of the day, nearly every day

2. Diminished interest or pleasure in almost all activities of the day, nearly every day

3. Significant weight gain or loss when not dieting, and decreased appetite nearly every day

4. Insomnia or hypersomnia (sleeping too much) nearly every day

5. Abnormal restlessness or a drop in physical activity nearly every day

6. Fatigue or loss of energy nearly every day

7. Feelings of worthlessness or excessive or inappropriate guilt nearly every day

8. Diminished ability to think, concentrate, or make decisions nearly every day

9. Recurrent thoughts of death, or recurrent suicidal thoughts without a specific plan; or a suicide attempt; or a specific plan for committing suicide

In addition to exhibiting the initial five symptoms, the following must also be true:

1. The disturbance is not being caused by another illness.

2. The disturbance is not a reaction to the loss of a loved one.

Symptoms of Bipolar Disorder

Two separate and opposite states comprise bipolar disorder, in which depression alternates with mania. During the manic phase of a bipolar condition, a person can appear to be positive, excited about life, even euphoric. An unusually high sense of self-esteem may be evident. This person may seem conspicuously active and brimming with ideas, one after the other. Many projects may be started, and many quests launched. Friends or acquaintances may be aware that something is amiss: after all, the person in the midst of a manic phase seems different than usual. But the hazards of the opposite pole—depression—would probably be the furthest thing from a lay observer's mind. Once the manic stage wanes, and the depression stage emerges, the Jekyll-Hyde nature of this disorder becomes apparent.

Switching from one state or pole to the other, from mania to depression and back again, is called *cycling*. Characteristics of cycling vary from person to person. In some, the cycles last for long periods and switch infrequently. Others switch from depression to mania and back relatively often. This quick switching from one emotional state to the other is known as *rapid cycling*. A one-to-one ratio (one period of depression to one period of mania) rarely occurs; usually, one cycle is more prevalent than the other. In general, men tend to experience manic periods more often than episodes of depression, and women have more depressions than manic episodes. Long periods during which the bipolar sufferer feels neither manic nor depressed can exist between cycles. During these times, the person seems and feels all right.

There are several criteria that must be met before a condition is considered mania.

First, a person's mood must be elevated, expansive, or irritable. This mood must be different from a person's normal personality. The change must be unusually intense, and must last for a considerable period of time. While exhibiting this elevated mood, a person can become very expansive and grandiose. In some cases of mania the mood that is expressed may be irritated and angry, and the person may act with arrogance and belligerence.

The second criterion states that at least three of the following symptoms must have been present to a significant degree:

1. Inflated sense of self-importance

2. Decreased need for sleep (for example, the individual feels rested after only three hours of sleep)

3. Unusual talkativeness

4. Flight of ideas or a subjective feeling that thoughts are racing

5. Distractibility (the person's attention is too easily drawn to unimportant external stimuli)

6. Increase in goal-directed activity (for instance, social or sexual) or physical activity

7. Excessive involvement in activities that bring pleasure but have a high potential for painful or harmful consequences (for example, the person engages in unrestrained buying sprees, sexual indiscretions, or unwise business investments)

These criteria help differentiate mania from other excitable states. Individuals in the midst of mania almost always have an overconfident and exaggerated opinion of themselves or their abilities. They will talk too loudly, too often, and too quickly. Their thought processes are accelerated; many thoughts occur almost simultaneously and are verbalized about as quickly. This rapid train of thought is easily derailed, and the manic person will often find it difficult to follow a single subject for very long. Activity can increase both in terms of multiple projects and physical activity, such as fidgeting, pacing, or exaggerated sexual behavior. Finally, manic individuals tend to pursue their goals with great abandon and almost total disregard for consequences.

The third criterion states that a mood disturbance must be severe enough to affect an individual's job performance, participation in regular social activities or relationships with others; or to necessitate hospitalization in order to prevent injury to self or others. This criterion is designed to distinguish full mania, which is potentially very harmful, from hypomania (or "lesser" mania), which does not necessarily have the potential for harm.

How the Brain Communicates

The part of the brain responsible for regulating emotions is called the limbic system. This area lies deep within the brain, below the cerebrum, which is the "thinking" part of the brain. In addition to emotions, the limbic system controls such functions as body temperature, appetite, hormone levels, sleep, blood pressure, and behavior.

Information is transferred from one part of the brain to another with the help of a particular group of chemicals called *neurotransmitters*. This communication network is very delicately balanced. For the limbic system to perform properly, it is essential that this balance be maintained.

Two mechanisms within the neural system allow signals to be passed from cell to cell. The first mechanism is *electrical stimulation*. An electrical impulse is generated in one nerve cell, or neuron, and travels down the length of the cell until it reaches a very small space, or gap, between that cell and the next (neurons are not really connected to each other). This gap between neurons is called a *synapse*. For information to be transmitted, the electrical impulse from the first cell must somehow get across the synapse to the next cell. But it can't jump across this space. Another mechanism is needed to transfer the electrical charge to the next cell.

Here a second chemical mechanism comes into play. As the electrical impulse reaches the end of the first cell, it initiates a chemical reaction. Small sacks, or vesicles, containing neurotransmitters fuse with the cell wall. The sacks then open and empty the chemicals they contain into the gap between the cells. These chemicals float over to the second cell, attaching to the cell wall at specific places called *receptor sites*. Each receptor site will only accept a chemical that is the right molecular shape to fit that site. When enough of the receptor sites are filled on the second cell, an electrical impulse is generated which travels down this cell until it reaches the next synapse. There the process is repeated. Electrical impulses, passing from cell to cell, travel in this manner throughout the limbic system and the rest of the central nervous system as well. The hypothalamus, located within the limbic system, serves as a sort of traffic controller.

Exactly what information is transmitted depends on which neurons are electrically activated, and what part of the brain is stimulated by these neurons. For instance, a particular series of neural firings will stimulate the area of the brain that tells you that you're tired. If another series of neurons fire and stimulate a different part of the brain, you may feel that it is time to eat. Still another series will let you know that you're angry at your boss, or delighted with your child's A in math. Each series of neurons that stimulates a different area in the brain is called a *neural pathway*.

A Brief History of Treatments for Depression

Until recently, mood disorders have been shrouded in secrecy and shame. People suffering from these illnesses have consequently been denied the compassion and access to treatment that are normally available for patients with so-called "physical" complaints.

Early treatment strategies rival each other for bizarreness and cruelty. Contemporary accounts from ancient Greece describe a particularly brutal treatment that was perhaps a precursor to electroconvulsive therapy. Temple priests on an Aegean island threw depressed patients into the sea from a high cliff. Other priests waited in boats in the water below to rescue the "patients" from drowning. The accounts say that many of the subjects of this unorthodox procedure recovered, perhaps cured by the shock of the harrowing experience.

In ancient Phoenicia, the mentally ill were sequestered aboard a "ship of fools" and set adrift to roam the seas in search of more hospitable harbors. During the Middle Ages in Europe, exorcists coaxed the "demons" from the bodies of those who acted strangely. "Shock treatments" were administered to eighteenth-century patients by twirling them on stools until their ears bled or by dropping them through trapdoors into icy lakes.

As late as 1806, a prominent thirty-year-old attorney from Vermont was treated for depression by having his head held down in a bucket of water. When the first treatments proved unsuccessful, his head was held under for increased lengths of time until he finally drowned.

The Shift in the Twentieth Century to Chemical Interventions

The greater part of the twentieth century in American psychiatry was dominated by Freudian thought. Freud promulgated the belief that depressive disorders are the result of internalizing a lost object or relationship, then turning the anger about the loss against the self. He taught that the environment and early childhood experiences were responsible for all mental disorders, including depression and bipolar illness. If you were depressed, you needed to enter psychoanalysis and talk about past traumas from your infant and childhood periods.

It is now believed that psychoanalysis alone is not a useful treatment for depression or bipolar disorders. Depression and mood instability may be due, in part, to psychological stress; but there are many other possible components to these disorders. In 1937, Freud himself said, "The future may teach us how to exercise a direct influence, by means of particular chemical substances, upon the amount of energy and its distribution in the apparatus of the mind. It may be that there are other undreamed-of possibilities of therapy."

Based on Freud's theories, people generally viewed depression and bipolar illness as if they were the result of a character flaw within the victim, rather than illnesses like diabetes and tuberculosis. In reality, though, mood disorders are also medical illnesses and should be regarded as such. There is no shame involved in having them: consciousness-raising organizations and nationwide educational campaigns are doing much to erase the social stigma of depression and manic depression.

In 1938, electroconvulsive therapy (ECT) was introduced as a treatment for mood disorders. Today this procedure is often considered the treatment of last resort, because it is the most invasive among the various interventions available. Electroconvulsive therapy uses electrodes attached to the patient's head to induce a seizure in the brain. This type of seizure seems to increase the level of certain neurotransmitters, the chemicals that transmit nerve impulses from one cell to another. After a short series of treatments administered during a two-week period, depressed patients are often able to regain a normal range of emotions. Confusion and memory loss are also frequent by-products of this type of therapy. Although both these effects are usually short term, full memory restoration can take up to two weeks and, in some cases, the loss can be permanent.

Although not a cure for depression, ECT can be an effective treatment for those patients who don't respond to medication. Such individuals have an 80 to 90 percent chance of responding positively to ECT, which also elicits a much quicker response than drug therapy. Research indicates that ECT can reduce the time required for recovery from depression; but the invasive nature of shock treatment, and its possible side effects, still make it an undesirable treatment for most people.

In 1949, John F. J. Cade, an Australian psychiatrist, discovered that doses of the drug lithium given to frightened guinea pigs changed their behavior from severely agitated to calm and docile. Cade then administered lithium to several psychiatric patients with manic disorders. The patients became emotionally stable. Lithium gradually came to be recognized as a highly effective treatment for mania.

In 1952, French psychiatrists Jean Delay and Pierre Deniker tested and used chlorpromazine (Thorazine) to calm psychotic agitation. Soon afterwards, the family of drugs known as tricyclics were developed in a further attempt to treat psychotic behavior. Although ineffective when used for psychosis, these drugs did seem to raise the spirits of many people in the throes of chronic depression. The commercial development of tricyclics and other antidepressants soon followed.

The problem of how to medically treat mood disorders was basically solved backwards. Neurotransmitters are difficult to isolate and study, since these chemicals are released in extremely small quantities, and any extra amount released is broken down by enzymes and reabsorbed into the cell. At the time when the first antidepressant was discovered, very little was known about neurotransmitters. In fact, the first antidepressant was discovered by accident in the course of an attempt to manufacture an antipsychotic drug. It was only after the antidepressant had been administered to patients and found to be an effective treatment for depression that the biological changes in patients could be analyzed.

Researchers discovered that when one of several types of neurotransmitters malfunctioned, the patient experienced mood fluctuations. The primary neurotransmitters linked to mood instability were norepinephrine and serotonin. The neurotransmitter dopamine has also been linked to mood disorders. Subsequent research has found that increasing levels of serotonin cause elevation of mood, while extremely high levels of serotonin cause manic states. Low levels of serotonin have been linked to depression.

Psychological Therapy for Mood Disorders

Mood disorders—especially depression—usually respond to the use of certain kinds of psychotherapy. Interpersonal therapy and cognitive-behavioral therapy are the two types that seem to work best. Instead of focusing on probable causes of the depression, which may have originated in the patient's childhood, each of these therapies deals directly with how depression makes one think and act, and what needs to be done to bring about change. These are often short-term approaches designed to alleviate only the existing depressive episode, not to solve the deep, hidden secrets of the psyche.

Cognitive-behavioral therapy is based on the theory that patients suffering from depressive disorders see themselves, their family and friends, and their surroundings in a negative light. Negative thoughts usually breed negative emotions. More often than not, a depressed person's assessment of his or her situation is inaccurate. Cognitive therapies help depressive patients see the errors in their thinking and recognize the feelings and behavior that result from their distorted view.

Interpersonal therapy is based on the premise that people in the midst of a mood disorder are also having problems with the primary relationships in their lives. A depressed person's relationship with his or her spouse, children, parents, and friends will most likely be strained. It is considered immaterial whether these relationships became difficult because the patient developed a mood disorder, or whether the difficult relationship was the original cause of the depressive episode. The interpersonal therapist helps the patient discover the exact problem and its possible solutions within each troubling relationship.

Drugs versus Talking Therapies

Various independent studies have shown that psychotherapy can be an effective treatment in dealing with mood disorders. Does drug therapy or psychotherapy work best? Some studies have shown that psychotherapy performs better in the treatment of depression. For example, one National Institute of Mental Health study showed that cognitive and drug therapies had about the same success rate, but fewer patients treated with cognitive therapy relapsed. Other studies have suggested that for severely depressed people, cognitive and drug therapies are most effective when combined. Most clinicians agree that bipolar disorders are rarely responsive to a course of therapy that does not include drug treatment. Psychotherapy is therefore only adjunctive in treating bipolar conditions. The psychological makeup of each individual can also have a bearing on whether a particular patient will respond better to drugs or to talking therapy. For patients who are not particularly self-aware, or who cannot separate themselves from their feelings or actions, drugs are often more helpful.

The important point here is that different types of mood disorders can be helped by different kinds of therapy. If the first therapy tried doesn't work for you, don't give up altogether. Try again with a different therapy, a different therapist, or a different doctor.

Diagnosing Depression and Bipolar Disorders

Like fever, depression and other mood disorders are the final outcome of a range of causes. There are many ways you can contract a fever, such as through bacterial infections, dehydration, and excessive exposure to the sun. There are likewise many ways in which you can become clinically depressed.

It's useful to divide these mood disorder pathways into two main categories. The first category of causes contains those that are psychological in nature. Stress is the key factor in psychologically induced depression, particularly stress that results from some sort of trauma or loss. The second group of causes are those that arise from a biological source. These physical illnesses, hormonal malfunctions, and genetic factors are all capable of generating the symptoms of major depression by themselves or in tandem with a psychological cause. Mood disorders often arise from a combination of causes that are both biological and psychological in nature. Let's now look at the psychological causes of depression and how these factors can contribute to mood disorders.

Psychological Causes of Depression

About 25 percent of people with depressive disorders report that they are experiencing some sort of serious stress, while only 5 percent of the general population report a similar phenomenon. Studies also show that people who had a loved one die when they were young are at least twice as likely to suffer from major depression in their adulthood as those who have not experienced a similar grief. Although there seems to be a clear linkage of some sort between stress and mood disorders, these facts fail to provide real evidence that stress is the causal agent.

A study carried out jointly at the University of Oregon and the University of Pittsburgh concluded that stressful life events do tend to precede depression. Each group of researchers interviewed five hundred to eight hundred women at two different times, eight to twelve months apart. These women were questioned about major stresses relating to loss, and minor stresses such as job satisfaction and social support systems. The statements from women who did not report depression during the first interview, but who had clearly become depressed by the time of the second interview, were analyzed. Both groups of investigators concluded that the existence of stressful circumstances during the first interview greatly increased the odds that depression would occur by the time of the second interview (Lewinsohn 1981). This study clearly suggests a causal link between stress and depression.

One kind of stress that can be particularly debilitating is known as post-traumatic stress disorder. A stressful event may take place at a time when, as a matter of survival, the individual experiencing it must postpone the mental and emotional processing of the event. After the imminent danger has passed, the trauma of the event is free to rise to consciousness, although it does not necessarily do so immediately. The conscious or emotional memory may not become manifest for many years.

Post-traumatic stress disorder is often linked to wartime trauma, natural disasters (such as hurricanes or fires), childhood sexual abuse, and such violent crimes as rape. When emotions from past traumas surface, the feelings may seem to have no cause in the individual's present context, since they are temporally dissociated from the actual causal event.

Fifty percent of all people who suffer from post-traumatic stress disorder also suffer from depression. This type of depression is difficult to diagnose until the traumatic event, and the emotions that it elicits, are remembered and felt.

Biological Causes of Depression

Biological factors contribute to or cause a large percentage of the cases of mood disorder. Emotional stability is closely related to the normal formation and function of a number of vital chemicals that exist in the brain. These chemicals, the neurotransmitters, are an integral part of the system that transmits information from one central nervous system cell to another. When neural cells lose the ability to make the proper amount of a neurotransmitter, store it properly, or bind it efficiently, a chronic mood disorder may result.

Three physiological conditions affect neurotransmitter production and can inhibit chemical functioning. They are:

1. Specific diseases

2. Hormonal imbalances

3. Genetic factors

Specific diseases that affect neurotransmitter production. You seldom feel ill the precise moment when bacteria or a virus enter your body. It takes time for the bacteria to spread or for the virus to multiply until there are enough foreign bodies present to activate your immune system. As many illnesses progress, they can slowly, almost imperceptibly, change the chemistry of your body. The delicate balance of neural chemistry can be altered enough to generate a mood shift, even before physical symptoms are apparent.

It is easy to understand how diseases of the central nervous system can affect brain chemistry since these diseases are actually located in the brain itself. Alzheimer's disease is a common cause of severe mental impairment in older adults. Epilepsy has often been misdiagnosed as schizophrenia. Multiple sclerosis, a degenerative disease of the central nervous system, is thought to be caused by a virus or a defect in the immune system. All of these illnesses are associated with the common symptom of depression.

Many infectious diseases can generate psychiatric symptoms, including mononucleosis and infectious hepatitis. A wide array of mental symptoms, ranging from depression to psychosis, can accompany such illnesses.

Diseases of the immune system can also be the source of a wide array of psychiatric symptoms. Lupus, allergies, and AIDS are just three examples (all three can cause depression).

Various types of cancerous tumors can generate mood instability before the nature of the disease has been diagnosed. Nutritional deficiencies can alter brain chemistry. Chronic overgrowth of yeast, otherwise known as candida albicans, may result from eating too much sugar, taking antibiotics, or an imbalance of hormones. Yeast infections have been implicated in mania, depression, and malfunctions in the thyroid. This condition can be controlled by eating properly, particularly by restricting sugar in the diet.

Hormonal imbalances. Hormones are secreted into the bloodstream by structures throughout the body called endocrine glands. Hormones help keep the body in a state of balance by regulating metabolic processes such as growth, sexual development, reproduction, sexual activity, energy production, heart rate, and blood pressure. The entire endocrine system is intimately linked to the nervous system. For instance, norepinephrine, a neurotransmitter that is crucial to mood stability, doubles as a hormone secreted by the adrenal gland. The hypothalamus regulates the endocrine glands by using the same neurotransmitters that regulate moods.

The thyroid gland, which secretes two crucial hormones, is perhaps the most common biological cause of depression. It is estimated that 10 to 15 percent of depressed patients have some form of thyroid malfunction. The usual tests that are given to check thyroid function often yield a false negative, necessitating the use of a more exhaustive panel in all cases where mood instability is an issue. Hyperthyroidism, or an overactive thyroid, causes an overabundance of the hormones to be produced. Resulting symptoms can include nervousness, sweating, racing pulse, anxiety, and insomnia. Symptoms of mania sometimes result from this condition. Hypothyroidism, or an underactive thyroid, often results in tiredness, weight gain, mental sluggishness, dry and coarse hair, and an intolerance to cold. It can cause either depression or bipolar disorder. If a bipolar condition is produced by hypothyroidism, it is usually of a rapid cycling nature. Lithium, the usual treatment of choice for bipolar disorders, weakens the thyroid and slows down hormone production. If the underlying cause of a bipolar disorder is a low-functioning thyroid, lithium can actually worsen the mood disorder.

Diseases of the adrenal glands are not as common as those of the thyroid, but can produce symptoms that are psychiatric in nature. The entire endocrine system can be affected by malfunctions of the pituitary gland, and psychiatric symptoms are present in three-quarters of all cases. Since this gland is directly linked to the hypothalamus and the limbic system, anything that alters its function is likely to affect one's emotional state in some way.

Sex hormones, particularly the female hormones estrogen and progesterone, are often implicated in depression and bipolar illness. Severe depression is frequently recorded in women during times when their sex hormones are changing radically. Depressive symptoms are common among women who are premenstrual, pregnant, postpartum, or premenopausal. Few studies have actually pinned down the biological interrelation between mood and these hormones. However, it's known that two-thirds of women with significant premenstrual depression have a history of chronic depression, and that women with a history of premenstrual depression are prone to have a family history of chronic depression. Hormones clearly play a major role in depression, but a precise description of this role has yet to be made.

The pineal gland in the brain produces a hormone called melatonin. The function this hormone serves in humans is still a mystery. In animals, melatonin is related to the seasonality of conception and giving birth. Even though humans don't follow these reproductive rhythms—at least not at this stage in our evolution—our bodies still secrete melatonin at night. Bright light suppresses its production. People who become seasonally depressed—who feel down in the winter because there is less sunlight—may be reacting to their increase in melatonin production. Other researchers have suggested that serotonin levels are the real culprit in seasonal depression. Regardless of its cause, this condition, called seasonal affective disorder, is very common and easily treatable. Exposure to full-spectrum light, either natural or artificial, will decrease melatonin levels and raise your spirits. If you suffer from this condition and a three-month winter vacation to the equator is impossible, keep in mind that artificial light used for treatment needs to be five to ten times brighter than normal indoor lighting.

Genetic factors. The fact that depression and bipolar illness tend to run in families suggests that genetic inheritance for these disorders plays a role. The role is not absolute: not all children of depressed parents contract depression. However, various studies have concluded that the tendency for mood instability is passed from one generation to the next.

Twins have been a prime group of subjects studied in attempts to discern the nature of mood disorders. In these studies, when both twins express a genetic trait, they are said to be concordant for that trait. When only one individual exhibits the trait, the twins are said to be discordant for the trait. Studies investigating the occurrence of both unipolar and bipolar disorders in twins have determined that the concordance for unipolar disorders in identical twins, where genetic material is the same in each individual, is about 40 percent. When identical twins were surveyed for bipolar disorders, that number jumped to 70 percent. The concordance for both types of disorders in fraternal twins, who have dissimilar genetic material, is the same as that for normal siblings, about 0 to 13 percent. These studies show that mood instability is at least to some extent genetically based; the genetic predisposition for bipolar illness is almost twice that for depression alone (Kield and Weissman 1978).

It is not yet known whether all genes that affect mood are located on one chromosome or on several. Early research suggests that bipolar illness might be a sex-linked characteristic, and that the genes that govern it might be located on the X chromosome (one of the two chromosomes that define our gender). If bipolar illness is determined by a sex-linked gene, and if this type of mood disorder is a dominant trait, this could explain the reason why depression occurs more often in women than in men. Since women are genetically composed of two X chromosomes, they would have a greater chance of contracting a mood disorder; the genes for the condition could be carried on either of the two X chromosomes. It would be less likely for men, who genetically have one X and one Y chromosome, to contract the disease. However, the relationship of depression to sex-linkage has not been firmly established and at present is still a theory.

It needs to be mentioned that separating genetic factors from environmental ones is difficult at best. If depression is observed in individuals belonging to three consecutive generations, does this absolutely mean that the disorder is transferred genetically? Could a child become depressed because the depressed parent is not able to nurture the child adequately? What about conditions such as poverty and other high-stress factors? Could the same factors exist in each generation, thereby contributing to, or causing depression? And where does learned behavior fit in? Could a child learn, for example, poor nutritional habits and carry on the tradition of depression in this way?

No one knows the answers to these questions yet. The strongest evidence points to the source of depression and bipolar disorders being an admixture of inherited traits and environmental factors. Genetic makeup can lend a predisposition for these illnesses; but it may well be that they only come into existence when those so born are exposed to an environment which, for whatever reason, causes the condition to manifest itself.

The Mind-Body Connection

Chronic negative thoughts, guilt, early trauma, post-traumatic stress disorder, deprivation, emotional losses, and the feeling that your life has no meaning are all psychological states that affect brain chemistry and neurotransmitter effectiveness. Conversely, an imbalanced neurotransmitter system can exacerbate negative thinking, guilt, and reactions to trauma, and rob you of the energy you need to meet important challenges and goals.

Drug therapy and psychotherapy are both viable methods of initiating intervention for depressive disorders; each starts at the opposite end of the mind-body continuum. Drugs chemically alter brain cell function in an attempt to "fix" the biological apparatus. Psychotherapy targets thought and behavior in an attempt to initiate similar chemical changes.

There is a constant interaction between your biological and psychological self, between your mind and your body. Either type of treatment can be an effective way to restore emotional health (although, as mentioned before, bipolar illness is much more susceptible to drug therapy than to psychotherapy alone).

Specific Drug Therapies

Antidepressants

Antidepressants are a class of drugs that increase the amount of the neurotransmitters norepinephrine and seratonin. These neurotransmitters act to decrease a certain type of neural cell function called reuptake. In reuptake, a cell not only releases the neurotransmitter into the synapse, but also reabsorbs much of the chemical before it is able to link with a receptor on the postsynaptic cell. Antidepressants decrease the reuptake and increase the time that neurotransmitters are in the synapse, thereby increasing the stimulus across the synapse.

Tricyclics. There are two types of antidepressants. The first group is called tricyclics. These work by increasing the amount of either seratonin or norepinephrine in the synapse. Some tricyclics block the reuptake of norepinephrine, and others prevent the reuptake of seratonin. Still other tricyclics inhibit the reuptake of both neurotransmitters. Here is a list of tricyclics and the neurotransmitters affected by them. (Adapted form *Clinical Psychopharmacology Made Ridiculously Simple* by Preston and Johnson.)

Name	Norepinephrine	Serotonin
Imipramine	yes	yes
Desipramine	yes	no
Amitriptyline	slight	yes
Nortriptyline	yes	yes
Protriptyline	yes	slight
Trimipramine	slight	yes
Doxepin	slight	yes
Maprotiline	yes	no
Amoxapine	yes	slight

For most patients, the use of tricyclics improves the likelihood that depression will cease by about 50 percent. In those individuals who respond to tricyclics, every symptom caused by depression is relieved to some extent. Not only do patients regain the desire for food and the ability to sleep soundly, but mental outlook also turns around. Those who previously felt hopeless, guilty, and confused feel more clear and content after adhering to a regimen of tricyclic medication. They find that they are able to make decisions more readily, think more positively, and remember things more accurately than they could when they were depressed.

If you are taking tricyclics, remember that two to four weeks are needed before the symptoms of depression will start to lift. First, the physical symptoms will subside. Your normal appetite and sleeping habits will return. Eventually, your mood will begin to shift. Altogether, it could take up to eight weeks for depression to entirely subside. In most cases, treatment needs to continue for an additional six months or longer. Without further treatment, 50 percent of all depressive patients will relapse within a year. In 15 to 20 percent of patients with depression, the depression is chronic, and medication must always be taken to control it. Antidepressants are not addictive: they will not intoxicate, stimulate, or make you "high" in any way.

However, tricyclics aren't for everyone. One-third of all depressed patients don't respond to tricyclics at all. Still others find that some of the side effects are too onerous to make continuation of the drug desirable. And for those who suffer from bipolar disorder, tricyclics can have the effect of bringing on episodes of mania.

In addition to increasing the synaptic concentration of seratonin or norepinephrine in your brain, tricyclics also block certain acetylcholine synapses. This action is responsible for a group of so-called anticholinergic side effects. These include dry mouth, blurred vision, urinary retention, sexual dysfunction, and constipation. Most of these side effects are not life-threatening, but urinary retention and constipation can be serious.

Tricyclics can also cause various abnormalities to occur in the cardiovascular system. Rapid changes in blood pressure can cause stroke. The heart may display abnormal electrical activity and arrhythmias. Dizziness caused by low blood pressure in the brain (*orthostatic hypotension*) can occur. Sometimes the heart can lose its ability to pump blood, causing cardiac arrest.

Other side effects include fatigue or decreased energy, excessive sleeping, weight gain, tremor, and tinnitus (ringing in the ears); occasionally, seizures occur. Tricyclics that have sedating effects will reduce memory somewhat and inhibit psychomotor performance.

Obviously, no one should undertake drug therapy without careful consideration and the oversight of one or more competent physicians.

MAOIs. The second kind of antidepressant is called monoamine oxidase (MAO) inhibitors, or MAOIs for short. MAO is an enzyme that breaks down the neurotransmitters. If a cell malfunction results in an overabundant production of MAO, there will not be a sufficient amount of neurotransmitters in the synapses. By inhibiting production of the enzyme that breaks down neurotransmitters, MAOIs increase the amount of neurotransmitters retained in the synapse.

People who suffer from atypical depression often respond more readily to MAOIs than to other antidepressants. Atypical depression is a condition in which patients, instead of having difficulties with appetite and adequate sleep, find that they are oversleeping and overeating. They also feel extremely fatigued and are overly sensitive to rejection. People who don't respond to tricyclics will also sometimes be helped by the MAOIs. Others who cannot tolerate the side effects of tricyclics will more readily be able to deal with the side effects of MAOIs.

MAOIs cause many of the same anticholinergic side effects as tricyclics, but the MAOIs' side effects are much less severe. Side effects in sexual function also appear while taking MAOIs. However, the most serious side effect involves the MAOIs' effect on metabolism. Just as the enzyme MAO is used to break down certain neurotransmitters, it also breaks down certain compounds in food, specifically the amino acid tyramine. Since the patient taking these drugs cannot metabolize tyramine, if the amino acid is ingested, it will enter the circulatory system. Tyramine releases norepinephrine from the nerve cells that regulate blood pressure, and the result can be a sudden surge in blood pressure and possibly stroke. This amino acid is found in many foods, such as aged cheese, beer, wine, chocolate, and liver. Individuals taking MAOIs must strictly avoid these foods.

For the same reason, nose drops and cold remedies should not be taken with MAOIs. These drugs are chemically similar to the catecholamines that are normally metabolized by MAO. When MAOIs prevent the breakup of cold medications, the drugs' concentration in the blood rises and may dangerously increase blood pressure.

Other antidepressants. Since the discovery of tricyclics and MAOIs, many newer antidepressants have been synthesized. The most popular by far is fluoxetine, more commonly known as Prozac. As effective as tricyclics, Prozac seems to have an advantage in that it causes fewer and milder side effects. No anticholinergic or cardiac side effects appear at all. Mild bouts of nausea, headache, insomnia, and nervousness may be noticable. All of these symptoms, however, should decrease over time. It has also been suggested that Prozac may be more effective than tricyclics at preventing depressive relapses. For more on drugs, see the chapter on Psychiatric Drugs in part VI.

Drug Therapies for Bipolar Illness

Lithium is unparalleled in the treatment of bipolar disorders. Unlike tricyclics, MAOIs, and Prozac, lithium is not a complex molecule, but rather a simple metal ion in the form of a salt. Lithium works by inhibiting the production of *second messengers*, molecules that are produced when certain neurotransmitters bond with certain receptors. These molecules activate enzymes that affect the neurotransmitter-receptor bond, perhaps altering the amount of neurotransmitters, or altering the number of receptors that are sensitive to that neurotransmitter, or affecting the electrical charge that builds in the postsynaptic cell. The exact chemical process is not yet understood. It's thought that lithium prevents the manufacturing of a particular second messenger called PIP2, stopping the cell from responding to certain neurotransmitter signals.

The condition of mania is produced when certain neurotransmitter-receptor bonds send signals to various neurons, causing them to become overactive. Likewise, depression can be triggered by cells becoming overactive, but in response to signals sent by a different set of neurotransmitter-receptor couplings. If the second messenger is not produced, the cells' response to signals that elicit mania, and to signals that elicit depression, will decrease. Lithium turns down the response to any stimulus that depends on the presence of the PIP2 enzyme.

The most common side effects of lithium are weakness, tremor, fatigue, nausea, abdominal cramps, diarrhea, weight gain, lethargy, and increased thirst and urination. All of these side effects, with the exception of the tremor, will disappear within a month. No sedating effects occur with lithium.

The problem with lithium treatment is that there is a fine line between therapeutic and toxic levels of this drug. If the prescribed dose is too high, lithium poisoning can occur. Lithium poisoning affects the brain. Symptoms are slurred speech, drowsiness, loss of balance, tumors, vomiting, diarrhea, and, ultimately, coma and death.

In order to find the right dosage, frequent blood tests must be taken to check the lithium concentration in the bloodstream. During the first week of lithium therapy, lithium blood concentration rises rapidly. After the lithium blood concentration stabilizes, the number of tests can be reduced. However, it is important that these tests continue to be steadily administered, as lithium concentration can change when diet, healthiness, or activity levels alter.

Lithium is often ineffective for bipolar disorders that involve rapid cyclers—patients who experience four or more manic-depressive cycles per year. About 25 percent of manic patients don't respond to this treatment. For these patients, the anticonvulsant drugs tegretol and *volproic acid* sometimes prove effective. Our understanding of how these two drugs alleviate bipolar illness is still very limited.

The Way Out of Depression

I have developed a program that includes reading anything current on depression, forcing myself into self-help to slowly reverse the depressive cycle, using self-practiced cognitive therapy, and forcing myself to return slowly to life's surroundings and functions. I must use all of these techniques; they work together. I have spent many years developing these techniques and I know how important they all are: it's like being a world-class chef who would never leave any ingredient out of his best recipe.

Early Warning Signs

As you become more aware of the subtleties of your depression through research and by charting your moods, you will become familiar with your own early warning signs of depression. These may be quite subtle indeed: for instance, an early warning sign of depression for me is that I don't look both ways before I cross the street.

When you notice such signs, there are simple, noninvasive, safe, and inexpensive techniques you can use to slow or halt the downward spiral. By being aware of your early signs of depression and taking action early, you may be able to avoid plummeting to the depths of depression.

What are your early warning signs that you are on a downward spiral?

☐ withdrawal

☐ not wanting to do anything

☐ inactivity

☐ inability to function

☐ tire easily

☐ low energy level

☐ excessive sleep

☐ talk little

☐ slow speech

☐ insomnia

☐ premature awakening

☐ stay in bed for long periods

☐ poor appetite

☐ nausea

☐ irritability

☐ negative attitude

☐ poor ability to concentrate

☐ mind slows down

☐ confused

☐ low self-esteem

☐ cry easily

☐ lack of interest in everything

☐ despondent

☐ suicidal ideation

- ☐ self-destructive thoughts
- ☐ feel no one understands me
- ☐ inability to experience pleasure
- ☐ feel like giving up on life
- ☐ unable to do what I normally do
- ☐ boredom
- ☐ insecurity
- ☐ fear
- ☐ anxiety
- ☐ desire to be taken care of
- ☐ agitation
- ☐ ache all over
- ☐ sore shoulders and neck
- ☐ headache
- ☐ low back pain
- ☐ trembling
- ☐ low libido
- ☐ senses shut down
- ☐ extreme grief-type emotions
- ☐ paranoia
- ☐ overeating

- ☐ eat a lot of salty foods
- ☐ eat junk foods
- ☐ craving for carbohydrates
- ☐ inability to show affection
- ☐ easily frustrated
- ☐ void of emotions
- ☐ avoid people
- ☐ everything seems disorganized
- ☐ feel clumsy, drop things
- ☐ hair becomes wiry
- ☐ I start wearing a coat all the time
- ☐ my learning disabilities are more pronounced
- ☐ as my eyesight does not seem right, becoming sure I need new eyeglasses
- ☐ eczema
- ☐ swollen thyroid
- ☐ see white spots
- ☐ increased consumption of alcohol
- ☐ have trouble getting dressed
- ☐ skin problems
- ☐ feelings of regret for past decisions

Other early indications of depression you have noted:

_____

_____

Learn what your early warning signs of depression are. Take appropriate action when you notice these signs.

Strategies for Alleviating or Eliminating Depression

I studied 120 people with depression and manic depression. Below is a checklist of ways in which the study respondents alleviate their depression. These strategies are divided into five categories: activities, support, attitude, management, and spirituality. Which strategies have you used successfully? Which ones do you feel you should use more often? Which methods have you never used that you would like to try? Remember—what works for someone else may not be the right thing for you. Cleaning is such an example. For some people it is depressing and discouraging. Others are uplifted by it.

Activities	Have tried successfully	Should use more often	Would like to try
Exercise			
Sports (such as basketball, soccer, volleyball)			
Long walks			
Yoga			
Dancing			
Reading			
Listening to music			
Long, hot baths			
Making love			
Gardening			
Long drives			
Needlework			
Working with wood			
Working with clay, pottery			
Drawing, painting			
Journal writing			
Writing poetry			
Writing letters			
Canoeing			
Horseback riding			
Shopping			
Relaxing in a meditative natural setting			
Day trips			
Playing a musical instrument			
Spending time with young children			
Cleaning			
Watching a funny movie			
Watching TV			
Watching videos, a movie, or a play			
Buying something I've been wanting			
Helping others			

What other activities have you used successfully to help alleviate your depression?

_____

_____

_____

_____

_____

Support	Have tried successfully	Should use more often	Would like to try
Talking it out with an understanding person			
Getting emotional support from a person I trust			
Talking to a therapist or counselor			
Peer counseling			
Talking to people who validate my feelings			
Spending time with good friends			
Talking to staff at a crisis clinic or hotline			
Arranging not to be alone			
Reaching out to someone			
Being held by someone I love			
Going to a support group			
Spending time with and taking respoinsibility for a pet			

What other kinds of support have been helpful to you in alleviating your depression?

_____

_____

_____

_____

_____

_____

Attitude	Have tried successfully	Should use more often	Would like to try
Changing negative thought patterns to positive ones			
Waiting it out			
Staying active			
Remembering that depression ends			
Recalling good times			
Being good to myself			
Diverting my attention			
Being gentle with myself			
Refusing to feel guilty			
Focusing on living one day at a time			
Endorsing and affirming my efforts			
Laughter			

What other attitudes have you developed and used to help you alleviate your depression?

_____

_____

_____

_____

_____

Activities	Have tried successfully	Should use more often	Would like to try
Medication			
Full-spectrum light			
Spending time outside			
Keeping busy			
Eating a diet high in complex carbohydrates			
Eliminating foods that worsen my depression			
Resting			
Forcing myself to get up in the morning			

	Have tried successfully	Should use more often	Would like to try
Forcing myself to go to work			
Doing whatever I need to do to meet my needs			
Maintaining a balance of rest and good times			

Study participants wrote:

"If my depression gets to be too much to handle, I should have the right to use hospitalization without feeling guilty. I like to try and use the most conservative treatment possible."

"I use activity and exercise together. Using the body fully stimulates the brain."

What management strategies have you found for alleviating your depression?

_____

_____

_____

_____

_____

Spirituality	Have tried successfully	Should use more often	Would like to try
Praying			
Getting in touch with my spirituality			
Meditating			
Keeping up with a 12-step program			

What other spiritual practices help to alleviate your depression?

_____

_____

_____

Use Scheduling and Planning to Help Alleviate Depression

A person who is experiencing depression may spend a whole day or many days literally doing nothing. This inactivity and lack of accomplishment can deepen your depression and lower your self-esteem. If you accomplish anything, you may belittle it as "insignificant."

People with whom I talk and work find that the following strategies can help break this cycle and help the depressed person feel better.

- make and stick to simple plans

- break tasks down into smaller componants

- learn to give yourself credit for whatever you accomplished

The success of this approach is corroborated by Dr. David Burns in *Feeling Good* and by Dr. Aaron Beck in *The Cognitive Therapy of Depression*.

Make and Stick to Simple Plans

In everyone's life, there are some things you have to do—such as washing the dishes or vacuuming; and other things you really enjoy—such as going for a walk or listening to good music. When planning the day's schedule, it is important to include some things you "have to do" (so you come out with a sense of accomplishment) and some things you "enjoy doing" (to increase your good feelings about being alive). Referring to the lists on the previous pages, make a list of things you must do on a daily basis and things that you really enjoy doing. These lists will be different for everyone. Before you start your list, take a look at these examples:

Things I have to do *Examples:*	**Things I enjoy doing** *Examples:*
wash the dishes	take a hot shower
vacuum	pet the dog
mow the lawn	pick some flowers
go to work	paint
make my bed	chat with a friend
balance my checkbook	play with a baby
shovel snow	go to a movie
organize my closet	watch TV

What do I have to do?   **What do I enjoy doing?**

_____   _____

_____   _____

_____   _____

_____   _____

Keep these lists in a handy place so you can refer to them when you need to. Build activities from each list into your daily plan. Avoid spending the whole day doing things that "must be done," as that is a recipe for failure.

As you develop your daily plan, assess your expectations of that activity by rating it on a scale of 0 to 5, with 0 being that you expect you could do it or could enjoy it, 3 being that you think you could do the activity and/or would enjoy the activity, and 5 being that you expect to be able to do the activity very well or that you would enjoy it immensely. For instance, if the activity is something you have to do, such as washing the dishes, and you think you will be able to do it, you could rate the activity H (for "have to do") 3, meaning that you expect to be able to do the task. If the activity were something you usually enjoy, such as going to a movie, but you don't think you'll be able to enjoy it now, you could rate it E (for "enjoy") 1, meaning that you don't think you'll have a good time. When you complete the activity, rate how well you did it or how much you actually enjoyed yourself. You will discover that your expectations and what actually happens can be very different!

Example of a Schedule for a Person Who Is Depressed but Able to Work

(Note that even on a workday, activities for enjoyment are included.)

Time	Planned Activity and Expectations	Actual Activity	How It Felt
7–8 a.m	Get up; shower; make and eat hot cereal **H1**	Got up; took a shower; had tea and toast	Better than if I had stayed in bed **H3**
8–9 a.m.	Walk to work, picking up the mail on the way **H3**	(As planned)	Exercise lifts my spirits **H4**
9–10 a.m.	Open and sort mail; return two phone calls **H1**	Opened and sorted mail; made one phone call	At least it feels better to be doing something **H3**
10–11 a.m.	Attend office meeting **H0**	(As planned)	Hard for me to be with a group, but I did it **H2**
11–12 Noon	Write press release **H1**	(As planned)	Glad I got it done **H3**
12–1 p.m.	Have lunch with Jane in the park; take a 15-minute walk with her **E1**	Ate lunch with Jane at park	It felt good to share how I have been feeling **E4**
1–2 p.m.	Watch a management video **H1**	(As planned)	OK, but I fell asleep for part of the time
2–3 p.m.	Interview a candidate for a data entry position **H1**	(As planned)	Hard, but I did it **H3**

Time	Planned Activity and Expectations	Actual Activity	How It Felt
3–4 p.m.	Enter data in computer *H2*	(As planned)	Felt slow *H4*
4–5 p.m.	Walk home from work; stop at store for milk *H3*	Walked home, but did not stop at store	Tired *H3*
5–6 p.m.	Relax, meditate *E2*	(As planned)	Helped me feel better *H4*
6–7 p.m.	Cook frozen pizza and eat *H2*	Had a peanut butter sandwich instead	Wish I had cooked the pizza *H0*
7–8 p.m.	Do the dishes; straighten up the house *H0*	Did the dishes	Fine; the housework can wait *H3*
8–9 p.m.	Watch *Nature* on PBS *E2*	(As planned)	OK *E4*
9–10 p.m.	Call a member of my support team for a talk; read a light novel, go to bed *E2*	Talked to Claire for 15 minutes; read and went to bed	OK *E4*

Review these charts after you have completed them. When people are depressed, they often feel quite negative prior to undertaking an activity. Upon completion of the activity, you may realize that you actually had a better time, or did a better job, than anticipated. Being tuned in to this can encourage you to have more realistically optimistic expectations.

Make copies of this form to plan daily schedules for yourself when you are depressed

Excerpted and adapted with permission from *The Depression Workbook: A Guide for Living with Depression and Manic Depression* by Mary Ellen Copeland, M.S. For more information on this and related books, see the "Further Reading" section in the back of the book.

Time	Planned Activity and Expectations	Actual Activity	How It Felt
7–8 a.m			
8–9 a.m.			
9–10 a.m.			
10–11 a.m			
11–12 Noon			
12–1 p.m.			
1–2 p.m.			
2–3 p.m.			
3–4 p.m.			
4–5 p.m.			
5–6 p.m.			
6–7 p.m.			
7–8 p.m.			
8–9 p.m.			
9–10 p.m.			

CHAPTER 42

Suicide Prevention

Are you feeling suicidal? Does killing yourself sometimes seem like the only way out? If so, there are three things you need to do:

1. *Get rid of the stigma.* Nothing interferes with therapeutic progress quite like shame. This isn't surprising. If a tennis player believes that it's shameful to need lessons, he'll have a tough time improving his game. Women who are ashamed to see a gynecologist and men who are ashamed to get a prostate exam place themselves at greater risk for undetected cancer. And if you're ashamed of your suicidal thoughts and behaviors, then you aren't very likely to address them through self-help or therapy. Because of this, you could risk losing the opportunity, literally, to save your own life.

Practice thinking of the term *suicidal* in a nonjudgmental way, just as you might think of your friend as being a procrastinator or a couch potato. These are human imperfections that carry with them distinct disadvantages, but they certainly are no cause for condemnation. And these problems all are definitely solvable. This brings us to our second suggestion.

2. *Adopt a problem-solving point of view.* Convince yourself that being suicidal is no more nor less than an attempt (however disadvantageous) to solve a problem—a desperate attempt, when no other viable options are apparent. (Think about it: It makes no sense to believe that an otherwise sane, intelligent person would contemplate self-harm when effective, less painful approaches to problems were apparent.) Whether the predicament is physical pain or the emotional pain of loneliness and loss, painful problems cry out for relief. Is a person to be condemned simply because he or she is having trouble finding a less desperate solution than self-harm?

Also, consider that, unlike shame, the problem-solving view points directly to a solution: The solution to maladaptive problem solving is, quite simply, improved problem solving. At this point, you might be thinking, "Easy for you to say. My problems don't have solutions. If they did, I wouldn't be suicidal!" This leads us to a third suggestion.

3. *Keep an open mind.* Perhaps it's not that your problems have no solutions, but just that the solutions are not apparent to you. This is not to suggest that you are missing easy, obvious solu-

tions. If the solutions were easy, you'd have discovered them long ago. Consider the possibility that even intelligent, responsible people occasionally benefit from outside input. Successful businesspeople, major corporations, governmental agencies, and star athletes all use consultants to great advantage. Far from being ashamed, you have every reason to take pride in your openness and willingness to grow by listening and learning.

Suicide Risk Factors

Although suicidal risk is often clear-cut (for example, you may be fully aware of the seriousness of your wish to die, or your loved one may have made a life-endangering attempt), there also exists a gray area. How can you distinguish between what are simply passing thoughts in a moment of pain or an angry but superficial outburst versus suicidal thoughts and behaviors that are cause for major concern? These risk factors have been shown to be associated with suicide:

Psychological disorder. Depression, substance abuse, and schizophrenia are the illnesses most often associated with suicide risk, but any psychological disorder raises suicide risk to some extent. Niney-five percent of people who kill themselves suffer from some psychological disorder. Both depression and schizophrenia have eventual suicide rates as high as 15 percent.

History of suicide attempts. One of the best-known principles in behavioral science is that future behavior tends to be consistent with past behavior. In the area of suicide, studies have shown that the best predictor of death by suicide is a history of previous suicide attempts.

Hopelessness. Research has demonstrated that hopelessness is a critical connecting link between depression and suicide. If you or your loved one experiences difficulty imagining when and how things will get better, this is a sure sign that professional help is needed.

Family history of suicide. Studies have shown that suicide often runs in families. Whether this is due to a genetically transmitted biological vulnerability, behavioral modeling effects, or some combination of factors is not known, but thoughts or talk of suicide in a person with a family history of suicide should be taken very seriously.

A specific plan. If suicidal thinking has proceeded from vague abstraction to a specific plan, immediate attention is required. The more specific the plan, the greater the risk. Someone who has considered a method of committing suicide, and even thought of a time and a place to do it, is at much greater risk than someone who has not considered a specific plan.

Making preparations. When suicidal thinking proceeds from a plan to actual preparations, suicide risk increases significantly. Preparations may take the form of composing a suicide note, putting things in order (such as writing a will or taking out life insurance), storing up pills, obtaining a weapon, or mending fences with relatives. Suicidal teenagers sometimes give away prized possessions as a way of preparing for death.

Severe symptoms of depression and anxiety. These include hopelessness, agitation, sleep problems, loss of appetite, chronic anxiety and worry, panic attacks, loss of interest, abuse of alcohol or other substances, and severe self-criticism. These symptoms almost always respond well to psychological or pharmacological intervention. However, when left unchecked, sufferers sometimes conclude that they can no longer stand the burden life has placed on them.

Isolation and withdrawal. Hopelessness and despair tend to grow stronger in the absence of support from caring others. Isolation and withdrawal increase suicide risk because cutting off ties with other people magnifies feelings of aloneness and precludes many problems from being solved.

Perception of insufficient reasons for living. Dr. Marsha Linehan (1993) has shown that suicidal people have considerable trouble listing reasons for staying alive. This is probably not because the reasons weren't there, but because emotional distress had made it difficult for them to see or remember those reasons. People in comparison groups, on the other hand, waxed eloquent, listing everything from family ties, career goals, and spiritual beliefs to ice cream and flowers in the spring. Lack of perceived reasons for living is exactly what common sense tells us it is, a symptom of depression and a sign of suicide risk.

Presence of a firearm in the home. Dr. David Brendt and his colleagues at the University of Pittsburgh showed in a study of suicide attempts that a potent predictor of which teenagers died from their suicide attempt was the presence of a firearm in the home. In addition to viewing this as a risk factor, *you must remove all firearms from your home if any family member shows signs of suicidality*. This is not optional! Safe firearm practices, such as locking guns away, have not been shown to be helpful; however, solid research does show that lack of availability in the community effectively reduces the suicide toll.

If you or a loved one are free from these risk factors, then passing thoughts of suicide are probably no cause for alarm. On the other hand, you should seek help immediately if you or a loved one is experiencing suicidal thoughts in combination with risk factors on this list. Trying to rationalize or explain away suicidal thoughts or impulses in the presence of known suicide risk factors is dangerous and unwise.

Prevalence of Suicide

As you reconsider thoughts and feelings about your suicidality, you might wonder whether you have any company. Suicidal individuals often struggle with feeling alone and lonely, different and defective. When they take part in group therapy, they often express amazement that others have had similar thoughts and feelings.

Suicidality in its various forms is surprisingly common. Consider these facts:

- Suicide is the ninth leading cause of death in the United States, accounting for 14 out of every 1000 deaths (1.4 percent).

- More than 30,000 people kill themselves in the United States every year; this is greater than the annual number of homicides.

- More than half of people who commit suicide have never received mental health services.

- Suicide is the number three killer of young adults, ages 15 to 24, third only behind accidents and homicide.

- About 17 percent of people suffer from clinical depression at some time in their lifetimes. If untreated, as many as one-sixth of these individuals eventually kill themselves.

These figures don't include people thinking about suicide, threatening suicide, or engaging in nonfatal suicidal behaviors. Knowledge of nonfatal suicidal events is less complete because they are much less public than suicide fatalities. However, surveys have asked people whether they ever attempted or seriously considered suicide. Results show that up to 16 percent of the population have thought about ending their own lives, and up to 4 percent have made actual attempts.

We do not present these statistics to frighten you or to present gloom and doom, but merely to emphasize this: *Suicidality is not a rare, bizarre phenomenon, and you are not a freak.* Having suicidal thoughts and feelings, while certainly undesirable, is not uncommon. So if you find yourself feeling ashamed and thinking thoughts such as "I'm all alone," "This is too terrible to talk about," or "No one would understand this," think again. Remembering the prevalence of suicidality is one way to give yourself the compassion and understanding you need so you can do something about your suicidal feelings.

"Rational" Suicide

People often ask us about rational suicide. The question usually goes something like this: "Don't you think that some peoples lives are so terribly miserable—either from agonizing, terminal illness, or desperate life circumstances—that suicide truly is the best solution? And aren't we rather presumptuous to suggest that someone else should go on living, when we haven't taken a walk in their shoes?"

The question of rational suicide is a legitimate one. Our world is changing rapidly and becoming more complex. One example of change is that people are living longer now than ever before. While this usually is seen as a blessing, there is a dark side: The older a person grows, the more losses he or she suffers in the form of deaths of friends and loved ones, loss of status in a youth-oriented culture, and loss of function due to declining health.

Our new age presents other double-edged swords. For example, medical science understands disease processes, such as Alzheimer's disease and AIDS, better than ever before. By the same token, patients with such illnesses are also better informed and are well aware that their medical future is bleak. They know that, in all probability, they can expect a difficult decline and eventual death from their illness.

All around us, we see society trying to respond to these maddeningly complex issues. We see movies like *Whose Life Is It Anyway?*, in which Richard Dreyfuss plays the part of a formerly healthy, vital man paralyzed from the neck down from an auto accident, who pleads with his caretakers to let him die. We witness the growth of a significant "Right to Die" movement, led by groups such as the Hemlock Society, which makes available information on how to end one's life. Medical societies debate "physician-assisted suicide" at meetings and in journals to address cases in which terminally ill patients can be helped to die rather than live a few more days or weeks in severe, intractable pain. At the other extreme, we follow the exploits of Jack Kevorkian, the retired pathologist carrying on a one-man crusade by granting desperate people's requests that he help them commit suicide.

What are we to make of all of this? After acknowledging that these are genuinely complex issues, let us remember the words of H. L. Mencken, who said, "For every complex problem there is a simple solution . . . which is wrong." Consider some facts that, while well established, are often lost in the din of this controversy:

- Rigorous studies have shown that, whereas some (though not most) people who committed suicide were terminally ill, almost all (at least 95 percent) were suffering from a treatable psychiatric disorder. Unfortunately, most of these people did not receive treatment for their disorder.

- Studies also show that suicidal individuals, terminally ill or not, are almost invariably clinically depressed. Because depression interferes significantly with rational thinking, the concept of "rational" suicide loses meaning.

- Depression can be treated successfully in the vast majority of cases; and when the depression is treated, suicidal wishes fade away along with other depressive symptoms.

In other words, even though the case for rational suicide can theoretically be made in rare cases, in the overwhelming majority of cases the problem is not the illness or life circumstances, but the depressive disorder itself. *As long as you are depressed or otherwise emotionally distressed, it is virtually certain that your suicidal thoughts stem from distorted, unrealistically negative thinking. Until and unless this is remedied, "rational" suicide is a virtual impossibility.*

The decision to die is too important to be made by any one person, especially one in the grips of dire circumstances. In cases when suicide (or euthanasia) *might* be an appropriate option, the decision must be made in close consultation with the individual's family and care providers. A team of responsible health care professionals must be involved to assess for depression and ensure that any psychiatric disorder receives appropriate attention. When depression is found and treated, the vast majority of patients feel better and express relief that they did not act on what seemed, at the time, to be rational suicidal ideas.

Are You a "Suicidal Person"?

Do you find yourself wondering whether the word suicidal really applies to you or your loved one? Perhaps you wonder whether you even need to be reading this. If you feel at all confused, you're not alone—in fact, you're in pretty good company. Even world-renowned experts have trouble agreeing on what is meant by the terms suicide and suicidal.

Although some of our patients are very clear about their suicidality, others show considerable confusion. Some say (or worry) that they are suicidal when actually they are not, while some people who are clearly suicidal deny it. It is not necessary to get into the technicalities of suicidology to do your own assessment (although it is essential that a mental health professional be consulted anytime suicidality is suspected).

Am I Serious about Suicide or Not? (Answer: Neither and Both)

Part of the confusion in identifying suicidality arises from black-and-white thinking. This is the false belief that you must be either one or the other: smart or stupid, attractive or ugly, good or bad, suicidal or nonsuicidal. The truth of the matter is that human beings almost always either fall between two extremes (such as "moderately good looking" or "fairly smart") or show some mixture (such as "good and bad").

This also applies to people with self-destructive thoughts. Almost without exception, suicidal people either say or show that they have mixed feelings about living or dying. For example, the individual who insists that he only wants to die often shows in various ways that part of him still wants to live. This may be reflected in certain aspects of a suicide attempt—perhaps the attempt was timed, with or without awareness, to coincide with the arrival of someone who would rescue him. The mere act of communicating suicidal thoughts to someone else suggests that some part of this person wants help so that he can go on living.

The reverse is usually true for the individual who insists that he or she has no desire to die, despite having engaged in dangerous self-harming behavior. We have seen such individuals—from those who have engaged in behaviors as "harmless" as threatening suicide or writing suicide notes to those who have seriously injured themselves or taken potentially lethal overdoses and were rescued only by accident—insist in earnest that they were definitely not suicidal and would never engage in such behavior again.

These individuals typically are not being dishonest. They sincerely believe what they are saying. They simply show by their behavior that they have ambivalence—the human capacity to feel two apparently contradictory feelings at the same time. For example, we may simultaneously feel happy for a close friend who has taken a job in a distant city, but also sad or angry that she is leaving. In a similar way, suicidal people almost always have a mixture of a wish to die and a wish to go on living. We have seen people near death from a suicide attempt still gamely cooperating with helpers; and we have seen people who claim to have a great desire to live resist mightily when we ask them to flush their stockpiled pills or remove a gun from the house.

Exercise: Exploring Your Two Sides

Use the following form to explore your own ambivalence. In a column labeled "The Hopeful Side," begin listing all of the arguments against committing suicide (such as "My family needs me," "It's against my religious beliefs," or "Brighter days might lie ahead"). In the column labeled "The Dark Side," list all of the arguments you can think of in favor of committing suicide (in other words, all the reasons why life might not be worth living). There are no right or wrong answers; this portion of the exercise is strictly for getting in touch with where you are.

The second portion of the exercise will help you further expand your awareness. If The Dark Side is the longer or more compelling of your two lists, go back and work on The Hopeful Side. Search for your ambivalence. Think of better times; imagine you're an outside observer, looking at your life objectively. Do whatever you have to do, but add to that list! The goal here is to begin connecting with the life-affirming part of you that you may have lost touch with.

If The Hopeful Side is your longer list, we suggest that you first congratulate yourself, but then search for your ambivalence as well. Although having a long life-affirming list puts you a step ahead, we assume that you're reading this for a reason. So take yourself in your imagination to past (or predicted future) dark periods and write any reasons you find there why life may not be worth living after all. We are not asking you to make things up—only to get in touch with what's already there (or may be there in the future). The purpose here is not to change anything yet, but to dig for what's there as a way of mapping out what you will need to focus on.

Knowing about ambivalence can help you in many ways. Knowing that a subtle but significant wish to die is lurking behind your current positive outlook can help you to make that outlook more solid (for example, if you were to find that part of you believes that being dead would solve all of your problems, this exercise would give you the opportunity to remind yourself that being dead prevents you from enjoying your problem-free state). On the other hand, recognizing a persistent glimmer of a stubborn wish to live, even in the face of severe suicidal thinking, can give you a place to start rebuilding your passion for life.

Two Types of Suicidal People

Perhaps this explanation of ambivalence has helped clarify suicidal states, but one additional source of confusion remains. You may have found yourself thinking, "I know what a suicidal person is like and I don't (or my loved one doesn't) fit that mold."

This brings us to another vital piece of information about suicidality: Suicidal people come in many different forms. If you think that all suicidal people are crazy, or smart or stupid, or old or young, or divorced, or alcoholic, or any combination of these, then think again. In fact, it's not even true that all suicidal people are depressed.

Although researchers and therapists sometimes talk about suicidality as if all suicidal persons are alike, experienced clinicians know better. Just as the term cancer can mean totally different things for different patients, so too does suicidality vary greatly from one individual to another. Unfortunately, modern science has not yet brought us to a place where we can say, "You are a Type XYZ suicidal person, and here's the treatment program for you." However, we can say from clinical experience that suicidal people seem to fall generally into two categories.

The first category is the Depressed/Hopeless type—the group most often referred to in literature about suicide and probably most often thought of when one hears the word suicide. This group is exemplified by Randy. He had suffered from depression for many years and reached the point where he was unable to derive pleasure from life. He suffered from sleep problems and loss of appetite and lost interest in things that were important to him. Even more important, he

Exploring Your Two Sides

The Hopeful Side	The Dark Side
1.	1.
2.	2.
3.	3.
4.	4.
5.	5.
6.	6.
7.	7.
8.	8.
9.	9.

became hopeless—he was convinced that his misery was permanent and that nothing he nor anyone else could do would change this. His thoughts of suicide were motivated by a wish to end his suffering in the only way he thought was left: self-annihilation.

The other category, the Communication/Control type, looks similar on the surface to the Depressed/Hopeless type, but is quite different when we look beneath the surface. True, people in this group express wishes to die and sometimes act on these wishes by harming themselves, but several characteristics set them apart. Jennifer, for example, was brought to an emergency room by her mother and stepfather. In the midst of a loud argument about her choice of friends, she had swallowed several different medications that she found in the medicine cabinet. At age 16, she had endured many years of family conflict and had in fact been physically abused by her biological father prior to her parents' divorce two years earlier. Things seemed better after her mother remarried, but they deteriorated after her mother gave birth to another child one year later. In a therapy session following her suicide attempt, Jennifer said that she had not wanted to die, but that she had tried everything else to make things better at home and failed, and taking the pills was the only way she knew to communicate her desperation.

The following table lists other ways that these two groups of suicidal individuals differ. If you wish, you can use it as a checklist to assess which set of characteristics seems to fit you or your loved one better. Some items from both lists might ring true to you, but you probably will find that one list seems more characteristic than the other. Remember that neither of these groups is better or worse, or more or less deserving of care and concern than the other. Research shows that both groups are at a significantly elevated risk for eventually killing themselves. The reason for making the distinction is to help you see how you fit into the big picture we refer to as "suicidal." It also can help therapists and clients in planning what therapy strategy might be most beneficial for a specific individual.

Two Types of Suicidal People

Depressed/Hopeless	Communication/Control
Typical individual is male and middle aged or elderly	Typical individual is female and young
Suicidal episodes often triggered by loss	Suicidal episodes often triggered by conflict
Primary emotional state is despair	Primary emotional state is desperation
Main motivation behind suicidal behavior is to end life	Main motivation behind suicidal behavior is to communicate pain, in hopes of making life better
Attempts are typically secretive and planned well in advance	Attempts are often communicated and may be highly impulsive
Attempts tend to be violent and highly lethal (often guns or hanging)	Attempts tend to be less lethal (usually drug overdoses or cutting)
Typically regrets surviving a suicide attempt	Typically relieved to have survived a suicide attempt
Main focus of therapy is restoration of hope and reduction of negative thinking errors	Main focus of therapy is reduction of conflict and enhancement of problem solving

You're Probably Not Suicidal If . . .

In case it's beginning to seem as if everyone on the planet is suicidal, let's consider some groups of people who may worry about being suicidal (or whose loved ones worry they may be), but who probably are not. One such group is persons with **panic disorder**. This is an anxiety disorder characterized by sudden, unpredictable bursts of severe anxiety that produce physical arousal (pounding heart, breathlessness, etc.) and extreme fear of dying or going crazy. In addition to their other concerns, these patients worry that they might go out of control and kill themselves. This fear is sometimes fueled by occasional passing thoughts that they would rather be dead than suffer through another panic attack. Some research evidence does suggest that people with panic disorder attempt suicide at a higher rate than the general population, but this is still a controversial issue.

Several points are worth noting here. First, although people with panic disorder fear that they will lose control, they almost always report that this has never actually happened, even after dozens of high-intensity panic attacks. Moreover, when asked, these patients say that, far from wanting to be dead, they are fearful that they *might* kill themselves. Also, studies about these people when examined closely, reveal that the researchers did not take into account some reasons other than the panic disorder for the patients' greater tendency toward nonfatal suicide attempts. Judging from later published reports showing that people with panic disorder had a suicide rate no greater than the general population, it appears that suicidal behavior is driven by something other than panic disorder.

A caveat: One line of research that has implicated panic disorder as a risk factor for suicide looks at the relatively common combination of panic disorder and depression. As bad as depression is, it doesn't take much imagination to realize how much more miserable a person would be if suffering from both depression and panic attacks (or any other form of severe anxiety). If this describes you, we encourage you to seek help immediately. Anxiety, as well as depression, responds very well to therapy, medication, or a combination of the two. See also the chapter on Panic Attacks earlier in part V.

Another group of people who are sometimes unnecessarily concerned about suicide is people with **obsessive-compulsive disorder (OCD)**. People with this anxiety disorder feel compelled to perform certain nonsensical behaviors (such as washing their hands dozens of times a day or repeatedly checking to make sure the oven is turned off); or they think certain thoughts (such as extreme worry that they might hurt their child, though they have no history of violence). If you have OCD and are not depressed, your worries about committing suicide may merely be a manifestation of your anxiety disorder and not true suicidality. This will likely be a difficult determination for you to make alone, and we recommend a consultation with a mental health professional to sort it out. This anxiety disorder, too, is highly treatable. See also the chapter on Obsessions and Compulsions earlier in part V.

We are often asked about people with **unhealthy lifestyles**. Certainly, we all wonder what is going through the minds of loved ones who continue to smoke cigarettes after a heart attack, kids who ride motorcycles recklessly and without helmets, and alcoholics who drive drunk. Indeed, some suicide theorists have proposed *subintentioned* suicide to explain such self-destructive behaviors in people who may not be depressed and who deny that they wish to die.

The problem with this line of reasoning, and the reason we reject it, is that following it to its logical extreme makes the entire concept of suicide practically meaningless; for if a person who smokes cigarettes is suicidal, what about the person who eats too many fatty foods? Those who don't get enough exercise? People who live in cities with air pollution and high crime rates? As you can see, before long we end up believing that practically everyone in the population, in one way or another, is suicidal.

Some people make unwise and unhealthy choices in the way they live their lives; and while therapy might be helpful to them, suicidality is probably not the most useful explanation for their behavior. We maintain that a person is suicidal only if he or she expresses, through words or behavior, extreme emotional pain and an inclination to relieve that pain through self-inflicted harm or death.

Finally, let us consider the issue of brief, **passing thoughts of suicide**. Some patients we have talked to have expressed great concern about the meaning of occasional thoughts such as, "Maybe I'd be better off dead" or "They'd be sorry if I weren't here." Family members sometimes feel grave concern when they hear mention of death, perhaps by a teenage child or elderly family member.

First, you should know that such thoughts are extremely common: Some studies have indicated that half of the population has had such thoughts at one time or another. What's important is to remember that a thought does not equal an act, whether we are talking about suicide, hostile and violent thoughts about an obnoxious coworker, or sexual feelings toward a married neighbor. Suicidal thoughts become important only when they persist, contemplation sets in, or other suicide warning signs are present. If this is the case, immediate action is warranted; if not, concern is probably not necessary.

Assessment by a Mental Health Professional

Although we have shown in this chapter how you can assess signs and symptoms of suicide risk in yourself or a loved one, a valid suicide assessment, like any examination with life-and-death implications, should be done by a professional trained in what to look for and what interventions to pursue. Although most mental health professionals (psychologists, psychiatrists, social workers, and counselors) are competent to conduct a suicide risk assessment, we must tell you that, as among doctors, lawyers, stockbrokers, and other professionals, competence levels vary. Often, nonpsychiatric physicians, ministers, and lay counselors are unprepared to explore for suicidality or to ask the detailed questions necessary for a thorough assessment.

Therefore, we encourage you to exercise intelligent self-interest. If you visit a counselor, doctor, clergyperson, or any other helper to talk about your problems, and he or she fails to inquire about suicide, *bring it up yourself*. There is no law that says you must wait to be asked or cannot volunteer information. If you feel that suicidality is brushed over too lightly, seek out someone who gives the matter its due. Remember, your life or that of your loved one might be at stake.

Guide for Concerned Family Members and Friends

The topic of suicide remains a rather taboo subject in our society and time. As a result, many people who are considering suicide are loath to discuss their feelings with the people in their lives who might otherwise be most concerned and anxious to know. Similarly, many people who become aware or who suspect that a friend or loved one is thinking about taking his or her own life are hesitant to express their suspicions or fears to the suicidal person. Conversely, some suicidal individuals talk at great length and with great frequency about their self-harming ideas and intentions, leading others to be anything from alarmed to constantly on guard, exasperated, or exhaustedly detached.

The upshot of these examples is that communication between suicidal persons and their friends and relatives often is deficient or problematic. At the very time when accurate, direct, facilitative communication is most needed between the deeply depressed person and others in his or her life, such communication typically is lacking. This is not to imply that it's the "fault" of one party or the other. Rather, it is to point out that an important resource—communication—needs to be attended to, worked on, and encouraged in order to maximize the chances that the suicidal person can be helped in time.

What Warning Signs Should I Look For?

People who experience suicidal feelings come from all walks of life, in all shapes and sizes, and have all manner of personality characteristics. Therefore, we cannot present you with a standard profile of someone who is suicidal. It can happen to anyone. However, there are some behavioral signs that are more common than others in identifying someone who may be suicidal. Additionally, there are some life situations that are more apt than others to trigger depression and suicidality in some people.

Review the "Risk Factors" covered above. In addition, here are other signs and situations to look for:

The person talks about suicide. The talk may seem to be in jest at first, but it persists. The person talks about "not being around anymore," or reflects on the time "when I'm gone," or comes right out and says, "I don't think I can go on anymore." When you hear this kind of talk, take the hint and ask (in as sympathetic and unintimidated a tone as you can muster) whether the person is thinking of committing suicide. Then be willing to sit down and engage in more lengthy dialogue, in a caring way. At worst, you may feel embarrassed when the person says that he or she is not talking about suicide and that you shouldn't worry. At best, you will start a process that might help save a life. More likely, you will simply show that you care, and this will be of help in and of itself, even if the person's mood is not serious.

The person's behavioral patterns change in disturbing ways. For example, a previously gregarious person begins to isolate himself or herself. Or, the person's moods change, with irritability, sadness, and apathy becoming more predominant. Of course, these may be signs of drug or alcohol abuse, or other emotional disturbances, and may not entail suicidality. However, since these problems sometimes coexist with (or are early warning signs of) suicidality, it is important to note these sorts of behavioral changes.

The person behaves in ways that are self-injurious or seem to invite danger and harm. This may involve driving recklessly, abusing substances, associating with dangerous people, disregarding his or her medical health (for example, neglecting to take insulin), and being cavalier about safety. Again, these behaviors are often associated with problems other than suicidality. However, if such behaviors represent a marked departure from the way the person usually acts and are accompanied by comments such as "I don't really care what happens to me anyway" or "Who cares if I die?" it would be prudent for you to consider the possibility that this person is suicidal.

The person has experienced significant losses in a short period of time. In this case, he or she may be vulnerable to severe depression and perhaps suicidality. This is especially true if the losses have to do with the person's sense of identity and self-worth (for example, losing a career path unexpectedly) and the sense of meaningful connection to other people (for example, the death of a spouse). A tragic illustration of this phenomenon can be found in the case of a young woman at the University of Pennsylvania who took her own life in the months following her boyfriend's murder. Her suicide note indicated that she could not bear to go on without him.

The person suffers from a chronic illness. A person who is medically ill, experiences constant physical pain, and believes (rightly or wrongly) that the illness or condition will never get better is at increased risk for suicide. The combination of ceaseless pain with a sense of hopelessness is a very serious condition. In such cases, it is critical to offer realistic support and hope and to help with the provision of appropriate pain management.

The person has suffered extreme social humiliation. We have seen persons become suicidal in the aftermath of such events as a high-profile bankruptcy (splashed all over the business section of the local newspaper), public accusations of professional misconduct, or their family's discovery that they are homosexual.

The person abuses mind-altering substances and has access to firearms. Certain situations, in and of themselves, do not necessarily bring about a person's suicidality. However, their presence in the suicidal person's life makes the risk that much greater. The abuse of mind-altering substances such as alcohol, illicit drugs, and prescription painkillers, as well as the possession of firearms are two examples. It is routine procedure when treating a suicidal individual to assess whether the person has easy access to drugs or weapons and to take all reasonable steps to remove these instruments of self-destruction from the hands of a deeply depressed person.

Is This My Fault?

When you become aware that someone you love is contemplating taking his or her own life, you will naturally be concerned and scared. You may also feel guilty, wondering what you may have done to cause this, or what you have failed to do to prevent it. While this might be an understandable reaction to an extreme situation, it is useless to think that you are to blame.

Many factors come together to cause a person to consider suicide, as we have discussed throughout this book. To try to assess personal responsibility and blame likely will yield little insight or practical benefit, either for the person who feels guilty or the person who is suicidal. At the very least, blaming yourself will be a waste of time and energy at a moment when you need to summon up all the strength you've got. At worst, you will render yourself depressed as well, and you will be less apt to be of help in the days ahead, when the suicidal person may need your support and presence most of all. In absolute worst-case scenarios, we have seen people become suicidal themselves over a loved one's suicidality. Nobody benefits from this state of affairs.

What should you do if someone else blames you? This is a very painful situation, especially if it is the suicidal person who is holding you responsible for the suicidal feelings or attempt. Your first reaction might be extreme, either buying into the notion that it's all your fault or feeling unjustly accused and indignant and possibly responding with anger.

Extreme reactions like these are to be avoided whenever possible. Therefore, we suggest a middle-ground approach—do your best to ignore the entire issue of who is to blame, while you make yourself available to be as much help to your suicidal loved one as can be reasonably expected. If someone blames you, a good response might be, "That's neither here nor there. Right now, my main concern is [the suicidal person's] well-being." If the other person retorts, "You should have thought of that before," you can reply, "We'll never know for sure what anyone could have done, but right now I'm determined to help as much as I can." In other words, don't get backed into a defensive posture. Remain a levelheaded, caring problem solver, if possible.

She's Threatening to Kill Herself: What Should I Do?

The rule of thumb here is to seek middle ground between under- and over-reacting. You should neither ignore the threat, hoping that it will go away, nor become agitated and overwrought. A serious, levelheaded demeanor is most helpful at this time.

In addition, we strongly suggest that you attempt to engage in dialogue with the person who is making the suicidal threat. Some people think that talking never solves anything, but we completely disagree. While it may be true that a single conversation is not a panacea for all major problems, it does serve a number of valuable functions. It helps to make a connection with a person who otherwise may be trying to disconnect from life. A conversation also gives you the opportunity to provide the suicidal person with a new perspective.

For example, "Lanny" became suicidal when he was not accepted into medical school. He believed that his father would be ashamed of him, and the young man became convinced that his life was worthless. By talking with him, his father convinced Lanny that he was not ashamed of him and that, in fact, he was proud of his son in many respects. This offered the young man a perspective he had not been able to gain on his own, and his sense of desperation abated, even though he remained understandably disappointed.

Communicating with the suicidal person also stimulates thinking and reasoning. People who are depressed and hopeless often evidence thinking patterns that are negatively biased. They show a lack of reasoned thinking, and they often act primarily on their emotions. When it's a matter of life and death, as it is in cases of suicidality, it is imperative that the suicidal person be encouraged and stimulated into thinking things through. A conversation helps this process significantly.

What if the suicidal individual possesses the means to kill himself or herself and threatens to use it? If your loved one is not actively wielding a weapon or a bottle of pills, you can take your time and try to negotiate the surrender of these instruments of potential suicide. Make a strong point that your loved one should not have the means by which to die on the spur of the moment, but don't be so heavy-handed that it makes the other person defensive or combative. Show respect for the other person's point of view, and for his or her right to make an autonomous decision, even as you make a plea for that person to consider another way. Do what you can to make the relinquishing of pills, poisons, or weapons a collaborative process. This makes it possible for the suicidal person to have an active say in his or her own decision to live, which is a more secure and enduring state of affairs than the coercive alternative.

We understand that, at times, it may be necessary for you to make a decision for the suicidal person, but no human being can do this forever. No matter how good your intentions are, and no matter how vigilant you are in watching over the suicidal person like a hawk, you cannot be a guardian angel twenty-four hours a day, seven days a week, for all of your life. At some point, it will be necessary to rely on your loved one's acceptance of life, and rejection of suicide. The other person's life is not solely your responsibility. This fact is often difficult and scary to accept. We want to do everything we can to help our loved ones to overcome crises and get on with their lives, and sometimes we can make a difference for the better. In the end, however, the decision to live or to commit suicide lies with the individual.

Finally, you should not try to face the crisis of a suicidal loved one alone. Other people need to know, so that they may offer assistance. Sometimes these "others" are friends or family members. More often, they are professionals. For example, if your loved one calls to tell you that he or she has just taken an entire bottle of medication, you will need to call for an ambulance right away. Before you call for the paramedics, ask the suicidal person the following questions, and try to keep your head about you enough to take coherent notes:

- Where are you? (address, if possible)

- What action have you taken to harm yourself?

- (If applicable) What substance have you ingested, and how much?

- How long ago did you do this?

- Can you hold while I make a call? (or) Can I call you right back after I call for help? I want to talk to you until the ambulance gets there.

There is no guarantee that the person will give you this information, but it is most prudent for you to make an attempt to get these facts as quickly as possible so that you can communicate meaningful information to the professionals who will soon be attending to your loved one.

Other ways of enlisting the help of professionals is facilitating the suicidal person's involvement in psychotherapy (and perhaps medication treatment as well) and (in more immediately serious instances) admission to a hospital. Never make therapy or hospitalization sound like a threat or punishment. The purpose of treatment is to protect, preserve, and improve the life of your loved one. It is decidedly not to take away his or her freedom, to "dump" him or her on someone else, or to win an interpersonal power struggle.

One way to make this point effectively is to volunteer (to both the suicidal person and the professional in charge of his or her therapy) your appropriate involvement in the treatment. What constitutes "appropriate" involvement will vary, but it can range from daily visits, to taking part in couple's or family therapy, to monitoring the person's compliance with medications, to getting individual professional help yourself.

What can I do if he refuses to be helped?

As difficult as it might be to cope with a loved one in distress, it is even more stressful when your efforts of help are not accepted. Clinicians often hear from family members wanting advice about what to do for a loved one who seems suicidal but refuses to get help.

It is important to realize that people who are considering suicide often have very mixed feelings: they may experience a wish to die, but some desire to live remains. If you express your concerns compassionately and make your suggestions about "getting professional help" respectfully, your loved one may not accept your comments right away. However, he or she at the very least might think over what you have said and may eventually seek help. The key here is to give the individual room to draw his or her own conclusions, without feeling as if he or she is being coerced or "committed." In the meantime, you might wish to consider whether to seek professional help for yourself. Coping with a suicidal loved one is not easy. Support and wise counsel from a caring professional can provide great relief for you, as well as setting an excellent example for your loved one to follow.

However, in an emergency situation, it may not be possible to stand by until your loved one chooses to seek help. In such situations, it may be possible to involuntarily commit the suicidal individual to a treatment facility. Involuntary commitment is (and should be) a difficult process and it should be pursued only as the option of last resort. It is no longer possible in most places for a family member alone to commit a distressed loved one to an institution. In fact, in some situations it is not possible to do this at all, because most state laws demand that the committable person be clearly dangerous to themselves or others. Although commitment criteria vary from one state to another, in most places this is a legal decision that must be made by a judge in consultation with mental health professionals.

One time when involuntary hospitalization might become a consideration is in the aftermath of a serious self-harming incident, such as a potentially lethal medication overdose leading to emergency medical care. In such as situation, hospital personnel typically will conduct a suicide risk assessment and may begin the commitment process themselves, if they believe that failure to do so would put the patient's life in danger. However, you can play a major role in making this procedure go more smoothly if you can provide the professional staff with information, cooperate with them, and help your suicidal loved one to deal with the situation. You will continue to be of significant assistance if you play an active role in the suicidal person's care and if you are a positive presence during hospital visits.

In a perfect world, involuntary hospitalization would never be needed—everyone who needed help would seek it freely on their own. Given that we live in the real world, you may need to take this difficult step in order to provide your loved one with the medical treatment and supervision he or she needs. Hospitalization is not a cure-all, and it does not substitute for long-term solutions to the problems of depression and suicidality, but it can save a life in some critical situations.

References

Linehan, M. 1993. Cognitive-Behavioral Treatment of Borderline Personality Disorder. New York: Guilford.

Excerpted and adapted with permission from *Choosing to Live: How to Defeat Suicide Through Cognitive Therapy* by Thomas E. Ellis, Psy.D., and Cory F. Newman, Ph.D. For more information on this and related books, see the "Further Reading" section in the back of the book.

PART VI

GETTING HELP

A self-help book in the hands of a motivated reader is a powerful combination that can make profound changes for the better. But sometimes you may need more help—a real live expert to talk to or medication to correct a biochemical imbalance. This section covers the two kinds of help most commonly available today:

Brief Therapy outlines the differences between various kinds of therapists, how to identify a good therapist for your situation, how to get the most out of therapy, and where to start looking for a therapist.

Psychiatric Drugs explains the pros and cons of various medications that have been developed to treat emotional disorders, often with striking results and very minor side effects.

CHAPTER 43

Brief Therapy

When you're really sick, you probably make an appointment with your physician. The physician examines you, prescribes medicine, and—with time and good fortune—you're well again.

Psychotherapy began with a similar model: the "powerful doctor" healed the "sick patient." The patient may not have chosen to see a therapist, but was too ill to resist. It was generally assumed that a mentally ill patient would need treatment for a long time, if not forever. The relationship between the therapist and the patient reflected an unequal division of power, with the patient holding the short straw. Those earlier patients saw a therapist because they were "sick," not because of the problems of daily living.

Today people often make the choice to see a professional therapist—counselor, clinical social worker, marriage and family therapist, pastoral counselor, psychologist, or psychiatrist—when life feels too hard to deal with alone.

Today's clients know they won't be in therapy for twenty years or have to recount every detail of childhood. This is not to say that long-term therapy doesn't have its place. Brief therapy is not for everyone, nor is it appropriate for every problem. But for many people, a brief intervention can offer much needed help, support, and emotional relief.

Hire a Consultant!

If your finances are complex, or if you're having financial problems, you might decide to hire an accountant. The accountant would assist you in creative problem solving, show you how to work out your difficulties with income, expenses, and taxes. And ultimately help you to make the best choices.

Similarly, if you were physically out of shape and decided to get healthy, you might go to a gym and hire a fitness instructor. A fitness professional would assess your condition, guide you through exercises appropriate to your current abilities and physical state, and help you choose exercises suited to your particular needs and goals.

When living gets hard, you could go shopping (some folks call this "retail therapy"). You may find temporary relief—or escape—this way. However, short-term solutions are often not the answer. It is likely that you'll get more in the long run if you hire a mental health consultant.

Is your mental health as important to you as your physical well-being? You don't stay in shape by being lucky, you have to work at it. A strong marriage is the result of hard work. And a healthy mind and attitude may at times require a little outside help and maintenance—a "tune-up" for how you think and feel.

When you view a therapist as your mental health consultant, the unequal division of power seen in earlier years is gone. You alone made the decision to enter therapy—no one made that decision for you. You may be in pain and seeking relief, but that doesn't mean that you can't be an educated and informed consumer.

Your mental health consultant is there for you as a facilitator of change, healing, and growth. Like the fitness consultant who doesn't "cure" but provides direction, guidance, and support, the mental health consultant is an agent of change working with you to help you through difficult times. A therapist can, for example, help you to learn more effective problem-solving skills, resulting in greater self-confidence and increased ability to cope with your current problems.

Maybe you'd prefer to be your own mental health consultant? Here are a couple of things to keep in mind: emotional pain is considerably more intense when it is experienced alone and none of us can be completely objective about our own circumstances.

Your mental health consultant won't and can't do the work for you, but will listen objectively and help guide you toward the results that you choose. Each life experience gives you and your consultant the chance to examine your thoughts, beliefs, perceptions, and attitudes and how they work for and against you in your daily living.

Your therapist isn't there to "fix" or "change" you, but to build on your strengths. A consultant is your guide to understanding the complex nature of stressful events and how they are related to your thoughts, attitudes, and beliefs about yourself and your world.

A therapist/consultant can help you reduce your pain, minimize future disasters, and develop action plans and strategies for growth and healing, now and in the future. The emphasis in brief therapy is not on "sick patients" and "powerful doctors." It's on people in distress making wise choices so they can take charge of their lives.

Why Brief Therapy?

Since psychotherapy arrived on the scene in the early part of the twentieth century, this form of treatment has been considered a lengthy endeavor. Therapists advocating traditional Freudian analysis insisted, for therapy to be beneficial, it had to be intense and long-term. Those few who were able to afford it entered analysis and visited their therapist three to five times a week for many months, and often many years. Psychoanalysis was often helpful for this small group of clients, and, because it was the treatment of choice for the "rich and famous," it became the approach glorified by the media and desired by the rest of the population.

What's wrong with this picture? First, long-term psychotherapy is extremely expensive and therefore out of reach for most people. Human emotional suffering is widespread and affects people from all walks of life, rich and poor alike. Second, extensive research finds little compelling scientific evidence that, overall, long-term psychotherapy is more effective than brief therapy. In fact, the majority of people looking for therapy prefer short-term psychotherapy and greatly benefit from the experience.

What Is "Brief Therapy"?

Generally brief therapy is defined as psychotherapy lasting from one to twenty sessions. In the contemporary "managed care" environment, and in most public treatment settings (community mental health, university counseling centers), brief therapy averages between three and twelve sessions.

This shorter course of treatment—fewer sessions and significantly lower costs—makes psychotherapy available to more people.

Sometimes therapy must be brief because insurance companies, mental health clinics, counseling centers, and HMOs have limits on the mental health benefits that they offer. However, short-term psychotherapy is often brief by design. Short-term therapy includes special techniques that can speed up the process, and the results are often better than for long-term therapy.

Brief therapy, however, is defined not only by the length of treatment. There are a number of goals and characteristics of brief therapy that set it apart from longer forms of psychological treatment. The key elements include:

- Focus on a *specific problem*, not on "reshaping your personality"

- *Active involvement* of both client and therapist

- Emphasis on *solutions*, not causes to life problems

- *Time-limited* course of treatment

Off the Couch and into Action

Most brief therapy approaches are "action oriented." Every session really does count. With only a few sessions available clients cannot afford to be passive or to gradually explore their concerns, feelings, and past and present experiences. The process requires rapid identification of and attention to the primary area of greatest current concern. Therapists call this establishing a focus.

It's not that other issues or life experiences are unimportant. In brief therapy, you and your therapist together will identify and agree to work on the most important or urgent concerns in your life right now (this may be, for a particular symptom, such as depression or panic attacks, a particular life struggle, such as resolving conflicts with an employer, or learning more effective ways to resolve marital problems). Once you and your therapist have clearly identified "the problem," this focus becomes the central issue to be discussed in therapy sessions.

- A second way brief therapy is "active" is that the therapist is more likely to speak out in therapy sessions. In some forms of therapy the therapist stays pretty quiet; in brief therapy there generally are more questions, answers, feedback, and active problem solving.

- A third way brief therapy is lively is that it really encourages the client to take action. This may be in the form of between-session homework assignments (keeping a personal journal, monitoring progress using self-rating checklists, trying out new behaviors in life situations). A lot goes on outside the therapy room and between sessions. Many clients enjoy these activities that make them active participants in their treatment, feeling that they are better able to "take charge."

- Another way that brief therapy is action oriented is through developing the client's "tool kit" for dealing with stressful situations, including life skills for:
    - Interpersonal coping—more effective and practical ways to problem-solve and resolve conflicts with friends, relatives, co-workers, and important others

- Internal stress reduction—powerful ways to reduce anxiety, sadness, despair, and irritability

One important benefit of increasing your coping skills is that you may discover these skills offer you a greater sense of control and mastery in everyday life situations, reducing feelings of helplessness and powerlessness. Coping skills may be taught in individual or group therapy sessions, or with the use of self-help books.

Living life, meeting challenges, surviving hard times, and growing are lifelong processes. Brief therapy can best be seen as an important experience or tool that helps people as they hit those inevitable hard times throughout life. The goal of brief therapy is not to cure, but to provide support, facilitate growth, and increase effective coping.

Research shows that people can change and experience benefits while in brief therapy, but it doesn't end there. A good deal of growth and "work" continues after therapy has ended. The last session of brief therapy, in a very real sense, is not the end. After the final session, clients put newly learned skills into action, acting as their own "therapist." Following a course of brief therapy, one of the authors received a note from a woman client stating:

"I stopped coming to therapy sessions three months ago, but it's like I'm still in treatment. I often hear your voice in my mind saying, 'Remember to be decent to yourself' or 'It's okay to give yourself permission to be who you are and to feel what you feel.' . . . I also kinda do therapy with myself . . . and it helps a lot."

The time spent in therapy may be "brief," but life doesn't stop handing us challenges, frustrations, joys, and hopes. No one ever stops growing; no one ever has it all figured out.

It is not uncommon for clients to go through two or more courses of brief therapy, at various times in life. At twenty-four, Sara saw a therapist seven times for help as her marriage floundered and she and her husband became more distant with each other. She also attended a group for couples. The therapy and support group helped Sara and Ken find new ways of balancing their relationship, and they stayed together. Nine years later, following the death of her mother, Sara returned to her therapist to help her deal with her loss. They met for six sessions, though her grieving continued well past the time of her last session. However, therapy helped her to accept the reality of her mom's death and the depth of her sorrow. She began to feel more "okay" about expressing her sadness to her husband and her kids. She was clearly on the road to emotional healing from this painful life event.

Therapy is not a magical solution or a cure-all for the painful things that happen to us as human beings. Brief therapy can, however, be a tremendously important resource during painful times, and a foundation for successfully handling the tough times that may come later.

What's Therapy Like?

It's not what you think.

You've had glimpses of psychotherapy in books, in the movies, and on television. Forget that. It's not likely that what you've seen has prepared you for what really goes on.

If you're like most folks, you're thinking about therapy because you're experiencing significant distress or emotional pain—perhaps desperation—in your life. (Almost no one goes to therapy for the small stuff.) Under such times of great stress and personal uncertainty, everyone wants and needs to feel safe, and to feel some assurance that the decision to see a therapist was the right one.

Most people have lots of questions about this business of telling their troubles to a total stranger:

"What actually happens in therapy?"

"What can I expect to get from therapy?"

"What are realistic and attainable benefits I might gain from therapy?"

"Is there a reasonable chance of getting the help I need?"

"Will it be worth the time, money, effort, and emotional investment to become involved in a course of brief therapy?"

Good questions! We are going to offer you some straight talk about psychotherapy, and present how some people benefit from their experience of brief therapy. We'll focus on two topics: what's expected of you, and what actually happens during therapy sessions.

What's Expected of You

You may be asked to fill out a background questionnaire to help the therapist determine if treatment with you is appropriate, and as a means of learning details of your history (educational history, number of people in your family, prior psychotherapy experiences, medical history . . .).

- You will be asked to do your best at sharing openly your particular concerns, thoughts, and feelings.

- You may be asked to complete assigned and agreed tasks—homework assignments—outside the therapy hour.

- You will be expected to show up for sessions as scheduled and to pay agreed-upon professional fees. And to give advance notice in case of a cancellation (except in cases of last-minute emergencies).

- You may be asked to complete one or more psychological tests to help your therapist assess your personal situation and needs.

What Actually Happens during Therapy Sessions?

Therapy sessions vary, depending on who you are, what current problems you're experiencing, and the kind of therapist you hire. We can, however, give you a summary glimpse of the "typical" course of brief therapy.

PHASE ONE: Getting Acquainted and Discussing What Concerns You Most. Effective therapists often help the therapy process get under way by asking their clients, "What are the main reasons you've decided to come to therapy?" or "I'd like to know what's most on your mind and what you'd like to accomplish in coming to therapy." The early sessions generally are designed to help you feel more at ease and begin discussing your main problems or concerns. At this beginning phase, many people entering therapy are unclear about what they are feeling, or they may be self-critical, for example, "I shouldn't be feeling this way." You and your therapist will be forming a "therapeutic alliance"—a working partnership that will help you get past your uncertainty and reach your goals in therapy.

PHASE TWO: Finding a Focus. As the discussion continues in further sessions, your therapist will do a lot of listening and ask questions to help you pinpoint a major focus—the major issue or problem you'll be dealing with in therapy. You and your therapist will identify specific problems, and find out in what ways these issues are especially important to you at this time in your life.

Psychotherapy (brief or long-term) doesn't provide a quick fix. In fact, people may find that they feel somewhat worse during the first couple of sessions—at least more keenly aware of distressing feelings. And the reality often is that once a person begins to take a close look at difficult issues, emotional pain may be felt more intensely. If this happens to you, don't bail out! It's natural, normal, and fairly predictable—but an essential part of coming to terms with life issues that hurt. Fortunately for most, emotional distress at some point subsides as they begin to get a handle on life problems and cope more effectively.

PHASE THREE: Refocusing or Tuning into the Problem. A common experience during the third phase of brief therapy is for clients to begin to understand their problems, and themselves, in a new light. Many times this involves a change of perspective and attitude. Such "problems" as being oversensitive to criticism, feeling taken advantage of by others, missing a loved one who has died, feeling overwhelmed and frustrated at work, start to seem more "understandable." The problems may seem just as painful, undesirable, or frustrating; however, many folks start to think, "My feelings make sense to me now" or "Of course I feel this way." The volume gets turned down on harsh self-criticism.

Attitudes Can Shift during Therapy

From	To
This is crazy. I shouldn't be so upset.	I don't like the way this feels. I'm upset. What can I do about it?
This shouldn't be happening!	I don't want this to happen, but it is and it's upsetting.
I'm confused. What the hell is the matter with me?	Of course I feel this way!

PHASE FOUR: Action-Oriented Skills . . . Practice, Practice, Practice. "I am more aware of what I feel and I don't condemn myself so harshly. But I still feel bad. What do I do next?"

Often in brief therapy, once the major problems or concerns have been clarified, the focus is shifted toward active problem solving. Kimberly, for example, learned ways to reduce anxiety by providing inner support for herself prior to taking an exam at school. Roberto developed assertive ways to communicate his feelings and needs to his wife. In one of his therapy sessions, Doug carefully planned out just how he was going to approach his shop foreman to share concerns he had about his work environment. Sherri began to write in her personal journal, discovered more about her own feelings, and learned to give herself permission to grieve the loss of her brother.

Brief therapy became a place for these people to think things through, come to conclusions regarding actions they wanted to take, learn some new coping skills, and practice these skills during the session. As Roberto said, "Having a therapist is kinda like having a coach. You can plan out what you want to do, practice it, get some feedback, refine it, and then get the extra push you need to do it for real in your life."

PHASE FIVE: Fine Tuning. In the final stages of brief therapy, it is often helpful to summarize what's happened. It helps to be clear about several points:

- This was my problem

- I came to see it as understandable . . . not "crazy"

- I felt okay about wanting to make a change

- I figured out which approaches work for me and which don't
- I felt supported by my therapist
- I put coping skills into action
- I got some results

Getting better and feeling better usually aren't just due to fate or good luck. You have to work at changing and discovering what helps.

Once you know how to cope more successfully you're better prepared for the next time life becomes difficult.

Of course, it's not all this simple! Experiences vary. But the phases we've talked about here describe a common experience in brief therapy. Most people who succeed in therapy typically don't feel ultimately "cured" or "fixed," but they do feel better. They leave therapy knowing that they've done some real work, and it was their effort that paid off. In particular, the most common outcome of successful brief therapy is feeling okay about who you are!

What Are Therapists Like?

Therapists are human beings.

"Obviously," you may say. But some folks seem to think that therapy is an art, practiced by individuals with X-ray vision and wise advice for every problem. The fact is that therapists are highly trained experts in human behavior who are just as vulnerable as the rest of the population to all of the realities of being human.

What Makes Therapists Different?

- *Therapists generally don't give advice.* Many people can benefit from helpful suggestions and good advice from time to time, but such input is readily available from friends and relatives (even when you don't want it). Truth be told, most therapists aren't really any better at giving commonsense advice than anyone else. But they can and do provide a kind of help not readily found in your ordinary network of family and friends.

- *Therapists are trained to understand emotional distress and the process of emotional healing.* In a sense they are people who understand the general terrain of the human landscape, and can help guide people through painful times toward growth and healing.

- *Therapists are willing and able to face very strong emotions.* It's hard to really be with someone when they are experiencing intense feelings. To witness a human suffering in itself is difficult. It is also hard for many people to experience another's pain without it touching on their own inner feelings. Good therapists have learned to handle these issues: to be fully present with their clients, resonate with their pain, but also maintain an appropriate objectivity. A client is able to express strong feelings and knows that the therapist cares without being overwhelmed or blown away by the client's powerful emotions. This provides a considerable amount of stability and safety within the therapy hour.

- *Good therapists tend to be nonjudgmental.* They understand that most interpersonal and emotional problems can be seen as attempts to emotionally survive the common problems in living. Effective therapists transmit an attitude of respect, understanding, and acceptance. In psychotherapy outcome studies, the most commonly reported factor judged to have been helpful to clients was the therapist's ability to genuinely care and to understand the client. The therapist's compassionate attitude helps the client to reduce excessive self-criticism and develop an enhanced capacity for self-acceptance.

- *Therapists provide support for self-expression.* Support and encouragement of honest expression helps shore up and solidify the development of the self. To use an analogy, when building a concrete wall, boards are used to provide support for the concrete as it begins to harden. At some point the boards can be removed and the wall is solid; the concrete has developed its own strength and it can stand on its own. In therapy, it begins to feel okay to talk openly about how things really are. Although reduction of emotional distress (decreased depression, anxiety, tension, etc.) is a primary goal for most people entering treatment, one of the most common results of psychotherapy is an increased sense of self and self-esteem. "When my therapist really listens, I know it's okay to be me!"

- *Therapists help clients to maintain a sense of realistic hope during difficult times.* Not the phony "Everything will be all right" hope, but a realistic perspective and trust in the process that psychotherapy will very likely lead to healing or better coping skills.

- *Therapists do not repeat maladaptive patterns of interaction.* Many relationships involve patterns. A dependent, seemingly helpless person may frequently enter into relationships where her behavior leads others to treat her like a child. This repetitive "interpersonal dance" may feel good at first (because it is familiar), but ultimately contributes to keeping her stuck; she never grows up. The tendency for others to rush in and rescue this "helpless" person keeps her stuck in an infantile position. A good therapist would empathize with her distress, but would resist the urge to treat her like a helpless child. The therapist's refusal to perpetuate the dance allows this client to grow and come to feel her own strength.

What You Can Expect from the Therapist

All competent psychotherapists are committed to a code of ethics and a standard of practice that attempts to assure the following (essential ingredients in a helping relationship):

- Provide privacy and confidentiality.

- Treat clients in a decent and respectful manner.

- Gain the client's informed consent for any procedures undertaken in the course of therapy.

- Provide realistic emotional support.

- Help you feel at ease during the first meetings. Many people are worried about the first session: "I won't know what to say or where to start," "I feel anxious about talking to someone I don't know." These concerns are common and understandable; it's normal to feel nervous during the first session. Effective therapists know how to help people get started talking.

- Provide a "neutral," noncritical, and nonjudgmental environment. An important goal in therapy is not to judge people, but to understand and be helpful.

- To be honest. Your therapist is there to help you fully understand yourself, your patterns of behavior, and your feelings. The therapist's function is to provide honest and objective feedback about your attitudes and actions. The feedback will feel good when it recognizes your strengths and it may feel uncomfortable when it points out your weaknesses. Brief therapy can help you capitalize on your strengths and transform your weaknesses. The process may be uncomfortable at times, but the outcome may be positive, even more than you expect.

- Maintain a professional relationship. This is what psychotherapists refer to as "maintaining appropriate professional boundaries." It is a part of the therapists' ethical codes to assure that therapy remains safe. In the practice of psychotherapy, relating to a patient in other-than-professional ways—socially, romantically, or entering into a business relationship—is inappropriate, and may be unethical or illegal. Sexually intimate relationships are absolutely prohibited by the professional codes of ethics (and the law in most states). Social friendships outside the therapy hour and business deals are unwise, and may also be unethical.

- Make appropriate referrals. Sometimes your therapist may need to refer you to a medical doctor, for a psychiatric evaluation and possible medication treatment. They may refer you to another therapist who offers particular services (marital counseling), or support groups or programs when appropriate (Alcoholics Anonymous, bereavement support groups, etc.). Your therapist may even refer you to another therapist if both of you feel that the current therapy isn't working.

- Provide information about the therapist's education and training, fees, type of services offered, and responses to any number of relevant questions regarding the treatment they provide.

Types of Mental Health Therapists

Psychiatrists (M.D.): Psychiatrists are medical doctors who have received specialized training in the treatment of emotional problems, including both medication and psychological treatments. (It is possible for a physician to practice psychiatry without specialized training; however, very few do so.) Most psychiatrists treat emotional disorders with medications. Some psychiatrists also provide psychotherapy, behavior therapy, or cognitive therapy.

Psychologists: Almost all hold a doctorate degree in psychology (Ph.D., Psy.D., Ed.D.), have a number of years of postgraduate training in psychological methods, and in most states are licensed or certified to practice. They also have specialized training in the administration and interpretation of psychological tests.

Clinical Social Workers: Generally hold a master's degree (M.S.W.), have considerable supervised experience, and are usually licensed by the state ("L.C.S.W."—Licensed Clinical Social Worker).

Marriage Family and Child Counselors/Therapists: A number of states grant a license or certificate to marriage, family and child counselors (or marriage, family, and child therapists). Such therapists generally have at least a master's degree in counseling (M.S. or M.A.), usually with specialization in treatment of marriage and family problems and the treatment of children and adolescents.

Pastoral Counselors: Some clergy have received training in counseling and may provide supportive therapy to members of their church or to others desiring a therapist who addresses both emotional and spiritual concerns.

Getting the Most from Your Therapist

- *The chemistry has to be "good enough."* You need to feel a degree of comfort and compatibility with your therapist. Not all people are going to make a good connection. It may not be essential to feel 100 percent comfortable with your therapist, but it is quite important to feel the following: a basic sense of trust, the perception that you and your feelings are being treated with respect, and some degree of confidence that your therapist is competent. First and foremost competent therapists, beyond being well-trained and skilled, need to be good, decent people.

- *The type of treatment must be appropriate.* Not all problems are best approached in the same manner. A good therapist will evaluate your situation and within the first session or two talk with you about what kind of treatment they recommend. Some types of emotional problems are due, either in part or in full, to medical/biochemical disturbances. Medical treatment and/or psychiatric medication treatment may be helpful or even necessary.

- *The treatment must do no harm.* Any approach that is powerful enough to help can be powerful enough to cause harm, if in the hands of an incompetent or destructive therapist. Most licensed therapists are well trained and are helpful to most of their clients. However, as in any other profession, incompetence and/or unethical behavior does exist. You are entitled to competent and ethical treatment. Anything else should be reported to appropriate institutional or regulatory agencies.

Where to Find a Therapist

Most people find therapists through personal referral. They go to someone who has helped a friend, family member, acquaintance, or colleague. Your family doctor or primary health care provider is another good source of information. If you belong to an HMO or other health care plan, there may be a list of local therapists approved for reimbursement under your plan.

Another way to find a therapist is to contact an organization devoted to research in and support of those suffering from a particular emotional disorder. A search of the Internet or visit to your local library will turn up groups such as the Anxiety Disorders Association or the Obsessive Compulsives Association.

Finally, you can simply consult your local yellow pages under such headings as:

Marriage, Family & Child Counselors

Mental Health Services

Physicians—Psychiatry

Psychologists

Psychotherapy

Social Workers

Excerpted and adapted with permission from *Make Every Session Count: Getting the Most Out of Your Brief Therapy* by John Preston, Psy.D., Nicolette Varzos, Ph.D., and Douglas S. Liebert, Ph.D. For more information on this and related books, see the "Further Reading" section in the back of the book.

CHAPTER 44

Psychiatric Drugs

During the nearly five decades since their inception, psychiatric medications have undergone significant changes. The development of new medical and scientific technologies has provided researchers with a much clearer understanding of the functioning of the brain and the biology of mental illness. Newer, safer, and more effective medications have been developed. A great deal of information has been acquired about how to prescribe treatments appropriately and how to avoid or minimize problems with side effects. Recently, new vistas have opened regarding the use of psychiatric medications for what are considered to be the less severe emotional disorders.

In most states the only people who can prescribe psychiatric medications are physicians and dentists. In a few states such medications may be prescribed or furnished by appropriately trained nurse practitioners. Having the legal right to prescribe, however, does not imply that all such professionals are trained in the treatment of emotional and psychiatric disorders.

Many prescriptions for psychiatric medications are written by primary care and family practice doctors. Some of these physicians are well trained in the diagnosis and treatment of emotional problems, and have years of experience carrying out such treatment. In fact, primary care physicians see between two and three people daily who are suffering from major depression.

Although many people do seek psychiatric treatment from their primary care doctors, the ability to accurately diagnose psychiatric disorders in this setting is not good. This is the case primarily because of the fast-paced and brief nature of visits in a general medical clinic.

If you suspect that you (or a relative) are suffering from a psychiatric disorder and you want to consult your primary care doctor, it is strongly recommended that you first contact him or her and ask directly if they have experience in treating emotional disorders (e.g., depression or anxiety). Should your physician not have that experience, he or she is very likely to offer you a referral to a mental health specialist. If you are treated by your family practice doctor, we highly recommend that you also ask for the name of a psychotherapist. Psychiatric medication treatment is almost always more effective if taken in conjunction with psychotherapy.

The material presented in this chapter is very general. By no means does it describe all of the complex interactions that take place within the human body when medications are taken. Our intention is not to provide detailed information as a textbook would, but rather to describe and explain some extremely important principles that you can use to make sure you get the most benefit out of your medications.

To better understand and benefit from medications of any type it is important to have a working knowledge of some of the processes that take place when medications are ingested.

Once a drug enters the body, a cascade of actions is set in motion. Certain bodily organs or systems can affect the action of a medication. There are four basic processes that occur: *absorption, distribution, metabolism,* and *excretion.*

Absorption

Most drugs are absorbed in the stomach or small intestine. The presence of food, milk, or other medications in the stomach can affect a given medicine. It is important to find out how your medication should be taken with regard to meals. If the absorption of a medicine is known to be impaired when food is present in the stomach, then it might be advisable to take that medicine on an empty stomach. On the other hand, the presence of food sometimes increases the amount of a drug that is absorbed, in which case it might be preferable to take the medicine at mealtimes. Certain medications can irritate the stomach and should be taken with food or milk to lessen this effect and prevent damage to the stomach lining.

As a drug travels throughout the body it encounters various membranes that it must cross. One of the most important of these barriers is called the *blood-brain barrier*. This barrier serves to limit the substances that pass into the brain. It is one of the ways the body protects the brain from damage caused by chemicals or other toxins. Some medications pass freely into the brain, while others have more limited accessibility.

The total amount of a medication that is ingested may not equal the amount that ultimately becomes available at the place in the body for which it is intended. This is a principle called *bioavailability*. For example, if a medication is known to break down and be inactivated by the acidic environment of the stomach, only a certain percentage of the original dose will reach the bloodstream. In this case, less than 100 percent of the drug will be bioavailable. In contrast, a drug injected directly into the bloodstream is considered to be nearly 100 percent bioavailable because it reaches the bloodstream intact.

Bioavailability is also the benchmark measure used to compare products made by different manufacturers, or between generic and brand-name products. With most generic drugs, bioavailability closely matches that of the original brand-name product. Such generic products can provide an economical advantage over higher-cost brand-name drugs. Certain medications, however, are not readily formulated into generic products and the brand-name product may be superior. From a practical standpoint, it may be more important not to make frequent switches between products.

Distribution

Once a medication reaches the bloodstream it is then distributed to various areas or organs in the body. The distribution pattern varies from drug to drug. For most medicines, the distribution process is very straightforward; for others, the pattern is more complex. For example, more complicated processes apply to medicines that are preferentially stored in fatty areas of the body. A drug can remain for long periods of time in fatty areas, somewhat like being stored in a reservoir. When in these storage areas, the drug is not readily available to produce any action; rather, it has been deposited and is inactive.

The amount of medicine in the reservoir will vary in order to reach a balance with the amount that is in the bloodstream. If the amount in the bloodstream drops, then some of the medicine will be released from the storage area. If the amount in the bloodstream is stable and adequate, none will be released from the storage area, and the amount in the reservoir can continue to accumulate.

For people taking antidepressants and antipsychotics, understanding how drug distribution works can be very important. To a large degree, these types of medicines are stored in fatty areas. This means that even after a medication is discontinued, because some of it has been stored, it will gradually re-enter the bloodstream until all of it is eliminated from the body. In such instances, there can be continuing effects from the medication for several weeks or longer after it has been discontinued.

This is very important information to remember about stopping antidepressants or antipsychotics. In essence, a person can continue to experience the benefits, or side effects, of the medicine even though it is not being taken as a daily dose. After stopping, the symptoms may return several weeks down the road. It is important to watch out for signs that symptoms might be returning, not just in the first few days after stopping a medicine, but for as long as eight weeks after discontinuing.

Metabolism

This process, which occurs primarily in the liver, is also known as *biotransformation*. Most medications are metabolized, or chemically altered, to varying degrees by the liver. The actual process takes place through the action of enzymes that break down molecules from their original size to smaller ones that then can be eliminated by the kidney more easily.

The extent and rate of metabolism for a given drug is generally consistent, within a range, from person to person. However, some people may be exceptionally fast metabolizers while others may be especially slow. In these instances, there is less predictability when determining the dose or frequency of a given drug, and adjustments are often necessary. Slow metabolizers, for instance, might be extremely sensitive to the side effects of a medication, even at a low or average dose. Antidepressants and antipsychotics are classes of medications that are especially prone to differences in metabolizing capability. There is some evidence that there may be a genetic influence in those who are slow metabolizers.

People who have damaged livers may have impaired metabolic ability, which can lead to a buildup of medication in the body. To prevent serious side effects from excessively high levels of a medication in the blood, it may be necessary for such people to take smaller amounts of medicine, or less frequent doses.

Because the liver is called upon to metabolize most medications, there are times when multiple drugs will compete for the same enzymes. This competition is the source of one of the most common types of drug interactions. Usually one drug wins this contest over the other. The result is that one medication will build up in the body because the liver is busy metabolizing the other. Adjusting the dose of one or both of the interacting medications may become necessary.

Excretion

Excretion is the second step in the process by which drugs are eliminated from the body. The first step, metabolism, happens via the liver as described above. Excretion takes place primarily through the kidneys. If there is kidney damage, medications can accumulate to higher than desired (or even dangerous) levels. If the kidneys are working in a less than ideal manner, adjustments in medication may be necessary to avoid unnecessary or dangerous side effects.

Half-Life

A measure of a medication's action that is related to excretion is called *half-life*. The half-life is the amount of time required for the blood level of a drug to drop by 50 percent. A drug's half-life is used to decide how often it should be taken and also to determine correct dosages. For instance, drugs with short half-lives will require more doses throughout a twenty-four-hour period because they will leave the body faster. Medicines with longer half-lives will not need to be taken as frequently because they will stay in the body longer.

Getting the Most out of Your Medications

Getting the maximum benefit from your medicines requires that you and your doctor work together. Your doctor will ask many specific questions before prescribing a medication. The following list highlights some of the key steps you can take to work effectively with your doctor in managing your medicines.

Inform Your Doctor. Your doctor will need the following information: Your complete medical history; everything to which you are allergic; the names and dosages of all the medicines you take, including over-the-counter products; your past experiences with medicines, positive and negative; how much alcohol you drink on a daily or weekly basis; all the recreational drugs that you use.

Take the medicine exactly as prescribed. Taking more than prescribed can be dangerous. Missing doses can mean you don't get better. If you do not understand the directions, ask your doctor or pharmacist to clarify them for you. If you have trouble remembering to take your medicine, ask someone like a family member or health care provider to help you set up a system.

Be sure you understand exactly why you are taking a given medication. If your questions are not answered to your satisfaction, be persistent with your doctor or pharmacist to get the information you need. This is your right.

Understand how long it should take to begin to feel better. Do not hesitate to contact your doctor if you experience unexpected side effects or if you are not getting better in a reasonable time.

Avoid seeing too many different doctors who might prescribe many kinds of medicine. If you have an established need to see several physicians, be sure each doctor is aware of what the other doctors are prescribing for you.

If you are having difficulties taking a medicine because it is hard to swallow, find out whether it is available in a liquid form. Also, some tablets are suitable for crushing, and the contents of some capsules can be mixed in a liquid. Check with your doctor or pharmacist first.

Read the label on the medicine bottle every time you take a dose to be sure you are taking the correct medication. Some people have many bottles of medicine and they can be mixed up easily. Become familiar with what your medicine looks like. If you receive a prescription that doesn't "look right" to you, be sure to double-check it with your pharmacist. Never take your medicine in the dark when you cannot see exactly what you are swallowing.

Do not switch medication bottles. Keep your medicine in the original bottle in which it came. Never put all your medicines together in one bottle. If you need help in keeping your medicines straight, there are pill reminder boxes that you can purchase to help you keep track.

Make sure you put the lids back on tightly. By law, child-resistant lids are required for prescription medicines to protect children from accidental poisonings. Some adults find these hard to use and will compensate by not putting the lids on securely. Such people can ask for a waiver and receive lids that are not child-resistant. In any case, it is essential to prevent ingestion by children because accidental overdoses can be fatal to them.

Know whether your prescription has refills. Sometimes your doctor will want to check with you before authorizing your refills. Keep track of when you are close to running out of your medicine and allow ample time to get your refills. Be familiar with how to get your prescriptions refilled. Sometimes people run into problems getting refills and will go for several days without taking their medicine. In that amount of time it is possible for symptoms to return. Taking medicine consistently, without any lapses in treatment, is the best way to ensure that you (or your loved one) will get better—and stay that way.

Follow the storage instructions. In general, most drugs should be kept in a cool, dry place, away from high temperatures, in an area of low humidity and out of direct light. In actuality, the bathroom "medicine" cabinet is one of the worst places to store your medications because of the humidity and temperature of the bathroom. If you have not stored your medicine appropriately, it may deteriorate or undergo a physical change to become a harmful chemical.

Do not take medications past the expiration date on the bottle. The expiration date is accurate, assuming that proper storage instructions were followed.

Keep taking your medicines as prescribed. Sometimes people decrease their dosage or discontinue their medication altogether because the cost is prohibitive. However, taking less that an adequate dose won't provide the relief that is sought. If you are unable to afford an expensive medicine, your doctor and pharmacist will often work with you to find a more affordable drug. If you do not have insurance that pays for your prescriptions, try to get an idea of how much your medicines will cost you each month.

Antidepressants: What They Are and How They Work

It is very important to note that antidepressants are a specific and unique class of psychiatric medications; they are not tranquilizers and they are not stimulants. Antidepressants are believed to have their main effects on the aforementioned nerve cell chemicals—serotonin, norepinephrine, and/or dopamine. *As a rule, after several weeks of continued treatment, antidepressant medications restore these nerve cells to a state of normal functioning.* This point is worth emphasizing.

Some other drugs (like alcohol or tranquilizers) also can produce rather quick changes in one's feelings. However, such changes are truly "drug-induced effects"; and typically people feel "drugged" or at least know that "This feeling is not me—it's the drug." This is not the case with antidepressants. The changes experienced by those who respond to antidepressants occur because the medication has actually restored particular nerve cells to a state of normal functioning. When this takes place, normal brain function is restored and the experience generally does not feel like a "drug effect." In fact, most people report that they begin to "feel like themselves again."

When brain functioning is restored, the most notable symptomatic changes are seen in the biological symptoms of depression (sleep, energy, etc.). Feelings of sadness, irritability, negative thinking, low self-esteem, and others of the "core symptoms" also respond; however, the most significant changes are seen in biologically based symptoms.

Unfortunately, antidepressants do not work rapidly. In almost every case in which the drugs eventually resolve the depression, it will require somewhere between two and four weeks of treatment to begin to see positive results. Furthermore, for these medications to work, they must be taken as prescribed and on a regular, daily basis. Much in the same way that antibiotics need some time to knock out an infection gradually, antidepressants require this amount of time to gradually restore the brain to a state of normal functioning.

Classes of Antidepressants

Not all antidepressants are alike. They all treat depression, but differ considerably in their chemical makeup and particular side effects. There are two broad classes of antidepressants that we will look at first: MAO-inhibitors and standard antidepressants.

MAO-Inhibitors

First developed in the 1950s, MAO-inhibitors are a specific class of antidepressants that work by inhibiting the action of a particular enzyme (monoamine-oxidase) in the brain. This enzyme metabolizes (or chemically degrades) the neurotransmitters serotonin, dopamine, and norepinephrine. Thus, MAO-inhibitors are able to block this process and thereby prevent the enzyme from lowering the level of these important brain chemicals. The particular action MAO-inhibitors use to normalize brain chemical levels is different than the action of standard antidepressants.

MAO-Inhibitors "No No" List

MAO-inhibitors are very effective antidepressants but, unfortunately, they may have some potentially dangerous drug-drug interactions (i.e., if combined with certain other medications, they can cause life-threatening reactions). Also, these drugs may have adverse interactions with a number of foods and alcoholic drinks (some of these interactions can be fatal). For this reason, when people are prescribed a MAO-inhibitor, they are advised about the potential risks and given a list of drugs and foods to avoid. Because of these potential problems, MAO-inhibitors are not widely prescribed, although for some individuals they are the treatment of choice.

Standard Antidepressants

The second broad class of antidepressants is referred to as standard antidepressants (this list includes all non-MAO-inhibitor antidepressants). This group is comprised of the earliest generation of antidepressants (most were developed in the 1950s and 1960s) called *tricyclic antidepressants* and a number of newer agents commonly referred to as *second generation antidepressants* (developed in the late 1980s and in the 1990s). The currently available antidepressants are listed in the table below, along with additional information about typical doses and side effects.

The standard antidepressants differ from each other in two ways. First, each has its own particular side effect profile. Second, each has a somewhat different effect on the various key neurotransmitters, serotonin, dopamine, and norepinephrine. As can be seen in the table below some of these medications specifically target serotonin (5-HT) nerve cells (e.g., Prozac, Paxil). These antidepressants often referred to as SSRIs (selective serotonin reuptake inhibitors). The term "reuptake" refers to the reabsorption of the neurotransmitter by the neuron that originally produced it.

Other standard antidepressants focus their actions exclusively on norepinephrine (NE) nerve cells (e.g., Norpramin, Ludiomil). Still others have an impact on two groups of nerve cells (e.g., Wellbutrin focuses on NE and dopamine [DA], and Remeron focuses on NE and 5-HT).

Antidepressants at a Glance

| ANTIDEPRESSANT | | | | | Selective Action On Neurotransmitters[1] | | |
Generic	Brand	Usual Daily Dosage Range	Sedation	Weight Gain	ACH[2]	NE	5-HT
imipramine	Tofranil	150–300 mg	mid	mid	mid	mid	mid
desipramine	Norpramin	150–300 mg	low	low	low	high	none
amitriptyline	Elavil	150–300 mg	high	high	high	low	high
nortriptyline	Aventyl, Pamelor	75–125 mg	mid	low	mid	mid	mid
protriptyline	Vivactil	15–40 mg	mid	low	mid	high	low
trimipramine	Surmontil	100–300 mg	high	high	mid	mid	mid
doxepin	Sinequan, Adapin	150–300 mg	high	high	high	mid	mid
maprotiline	Ludiomil	150–225 mg	high	mid	mid	mid	none
amoxapine	Asendin	150–400 mg	mid	low	low	high	low
trazodone	Desyrel	150–400 mg	mid	low	none	none	high
fluoxetine	Prozac	20–80 mg	low	nore	none	none	high
bupropion-S.R.	Wellbutrin-S.R.	150–300 mg	low	nore	none	none	none
bupropion	Wellbutrin	150–400 mg	low	nore	none	mid	none
sertraline	Zoloft	50–200 mg	low	none	none	none	high
paroxetine	Paxil	20–50 mg	low	none	low	none	high
venlafaxine-X.R.	Effexor-X.R.	75–300 mg	low	none	none	mid	mid
venlafaxine	Effexor	75–375 mg	low	none	none	mid	mid
nefazodone	Serzone	100–500 mg	mid	none	none	low	high
fluvoxamine	Luvox	50–300 mg	low	none	low	none	high
mirtazapine	Remeron	15–45 mg	mid	high	mid	mid	mid
MAO-INHIBITORS							
phenelzine	Nardil	30–90 mg	low	mid	none	mid	mid
tranylcypromine	Parnate	20–60 mg	low	low	none	mid	mid

[1] Action on neurotransmitters. NE: Norepinephrine; 5-HT: Serotonin.
[2] ACH: Anticholinergic effects: dry mouth, constipation, blurry vision, urinary hesitation.

How do these actions on the activities of various nerve cells relate to the treatment of depression and the choice of medications? The research to date indicates that some people with depression suffer from a malfunction primarily in the serotonin system in the brain, while others' depression may be traceable to a disorder in the norepinephrine system. Furthermore, some depressed people may have biological disturbances in their dopamine system, or combined disturbances in any of the three nerve cell systems. This is an important point, because there are those who are treated initially with an antidepressant that targets serotonin, and who exhibit either no response or only a partial response. If this occurs, it is important to know that it absolutely does not mean that antidepressants in general will be ineffective. Many of these patients will be switched to another class of antidepressants (e.g., one targeting norepinephrine) and then go on to have a very good response.

Here is the problem: It is often difficult for doctors to know which group of antidepressants ultimately will prove effective. There are some guidelines that can aid the physician in choosing a medication, but often the choice must be made on a trial and error basis, starting treatment with one medication and being prepared to switch to another should the patient fail to show a good response.

Bipolar Disorders

In the most general sense, bipolar disorder, which is also known as manic depression, is characterized by wide swings in mood that alternate between mania and depression. These two emotional states can be viewed as opposite ends, or "poles," of a continuum, hence the term *bipolar* (*bi* is the Latin term for two). During an episode of mania a person's mood is abnormally elevated or euphoric. The depression associated with bipolar disorder can be equal in severity to major depression and is recognized by feelings of intense sadness and hopelessness. Actually, there are several different types of bipolar disorder; however, central to all types are the swings between an elevated mood and a depressed mood.

On average, one percent of the U.S. adult population is afflicted with bipolar disorder (American Psychiatric Association 1994b). It often first appears in adolescence or early adulthood and is considered a long-term illness, characterized by patterns of multiple episodes.

Medications used in bipolar disorder are intended to treat acute episodes of mania or depression, and also to prevent future episodes from occurring. These medications are referred to by various terms: mood stabilizers, antimanic agents, or anticycling agents. In general, these are interchangeable terms.

Mood Stabilizers and How They Work

The three most widely used mood stabilizers are lithium, carbamazepine, and valproate. Carbamazepine and valproate are anticonvulsants. Two newer anticonvulsants, gabapentin and lamotrigine, are currently being evaluated for potential usefulness in treating bipolar disorder. All of these medications work differently from each other. This means that for some people it will be necessary to try different medicines until the best one can be determined. It can also mean that if one mood stabilizer does not work well, there is a good chance that another one will. The mood stabilizers may begin to take effect within the first week of treatment. However, full stabilization of mood and behaviors can take up to eight weeks.

Most people experience some symptom relief with mood stabilizers. In the United States, lithium is the medication that has been most widely used since the early 1970s. There are many more studies on its effectiveness than there are for the other mood stabilizers. In general, about 60–80 percent of all people on lithium experience a significant reduction in their symptoms.

Of the anticonvulsants, valproate and carbamazepine have been used for a much longer period and have been studied more intensively than gabapentin and lamotrigine, which have been available only for a short time. Valproate and carbamazepine are very effective medications, especially for rapid cycling bipolar disorder or other difficult to treat cases.

It is becoming more common to see combinations of mood stabilizers used. There is also increasing evidence that the effectiveness of a mood stabilizer, or a combination, may change over the course of the disease for a given person. A medication that previously worked well for someone may begin to lose effectiveness for reasons that are not clearly understood.

As with all medications, side effects, drug interactions, or effects of the particular drug on an existing medical condition must be considered. With the mood stabilizers it is these factors that often determine which medication will work best for a given individual. Because the mood stabilizers differ so much from each other, we will discuss each one individually.

Lithium

Lithium is a basic element found on the Periodic Chart of Elements, in the same chemical family as sodium and potassium. Lithium shares some, but not all, of the properties of the other elements in its family. Although widely found in nature, a physiological function for lithium has not been discovered.

The exact way in which lithium works is not completely understood. Current research suggests that it works inside the nerve cells in the brain to stabilize overactive systems that regulate mood. These overactive circuits can lead to either mania or depression, depending on which system is affected. It appears that lithium can interrupt several overactive pathways, which may explain its effectiveness in treating both mania and depression.

Medication Treatment: What to Expect

When lithium is initiated, the starting dose will be in the range of 600–900 mg per day. The dose will be gradually increased over the first seven to ten days. During, and immediately following, the acute manic phase, the dose will be kept at about 1200–2400 mg daily. After the acute episode has resolved, many patients will not need as much lithium. The dose during the maintenance phase will be between 600–1800 mg per day. Lithium is available as the following products:

Tablets or capsules, as lithium carbonate (not extended release)

- Eskalith 300 mg tablets and 300 mg capsules

- Lithonate 300 mg capsules

- Lithotabs 300 mg tablets

- Various generic products available in 150 mg, 300 mg, and 600 mg tablets or capsules

Extended release tablets, as lithium carbonate

- Eskalith CR 450 mg tablets

- Lithobid 300 mg tablets

Syrup, as lithium citrate

• Cibalith-S 300 mg/teaspoonful (sugar free)*

• Various generic products 300 mg/teaspoonful*

*Contains alcohol.

The best way to ensure that the dosage of lithium is correct for someone is to measure the amount of lithium in the blood. This is necessary because lithium can have some very serious side effects, which are often related to its level in the bloodstream. The amount of lithium required to produce symptom relief is very close to the amount that can be dangerously high, or toxic. To avoid problems with a high blood level of lithium, laboratory tests are performed periodically to make sure the range is both safe and effective. It is important to discuss the frequency of these laboratory tests with the doctor who is prescribing lithium. The dosages and blood level values for lithium are summarized below:

	Dosage Range	Blood Level
Acute mania	1200–2400 mg/day	0.8–1.5 mEq/L
Maintenance	600–1800 mg/day	0.6–1.2 mEq/L

Side Effects

To get the most benefit from treatment with lithium it is extremely important to have an understanding of the side effects. Many side effects are not serious and can be effectively managed. Others can be more serious. All side effects should be reported to the doctor. If the side effects are severe, they should be reported immediately. The following information is not inclusive and is intended to give only a general idea of what to watch for.

• *Nausea, vomiting, diarrhea*—These can occur to varying degrees and at any time during treatment. These side effects can be minimized by taking lithium with food or meals. Sometimes the long-acting forms of lithium will produce fewer of these gastrointestinal symptoms. *However, if these symptoms are severe, or arise suddenly after someone has been taking lithium for some time, who has not previously been bothered by these side effects, the doctor should be notified immediately.*

• *Tremor of the hands*—Many people will experience a slight tremor in the hands when lithium is first started. This usually goes away with time. Limiting or avoiding caffeine helps lessen this tremor. Other medications can sometimes be added to help reduce a tremor. *If this hand tremor becomes more noticeable or appears suddenly, the doctor should be notified.*

• *Drowsiness, fatigue*—When people first start taking lithium they may experience some degree of drowsiness or sedation. Usually, this is not severe, although caution is advised when driving. For most people, this side effect disappears. *However, if a person is noticeably sedated, appears confused, has slurred speech or difficulty walking, the doctor should be notified immediately.* People often report feeling "slowed down" while taking lithium. This is a different sensation than the drowsiness described above. Sometimes this just means that the symptoms of mania or hypomania are responding to treatment. As mentioned earlier, some people do not like to lose the manic high and will use this effect as a reason to stop taking lithium.

- *Effects on kidneys*—Lithium relies on the kidney to be removed from the body. Keeping the kidneys functioning well by drinking lots of fluids helps to ensure that lithium is removed from the body properly. Lithium can cause increased urination and thirst, which go away for most people. *Anytime a person becomes dehydrated, or loses sodium from the body, there is a potential for lithium levels to increase. People can become dehydrated from having the flu, running a fever, sweating excessively, or taking certain medications. The doctor prescribing lithium should be informed of any of the above-mentioned situations.*

- *Effects on the thyroid gland*—Lithium can cause a change in some laboratory tests that are used to measure thyroid function. For most people, this is not significant. A small number of people experience a decrease in the functioning of the thyroid gland (hypothyroidism). The doctor may decide that supplementing the lithium with a thyroid medication is the best approach, or may try another mood stabilizer.

- *Weight gain*—Weight gain, from five to twenty pounds, may occur while taking lithium. This side effect will cause some people to want to stop the medication.

- *Rash or acne*—Either or both can result from taking lithium. If the rash and/or acne are severe enough, the lithium may need to be stopped.

Carbamazepine

Carbamazepine (brand-name Tegretol) has been used for more than twenty-five years to treat bipolar disorder. This medicine is chemically related to the tricyclic antidepressants. The exact way in which carbamazepine works has not been identified. It has been widely studied, without yielding conclusive results, to support the theory that it works by reducing the kindling process. As described previously, kindling is a process by which the brain becomes increasingly sensitized to various stimuli and, eventually, spontaneous abnormal brain activity occurs. Carbamazepine also affects the regulation of the movement of sodium and potassium in and out of nerve cells. And, like lithium, it can stabilize malfunctioning neurotransmitter circuits inside cells.

Medication Treatment: What to Expect

When carbamazepine is initiated, the starting dose will be in the range of 200–400 mg per day. Over the first two to three weeks, the dose will be increased to a range of 600–1600 mg daily. Smaller, more gradual increases in dosage can help keep side effects to a minimum. The amount of carbamazepine in the bloodstream must be measured periodically. The level that is safe and effective for most people is 4–10 mcg/ml. This drug is available as the following products:

- Carbamazepine 100 mg chewable tablets (as common brand-name, Tegretol)

- Carbamazepine 200 mg tablets (as generic and common brand-name, Tegretol)

- Tegretol XR (extended release) 100 mg, 200 mg, and 400 mg tablets

- Liquid, 100 mg/teaspoonful

Side Effects

- *Stomach upset*—Nausea, vomiting, diarrhea, and stomach cramps can occur. These side effects can be minimized by taking the dose with food or milk.

- *Sedation and drowsiness*—Most noticeable when the drug is first started; for most people, these side effects go away. *Dizziness* and *blurred vision* are also possible.

- *Skin*—A red, itching rash, or hives, may develop. Sometimes it does not go away and the drug must be stopped. Carbamazepine also can increase the skin's sensitivity to sunlight, leading to sunburn or discoloration. The use of sunscreen is recommended.

- *Heart rate*—The heart rate can become slowed with carbamazepine. This is most likely to be a problem for older people.

- *Effects on blood*—Although rare in adults, carbamazepine can cause anemia, or lower the red blood cell or white blood cell count.

- *Effects on the liver*—Carbamazepine can cause damage to the liver, but this is a rare occurrence. Laboratory tests can be done to monitor for this.

Valproate

Valproate, also called valproic acid, and known by the brand-names Depakote and Depakene, has been used for about twenty years in the treatment of bipolar disorder. The precise manner in which valproate works has not been determined. One of its strongest effects is on a neurotransmitter called GABA. It is thought that valproate increases the GABA levels in the brain, which leads to decreasing manic symptoms.

Medication Treatment: What to Expect

When valproate treatment is initiated, the starting dose will be in the range of 500–750 mg per day. Sometimes the starting dose can be higher as long as the person does not experience serious side effects, especially stomach upset. The dose will be increased over the first one to two weeks to 750–1500 mg daily. The amount of valproate in the bloodstream will be measured periodically. The level that is safe and effective for most people is 50–100 mcg/ml. This drug is available as the following products:

- Divalproex sodium, 125 mg, 250 mg, 500 mg delayed-release tablets (brand name Depakote)

- Divalproex sodium, 125 mg sprinkle capsules (brand-name Depakote)

- Valproic acid 250 mg capsules (generic and brand-name Depakene)

- Valproic acid, liquid, 250 mg/teaspoonful (generic and brand-name Depakene)

Side Effects

- *Stomach upset*—Nausea, vomiting, and indigestion are common, although usually not severe, and diminish with time. The delayed-release tablet form is less likely to cause stomach upset than are the capsules. Rarely, valproate can cause pain and inflammation in the pancreas. The sign that this may be occurring is severe abdominal pain. *Notify your physician immediately if you experience sudden, very intense abdominal pain.*

- *Dizziness, moderate drowsiness, hand tremor*—These side effects are usually not significant and will go away with time. *However, if a person is noticeably sedated, appears confused, has slurred speech or difficulty walking, the doctor should be notified immediately.*

- *Tremor of the hands*—Many people will experience a slight tremor in the hands when valproate is first started. This usually goes away with time. Limiting or avoiding caffeine will help to lessen this tremor. Other medications sometimes can be added to help reduce a tremor.

- *Weight gain or loss*—This is usually accompanied by an increase or decrease in appetite.

- *Hair loss*—This may be a short-term effect.

- *Effects on blood*—Although rare, sometimes the normal manner in which blood clots may be inhibited. The result can be increased bleeding and/or bruising.

- *Effects on the liver*—Rarely, valproate can cause damage to the liver. Laboratory tests should be done to monitor for this possibility.

New Anticonvulsants

A brief discussion of two new drugs, gabapentin and lamotrigine, follows. Time will tell whether either or both of these will play an important part in the treatment of bipolar disorder.

Gabapentin

This medication, marketed under the brand name of Neurontin, is thought to have an effect on the GABA neurotransmitter system. It is not clear whether this action explains how it might be helpful in bipolar disorder. The dose of gabapentin is usually 300–2400 mg per day. Blood level monitoring is not necessary for this drug. Common side effects are drowsiness, tremor, and blurred vision.

Lamotrigine

This medication, with the brand-name of Lamictal, is assumed to work by decreasing the effects of an excitatory neurotransmitter called glutamate. This may or may not explain how it works in treating bipolar disorder. The dose of lamotrigine is 200–500 mg daily. Blood level monitoring is recommended. The common side effects are drowsiness, headache, blurred vision, stomach upset, and skin rash.

Anxiety Disorders

There are several types of anxiety disorders, including situational anxiety, phobias, social phobia, panic disorder, generalized anxiety disorder, and obsessive-compulsive disorder.

In the initial evaluation of an anxiety disorder, it is always a good idea to have a physical examination, including appropriate laboratory tests, and to give a thorough drug history, including prescription, over-the-counter, and street drugs. If a medical condition or drug usage is found, it is important to first treat the underlying disorder that may be causing the anxiety or to address the drug use. Then, if necessary, treatment targeted specifically at anxiety can begin.

The most common medical treatment for anxiety is antianxiety medication, also called "minor tranquilizers." These medications have been used since the mid-1950s to treat anxiety. They are usually very effective at relieving it and have few side effects. The main side effects they do have are sedation and a tendency to increase the effects of other drugs, such as alcohol. They also can be habit-forming if used for more than a few weeks. Some of these medications have achieved notoriety because of this side effect, as described in the book *I'm Dancing as Fast as I Can* (Gordon 1990). The following chart shows a list of the drugs in this class.

Dosages of Antianxiety Agents

Generic Name	Brand-Name	Single-Dose Dosage Range (mg)	Usual Dosage Range (mg/day)
Minor Tranquilizers			
Diazepam	Valium	2–10	4–40
Chlordiazepoxide	Librium	10–50	15–100
Flurazepam	Dalmane	15–60	15–60
Prazepam	Centrax	5–30	20–40
Clorazepate	Tranxene	3.75–15	7.5–60
Clonazepam	Klonopin	0.5–2	1–8
Temazepam	Restoril	15–30	15–60
Lorazepam	Ativan	0.5–2	1.5–6
Alprazolam	Xanax	0.25–2	0.5–6
Oxazepam	Serax	10–30	30–90
Triazolam	Halcion	0.125–0.5	0.125–0.5
Midazolam	Versed (injectable only)	1–2.5	1–15
Quazepam	Doral	7.5–30	7.5–30
Other Antianxiety Medications			
Estazolam	ProSom	1.0–2.0	1.0–2.0
Zolpidem	Ambien	5–10	5–10
Buspirone	BuSpar	5–20	10–40
Hydroxyzine	Atarax, Vistaril	10–50	30–200
Diphenhydramine	Benadryl	25–100	75–200
Propranolol	Inderal	10–80	20–160
Atenolol	Tenormin	25–100	25–100
Clonidine	Catapres	0.1–0.3	0.2–0.9

Often, someone will be prescribed a minor tranquilizer to be taken when the anxiety is particularly severe. Thus, several doses may be taken on some days and none on others. Usually, these antianxiety medications can be used safely for two to five months without significant dependency developing, depending upon the individual. However, when used for more than six months, dependency is likely to develop. Over time, as the anxiety gradually diminishes, the medication can be used less frequently, and eventually discontinued.

Minor tranquilizers work by binding to certain receptor sites in the brain associated with the neurotransmitter GABA. When they bind to this receptor they seem to reduce the reactiveness of the limbic system.

Caution: If these medications have been taken daily for several weeks or more, they should never be stopped abruptly because of the risk of serious withdrawal symptoms.

Treatment Considerations: What to Expect

In cases of situational anxiety, initially a low dose of medication may be prescribed. Typically, 0.5 to 1 mg of lorazepam, or the equivalent, is an effective starting dose, taken up to two to three times daily. For situational anxiety, however, it is usually not necessary to take the medication routinely. It can be taken when anxiety increases, or when an increase is anticipated. Sometimes, after a few weeks of use, the medication doesn't seem to work quite as well, and a small dosage increase may be necessary. This reduction in anxiety helps people to function better and thus allows time for them to address the situation that caused it. Then, over time, use of the medication can be gradually tapered off. The average length of treatment is a few weeks to a few months. In situational anxiety, insomnia, especially a difficulty in falling asleep, is often a problem. These medications have proved useful for dealing with this problem (on a short-term basis).

Side Effects

As a rule, if taken in the correct dose, minor tranquilizers are relatively free of side effects. However, the correct dose varies from person to person. It the dose is too low, the anxiety will still be noticeable. If the dose is too high, the person may feel drowsy or even drunk, talk with slurred speech, and walk unsteadily. Obviously, driving a car or operating machinery should not be attempted under these circumstances. If the dose is correct, however, people are usually able to drive, and do all of their customary activities. As with all medications, other reactions are possible. Some people may develop a rash. On very rare occasions some people react "paradoxically" and become more agitated instead of calmer.

Addiction Potential

Minor tranquilizers have an addiction potential similar to that of alcohol. When taken, they can create feelings that are like those experienced when drinking alcohol. They also have a withdrawal syndrome similar to alcohol. (Contrary to popular belief, alcohol can be habit-forming, but not everyone becomes dependent on it.) Most people can use minor tranquilizers in a controlled fashion, but some tend to become hooked on them. Fortunately, minor tranquilizers are not toxic to the brain, liver, and other organs as alcohol is. In general, they are very helpful for reducing suffering and they are safe, but must be used with caution.

Other Antianxiety Medications

These include the antihistamines and beta-blockers. The main antihistamine used for anxiety is hydroxyzine (Vistaril or Atarax). It is sedating and has some antianxiety effect. It is not habit-forming. The main problem with it is that often, in order to take enough to reduce anxiety, significant drowsiness may be produced. The usual starting dose is 10–25 mg three to four times daily. Beta-blockers are blood pressure medications that block the effects of adrenaline. They are better at reducing the physical symptoms of anxiety than the emotional feeling of anxiety. They can cause low blood pressure and light-headedness. The usual starting dose is 20–40 mg of propranolol, or the equivalent. They are not habit-forming, but should not be stopped abruptly because of the possibility of temporarily raising the person's blood pressure.

Antipsychotic Medications: What They Are and How They Work

Antipsychotic medications help to reduce psychotic symptoms. They are often used in schizophrenia, but they will treat psychotic symptoms regardless of the cause of the psychosis. They are somewhat sedating, but this is not how they work. Antipsychotic medications specifically target psychotic symptoms, especially delusions, hallucinations, and disorganized thinking. Until recently, they all worked by blocking dopamine in certain parts of the brain. Now, there are newer agents, the atypical antipsychotics, which have a somewhat different mechanism of action.

Types of Antipsychotics

The older medications traditionally have been divided into high-potency and low-potency types. They all work basically the same way, but each type has a significantly different side-effect profile.

The high-potency medications, such as haloperidol, require lower doses and produce less sedation. However, they have more of a tendency to produce extrapyramidal (neurological) side effects, such as Parkinsonian-like behavior (tremors, lack of facial expressions, stiff gait).

One problem with the older medications is that they tend to work very well for the positive symptoms of schizophrenia but they often have little or no effect on negative symptoms. This has meant that although the floridly psychotic symptoms were controlled, so that schizophrenics could function outside of hospital settings, they often continued to feel listless, be very isolative, and lead very restricted lives. The newer, atypical agents may help treat the negative symptoms, as well as the positive ones, so that people not only think better, they may also feel better, e.g., they may experience more vitality and a greater sense of "aliveness."

Medication Treatment: What to Expect

Once the diagnosis of schizophrenia or schizophreniform disorder has been made, the physician will probably recommend treatment with an antipsychotic medication. Average doses are shown below.

Dosages of Antipsychotic Medications

Generic Name	Brand-Name	Dosage Range (mg/day)	Equivalence[1] (mg)
Low Potency			
Chlorpromazine	Thorazine	50–1500	100
Thioridazine	Mellaril	150–800	100
Clozapine[3]	Clozaril	300–900	50
Mesoridazine	Serentil	50–500	50
Quetiapine[3]	Seroquel	300–750	50
High Potency			
Molindone	Moban	20–225	10

Perphenazine	Trilafon	8–60	10
Loxapine	Loxitane	50–250	10
Trifluoperazine	Stelazine	10–40	5
Fluphenazine	Prolixin[2]	3–45	2
Thiothixene	Navane	10–60	5
Haloperidol	Haldol[2]	2–40	2
Pimozide	Orap	1–10	1
Risperidone[3]	Risperdal	4–16	1–2
Olanzapine[3]	Zyprexa	5–20	1–2
Ziprasidone[3]	Zeldox	80–160	15

Antiparkinson/Anticholinergic Drugs[4]

Trihexyphenidyl	Artane	5–15
Benztropine mesylate	Cogentin	1–8
Biperiden	Akineton	2–8
Amantadine	Symmetrel	100–300

1 Dose required to achieve efficacy of 100 mg chlorpromazine.
2 Available in time-release IM formulation.
3 Atypical antipsychotic.
4 Used to treat some antipsychotic side effects.

References

American Psychiatric Association. 1994. Practice guidelines for treatment of patients with bipolar disorder. *American Journal of Psychiatry* 151:(Suppl)1–35.

Gordon, B. 1990. *I'm Dancing as Fast as I Can*. New York: Bantam.

PART VII

OPTIMIZING YOUR LIFE

Emotional wellness is more than just putting out psychic fires. Beyond crisis management, you need to seek positive enrichment of your emotional life through relationships, learning, and self-exploration. This section opens up four paths to optimizing your life:

Relaxation emphasizes the important of daily relaxation and stress relief, offering a dozen simple exercises that can be mastered in ten minutes each.

Meditation gives a sampling of the meditation practices that have calmed, enriched, and deepened the lives of millions of people all over the world.

Visualization teaches the basics rules for effective imagery, special place visualization, and consulting your inner guide.

Dreams provides practical advice in interpreting your dreams and applying the lessons learned to your daily life.

CHAPTER 45

Relaxation

Daily Relaxers

This is a simple section with only one purpose—to help you relax with varied techniques that you can learn in five minutes.

For each technique you'll find a short explanation first, followed by the instructions. The explanation tells you how the technique works, why it works, and what it's particularly good for. The instructions are clear and simple. You should be able to read and understand the technique in a few minutes, and practice it with positive results right away.

Body Check-In

How relaxed are you at this moment in time? Where is the tension in your body? If you're like most people, you're probably more aware of your bank balance or the time of day than you are of your own body, even though you're riding around in it. And that's the problem, isn't it? You've been treating your body like a junk car that gets you from one place to another, instead of treating it like a precious temple enshrining your existence.

Your body can actually tell you more about relaxation than any book can. It knows volumes about your unique states of tension and release. All you have to do is turn your attention within, and quietly listen.

Remember to thank your body for keeping you alive and informed, for serving you despite all the times you've ignored its needs. Do something special for your body today: take a bubble bath, get a manicure, use some hand lotion, or wear your most comfortable clothes. Keep checking in with your body. It will tell you truths you need to know, secrets you cannot hear from any other source.

From time to time today, pause in a quiet spot and close your eyes. Allow your breathing to slow and deepen. Ask your body, "Where are you tense?" Scan your body for any tight neck or back muscles, sore joints, tiny aches and pains in your arms or legs, little twitches around your eyes, or places where you are hunched up to protect tender spots.

As you find each twitch, contraction, or distortion, thank your body for showing it to you. Remember that all tension is muscular tension, and all muscle contraction is self-produced, even if you aren't aware of producing it. So, once you become aware of the tension, you can begin to let the tension go. Focus on each area for a moment, exploring the tightness or soreness, even exaggerating it a little if you can. Exhale slowly and allow your tight back muscles to relax, your eyelids to stop twitching, your knees to stop aching. Tell your body, "It's okay, we don't need this tension or this soreness anymore. We can let it go."

Paying Attention

Paying attention to a problem will sometimes solve it. If your son is getting Ds in math and you start paying more attention to his homework, the grade may come up. A spouse who is feeling neglected can be cheered up by more attention. Writing down every cent you spend can curb overspending.

Likewise, tension in your body is a problem that you can start to fix by just paying more attention. When you feel tense or nervous, it's a big help to simply notice and list your physical sensations. For example:

I have a slight headache.

My lower back hurts.

My neck muscles are tight.

I'm breathing in short, shallow breaths.

I feel hot.

Of course, it's difficult to remember in the middle of rush hour or an exam that you're supposed to notice and list your physical sensations. In those situations, you're usually oblivious to your bodily state.

You can improve your chances of remembering to focus on your body and your ability to do it well by practicing this simple exercise in private, when you aren't under stress:

Sit in a comfortable position and close your eyes. Take several deep breaths. Bend your right arm at your elbow, out to the side, and lift the arm so that the tips of your fingers are about even with the top of your head. In other words, raise your hand as though you want to ask a question. Hold it in this position for a while.

As your right arm begins to tire, focus on the sensation of tiredness. Which muscles are actually holding the arm up? Can you find a way to relax them somewhat without letting the arm fall? Scan your body and see if other muscles are tightening. Are your legs tensing because your arm hurts? If so, can you relax them? Focus on your heart, stomach, and lungs. Are you beginning to feel a little anxious? If so, can you find a way to calm yourself? Take several deep breaths and say to yourself gently, "Relax," or "Let go."

After three or four minutes, lower your right arm slowly until it rests in your lap. As you lower it, focus on the sensations. Which muscles are strained and which are not? Can you identify the moment at which the muscles that held up the arm relax? How does the discomfort change? Does it go away as soon as the arm moves? Does it go away gradually? Is there any discomfort as your hand rests on your lap? Can you still feel the muscles you were so aware of when your arm was raised?

Instant Relaxer

Once you've learned Progressive Muscle Relaxation (see the chapter on stress in part V) you're ready for the big league of stress reduction. Soon you'll be able to relax anywhere, anytime, with almost instant effectiveness.

Forget Valium. You don't have to wait for that trip to Hawaii. You will soon have a way to relax even in crisis—even if your mother-in-law stops by for an impromptu visit.

The technique, called *Cue-Controlled Relaxation*, hinges on a well-known principle that governs learning: When two unrelated events occur at the same time (for example a chime rings every noon while a monk is saying his prayers) the events become linked in the mind. Eventually, if they occur together often enough, one event can trigger feelings and reactions associated with the other (the mere sound of the noon chime can stimulate peaceful feelings associated with the monk's prayers).

In the next exercise, you'll choose a cue word or phrase that will become linked to feelings of deep relaxation. With a little practice, the mere thought of your cue word, like the monk's chime, will trigger a simultaneous muscle release throughout your entire body.

The first step is to choose your cue word or phrase. Make it something that pleases you, but it also helps if the cue phrase tells you exactly what to do. Here are some examples:

Relax and let go

Breathe and release

Calm and relaxed

Relax now

Peace

You might even choose a favorite color or place as your cue word. Anything will work as long as it is linked, through practice, to feelings of relaxation.

The second step is to relax using the same sequence of muscle groups that you learned for Progressive Muscle Relaxation—but this time don't tighten anything. Just relax each muscle group by deliberately releasing all tension in the area. At the same time, take a deep breath and in your mind, say your cue word or phrase. Here is the sequence:

1. Take a deep breath. Say your cue phrase.

2. Relax your forearms, biceps, and pectoral muscles. Take a deep breath. Say your cue phrase.

3. Relax your forehead. Take a deep breath. Say your cue phrase.

4. Relax your eyes, cheeks, lips, jaw, neck, and shoulders. Take a deep breath. Say your cue phrase.

5. Relax your back and chest. Take a deep breath. Say your cue phrase.

6. Relax your abdomen. Take a deep breath. Say your cue phrase.

7. Relax your calves, thighs, and buttocks. Take a deep breath. Say your cue phrase.

8. Briefly scan your body for any remaining tension. Release it while taking a final deep breath. Say your cue phrase.

Practice Cue-Controlled Relaxation daily for a week. Only when you feel confident in your ability to release tension by willing yourself to relax, should you go on to the final step.

In this step, you relax all muscle groups *simultaneously*, while taking a deep breath and thinking of your cue phrase. You continue to breathe deeply, thinking of the cue phrase with each exhale, and scanning your body for any tightness. Focus on muscles that need to relax and empty them of tension. You should soon be able to achieve significant levels of relaxation in thirty to sixty seconds.

Practice Cue-Controlled Relaxation at first when things are quiet and peaceful. Then begin using your cue phrase in slightly tense situations at home or work. Keep practicing until you can cue relaxation even while your boss looks steamed or your children are fighting in the backseat. And remember, as with any technique, you must invest the time to master this skill. It works!

Withdrawal into Blackness

It may surprise you that a lot of stress enters through your eyes. Bright sun or car headlights make you squint. Clashing colors can make you irritable. Sudden movements make you flinch. Wind and dust make your eyes water and blink. Long hours reading make your eyes sore.

Fast-paced TV commercials can exhaust your eyes. The brash ads on signs, billboards, and magazine ads are all brightly competing to grab your attention and hold it. We've created a frenetic modern visual environment that is a continuous assault on eyes that evolved to scan peaceful green and gold savannahs.

There are also emotional stressors that involve the eyes. Urban clutter or household mess—the visual equivalent of noise—can wear you down. Overwork can not only tire your eyes but make you "sick of looking at" your papers. Some days, everywhere you look you see reminders of jobs undone, hopes dashed, obligations unfulfilled, opportunities lost, defeats suffered.

Your eyes are pointed outward because they are your primary tool for observing and comprehending the external world. Your eyes are literally your "lookouts," constantly scanning the horizon for approaching danger or opportunity.

Tired eyes seek blackness as a rest from vigilance and the daily image assault. Blackness shuts you off from the real world and forces you to "look in" on yourself—a physical impossibility and a spiritual necessity.

Try enjoying blackness a couple of times a day. It just takes a minute. Seated at a desk or table, put the heels of your palms directly over your closed eyes. Block out all light without putting too much pressure on your eyelids.

Try to see the color black. You may see other colors, or images, but focus on the color black. Use a mental image to remember the color black: black cats, black holes in space, the back of a dark closet.

Tell yourself you don't have to look at anything right now. Let the muscles around your eyes relax—your eyelids, under your eyes, the crease between your brows, your forehead, your cheeks.

After a minute, slowly lower your hands and gently open your eyes. Remind yourself throughout the day that at almost any moment you can close your eyes and escape into blackness.

Pencil Drop

When localized areas of high-pressure air meet low-pressure air they can spawn a whirlwind that sucks up dirt and trash and moves across the landscape spreading disorder and destruction.

When your high-pressure lifestyle meets a low ebb in your energy level, together they can stir up an emotional whirlwind that makes everything you value—your loved ones, your work, your hopes and dreams—seem like debris swirling around you.

Before you take off across your emotional landscape spreading disorder and destruction, take a moment to relax and center yourself. When your life seems like a whirlwind, the image of the calm center is important. At the exact center of a whirlwind, there is a spot of perfectly calm air.

Tell yourself, "I am the calm center of the whirlwind. I can take a moment to right myself, to return to center. At my core is a calm spot that does not turn with every gust of wind." Paradoxically, when you take your place as the calm center, the whirlwind slows, the dust settles, and your life seems more orderly and manageable.

An ordinary pencil can help you find your calm center. This is something you can do at a desk or table, when you're working on the bills or homework, and you need to return to your calm center quickly and get on with your work.

Pick up a pencil by the point end. Hold it very lightly between your thumb and fingertip, letting the eraser end hang down a couple of inches above the tabletop. Cradle your head in your other hand and get as comfortable as you can.

Close your eyes and consciously slow your breathing. Tell yourself that when you are sufficiently relaxed, the pencil will slip out of your fingers and drop. That will be your sign to let go completely, to just relax and feel peaceful for two minutes.

Imagine you're at the calm center of a whirlwind. You can hear the cold wind whistling, but right where you are it is calm. The sun is shining and you feel warm and secure. Imagine all your cares and worries receding. The whirlwind expands and slows down. The calm center gets larger and more relaxed.

Continue breathing slowly, thinking about calming and relaxing all your tight muscles. If a worry or doubt intrudes, just tell yourself, "That's okay, I can let that go for now and relax. I'll just sit here, calm and centered, deeply, deeply relaxed."

After the pencil drops, continue to enjoy your calm center for a couple of minutes. Then return to what you were doing with renewed energy, feeling calm, relaxed, and focused.

Going Deeper and Deeper

Self-hypnosis is perhaps the most effective, most pleasurable relaxation technique ever devised; your mind and body begin to feel free, your muscles relax, your attention narrows, and you become more open to suggestion.

You've already been hypnotized many times without knowing it, going into a trance state while driving or daydreaming. Even trying to remember a shopping list or lounging in front of the TV can induce a temporary hypnotic state. You may also have been in a shock-induced trance following a scary experience.

When you learn to hypnotize yourself, you're harnessing a power you already possess: your mind's capacity to disconnect from the pain and pressures of the moment. Hypnosis can offer you a vacation from stress while it refocuses your mind on healing and relaxing imagery.

Before trying the following induction, you'll need to do two things in preparation. First, create an image of a safe and peaceful place. It should be a place that's comfortable and calm, and beyond the reach of anything stressful or threatening. You can use the Special Place exercise in the chapter on Visualization later in part VII. Second, develop one or two posthypnotic suggestions that will help you stay relaxed when you come back to the real world. Make suggestions for the immediate future (so your subconscious has time to put them into practice). The following list might give you some ideas:

I can awake refreshed and rested.

My body is feeling more and more healthy and strong.

My mind will remain cool and relaxed throughout the day.

Whenever I start to worry, I can take a deep breath and let go.

I feel relaxed, secure, and at ease with myself.

I move calmly and assertively through the world.

1. **Deep Breath.** Start by closing your eyes and taking a slow, deep breath. Take a second deep breath and focus on relaxing your body as you exhale.

2. **Muscle relaxation.** Relax your legs, arms, face, neck, shoulders, chest, and abdomen in that order. As you relax your legs and arms, say to yourself the key phrase, "heavier and heavier, more and more deeply relaxed." As you relax your forehead and cheeks, say the key phrase, "smooth and relaxed, letting go of tension." As you relax your jaw, say the key phrase, "loose and relaxed." Your neck, too, becomes "loose and relaxed." Your shoulders are "relaxed and drooping." You relax your chest, abdomen, and back by taking a deep breath. As you exhale, say the key phrase, "calm and relaxed."

3. **Staircase or path to a special place.** Count each step going down to a peaceful place, and with each step you will become more and more deeply relaxed. Count slowly backwards from ten to zero. Each number you count is a step going down. Imagine that saying each number and taking each step help you feel more and more deeply relaxed. You can count backwards from ten to zero once, twice, or even three times. Each complete count will deepen your relaxation.

4. **Your special place.** In this place you feel total peace and complete safety. Look around and notice the shapes and colors. Listen to the sounds and smell the fragrances of your special place. Notice the temperature and how your body feels there. If you are at the beach, make sure you can hear the waves crashing and the hiss of foam as the waves recede. See and hear the seagulls overhead. Notice the salty sea breeze, the warmth of the sun on your body, and the feel of the sand beneath you. Try to involve all your senses in building the scene: sight, sound, taste, smell, and touch.

5. **Deepen hypnosis.** Now use the following four key suggestions over and over, in varying orders and combinations, until you feel a deep sense of calm and letting go.

    Drifting deeper and deeper, deeper and deeper

    Feeling more and more drowsy, peaceful, and calm

    Drifting and drowsy, drowsy and drifting

    Drifting down, down, down, into total relaxation

6. **Posthypnotic suggestions.** After spending some relaxing time in your special place, give yourself a posthypnotic suggestion. Repeat each suggestion at least three times. And

7. **Coming out of hypnosis.** When you're ready to come out of your trance, count back up from one to ten. In between numbers, remind yourself that you are becoming "more and

more alert, refreshed, and wide awake." As you reach number nine, tell yourself that your eyes are opening; at ten suggest that you are totally alert and wide awake.

Memorize the basic idea behind each of the seven steps. When you can generally recall each step, you're ready to try your own induction. Imagine your own voice saying each hypnotic suggestion slowly, clearly, and calmly. Take the time to let each suggestion sink in before moving on to the next one. It won't take long before you begin to feel the deep relaxation that hypnosis can give you.

Looking Back from the Future

Each separate detail of your life is like a sticky strand of a spider web attaching you to the present. Your attention is fragmented in a thousand directions as you try to keep an eye on the kids, the mortgage, the bills, the appliances, the laundry, the grocery shopping, the cars, the boat, the lawn, the school, the job, the promotion, the raise, the spouse, the trip, the vacation, the parents, the wedding, the funeral, and so on.

It's a full-time job worrying about it all, responding to the sticky tug of every strand of your life. It seems impossible to escape the present situation, to fly out of the web and get some perspective.

But you can escape from the web of the present. You just need to use your imagination.

Just let yourself daydream. Think about the future. But instead of thinking about the near future and whether you can afford a new car next year or what to wear to the Christmas party, think about the far future.

Imagine that you are very old—still healthy and alert, but very old. You've had a long and full life. You are comfortable and secure. You are surrounded by friends and family.

From this perspective, let yourself dimly remember the myriad concerns and worries and doubts that trap you in the web of the present. What will it all matter twenty or thirty or fifty years from now?

When you are old, near the end of a full life, how much will it matter what college your daughter attended? How much will it matter whether you got your teeth capped or moved to a bigger apartment? How much will it matter that your son had a reading problem in third grade? How much will it matter that you had a big fight with your spouse over the credit cards?

Remember that the web that binds you to the present is largely an illusion. Most of the strands are fleeting and ultimately unimportant.

When you imagine looking back from the perspective of old age, focus on the truly important stuff that's going on in your life now. Focus on the love, the hugs and kisses, the quiet moments in the garden.

When you return to your present point of view, try to keep your eye out for those precious moments, and let some of the minor annoyances blow away like cobwebs.

Empathy

A wise old proverb says that you cannot understand a man unless you walk a mile in his shoes. But it's not easy to leave your own beliefs, needs, and fears behind, let alone to see the world through the lens of someone else's experience.

This action is a form of surrender, a letting go of self. But it's also as precious as gold, for without it families, tribes, and nations turn against each other. It is a thing called empathy.

Empathy protects us from the corrosive effects of judgment and contempt. It's the antidote for anger. It's the binding force of friendship and marriage. And it is something you can strengthen in yourself with a few minutes of meditation each day.

Sit with your arms and legs resting comfortably. Close your eyes and take several deep breaths. Think the word "peaceful" as you inhale and the word "relaxed" as you exhale. Scan your body for tension and relax any muscles that seem tight. Let your breathing slow as you allow yourself to relax more and more deeply.

Now imagine a chair in front of you. You have negative feelings for the person sitting in it—feelings of anger, disapproval, or hurt. Visualize the face and expression of the person before you; notice how big or small the person is, the clothes, the colors, the posture.

Now make a conscious decision to suspend your judgments and negative thoughts. Take another deep breath and put those judgments aside; for a brief moment just let them go. See the person in front of you as a human being, just like yourself, who is trying to survive and lead a happy life. Meditate briefly on each of these questions:

What needs might influence his or her behavior?

What fears might affect this person?

What beliefs or values are influencing this person?

What lack of knowledge or skills could have an impact on this person's behavior?

What situational limits, problems, or conflicts might be affecting his or her behavior?

And the most important meditation: How is this person sitting across from you doing the best he or she can? How has this person chosen what seems the highest good, given his or her needs, fears, beliefs, and abilities?

Really think about these questions. See the person as struggling to cope, despite fears and longings, limits of knowledge and ability, despite conflicts and problems. Try to see the world through this person's eyes.

Practice this meditation once a day, perhaps after things quiet down in the evening. Each time you do it try to hold the meditation long enough to feel some of your judgments melting away. As anger and judgments dissolve, you are making room in your heart for empathy, even compassion. Notice the difference in the way you feel about that other person—and about yourself.

Changing Channels

Sometimes your mind gets stuck and you can't stop thinking about your back trouble, your bank balance, or your failed love affair. When this happens, your worries make your body tense up, which worsens your negative mental state, which leads to even more tension, and so on, creating a vicious cycle.

When your mind is stuck, it's not enough to physically relax your body. You have to change channels in your mind as well.

But that's not so easy. Has anyone ever told you, "Just don't think about it?" If so, you know how difficult it is not to think about something that's preying on your mind. You need to not only decide to stop thinking about your worries, but also to replace your worries with something else to occupy your mind.

The exercise that follows offers three different ways to change channels. You can change your negative thoughts to positive images, positive actions, or positive affirmations.

When you notice the same old worries haunting your mind, mentally shout, "Stop!" to yourself. Imagine that you hear the word and it startles you into suspending the monotonous chain of rumination that was causing you stress.

As soon as you have interrupted the stressful thinking, replace it with a pleasant daydream. Pick something that you normally daydream or fantasize about—sex, vacation, hobbies, past successes or pleasures, and so on. Pick something you can see yourself doing that is both easy to imagine and pleasant.

If the visualization of a pleasant daydream doesn't work or "wears out" after a while, try swinging into action. Turn on the radio, play a favorite CD, go for a walk, look through your picture album, do some aerobic exercise, pick up a book or magazine, sing a song, or play an instrument. Try to find an activity that is interesting to you and has high "distraction value."

The third method of changing channels is to replace your worrisome thoughts with affirmations. These are short, positive self-statements that you prepare ahead of time. They both distract from and refute negative thoughts.

Affirmations tell you that you are safe, you are okay the way you are, and you can handle any stress that comes along. Here are some examples:

I am well.

I am safe and calm.

I trust my ability to cope.

I am surrounded by support and love.

I can relax my body and my mind.

I can relax now and make plans later.

These are just stomach cramps.

Tests show my heart is strong and healthy.

I can ask for help.

It's okay to say no.

It's normal for couples to quarrel.

This is the same old neck pain, it always passes.

Can't Lose

Do you worry about the future? Do you agonize about conflicts on the horizon? Are you stressed out by the daily hassle of little things going wrong?

If you listen to politicians on the news or read self-improvement business books, you hear about "win-win" solutions to problems. You hear about clever compromises whereby both sides to a conflict get something positive and nobody loses.

Workers get health insurance and management gets higher productivity. Renters get rent control and landlords get tax credits. Teens get midnight basketball and the community gets less graffiti.

But often, the most stressful hassles in life aren't susceptible to the win-win approach. Many situations are just up to chance: It's either going to rain on the day of your daughter's wedding or it's not. You are either going to win the lottery or you're not. Other situations aren't up to chance, but you personally have little power to influence their outcome: Your company is either going to move to Chicago or not. Your son's application to college is either going to be accepted or not.

When you're worrying, hoping, and fretting about these types of situations, you can't negotiate a win-win approach. But you can reduce your stress by adopting a "can't lose" attitude toward the possible outcomes.

The Can't Lose exercise works like this: you say to yourself, "I can't lose because . . ." and you look for the positive benefits of all possible outcomes.

For example, you can't lose because if it doesn't rain, your daughter will have a splendid outdoor wedding, and if it does rain, she'll have a more intimate, cozy indoor affair, more like your own wedding.

You can't lose because if you win the lottery you'll be rich, and if you don't win the lottery you'll be spared the envy of your friends and the greedy attention of strangers.

You can't lose because if your company moves to Chicago you can move with them and have the excitement of a new city to live in (or quit and have the security and familiarity of staying put), and if your company doesn't move to Chicago you won't have your life disrupted.

If your son gets accepted to college out of state, you'll be proud and excited to see him leave the nest and go out into the world. But if he doesn't get accepted and goes instead to the local community college, you will get to hang on to him a little longer.

Is this just positive thinking in advance? Yes. Is it an impossible abandonment of your desire for your preferred outcome? No. You can't really stop wanting what you really want. You'll still prefer winning over losing, sunshine over rain, security over risk, and so on. But if you even half-heartedly try this exercise, you will reap two enormous benefits: First, you'll reduce the present anxiety associated with wishing, hoping, and worrying. Second, you'll reduce the disappointment you feel when you don't get what you want.

Nourishment from the Past

Memories can be painful—lost loves, moments of embarrassment or fear, times of struggle. But your past can also be a source of strength and inner calm. It's all a matter of knowing where to look, then doing some armchair time travel to reexperience the truly nourishing moments in your life.

The Five-Finger exercise was developed by Dr. David Cheek as a way to achieve deep relaxation and peace, while simultaneously affirming your human worth. The exercise can take less than five minutes. All you have to do is imagine four scenes from your past—using visual, auditory, and kinesthetic (touch) images. It's simple, it's pleasurable, and it works.

Take a deep breath, and as you exhale let your whole body begin to relax. Take another deep breath, and now as you exhale let your eyes close and allow the relaxation to deepen.

Continue to breathe slowly and deeply, counting your breaths on the exhale. Now touch your thumb to your index finger. As the fingers touch, go back to a time when your body felt healthy fatigue. Maybe it was after playing a strenuous sport, or digging in the garden, or hiking a steep trail. Feel how heavy and relaxed your muscles are, feel the warmth and well-being throughout your entire body. Dwell for a minute or two in the scene, enjoying the feeling.

Now touch your thumb to your middle finger. As the fingers touch, go back to a time when you had a loving experience. It might be a warm embrace, an intimate conversation, or a moment of deep sexual connection. Take some time to see, hear, and feel the experience.

Touch your thumb to your ring finger. As the fingers touch, remember one of the nicest compliments you have ever received. Hear it right now; listen carefully. Try to really let it in. By accepting the compliment, you are showing your high regard for the person who said it.

Touch your thumb to your little finger. As the fingers touch, revisit the most beautiful place you have ever been. See the colors and shapes; see the quality of light. Hear the sounds of that beautiful place—the whisper of the wind through the trees or the roar of the waves. Feel that place—the texture, the warmth or coolness. Stay there for a while.

Accepting Yourself

What do you have to work with in your life? What are your tendencies? What are your strengths? What interests you? It's terribly stressful and ultimately self-defeating to go against your own grain, to try to make yourself into a totally different person than you naturally are.

If you're shy and tend to make only a few important friends, you will suffer if you want to be more like someone you know who's naturally gregarious and has a lot of casual acquaintances. If you're a hardworking go-getter, you'll probably never have a poet's ability to stop and extract sonnets from the sunset. If you're genetically inclined to be a sedentary, thoughtful, large person, you'll only beat yourself up needlessly by wanting to be like your physically active, high-strung, skinny-as-a-stick cousin.

That's not to say you shouldn't aspire to self-improve. It's just that you need to honestly assess your starting point and accept what you have to work with as basically okay.

So if you have a chronic illness, or you're short, or you don't earn as much money as some people you know—that's okay. It's what you have to work with. The next time your favorite self-deprecating thought crosses your mind, remind yourself to take a break for a little self-acceptance.

The following exercise is a powerful way to quiet internal self-criticism, reestablish contact with your body in the present moment, and raise your self-esteem by simple self-acceptance.

In a quiet moment, just close your eyes and clear your mind of all the negative, obsessive chatter that tends to go on and on. Let it get quiet inside. Let the echoes of your usual monologue die away. If a negative thought surfaces just tell yourself, "It's only a thought" and let it go.

Notice how you're breathing and consciously try to slow it down. See if you can sense your own heartbeat. Listen to the sounds around you. Sense how each part of your body feels: your arms, your legs, your head, your torso.

If you feel a pain, an itch, or a tingle, tell yourself, "That's all right. That's just how it feels right now. I can accept that."

As you feel more and more relaxed, make some positive, self-accepting suggestions to yourself, such as

I accept myself, whatever good or bad happens.

I can let go of the shoulds, doubts, and worries.

I'm only human, I accept my human nature.

I breathe, I feel, I do the best I can.

End your exercise with a promise to yourself to focus on your positive traits and accomplishments.

Excerpted and adapted with permission from *The Daily Relaxer* by Matthew McKay, Ph.D., and Patrick Fanning. For more information on this and related books, see the "Further Reading" section in the back of the book.

CHAPTER 46

Meditation

General Instructions

There are really only three important general instructions for meditation.

The first is to remember that you are meditating, and that your attention is supposed to be focused on the object of meditation, be it your breath, your steps, your feet, a sound, or a candle. Whenever any other thought intrudes, as soon as you notice that you are no longer focused on the meditation, bring your attention back to the meditation.

The second is to be *compassionate*. Spending time berating yourself for not focusing on the meditation (because you momentarily thought of lunch, or work, or sex) is just more time spent not focusing on the meditation. No need to be critical—just go back to the meditation.

The third (which may help you with the second) is to realize that the thoughts which distract you from the meditation are actually *helping* you. They give you the opportunity to notice that you're no longer focused on the meditation, so that you can return your attention to it.

Think about trying to paper-train a puppy. It looks as though it has to pee. You place it on the newspaper. It wanders off. You gently, patiently bring it back. It wanders off again. *It is the act of being returned* to the newspaper that paper-trains the pup. If the foolish little thing never left the paper, you wouldn't have the opportunity to train it. So you don't kick it when it wanders off, nor give up in disgust. It's just the nature of a puppy to wander.

Likewise, it's the act of noticing the mind has wandered, and returning the attention to the meditation that helps us learn to focus the mind . . .

An Example

When I began to meditate, I was "plagued" by distracting thoughts. I'd try to focus on my breathing, but a typical meditation session might have gone something like this: "breathe in, breathe out . . . wow, I'm meditating . . . uh-oh, I'm not supposed to be thinking about meditating, I'm supposed to be focusing on my breathing . . . in, out . . . hungry . . . uh-oh . . . drat, I can't do this, I'm no good . . . in, out, in, out, in, out . . . hey, I've got it now! . . . feelings of pride . . . uh-oh, better go back to breathing . . . in, out, in, out . . . wonder what's for lunch . . . darn . . . in, out, in, out . . . wonder if it's time to stop yet . . . and so on." Sometimes I'd get lost in a daydream of some sort, and my period of distraction would last for minutes at a time, far longer than I was ever able to concentrate on my breath!

Now that I'm more experienced, I still have plenty of sessions like that! But many times, I can just quickly notice that a thought has crept in, and go right back to my preferred business at hand, which is meditating. So a current session might look more like this: "breathe in, breathe out, in, out, in, out . . . ahh, a lunch thought . . . in, out, in, out . . . Doing Well! . . . ahh, that's a pride thought . . . in, out, in, out. . . ." Of course, sometimes I still spend more time being distracted, than being focused! But I notice the distractions more quickly, and return to the meditation!

On Diligence

It is important to be diligent in your attention to the meditation. That means that *as soon as you notice* that your attention has strayed from the meditation, you bring it gently but firmly back. That means not spending even an extra second on that daydream, no matter how exciting it is (so forget the old "but wait—this is a really important thought I'm thinking—I'd better stick with it, and meditate later" trick). Don't waste even a second on self-critical thoughts like, "Darn it! There I go, thinking again." Simply *let go* of whatever thought it was that passed through, and come back to the meditation. Just for these three minutes, the meditation is your *preferred* thought—any others can wait.

It's a bit like training yourself to wear a seat belt. As soon as you notice that it isn't buckled, you put it on, *every time*, even if you're only three blocks away from your destination. Soon it becomes a habit.

On Body and Hand Position

Luckily for you, I don't require a full lotus position for meditation (can't do one, myself, without enriching my chiropractor)! I think that it's probably best to meditate (except for the walking-based meditations) while sitting up straight. Not ramrod rigid, but not slouching either, with your feet flat on the floor. Then again, you'll sometimes want to meditate while laying down, on the bus, in the bathroom, or standing in line. So don't worry much about body position. Sit up straight when it's convenient, and see if it makes any difference to your concentration.

However, for many people it is useful to maintain a particular and *consistent* hand position while doing most of their meditating. I favor having the thumb tip and forefinger tip of each hand very lightly touching, with the other fingers either curled or extended out.

Learning to maintain a standardized hand position can help to act as a "memory cue" or "trigger" for meditation. Once you get used to meditating, and begin to associate the hand position with meditating, just re-creating the hand position will help you to enter into a meditative state of mind.

This can be especially useful in stressful situations, like a job interview, where you cannot take "time out" to go and meditate (unless you fake a bathroom break—a useful tactic at times). But simply touching thumb to forefinger while taking a deep and mindful breath can help to remind you of the peaceful place that you find in meditation, and give you energy to continue the interview with confidence.

What to Do with Feelings of Doubt and Resistance

Minds being what they are, at some point yours is going to say to you: "This just won't work" or "Why bother?" And if you can learn to use the mind-watching exercises described later, you'll be able to use these thoughts as objects of focus for your attention. Just as smelly old manure can be turned into valuable fertilizer, you can use even thoughts of doubt and resistance to hone your meditation skills, merely by watching them. They will then become your teachers, instead of your tormentors.

Competitive Meditation

It's easy to get competitive, or goal-oriented, with meditation (or with anything else, in this high-pressure culture of ours). The late Tibetan guru Trungpa Rimpoche used to call this "spiritual materialism"!

Try to think of meditation as dance, rather than a race. In a race, the goal is to reach the end faster than anyone else, or faster than you've ever done it before. In a dance, the goal is to enjoy what you're doing while you're doing it. So try not to worry about whether your meditations are "improving," or about whether you're "doing it right." Just do it! Even in a race situation, excessive concern about how you are doing (looking back over your shoulder too much) will actually decrease your performance!

Clearing the Mind

Most of the following exercises operate on what I call the "distraction/subtraction" principle. By giving the mind a very simple but consuming set of instructions to follow, the "normal" mental monologue of fears, desires, memories and predictions can be stilled. The mind becomes just too busy to keep up its usual chatter.

After subtracting these above unwanted thoughts from the contents of the mind, you will gradually be able to directly observe the thought processes of the mind, with the mind-watching exercises. But for now, merely removing these "excess" thoughts from the mind will be your goal.

When asked how he could carve an elephant from an immense block of stone, the master sculptor replied: "I simply cut away everything that doesn't look like an elephant . . ." Carving away the excess thoughts from your mind will leave you with a clear and peaceful feeling, and eventually allow you to understand what really goes on in there!

If not otherwise indicated, at first practice each meditation for three minutes, or longer if you prefer. Once you've learned the exercise, do it for as long or short as you like, from three seconds to three hours!

This first Three Minute Meditation involves our most basic need. We can live for days without water, weeks without food, and perhaps years without sex or a job. But one scant minute without breathing is a long time, for most of us. Yet how often do we really focus our attention exclusively on this most crucial of functions? Fortunately, for a person in good health, breathing doesn't take much thought—and we haven't usually given it much—until today.

Breath-Counting Meditation

Begin by practicing this meditation while sitting comfortably in a quiet place, with your hands in the thumb to forefinger position.

Simply *count* the exhale of each breath, mentally: "Inhale . . . one, Inhale . . . two, Inhale . . . three, Inhale . . . four" then begin again with "Inhale . . . one." Strive not to lose your count, and also try not to alter or regularize your breathing in any way. Try to feel the physical sensation of each breath, both inhale and exhale, as it passes through your nose or mouth.

If you find yourself thinking about *anything* except the feel of your breath and the number of that breath, return to focus on the sensation of breathing, and on the number of that breath. If you are not absolutely sure what number breath you're on, begin again with "In . . . one." No judging, no "I blew the count" thoughts, just back to "In . . . one."

Right now, consider the breath focus and count to be your "preferred" thoughts. Thoughts of lunch, memories, or other intruders will just be gently replaced by "In . . . one, In . . . two" and so on, *as soon as you notice them* creeping in. And they will! Of course it's difficult to stay focused! But with practice, it just gets easier and easier.

The beauty of this meditation is that, once learned, you can do it *anywhere*! Try it while waiting in line, or at the laundromat. No one can even tell that you're doing anything unusual!

Experiment, if you like, with extending each count up to eight or ten. Is that easier or harder to do than a count of four? Want to be meditationally macho (or macha)? Every once in a while, see how many consecutive exhales you can count without losing yourself, and your count, in a thought. My personal record to date is 442, reached one competitive afternoon during a ten-day retreat.

Pride was my downfall: "Inhale . . . 439, Inhale . . . 440, Inhale . . . 441, Inhale . . . 442, Wow, I'm really doing great! I bet I've gotten further than anyone else here, me! David!—Uh oh, what number breath was that last one?—#%X@!!! . . . . . . Inhale . . . one, Inhale . . . two, Inhale . . . "

The Chore-Based Breath Count

Try this meditation after you've practiced at least a few sessions of the Breath-Counting Meditation. You'll be doing this one in conjunction with a specific task or chore that you do at least on a daily basis (preferably something short, and more or less mindless). For me, taking a short break to get a drink of water (average count, four breaths), putting paper into my computer printer (average count, six or seven breaths), or making popcorn in the microwave (average count, twenty breaths) work well.

I simply count the number of breaths it takes me to do the task (numbering each exhale, and without, of course, trying to control the speed or regularity of my respiration). Naturally, thoughts try to intrude, but for the duration of this particular task, my "job" is to get an accurate count of my breaths.

Some people seem to find this meditation slightly easier, or more compelling, than the more basic Breath-Counting Meditation. It has the added advantage of helping you integrate your meditation practice right into your daily life.

If you like this one, you may eventually want to try doing it with more complex tasks. When I'm in good meditating shape, I sometimes try (and often fail) to keep an accurate breath count while I drive to town, do an easy errand, and drive home. But start out with short, simple tasks, and if you lose count, you know what to do: Go directly to breath number one, without spending time on self-judgment or other thoughts!

The Walking Breath Meditation

Walk a bit more slowly than usual, focusing your attention on the ins and outs of your breath. Begin each inhale and each exhale with a mental label of "In" or "Out." Maintain a thumb to forefinger hand position, unless that feels unnatural now.

Without trying to control the breath too much, see if you can begin each in and each out breath exactly as one of your feet hits the ground. Notice how many steps you take during each inhalation, and how many steps you take during each exhalation.

Then count each step as you walk and breathe, so that in your mind you are saying "In two, three, four . . . Out two, three, four...In two, three, four . . . Out two, three, four" or perhaps "In two, three . . . Out two, three." Continue to substitute "In" or "Out" in place of each count of "one," to help you stay focused on the breathing as well as the walking.

Your own personal breathing rhythm may be different from the above. Your exhales may take longer than your inhales as in: "In two, three . . . Out two, three, four." Or your inhales may take longer than your exhales as in: "In two, three, four, five . . . Out two, three." The step count may vary from one breath to the next—just pay close attention, so that you can accurately count your steps during every inhale and every exhale. Just breathe, and walk, and count. As in all meditations, if your mind wanders, gently bring it back as soon as you notice that it's gone.

Using the Walking Breath Meditation in Real Life

I always use this meditation at the national publishing and music conventions, which tend to be hectic and stressful for me. Instead of scurrying and worrying from one appointment to the next, I walk and breathe, walk and breathe—so that each step soothes and centers my mind. Then, when I arrive at my next meeting, I'm more relaxed, and ready to deal with whatever may arise. Try it yourself, whether on a quiet walk in the country or in between errands on the job!

More Complex Clearing the Mind Meditations

In these following exercises, you'll be focusing your attention on a physical sensation, rather than merely labeling a physical action with a number as we've already done. Since this is a slightly less cut-and-dried thing to focus on, your attention is apt to wander more. So you must be diligent in noticing that the "puppy" of your attention is wandering off, and gently bring it back to the sound, or the foot, or the flame.

These meditations are somewhat harder to do during that boring meeting, or at the convention, since they require a bit more action than the simpler mind clearers. But with ingenuity, you'll find moments of privacy to practice the chant and slow walk, and candlelit restaurants are natural places to do a flame meditation (while your new date is in the rest room!)

About the Simple Chanting, or "Mantra," Meditation

This simple chanting, or "mantra" (a repeated sound used as a chant), exercise is probably the world's most widely used meditation. It's somewhat similar in nature to Maharishi Mahesh Yogi's Transcendental Meditation™, or "TM" system that The Beatles helped bring to the Western world in the late 1960s (except that it won't cost you $385, or require you to bring a white flower to the TM trainer). Dr. Herbert Benson further popularized this style of meditation in his "scientific" meditation book, *The Relaxation Response*. As I've mentioned, TM was my first organized meditation experience, and even though I no longer practice it, I'll always feel a debt of gratitude to both the Beatles and the Maharishi, for popularizing and publicizing this age-old technique in the West.

The Simple Chanting Meditation

Sit in a comfortable, upright position, in a quiet place. Place thumbs and forefingers together. Now focus your attention on a pleasant-sounding one- or-two syllable word. Yogis seem to prefer OM or AUM. Dr. Benson likes ONE. AMEN may be especially appropriate for those of a Christian persuasion. The TM folk also like two-syllable mantras (many of theirs sound quite like AMEN). Choose any one of these to use right now.

Begin by slowly whispering the word (let's say you've chosen OM) to yourself. Stop whispering "OM," and just think "OM." Perhaps you'll picture the word OM, written out in your mind. Perhaps you'll imagine hearing it in your mind, or imagine saying it. Keep your attention focused on that OM, in whatever form it may seem to appear.

Of course, your mind will wander. You'll find yourself thinking about tomorrow, or about how well-focused you are on the OM. Maybe you'll have a doubtful thought ("I can't do this") or a pleasant daydream.

When Attention Strays

When your attention strays from the OM, bring it gently but firmly back. Let go of the daydream, or the doubtful thought, or the desire thought for now. You can think about those things all you like, later. Now, you're just thinking OMMMM . . .

That's all there is to it. The more you do it, the longer you'll be able to stay with the OM. A few seconds at first, then ten, or fifteen, or half a minute. For many meditators, mantras seem to be an especially powerful focus for the attention. That's why they're so popular!

Christian, Jewish, and Buddhist Chants

If you enjoy practicing the Simple Chanting Meditation, you might eventually like to try repeating a longer chant. Some people find that a longer chant holds their attention more. Any short Christian prayer that you've memorized will work, like the "Prayer of the Heart": "Lord Jesus Christ, have mercy on me." If you come from the Hebraic tradition, try the most important prayer of the Jewish faith, the "Shma": "Hear oh Israel, the Lord our God, the Lord is One." (Pronounced: Shma' Yis-roy-el' Ah-doh-noy' Eh-lo-hay'-nu, Ah-doh-noy' Eh-chord').

The Buddha's last instructions to his disciples were to repeatedly chant the phrase "Nam Myoho Renge Kyo" (Pronounced: Nahm Me-yo'-ho Reng'-yay Ke-yo'). A greatly oversimplified translation of this might be, "I devote myself to the law of the Universal Consciousness." This form of meditation is now known as "Nichiren" Buddhism, and has proponents and groups worldwide.

Consult your local priest or rabbi to obtain additional Judaic or Christian chants, which will add greater depth to the practice of your chosen religion. You might also look up Jim Cowan's book on Nichiren Buddhism, or create a meaningful chant of your own.

The Slow Walking Meditation

You'll probably want to begin practicing this one in a private place, since it looks a bit funny. Pick a spot where you can walk for at least eight or ten feet in a straight line.

Now walk *very* slowly, so slowly that you have enough time to mentally label *every part* of every step.

Say "lifting" as you pick your foot up. Say "moving" as your foot travels through the air. Say "placing" as you put that foot down again. Say "shifting" as you shift your weight onto that foot. Say "lifting" as you begin to pick up the other foot. And so on. Lifting, moving, placing, shifting . . . lifting, moving, placing, shifting. . . .

At first, take a minimum of eight to ten seconds to complete each four-part (lifting, moving, placing, shifting) step. This is truly life in the slow lane! Whenever your attention wanders, bring it back to your walking process.

As you get used to focusing on your feet, you can try sometimes walking faster, labeling only the lifting and placing portions of each step. If you prefer, you can say "up" and "down" instead of "lift" and "place." Or try slowing it way down, and take thirty to forty seconds (some people call this "the Zombie Walk") for every complete step.

Other thoughts intruding? Get right back to that focus on the active foot!

The Flame Meditation

In a darkened room, from ten or fifteen inches away, stare intently at a candle's flame for one or two minutes. Whenever your attention wanders, return your gaze to the heart of that tiny fire. Try not to think about the candle, or this exercise, or why fire looks as it does, or politics. Just keep returning your attention to stare at the flame.

Abruptly blow the candle out, and close your eyes. Within a few seconds, you'll begin to see the image of the flame again, apparently projected onto the inside of your eyelids. Watch that image for as long as you can. It may change color, or shape, or seem to slide around. It may disappear, and then come back in a slightly different shape, color, or form. But you'll recognize it, if you concentrate. With practice, you'll be able to perceive the image for at least as long as you watched the actual flame.

I find the combination of focusing on both the real flame and then the afterimage exciting and challenging. Artists and other people who are visually oriented may achieve an exceptionally strong concentration with this exercise.

For Friends and Couples: The "Ahhh" Breath

For a very intimate experience with a close friend, relative, or lover, try this exercise. I learned it from Stephen Levine, who learned it from Richard Boerstler, of The Clear Light Society. I don't know who Richard learned it from, but it's a wonderful thing to do!

Decide which of you will be the active partner. The inactive partner simply sits or lies comfortably, eyes closed, and breathes normally. The active partner sits nearby, close enough to see the rising and falling of the inactive partner's chest as they breathe, close enough to hear each in and out breath.

The active partner tries to match as exactly as possible the breathing rhythm of the other, to begin the in breath exactly as they do, to inhale exactly as long, to hold the breath exactly as long, to exhale for the same amount of time. It's not easy to do, and requires intense concentration! On each exhale, the active partner will release the breath with a sigh . . . "ahhh."

The inactive partner should try not to "help" the active partner by making breaths unusually regular or loud, neither should they try to hinder the other by holding their breath or breathing especially softly.

This exercise promotes a strong feeling of connection, compassion, and love between the partners. It's almost as though one breath is being shared between two people—sometimes it actually feels as though the two bodies are somehow merged. Couples will find this a lovely trust-builder, and especially powerful if eye contact is maintained. You can even do the "ahhh" breath with a pet (you'll probably need to take the active role).

Many nurses, therapists, and some physicians use this meditation with their patients. It can be done with the inactive partner sleeping or comatose, and may be very calming and soothing for someone who is ill, as well as for the healer.

The Heartbeat Meditation

Every second your heart beats at least once. If it stops beating for very long, you're history. So counting or labeling each beat is an amazingly powerful attention focuser, even if you only do it for one minute or less. If you are a hypochondriac, or have any heart problems, don't do this exercise until you feel very comfortable with the mind-watching exercises that follow.

Put your hand over your heart, or locate the pulse in your wrist with a few fingers. Count each beat or pulse to four, or ten, like you've done with the breath. If you lose count, start again.

Or label each beat or pulse by mentally saying "beat" every time you feel one. This is similar to what you did with the four-part walking meditation.

For me, the exciting (and scary) part of this meditation is that my heart skips a beat every minute or two. I'm never absolutely certain whether the next beat will happen, or not. So I have to pay very close attention.

Doctors tell me that unless you average more than four or five per minute, skipped beats are not necessarily indicative of heart problems. But it's still a bit unnerving, when it occurs. If a fear thought comes up after a skipped beat, just notice it, notice that you've stopped counting or labeling, then go back to focus on the heartbeat. You can always worry later, after you're done meditating. Or, perhaps, with sufficient meditation, you won't even want to worry quite as much!

Harder Walking and Breathing Meditations

These next two mind clearers involve the focus of attention directly on physical sensations, no counting or labeling. They are the mainstays of the Vipassana meditative tradition. If they seem hard to concentrate on, alternate them with exercises that you find easier, like the meditations above.

The No-Label Walking Meditation

Walk slowly, and focus your attention carefully on your feet. What does walking really feel like? Which muscles in your calves, ankles, or toes do you use? What is the consistency of the ground—is it hard, or rough, or spongy? Go barefoot, and feel each pebble, twig, or crack in the floor.

You may find it easier to begin with this meditation by doing the Walking Breath or the Slow Walk (labeling) Meditation. After a minute of those, stop counting breaths or labeling, and focus on your feet and the ground. As usual, when thoughts intrude, gently return your attention to your feet.

The No-Label Breath Meditation

Breathe normally, and focus your attention on the sensation of breathing. In what part of your body do you feel each inhale most clearly? Some people feel the breath best at the nostrils, right where it flows in and out. Others find it easier to concentrate on the rise and fall of the stomach or chest. Mouth breathers might be very aware of the breath at the back of the throat. Choose one of these areas, and concentrate on it.

Do not try to control your breathing at all, to make it slow, or even, or otherwise meditative. Just let every breath be exactly as it is.

Observe *each* breath as though it were a strange and unique creature passing in front of you. Is this breath long, or short? Smooth and continuous, or jerky? Feel cool, or hot? Does it go directly from inhale to exhale, or is there a point at which the breath is held immobile? Was there a cough, burp, or hiccup experienced as part of this breath? Or even a sneeze? A sighing or wheezing quality to it? As always, if your attention wanders off, return it diligently but gently to the breath.

Helpful Hint: Wavy Gravy (clown, prankster, and sixties holdout) works with dying children in San Francisco. His meditation practice helps him to stay calm and loving, in the hospital or in the circus. He likes to put a touch of "Tiger Balm" liniment (or Vicks Vaporub) inside the big red ball of his clown nose as an aid to concentrating on the sensation of the breath at the nostrils. Try it!

The Tongue-Block Breath Meditation

This easy but effective meditation comes out of both the harmonica and the yogic traditions. When playing harmonica, "tongue blocking" is a method of playing low and high notes simultaneously by blocking out the middle notes with the tip of the tongue. In my "Zen and the Art of Blues Harmonica" workshops, I've noticed that many students find tongue blocking to be an excellent attention focuser. In the popular Kriya yoga style, an important technique involves placing the tongue tip so that it partially blocks the incoming air, which helps emphasize attention on the breath.

Just touch the tip of your tongue to the roof of your mouth, less than an inch behind your upper front teeth. As you inhale, you'll feel the coolness of each breath on the sensitive underside of your tongue. You can apply this new tongue position to any of the breathing meditations: the basic, the chore-based, or the no-label (for which it may be especially useful). And it's inconspicuous enough to do anywhere or anytime (which, of course, is where you *should* be doing it!).

Looking and Listening Meditations

Our last (and perhaps most difficult) type of mind-clearing exercise is to watch clouds, or the flames of a fire, or the foaming waves at the ocean's shore. Don't try to make sense of what you see. Don't try to look for patterns. Don't judge what you're seeing. Do nothing but see. Just seeing. As soon as you notice a thought creeping into your mind, go back to just seeing.

It's easiest to begin Looking Meditations with natural objects like those mentioned above, as they are slightly less likely to inspire thoughts in your mind than visual objects like faces or bodies are. But with practice, you will be able to look at anything and "just see." Cars or people passing by, a blank wall, or your own hands can provide visual objects for the focus of your attention.

You can practice *listening* in the same way. No thought, no judging, no attempts to make sense. Just listening. If thoughts intrude, notice that you're thinking, then focus your attention back to the music. Instrumental music is usually the easiest type of meditative listening to begin with, as any music that contains words tends to inspire thought when you hear the lyrics.

Of course, when you've *really* gotten the hang of it, everywhere that you go and *everything* that you do can become the basis for a mind-clearing meditation. We can call this rather advanced state "Living in the Now."

Watching the Mind

If you've begun doing the mind-*clearing* exercises, then you're probably ready to try some mind *watching*. In these exercises, *thoughts in the mind* will provide the focal point for our attention. In other words, we'll be using thoughts as our meditation objects, just as we've already used breathing and walking. As with the breathing and walking exercises, we'll begin by counting, and then by labeling, our thoughts. Finally, we'll be able to focus on the direct sensations that our thoughts produce, without counting or labeling.

The Thought-Counting Meditation

This exercise will help you to start withdrawing your attention from the *content* of your thoughts.

Sit comfortably, with some type of timer or alarm clock handy. If none are available, make sure you can see a clock. Set the timer for one minute, or time yourself by the clock.

Now close your eyes, and begin to count your thoughts. As soon as a thought appears in your mind, count it, but don't "get into" the content of that thought. If you do, you may only end up with a count of one thought for your entire minute!

Think about a bird-watching competition. Competitive bird watchers go out, armed with binoculars, to try to identify as many species of bird as they can in one day. They don't study each bird for hours, or even minutes. As soon as they see one—that's it—on to look for the next. And you're a thought watcher, for these sixty seconds!

You've already gained some skill at returning the focus of your attention to a meditation (from practicing the mind-clearing meditations). So you'll probably be able to let go of each thought after counting it, unless it's one of those particularly stubborn thoughts, which we'll deal with below. And then return the focus of your attention toward looking for another thought to count. If no thoughts seem to come up, either say to yourself "no thoughts" (which is a perfectly valid thought itself, and should be counted), or else just relax and enjoy a moment of spontaneous mind clearing!

So keep a count of your thoughts. This will include thoughts such as "gee, I haven't had many thoughts yet" or "uh-oh, was that thought number seven or number eight?" Some thoughts will flash by like speedy and exotic birds, perhaps as quick mental pictures or even as single words. Others will lumber like penguins into sight of your mind's eye, and take their time leaving as well.

If a thought arises, and its content is so "grabby" for you that you just "can't" let go of it, try to remember what thought it is. That information will be useful, even though it seems to be preventing you from doing this exercise right now. Write the stubborn thought down, then try the exercise again later on. Fear thoughts and desire thoughts tend to be the hardest to let go of, for most people. But remember—it's not the fear or the desire thought that's the problem—it is the inability to control your reaction to that thought that may create a problem.

This isn't an easy exercise, but there is no way to do it wrong. It's sole purpose is to learn to look, for this moment, at your thoughts as objects, like birds, or rocks, or other people. Nothing to take personally—just thoughts.

About the Thought-Labeling Meditation

In the last meditation, we paid no attention to the content of the thoughts that we were counting. Now, we are going to pay just barely enough attention to thought content so that we will be able to label each thought.

Now make a brief mental or written list of the types or categories of thoughts that are commonly featured in the movie of your mind. I have about eight perennial favorites, which I'll list below, in general order of popularity. Is your list as high-minded and spiritual as mine?

Planning thoughts are those in which I try to decide exactly what to do, specifically ("I'll write to John, then have lunch") or generally ("perhaps I should go to law school"). Desire thoughts include wishes for anything, from sex to world peace. Fear thoughts include any type of worry: hypochondria, money, work, you name it. Happy or appreciative thoughts are often noting pleasurable sensations such as the sun on my face, or the smell of potatoes cooking. Judging thoughts are those in which I approve or, more likely, criticize anything or anyone. Righteous thoughts are those in which I am right, and someone else is wrong. Angry thoughts could be those directed at myself, in which case I consider them as falling into the specialized subcategory of self-hating thoughts, or at anybody else.

The Thought-Labeling Meditation

Sit comfortably, and observe each thought as it swims into awareness. Observe it only long enough to decide which one of your categories it fits into, then go on to look for the next. If absolutely no thoughts seem to be forthcoming right now, simply relax and enjoy a few seconds of effortless mind clearing.

If a thought doesn't seem to fit into any of your categories, just make up a more or less appropriate new category, ("ahh, that's one of those 'What-If-I-Had-Been-Born-an-Eskimo' type of thoughts") and go back to looking for the next thought.

As in the last exercise, if a "grabby" thought arises, just notice what thought, and type of thought, it is.

After the meditation, see if you can tell which thoughts occurred most often. Which thoughts were easy to let go of? Which ones were hard to let go of?

The Particular Thought-Counting Meditation

You can choose any thought, or category of thought, to notice in this exercise. You will probably get the most benefits by choosing one of those "grabby" thoughts, as they are the thoughts that you most need practice working with.

In this exercise, you are going to try to remember to count the number of times in the course of an hour or a day that a particular thought arises. That's all there is to it. You may want to keep count on a piece of paper, so that you don't forget your score. Try not to get angry with yourself for having these uncontrollable thoughts. The Compassion exercises later on will help you to treat even your own mind with a touch of mercy . . .

I usually do this exercise with my righteous thoughts, since they are, for me, the grabbiest. I love to be *right*, and it's hard for me to let someone else be wrong without their admitting it, to just let go of me being right and them being wrong. On a seriously righteous day, I can count dozens of righteous thoughts! Doing so helps me to be aware of the hold that this particular thought has on me, and to diminish it.

The "Rube Goldberg" Thought Chain Meditation

In a Rube Goldberg cartoon, strange events are chained together to cause a final event. To create a Goldberg alarm clock, for example, the sun comes up, and its rays through a magnifying glass burn the rope that holds up the cheese, the cheese falls down so that the mice come out, the cat goes after the mice, the dog goes after the cat from under the bed where he was sleeping, which pulls out a slat so that the farmer falls on the floor and is woken up in time for milking!

Our minds often work similarly, chaining together thoughts in strange ways. As I began to observe my thoughts more carefully, I found that my frustration or fear thoughts usually bring up anger thoughts.

After you've spent some time with the Thought-Counting and Thought-Labeling Meditations, try a Thought-Labeling exercise in which you specifically look for two or more thoughts which often occur together. You may find, for example, that the guilt thoughts that you had perceived as happening spontaneously are actually a result of prior angry thoughts, which themselves are a result of helplessness thoughts. Becoming aware of your thoughts in this manner can really help you to understand why you feel the way you do.

The Experiencing Thoughts Meditation

Just as with breathing and walking, we began by counting our thoughts, and then labeling them. Now it's time to just experience the sensation of thoughts, rather as we experienced the physical sensations of walking and breathing in the "no-label" walking and breathing exercises.

Begin with a moment of your favorite meditation, just to relax and clear your mind a bit. Then call one of your "grabby" thoughts, perhaps a fear, or a desire, or an anger into your mind. Observe the thought, and ask yourself, "What does anger (or whatever) feel like?" Is it a hot feeling, or a cool feeling? Does my body feel tighter, or looser? Is there an enjoyable element to this feeling, or is it only painful?

Just watch the thought—step back, and turn it around in your mind like an object that you are investigating. Does looking at the thought in this way change your reaction to the thought? In what way?

If you find yourself getting caught up in the content of the thought ("I have a right to be angry, they shouldn't have . . ."), watch the caught-up-ness. How does it feel to be caught up in a thought like that? And if you cannot back off and relate to this particular thought, try one that's not so grabby for now!

Living in the Now

Most of us live most of the time in either the past or the future. Only rarely is our attention focused on what is happening in the "Right Now." Is yours? You think so? Then quick—without thinking about it—are you inhaling or exhaling? You probably had to refocus your attention onto the breath to answer that question. Where had it been?

Thoughts about what we just did, or didn't do, and thoughts about what we should do, or shouldn't do, or might do, continually clutter our minds. How often we use past thoughts in a self-hating way, "I should have done it differently," or "I sure messed that one up." How often we use future thoughts to upset ourselves, such as "What if that happens?" or "It probably won't work out."

Virtually all of our thoughts are either based in past or future, and absolutely all of our fears and desires. Desires are usually remembrances of past pleasures that we plan and hope to recreate in the future. Fears are usually memories of past pain that we plan and hope to avoid in the future.

In a way, all of the exercises are "Living in the Now" exercises. When we are Thought Counting or Slow Walking, there just isn't much time to think of the past or the future. We learn to let go of such thoughts, as soon as we notice them.

There is something very satisfying about keeping your mind in the Now, but it's hard to describe it precisely. All I can say is that the bite of food that you are savoring right now, is somehow quite different from the mouthful that you just ate (which you can only remember) or the mouthful that you plan to eat next (which you can only anticipate). Of course, thinking about either the past or future mouthful does bring it into the Now as a thought in your mind. But the actual food that's in your mouth can clearly be more satisfying than the thought of past or future food which may be in your mind right now. Better to be present with a potato than lost in thoughts of past or future banquets!

As a small press publisher, I often need to plan books, advertising, or marketing strategies far into the future. So my Now may involve initiating events that will not be completed for many months. It's confusing for me to separate the reality of the "publisher's Now" (which includes the next six to twelve months) from my "personal Now." In my personal Now I wish to savor the events of the present—smells, tastes, feelings—without overinfluence by future and past related fears and desires. It's a delicate balance, and one that I don't yet clearly understand. But I do know that the following "Living in the Now" exercises help! And, speaking of a delicate balance . . .

The Centering Balance Meditation

Stand up straight, arms at your sides, with your feet no more than six inches apart. Focus your attention on your sense of balance, your sensation of standing upright with your body weight centered over your feet.

Lean forward an inch or two, and feel the tension as your toes dig deeper into the ground to compensate for the forward incline, as you become a human Tower of Pisa. Lean backwards an inch, until most of your weight is on your heels. Lean slightly left and then right, noting the weight shift from foot to foot.

Do the forwards, backwards, left, and right leaning motions again, but more subtly, with less movement. See just how little you need to lean in order to feel not quite perfectly upright, not quite perfectly balanced. See how easy it is to overcompensate, in one direction or another. Is there any one position in which you do feel in complete equilibrium, when you really focus your attention on it? There may not be one.

You can do this exercise anywhere, without attracting much attention to yourself, if you use the more subtle motions of the second part. Since "feeling balanced" is often used as a metaphor for mental stability, this exercise is a useful one to do anytime you feel off-balance. The few moments' respite that you'll get from the tensions of past and future thoughts will help you to restore both your mental and physical equilibrium!

Other Living-in-the-Now Meditations

We can also take commonplace daily activities and easily convert them into effective and interesting Living-in-the-Now Meditations. In effect, we've already done this with walking and breathing. As I've said before, anything done with a high degree of focused awareness is, by definition, a meditation.

The Zen Buddhist tradition of Japan often utilized this approach. Flower arranging, the tea ceremony, Zen archery, and most of the Japanese martial arts are used as forms of meditation. Their practitioners focus exclusively on the flowers, or tea, or bow, excluding all other thoughts. Sound familiar?

The Conscious Eating Meditation

Our society gives us many mixed messages about food. We use it to give ourselves love by eating exotic chocolates, tantalizing treats, and tempting tidbits. Yet we also punish ourselves and use food to withhold self-approval, with crash diets and lifelong obsessions about those few extra pounds of flab. We pay lots of attention to what we eat, but little to how we feel while we eat. Often we avoid feeling entirely while eating. We do this by eating and conversing in the company of others, and when alone will eat while reading, or in front of the television set. Or we may stuff ourselves compulsively without even tasting the food.

A conscious focus of attention on feeling and eating can be a most powerful experience. Someday, perhaps when eating by yourself, try this Conscious Eating Meditation.

Once your food is in front of you, spend a moment with a mind-clearing exercise, perhaps one of the breath-based meditations. Then, slowly, begin to eat. Focus your attention on each part of the eating process, lifting the fork or spoon, choosing which forkful of food to pick up, lifting the food to your mouth, placing the food in your mouth, lowering the fork, chewing the food and noticing the taste, swallowing the food, then lifting the fork once again.

If you like, label each action, as you did in the Slow Walking Meditation: lifting, choosing, lifting, placing, lowering, chewing, tasting, and swallowing. If other labels seem more appropriate to you, by all means use your own.

Perhaps you would prefer to concentrate on how each action feels, rather than labeling them, as you did in the No-Label Walking Meditation. Simply slow down and concentrate on your eating. Some people find that this is easier to do if they hold their fork in the hand that they don't usually use, as this will increase your concentration on your fork hand.

Notice the sensation of metal against mouth, the muscular actions involved in lifting, chewing, swallowing. Feel each motion of your tongue, your lips, your throat. Concentrate on the texture and taste of each food. Be as specific as possible in your investigation. Do the skins of peas taste different from the insides? How close to your mouth is the food before you smell it? What else can you notice?

As usual, be aware of thoughts as they arise in the mind, and then return your attention to your food. I often notice a desire to choose and lift the next forkful before I'm done chewing and swallowing the one in my mouth. This desire is then usually followed by a guilty thought about greediness. If similar thoughts occur to you, note them, perhaps label them ("aha, there's greed . . ."), then let them pass, and return mindfully to your dinner.

An interesting duo exercise for friends or couples is to take turns feeding each other, while silently focusing on physical or mental sensations. For me, this usually stirs up compassionate feelings as the feeder, and vulnerable or infantile feelings as the one being fed.

Conscious Driving

Driving is one of the most hazardous things we do on a daily basis. Yet often, as we drive, our mind is lost in the past or the future, far from a clear focus on the manipulation of tons of iron at high rates of speed. We talk, listen to the radio, eat, drink or smoke, keeping "half an eye" on the road and other traffic.

In conscious driving, we focus our attention exclusively on the elements important to automotive safety, as intently as though we were Monte Carlo racing drivers, participating in the race of our lives. But instead of concentrating on speed alone, we pay attention to many factors: the road in front of us, the positions of other cars near us, our speed, driving conditions, and road conditions.

Should any thoughts not germane only to safe driving enter, we notice them and gently return our attention to our driving. If this exercise seems, for any reason, to be unsafe, please don't do it. But I am convinced that if more people did focus their attention exclusively on their driving, that the highways would be much safer places.

More Living-in-the-Now Meditations

We can make any activity a meditation simply by steadily focusing our attention on it. Try doing this with shaving, brushing your teeth (I find that switching hands here really forces me to focus on my hand movements, and makes the toothbrush meditation a challenge), washing your hands, dishes, or any other simple daily task.

Just make sure that you are thinking only of the task at hand, and gently return your awareness to it as soon as you notice other thoughts entering the mind.

I like to try to make hand washing into a meditation, each time I do it throughout the day. Instead of using those thirty or forty seconds to plan, or worry, or daydream, I focus on the sensations of warmth, wetness, slipperiness, rinsing, drying. And feel better centered and more relaxed afterwards. Perhaps cleanliness is next to godliness, after all!

Excerpted and adapted with permission from *The Three Minute Meditator* by David Harp, with Nina Feldman, Ph.D. For more information on this and related books, see the "Further Reading" section in the back of the book.

CHAPTER 47

Visualization

Visualization for Change

"The greatest discovery of my generation is that human beings, by changing the inner attitudes of their minds, can change the outer aspects of their lives."

—William James

Visualization is a powerful tool for changing your life. Five minutes of visualization can cancel out hours, days, even weeks of negative thinking or acting. Three five-minute sessions a day can change a habit that took years to form and reinforce.

Everybody visualizes. You visualize whenever you daydream, remember a past experience, or think of someone you know. It's a natural, largely automatic activity like breathing or walking. You can improve your existing powers of visualization to harness this automatic activity and use it consciously to help keep yourself sane, fit, healthy, and happy.

You probably have a lot of questions about visualization: What is it exactly? Is it like dreaming or meditation or hypnosis? Is it a mystical or religious kind of experience? How do you do it? Is it difficult? What can it be used for?

Visualization is defined as *the conscious, volitional creation of mental sense impressions for the purpose of changing yourself.*

Almost every word in this definition is important for understanding exactly what I mean, and don't mean, by visualization.

The word "conscious" sets visualization apart from dreams, which occur in an unconscious state. Many people who study visualization are also interested in dreams and dream interpretation, and indeed there do seem to be some real connections between visualization and dreaming. See also the chapter on Dreams next in part VII.

"Volitional" means that you choose the time, place, purpose, and general content of your visualization. This aspect distinguishes visualization from hallucinations or visions. The visualization skills you will learn in this book work without having to take drugs or believe in any particular religious or mystical system.

"Creation" means that the process is creative. Your visualizations will often be fantastic or impossible. This sets visualization apart from normal perception or cognition, which is, hopefully, based in reality. Work on a problem using visualization is very different from just thinking about it.

"Mental sense impressions" reminds you that visualization is not all visual. Besides mental pictures, you will also create mental sounds, tastes, smells, sensations of temperature, texture, and so on. The visual component is usually the strongest, but all the senses must be brought into play to get the most from visualization. It's unfortunate that terms such as "visualization " and "imagery" and "imagination" stress the visual aspects of the process. But no other satisfactory term seems to exist in English, so you just have to keep in mind that "visualization" includes the use of all the senses.

"For the purpose of changing" is included because this is about visualization *for change*. It doesn't deal with visualization used solely for entertainment, for relieving boredom, for generating pure insight, for exploring past lives, for communicating with the dead, for recovering lost memories and objects, for enhancing mystical experiences, or as part of the study of psychic phenomena. These endeavors are omitted not because they are unworthy of consideration, but because they are usually not concerned with the kind of changes covered in this book: self-improvement, therapy, healing, and pain control.

"Yourself" means that this book doesn't have much to say about using visualization to change *others*. Many people have pointed out the similarities between visualization and some of the techniques employed by shamans or witch doctors in primitive societies. These healers often visualize an imaginary journey for the purpose of healing their patients. The subject of the shamanistic healing of others is interesting, but beyond the scope of most people. You will learn to "change" others only by changing yourself and how you interact with people.

Types of Visualization for Change

Receptive Visualization

Receptive visualization is listening to your unconscious. In its purest form, you just close your eyes, relax, and wait to see what comes into your mind. You might set a minimal scene first, or ask a question and wait for the answer.

This kind of visualization is good for exploring your resistance to some change in your life, for uncovering your true feelings when you're ambivalent, for unearthing your personal images or symbols of change, or for clarifying what you really want to do when faced with several confusing alternatives. The information that comes up during receptive visualization is sometimes vague, like dream images. It often requires some interpretation before the meaning becomes clear.

Jennifer was a pediatrician just finished with her residency. She didn't know whether to look for a secure job on the staff of a big hospital or to join a private practice being started by someone she knew in school. Jennifer lay down on the couch one day and closed her eyes, with the intention of just clearing her mind and letting her true desires surface. She saw herself in a fog, and heard twittering noises like birds. She drifted forward and two buildings came into sight: a gray concrete structure and a cute little cottage. The cottage seemed welcoming and the concrete building seemed cold. At this point she opened her eyes and realized that the warmer, more personal environment of the private practice was more important to her than the security and excitement of a big hospital.

Programmed Visualization

If receptive visualization is listening to your unconscious, programmed visualization is talking to it. You create what you want to see and hear and feel in great detail and manipulate it according to a predetermined script. You stay in conscious control.

Programmed visualization is good for achieving goals, improving athletic performance, speeding up the healing of injuries, and intensifying images in general.

Bill was a carpenter who broke his leg on the job. While he was laid up, he used visualization to speed the healing of his leg. He would spend several minutes each day visualizing his leg bone as a splintered piece of wood. He saw himself straightening out the wood, pressing the jagged edges into place, spreading glue on the break, and clamping splints around it. He would make himself very small and go inside the bone, plastering over microscopic cracks as though he were fixing an old plaster wall. He saw the cells of his leg bone knitting together like the frame of a house being built. In this way he used very detailed, familiar images of construction and repair to enhance the natural healing process. Bill was back on the job a full two weeks before his doctor had predicted he might be.

Guided Visualization

Guided visualization is actually a combination of receptive and programmed visualization. You set a scene in detail, with certain crucial elements left out, and then let your subconscious fill them in.

Most visualization is of the guided variety. In fact, it's nearly impossible to create a visualization that is purely receptive or totally programmed. Your rational mind is likely to add conscious detail to the former, while your unconscious mind tends to toss unexpected images into the latter.

Marilyn's visualization about weight loss is a good example of how planned and unplanned elements make up a guided visualization. As part of her campaign to lose forty pounds, Marilyn practiced seeing herself having fun in the future in her slim new body. One time she was visualizing herself dancing at her older sister's wedding, which was coming up in six months. She concentrated on hearing the music, feeling her handsome partner's arms around her, seeing the swirling lights, and feeling happy and attractive—all as planned. Then she "zoomed back" from the scene to get a look at her slimmer self, and was surprised to find that she was not only slimmer, but shorter. She looked like a midget. This surprised her and she snapped out of the scene.

Later she decided to explore the scene by re-creating it in detail. She asked her shorter self what had happened and received the reply, "I've lost so much weight, I'm disappearing." This unplanned, unsought-for information made Marilyn realize that one reason she had been overweight for so long was that it made her feel "substantial" in the world. Her weight made people notice her. Marilyn used this realization to reprogram her vision of the future to include a full-sized, substantial, noticeable Marilyn who happened to be thinner. She did start losing weight, and danced at her sister's wedding in a two-sizes-smaller dress.

The Possible Changes

Visualization is good for self-improvement, therapy, healing, and pain control.

Self-improvement covers a lot of ground. On the one hand, it involves getting control of or getting rid of negative aspects of your life such as smoking and overeating. On the other hand, self-improvement means acquiring or increasing positive aspects of your life by fostering creativity, solving problems, achieving goals, improving study habits, and excelling at sports.

Therapeutic change runs the gamut from reducing stress, bolstering self-esteem, and conquering insomnia to relieving painful emotions such as depression, anxiety, anger, and shyness.

Visualization techniques for healing and pain control work for a wide range of injuries, diseases, infections, and immune system disorders.

Visualization for change is a powerful skill that works in harmony with other agents for change in your life. It augments and enhances everything you do, but it doesn't *replace* anything. Visualization can ease the pain of a serious sinus infection and maximize your body's natural defenses—but antibiotics are still the treatment of choice. Likewise, you can imagine yourself breezing through a job interview, and it will probably help relax you—but success is more likely if you also practice your self-presentation with a friend, bone up on relevant facts you'll need to know, and talk about your fears with a professional counselor.

If you feel seriously sick, see your doctor. If you feel seriously disturbed, see a therapist. You owe it to yourself to muster all the help available.

Guidelines for Effective Visualization

"Everything should be made as simple as possible, but not simpler."
—Albert Einstein

These guidelines are drawn from many sources: from the history of visualization as practiced throughout the world for hundreds of years, from various theories of how and why visualization works, from my own experience of visualization, and from discussions with many people who use visualization for different purposes.

These guidelines are a consensus, a distillation of the really important facts about visualization that most "experts" accept, regardless of their point of view. For example, the importance of employing positive as opposed to negative images is stressed by scientists studying pain control, by gurus teaching meditation, by therapists helping disturbed children, and by career consultants training executives in how to conduct a job interview.

In terms of changing your life and healing what ails you, the guidelines are listed in order of importance. If you just lie down, close your eyes, and relax a little bit three times a day, without doing any formal "visualization," you'll go a long way toward reducing stress and getting a refreshed outlook on life. Follow the next three guidelines—creating, manipulating, and intensifying positive sense impressions—and you will have mastered the basics of visualization. Following the remaining guidelines should come naturally after that, and you will become really adept.

For easy reference, the guidelines are summarized immediately below, followed by detailed explanations of each guideline.

1. Lie down

2. Close your eyes

3. Relax

4. Create and manipulate sense impressions

5. Deepen and intensify

6. Accentuate the positive

7. Suspend judgment

8. Explore resistance

9. Use affirmations

10. Practice often

11. Be patient

12. Use aids if they help

I. Lie Down

Lying down is best for visualization because it is the most relaxing position. Lie flat on your back on a bed, couch, or carpeted floor. Keep your hands and feet uncrossed. Try to tilt your pelvis a little to flatten the small of your back against the floor. Putting a pillow under your knees can help to take the strain off your back. The goal is a lying position that lets you release tension in all your muscles. None of your muscles should be working to hold you in a particular position. Your arms can be at your side, or your hands can be resting lightly on your chest or stomach. Wiggle around and experiment until you find the most comfortable position for you.

If you notice that your belt or collar is too tight, loosen it. If it crosses your mind that you should have gone to the bathroom or brushed your teeth or unplugged the phone, get up and do those things so you won't be distracted. Make sure it's warm enough. The object is to get as comfortable as you can.

It's possible to do visualization sitting or even standing up, especially after you've had some practice. But an upright position is not the preferred way. Some people find that visualizations done while sitting up seem dull and unimaginative, somehow contrived. Perhaps this is because they associate sitting with desk work, a very rational, linear, left-brain function.

2. Close Your Eyes

Let your eyes slide shut gently. Don't clamp them down with clenched eyelids. You might try rotating your eyeballs upward slightly and inward, looking toward the center of your forehead. This rotation of the eyes is recommended in several methods of meditation. Schultz and Luthe also used this upward and inward rotation as part of their Autogenics instructions. In 1959 they performed an experiment that showed an increase of alpha brain waves when the eyes were rotated in this manner.

But nothing is gospel. Some people find that the muscular effort required to keep looking upward interferes with their efforts to relax. So try several positions and do what feels best. You may even want to try looking downward. This method is recommended by some Yoga teachers, who use it as a way of getting in touch with the heart chakra. Do whatever works for you.

The obvious reason for closing your eyes is to shut out the real world, with all its myriad objects to look at. Shutting your eyes is also a signal to your mind that it's time to look inward. The mind makes automatic association with night, relaxation, sleep, and dreams.

You can't close your ears as well, but you should make sure you're in a quiet place where you won't be disturbed by noises like ringing phones, doorbells, and so on. Tell the people you live with that this is your quiet time, and ask them not to disturb you. Earplugs or headphones may help to shut out distracting noises.

3. Relax

This is the single most important guideline. More than half of the benefits of visualization come from simple relaxation. Relaxation by itself has been shown to be an effective way to reduce anxiety, depression, anger, fear, and obsessive thinking. Relaxation training is the obvious prescription for muscular tension and muscle spasms, but it is also highly effective in the treatment of headaches, ulcers, chronic fatigue, insomnia, obesity, and many other physical disorders.

When you relax, your brain produces alpha waves, which are associated with feelings of well-being, heightened awareness, creativity, and openness to positive suggestions. In a relaxed state, your conscious images will be sharper and easier to retain and manipulate. Spontaneous images will tend to come from deeper, more basic and authentic levels of your unconscious. There is a synergistic relationship between visualization and relaxation—they depend on and augment each other. You need to be relaxed to visualize, and visualization is very relaxing.

You are naturally most relaxed just before you fall asleep at night and immediately upon awakening, so those are good times to do visualization. If your goal is to visualize three times a day, you can get two of your sessions accomplished in bed, leaving only one to fit into a busy schedule. For detailed instructions for Progressive Muscle Relaxation, see the chapter on Stress in part V.

4. Create and Manipulate Sense Impressions

Involve All Your Senses

Vision is the predominant sense in humans, so most people find that visual images are the easiest to imagine. When I say, "Think of an apple," you probably get a visual picture of an apple. A few people will get a sound first, such as the crunch of biting into an apple, the wind in an apple tree, or some other sound they associate with apples. Such people are rare, and not at all to be pitied. They have much in common with great composers like Mozart and Beethoven, both of whom reported having a primarily auditory experience of the world.

It doesn't matter whether you are predominantly visual or auditory. You just take what you do naturally and build on it. Practice improves both the intensity of images in one modality and your ability to get impressions in other modalities. So if the word "apple" creates only a dim visual image in your mind, you can sharpen the image and add details to it with practice. After you have worked on the visual image for a while, you'll find that elements of sound or taste or smell or touch will be easier to add.

When you start to create images in your mind, they may seem to float in space in front of your eyes. They may also seem to be in the back of your head, the front of your head, on a movie screen, or even arising from your solar plexus or some other part of your body. There is no single "right" way to experience images.

Transform Abstractions and Language Into Images

In general, it's best to find a distinct, concrete image or sound to represent sent words and ideas in a visualization. This can be very challenging. For example, it's possible to explore an abstract idea like "justice" by translating the concept into sense impressions: Try seeing "JUSTICE" written on a sign or a blackboard. Hear a voice say it. Associate a color like the black of a judicial robe, or visualize a symbol like the scales of justice. Make up a story and run it in your mind like a movie. Play around with your associations until you get some concrete images that you can manipulate. Be sure to pay attention to the emotional overtones of your images.

Sometimes seeing or hearing words in a visualization can evoke strong sense impressions. When this happens, language is functioning on an early, primitive level, at which a word stands for a real thing and calls that real thing clearly to mind. For example, I once made a harpsichord from a kit. It took a long time and I really got involved in the details of authentic keyboard instrument construction. I came to know every inch of that harpsichord, until I could just sound one chord and know its state of tune and adjustment. Now if I see or hear the word "harpsichord" in a visualization, it evokes a rich stew of images and full body sensations of making and playing my harpsichord.

On the other hand, nonmusical people may hear "harpsichord" and get no image at all. For them, the word is operating at a later, more "advanced" level, at which language is a set of abstractions or labels for conveniently categorizing objects and experiences. This kind of language is essential for getting by day to day, but it's pretty useless in visualization. You have to transform it into detailed images.

Trust Your Intuition

In deciding how to structure a visualization—figuring out what techniques to use, images to select, or sequences to follow—nothing is so important as following your heart. Choose the techniques and images to which you feel drawn. I may suggest that images in full color are best for vivid visualization, but you may find that the dramatic black and white tones of an old movie are sometimes just right. Or always right for you. You are an individual and have your own individual best style of visualization.

5. Deepen and Intensify

Deepen Relaxation

This happens naturally, as you get more and more involved with your images. But you can be distracted, or tense up due to negative images. So take a moment to deepen relaxation by throwing in some deepening images: going down staircases or elevators, sinking deeper through water, melting, lying in the sun, or whatever fits in with the rest of your visualization.

Hypnotists know that the trance state should be deepened in stages. You get relaxed, let the trance stabilize, then relax some more, stabilize, go deeper, and so on. Visualization works the same way.

Intensify Sense Impressions

Add details. Vividness comes from realistic details. If you are visualizing a steam locomotive, you might start with a vague cylinder for the boiler, and several big steel wheels, and some sort of cab at the back where the engineer rides. To intensify the image of your locomotive, add a big headlight, a funnelshaped smokestack with a red band around the top, lots of shiny nickel-plated knobs and levers and handles, the sound of the steam chuffing and hissing, the blast of the whistle, the clang of the big brass bell. Sprinkle coal dust inside the cab, and include the engineer's lunch pail and the fireman's shovel. Really see the gauges and dials with their quivering needles inching toward the red danger zone as the train pounds on through the night. You add details for realism the same way a novelist or a movie director does.

Add movement. Your real eye and your mind's eye are both attracted to movement. Move both the object you're looking at and also your imaginary point of view. To make your dream car come alive, see it from several angles, as if you were walking around it in the showroom or it is rotating on a pedestal. Then see it zooming down the highway or climbing a mountain road, with you in a helicopter above. Move your point of view into the car and see the road streaming toward you. Glance at the instruments and watch your hands move over the gearshift and steering wheel. Creating a vivid scene in your mind is like creative writing: verbs and action words have more impact than nouns.

Add depth. As in normal perception, nearer details are seen first in visualization. Many people visualize images on one plane, as if each scene were displayed on a movie screen at a set distance in front of their eyes. Add depth by deliberately creating a foreground, a middle ground, and a background. Your eyes, even though shut, will change focus as you imagine images at different distances, giving you a much more vivid sense of reality. It's like the difference between a snapshot and a stereopticon view, or a regular movie and a 3-D movie.

Add style. Visit art galleries or look at books, magazines, billboards, and other graphics to see the many possible styles that vision can take. Your visualization can be realistic, cubistic, cartoonish, surrealistic, impressionistic, and so on. It can look like your favorite movies, magazines, or album covers.

Increase contrast. In normal perception, your eye is drawn toward sharp contrasts and the edges of things, as opposed to dull contrasts and the middle of things. When you're trying to visualize a particular object with great clarity, take advantage of this fact. First picture a black outline on a white background, and let your mind's eye roam over the boundary. Then fill in the middle and add natural color, but keep the shape against a background that provides sharp contrasts.

Switch among different senses. In real perception, all your senses work together. You often hear of the "five senses," but for visualization, it helps to think of over a dozen senses or kinds of sensing:

1. Sight

2. Hearing sounds

3. Hearing the direction of sounds

4. Taste

5. Smell

6. Touching hard versus soft

7. Touching rough versus smooth

8. Touching hot versus cold

9. Touching wet versus dry

10. Touching yourself versus anything else

11. Feeling pain of various types

12. Kinesthesia—sensing your body's movement and position in space (including your sense of balance and the feeling of dizziness)

13. Internal sensations—nausea, hunger, fatigue, and the distinct bodily sensations associated with emotions such as fear, anger, depression, or excitement

Take advantage of the fact that all your senses work together to confirm and round out impressions. In the chapter on warmup exercises, you'll get a lot of practice starting with a visual image, adding sound, touch, taste, smell, and so on.

Include appropriate emotions. Don't just see yourself as president of the club. Feel in your body the pride, the excitement, the sense of power and accomplishment. Furthermore, create the outward signs of the emotions you expect to feel: images of yourself smiling, receiving congratulations and compliments, giving advice to grateful members—make the experience real and concrete by translating the abstraction "pride" or "success" into observable actions.

If contradictory or negative emotions come up while visualizing, allow yourself time to experience and explore them for a while. These feelings may be a form of resistance, or a message about your conscious goal—that it may not be what you really want or need at this point in your life. For example, if you see yourself receiving a long-awaited diploma, but feel sad or anxious during the visualization, explore the feeling. Give your sadness or fear a shape and a color. Make an imaginary character the spokesperson for your feeling and ask this character about it. You may find that graduation means more than simple success to you. It may mean sadness at leaving your school friends or fear of having to look for a job.

If negative emotions get very strong, pull back from the scene and visualize something else. If painful images persist, terminate the session.

Create metaphors. This technique is at the heart of visualization. Effective visualization does not progress rationally like a syllogism or a doctor's logical prognosis:

A. I have a tumor.

B. Some tumors grow smaller.

C. Therefore, my tumor may grow smaller.

This is a bleak statement. The only thing it has going for it is that it is positive (after all, proposition B could state that "some tumors grow larger"). This sort of verbal, linear thinking inspires few images and has no power. To make such a truism into a powerful visualization, you must use your imagination to make a metaphor.

The verb "grow" can inspire you to make an organic metaphor: a tumor is like a plant in that it grows. That's all a metaphor is—an example of the likeness between one thing and another. The better-known thing teaches you about the lesser-known thing. In this case, you probably know a lot more about plants than you do about tumors. So you use what you know about plants to make a series of comparisons, or metaphors, between plants and your tumor.

For example, plants need sun and water and fertilizer to grow. They are green when healthy, yellow when dying, and brown when dead. You cultivate the plants you want, and pull the weeds you don't want. From this simple knowledge of plants you can construct a very effective metaphorical visualization:

My tumor is like a plant. I am shading it out, shutting off the sunshine of my worry and the water of my tears. I am shutting off the faucet of its blood supply, starving it. My tumor is turning yellow. It's dying. I chop at its roots with a hoe, dig it out like a weed. It shrivels up and turns brown. It dries up and blows away. Healthy, normal tissue like vibrant bean plants grows in its place.

Metaphors elaborate. They turn abstractions into visual and auditory footage you can screen in your mind and spend substantial amounts of time viewing, editing, and reviewing. Metaphors give you firm handles on otherwise slippery concepts.

Metaphor dressed up to go out is symbol. Goethe said that "symbols are the visible standing in for the invisible to reveal the unknowable." Gone are "like" and "as." The tumor is a weed, your blood is life-giving water, you really are chopping with a hoe.

This is the rich patois of the unconscious, the language of dreams. If you are skilled, you can master a conscious facility at simulating this language. You can come to speak a pidgin dialect of symbols in which you can couch many fruitful suggestions to your unconscious self.

6. Accentuate the Positive

In the Present

Approach each visualization session with a positive attitude. Expect success and expect to have a good time. If you don't see or sense something that you're seeking, assume it's there anyway. If you're looking for a way to solve a tough problem, and receptive visualization is not presenting any inspiring images, assume that the answer is there. Now just isn't the right time for it to come clear.

When you visualize yourself, *see yourself as basically OK and lovable in the present*, right now. Sure, maybe you smoke, maybe you're too anxious, or maybe you're unemployed at the moment. But none of that takes away from your intrinsic human value. See yourself as having high self-esteem in the present, before you even begin work on any of your problems.

During an ongoing visualization, negative thoughts may pop up: "This won't work . . . This is stupid . . . This'll never happen," and so on. Put these thoughts aside and keep your positive images before you. If negative statements persist, visualize them written on a blackboard, and erase them. Keep visualizing the blackboard and erasing the negative thoughts until they fade away.

In the Future

Include the positive consequences of attaining your goals. See yourself enjoying favorite activities in your newfound leisure, running, dancing, swimming, or whatever you would like to do. See yourself surrounded by loved ones and friends, popular and relaxed, having a good time. See yourself out of the hospital, enjoying a healthy, normal life. See yourself wearing new, stylish clothes, driving a new car, playing with a new tennis racket or skiing on new skis.

The Global View

It helps greatly to see the universe as a benevolent system in which there are plenty of material, emotional, spiritual, professional, and intellectual goodies for all. See humankind as perfectible. Assume that right can win over might, that you can always get what you need. In *Creative Visualization*, Shakti Gawain says, "Unless you can create a context that the world is a good place to be that can potentially work for everyone, you will experience difficulty in creating what you want in your personal life."

What if you just don't believe in a benevolent universe? What if you think it's a dog-eat-dog world, that only the fittest survive, or that the human race is basically greedy, petty, or weak? Visualization will still work for you. Maybe not as well, maybe not as fast, but it will work. Your mind is wired to your body in such a way that visualized changes tend to come to pass, regardless of your rationalized beliefs.

Many "New Age" teachers of visualization take the view that visualization taps some creative, universal force for good and growth in the universe. They say that it cannot be used for evil, ignoble, or selfish ends. I think this isn't so. You can use visualization to help you accomplish evil, and it will work just fine. It's a tool, not a virtue, and like any other tool it can be used for creation or destruction.

Thus visualization is a double-edged sword. It not only gives you the power to heal yourself, but also gives you the power to make yourself sicker. All the more reason to accentuate the positive. For example, don't create visualizations involving negative feelings about your body. Bernie Segal, author of *Love, Medicine & Miracles*, tried to eat less by imagining seasickness before meals. He actually started to experience severe nausea and vomiting.

7. Suspend Judgment

Expect the Unexpected

Visualization is a right-brain activity—nonrational, nonlinear, intuitive, and so on. You can expect the unexpected. You try to visualize a red square and you keep getting a green Oldsmobile. You try a receptive visualization to uncover your deepest feelings about yourself, and you get nothing but old Roadrunner cartoons. Funny images make you cry and tragic images give you a chuckle.

Your rational, logical, left-brain self will get in the way all the time, with doubts and intellectual interpretations that throw you off the track. You will tend to want to censor images that put you in a bad light or seem too violent, too weak, too sexual, too crazy, or whatever.

Through all this, you must remember to expect the unexpected, and go with the flow of spontaneous images. When you begin to tap your intuition, it will push you toward areas that seem foreign to you. If you are a shy, retiring, contemplative type, your visualizations may well be full of action and conflict. If you are a competitive go-getter, your unconscious might serve up images of contemplation and acceptance.

Not only should you expect the unexpected, you should suspect the expected. Kenneth Pelletier, author of *Mind as Healer, Mind as Slayer*, says that during a receptive visualization, if you first come up with an image that is exactly what you expected, it's wrong. It's probably a cover-up. Look deeper.

Time is simultaneous in the imagination, not sequential. For example, in sexual fantasies the mind keeps jumping ahead toward the climax, then flashing back to fill in the arousing details. When you're visualizing, don't worry if the sequence of events or cause and effect get mixed up. Your imagination is not linear, not sequential, not causal. Even if you are doing a carefully programmed visualization with a plot and dialog and everything, don't worry if you keep skipping ahead in the story or flashing back to earlier parts of the script. In fact, rejoice when this happens. It means that your intuitive side is getting into the action and making its timeless connections.

Take What You Get

Everything you get in a visualization comes from some part of you. It's all genuine, all you. Some parts are probably more important or interesting than others, but none of it is bad or wrong.

There is no right way or wrong way to do it. Only your way. Take what you get in an interested, nonjudgmental way. If you continually pass judgment and censor what goes on in a visualization, your imagination will dry up. Your creative, intuitive side will be laboring under a heavy load of critical static from your logical, judging side. This is especially important in receptive visualization, where you want to open clear channels to your unconscious.

Trust Yourself

All the experts give examples of images to use for various purposes, just like I do. Then we all say the same thing: Your image is the best. The best image for curing colitis is the patient's image. The best image for increasing sales is the salesperson's image. The best image for countering a phobia is the client's image. Even if these images don't make sense to a doctor, a sales manager, a therapist, or anyone else.

Trust yourself. Your mind is connected intimately with your body and your history. You know in every cell of your body, in every chemical and electrical shift in your brain, exactly what images to generate to perfectly represent and foster change.

8. Explore Resistance

Each time you use visualization to answer a question or solve a problem, ask yourself whether you really want the answer or really want to solve the problem. Do you feel you really deserve what you're seeking? Are you willing to take whatever comes up, even if it doesn't look like what you expected? If you have resistance to these questions, explore and resolve the resistance first. You need to be positive and single-minded to get the best results.

If you feel reluctant or ambivalent about visualizing a particular goal or other change, you may be afraid of confronting pain, finding a hard answer, or having to pay too high a price for what you want.

During visualization, you may "wince" inside or sense a voice saying no to something you want. Explore the no. Find out why you are conflicted. Finding out exactly what you want and if you really want it are the first steps to getting what you want.

9. Use Affirmations

To affirm something means to make it firm, to give it shape and substance and permanence. An affirmation is a *strong, positive, feeling-rich statement that something is already so.*

Strong means simple, short, and unqualified. *Positive* means that it contains no negative words for your unconscious to misconstrue. *Feeling-rich* means that the affirmation is couched in emotional language, as opposed to theoretical or intellectual terms. It is a *statement* in the form of a simple, active, declarative sentence. It is in the present tense to show that the desired result is *already so*, reflecting the timelessness of your imagination.

Here is an example of a very poor affirmation:

Except insofar as it is necessary to maintain a baseline of ethical conduct, I will not be self-critical, will not harm myself by staying up too late and working too hard, and will not dwell on my past mistakes.

This breaks all the rules. First, it's weak. It needs to be simpler, shorter, without qualifiers. Eliminating the qualifying first phrase would help a lot:

I will not be self-critical, will not harm myself by staying up too late and working too hard, and will not dwell on my past mistakes.

This is better, but it's negative. A positive version would go something like this:

I will be self-accepting, will take care of myself by going to bed early and working reasonable hours, and will let go of past mistakes.

We're getting there, but the affirmation still lacks feeling and it's still too long. One solution is to break it up into three affirmations, getting rid of the mention of bedtime and work hours, which are just examples of taking care of yourself:

I will accept myself.

I will take care of myself.

I will forgive myself.

We're almost home free. All that remains is to switch to the present tense, to show that the change is already so:

I accept myself.

I take care of myself.

I forgive myself.

Can this be improved even further? That depends on your personal, internal vocabulary—the way you habitually talk to yourself. You might prefer to make the obvious conceptual leap and reduce these three affirmations to an underlying truth:

I love myself.

On the other hand, maybe not. You may prefer to be more specific and stick with three affirmations that spell out what it means to love yourself.

How Affirmations Work

Affirmations reprogram or replace the negative self-statements that float around in your mind. They also function as reminders to suspend your judgments and set doubt aside.

During visualization, affirmations can be made silently, spoken out loud, written down in imagination or on actual paper, or even chanted.

Here are some affirmations that have worked for others. Pick out several that you like and rephrase them in your own internal language.

Every day in every way I'm getting better and better.

I have everything I need within me.

I accept and love myself.

The more I love myself, the more I can love others.

I am right here, just now, doing exactly what I'm doing.

My relationship with _____ is more and more satisfying. I can close my eyes and relax at will.

I accept my feelings as a natural part of myself.

I am getting stronger and healthier every day.

If you believe in Christ, God, Buddha, Universal Love, a Higher Power, or another spirtual deity, use them in your affirmations. Mention of spiritual matters can strengthen affirmations. Here are some examples:

Christ is manifest in my actions.

I am following God's plan for me.

I am in harmony with the Higher Power.

Divine love is guiding me.

Shakti Gawain makes much of affirmations. She says that they have three elements: *desire* (you must truly want change), *belief* (you must believe change is possible), and *acceptance* (you must be willing to have the change take place). All three add up to intention. She summarizes this notion in the affirmation:

I now have total intention to create this here and now.

Affirmations are especially important at the end of a visualization, where they function like posthypnotic suggestions. Shakti Gawain likes to end a session with:

This, or something better, now manifests for me in totally satisfying and harmonious ways for the highest good of all concerned.

This affirmation allows for an unforeseen, better change to come about. It eliminates the chance of "devil's deals," where you get what you ask for but aren't satified. And it purifies your motive, eliminating selfishness.

You should remember and repeat your affirmations throughout the day, when you aren't actively visualizing. Repeating affirmations during the day is like visualizing all day long. It keeps your unconscious focused on the change you are making. It reminds you to notice images in your everyday life that can become part of your visualizations. For example, when you're washing the car, you can think of washing all your tiredness away. When you put out the trash, you are setting aside your troubles and limitations so they can be picked up and hauled away.

10. Practice Often

Visualization is a tool for change that sharpens with use. You should use it daily and for many kinds of change.

Your early images may seem dull and lifeless, like mere verbal descriptions running through your mind. You'll feel like you're "making it all up." Later, with practice, your images will get more vivid, more like real seeing and hearing and touching.

Likewise, your first attempts to relax and shut out the outside world will probably be only partially successful. You'll only achieve a shallow relaxation and you'll be easily distracted. With practice, you will go deeper, faster. Soon you will be able to drop into an altered state of consciousness, with its profound relaxation and focusing of attention, almost at will.

Part of your practice should include fading out and turning off images, in case negative or unpleasant images arrive and need to be banished. For example, suppose you are creating a Garden of Eden setting as a special place in which to relax, and an unwanted snake slithers into view. You can have the snake fade out like a scene in a movie, or "beam" it someplace else, like an unwelcome visitor to the Starship Enterprise. Or you can delete it like a line in a word processor, or paint it out like an image in an acrylic painting. Or freeze it into immobility and turn it into a stuffed snake. Use your imagination. Practice changing and erasing images and you'll be ready for the rare unpleasant image that turns up.

11. Be Patient

Visualization is a skill that takes time to learn. It's like learning to ice skate. The first time out on the ice, you wobble and fall. The second time you have a little bit more control, and by the third or fourth time you can actually get around without falling so much. Then, if you get some coaching, you can refine your technique and start looking graceful and going faster. With further practice and coaching, you can begin cutting figures, racing, or playing hockey.

All this inevitably takes time, and proceeds in a series of steps, not in a straight-line progression. Athletes frequently find that they reach a "plateau," a level of skill at which they must perform for a while before they begin to improve further. Sometimes the plateau becomes a slump, and skill actually seems to decline for a while. The same applies to visualization. You have natural abilities that will improve with practice to a point where you "plateau out." Then books like this one or a teacher can be your coach. Over time, with coaching and practice, you become an expert.

However, there is a danger in approaching visualization in the same way you would learn to ice skate. Learning to visualize effectively is a matter of letting go of something, not forcing it to happen. This is when patience becomes of paramount importance—when you have to sit back and patiently take what you get, even when it's not what you expect or want, even when your internal critic is whispering to you, "This is dumb. . . . You'll never get it. . . . Give it up."

Patience must also be exercised during a visualization session. Often the first image that comes to your mind in a receptive visualization is an easy, "cover-up" image, hiding your real, less acceptable feelings about a person, place, or event. Keep open, be patient, and see what else comes up.

Like any growth process, visualization makes changes happen over time. A strong visualization experience needs to be integrated and resolved just like a strong waking experience. Your reaction to this morning's visualization may change by the end of the day or next week. Often, the answer you seek in a visualization may not come during the session, but surface spontaneously hours or days later.

12. Use Aids If They Help

There are many aids that can enhance visualization while it is going on: music, tape-recorded instructions, sounds of nature like surf or birdsong, sleep masks, ear plugs, rhythmic rattling or drumming, focusing on a yantra image, or chanting a mantra. In addition, you can enrich your visualizations by incorporating images or stories gleaned from reading fairy tales, primitive folklore, psychology, sociology, mythology, archeology, comparative religion, inspiring literature, and so on. You can use literature as a guided imagery exercise, living out parts of your favorite stories or changing the plots to suit yourself. You can also attend consciousness-raising events and discuss your visualizations with like-minded friends, steeping yourself in the life of the mind.

There is a long tradition of having a teacher, counselor, guru, or fellow student help you master a mental discipline. Whatever you call them, such guides and fellow travelers can be invaluable. It helps to have someone to talk to, to share difficulties, to keep you practicing, and to help you reach depths of understanding and heights of inspiration that might be out of reach for you on your own.

Another powerful aid is keeping a journal of your visualizations. You can record your experience and your thoughts and feelings about them while they are still fresh in your mind. Later you can go over your journal to glean ideas for future visualizations. Even if you don't go back over your entries, the mere act of writing in a journal is powerful. It will increase your ability to visualize in detail, develop your powers of introspection, and help you remember your visualizations. If you don't write your images down or tell them to someone, they can fade quickly from conscious memory.

It's important to mention one traditional aid that is not recommended: drugs. Some primitive societies and some holdovers from the late '60s and early '70s use drugs to loosen the imagination and provide extremely vivid or surreal visions. It's my conviction that in the long run, everyday drugs like alcohol, coffee, tobacco, tranquilizers, and marijuana only dull the intuition. Stronger drugs like LSD can indeed induce strange and vivid images, but these images are more properly classed as hallucinations. They are not volitional and not oriented toward change, and therefore not visualization as it is practiced in this book. So lay off drugs if you want to really get the most out of visualization for change.

Contraindications

Visualization is one of the most natural, gentle, and safe self-help disciplines. There's not much that can go wrong. However, there are people for whom visualization is not recommended, and situations in which it won't work well.

For example, if you have persistent visions of blood, death, violence, or hurting people, you have a problem. See a therapist right away.

You have a problem if you spend so much time daydreaming that you have trouble getting along in the real world. If your fantasies keep you from getting places on time, keeping commitments, getting schoolwork done, making simple plans for the future, and so on, then visualization may not be for you. You must be able to confine your visualization sessions to a reasonable amount of leisure time.

You have a problem if you put all your energy into visualizing impossible goals that you can never reach. The goals you set should be a stretch for you, but not entirely out of reach. Measure what you want against what is possible for someone in your situation to get. If you're not sure about a goal, talk to someone about it.

You have a problem if you find yourself investing a lot of energy in unrealistic fantasies in which you find the perfect lover or the ideal romantic relationship, get even for ancient injuries, or perform incredible feats of strength, daring, or invention that you don't possess. Visualization cannot help you attain the unattainable.

If your self-esteem is low and you don't believe you deserve good things, then you will have trouble visualizing them into becoming real.

Creating Your Special Place

"Chance favors only the prepared mind."
—Louis Pasteur

A special place is an imaginary setting to which you can return again and again in your visualizations.

In this section you will be guided through the creation of two of these special places, one outdoors and one indoors. The places you create will be exactly the way you want them, tailored to your unique personality, preferences, and expectations.

Uses of Your Special Place

Your special place has several uses. First of all, its creation is a good exercise in controlling mental images. It will give you essential practice in creating and revising scenes to get them exactly the way you want them.

Second, and most importantly, your special place will be used for relaxation. It's a safe, secure retreat where you can let go of all tension. You can let your guard down and relax totally. You will automatically associate your special place with deep levels of relaxation and peace, so that even a brief thought about it will begin to relax you.

Your special place can provide a quick release from anxiety. For example, June was a clerk at a title company. She often had to deal with people who were tense and angry with her because they were borrowing large amounts of money and didn't understand something about the loan fees or other expenses. When June felt very anxious after such a confrontation, she would go to the ladies room, lie down, and spend a minute visualizing her special place to calm herself. She would see herself lying on the beach in front of her grandfather's house at the lake. She hadn't actually been to the lake for years, but it represented peace and contentment for her. A minute on the beach eased June's anxiety and made her ready to go on with her job.

Your special place is also where you go to meditate, to mull things over, and to solve problems. In your special place you are a deep and clear thinker. You can penetrate to the core of a problem. You can enter into and understand complexities of feelings and motivations that are opaque to you elsewhere. You are in touch with your own unconscious, able to remember and know things that in ordinary places are hidden from you.

You'll go to your special place to do receptive visualizations. Once you have found your inner guide (discussed later in this chapter) you may invite him or her to join you in your special place to answer important questions you have about your life. For example, Richard agreed to help his mother run a flea market for her church group, even though he would rather have done something else that weekend. He was irritable and got very angry with his mother on the phone Friday night, for no apparent reason. Before going to sleep that night, he went to his special place—a meadow by a mountain stream. He reviewed his phone conversation with his mother, then invited his inner guide to join him and explain what had gone wrong. Richard's inner guide—a bearded old man named Oscar—stepped out from behind a tree. Oscar had a roll of stickers like kids buy at the candy store. Each sticker was printed with a big "YES" in bold letters. Oscar was pasting these stickers all over Richard's face. It was very uncomfortable and annoying. Richard said, "Stop it! Stop it! No!" At once the stickers disappeared and Oscar smiled. He held up one last sticker that read "NO" and said, "No is your magic word," and walked away behind the tree. Richard realized then the source of his conflict with his mother. He should

698 FAMILY GUIDE TO EMOTIONAL WELLNESS

have told her no, he couldn't help with the flea market that weekend. It was too late to back out, but at least he understood the source of his resentment and could cope with it. He would remember it the next time he felt uncomfortable with one of her requests.

Characteristics of Your Special Place

Most often a special place is a nature scene: a beach, forest, mountain, desert, meadow, or other pleasant outdoors area. It can also be indoors: a study, den, library, castle, dream house, teepee, cabin, cave, or some other enclosed area, either man-made, natural, or some combination of the two. In this chapter you'll make up an outdoor and an indoor place that you can visit as the mood strikes you.

A special place can be based on a real place you've visited, such as a national park where you went on vacation or someplace you spent a lot of time in as a child. Or your special place can be entirely made up, a pure work of imagination. It's likely that it will have elements of both reality and imagination.

Your special place can be based on a fictional, historical, or legendary locale. You can go to Alice's Wonderland, Marie Antoinette's palace at Versailles, or the Hanging Gardens of Babylon.

There are certain characteristics that you should be sure to incorporate into your special place. First of all, it should be quiet. Avoid crashing surf if you choose a beach scene, and don't include a roaring waterfall as part of your stream setting. Likewise, your place should be comfortable: not too hot, cold, windy, bright, dark, and so on. If you choose a desert scene, make it warm but not hot. If you want to be on the top of a mountain, go easy on the snow and wind. Since you're making it all up, you can do away with the sunburn and mosquitoes that you usually can't escape in a real natural setting.

Your place should be safe, secure, and relaxing. If it's in the woods, there needn't be any bears or mountain lions. However rugged and picturesque, it should have a place for you to sit comfortably and a place to lie down.

Include some means for another person or animal or object to appear. This can be a rock or tree to hide behind, a path down which somebody could walk, a door that can be opened and shut, or a treasure chest that you can open and find something in. These are all mechanisms by which your unconscious can send messages.

To make your special place more realistic, it should have perspective and be stocked with many details. Make sure there's a foreground, a middle distance, and a background. Include flowers, plants, rocks, furniture—whatever seems appropriate. Especially include any favorite things of your own or that you'd like to have. There aren't any logical limits, so you can have a color TV in the Middle Ages or a big, four-poster bed in a redwood grove.

Some handy things to have in your special place are a mirror or reflecting pool for looking at yourself, paints and canvas, paper and pencil, musical instruments, clay for making statues, and any other aids you can think of for self-expression or discovery. For imagining the future or visualizing goals within your special place, include a natural stage area, a TV, movie screen, or a crystal ball.

Nature Scene Exercise

Lie down, close your eyes, and relax. You are going to gradually create a special place for yourself in nature. The instructions will be necessarily somewhat vague, since you have to fill in details with special meaning to you.

Imagine a path. It can be in the woods, at the seashore, in the desert, or in the mountains. It can be a place you know or would like to know. Imagine that you are standing on the path, looking down it. Notice the surface of the path: the dirt or sand, the rocks, the color and texture. Begin walking on the path and notice how it feels against your feet. You can be barefoot or wearing comfortable shoes, boots, or sandals.

As you stroll down the path, look up and notice the countryside. See the colors and shapes of the trees, rocks, mountains, or whatever. Listen and hear the birds, the sound of water, of wind, and of your own steps. Notice how quiet and peaceful it is here in this special place. Take a deep breath and smell the fresh air. Take in the smells of earth, water, and green growing things. Feel the sun shining and a gentle breeze blowing against your face.

Continue down the path until you come to some sort of enclosed area. This will be your special place. If it doesn't seem inviting, change the aspects you don't like, or go a little further down the path until you come to a spot you like more.

Take a look around this special spot. It can be a meadow, a clearing, a cove, a glade, a hollow, a peak—whatever feels right to you. Notice its shape and general layout. Take in the sights, sounds, and smells. Notice the ground, rocks, grass, bushes, and so on. Are there any little animals like birds or squirrels? Is there water nearby that you can see or hear?

This is your place, special for you alone. You can come here any time you want. No one else can come unless you invite them. It's safe and secure, a quiet place of relaxation and peace.

Walk around your special place and notice the quality of light. Make it comfortable, not too bright or too dim. You are in control. You can make the temperature warmer or cooler, make the wind stronger or cause it to die away entirely. Notice what you are wearing—the colors and style and how it feels against your skin. Change to something else if you want. You can dress any way you choose here.

Find a comfortable place to lie down. It could be a bed of dry moss, a patch of sun-warmed sand, or even a real bed with sheets and blankets and everything. You can have it just the way you want it. Lie down and try it out. Make sure it's a good place to rest. What do you see when you look up?

Get up and go to the center of your special place. Turn in a circle and notice what you see, first right in front of you. Then raise your eyes and fill in the middle distance. Then look out as far as you can see. Make sure that there are near and far things to look at.

Look around and find a place where someone else could be, nearby yet hidden from you. This is where you will have your inner guide and other visitors appear. It can be a rock outcropping, a big tree, a bend in the path, or even a cave or hole in the ground.

Next make a place in which you can store things: a hollow tree, a cupboard, a hole under a rock, a treasure chest, a niche in a cliff face. Into this space, place some paper and a pen or pencil. Make it the kind of art paper you loved as a child, and your favorite kind of pencil or pen. Include some paints and some modeling clay. If you play or would like to play a musical instrument, put that in too. If your instrument is a grand piano or something else that won't fit in the storage space, put it in a convenient corner of your special place. Remember, you can do anything in your special place, including playing an instrument on which you have had no training.

Look around and find a reflecting surface where you can see your face. Create a mirror or a reflecting pool. Also make some provision for a place to watch imaginary scenes: a spot in the middle distance that seems like a stage, or a crystal ball on a pedestal, or even a TV monitor. Perhaps your reflecting pool can double as a viewing screen.

Go around your special place experiencing and refining all the things you have created. Look at them, smell them, touch them, even taste them. Fill in details. Change colors or textures. Make your special place just as perfect as you can. Remind yourself that this is your place, to come to any time you want. It is peaceful and serene, a safe refuge from the cares of the world.

Take a last look around, then walk out of your special place, down the path the way you came. Entering and leaving your special place by the same path is a way to heighten its reality for you.

Stop walking on the path and begin to remember your actual surroundings at this moment. When you are ready, open your eyes, get up, and stretch. During the day, think back on your special place. It's your place. You can go there any time.

Indoor Scene Exercise

Once again, lie down, close your eyes, and relax. You are going to create another special place, this time indoors. This can be based on a real room you know, a setting from a favorite book or movie, or a totally imaginary room of your dreams. You are the architect, and you can design your room any way you want.

Start by imagining that you are in your outdoor special place. Leave it and walk down a path. Take a moment to notice the sights, sounds, smells, and temperature of your surroundings. What kind of vegetation and terrain do you see? What is the weather like? What are you wearing?

Come around a bend in the path and encounter a building. What kind of building is it? It can be a modern house with lots of natural wood and glass, a Victorian mansion, a hide yurt, a stone cottage with a thatched roof, a circus tent, a crystal palace, a teepee, or a pyramid—whatever you want to contain your indoor special place.

Enter the building and find your special place inside. Notice what the door is made of. Make sure it has a lock if you want one, and a peephole to look through. Close the door and go into the center of the space.

Look around you and see the doors, walls, and windows (or whatever kind of surface and openings your space has). If things are unclear, take some time to experiment with wall coverings and window positions. You can alter things until they seem right. Try changing the floor plan around, so that you have interesting nooks and crannies to give scale and comfort.

What kind of flooring do you like? Carpet, rugs, hardwood, tile, earth, even growing grass? Make up a good floor. Then look up and see how high you want the ceiling. Maybe you want it low in some places and high in others.

Put in some furniture. Make sure you have a comfortable chair, a table or desk to work on, a bed or couch of some kind to lie down on, bookcases and other places to store your art supplies or musical instruments, and so on. The furnishings should be exactly what you've always wanted, precisely to your taste. Don't forget purely decorative items like plants, flowers, sculpture, paintings, photographs, or wall hangings. If you like small pets, throw in a tank of fish or a parrot in a cage. Make this the room you always wanted.

If a view is important to you, go around to each window and look out. Create what you want to see: an ocean, a forest, the city at night, fields of grain, or whatever.

Pay some attention to the means of lighting—overhead, table lamps, track lighting, indirect, skylights, and so on. Notice where the switches are.

Make a closet with a door or a niche with a curtain where you can "discover" messages from your unconscious. Also, you should have a TV, mirror, movie screen, stage, or some other means of viewing imaginary scenes.

Look around you and coordinate the visual style of your special place. It can be as plain and ascetic as a monk's cell, or as barbarically splendid as a sultan's throne room. Just make sure the colors, shapes, and textures all work together visually in a way that pleases and excites you.

Now add some sound. Create a stereo system to play your favorite music. Consider warbling birds, a tinkling fountain, wind chimes, wind or water sounds from outside.

This is your special place. It belongs to you alone. You can do anything in this room, and no one will care. No problem or other person can bother you in this special place. Here you are relaxed, content, creative, and fully alive. This is a room where you can come any time you want to rest or think.

Walk around and touch the things in your space. Feel the unique textures of fine wood, fabric, paper, brass, and glass. Switch the lights on and off. Open and shut doors and windows, get the tactile feel of the place as you sit in different chairs and flop on the bed.

Smell the scent of your cut flowers, or create a bowl of exquisite fruit and sample the taste.

Continue looking and walking around your special place, changing and refining details until you're satisfied with it. You will come back to this space many times to solve problems, answer questions, or just escape daily stresses and relax.

When you're ready, recall your immediate surroundings and open your eyes. Get up and go about your usual routine, remembering from time to time that you now have a special place you can enter whenever you like.

Finding Your Inner Guide

"It is easier to go to Mars or to the moon than it is to penetrate one's own being."

—Carl Jung

Your inner guide is an imaginary person, animal, or other being that you create to help you solve problems or answer questions. Your inner guide is the personification of your inner wisdom. It's your unconscious, all-knowing mind given a form and a voice.

Inner guides can take many forms: wizard, priestess, old woman, circus ringleader, angel, Greek goddess, stag, space alien, grandfather, old childhood friend, movie star, and so on.

Your inner guide answers questions and gives you advice. He or she or it can be of great help in resolving dilemmas—when you are stuck between two or more mutually exclusive choices. Your inner guide helps by being a channel for messages from your unconscious. Consulting your inner guide is really a matter of uncovering feelings you may not be fully aware of and clarifying what you really need or want.

Characteristics of Your Inner Guide

An inner guide can be someone you know or have met, someone who is now dead, a character in a book, play, or movie, someone out of myth and legend, or an entirely imaginary being who just feels right to you. It doesn't matter whether your inner guide is of the same or opposite sex.

The most important characteristic is that your inner guide is wiser and smarter than your conscious mind. Your inner guide knows everything you have ever experienced or thought, even things you didn't consciously notice at the time. Your inner guide isn't confused by emotions or complexity. Your inner guide can arrive at correct conclusions and decisions directly by intuition, without having to go through a long chain of logical reasoning and rationalizations.

You can communicate verbally or nonverbally with your inner guide. When you ask a question, your guide may say yes or nod or smile as an answer. If your guide is an animal, it may purr, smile, lick your hand, or whatever—you decide the meaning and the means of communication. Sometimes your inner guide may show you visions—little visualizations within a visualization—that provide you with insightful answers. Or your guide may give you something, a symbolic gift that represents the answer you seek. For example, you may be considering whether to go back to school and finish your degree, and your guide gives you an academic robe or a pencil box like you had on your first day of school. Or your guide may give you a tool or some other item that means, "Better keep working at what you're doing."

Like the ancient Greek oracle at Delphi, your guide may sometimes be cryptic or silent. This might mean that the information you are seeking is just not available to you at this time. For instance, you may be trying to clarify your true feelings about another person, but it's actually too early to tell how you feel. A cryptic answer might also mean that the information you're seeking is something you really don't want to know, some truth that you're not yet ready to face. For example, an art student was considering dropping out of school. She asked her guide, "Is my art any good? Am I really an artist, or just pretending?" Her guide, an incredibly old Indian chief who resembled Picasso, just looked confused and gave a Gallic shrug. Months later she decided that she wasn't really committed to art, but at the earlier time, she wasn't ready to face that evaluation.

Your inner guide can show up anywhere in your visualizations. You can call your guide into your special place for a consultation, or take your guide along on any kind of imaginary exploration, or encounter your guide somewhere along the way, either by plan or unexpectedly.

Treat your inner guide like a trusted friend. Your guide has your best interests at heart. Don't make a commitment to your guide unless you mean it. Be honest in what you say to your guide. Remember, your guide is your wiser self. If you try to fool your guide, you're fooling yourself.

Treating your inner guide like your best friend is a way to build your self-confidence and self-esteem.

Since he or she is really you, your inner guide reflects your personality. Your guide's timidity reflects your own fear. Sarcasm reflects your own cynicism. Dire warnings reflect your own negativity.

Your inner guide will change over time as you change. He or she may get older or larger or more outgoing, reflecting changes in your own life. Your original inner guide may disappear and be replaced by a different one that better suits your current circumstances and feelings. If you notice changes in your inner guide, ask about them. It may give you some valuable information about how you're changing.

You may choose to have more than one inner guide. For example, it makes sense to have a child guide, a man guide, and a woman guide. This is recommended by David Bresler, a pain control expert. He reasons that you have all three elements in your personality—the child, the male, and the female. Having three guides provides all three elements of your personality a clear channel of expression.

Or you may have a guide that has many moods. For example, you could create a Zen monk who can be very serious, very funny, very earthy, or very mysterious, depending on what you need from him at different times.

By the way, humor is very important. Consulting your unconscious self sounds like a very serious and formal enterprise, but the results are often funny. Your inner guide may even take the form of a clown or a comedian. Humor often has its roots in unconscious desires that are too powerful or threatening to be allowed any other kind of expression. Along these lines, you may find that your inner guide communicates to you by using puns or riddles. This is just another way you protect yourself by expressing unconscious desires in a coded or disguised form. Figuring out what your guide is really saying is often like interpreting a goofy dream.

Finally, you must pay attention to the rule of visualization that says, "Take what you get." Your inner guide may not live up to your expectations. You may start the exercises below expecting to find a beautiful Indian maiden or Gandalf the Wise, only to end up with the nerd who broke your bike in fifth grade or a dwarf smoking a cigar. Your unconscious will be doing the choosing in the next exercise, and it's not predictable, reasonable, or literal in its creations. So don't be surprised, and take what you get.

Inner Guide Exercise

Before you begin this exercise in discovering an inner guide, prepare a question to ask. For this first experience, the best question is, "Are you my guide?"

This is simple, with no negatives to confuse your unconscious. The rules for making up good questions for your guide are the same as the rules for making up good affirmations: Keep them short, simple, positive, rich in feeling, and in the present tense whenever possible.

Begin the exercise by lying down, closing your eyes, and relaxing. Go to your outdoor special place and settle in. Notice all the details of sight and sound, touch and taste and smell that define your place and make it real to you.

From your special place, look off into the distance. See a tiny figure there. It's so far away that you can only see a speck moving in the haze. Imagine that this figure is your inner guide, approaching very slowly, getting larger very slowly. Soon you will be able to make out some details.

By now you can see the general shape of the figure. Is it a person or an animal? Wait until you can see this. Then try to tell if it's a man or a woman, or what kind of animal it is.

As the figure gets closer, see more and more details. How is this figure dressed? In regular clothes, in robes, not dressed at all? Any hats, staffs, bags? What colors and textures do you see?

You can see small details now: the color of the eyes, the texture of skin, the shape of nose and chin and brow. You can hear the figure's steps. Let this being, this possible guide, get closer, right up to the edge of your special place, then stop.

Does this figure look friendly? This is an important question. If the figure you've called up looks angry or dangerous, there's no need to invite it into your special place. Turn it around and have it walk away into the distance and disappear.

If you're confronting an animal figure, it may be hard to tell what "friendly" means. If you feel afraid of the animal, send it away. If you are in doubt, offer it some food and see if the feelings warm up.

In shamanistic teachings, there are stern warnings about dealing with figures in the shape of snakes, lizards, fish, dragons, or beings who have the features of these scaly, cold-blooded creatures. So if you have conjured up some kind of reptilian figure, you might want to send it away and try again. On the other hand, maybe you have warm memories and a strong identification with Puff the Magic Dragon or Cecil the Seasick Sea Serpent, and a scaled, friendly guide is just right for you, however cold-blooded and serpent-like. In the final analysis, choose what feels right.

You can have several figures in turn approach from the distance and keep sending away the unfriendlies until you find a friendly one that you like. But don't send away a possible guide just because he or she doesn't meet your expectations. You may find that the same weird figure returns over and over. This is an indication that you have the right figure, even though it seems odd to your conscious, critical mind.

When you're satisfied that your guide is friendly, invite it into your special place. You can speak out loud and say, "Come in," or gesture, or use mental telepathy to communicate your desire. Greet your guide in an appropriate way: say hello or shake hands or embrace.

Grasp hands or look deep into the figure's eyes and ask your prepared question: "Are you my guide?" Your guide should say yes or nod or indicate in some other way that he or she is indeed your guide. If the answer is ambiguous, ask again until you get a clear answer.

If no clear answer comes or the answer is no, send the figure away with the instruction, "Please send me my guide." Then try again with another figure approaching from the distance.

Once you are satisfied that you are in the presence of your authentic guide, take a walk together and notice what you see. Hold hands during the walk, if that feels right. Return to your special place and show your guide around, as if you were showing off a new apartment or garden.

If your guide is an animal, pet or groom it. Ask for a gift or give something to your guide. If a simple question pops into your mind, ask it. Tell your guide that you trust him or her, and are glad to have your guide in your special place.

Finally, say good-bye. Promise to keep in touch. Have your guide promise to visit you whenever he or she is invited into your visualizations. Suggest to your guide that he or she should "drop in" on you whenever there is something important for you to know.

Rest for a moment alone in your special place. Know that you have an inner guide that you can trust. Your guide comes to you whenever you need it. Your guide is wise, all-knowing, and has only your best interests at heart.

When you are ready, remind yourself of your actual surroundings. Open your eyes and end the session.

In the next day or two, do this exercise again. This time, have your inner guide visit you in your indoor special place. Your guide can come to the door or appear in one of the places you have prepared for such visits. Repeat the question, "Are you my guide?" and interact in the same way you did outdoors.

When you're exploring particularly complicated or confusing issues, try meeting your inner guide deep within a cave or maze. Imagine finding the end of a thread at the mouth of a cave. Pick up the thread and follow it into the cave. Go deeper and deeper into the cave, following the thread as it leads down different tunnels, through tight spots, across great open chambers, and so on. Gradually come to a small, dark chamber deep within the cave. Your inner guide is there, holding a small light. In this special setting, ask for enlightenment. The cave imagery symbolizes the descent into your unconscious and a delving beneath the superficial surface of your situation. If the idea of going into a cave makes you nervous, imagine walking into a maze of hedges or a building with many corridors and doors.

References

Schultz, J. H., and W. Luthe. 1959. *Autogenic Training: A Psychophysiological Approach to Psychotherapy.* New York: Gruen & Stra Hon.

Excerpted and adapted with permission from *Visualization for Change* by Patrick Fanning. For more information on this and related books, see the "Further Reading" section in the back of the book.

CHAPTER 48

Dreams

Dreams consist of thoughts and feelings you experienced during the day but which were not within your direct awareness. They tell you what you don't know you know. They help you see more clearly, bringing to your attention strengths and talents you didn't know you had, as well as pointing out how you might be undermining yourself. By *experiencing* behavior in your dreams, you can rehearse for future behaviors and release pent-up emotions. In addition, studies have shown that dreams can help you maintain your psychological balance. Your dreams also assist in solving problems and making decisions. They are messages from yourself to yourself and derived from your own inner wisdom.

Dream interpretation is translating a dream message from one level of consciousness to another, from dream language to everyday language. Dream language is a visual language, using concrete pictures, images, and scenes to depict complex thoughts and ideas. We don't dream in the abstract—we *experience* feelings. Symbols are the vocabulary of this language. Symbols share common traits with the objects they refer to. These traits are the key to understanding a symbol's meaning.

The meaning of any symbol is unique to the dreamer. Both objects and actions are symbolic in dreams. Since everything in a dream is symbolic, it is important to carefully look at every detail in a dream.

Dream language is also a metaphorical language and uses plays on words. It is a humorous, playful, clever language where the mind becomes creative and inventive when freed of mental restraints. It is also an economical language, condensing several ideas into one.

Just as dream language has its own vocabulary in the form of symbols, it also has its own rules of logic. Once you understand the dream mechanisms comprising this logic, the dream becomes coherent. Dream language draws upon your inner wisdom, providing you with messages based on your inner knowledge.

Dreams are fleeting and vanish into thin air unless you have a net with which to catch them. *To recall your dreams*, keep a journal and a pen by the bed to remind you to have dreams and to record them. Once you awaken, close your eyes and try to get back into the dream state.

Write down your dreams as soon *as you wake up*. Don't judge them. Even a small fragment can be significant. You don't need to remember all of your dreams—one or two a week is enough.

To incubate a dream, have a discussion with yourself—preferably on paper—regarding the problem you want to dream about. Select a specific phrase that summarizes your question and repeat it over and over before going to sleep. Write down the dream immediately after waking.

Here are some *attitudes that interfere with dream recall*. If you have difficulty remembering your dreams, ask yourself if any of these may describe your situation.

- "I'm too busy."

- "I don't have time."

- "I'm already stressed out."

- "I need my sleep."

- "It's too much trouble."

- "I must have a dream."

- "I don't want to know what's going on because I'll have to deal with it."

- "I'm afraid my dreams will be too painful."

- "Dreams are not important."

Remember, dreams are like relationships: the more you put into them, the more you get out of them!

Interpreting Your Dreams

So how do you go about translating a dream back into everyday language? Dream interpretation is a translation from one level of awareness to another, from the obvious dream story to its underlying meaning. To translate dream language into everyday language, you need to find the common denominator of the dream and its waking counterpart. The common denominator serves as the bridge or link between the dream symbols and what they stand for. The following diagram illustrates this relationship:

Dream Language	*Common Denominator*	**Everyday Language**
	(Bridge) $\longrightarrow$	

This common denominator is usually a trait that is shared by both the symbol and the object it refers to. For example, in a dream, a dog could represent a loyal husband because they both share the common trait of loyalty. *To interpret a dream we must find the common features shared by the two levels of consciousness so that we can translate the dream story into its original form.* The following diagram makes this clear:

Symbol	*Common Features*	**Meaning**
	$\longrightarrow$	
Dog	*Loyal*	**Husband**
	$\longrightarrow$	

Interpreting a dream is very much like doing a jigsaw puzzle: there is no single way to do it. You have to start somewhere, and every piece you fit together makes it easier to make the next piece fit, until all the pieces are connected. This is how you do dream analysis, slowly and patiently, piece by piece, until you see the whole picture. Sometimes you can't find all the pieces, and you have an incomplete puzzle. That is okay. Even if you can only interpret part of a dream, you get something. You might still find the missing pieces the next day, or even in a later dream. An incomplete interpretation is always better than an incorrect interpretation.

The ideal situation for analyzing a dream is with the help of another person, usually a therapist, to ask the questions and trigger the associations. This process allows for a clear distinction between the analytical side of the dialogue (which stays on track and asks the questions) and the intuitive side (which makes the metaphorical connections).

We can also learn to perform this question-and-answer process by ourselves. What follows are a series of steps you can do on your own that will make the process of dream interpretation easier. Included are a number of questions you can ask yourself that can help clarify the meaning of a dream. I have found in my own experience that this process works best when I am in that receptive state of mind directly upon awakening, when I am still operating in a state of consciousness where I am open to new ideas and make connections easily, when my right brain is in full swing. The left brain is necessary to ask the questions and to keep me on track, but I don't want it to interrupt the free-flowing state of the right.

When doing the interpretive process alone, write down your dream, because you may forget important details later on. This will free up your mind for the interpretive work; writing the dream in full allows your right brain to come up with the associations spontaneously since your left brain doesn't have to work at remembering the details. This means you don't have to constantly shift between your analytical and intuitive modes of thinking.

In order to illustrate the step-by-step interpretation process, I will use a dream I had many years ago:

> I am taking my colleagues to lunch in a restaurant. I look at my salad plate and realize that there is a comb in my salad. I am somewhat embarrassed as it may reflect on me since I brought my co-workers to this restaurant, and I wonder if I should call attention to it. I decide to confront the server. "There is a comb in my salad," I say. She looks very unconcerned and nonchalant and doesn't take the complaint seriously. I decide this is unacceptable service and that I will never frequent that restaurant again.

Before going through the basic steps, it is usually best to try to figure out what the dream is about.

- Do I have any idea what the dream is about?

Sometimes you already know the meaning of the dream and have a notion what the different symbols refer to. In the case of an obvious dream, we can skip some of the steps later on. In the case of my restaurant dream, I simply had no idea.

Summarize the Dreamer's Actions

The first step in dream interpretation is to summarize your actions in the dream in a couple of sentences.

- What were you doing in the dream?

- What were you feeling?

This step focuses not only on your actions in the dream, but also on your thoughts and feelings. You are trying to get the general theme or plot of the dream. Just as in a puzzle, it is usually easiest to start with a frame and then fill it in with the missing pieces.

- Describe the dream in the third person, as though it were a story.

- What is the plot or story line?

- Try to put the plot into one or two sentences.

It can be helpful to describe the dream in the third person as a story happening to someone else. Why only a sentence or two? If you try to capture the entire dream, you might get bogged down describing everything you did in minute detail, thereby missing the forest for the trees. Why the third person? This way you get some distance between yourself and the dream, which helps you see it more objectively. For example:

> This is a story about a woman who takes her colleagues out for lunch, is embarrassed by the poor service she is getting, complains but is met by nonchalance, so she decides never to go to the restaurant again.

When telling the dream story, it's helpful to stay away from the nouns—the objects and symbols—and focus mainly on the verbs—the actions. You will get to the "comb" and the "server" later on. For the time being, concentrate on the action alone. By focusing on the action, you can summarize this dream even further:

> The dreamer is getting poor service and is met by nonchalance when she complains.

Relate the Actions to Your Waking Life

Once you know what the main action of the dream is, you can try to figure out the relationship between the dream and your waking life.

- Where in my waking life am I experiencing the same feelings as in the dream?

- Are the actions in the dream similar to any situation in my everyday life?

This question links the action in the dream to the action in your waking life. Where in my life am I getting poor service which embarrasses me in front of my colleagues. Where are my complaints being met by nonchalance? As soon as I asked myself this question, I recalled that the previous day, a colleague had mentioned to me that the answering service which took my calls had acted in a rude manner. When I had called the woman at the service to complain, she had shown the same nonchalant attitude as the woman in the dream. By discovering what part of your waking life the dream refers to, you are able to put the dream in context.

Find the Focal Point

Once you know the context of the dream, you can then define the symbols *within that context*. You have the frame of the puzzle, and now you can begin to fill in the different pieces. As with a jigsaw puzzle, a good starting point is a piece that stands out, the focal point.

The *focal point* is the part of the dream that stands out, is out of context, doesn't fit, or doesn't make sense.

- What stands out for me?

- What is not clear?

- Is there anything that doesn't fit or doesn't make sense?

Which part of the restaurant dream is least understandable? As I looked at the dream, I saw that the comb was clearly out of place. What is a comb doing in a salad? The comb is the focal point.

Some dreams don't have anything particular that stands out. If this is the case, we can go to the next step and define all the symbols in the dream and your own experiences with them.

Define the Symbols

To arrive at the meaning of a symbol, you have to define it. You don't ask, for example, "What is a comb to me?" You ask, "What is a *comb*?" Next you need to uncover your own unique associations to the symbol. You then use the words in the definition and the associations to get at the symbol's meaning.

- What is _____ (symbol)?

- What am I reminded of when I think of the words I used to define _____ ?

- What have been my own associations and experiences with _____ ?

- What part has _____ played in my life?

- Is there a part of me that's like _____ ?

I begin with the focal point of the dream, the comb, defining the symbol and uncovering my own particular associations to it. A comb is something I use on my hair to make me look good. It belongs in the bathroom, not the kitchen. A comb is clearly unacceptable in food. The words used in the definition and the specific associations to the symbol are the common denominator, the link between the symbol and the object it refers to. What was I reminded of when I thought of something unacceptable that made me look bad in front of my colleagues? The comb reminded me of rudeness to my callers, which was unacceptable and made me look bad to my callers.

I went on to define the other symbols in the dream: the *server*—someone who is giving me service but seems nonchalant—reminded me of the woman I had complained to; my *colleagues* represented my colleagues who have to interact with my service; the *restaurant*—a place that offers you service that you often provide for yourself—reminded me of my answering service. In dream analysis, we try to find the common features between the symbols and what they represent. As we define the symbols and give our associations to them, we discover the common denominator of the dream language and the situation it relates to in our waking life. By defining these symbols and their associations, we get the new meaning. The diagram below shows the relationship between the symbols and the objects they refer to.

Anatomy of a Dream

Dream Language	Common Denominator (Bridge)	Everyday Language
Comb salad	Unacceptable service	Rudeness to callers
Server	Person I complain to: nonchalant; unconcerned	Person at answering service
Colleagues	People I work with; peers	Colleagues
Restaurant	Place I use to provide service for colleagues; reflects on me	Answering service

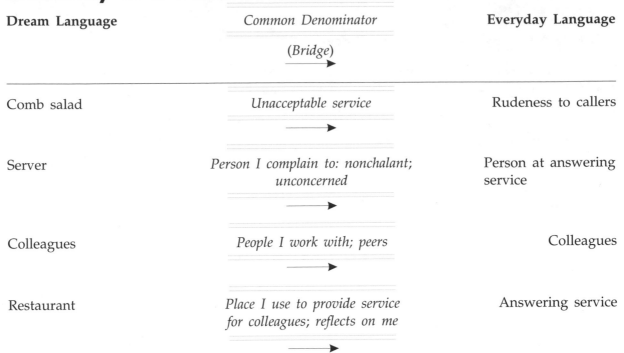

Rewrite the Dream Story

Now you can rewrite the dream story, using the new meanings. In this step, you simply substitute the new meanings for the symbols in the dream story as in the diagram.

Note that the verbs—the dreamer's *actions*—remain the same. Only the nouns—the *symbols or objects*—change. The actions are "getting poor service," "being embarrassed," "complaining," "being met by nonchalance," etc. The symbols—the restaurant, the comb, and the server—stand for objects in my life—my answering service, rudeness to my callers, and the person I complain to.

Rewriting the Dream Story

Dream story

*In the **restaurant**, I notice a **comb in my salad**. I am embarrassed in front of my **colleagues** as it makes me look bad. I wonder whether to call attention to it. I confront the **server** and complain. She is nonchalant and unconcerned and doesn't take the complaint seriously. I decide not to give them my business.*

Just change the symbols to their new meaning.

New story

*In the **answering service**, I notice **rude behavior**. I am embarrassed in front of my **colleagues** as it makes me look bad. I wonder whether to call attention to it. I confront the **woman at the service** and complain. She is nonchalant and unconcerned and doesn't take the complaint seriously. I decide not to give them my business.*

Unlock the Dream Message

Once you have the new story, you can find out what the message of the dream is for you.

- What is the message of the dream?

- What is it trying to tell me?

- What is the moral of the story?

- Why do I need to remind myself of this now?

The message seems clear: The service I was getting was unacceptable and I should not use it any longer. The dream highlighted this reality and brought it to my attention. I realized that being rude to my colleagues was as unacceptable as having a comb in my food.

Apply the Message to Your Waking Life

- How can I apply the message to my waking life?

- I decided to switch to another service.

Excerpted and adapted with permission from *Practical Dreaming: Awakening the Power of Dreams in Your Life* by Lillie Weiss, Ph.D. For more information on this and related books, see the "Further Reading" section in the back of the book.

Further Reading

Part I: Getting Along

COUPLE SKILLS: Making Your Relationship Work

This is a book that can change your relationship. It will change how you communicate, how you think about your partner, how you behave, and how you cope with problems and conflicts.

    Couple Skills differs from other relationship books because the focus is on action and change, rather than theory. It's also different in that each chapter is designed to stand alone. You can begin with the exercises suited to your needs and focus on just the skills that are relevant to you. By Matthew McKay, Ph.D., Patrick Fanning, and Kim Paleg, Ph.D. 6 x 9, 288 pages, 1994, ISBN 1-879237-66-0 (paper). Item SKIL $14.95

A WOMAN'S GUIDE TO OVERCOMING SEXUAL FEAR AND PAIN

This workbook provides a series of exercises designed to help women map the terra incognita of their own bodies and begin to overcome the fear or pain that inhibits or blocks their sexuality. By Aurelie Jones Goodwin, Ed.D, and Marc E. Agronin, M.D. 7 x 10, 288 pages, 1997, ISBN 1-57224-089-X (paper). Item WGOS $14.95

WHEN ANGER HURTS: Quieting the Storm Within

When Anger Hurts is a complete, step-by-step guide to changing habitual, anger-generating thoughts while developing healthier, more effective ways of getting your needs met. It is ideal for therapists who work with families or teach anger control and helpful for health professionals who treat the effects of Type A personality. By Matthew McKay, Ph.D., Peter D. Rogers, Ph.D., Judith McKay, R.N. 6 x 9, 325 pages, 1989, ISBN 0-934986-76-2 (paper). Item ANG $15.95

MESSAGES: The Communication Skills Book, Second Edition

Messages is the most complete and accessible guide for building communication skills available. Highly recommended for therapists who wish to provide a structured training program in specific communication skills for clients. By Matthew McKay, Ph.D., Martha Davis, Ph.D., and Patrick Fanning. 6 x 9, 310 pages, 1995, ISBN 1-57224-022-9 (paper). Item MES2 $15.95

STEPFAMILY REALITIES: How to Overcome Difficulties and Have a Happy Family

Explores setting boundaries and personal space, blending habits and values, family rules, jealousy among stepsiblings, discipline, and other special problems. By Margaret Newman. 6 x 9, 264 pages, 1994, ISBN 1-879237-9-5 (paper). Item STEP $15.95

INFIDELITY: A Survival Guide

An affair is a major crisis, but it can be survived. Psychologist Don-David Lusterman provides step-by-step guidance to help readers deal with the shock of discovery and cope with the emotional impact of the affair, decide what it tells them about their marriage, and either choose to break up or begin to rebuild with a new ability to acknowledge and support each other. 6 x 9, 207 pages, 1998, ISBN 1-57224-087-3 (paper). Item INFI $13.95

I'LL TAKE CARE OF YOU: A Practical Guide for Family Caregivers

Helps family caregivers cope with uncomfortable thoughts and feelings, avoid burnout, access resources and negotiate with unhelpful health care and social service systems, and set boundaries and find ways of meeting their own needs. By Joseph A. Illardo, Ph.D., L.C.S.W., and Carole R. Rothman, Ph.D. 6 x 9, 220 pages, 1999, 1-57224-165-9 (paper). Item CARE $12.95

Part II: Kids

THE POSTPARTUM SURVIVAL GUIDE

Offers detailed and practical techniques for preventing and recovering from the entire spectrum of postpartum adjustment problems. Includes special considerations for single mothers, older mothers, adoptive mothers, and women who have struggled with infertility. By Anne Dunnewold, Ph.D., and Diane Sanford, Ph.D. 6 x 9, 288 pages, 1994, ISBN 1-879237-80-6 (paper). Item POST $14.95

KID COOPERATION
How to Stop Yelling, Nagging, and Pleading and Get Kids to Cooperate

This is an empowering work, filled with practical skills that will help end sibling fights, boost children's self-esteem, and let parents handle discipline with understanding and authority. By Elizabeth Pantley. 6 x 9, 208 pages, 1996, ISBN 1-57224-040-7 (paper). Item COOP $13.95

THE TEN THINGS EVERY PARENT NEEDS TO KNOW

Describes in detail the skills parents most need to learn, including advice on how to nurture a child emotionally, listen and foster self-esteem, solve problems and handle discipline issues, cope with anger, and take care of themselves as well as the child. By Kim Paleg, Ph.D. 6 x 6, 168 pages, 1997, ISBN 1-57224-065-2 (paper). Item KNOW $12.95

UNDERSTANDING YOUR CHILD'S SEXUAL BEHAVIOR: What's Natural and Healthy

Puts parents' minds at ease by showing them how to differentiate between worrisome and natural or healthy behavior and freeing them from misconceptions about sexual abuse. By Toni Cavanagh Johnson, Ph.D. 6 x 9, 199 pages, 1999, 1-57224-141-1 (paper). Item CSB $12.95

THE DIVORCE BOOK: A Practical and Compassionate Guide

Two psychologists team up with a lawyer and a relationships expert to help you cope with all the issues involved in surviving a divorce, including advice to help you avoid the psychological traps, deal with the legal and financial issues, and create the best possible new life for your children and yourself. By Matthew McKay, Ph.D., Peter D. Rogers, Ph.D., Joan Blades, J.D., and Richard Gosse, M.A. 6 x 9, 330 pages, 1999, 1-57224-136-5 (paper). Item DIV2 $15.95

CHILDREN CHANGED BY TRAUMA: A Healing Guide

Shows parents and others what they can do to help children who have witnessed a traumatic event cope with emotions, learn to talk about what happened, and begin to feel safe again. By Debra Whiting Alexander, Ph.D. 6 x 9, 204 pages, 1999, 1-577224-166-7 (paper). Item CCT $13.95

HELPING YOUR ANXIOUS CHILD: A Step-by-Step Guide for Parents

Anxiety in childhood can result in tremendous personal suffering for the child and cause dramatic personal problems. Anxiety in children also frequently goes untreated, in part because parents don't know where to turn.

This book offers parents valuable practical advice to help you understand your child's anxiety and the options for dealing with it, with or without a therapist's help. Guided by a wealth of real-life examples and step-by-step instructions, you'll learn how to respond to your child's need for reassurance, avoid common pitfalls, and help your child overcome shyness and improve social interaction skills.

By Ronald M. Rapee, Ph.D., Susan H. Spence, Ph.D., Vanessa Cobham, Ph.D., and Ann Wiginall, M.Psych. 6 x 9, 160 pages, 2000, 1-57224-191-8 (paper). Item HAC $12.95

Part III: Consuming Passions

THE DEADLY DIET: Second Edition

Offering proven cognitive behaviorial techniques, this book's self-help program provides essential techniques for confronting the inner voice that's responsible for the shame, guilt, and low self-worth that fuels eating disorders. By Terence J. Sandbek, Ph.D. 6 x 9, 256 pages, 1993, ISBN 1-879237-42-3 (paper). Item DD2 $14.95

THE BODY IMAGE WORKBOOK: An 8-Step Program for Learning to Like Your Looks

This clinically tested program shows you how to transform a negative body image into a more pleasurable, affirming relationship with your appearance. By Thomas F. Cash, Ph.D. 8½ x 11, 224 pages, 1997, ISBN 1-57224-062-8 (paper). Item IMAG $18.95

THE ADDICTION WORKBOOK: A Step-by-Step Guide to Quitting Alcohol and Drugs

This comprehensive workbook explains the facts about addiction and provides simple, step-by-step directions for working through the stages of the quitting process. By Patrick Fanning and John O'Neill, L.C.D.C. 8½ x 11, 160 pages, 1996, ISBN 1-57224-043-1 (paper). Item AWB $17.95

CONCERNED INTERVENTION: When Your Loved One Won't Quit Alcohol or Drugs

Authors John and Pat O'Neill provide a compassionate and practical guide to the technique of group intervention, based on lessons learned from their experience with hundreds of families seeking counseling and treatment. 6 x 9, 208 pages, 1992, ISBN 1-879237-36-9 (paper). Item VENT $13.95

THE STOP SMOKING WORKBOOK: Your Guide to Healthy Quitting

If you know that it's time to quit, this workbook can give you the tools to change. Guided by challenging exercises, you start by learning how to assess your own smoking habit and lay a foundation for successful quitting. The authors cover the latest research on nicotine replacement therapies and other coping techniques, detail the best strategies for making it through the first weeks, and show you how to minimize your risk for relapse. By Lori Stevic-Rust, Ph.D., and Anita Maximin, Psy.D. 8½ x 11, 171 pages, 1996, ISBN 1-57224-037-7 (paper). Item SMOK $17.95

DON'T LEAVE IT TO CHANCE: A Guide for Families of Problem Gamblers

The devastating effects of problem gambling don't stop with the gambler: family members are often its biggest victims. Like any addiction, compulsive gambling takes its toll by causing instability and financial hardship and by fostering ineffective family dynamics that include denial, co-dependence, blaming, withdrawal, and isolation.

Based on extensive research at the Center for Problem Gambling in Bedford, Massachusetts, the authors of this guide provide family members with a step-by-step program of cognitive-behavioral strategies to help them overcome the negative hold gambling has on their lives. Easy-to-follow "action steps" help you learn new strategies to manage the problem, repair relations inside and outside the family, work toward a financial recovery, and develop a road map for the future.

By Edward J. Federman, Ph.D., Charles E. Drebing, Ph.D., and Christopher Krebs, M.A. 6 x 9, 220 pages, 2000, ISBN 1-57224-200-0 (paper). Item GMBL $13.95

VIRTUAL ADDICTION: Help for Netheads, Cyberfreaks, and Those Who Love Them

Is the Internet addictive? Psychologist David N. Greenfield lists the twelve warning signs of Internet abuse and suggests a variety of steps that Netheads can take, including help for those who can't seem to stop shopping or who find themselves compulsively trading stock. 5¼ x 7½, 228 pages, 1999, 1-57224-172-1 (paper). Item VRTL $12.95

Part IV: Coping with Physical Problems

BEING A MAN: A Guide to the New Masculinity

This practical guide for men who want to transcend male stereotypes provides clear instructions for understanding essential gender differences; relating to and reconciling with your father;

enriching your inner life with a spiritual practice; achieving integrity by clarifying and affirming values; finding meaning in work; thriving in personal relationships; and becoming a nurturing and supportive father. By Patrick Fanning and Matthew McKay, Ph.D. 6 x 9, 288 pages, 1993, ISBN 1-879237-40-7 (paper). Item BAM $12.95

PMS: Women Tell Women How to Control Premenstrual Syndrome

This self-care guide draws on the experiences of more than 1,000 women to show how to break the vicious PMS cycle of anger, guilt, denial, and depression. The authors explain how to record and chart symptoms and present the latest diet, vitamins, exercise, and hormone treatments. By Stephanie DeGraff Bender and Kathleen Kelleher. 6 x 9, 256 pages, 1996, ISBN 1-57224-052-0 (paper). Item PRE $13.95

PERIMENOPAUSE: Changes in Women's Health After 35

Beginning with subtle physiological changes in the mid-thirties and forties, perimenopause can encompass a bewildering array of symptoms. This self-care guide helps women cope with symptoms and assure health and vitality in the years ahead. By James E. Huston, M.D., and L. Darlene Lanka, M.D. 6 x 9, 416 pages, 1997, ISBN 1-57224-085-7 (paper). Item PERI $16.95

THE TAKING CHARGE OF MENOPAUSE WORKBOOK

A multidisciplinary team helps you ease the transition through this major life change. Covers the benefits and risks of hormone replacement therapy and the facts about hysterectomy and its alternatives. By Robert M. Dosh, Ph.D., Susan N. Fukushima, M.D., Jane F. Lewis, Ph.D., Robert L. Ross, M.D., and Lynne A. Steinman, Ph.D. 8½ x 11, 195 pages, 1997, ISBN 1-57224-060-1 (paper). Item PAUS $17.95

THE CHRONIC PAIN CONTROL WORKBOOK: Second Edition

Details the treatment strategies for managing and recovering from a broad range of chronic pain conditions. By Ellen Mohr Catalano, M.A., and Kimeron N. Hardin, Ph.D., together with an eight-person team of specialists in all areas of chronic pain management. 8½ x 11, 252 pages, 1996, ISBN 1-57224-050-4 (paper). Item PN2 $18.95

PREPARING FOR SURGERY

Details tested techniques that have been found to help reduce complications, lessen distress, and promote a quicker return to health. By William W. Deardorff, Ph.D., and John L. Reeves II, Ph.D. 8½ x 11, 232 pages, 1997, ISBN 1-57224-071-7 (paper). Item PREP $17.95

Part V: Coping with Bad Moods and Painful Feelings

THE RELAXATION & STRESS REDUCTION WORKBOOK: Fourth Edition

With over 400,000 copies sold, *The Relaxation & Stress Reduction Workbook* has become the American standard for relaxation training. Step-by-step instructions cover progressive muscle relaxation, meditation, autogenics, visualization, thought stopping, refuting irrational ideas, coping skills training, job stress management, and much more. Strongly recommended. By Martha Davis, Ph.D., Elizabeth Robbins Eshelman, M.S.W., and Matthew McKay, Ph.D. 8½ x 11, 256 pages, 1995, ISBN 1-879237-82-2 (paper). Item RS4 $18.95

SELF-ESTEEM: Third Edition

With over 550,000 copies sold, New Harbinger's classic *Self-Esteem* has long been the most comprehensive guide on the subject—and the only book that uses proven cognitive techiques for assessing, improving, and maintaining your self-esteem by talking back to the self-critical voice inside you. It's a book about stopping the judgments, healing the old wounds of hurt and self-rejection, and changing the perceptions and feelings you have about yourself.

Setting new goals is a profound means of changing old, self-limiting behaviors, and the third edition benefits from a new chapter on changing the core beliefs that hinder you from setting and achieving goals in your life. It covers the importance of goal setting in maintaining high self-esteem, how to set realistic goals and break them into manageable steps, and blocks to achieving goals and how to overcome them. By Matthew McKay, Ph.D., and Patrick Fanning. 6 x 9, 316 pages, 2000, 1-57224-198-5 (paper). Item SE3 $15.95

THOUGHTS & FEELINGS: Taking Control of Your Moods and Your Life
Second Edition

This is the most complete and useful guide to cognitive-behavioral techniques ever written—and the only client manual you'll ever need. Along with 14 new chapters, the revised second edition includes twelve step-by-step, research-based protocols that combine the most effective techniques for treating problems ranging from depression and panic disorder to obsessional thinking and anger control. By Matthew McKay, Ph.D., Martha Davis, Ph.D., and Patrick Fanning. 8½ x 11, 256 pages, 1998, ISBN 1-57224-093-8 (paper). Item TF2 $18.95

THE ANXIETY & PHOBIA WORKBOOK: Second Edition

This comprehensive guide has given real help to hundreds of thousands of readers—and it is the book therapists most often recommend to clients struggling with anxiety disorders. By Edmund J. Bourne, Ph.D. 8½ x 11, 448 pages, 1995, ISBN 1-57224-003-2 (paper). Item PHO2 $19.95

AN END TO PANIC: Breakthrough Techniques for Overcoming Panic
Disorder, Second Edition

A state-of-the-art treatment program covers breathing retraining, taking charge of fear-fueling thoughts, overcoming the fear of physical symptoms, coping with phobic situations, avoiding relapse, and living life in the here and now. By Elke Zuercher-White, Ph.D. Paperback, 8½ x 11, 230 pages, 1998, ISBN 1-57224-113-6 (paper). Item END2 $18.95

DYING OF EMBARRASSMENT: Help for Social Anxiety and Social Phobia

Clear, supportive instructions for assessing your fears, improving or developing new social skills, and changing self-defeating thinking patterns. By Barbara G. Markway, Ph.D.; Cheryl N. Carmin, Ph.D.; C. Alec Pollard, Ph.D.; and Teresa Flynn, Ph.D. 6 x 9, 204 pages, 1992, ISBN 1-879237-23-7 (paper). Item EMB $13.95

WHEN ONCE IS NOT ENOUGH: Help for Obsessive Compulsives

How to recognize and confront fears, use simple exercises to block rituals, keep going with positive coping strategies, and handle complications and relapses. By Gail Steketee, Ph.D., and Kerrin White, M.D. 6 x 9, 240 pages, 1990, ISBN 0-934986-87-8 (paper). Item ONCE $14.95

I CAN'T GET OVER IT: A Handbook for Trauma Survivors, Second Edition

This groundbreaking work helps survivors cope with memories and emotions; identify triggers that reactivate traumatic stress; relieve secondary wounding; and gain a sense of empowerment and hope. By Aphrodite Matsakis, Ph.D. 6 x 9, 395 pages, 1996, ISBN 1-57224-058-X (paper). Item OVER $16.95

BEYOND GRIEF

This is the complete guide for anyone surviving the death of a loved one. Written both for the bereaved and the helping professional, it combines supportive personal stories with a step-by-step approach to recovery. *Beyond Grief* acknowledges the path, reassures, and counsels. But most of all, it reassures grieving persons that they are not alone, that they can get through the pain, and that there is a path back to feeling alive again. By Carol Staudacher. Paperback, 6 x 9, 264 pages, 1987, ISBN 0-934986-43-6. Item BG $14.95

LAST TOUCH: Preparing for a Parent's Death

This gentle guide through the unfamiliar terrain of death and dying can help reduce fear and pain. By Marilyn R. Becker, M.S.W. 6 x 9, 160 pages, 1993, ISBN 1-879237-34-2 (paper). Item LAST $11.95

THE DEPRESSION WORKBOOK: A Guide for Living with Depression

This book is based on the responses of 120 survey participants who share their insights, experiences, and strategies for living with extreme mood swings. Interactive exercises teach essential coping skills such as building a strong support system, bolstering self-esteem, fighting negative thoughts, finding appropriate professional help, and using relaxation and exercise. By Mary Ellen Copeland, M.S. 8½ x 11, 320 pages, 1992, ISBN 1-879237-32-6 (paper). Item DEP $18.95

CHOOSING TO LIVE: How to Defeat Suicide Through Cognitive Therapy

Choosing to Live is the first self-help guide addressed to those who are considering suicide. A step-by-step program for change shows how to replace negative beliefs, feel better through coping, and develop alternative skills for solving problems in their lives. By Thomas E. Ellis, Psy.D., and Cory F. Newman, Ph.D. 6 x 9, 192 pages, 1996, ISBN 1-57224-056-3 (paper). Item CHO $12.95

Part VI: Getting Help

MAKE EVERY SESSION COUNT: Getting the Most Out of Your Brief Therapy

Sometimes therapy must be brief because of limits on mental health benefits. At other times short-term psychotherapy is all that is needed. If you are undergoing brief psychotherapy, this concise handbook offers special techniques that can help you and your therapist make the most out of each session. Included are exercises and strategies to help you stay motivated, solve problems, reduce stress, and choose a healthy, supportive lifestyle. By John Preston, Psy.D., Nicolette Varzos, Ph.D., and Douglas S. Liebert, Ph.D.; foreword by Simon Budman, Ph.D. 5¼x7½, 176 pages, 2000, 1-57224-190-X. Item SES2 $10.95

CONSUMER'S GUIDE TO PSYCHIATRIC DRUGS

The authors explain how each drug works, and offer detailed information about treatments for depression, bipolar disorder, anxiety and sleep disorders, and a comprehensive range of other conditions. By John D. Preston, Psy.D., John H. O'Neal, M.D., and Mary C. Talaga, R.Ph., M.A. 6 x 9, 340 pages, 1999, ISBN 1-57224-111-X (paper). Item CGPD $16.95

Part VII: Optimizing Your Life

THE DAILY RELAXER

The Daily Relaxer distills the best of the best to bring together the most effective and popular techniques for learning how to relax. Each relaxer presents a simple, tension-relieving exercise that you can learn in less than ten minutes and practice with positive results right away. By Matthew McKay, Ph.D., and Patrick Fanning. 7 x 7, 128 pages, 1997, ISBN 1-57224-069-5 (paper). Item DALY $12.95

THE THREE MINUTE MEDITATOR: Third Edition

If you don't think you have time to meditate, try this down-to-earth introduction to the basics of using meditation to cope with the stresses of daily life and treat yourself to the powerful benefits of self-acceptance and inner peace. By David Harp, with Nina Feldman, Ph.D., and a foreword by Ben & Jerry. 6 x 9, 208 pages, 1996, ISBN 1-57224-054-7 (paper). Item MED3 $13.95

VISUALIZATION FOR CHANGE: Second Edition

The updated edition of this classic includes applications for weight control, nonsmoking, creativity and problem solving, achieving goals, stress reduction, self-esteem, insomnia, depression, anxiety, anger, shyness, and healing and pain control. By Patrick Fanning. 6 x 9, 338 pages, 1994, ISBN 1-879237-84-9 (paper). Item VIS2 $15.95

PRACTICAL DREAMING: Awakening the Power of Dreams in Your Life

Practical Dreaming shares a step-by-step method that anyone can use to understand what dreams are trying to tell us. The author explains how dream language works, describes techniques to help remember dreams and ask them for guidance, and explains how to interpret a dream's symbols and relate the dream to your waking life. By Lillie Weiss, Ph.D. 5¼x7½, 154 pages, 1999, 1-57224-164-0 (paper). Item DRMG $12.95

Call **toll free, 1-800-748-6273,** or log on to our online bookstore at **www.newharbinger.com** to order. Have your Visa or Mastercard number ready. Or send a check for the titles you want to New Harbinger Publications, Inc., 5674 Shattuck Ave., Oakland, CA 94609. Include $3.80 for the first book and 75¢ for each additional book, to cover shipping and handling. (California residents please include appropriate sales tax.) Allow two to five weeks for delivery.

Prices Subject to change without notice

Patrick Fanning and Matthew McKay, Ph.D.

About the Editors:

Matthew McKay, Ph.D., is a founding director of Haight-Ashbury Psychological Services in San Francisco. Dr. McKay is the coauthor of thirteen popular books, including *The Relaxation & Stress Reduction Workbook, The Divorce Book, When Anger Hurts,* and several professional titles.

Patrick Fanning is a professional writer in the mental health field. He is the author of *Visualization for Change* and *Lifetime Weight Control* and coauthor of nine self-help books including *The Addiction Workbook.*

Self-Esteem, The Addiction Workbook, Self-Esteem Companion, Thoughts & Feelings, When Anger Hurts Your Kids, Prisoners of Belief, and *Couple Skills,* all New Harbinger classics, have been coauthored by the editors.

Some Other New Harbinger Self-Help Titles

Multiple Chemical Sensitivity: A Survival Guide, $16.95
Dancing Naked, $14.95
Why Are We Still Fighting, $15.95
From Sabotage to Success, $14.95
Parkinson's Disease and the Art of Moving, $15.95
A Survivor's Guide to Breast Cancer, $13.95
Men, Women, and Prostate Cancer, $15.95
Make Every Session Count: Getting the Most Out of Your Brief Therapy, $10.95
Virtual Addiction, $12.95
After the Breakup, $13.95
Why Can't I Be the Parent I Want to Be?, $12.95
The Secret Message of Shame, $13.95
The OCD Workbook, $18.95
Tapping Your Inner Strength, $13.95
Binge No More, $14.95
When to Forgive, $12.95
Practical Dreaming, $12.95
Healthy Baby, Toxic World, $15.95
Making Hope Happen, $14.95
I'll Take Care of You, $12.95
Survivor Guilt, $14.95
Children Changed by Trauma, $13.95
Understanding Your Child's Sexual Behavior, $12.95
The Self-Esteem Companion, $10.95
The Gay and Lesbian Self-Esteem Book, $13.95
Making the Big Move, $13.95
How to Survive and Thrive in an Empty Nest, $13.95
Living Well with a Hidden Disability, $15.95
Overcoming Repetitive Motion Injuries the Rossiter Way, $15.95
What to Tell the Kids About Your Divorce, $13.95
The Divorce Book, Second Edition, $15.95
Claiming Your Creative Self: True Stories from the Everyday Lives of Women, $15.95
Six Keys to Creating the Life You Desire, $19.95
Taking Control of TMJ, $13.95
What You Need to Know About Alzheimer's, $15.95
Winning Against Relapse: A Workbook of Action Plans for Recurring Health and Emotional Problems, $14.05
Facing 30: Women Talk About Constructing a Real Life and Other Scary Rites of Passage, $12.95
The Worry Control Workbook, $15.95
Wanting What You Have: A Self-Discovery Workbook, $18.95
When Perfect Isn't Good Enough: Strategies for Coping with Perfectionism, $13.95
Earning Your Own Respect: A Handbook of Personal Responsibility, $12.95
High on Stress: A Woman's Guide to Optimizing the Stress in Her Life, $13.95
Infidelity: A Survival Guide, $13.95
Stop Walking on Eggshells, $14.95
Consumer's Guide to Psychiatric Drugs, $16.95
The Fibromyalgia Advocate: Getting the Support You Need to Cope with Fibromyalgia and Myofascial Pain, $18.95
Healing Fear: New Approaches to Overcoming Anxiety, $16.95
Working Anger: Preventing and Resolving Conflict on the Job, $12.95
Sex Smart: How Your Childhood Shaped Your Sexual Life and What to Do About It, $14.95
You Can Free Yourself From Alcohol & Drugs, $13.95
Amongst Ourselves: A Self-Help Guide to Living with Dissociative Identity Disorder, $14.95
Healthy Living with Diabetes, $13.95
Dr. Carl Robinson's Basic Baby Care, $10.95
Better Boundries: Owning and Treasuring Your Life, $13.95
Goodbye Good Girl, $12.95
Fibromyalgia & Chronic Myofascial Pain Syndrome, $19.95
The Depression Workbook: Living With Depression and Manic Depression, $17.95
Self-Esteem, Second Edition, $13.95
Angry All the Time: An Emergency Guide to Anger Control, $12.95
When Anger Hurts, $13.95
Perimenopause, $16.95
The Relaxation & Stress Reduction Workbook, Fourth Edition, $17.95
The Anxiety & Phobia Workbook, Second Edition, $18.95
I Can't Get Over It, A Handbook for Trauma Survivors, Second Edition, $16.95
Messages: The Communication Skills Workbook, Second Edition, $15.95
Thoughts & Feelings, Second Edition, $18.95
Depression: How It Happens, How It's Healed, $14.95
The Deadly Diet, Second Edition, $14.95
The Power of Two, $15.95
Living Without Depression & Manic Depression: A Workbook for Maintaining Mood Stability, $18.95
Couple Skills: Making Your Relationship Work, $14.95
Hypnosis for Change: A Manual of Proven Techniques, Third Edition, $15.95

Call **toll free, 1-800-748-6273**, or log on to our online bookstore at **www.newharbinger.com** to order. Have your Visa or Mastercard number ready. Or send a check for the titles you want to New Harbinger Publications, Inc., 5674 Shattuck Ave., Oakland, CA 94609. Include $3.80 for the first book and 75¢ for each additional book, to cover shipping and handling. (California residents please include appropriate sales tax.) Allow two to five weeks for delivery.

Prices subject to change without notice.